Lecture Notes in Computer Science 9177

Commenced Publication in 1973
Founding and Former Series Editors:
Gerhard Goos, Juris Hartmanis, and Jan van Leeuwen

Editorial Board

More information about this series at http://www.springer.com/series/7409

Margherita Antona · Constantine Stephanidis (Eds.)

Universal Access in Human-Computer Interaction

Access to Learning, Health and Well-Being

9th International Conference, UAHCI 2015
Held as Part of HCI International 2015
Los Angeles, CA, USA, August 2–7, 2015
Proceedings, Part III

Springer

Editors
Margherita Antona
Foundation for Research and Technology –
    Hellas (FORTH)
Heraklion, Crete
Greece

Constantine Stephanidis
University of Crete
Heraklion, Crete
Greece

and

Foundation for Research and Technology –
    Hellas (FORTH)
Heraklion, Crete
Greece

ISSN 0302-9743   ISSN 1611-3349   (electronic)
Lecture Notes in Computer Science
ISBN 978-3-319-20683-7   ISBN 978-3-319-20684-4   (eBook)
DOI 10.1007/978-3-319-20684-4

Library of Congress Control Number: 2015942615

LNCS Sublibrary: SL3 – Information Systems and Applications, incl. Internet/Web, and HCI

Springer International Publishing AG Switzerland is part of Springer Science+Business Media
(www.springer.com)

Foreword

The 17th International Conference on Human-Computer Interaction, HCI International 2015, was held in Los Angeles, CA, USA, during 2–7 August 2015. The event incorporated the 15 conferences/thematic areas listed on the following page.

A total of 4843 individuals from academia, research institutes, industry, and governmental agencies from 73 countries submitted contributions, and 1462 papers and 246 posters have been included in the proceedings. These papers address the latest research and development efforts and highlight the human aspects of design and use of computing systems. The papers thoroughly cover the entire field of Human-Computer Interaction, addressing major advances in knowledge and effective use of computers in a variety of application areas. The volumes constituting the full 28-volume set of the conference proceedings are listed on pages VII and VIII.

I would like to thank the Program Board Chairs and the members of the Program Boards of all thematic areas and affiliated conferences for their contribution to the highest scientific quality and the overall success of the HCI International 2015 conference.

This conference could not have been possible without the continuous and unwavering support and advice of the founder, Conference General Chair Emeritus and Conference Scientific Advisor, Prof. Gavriel Salvendy. For their outstanding efforts, I would like to express my appreciation to the Communications Chair and Editor of HCI International News, Dr. Abbas Moallem, and the Student Volunteer Chair, Prof. Kim-Phuong L. Vu. Finally, for their dedicated contribution towards the smooth organization of HCI International 2015, I would like to express my gratitude to Maria Pitsoulaki and George Paparoulis, General Chair Assistants.

May 2015

Constantine Stephanidis
General Chair, HCI International 2015

HCI International 2015 Thematic Areas and Affiliated Conferences

Thematic areas:

- Human-Computer Interaction (HCI 2015)
- Human Interface and the Management of Information (HIMI 2015)

Affiliated conferences:

- 12th International Conference on Engineering Psychology and Cognitive Ergonomics (EPCE 2015)
- 9th International Conference on Universal Access in Human-Computer Interaction (UAHCI 2015)
- 7th International Conference on Virtual, Augmented and Mixed Reality (VAMR 2015)
- 7th International Conference on Cross-Cultural Design (CCD 2015)
- 7th International Conference on Social Computing and Social Media (SCSM 2015)
- 9th International Conference on Augmented Cognition (AC 2015)
- 6th International Conference on Digital Human Modeling and Applications in Health, Safety, Ergonomics and Risk Management (DHM 2015)
- 4th International Conference on Design, User Experience and Usability (DUXU 2015)
- 3rd International Conference on Distributed, Ambient and Pervasive Interactions (DAPI 2015)
- 3rd International Conference on Human Aspects of Information Security, Privacy and Trust (HAS 2015)
- 2nd International Conference on HCI in Business (HCIB 2015)
- 2nd International Conference on Learning and Collaboration Technologies (LCT 2015)
- 1st International Conference on Human Aspects of IT for the Aged Population (ITAP 2015)

Conference Proceedings Volumes Full List

1. LNCS 9169, Human-Computer Interaction: Design and Evaluation (Part I), edited by Masaaki Kurosu
2. LNCS 9170, Human-Computer Interaction: Interaction Technologies (Part II), edited by Masaaki Kurosu
3. LNCS 9171, Human-Computer Interaction: Users and Contexts (Part III), edited by Masaaki Kurosu
4. LNCS 9172, Human Interface and the Management of Information: Information and Knowledge Design (Part I), edited by Sakae Yamamoto
5. LNCS 9173, Human Interface and the Management of Information: Information and Knowledge in Context (Part II), edited by Sakae Yamamoto
6. LNAI 9174, Engineering Psychology and Cognitive Ergonomics, edited by Don Harris
7. LNCS 9175, Universal Access in Human-Computer Interaction: Access to Today's Technologies (Part I), edited by Margherita Antona and Constantine Stephanidis
8. LNCS 9176, Universal Access in Human-Computer Interaction: Access to Interaction (Part II), edited by Margherita Antona and Constantine Stephanidis
9. LNCS 9177, Universal Access in Human-Computer Interaction: Access to Learning, Health and Well-Being (Part III), edited by Margherita Antona and Constantine Stephanidis
10. LNCS 9178, Universal Access in Human-Computer Interaction: Access to the Human Environment and Culture (Part IV), edited by Margherita Antona and Constantine Stephanidis
11. LNCS 9179, Virtual, Augmented and Mixed Reality, edited by Randall Shumaker and Stephanie Lackey
12. LNCS 9180, Cross-Cultural Design: Methods, Practice and Impact (Part I), edited by P.L. Patrick Rau
13. LNCS 9181, Cross-Cultural Design: Applications in Mobile Interaction, Education, Health, Transport and Cultural Heritage (Part II), edited by P.L. Patrick Rau
14. LNCS 9182, Social Computing and Social Media, edited by Gabriele Meiselwitz
15. LNAI 9183, Foundations of Augmented Cognition, edited by Dylan D. Schmorrow and Cali M. Fidopiastis
16. LNCS 9184, Digital Human Modeling and Applications in Health, Safety, Ergonomics and Risk Management: Human Modeling (Part I), edited by Vincent G. Duffy
17. LNCS 9185, Digital Human Modeling and Applications in Health, Safety, Ergonomics and Risk Management: Ergonomics and Health (Part II), edited by Vincent G. Duffy
18. LNCS 9186, Design, User Experience, and Usability: Design Discourse (Part I), edited by Aaron Marcus
19. LNCS 9187, Design, User Experience, and Usability: Users and Interactions (Part II), edited by Aaron Marcus
20. LNCS 9188, Design, User Experience, and Usability: Interactive Experience Design (Part III), edited by Aaron Marcus

Universal Access in Human-Computer Interaction

Program Board Chairs: Margherita Antona, Greece, and Constantine Stephanidis, Greece

The full list with the Program Board Chairs and the members of the Program Boards of all thematic areas and affiliated conferences is available online at:

http://www.hci.international/2015/

HCI International 2016

The 18th International Conference on Human-Computer Interaction, HCI International 2016, will be held jointly with the affiliated conferences in Toronto, Canada, at the Westin Harbour Castle Hotel, 17–22 July 2016. It will cover a broad spectrum of themes related to Human-Computer Interaction, including theoretical issues, methods, tools, processes, and case studies in HCI design, as well as novel interaction techniques, interfaces, and applications. The proceedings will be published by Springer. More information will be available on the conference website: http://2016.hci.international/.

General Chair
Prof. Constantine Stephanidis
University of Crete and ICS-FORTH
Heraklion, Crete, Greece
Email: general_chair@hcii2016.org

http://2016.hci.international/

Contents – Part III

Universal Access to Health Applications and Services

Games for Learning and Therapy

Cognitive Disabilities and Cognitive Support

Universal Access to Education

Criteria for Designing Blended Learning Materials for Inclusive Education: Perspectives of Teachers and Producers

Ingo K. Bosse[✉]

Faculty of Rehabilitation Research, University of Dortmund, Dortmund, Germany
ingo.bosse@tu-dortmund.de

Abstract. Inclusion and learning with media are both global megatrends in 21st century education and both are stimulating profound changes for educational institutions. While there is consensus that media education offers special opportunities for inclusive classrooms, most of the blended learning platforms currently on offer are not accessible to and thus not usable for students with special needs. It is a challenge for both teachers and producers of media based learning materials to meet the needs of all students. The purpose of the exploratory study presented here was to collect qualitative data on the didactical requirements for inclusive learning materials from the perspectives of teachers and producers. The subject of the study was "Planet School", the most important blended learning platform available for schools in Germany. To include the perspectives of experienced teachers the first research module had a focus on their practical experiences in inclusive classrooms. Based on participatory observation and interviews it was possible to develop recommendations for the design of blended learning materials for inclusive education. The second module focused on the perspectives of the producers. Based on the results of module one the responsible public broadcaster developed criteria for the design of materials, modules, and activities for inclusive education. This article compares the different perspectives. This procedure will lead to the development of a blended learning platform that addresses the needs of different types of learners and offers accessible and usable materials including movies, television broadcasts, and interactive and multimedia content for students with different prerequisites for learning.

Keywords: E-inclusion · Blended learning · Broadcasters · Inclusive education · Inclusive multimedia learning materials

1 Introduction

The increased focus on inclusive education can be largely explained by the ratification of the UN Convention on the Rights of Persons with Disabilities (UN-CRPD). More than 150 countries had signed the contract as of 2014. They include almost all American nations, all European nations including the European Union, almost all Asian and African nations, Australia, and New Zealand. The contract describes high expectations to shape the process of inclusion by providing for appropriate representations of

© Springer International Publishing Switzerland 2015
M. Antona and C. Stephanidis (Eds.): UAHCI 2015, Part III, LNCS 9177, pp. 3–14, 2015.
DOI: 10.1007/978-3-319-20684-4_1

disability in the media as well as by using the media itself. Recent practical examples show how the combination of the global megatrends of media education and inclusive education create innovative approaches and that both trends can profit from each other [10, 18].

Before describing how to design digital learning materials for inclusive education, it is necessary to clarify the term 'inclusion'. UNESCO defines the term in the policy guidelines for inclusion in education as follows:

> "Inclusion is thus seen as a process of addressing and responding to the diversity of needs of all children, youth and adults through increasing participation in learning, cultures and communities, and reducing and eliminating exclusion within and from education. It involves changes and modifications in content, approaches, structures and strategies, with a common vision that covers all children of the appropriate age range and a conviction that it is the responsibility of the regular system to educate all children" [20].

"A key characteristic of 21st century education is that classrooms are more diverse than ever. [8] Students have very different needs due to their social and cultural backgrounds, their language backgrounds, and their physical and intellectual abilities. The central question with a focus on the use of learning materials and ICTs is:

"Do materials cater to the needs of all learners with learning difficulties"? [20].

UNESCO stresses the importance of the adequate design of learning materials. Education through the inclusion lens implies "Flexible teaching and learning methods adapted to different needs and learning styles. (...) Flexible teaching methods with innovative approaches to teaching aids, and equipment as well as the use of ICTs." [20].

Learning platforms can represent an essential aid for the individualization of ICT based learning materials and learning processes. One well known producer of web-based learning materials for schools in Germany is the public broadcasting station "Westdeutscher Rundfunk" (WDR). The WDR belongs to the ARD, a joint television network of nine state broadcasting organizations. It is the world's second largest public broadcaster after the BBC. The mission of all public sector broadcast networks is to speak to all groups of society, providing them with information, education, and entertainment as well as with innovative and alternative programmes, especially for minority groups. One of these is "Planet School" (www.planet-schule.de). Television broadcasts and movies can be downloaded and watched in real-time. Detailed information, worksheets for creative lessons, and multimedia (e.g. educational games) can be found in these "Knowledge Pools" also. The content of the different media complement each other. "The website is currently only available in German. Many schools already use the platform for a wide range of subjects. The platform however is not specifically designed for students with special needs" [6]. The purpose of this study was to find out how this platform can become appropriate for inclusive education and which design criteria for creating web-based learning materials are the most appropriate.

2   Research Design

The aim of this study was to show how to meet the challenges of creating media for inclusive learning. The main research questions were:

1. What distinguishes good inclusive digital learning materials?
2. Which quality criteria can be established?

Additional aims were to enable students to deal independently with media and to encourage cooperative learning. It was of key importance to link the perspectives of teachers and producers. The interpretative approach consists of three modules of qualitative research. These are outlined below (Fig. 1).

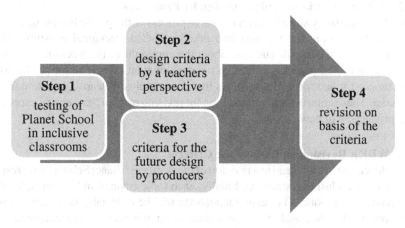

Fig. 1. Research design

Step 1 (Dortmund University): Testing of Planet School in Inclusive Classrooms
Analysis of international research shows seven essential factors for the creation of learning materials for inclusive education. The multi-method research design consists of participatory observation and semi-structured interviews with teachers. The main focus was on the practical experiences with the learning materials provided by "Planet School". Specifically, 11 experienced teachers at primary and secondary schools worked with different topics covered by "Planet School" in 2013 and 2014. The five schools belong to diverse German school districts and were randomly selected. All teachers had a wide range of students in their classroom. This included students with learning, intellectual, physical, emotional, and behavioural disorders. This also included students with dyslexia, dyscalculia, and special needs in language and communication. The sample contained 108 students. Twenty-six of them had special needs concerning learning and communication, as well as special social, emotional, and motoric development needs. A preliminary study ensured the quality of the interview guidance and the participatory observation.

Step 2 (Dortmund University): Design Criteria from the Perspective of Teachers
The interviews with the teachers were analysed to form guidelines for the revision of the website. The first step was to transcribe the audio recordings of the interviews

in full. Step two was to work on a summarizing content analysis with MAXQDA. The results were evaluated on the basis of core categories based on the desk research to create the interview guidelines. Finally, all interviews were summarised by core categories and interpreted in combination with the results of the participatory observation. This procedure led to scientifically sound guidelines for the revision of the website. The revisions were discussed with a focus group of television professionals from the editorial board for educational programmes.

Step 3 (WDR): Criteria for Future Design by Producers

The results of the study stimulated an intensive process at the public broadcaster WDR concerning how to put the findings into practice. Beside technical questions about accessibility and usability, discussions about the copyright of the worksheets were of high importance. The process resulted in the development of criteria for producers of WDR schools TV and for media agencies that create inclusive learning content for the broadcaster. These criteria are the foundation for revising parts of the website, especially for the production of new content.

Step 4 (WDR): Revision on Basis of the Criteria

The developed criteria will lead to a revision of the platform "Planet School "with respect to the needs of inclusive instruction. Finally, each topic covered in "Planet School" is to be revised one-by-one. The recommendations will be especially important for new productions. Beside the novelties for the website itself, it is necessary to include the new findings into teacher training that is offered by the public broadcaster to promote the use of "Planet School" in classrooms.

3   Results

The results of each of the steps are presented separately. The final results presented here are the criteria for the production of blended learning materials for inclusive classrooms, because the last step, the revision of the website is work in progress.

3.1   Desk Research: Basic Principles for Blended Learning Materials

The importance of the design of digital media for the learning success of students, especially of students with special educational needs, is often discussed among teachers and the scientific community [10]. Although there is little data, the following basic principles can be established by analysing the international research. The desk-based research identified seven factors that are essential for the creation of inclusive learning content with digital media. These include:

1. Text and language
2. Individualisation and personalisation
3. Same learning subjects

4. Respect for the complexity of lived-realities
5. Cooperative/collaborative learning
6. Activity-oriented instruction
7. Web accessibility and universal design

Text and Language. "Traditional textbooks can be difficult for print impaired learners to access" [14]. Web-based texts can also be difficult for print impaired learners to access. While offering content in a variety of modifiable media platforms is an important element of inclusive media didactics, the research shows that text and speech themselves are great barriers for students with learning difficulties. Accessibility does not only refer to the accessibility and usability of learning materials in a technical respect, but it also refers to language-related accessibility.

The language of instruction predominantly used in schools is still that of the middle classes. This often constitutes a barrier for students with learning difficulties. Similarly, the monolingual custom represents a barrier for young persons from migrant backgrounds. "All learning materials and media (e.g. textbooks, worksheets, and film documents) … should be critically examined with regard to their language related accessibility" [21].

However, alternatives should be offered. It should be considered that "… the needs of the large group of persons with learning difficulties … differ in terms of written texts. The discussion about inclusion in the modern foreign language classrooms provides helpful results as well. When creating web content, "easy to read on the web" is essential for users with intellectual disabilities [14].

Individualization and Personalization. "Not every student has to achieve the same level!" [4]. The same learning outcomes apply to all students. However, these may be achieved at different times, in different methodological ways, with different forms of support from teachers, and with different learning materials. Individualized learning processes will address different types of learners and offer accessible and usable materials, including movies, television broadcasts, interactive, and multimedia content for students with different prerequisites for learning. Personalized learning enables students to achieve suitable educational qualifications and individual learning at the same time. The general education learning content in schools is expanded, decreased, or modified according to special educational needs. In addition to selection and modification, the design of teaching methods also arises from the individual learning prerequisites. "Inclusive teaching enables both: goal-differentiated and content-differentiated learning" [22]. Different learning materials have to be offered for five different levels, reaching from learning difficulties to special interests and giftedness. It is preventive because it counts on early interventions in cases of emerging learning disabilities and it is curriculum-based in that it is geared towards the methods and contents of classroom instruction [22].

Same Learning Subjects. Although working on the same subject represents the didactic core of inclusive learning [3]. In inclusive learning, it is also important to lead all students towards the highest possible curriculum goals. This optimal support of all students is best achieved through joint and cooperative working on the same subject. This subject is determined by the students themselves, is derived from the general curriculum, and is offered in a differentiated way accordingly [9]. In the Index for Inclusion, the well-known tool for quality assurance in inclusive schools, this point is highlighted by the following question:

"Does teaching assume a shared experience that can be developed in different ways?" [13].

It is important to design learning methods in such a way as to enable students to discover for themselves what the "crux of the matter" is. The relationship between commonality and difference can therefore not be described on the basis of vertical levels from simple to complex. In planning, the issue revolves around the question of possible similarities among the students' approaches [17].

Respect of Lived-Realities. The individuality of students, including their diverse experiences outside of school, represents the starting point for education. School itself is a living space for growing ups. In the Index for Inclusion, this point is addressed by the following question:

"Do the teaching materials comply with the backgrounds, experiences and interests of the students?" [13].

Social orientation is made available for adults through lived-realities as well as through the media. The media also shapes identity construction and self-assurance in adolescents. In order to do justice to the different heterogeneity dimensions of inclusive didactics, images, texts, and films should be selected in a way as to enable individual diversity to be recognized. The issue of disability has moved into the mainstream during the past few years due to its more frequent depiction in the media and it is now perceived more clearly by the population. In inclusive education, films on the topic of disability can raise awareness among all students. However, in the sense of disability mainstreaming, disability should not always be highlighted explicitly. Instead, persons with disabilities should simply belong to all contexts. This is a topic just like any other, which is part of the lives of students.

Cooperative and Collaborative Learning. The Index for Inclusion tries to make clear that collective learning includes both cooperative as well as individual learning forms [5, 13].

In connection with cooperative learning, a helper system is referenced. For school-work in collective learning, there is a wide range of helpers to choose from. These include partner classes or students, parents, colleagues and special needs educators. However, cooperative learning means much more than establishing a helper system. It refers to the voluntary collective bundling of individual experiences, knowledge, responsibilities, and group activities towards a common goal. Cooperative learning is a form of interaction with a common goal in which knowledge and skills are acquired together through exchange [18]. Ideally, all group members participate equally and take over joint responsibility. Non-disabled students can thus practise their social skills without falling behind in their subject-related academic performance [22]. Good teaching is well-organized, clearly structured teaching with a high task-related activity level and intensive use of learning time on the part of the students. In addition, good teaching uses diverse methods and includes cooperative as well as individual learning phases [11]. Cooperative learning is intended to result in students supporting each other mutually to achieve results together. Cooperative learning is organized in the classroom whereas collaborative learning involves the whole school and additional partners. Collaboration is one of the successful factors that favor the inclusion of parents/guardians in the classroom and within the teaching team [2].

Activity-Orientated Instruction. Activity-oriented instruction is closely linked to cooperative learning. This student-oriented approach, developed from practical experience, is considered an alternative to traditional receptive teaching [1] or iconic and verbal-analytical acquisition processes. An understanding of environment and reality arises through an active dealing with reality because the idea of the origin of phenomena also determines the understanding thereof [12]. With action-oriented methods and practical approaches it is possible to create an "inclusive combination. This also includes product-orientation. Furthermore, students learn solidarity through goal-oriented work and to communicate and interact with others.

Web-Accessibility and Universal Design. "The convention on the rights of persons with disabilities (Articles 20 and 23), as well as the "Index for Inclusion" [5] call for accessibility. In the context of inclusion it is indispensable to implement suitable measures for accessible information and communication [22]. Aside from accessibility, universal design is a core principle for designing blended learning materials for inclusive education. The UN-CRPD addresses this issue in "Products, Environments, Programme and Services" [19]. Universal design is not only of importance for people with disabilities, but would benefit all citizens [14]. For example, the use of subtitles in films is useful for persons with hearing impairments as well as for migrants.

3.2 Perspectives of Teachers: Guidelines for Designing Blended Learning Materials

The aim of this module was to collect qualitative data on the didactical requirements for inclusive education from the perspective of teachers (for special and for mainstream education). The structuring of the individual interviews forms the basis for the systematic interview comparison. Finally, the results of the individual assessments are examined in context to core categories and are summarized in a table. By using this method we can make cross-case statements in which the specifics of the respective individual interviews are still explicitly considered. The overview shows the most frequently quoted statements (Fig. 2):

Code	Number of Codes	Percentage of all Codes
General learning arrangements	36	22%
Text and language	32	19%
Individualization and personalization	27	16%
Good presence of lived-realities	16	10%
Cooperative and collaborative learning	10	6 %
Activity oriented learning	10	6%
Accessibility	5	3%

Fig. 2. Most frequent codes

"The results of the summarizing content analysis underline the relative satisfaction of teachers with the usability of "Planet School" for inclusive classrooms. In general the teachers thought that "Planet School" is appealing to children and that "Planet School" is easy for children to understand" [6]. The teachers greatly appreciate the possibility of being able to exert direct influence across the revision. The systematic comparison of the individual interviews was made along the described core categories for the design of digital media for inclusive education.

Most of the remarks about the website concerned the general learning arrangements, an aspect that didn't play an important role in the desk-based research. The most common statement in this core category concerned the worksheets. The teachers stated that they would like to work with Word documents that they can adapt to the individual needs of their students, or at least work with barrier-free PDFs. The teachers also expressed a request for more clearly structured worksheets. In their opinion, the design should be simpler and exclude logos and captions or any visual clutter that is not absolutely necessary. One recurring opinion was that the materials should be kept simple, especially since the overwhelming number of elements can confuse the students. There is a strong wish to install a forum to share self-created materials.

Furthermore, the didactical instructions should be categorized in terms of activity-oriented learning, game, worksheet, etc. The teachers would generally like to see a greater variety of methods available for use within one lesson. Practical examples, exercises, and interdisciplinary ideas are required. Didactical instructions for teachers and working tasks for students on every worksheet are indispensable. The didactical instructions should be categorized in terms of activity-oriented learning, game, worksheet, etc. All-in-all "Planet School" promotes very receptive learning. There is a strong demand for more activeness including partner and group work.

From the teacher's point of view text and language are of high importance. The font type selected for the platform thus has to be a sans serif font such as Arial or Helvetica. It should also be possible to choose different fonts and font sizes. The platform should moreover offer short text with activity-oriented tasks for weak readers and alternative texts for strong readers. For complex topics like politics or history it would be helpful to have a version using simple language. Most of the students with special needs have learning difficulties. Thus, if writing is the main aspect, alternative tasks such as playful or physical exercises should also be offered.

The third most frequent quoted statements were about the individualization and personalization. The teachers identified a strong for different levels of learning concerning complexity, timeframe, and speed. There seems to be a need for the different levels to be labeled more clearly. Some of the expressions currently used (for all, for experts, for professionals) have stigmatizing effects. Neutral terms or the use of different colors would be more appropriate.

Design of Inclusive Blended Learning Materials. These recommendations were discussed in a focus group with television professionals who work at the editorial board for educational programmes. As such, a process of fundamental revision of the offer was initiated. This is still continuing. Since the WDR often has a large number of people involved in the design of materials, criteria (guidelines and checklists) was created for the design of inclusive learning and teaching materials specific to the different types of media. The checklists for the design of films and multimedia applications are presented below. They describe the individual measures in detail. These tools provide quality assurance.

3.2.1   Checklist Film[1]
"Content-Related Design

[ ] concentration on the essentials, no distracting elements
[ ] clear explanations
[ ] motivating background story
[ ] reference to the real world
[ ] clear character constellations and plots
[ ] make persons with disabilities visible without clichés

Formal Design

[ ] Essentials, no distracting elements: limit to one or two levels of action
[ ] simple, understandable language
[ ] no divergence of words and images
[ ] short, precise voice-over texts
[ ] calm imagery, no fast cuts
[ ] no clip-like cuts when conveying content; calm camera movements
[ ] structure films into meaningful units and chapters

Post-Processing

[ ] sub-titles for persons with impaired hearing
[ ] audio descriptions for blind and visually-impaired persons

3.2.2   Checklist Multimedia[2]
Design of Content

[ ] Universal Design: diverse forms of presentation, e.g. texts, images, audios
[ ] motivating elements (e.g. incentives, rewards)

---

[1] Copyright: Westdeutscher Rundfunk (WDR) Planet Schule 2014.
[2] Copyright: Westdeutscher Rundfunk (WDR) Planet Schule 2014.

[ ] content-related assistance (such as aids that are always indicated)
[ ] understandable language
[ ] short, simple texts
[ ] make persons with disabilities visible without clichés
[ ] offer different levels of difficulty

Formal Design
[ ] clear, simple symbols
[ ] essentials: avoid elements that have no content-related function
[ ] colour must not carry any meaning
[ ] clear contrasts
[ ] no automatically blinking, moving or scrolling elements
[ ] easily readable, scalable writing

Operability
[ ] simple, intuitive operability (no lengthy instructions necessary)
[ ] no need to work out all informational elements and not in a prescribed order

Accessibility
[ ] Compliance with WCAG 2.0 (Level AA)

Technical Functions
(…)" (WDR 2014, no page).

4 Conclusion

The megatrends of mediatisation and inclusive education can compliment each other. Seven decisive factors were identified from the analysis of the state of research on the design of inclusive blended learning materials. In guided interviews with teachers who worked with the website "Planet School" in inclusive classrooms, it became clear what concrete optimization requirements are necessary from their perspectives. From the analysis and interpretation of the interviews specific recommendations for the revision of media and materials became evident. The group discussion with producers initiated a process that ultimately led to the creation of criteria and checklists that the public broadcaster has set down as a quality benchmark for the design of appealing blended learning content for inclusive education. A number of revisions and new productions will still be necessary.

The broadcasting station is pursuing this emphatically. The subsequent embedding of the new materials in didactically meaningful teaching arrangements is a task for teachers. Even good blended learning materials do not automatically result in a meaningful learning environment. Further individualization and personalization must be accompanied. But the changes described here are important to reach equal learning opportunities with attractive digital media for every student.

References

1. Babel, H., Hackl, B.: Handlungsorientierter unterricht – dirigierter aktionismus oder partizipative kooperation? In: Mayer, O., Treichel, D. (eds.) Handlungsorientiertes Lernen und eLearning: Grundlagen und Praxisbeispiele, pp. 11–35. Oldenbourg, München (2004)
2. Beltran, E.V., Ciges, A.S.: The 21st century languages classroom – the teacher perspektive. In: Beltran, E.V., Abbott, C., Jones, J. (eds.) Inclusive Language Education and Digital Technology, pp. 67–83. Multilingual Matters, Bristol, Buffalo, Toronto (2013)
3. Bintinger, G., Wilhelm, M.: Inklusiven Unterricht gestalten: Creating inclusive Education. Behinderte in Familie, Schule und Gesellschaft **24**, 51–60 (2001)
4. Bönsch, M., Mögeling, K. (eds.): Binnendifferenzierung. Teil 2: Unterrichtsbeispiele für den binnendifferenzierten Unterricht. Prolog-Verlag, Immenhausen bei Kassel (2014)
5. Booth, T., Ainscow, M.: Index for Inclusion: developing learning and participation in schools. CSIE, Bristol (2011)
6. Bosse, I.K.: "Planet School": blended learning for inclusive classrooms. In: Miesenberger, K., Fels, D., Archambault, D., Peňáz, P., Zagler, W. (eds.) ICCHP 2014, Part II. LNCS, vol. 8548, pp. 366–373. Springer, Heidelberg (2014)
7. Bosse, I.K.: How to Design Blended Learning Materials for Inclusive Education? An Exploratory Study. In: Hogarth, A. (ed.): Blended Learning: Student Perceptions, Emerging Practices and Novapublishers, New York (2015) (in Press)
8. Edyburn, D.L., Edyburn, K.D.: Tools for Creating Accessible, Tiered, and Multilingual Web-Based Curricula, pp. 1–7. Intervention in School and Clinic, Austin (2011)
9. Feyerer, E., Prammer, W.: Gemeinsamer Unterricht in der Sekundarstufe I: Anregungen für eine integrative Praxis. Beltz, Weinheim (2009)
10. Florian, L., Hegarty, J.: ICT and Special Educational Needs: A Tool for Inclusion: A Tool for Inclusion. Open University Press, Berkshire (2004)
11. Green, N., Green, K.: Kooperatives LernenimKlassenraum und imKollegium: Das Trainingsbuch (2). Kallmeyer. Velber
12. Gudjons, H.: Pädagogisches Grundwissen: Überblick - Kompendium – Studienbuch. Klinkhardt, Bad Heilbrunn (2008)
13. Hinz, A., Boban, I.: Der "Index forInclusion" - eine Möglichkeit zur Selbstevaluation von "Schulen für alle". In: Feuser, G. (ed.) Integration heute - Perspektiven ihrer Weiterentwicklung in Theorie und Praxis, pp. 37–46. Peter Lang, Frankfurt am Main (2003)
14. McNaught, A., Featherstone, L.: Alternative Approaches to Alternative Formats – Changing Expectations by Challenging Myths. In: Miesenberger, K., Karshmer, A., Penaz, P., Zagler, W. (eds.) ICCHP 2012, Part I. LNCS, vol. 7382, pp. 43–50. Springer, Heidelberg (2012)
15. Probiesch, K. (n.d.). Barrierefreiheit im Web. http://www.rkw-kompetenzzentrum.de/fileadmin/media/Dokumente/Publikationen/FB_Barrierefreiheit_im_Web_280113.pdf
16. Richiger-Näf, B.: ICT und Sonderpädagogik. In: Schweizerische Zeitschrift für Heilpädagogik 16vol. 6, pp. 6–11 (2010)
17. Seitz, S.: Inklusive Didaktik: Die Frage nach dem "Kern der Sache". Zeitschrift für Inklusion, vol. 1, http://www.inklusion-online.net/index.php/inklusion-online/view/184/184article/ (2006)
18. Traub, S.: Kooperativ lernen. In: Buholzer, A, Kummer, A. (eds.): Alle gleich – alle unterschiedlich! Zum Umgang mit Heterogenität in Schule und Unterricht. pp. 138-150. Klett und Balmer-Verlag, Zug (2010)
19. UN – United Nations: Convention on the Rights of Persons with Disabilities and Optional Protocol. New York (2006)

20. UNESCO: Policy Guidelines on Inclusion in Education. http://unesdoc.unesco.org/images/0017/001778/177849e.pdf (2009)
21. Wember, F.: Herausforderung Inklusion: Ein präventiv orientiertes Modell schulischen Lernens und vier zentrale Bedingungen inklusiver Unterrichtsentwicklung. Zeitschrift für Heilpädagogik **10**, 380–387 (2013)
22. Wocken, H.: Das Haus der inklusiven Schule: Baustellen – Baupläne – Bausteine. Feldhaus, Hamburg (2011)

Interaction Design of Digital Teaching Improves Teaching and Learning Effectiveness

Tsung-Chou Chang[1(✉)], Ya-Fen Tsai[2], and Fong-Gong Wu[1]

[1] Department of Industrial Design, National Cheng Kung University, Tainan, Taiwan (R.O.C.)
deadpoet12@gmail.com, fonggong@mail.ncku.edu.tw
[2] Department of Product Design, Ming Chuan University, Taipei, Taiwan (R.O.C.)
lingocat@gmail.com

Abstract. With increasing penetration of mobile device like smart mobile phone, appropriate cloud system can be a good match for powerful teaching aid in classroom. Hu-man Computer Interaction is an important part of visual ergonomics and cognitive ergonomics. It focuses on mental process including perception, memory, inference and motor reaction, etc. The application of teaching is to expect that students can use active learning through interactive design to pay more attention on and complete various tasks instructed by teachers. Therefore, interactive teaching-aided software can not only make teaching activities vivid and variations but also increase students' attention and the willingness of active learning in classroom. The rise of "flipped classroom" in 2007 was also a teaching concept to propose that student should be returned to a learning body and interaction of teacher and student in classroom should be given attention. This study is to explore the relevant literatures for active learning, interactive design, action learning and flipped classroom, etc., supported by interactive design based on the concept of flipped classroom immediate feedback that how teaching media-Zuvio improves teacher's teaching skill through mobile APP and cloud system. The result of this study can be used as improvement of teachers' teaching effectiveness and students' learning outcomes.

Keywords: Human computer interaction · Visual ergonomic · Cognitive ergonomics · Active learning · Flipped classroom · Mobile APP · Interaction design

1 Introduction

Teacher's teaching method in Taiwan's education system is mostly one-way transmission of knowledge. Traditional teaching method, i.e. traditional lecture generally exists in the campus. Teachers give lessons with oral interpretation or repeat what books say and students absorb knowledge by listening to lectures, taking note and reading before/after class. Traditional lecture that has long been widely welcome in teachers is because teachers just follow simple and convenient process to interpret according to the textbooks. However, such a "duck-stuffing" type of teaching makes most of Taiwan's

© Springer International Publishing Switzerland 2015
M. Antona and C. Stephanidis (Eds.): UAHCI 2015, Part III, LNCS 9177, pp. 15–22, 2015.
DOI: 10.1007/978-3-319-20684-4_2

students dare not to express their ideas and lack of initiative. Once students show inattention, it may influence on their learning effectiveness.

Some studies show that few minutes after traditional lecture begins will cause distraction of students. 1094 students were surveyed on campus at Taiwan University for the change of classroom attention. The result is found that learning curve of 47.7 % students is indicated as Fig. 1 for a 50 mins class, meaning students stay focused upon the beginning of the class, showing distraction in the middle and refreshing shortly before class is over.

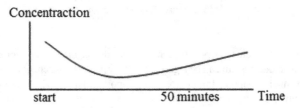

Fig. 1. Learning curve of NTU students (Source: http://goo.gl/wkXtXm)

Taiwan University also made 125 teachers self-appraisal for teaching concentration, indicating assessment results for 46.4 % teachers as Fig. 2, meaning teachers may give lessons with less concentration at the beginning, the more the lecture, the better the spirit, but will be exhausted shortly just before class ended.

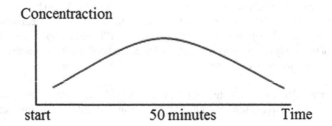

Fig. 2. Teaching curve of NTU teachers (Source: http://goo.gl/wkXtXm)

In terms of teachers, improving students' attention, assisting them to be good audiences and actively taking notes in classroom and making them active learners are essential responsibilities of educators. If teachers are able to make good use of inter-active teaching-aided software, students' attention in classroom can be improved other than lively and varied teaching activities. Consequently, this study is mainly to explore how interactive design of immediate feedback teaching media assists teachers in controlling students' learning status for more focus on learning in classroom, and improving more concentration and effectiveness within time limit for better interaction between teachers and students.

2   Active Learning

Learning is a kind of knowledge construction progress, in educational field, students enhance their memories or obtain skills and know-how by either passive or active learning. Active learning is an important learning strategy in a classroom. It is generally defined as any instructional methods that engage students in the learning process by meaningful learning activities [1]. The core components of active learning are activity and learners participation. Advantage of active learning is supported by research results of decades showing that active learning is generally better than passive learning in improving learning gain for students [1]. Active learning is generally defined as any instructional method that engages students in the learning process. In short, active learning requires students to do meaningful learning activities and think about what they are doing. While this definition could include traditional activities such as homework, in practice active learning refers to activities that are introduced into the classroom. Compare with the traditional lecture which passively receive in-formation from the instructor, Active learning is focused on learning effectiveness for students, such as collaborative learning, cooperative learning, problem based learning, and discovery learning [1].

3   Mobile Learning and Mobile App

For more and more penetrations of mobile phone and smart phone, the behavioral of people are changed. Mobile phones have been playing an increasingly significant role in pedagogy system for teaching and learning tests in the last years. The major affordances of mobile phone for learning include user mobility resulting from device portability, easily and movable battery charging, real-time interaction, and on-line connectivity. The smart phone users have more positive beliefs and behavioral intention to use smart phone for learning, and overall users will continue using smart phone for learning that would help educators to promote the use of smart phone for learning [3]. The result of the study by García Laborda et al. was extended prospective research for mobile APP interaction design includes following aspects: 1. task adaptation to mobile phones, smart phones and tablets; 2. user satisfaction; 3. external validity as compared to other delivery systems and other tests including similar pen and paper versions; 4. technical advances in software design for Multi-platform systems supported such as iOS and Android; 5. pedagogical benefits for both educators and students; 6. delivery reliability and 7. Functionality [2].

4   Flipped Classroom

"Flipped Classroom" was the first word used by Jonathan Bergmann and Aaron Sams, two chemistry teachers of senior high school to record the teaching video and uploaded online as extra class for students who missed a class, and general students also joined to view online afterwards, so as to generate a teaching mode of flipped classroom [4]. "Flipped Classroom" is a teaching concept to propose that student should be returned to a learning body. Students may view teaching video at home for preview before class or review after class, and make mutual discussion with teachers and classmates in classroom. "Flipped Classroom" is an interactive learning to adjust the time of teachers' explanation and students' homework, allowing teachers to have time for one-to-one instruction. It can enhance students' learning responsibilities and flexibilities to make classroom teaching become a mutual learning mode between teachers and students, which commands the attention of educational circles. The same concept as "Flipped Classroom" is Zuvio and Moodle platform. Zuvio cloud-based immediate interactive system is a teaching interactive system emerged at the right moment for improving problems among "teaching interaction", "students' learning habits" and "hardware limits" and combining students' learning willingness with digital mobile device and the trend of e-learning. Moodle platform initiated from 2010 has integrated learning contents, homework, quiz and answer sheet into the course website, expecting students to get help for learning with such a teaching video. So that, the entire class originally taken for content interpretation now only takes 15 min to play the video through design and preparation. Some studies pointed out students can get better grades in interactive teaching of "Flipped Classroom" than traditional lecture or the teaching video; however, students' satisfactions are needed for further improvement [5]. It shows the concept of "Flipped Classroom" is actually helpful for student achievements, but students' lower satisfactions come from extra tasks for preview before class.

In another study, some of the factors that may have contributed to students' improved scores included: student mediated contact with the course material prior to classes, benchmark and formative assessment administered during the module, and the interactive class activities. However, implementing a flipped classroom model to teach a renal pharmacotherapy module resulted in improved student performance and favorable student perceptions about the instructional approach [6].

5   Zuvio

Zuvio cloud-based immediate interactive system [8] is also an immediate feed-back system developed by Taiwan University educational group, in which students can communicate with teachers for immediate Q&A in classroom through various internet devices (e.g. smart mobile phone, tablet PC, notebook or desk computer), and then feedback real-time statistical information that teachers can adjust their teaching contents anytime depending on students statuses to improve teachers' teaching quality and increase students' learning motivation for promoting the popularization of digital education.

Zuvio system structure indicated as Table 1 mainly consists of the four parts: course account management system, multimedia item bank system, peer assessment system and results statistical system [7].

In the case of teachers, the operation of Zuvio system indicated as Fig. 3 Web picture can edit chapters and sections of such a course in the tabs of Chapter list after a new course is added; announced bulletins or topic discussions of such a course in the tabs of Bulletin board; adjusted semester and description of such a course in the tabs of Course information; management for students list or grouping of such a course in the tabs of Student management. It can also design TA limits of authority and statistical data for various learning statuses including students' attendance, class presentation and class response, etc. For example, teachers can make quizzes for the contents of specific chapters and sections in the course.

Table 1. Table captions should be placed below the table

System Items	Contents Description
Course account management system	Teachers can offer several courses each semester setting elective permissions to accept or refuse registration of students' accounts
Multimedia item bank system	Teachers can establish choice questions, question-response and question sets, including pictures that can make up for the lack of words and select grouping answer. Teachers can use it for Q&A process in class, the roll call, opinion survey and even quiz as well as homework and students instant the questions through IOS, Android and computer, etc. devices to achieve rapid interactive effect
Peer assessment system	Teachers can establish a group or individual peer assessment questions, also setting marking standards as well as proportion of each standard, and selecting if marking or discussion is open. Individual or each group's result and ranking should be immediately updated in the process at teacher's end while marking or discussion can be immediately given to others or other groups with IOS, Android and computer, etc. devices from student's end
Results statistical system	Teachers can dynamically view the current answer condition in the process and view detailed data analysis and chart analysis of answer results; it can support Excel file output for teachers' future score statistics while students can view their own answer records for course review

Fig. 3. The operation of zuvio system for teachers

In the case of students, they can login the system through smart mobile phone APP or digital mobile devices indicated as Fig. 4 the main operation picture. Students can answer the questions, send comments or view the relevant bulletins or discuss subjects for the main courses in discussion board after accessing such courses. If teachers have course notes, students also can select the files to download in bulletin board.

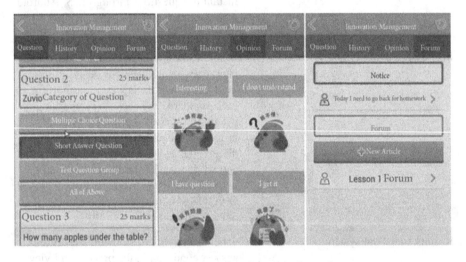

Fig. 4. The operation of zuvio system for students

6   Discussion

Zuvio's interactive learning is different from traditional lecture. It complies with emphatic core mentioned in Prince's [1] literature analysis that introducing activities into the traditional lecture and promoting student engagement has extreme significant effectiveness; meanwhile, Zuvio peer assessment system can facilitate collaborative learning and cooperative learning. Additionally, Zuvio's class presentation or quiz same as problem-based learning for active learning proposed by Prince actually provides a more challengeable, learning motivation and pleasure learning method.

Zuvio's student-end interface design is same as the study of García Laborda [2] et al. for mobile APP PAULEX that mobile APP can realize visual ergonomics with technology. The fundamental criteria for mobile App are accessibility, interaction, and the functionality or usability of the application according to the delivery, visual ergonomics, and content inclusion [2]. According to empirical study of Zek [3] et al., it explained interviewers are glad to use smart mobile phone for course learning and also improve learning effectiveness.

Besides, other relevant studies for flipped classroom [4–6] made further explanation that Zuvio integrates digital technology into classroom to provide teachers with assistive devices for teaching aids, valuing experiences of teachers and students to be helpful for teachers' teaching effectiveness and students' learning effect and to promote good interaction between teachers and students.

7   Conclusion

"Flipped Classroom" is an interactive learning to adjust the time of teachers' explanation and students' homework, allowing teachers to have time for one-to-one instruction. It can enhance students' learning responsibilities and flexibilities to make classroom teaching become a mutual learning mode between teachers and students, which commands the attention of educational circles

Based on the concept of flipped classroom for interactive designed teaching media, the way of how Zuvio improve teachers' teaching skill and students also can make good use of teaching software within limited time to pay more attention to classroom learning can be used to improve learning concentration and effectiveness; immediate interactive assessment and learning feedback are more likely to help teachers to control students' learning statuses for not only teaching the right candidates but also promoting good interaction between teachers and students.

To increase the teacher-student interaction and ease of use in the design of man-machine interface, the need to consider the people, the environment, user interface, and mobile multimedia products. In the design process, the need to understand the product itself by professionals (such as teachers) to lead, it must be in-depth analysis of the use of user behavior, so that interactive teaching media interface more consistent with human factors design.

While flipped classroom can improve student's learning outcomes, but there are still some issues to be resolved, such as: how to determine in advance prep students? Teachers how to teach in the classroom? School substitute teacher by the students, the teaching effect is better than the teachers to teach? In addition, learn how to improve the interface design of interactive systems? How to design more ergonomic interactive software to increase the flow of students and teachers in the operating convenience and fluency? Future researchers need to be further explored.

References

1. Prince, M.: Does active learning work? a review of the research. J. Eng. Educ. **93**(3), 223–231 (2004)
2. Laborda, J.G., Royo, T.M., Litzler, M.F., López, J.L.G.: Mobile phones for spain's university entrance examination language test. Educ. Technol. Soc. **17**(2), 17–30 (2014)
3. Sek, Y.W., Law, C.Y., Lau, S.H., Basri, A.S.H., Hussin, B.: Examining the behavior changes in belief and attitude among smart phone users for mobile learning. Int. J. Innovation Manage. Tech. **3**(4), 437–439 (2012)
4. Arnold-Garza, S.: The flipped classroom teaching model and its use for information literacy instruction. Commun. Inform. Literacy **8**(1), 7–22 (2014)
5. Missildine, K., Fountain, R., Summers, L., Gosselin, K.: Flipping the classroom to improve student performance and satisfaction. J. Nurs. Educ. **52**(10), 597–599 (2013)
6. Pierce, R., Fox, J.: Vodcasts and active-learning exercises in a "Flipped Classroom" model of a renal pharmacotherapy module. Am. J. Pharm. Educ. **76**(10), 1–5 (2012)
7. Zuvio. http://www.zuvio.com.tw/index.php
8. Design a wonderful course: use teaching curve for teaching procedures arrangement. http://ctld.ntu.edu.tw/_epaper/news_detail.php?nid=183

Exploring the Interactivity Issues of the Stereoscopic 3D Systems for Design Education

Li-Chieh Chen[1]([✉]), Yun-Maw Cheng[2], Po-Ying Chu[1],
and Frode Eika Sandnes[3]

[1] Department of Industrial Design, Tatung University, Taipei, Taiwan
{lcchen, juby}@ttu.edu.tw
[2] Graduate Institute of Design Science, Department of Computer Science
and Engineering, Tatung University, Taipei, Taiwan
kevin@ttu.edu.tw
[3] Oslo and Akershus University College of Applied Sciences, Oslo, Norway
Frode-Eika.Sandnes@hioa.no

Abstract. Stereoscopic 3D displays have been used by some research groups to present learning contents for education. However, in the highly interactive situations, the intertwined depth cues may result in symptoms that hamper the usability of such systems. In this research, an experiment was conducted to explore the interactivity issues. Thirty students were invited to participate in the experiment. The first task was to identify the differences between printed pictures and 3D virtual models. The second task was to point out ergonomic or design problems in a single piece of furniture or pairs of chairs and tables. Based on the analysis, discomfort caused by model rotation did contribute to the degree of overall discomfort. Even all participants had the background of using 3D modeling systems, some still experienced different levels of symptoms. Their comments indicated that adaptive adjustments of disparity and control response ratio were necessary in the highly interactive situations.

Keywords: Stereoscopic 3D displays · Design education · Interactivity issues

1 Introduction

Given the potential benefits of offering the binocular depth cue, Stereoscopic 3D (S3D) displays have been used by some research groups to present learning contents for design education. These examples included the systems for learning descriptive geometry through stereoscopic vision (Guedes et al. 2012), and displaying the process of learning to build a handmade PC (Mukai et al. 2011). Some systems even allow users to interact with the digital contents. It was reported that stereoscopic displays did improve the performance of depth-related tasks, such as judging absolute and relative distances, finding and identifying objects, performing spatial manipulations of objects, and spatial navigating (McIntire et al. 2014). However, depth cue interactions should not be neglected (Howard 2012; Mikkola et al. 2012). For instance, there were interactions among disparity and monocular depth cues, such as motion parallax, occlusion,

© Springer International Publishing Switzerland 2015
M. Antona and C. Stephanidis (Eds.): UAHCI 2015, Part III, LNCS 9177, pp. 23–30, 2015.
DOI: 10.1007/978-3-319-20684-4_3

shadow (or shading), linear perspective, and accommodation (Fig. 1). Especially in the highly interactive situations, the intertwined depth cues may result in symptoms that hamper the usability of such systems. In this research, an experiment was conducted to explore the interactivity issues.

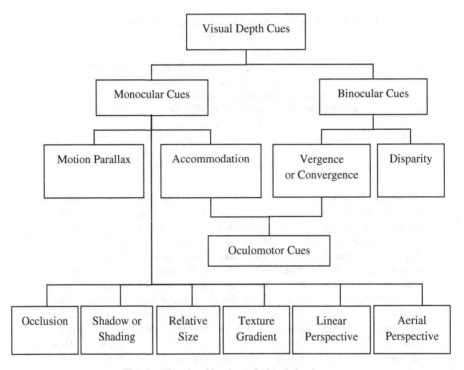

Fig. 1. The classification of visual depth cue

2   Literature Review

Although stereoscopic 3D displays were found to be useful for object manipulation tasks and for finding, identifying, classifying objects or imagery (McIntire et al. 2014), several content factors of stereoscopic 3D video could cause visual discomfort (Kim et al. 2013). For instance, large disparity and large amount of motion are two main causes of visual discomfort while watching stereoscopic 3D videos (Li et al. 2014). In addition, the in-depth motion generally induces more visual discomfort than the planar motion (Li et al. 2014). To reduce the visual fatigue in viewing rotational motions, it was suggested that a control of S3D exposure was required to enhance spatial recognition and reduce visual discomfort (Matsuura 2013). For highly interactive systems, the interaction-induced symptoms could happen due to virtual grasping and manipulation for object transport and 3D selection (Kim and Park 2014). While comparing the situations of cinema viewing versus video game playing using S3D TV, some research reported that video games present a strong conflict between vergence and accommodative demand. Therefore, people enjoyed cinema more than video games (Read 2014). However, other research reported that for game playing and film viewing, system-task combinations could cause mild eyestrain and small changes in visual functions. Using a stereoscopic 3D system for up to 2 h was acceptable for most users, including children and adults (Pölönen et al. 2013). For film viewing, age was negatively correlated with the symptom levels (Obrist et al. 2013). To resolve the issues of visual discomfort caused by interactive manipulations of S3D contents and increase the usability of such systems, in-depth studies and exhaustive experiments are necessary.

3　Learning Materials and the Stereoscopic 3D System

3.1　Learning Materials and Digital Contents

Understanding the features of masterpieces in design history and analyzing products from ergonomic aspects are the basic training in product design education. Among different categories of products, furniture is a representative product in daily life. Therefore, using furniture as a training example is widely adopted in the classroom. In the experimental S3D system, the digital contents consisted of 3D virtual models of chairs, tables, and sofa, some were classic design masterpieces. These models were allocated in a virtual room for investigation (Fig. 2).

3.2　The Stereoscopic 3D System for Experiment

In order to create an S3D system for experiment, Visual C ++ 2013 and Direct3D 11.1 was employed as the development tools. The authors modified and integrated the Direct3D stereoscopic 3D sample and Visual Studio 3D Starter Kit to construct a platform for importing 3D models in FBX format and displaying these models in either S3D or regular 3D mode. The program was running on the Windows 8 operation system installed in an Acer desktop computer with a GT640 graphic card. The images, with 1920 × 1080 pixels, were projected by a BenQ W1070 + projector on a 100-inch screen, and viewed by the shutter glasses, which were synchronized with the displays (Fig. 3). The left-eye and right-eye images were sequentially displayed at a frequency of 120 Hz. Therefore, the refresh rate of the display was 60 Hz for each eye. In addition, the experiment system allowed users to adjust the effect of disparity (from 0 to 2, with initial value set to 1.0), by pressing the up/down arrow keys. To offer minimal interactivity, the users could change the mode or the direction of model rotation (Fig. 4). At the beginning of program execution, the 3D models rotated in 1.0 rpm with respect to the vertical axis. The user could use the left button on the computer mouse to stop or regain rotation. In addition, the left and right arrow keys were used to control the clockwise or counter clockwise rotation, respectively. The "W" and "S" keys were used to control the zoom-in and zoom-out effects of the camera, respectively.

Fig. 2. Stereoscopic 3D displays and digital contents with different degrees of disparity

4   Design of Experiments

4.1   Participants

Thirty students, 17 female and 13 male, were invited to participate in the experiment. They were senior students in college or graduate students enrolled in the master program, all majored in industrial or media design. In previous education background, they took courses relevant to the subjects of design history, human factors, and user interface design. The average age was 23.1, with standard deviation 3.0. All had normal or

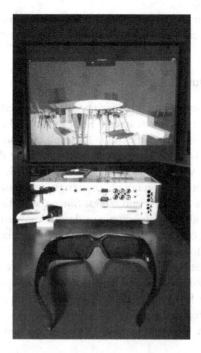

Fig. 3. The 3D projector and the shutter glasses for experiments

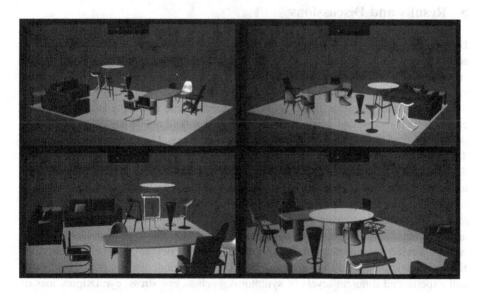

Fig. 4. Sample screen shots taken from different viewing angles and distances

corrected-to-normal vision and none reported stereopsis problems in prior experiences. They all had the experiences of using 3D modeling systems and playing 3D video games.

4.2 Tasks and Procedures

In a laboratory with illumination control, each participant seated in front of a desk, with four meters away from the projection screen. Prior to the S3D experiment, participants adjusted the disparity parameter to the value they felt comfortable for continuing the major tasks. The first task in the experiment was to identify the differences between printed pictures and 3D virtual models for seven classic design masterpieces. The second task was to point out ergonomic or design problems in a single piece of furniture or different pairs of chairs and tables. Since the participants needed to make the judgment based on both their ergonomic or design knowledge and the information from depth cues, the second task was more difficult than the first one. In order to perform these tasks and locate furniture design features or problems, the participants needed to control the rotation and zoom-in/zoon-out of the scene. During the experiments, they were allowed to re-adjust the disparity value whenever necessary to maintain the comfortable level. After completing the tasks, participants indicated the degree of overall discomfort and the discomfort caused by rotation or zooming using a 9-point Likert scale, with 1 indicating slightly discomfort and 9 indicating extremely discomfort, respectively.

5 Results and Discussions

Before conducting S3D experiment tasks, the participants took 127 s on average to adjust the disparity parameters (Table 1). The average disparity value was 0.72, with standard deviation 0.44. Among 30 participants, 4 participants re-adjusted the disparity value during the experiments. This indicated that the initial value (1.0) was still higher than the one they could accept. Participants needed time to be prepared for experiencing S3D contents, and the individual differences should not be neglected. As for the performance of tasks, the average task complete time was 1437 s (standard deviation: 482). In the task of locating differences between printed pictures and 3D virtual models, 5.33 features, on average, were correctly identified out of seven classic design masterpieces. In the task of pointing out ergonomic or design problems in a single piece of furniture or different pairs of chairs and tables, only 2.23 features were reported correctly. The discomfort levels were 2.17, 1.90, and 1.40, for overall, rotation operation, and zoom-in/zoom-out operation, respectively. Based on the regression analysis, discomfort caused by model rotation did contribute to the degree of overall discomfort. Even all participants had the background of using 3D modeling systems, 26 of them still experienced different levels of symptoms, such as eye stress, eye fatigue, loss of focus, or dizziness. The comments of participants included the requirements of adjusting the control response ratio of interactive manipulations.

Table 1. Measurements of experiments

Measurements	Mean	Standard deviation
Time		
Disparity parameter adjustment time	126	97
Task completion time	1437	482
Disparity parameter value	0.72	0.44
Degree of visual discomfort		
Overall	2.17	1.88
Due to Rotation operation	1.90	1.90
Due to Zoom-in or Zoom-out operation	1.40	1.48
Task performance		
Number of differences identified	5.33	2.72
Number of design problems identified	2.23	0.82

6   Conclusions and Recommendations for Further Work

Given the minimal interactions of S3D contents, such as rotating and changing the position of camera, visual discomfort was still reported by a group of participants who were familiar with 3D modeling systems and 3D video games. The comments indicated that adaptive adjustments of disparity and control response ratio were necessary to accommodate individual differences and enhance the usability of interactive and stereoscopic 3D systems. In this research, identifying image differences and locating ergonomic or design problems were the tasks performed by the participants. More active tasks, such as modifying the shape or the proportion of a S3D product model to fulfill the requirements for aesthetic or functional purposes, could be considered in future research works.

Acknowledgement. The authors would like to express our gratitude to the Ministry of Science and Technology of the Republic of China for financially supporting this research under Grant No. MOST 103-2221-E-036-019.

References

Guedes, K.B., Guimarães, M., Méxas, J.G.: Virtual reality using stereoscopic vision for teaching/learning of descriptive geometry. In: eLmL 2012: The Fourth International Conference on Mobile, Hybrid, and On-line Learning, pp. 24–30 (2012)

Howard, I.P.: Interactions between visual depth cues. In: Perceiving in Depth: Volume 3 Other Mechanisms of Depth Perception, Published to Oxford Scholarship Online (2012)

Kim, D.W., Yoo, J.S., Seo, Y.H.: Qualitative analysis of individual and composite content factors of stereoscopic 3D video causing visual discomfort. Displays **34**, 223–240 (2013)

Kim, Y., Park, J.: Study on interaction-induced symptoms with respect to virtual grasping and manipulation. Int. J. Hum. Comput. Stud. **72**, 141–153 (2014)

Li, J., Barkowsky, M., Le Callet, P.: Visual discomfort of stereoscopic 3D videos: Influence of 3D motion. Displays **35**, 49–57 (2014)

Matsuura, S.: Effective usage of stereoscopic visualization for the learning of a motional mechanism. In: Stephanidis, C., Antona, M. (eds.) UAHCI 2013, Part III. LNCS, vol. 8011, pp. 187–194. Springer, Heidelberg (2013)

McIntire, J.P., Havig, P.R., Geiselman, E.E.: Stereoscopic 3D displays and human performance: a comprehensive review. Displays **35**, 18–26 (2014)

Mikkola, M., Jumisko-Pyykko, S., Strohmeier, D., Boev, A., Gotchev, A.: Stereoscopic depth cues outperform monocular ones on autostereoscopic display. IEEE J. Sel. Top. Sig. Proc. **6**(6), 698–709 (2012)

Mukai, A., Yamagishi, Y., Hirayama, M.J., Tsuruoka, T., Yamamoto, T.: Effects of stereoscopic 3D contents on the process of learning to build a handmade PC. Knowl. Manage. E-Learning: Int. J. **3**(3), 491–505 (2011)

Obrist, M., Wurhofer, D., Meneweger, T., Grill, T., Tscheligi, M.: Viewing experience of 3DTV: an exploration of the feeling of sickness and presence in a shopping mall. Entertainment Comput. **4**, 71–81 (2013)

Pölönen, M., Järvenpää, T., Bilcu, B.: Stereoscopic 3D entertainment and its effect on viewing comfort: comparison of children and adults. Appl. Ergon. **44**, 151–160 (2013)

Read, J.C.A.: Viewer experience with stereoscopic 3D television in the home. Displays **35**, 252–260 (2014)

Enhancing Blended Environments Through Fuzzy Cognitive Mapping of LMS Users' Quality of Interaction: The Rare and Contemporary Dance Paradigms

Sofia B. Dias[1(✉)], Sofia J. Hadjileontiadou[2], José Alves Diniz[1], and Leontios J. Hadjileontiadis[3]

[1] Faculdade de Motricidade Humana, Universidade de Lisboa, 1499-002 Cruz Quebrada, Lisbon, Portugal
{sbalula,jadiniz}@fmh.ulisboa.pt
[2] Hellenic Open University, Praxitelous 23, 10562 Athens, Greece
shadjileontiadou@gmail.com
[3] Department of Electrical and Computer Engineering, Aristotle University of Thessaloniki, 54124 Thessaloniki, Greece
leontios@auth.gr

Abstract. Nowadays, higher education institutions (HEIs) are facing the need of constant monitoring of users' interaction with Learning Management Systems (LMSs), in order to identify key areas for potential improvement. In fact, LMSs under blended (b-) learning mode can efficiently support online learning environments (OLEs) at HEIs. An important challenge would be to provide flexible solutions, where intelligent models could contribute, involving artificial intelligence and incertitude modelling, e.g., via Fuzzy Logic (FL). This study addresses the hypothesis that the structural characteristics of a Fuzzy Cognitive Map (FCM) can efficiently model the way LMS users interact with it, by estimating their Quality of Interaction (QoI) within a b-learning context. This work proposes the FCM-QoI model, consisting of 14 input-one output concepts, dependences and trends, considering one academic year of two dance disciplines (i.e., the Rare and Contemporary Dances) of the LMS Moodle use. The experimental results reveal that the proposed FCM-QoI model can provide concepts interconnection and causal dependencies representation of Moodle LMS users' QoI, helping educators of HEIs to holistically visualize, understand and assess stakeholders' needs. In general, the results presented here could shed light upon designing aspects of educational scenarios, but also to those involved in cultural preservation and exploitation initiatives, such as the i-Treasures project (http://i-treasures.eu/).

Keywords: Blended learning scenarios · Moodle learning management system · Fuzzy Cognitive Maps (FCMs) · Quality of Interaction (QoI) · Rare and contemporary dance · i-Treasures

© Springer International Publishing Switzerland 2015
M. Antona and C. Stephanidis (Eds.): UAHCI 2015, Part III, LNCS 9177, pp. 31–42, 2015.
DOI: 10.1007/978-3-319-20684-4_4

1 Introduction

Human-Computer Interaction is a multidisciplinary field focused on human aspects of the development of computer technology, which combines the theories and practices from different disciplines (e.g., computer science, cognitive and behavioral psychology, ergonomics). In particular, computer-learning technologies, such as Learning Management Systems (LMSs), within an Online Learning Environment (OLE), can provide educators an environment to place their online course materials and for students to receive that education while interacting with other students/teachers; however, students' interactions, attention and communications are seen as relatively low in the LMSs [1].

Nevertheless, it seems fair to say that higher education institutions (HEIs) are facing the need of constant monitoring of users' interaction with LMS, in order to identify key areas for potential improvement. This could be expressed in terms of quality of interaction (QoI) through the LMS use within a blended (b-) learning environment [2–6]. The fundamental challenge would be to provide flexible solutions, where intelligent models could contribute, involving artificial intelligence and incertitude modelling, e.g., via Fuzzy Logic (FL) [7, 8]. In this line, a novel approach within the field of FL is proposed here, exploring the potentiality of the Fuzzy Cognitive Map (FCM) [9], in order to be used as a structural element of a new modelling scheme, namely FCM-QoI.

The proposed FCM-QoI model was drawn from a real-life LMS Moodle use case of a public Higher Education Institution (HEI), for effectively estimating the LMS users' QoI within a b-learning context. It involves a FCM with 14 input-one output concepts, dependences and trends considering the time period of the 51 weeks of the LMS use (one academic year), from two academic teaching of dance disciplines, including *rare* and *contemporary dances*, respectively. The latter are used as paradigms that comply with the educational scenarios of the i-Treasures project (www.i-treasures.eu), which is situated in the area of Intangible Cultural Heritage (ICH) education and it is aimed to: develop an open and extendable platform to provide access to ICH resources; enable knowledge exchange between researchers; and contribute to the transmission of rare know-how from Living Human Treasures to apprentices.

Two training/testing scenarios were explored, i.e., time-in/dependent, using pre-validated QoI data. Seen as a holistic and dynamic model, the FCM-QoI approach has the potential to explore possibilities and scenarios from different perspectives; for instance, pedagogical planners and decision makers can (re)adjust online tools, towards maximum use of the LMS Moodle within the teaching/learning practices.

The experimental results have shown that the proposed FCM-QoI model can provide concepts interconnection and causal dependencies representation of LMS users' interaction behaviour, contributing to the analysis and modelling of different ICHs (e.g., in the field of dance), thus, supporting learning of the rare know-how behind these cultural expressions and their passing down to new generations.

2 Methodology

2.1 The Fuzzy Cognitive Map (FCM) Concept

Originated from the theories of FL, neural networks, soft computing and computational intelligence techniques, FCMs can be understood as a modelling methodology based on exploiting knowledge and experience. In general, FCMs belong to the granular computing field, which refers to the conceptualization/processing of information granules (i.e., concepts). Based on binary values, Kosko [9] suggested the use of fuzzy causal functions considering numbers within [-1, 1], modifying, in this way, the Axelrod's cognitive maps perspective and introducing the FCM concept. In addition, a relevant update of cognitive maps combined with FL was examined by Kosko [10]. Basically, FCMs express causality over time and are intended to model causality, not merely semantic relationships between concepts, facilitating the exploration of the implications of complex conceptual models, with greater flexibility [11]. FCM is a qualitative modelling tool and can describe any system using a model with three main features, more specifically [11]:

- the signed causality, indicating positive/negative relationship;
- the strengths of the causal relationships, taking fuzzy values; and
- the dynamic causal links, where the effect of a change in one node influences other nodes (i.e., a feedback mechanism that captures the dynamic relationship of all the nodes).

Seen as a dynamic modelling technique, FCMs have gained considerable research interest in multiple scientific areas from knowledge modelling to decision making (e.g., [12, 13]). At the same time, FCMs have been studied resorting to data mining techniques for promoting user's expert knowledge ([14, 15]). In general, FCM is considered an efficient inference engine to easily model complex causal relationships in a qualitatively and quantitatively way, and to express the dynamic behavior of a set of related concepts.

2.2 The Proposed *FCM-QoI* Model

A schematic representation of the proposed FCM-based modeling approach, namely FCM-QoI model, is depicted in Fig. 1. From the Fig. 1(a), it is clear that the user interacts with the LMS Moodle and 110 metrics are acquired, exactly the same as the ones used in the FuzzyQoI model ([7] -Table 1). These metrics are then categorized into 14 categories, denoted as C1,C2,...,C14, corresponding to the 14 categories used in the FuzzyQoI model [7], i.e., C1: {Journal/Wiki/Blog/Form (J/W/B/F)}, C2: {Forum/Discussion/Chat (F/D/C)}, C3: {Submission/Report/Quiz/Feedback (S/R/Q/F)}, C4: {Course Page (CP)}, C5: {Module (M)}, C6: {Post/Activity (P/A)}, C7: {Resource/Assignment (R/A)}, C8: {Label (L)}, C9: {Upload (UP)}, C10: {Update (U)}, C11: {Assign (A)}, C12: {Edit/Delete (E/D)}, C13: {Time Period (TP)}, and C14: {Engagement Time (ET)}. These 14 concepts are considered the inputs of the FCM within the FCM-QoI model and the additional FCM-QoI concept is considered its output (see Fig. 1(b)).

The FuzzyQoI model (Fig. 1(a)) outputs the QoI^{FIS}, which is used in the training phase of the FCM within the FCM-QoI model (Fig. 1(b)). In the proposed FCM-QoI model, the Nonlinear Hebbian Rule (NHB)-based learning algorithm [16] is adopted. There, the $W : (Ci, Cj) \rightarrow w_{ij}$ is estimated, which is a function that associates a causal value $w_{ij} \in [-1, 1]$ to each pair of nodes of the connection matrix, denoting the weight of the directed edge from Ci to Cj, representing the causality degree between the interconnected concepts; hence, the weight matrix $W_{N \times N}$ gathers the system causality, usually determined by knowledge experts.

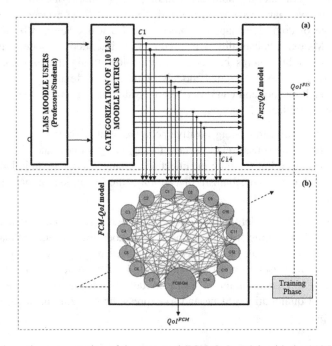

Fig. 1. A schematic representation of the proposed *FCM-QoI* model, with the 110 LMS Moodle user's interaction metrics, categorized into 14 input parameters (C1,...,C14) fed to: (a) the *FuzzyQoI* model [7] outputting the estimated QoI^{FIS} and (b) the *FCM-QoI* model as input concepts interconnected with the FCM-QoI as an output concept to estimate the QoI^{FCM}. Note that the estimated QoI^{FIS} is fed to the *FCM-QoI* model during the training phase only, to correctly adjust the interconnection weights of the latter towards the minimization of the error in the knowledge representation process.

During the iterative learning process ($k = 1, 2, \ldots, K$ maximum iterations), the weights $w_{ji}^{(k)}$, along with the corresponding concept labels $A_i^{(k+1)}$, are updated, towards the satisfaction of a convergence criterion [16]. When the latter is met, the FCM is considered trained and the updated weights (w_{ji}^{up}) are used in the testing phase of the FCM-QoI model, towards the final estimation of the QoI^{FCM} output of the FCM-QoI model.

As it is clear from the aforementioned description of the *FCM-QoI* model, the involved FCM plays the role of a system representation, dismantling the 14 inputs-1 output relations, as represented by the estimated W^{up} matrix. This actually reflects the expert's knowledge representation hidden in the IF/THEN fuzzy rules of the FuzzyQoI model, yet in a more quantitative way, i.e., in the form of the interconnection weight values. The efficiency of the proposed *FCM-QoI* model has been evaluated through its application to the same data used in the FuzzyQoI model [7], drawn from a real-life LMS Moodle use case from higher education, involving both professors and students, as thoroughly described in the succeeding section.

3 Validation of the FCM-QoI Model

3.1 Data Characteristics

The proposed FCM-QoI model was applied to LMS Moodle data from two dance disciplines, i.e., Rare and Contemporary Dances, drawn from the Faculdade de Motricidade Humana (FMH), Universidade de Lisboa (Portugal), where the corresponding dance disciplines are realized within the b-learning context. Rare Dances (RD) discipline belongs to the Social Dances at the FMH, aiming to provide and develop ways to dance, able to contribute to a students' education in a more complete, comprehensive and multifaceted way, through the diversity of approaches and multiplicity of perspectives developed in each dance form. Moreover, the social dimension and respect of the act of dance are taken into account to enhance the knowledge and extend the application domain with multicultural approaches, revealing the nature and specificity of their contents. The planning of this discipline aims to construct a place of experience and experimentation with different materials, choreographic and contextual, along with specific techniques for analysis, leading to "know-how" and the enlargement and consolidation of formal and expressive repertoire of the students. On the other hand, Contemporary Dances (CD) discipline is included in the Techniques of Theater Dances at the FMH, which aims to promote the analysis and study of motor vocabulary characteristic of modern and classical dance forms. The corresponding planning includes practice of standardized modeling steps organized in simple exercises with repetitions and chained in sequence dances increasing complexity. Moreover, training skills of observation in situations of mutual learning, are also considered, being consistent with the principles and quality of dance movements.

For each paradigm (RD and CD), the 110 LMS Moodle metrics data for one academic year (2009-2010) from Professors (P) (RD: 2; CD: 2) and Students (S) (RD: 29; CD: 43), were used and analyzed. In order to identify any possible changes in the users' interaction behavior correlated with a specific time-period section, a time-period segmentation was adopted. The latter has resulted in time-period sections (e.g., semesters (S1: 2-16, S2: 23-38 weeks), exam periods (1st: 18-23, 2nd: 38-46 weeks), interruptions (16-18, 24-25; 30-31 weeks)) that served as landmarks in 51-week total examined period.

3.2   Training/Testing Configuration

The whole dataset of the 14 input-1 output data from the FuzzyQoI model was randomly split into 75 % as a training dataset and 25 % as a testing dataset for the FCM-QoI model. Two training/testing scenarios were conducted, i.e., time-dependent and time-independent. In particular, in the time-dependent training scenario, the time unit of analysis of one week is taken into account, in order to obtain the best estimation of QoI^{FCM} per week. To this end, 50 randomized selections of the 75 % of the training set were considered and, for each random selection, the mean value across the users per input/output per week was estimated, setting, in this way, the initial concept values of the $A_i^{(1)}, i = 1, 2, \ldots, 15$, per week. The initial values of the W matrix $(w_{ji}^{(0)}, j \neq i$ per week were randomly selected from the range of $[-1, 1]$ (apparently $diagonal(W) = 0$). Consequently, the training process in the time-dependent scenario outputted a W^{up} *per week* ($W^{up,w}$). In the time-independent training scenario, the same process as in the case of the time-dependent scenario was followed, yet here, for each random selection of the 50 randomized selections of the 75 % of the training set, the mean value across the users per input/output and across the weeks was estimated. In this way, the training process in the time-independent scenario outputted a W^{up} per *academic year* ($W^{up,y}$). In the time-dependent and time-independent testing scenarios, the estimated $W^{up,w}$ and $W^{up,y}$ were used upon the initially selected testing set (25 % of the initial data) to infer the QoI^{FCM} per week and per academic year, respectively.

All above scenarios were applied to each RD and CD selected discipline. The evaluation of the performance of the FCM-QoI model was realized via the estimation of the Root Mean Squared Error (RMSE) between the estimated QoI^{FCM} and the QoI^{FIS} derived from the FuzzyQoI model [7].

3.3   Implementation Issues

The implementation of the whole analysis of the FCM-QoI model was carried out in Matlab 2014a (The Mathworks, Inc., Natick, USA), using custom-made programming code. The archived data in the LMS Moodle repository were exported from .xml to .xlsm (Microsoft Excel format) and imported to the Matlab environment and archived as .mat files. The values used for the updating process of the FCM were selected as the optimum ones that minimize the number of iterations for meeting the termination criteria ($K \leq 20000$).

4   Results and Discussion

4.1   Time-Dependent Scenario

Training Phase. The RMSE between the estimated QoI^{FCM} and the QoI^{FIS} across 50 iterations during the time-dependent training phase of the FCM-QoI model for the P and S cases and for the RD and CD disciplines are depicted in Fig. 2, with the corresponding horizontal lines denoting the mean RMSE, accordingly. Clearly, the low mean RMSE values and limited RMSE range across the 50 repetitions denote an efficient performance and consistency in the behavior of the FCM-QoI model during the time-dependent training phase.

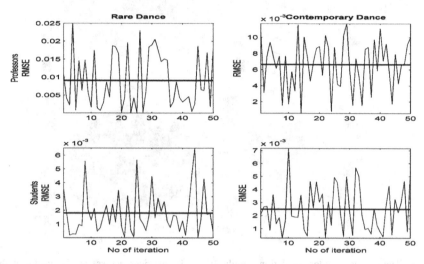

Fig. 2. The RMSE between the estimated QoI^{FCM} and the QoI^{FIS} across 50 iterations during the time-dependent training phase of the FCM-QoI model for the P (1st row) and S (2nd row) cases and for the RD (1st column) and CD (2nd column) disciplines (horizontal lines denote the mean RMSE).

The estimated $W^{up,w}$ matrices (corresponding to the minimum RMSE values of Fig. 2), for P/S and RD/CD are illustrated in Fig. 3. Due to the difference in the LMS interaction across the examined cases, some $W^{up,w}$ matrices show a degree of sparseness across the weeks-axis. Moreover, it seems that the CD discipline exhibits more negative than positive weight values (both in P and S cases), whereas the RD one shows mainly positive ones (both in P and S cases).

Testing Phase. Figure 4 illustrates the results from the testing phase of the time-dependent scenario of the FCM-QoI model, based on the $W^{up,w}$ 4D-matrices depicted in Fig. 3, displaying, in a superimposed, the estimated QoI^{FCM} (dashed thick line) and the corresponding QoI^{FIS} (solid thin line), estimated from the FuzzyQoI model [7]. From Fig. 4 it is clear that the estimated QoI^{FCM} efficiently captures the morphology of the QoI^{FIS}, showing an efficient generalization of the FCM-QoI model in predicting the QoI after a training procedure based on historical data.

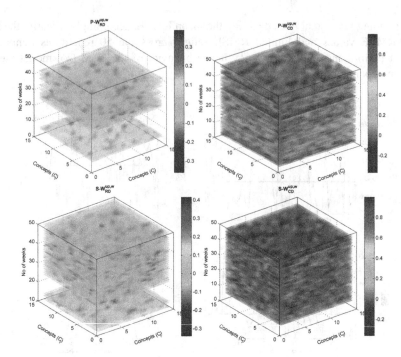

Fig. 3. The estimated interconnection weight $W^{up,w}$ 4D-matrices across the 51 weeks of the academic year between the 15 Ci concepts (14 input concepts and QoI^{FCM} as the output concept) of the time-dependent training phase of the *FCM-QoI* model, which correspond to the iterations of Fig. 2 that exhibit the minimum RMSE, accordingly. P (1st row) and S (2nd row) denote cases; RD (1st column) and CD (2nd column) denote disciplines.

4.2   Time-Independent Scenario

Training Phase. The RMSE between the estimated QoI^{FCM} and the QoI^{FIS} across 50 iterations during the time-independent training phase of the FCM-QoI model for the P/S cases and RD/CD disciplines are depicted in Fig. 5, with the corresponding horizontal lines denoting the mean RMSE, accordingly. Similarly to Fig. 2, low mean RMSE values (yet slightly higher than those of Fig. 2) and limited RMSE range across the 50 repetitions are derived, showing satisfactory training of the FCM-QoI model, based on the data across the whole academic year. Figure 6 presents the estimated FCMs with the interconnection weights $W^{up,y}$, which correspond to the iterations that exhibit the minimum RMSE in Fig. 5, between the 15 concepts (14 input concepts and QoI^{FCM} as the output concept) of the time-independent training phase of the FCM-QoI model, for the P/S cases and RD/CD disciplines, respectively. From Fig. 6, the interdependencies and causalities amongst the concepts can be identified.

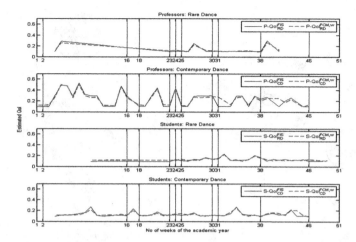

Fig. 4. The estimated QoI^{FCM} values (dashed thick line) during the testing phase of the time-dependent scenario, along with the corresponding QoI^{FIS} (solid thin line) derived from the FuzzyQoI model [7], for P/S cases and RD/CD disciplines. The vertical lines illustrate the time-period segmentation of Sect. 3.1.

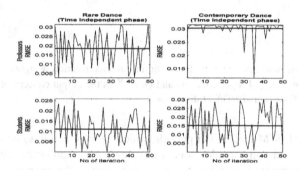

Fig. 5. The RMSE between the estimated QoI^{FCM} and the QoI^{FIS} across 50 iterations during the time-independent training phase of the FCM-QoI model for the P (1st row) and S (2nd row) cases and for the RD (1st column) and CD (2nd column) disciplines (horizontal lines denote the mean RMSE).

Testing Phase. Figure 7 illustrates the results from the testing phase of the time-independent scenario of the FCM-QoI model, based on the $W^{up,y}$ (not shown here), displaying, in a superimposed way, the estimated QoI^{FCM} (thick line) and the corresponding QoI^{FIS} (thin line), estimated from the FuzzyQoI model [7]. From Fig. 6 it is clear that, like in Fig. 4, the estimated QoI^{FCM} efficiently captures, in most cases, the morphology of the QoI^{FIS}, showing again satisfactory generalization of the FCM-QoI model in predicting the QoI, even after a training procedure based on historical data averaged across the whole academic year.

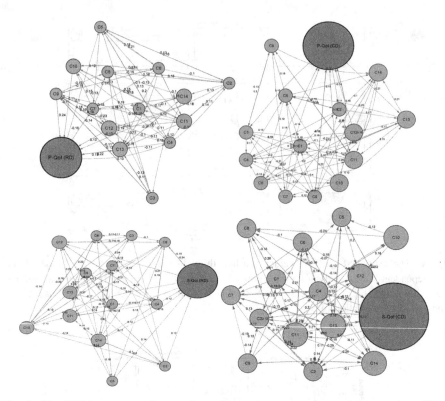

Fig. 6. The FCMs corresponding to the optimum interconnection weights matrices $W^{up,y}$ between the 15 concepts [14 input concepts and QoI^{FCM} as the output concept of the FCM-QoI model], for the P/S cases and RD/CD disciplines.

The described FCM-QoI model provides valuable information to both educational decision-makers and software developers towards more appropriate software development efforts, assisting to more effective management of the main activities that are essential towards optimization of the OLEs functionality. The FCM-QoI model allows dynamic monitoring of LMS users' QoI across the academic year; hence, contributing to the perspective of OLEs from a dynamic rather static view, taking into account the alterations in the QoI of the LMS users (both P and S) with time. Finally, the findings here support distinct perspectives between RD and CD disciplines, as reflected into the realization of the online component of the b-learning context. The latter could be very useful for effective designing of educational scenarios within the concept of sustaining the cultural heritage, such as teaching rare dances to young generations (New Millennium Learners) and build upon tradition to create a contemporary output, as in the case of the i-Treasures project (http://i-treasures.eu/). There, the RD and CD use-cases are realized via a LMS-based OLE platform, which supports sensorimotor learning, incorporating cutting-edge technology and pedagogical planning according to the experts; hence, combined with the FCM-QoI model output, more enhanced feedback could be provided to the users.

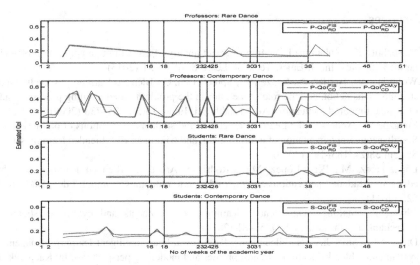

Fig. 7. The estimated QoI^{FCM} values (thick line) during the testing phase of the time-independent scenario, along with the corresponding QoI^{FIS} (thin line) derived from the FuzzyQoI model [7], for P/S cases and RD/CD disciplines. The vertical lines illustrate the time-period segmentation of Sect. 3.1.

5 Conclusion

A FCM-based estimation of the QoI of both professors and students, when interacting with the LMS Moodle within a b-learning context (RD/CD disciplines), has been presented here. The FCM-QoI model provided an easy way to represent LMS Moodle academic community understanding, in a form of scaled up mental modeling, as a kind of internal representation of external reality. The FCM-QoI model was validated on real data, proving its potentiality to represent the LMS users' attitude in terms of their QoI. This could facilitate the dynamic design of educational scenarios and strategies in many disciplines/courses/fields (e.g., engineering, social sciences) within advanced OLEs, such as the one of the i-Treasures.

Acknowledgements. This work has received funding from the EU FP7-ICT-2011-9-ICT-2011.8.2, grant agreement N°600676: 'i-Treasures' Project (www.i-treasures.eu). Dr. Dias acknowledges the financial support by the Foundation for Science and Technology (FCT, Portugal) (Postdoctoral Grant SFRH/BPD/496004/20) and the Interdisciplinary Centre for the Study of Human Performance (CIPER, Portugal).

References

1. Musbahtiti, K., Muhammad, A.: Improvement quality of LMS through application of social networking sites. Int. J. Emer. Technol. Learn **8**(3), 48–51 (2013)
2. Woltering, V., Herrler, A., Spitzer, K., Spreckelsen, C.: Blended learning positively affects students' satisfaction and the role of the tutor in the problem-based learning process: results of a mixed-method evaluation. Adv. Health Sci. Educ. **14**(5), 725–738 (2009)
3. Miyazoe, T., Anderson, T.: Learning outcomes and students' perceptions of online writing: Simultaneous implementation of a forum, blog, and wiki in an EFL blended learning setting. System **38**(2), 185–199 (2010)
4. López-Pérez, M., Pérez-López, M.C., Rodríguez-Ariza, L.: Blended learning in higher education: students' perceptions and their relation to outcomes. Comput. Educ. **56**(3), 818–826 (2011)
5. Oliver, K., Stallings, D.: Blended learning: core concepts and evaluation strategies. J. Technol. Teach. Educ. **22**(1), 57–81 (2014)
6. Dias, S.B., Diniz, J.A., Hadjileontiadis, L.J.: Towards an intelligent learning management system under blended learning: trends, profiles and modelling perspectives. In: Kacprzyk, J., Jain, L.C. (eds.) Intelligent Systems Reference Library, vol. 59. Springer-Verlag, Heidelberg (2014). ISBN: 978-3-319-02077-8
7. Dias, S.B., Diniz, J.A.: FuzzyQoI model: a fuzzy logic-based modelling of users' quality of interaction with a learning management system under blended learning. Comput. Educ. **69**, 38–59 (2013)
8. Dias, S.B.: Towards an Intelligent Online Learning Environment: A Systemic Approach. LAP Lambert Academic Publishing, Saarbrucken (2014)
9. Kosko, B.: Fuzzy cognitive maps. Int. J. Man Mach. Stud. **24**(1), 65–75 (1986)
10. Kosko, B.: Fuzzy associative memory systems. In: Kandel, A. (ed.) Fuzzy Expert Systems (135-162). CRC Press, Boca Raton (1992)
11. Papageorgiou, E.I., Stylios, C.D.: Fuzzy cognitive maps. In: Pedrycz, W., Skowron, A., Kreinovich, V. (eds.) Handbook of Granular Computing, pp. 755–774. John Wiley & Son Ltd, Chichester (2008)
12. Lee, S., Yang, J., Han, J.: Development of a decision making system for selection of dental implant abutments based on the fuzzy cognitive map. Expert Syst. Appl. **39**(14), 11564–11575 (2012)
13. Groumpos, P.P., Karagiannis, I.E.: Mathematical modelling of decision making support systems using fuzzy cognitive maps. In: Glykas, M. (ed.) Business Process Management. SCI, vol. 444, pp. 299–337. Springer, Heidelberg (2013)
14. Hong, T., Han, I.: Knowledge-based data mining of news information on the Internet using cognitive maps and neural networks. Expert Syst. Appl. **23**(1), 1–8 (2002)
15. Kotsiantis, S.B.: Use of machine learning techniques for educational proposes: a decision support system for forecasting students' grades. Artif. Intell. Rev. **37**(4), 331–344 (2012)
16. Papageorgiou, E., Stylios, C., Groumpos, P.: Fuzzy cognitive map learning based on nonlinear hebbian rule. In: Gedeon, T.D., Fung, L.C.C. (eds.) AI 2003. LNCS (LNAI), vol. 2903, pp. 256–268. Springer, Heidelberg (2003)

Once Upon a Tablet: A School Toy in the Making

Isabel Cristina G. Fróes[✉]

IT University of Denmark, Copenhagen, Denmark
icgf@itu.dk

Abstract. The current paper introduces the definitions of *playful literacy* and *multimodal hyper-intertextuality*, key concepts when researching children's use of digital tablets. The pilot investigation, which took place in spring 2014 in Denmark, is part of a larger cross-cultural comparative project exploring what emergent behaviors are present when preschool children use and play with tablets in their formal learning environments. In order to map the array of play and usage of such devices for this research, after the first round of observations, the tablet taxonomy was outlined and has been applied as a guide for the subsequent rounds of data collection. The proposed definitions are a valuable contribution to the field of multisensory interfaces, due to their pervasiveness on digital mobile platforms.

Keywords: Tablet · Play · Interaction design · Intertextuality · Literacy · Education

1 Introduction

Children are curious and natural explorers of their environment. They replay their routines and fantasize about their daily universes while playing with friends or with their toys. They become parents, children, pets and superheroes intertwined in stories and games aided by various toys or just plain imagination. The ubiquity of digital devices in the social sphere creates an environment where technology becomes a natural commodity in daily routines. In this context, children are no longer only observant of digital technologies, but they are players and users, with tablets becoming the digital toy of choice. In the case of Denmark, tablets and smartphones are present in over 75 % of all Danish homes [1].

The use of tablets and smartphones devices is enhanced by the growth of the application (app) market. As tablets joined the home environment, they were shared among all family members, including children. This shared feature propitiates specific customizations in ways that allow smooth use by their assorted clientele [2]. Tablets either joined other digital devices in the home environment, or became the primary digital tool. With the proliferation of these portable devices, daily activities, such as surfing the Internet, reading newspapers and magazines, listening to music, as well as playing games, have migrated from computers to tablets with little effort [3].

In order to map how 4-7 year old children in distinct cultures use and discover tablets' capabilities, this PhD research, which started in spring 2014, focuses on observing

© Springer International Publishing Switzerland 2015
M. Antona and C. Stephanidis (Eds.): UAHCI 2015, Part III, LNCS 9177, pp. 43–53, 2015.
DOI: 10.1007/978-3-319-20684-4_5

preschoolers' uses of these devices in three countries; Denmark, Japan and Brazil. Tablets, as the latest toy in the playground, raise a number of questions when studying children's digital knowledge: What is learned during tablet interactions? What kinds of skills are being developed with tablet play? How does the target group, which is still non-alphabetized, navigate digital literate interfaces? Does the concept of digital literacy cover preschoolers' tablet play? How can tablets promote social interaction? Which modes of interaction are present during tablet play?

More specifically, preschoolers' playful experimentation with tablet devices provides valuable information on future uses of technologies in educational institutions and how such technologies can be explored as learning aid tools. In order to complement learning and digital interactions fields of study, definitions of digital literacy are being revisited together with related theories, which help inform and define the current scenario of digital learning and digital play. Additionally, this research challenges notions of digital literacy by confronting how children's use of tablets is affording or complementing modes of learning, suggesting a definition of *playful literacy*. Supplementing *playful literacy*, the tablet taxonomy, which has emerged from the pilot study findings, has been defined and presents key topics towards upcoming researches that focus on children's interactions with tablets. Among the subtopics that emerged from the tablet taxonomy, the concept of *multimodal hyper-intertextuality* proves itself of relevance and it should serve as a valuable contribution to studies in the field of multi-sensory interfaces.

1.1 Digital Play

Digital play, on consoles and portable devices, has been an integral part of childhood for the past twenty years, through a combination of three key elements: technology, culture and marketing [4]. The playful trait of portable devices currently witnessed in society, with games amounting to 50 % or more of tablet use [5], is also of high significance. Following a trend of touch screen mobile devices initiated in 2007 with the success of smartphones, digital tablets have grown in popularity and slowly become the device of choice for both work and play [6]. There are several available apps with various purposes such as games, education, reading, etc. As of February 2015 [7] there were more than 80,000 educational apps available for the iPad, and they target both educational institutions and families. Notwithstanding that these apps do not necessarily target pre-school children, it is still of relevance to acknowledge these numbers in order to better assess how digital learning became highly connected to tablet devices as the educational tools of choice within a five-year timeframe.

From a tangible perspective, due to their lightweight and size, tablets are more portable than laptops, so they are easier to store and transport. Tablets and apps, which are also cheaper than computer and software packages, have become an attractive option for institutions. Another perspective relates to access of knowledge. As the Internet has grown to be a reliable information resource, its use in schools has become more prevalent, with students using an assortment of online software and search engines as learning tools. Following this Internet role in society and schools, it is pertinent to say that tablets entered the consumers' market when a large infrastructure was already in place to make them a desirable and useful device. It is therefore hardly surprising that schools world-wide are adopting them as educational tools [8]. In Denmark, following local ICT initiatives, tablets (primarily iPads) have been chosen to complement educational materials in the Danish school system [9]. Therefore studying what preschool children know and how they interact with tablet devices is key to informing and challenging future development of similar digital tools in educational institutions. During the pilot study, nineteen children were observed, with seventeen of the observations taking place at the partnering institution, a Danish kindergarten that is in the process of acquiring tablets, and plans to use them as one of the kindergarten's activities in the near future.

1.2 Child-Friendly Interface

A unique characteristic of tablets' shared access lies in its interface. Despite tablet app icons' static behavior [2], the fact that there are no 'important files floating on the screen' facilitates its sharing capabilities. The primary interface contains only apps, which according to the pilot study's results, tend to be recognized by the intended users. Users are less concerned about undesired file deletion or other similar problems. Besides this, as they are touch-sensitive devices, the need for a "mouse" is eliminated, giving tablets the advantage of easy and faster setup and use in both formal and informal settings (on tables, as well as on couches).

As young children swipe their little fingers across screens and figures, they appropriate tablet devices to their own needs by playing and exploring icons and images beyond their intended design parameters. One example is taking screenshots of the main screen and using them in a 'paint like' application, or just playing with the placement of app icons as if in a type of game involving 'arranging' toys. Although preschoolers (and even younger children) mostly choose children's apps, they are able to engage with a large variety of apps, even ones that have been developed for literate users, such as YouTube and Google search. Initial pilot observations have shown that these children, who are not yet schooled, take on the challenge of copying alphabet symbols from their favorite toys into search form fields in order to engage with videos, images and games featuring that same character. They are not intimidated by apps that require the use of letters, words or numbers in their game play. They also tend to skip any written or oral information in a game and discover or create the rules and goals of the game themselves by virtue of trial and error. In an almost decoding process, the observed children were quick and keen to learn, even though they were not familiar with many of the apps in the specific tablets used for the research.

During the observations, children were not interested in apps that did not seem like children's apps. This is of relevance as it informs about children's semiotic awareness in relation to digital interfaces. How do children classify and identify digital icons? What motivates a choice of one app rather than another? This semiotic trait is one of the skills being afforded by children's exposure to digital devices, it shapes children's expectations towards upcoming interactions and interfaces in the digital realm, thus it composes one of the categories identified in the tablet taxonomy.

2 *Toyblet* Taxonomy

The tablet taxonomy [10] definition was based on the first round of observations and it is briefly described below.[1] The taxonomy topics are divided into five categories: *vocabulary*, *design*, *play*, *interaction* and *emotion*, each covering three or more related subcategories. For example, the topics of *vocabulary*, *design* and *play* deal with learning sides of tablet play, including symbolic meanings and cultural expectations; *interaction* and *emotion* provide information about skills being developed and social qualities observed when talking about or playing on tablets.

The taxonomy topics are grounded on the pilot study findings and address some initial research questions: (a) What is learned during tablet interactions? (b) What kinds of skills are being developed with tablet play? (c) How does the target group, which is still non-alphabetized, navigate digital literate interfaces? (d) Does the concept of digital literacy cover preschoolers' tablet play? (e) How can tablets promote social interaction? Besides addressing these questions, the taxonomy expands them further into broader arenas.

The taxonomy topics are:

Vocabulary. Deals with themes of how adult mediation shapes and affects children's perceptions of their activities on tablet devices. The topic also deals with a lack of words that specifically define characteristics of the interface and types of activities, e.g. do we swipe to another 'screen', 'region' or 'app selection'? Apps are called games, even though they might be a read-aloud book app, or a full platform containing a wide range of activities, such as puzzles, sing-along or drawing.

Design. Relates to both graphical and interaction design features, such as tablet semiotics and how apps are designed. E.g. how children decode apps' symbolic meanings (what is available to use, what is 'locked', how they distinguish 'children's apps' from other apps, etc.); it also relates to what types of information app icons communicate during a first and subsequent encounters.

Play. Concerns the modalities of play taking place when using tablets. Both the modes of play afforded by a wide range of applications (solve a puzzle, listen to a story, draw or pop symbols, dress-up dolls, etc.), as well as ways in which children create and defy these modes through playing (not necessarily following the suggested solution, just playing for fun without following the app design). This category also deals with how digital play is intertwined with a broader culture outside tablets, which involves television programs, movies, toys, clothing, language references, etc. For example, users can choose an app based on a TV program, a brand or a movie, and choose clothing with app character icons. Together, this vast universe of play modes combined with the interlinked knowledge from distinct sources, define the subtopic of *multimodal hyper-intertextuality* that will be described in more depth in a later section of this paper.

---

[1] The tablet taxonomy is fully described at Fróes, I.C.G.: Toyblet: A Taxonomy to Children's Playful Interactions with Tablets. (Forthcoming).

Interaction. Covers what motivates and engages children's use of tablets. It also deals with how preschoolers tackle and explore unknown narratives and interfaces. For instance, every time children are confronted with unknown apps, they have ways of identifying and 'problem solving' during gameplay, either by trying things out or by comparing the app with previously experienced apps. Another aspect is playing on an app without expectations i.e. ignoring the game goal, besides not having to 'put toys away' after they have had enough of an activity– just choose another app instead.

Emotion. It includes subcategories covering notions of identity, privacy and attachment. They directly relate to social and emotional properties linked to tablet play: e.g. referring to app avatars and characters as 'I'; being able to join in conversations related to apps in their social environment, with peers, relatives and others; associations of playing on a tablet in specific circumstances, such as on holidays, together with friends or family, etc., which may shape emotional bonds and memories.

The tablet taxonomy contributed to acknowledging emerging patterns encountered during *tablet play*. The taxonomy also served as a guideline to review and challenge a number of theories connected to ways children use and play with digital media, as well as children's tablet literacy.

3   Playful Literacy

While the early concept of literacy is defined as the ability to read and write, and a number of scholars have already covered the area of how digital technologies can aid the processes of acquiring literacy skills [10–13], digital literacy has a broader perspective and covers a much larger learning spectrum beyond reading and writing skills. With the spread of computers and IT-related communication, digital literacy was initially defined as the ability to use computers [14–16]. Internet and Internet communication technologies (ICTs) helped outline new forms of literacy and due to technological advances, digital literacy is in continual change and development [18]. Additionally, the advent of mobile devices has brought a change in how literacy is attained and perceived [18, 19].

For the purpose of this study, I chose to use Martin's definition of digital literacy due to its comprehensiveness. He defines digital literacy as:

"The awareness, attitude and ability of individuals to appropriately use digital tools and facilities to identify, access, manage, integrate, evaluate, analyse and synthesise digital resources, construct new knowledge, create media expressions, and communicate with others, in the context of specific life situations, in order to enable constructive social action; and to reflect upon this process." [15].

Although Martin's definition covers an extensive ground in terms of digital literacy, other scholars have suggested parallel and sometimes complementary definitions, such as media literacy [17], and emergent literacies [20]. Media literacy broadens the scope of digital literacy and is described by Buckingham as the capacity not only to use media devices, but to also be able to assess and understand the breadth of media's cultural aspects and impacts [17].

The concept of emergent literacies predates the other concepts above, and according to Spencer [20], it is characterized by:

"The continuous incidental interaction of children and adults in a world of increasing semantic complexity, intercultural contact, common experience of media, and the possibilities of almost immediate communication systems ... have to be acknowledged as events in emergent literacies" [20].

Due to the ubiquity of portable devices, such as tablets, and even to the ongoing development of new interfaces of interaction (wearable, non-touch interfaces, etc.), it is relevant to reassess the roles of digital-related literacy currently witnessed in society. This assessment has to be complemented with investigating the modes of learning they are affording. By observing the types of literacy occurring outside specific apps that are present in digital device interaction as a whole, it is possible to identify the assets of some of these modes.

Based on the findings resulting from the pilot study observations, it became apparent that the ways preschoolers use tablets portrayed degrees of literacy; however they did not fit within existing digital literacy definitions. A simple example refers to the term *"appropriately"* and the *reflective* theme suggested by Martin [15] in his digital literacy definition. Neither of them applied in the context of the researched target group. E.g. children challenged the way apps were designed by tapping back buttons and playing in infinite loops rather than following the app design. Another example was trying to control an interaction by shaking the device instead of using a finger.

The styles of digital play that tablets afford, together with the knowledge of app characters and with the range of activities and possibilities within one device, have entered children's play discourse – either in drawings, or when talking about some of the games. However at this stage there is little reflection upon the whole process and even about perceptions of abstract topics such as "Internet". Even though there is a degree of reflection while playing on a device, these children, who were all younger than seven years old, saw the devices as a toy containing many games. They did not differentiate between distinct activities on the tablet, such as drawing, watching a cartoon, or playing a game. All of these activities were described as game like activities. However, when the children were asked to use a specific application (Book Creator app), this activity was not recognized as play time, even though the children were doing something they tend to recognize as play in other settings (drawing, telling stories and jokes to their peers, etc.).

Based on the playful characteristics that regulated the observed interactions, I have proposed the concept of *playful literacy*. **Playful literacy** is defined as **the ability to use, interact, relate, communicate, create, have fun with and challenge digital tools through playful behavior**.

This definition of *playful literacy* is intended to challenge and expand digital literacy perceptions, aiding future studies that address children and emerging digital technologies. Moreover, the concept of *playful literacy* acknowledges the role of 'having fun' as a key quality of successful digital interactions among preschoolers. *Playful literacy* can also be helpful in supporting forthcoming assessments of technologies among older target groups, due to the wide spectrum of playful multimodal interactions afforded by tablets and similar devices.

4   Playful Intertextuality

Despite the screen constrains, tablets afford a *playful literacy* by being versatile toys with diverse modes of play and topics of interest, and fitting in with children's curiosity and pace. As different apps are available in one device, and more apps can be downloaded through the devices' 'digital stores', tablets can be described as unique multipurpose toys that afford a subtle link between physical and digital experiences, e.g. actual payments for digital downloads. These exchanges between the digital and physical realms relate to notions of intertextuality [24–26]. In 1987, John Fiske defined the concept of intertextuality as:

"Any one text is necessarily read in relationship to others and that a range of textual knowledges is brought to bear upon it. These relationships do not take the form of specific allusions from one text to another and there is no need for readers to be familiar with specific or the same texts to read intertextually. Intertextuality exists rather in the space between texts." [26].

This definition of intertextuality has been expanded to delineate the ways in which a variety of media interrelate, shaping the later concept of transmedia intertextuality [24, 25, 27], when characters or stories converge throughout various media, creating an intertextual narrative. The narrative from one medium suggests the consumption of the next medium, such as read the story, play the game, watch the movie, etc. In tablets, this type of narrative can occur from within one app, where a child can listen to the story while playing a game with one of the characters, followed by a small video, which can then lead to an online store or website where the child can be exposed to existing merchandise (physical or digital) related to the character or brand. The notion of intertextuality is very much connected to hypertext, hypermedia and hyper-intertextuality theories. Hypertext [28] was regarded as a live reference to distinct pieces of textual information, hypermedia [28] was defined as complexes of branching and responding graphics, movies and sound as well as text, and hyper-intertextuality [29, 30] has been portrayed as the multimedia version of hypertext. However, the intertextuality and intertwined features of tablet applications afford a new paradigm that I am currently proposing to define as multimodal hyper-intertextuality.

Multimodal hyper-intertextuality refers to the wide array of media and modes of use in which users rely on and experience the interaction and interdependence of applications on mobile platforms, tablets and smartphones.

One example is encountering or being exposed to a specific topic at a static location, such as at home, or while on the go, and picking up the portable device in order to search for related information on a browser. As you click on one of the images, you are redirected to another application that will allow you to access the information, for example tapping on a video icon that will open YouTube and possibly redirect you to the "store" app, where you can then download the app in order to see and explore the searched content in more detail. If the information related to a cartoon character, you might be led to a book, movie or game app and so forth. If the content searched was related to music, you could watch a video, listen to a song, and if you like it, add it to a playlist.

Preschoolers are growing up with this vast realm of possibilities and continuous technology developments. When asked why they liked playing on tablet devices, all the children observed mentioned "fun" as the main reason. Tablet devices' *playful literacy* and *multimodal hyper-intertextuality* are shaping children's learning skills and perceptions of their everyday life. This trend not only shapes children's experiences with digital devices, it also prompts other interactions to follow suit, and to contain a multitude of perceptions in every interaction, which will feed into another experience.

The theme of *multimodal hyper-intertextuality* complements that of *playful literacy* and both contribute to the field of multisensory interfaces informing current modes of experiencing and interacting with tablet devices, i.e. adding characteristics of fun and intertwined app interaction together with diverse inputs (touch, voice) and outputs (visual, sound, tactile), as some of the ways that digital events can be experienced. Furthermore, even though the definition emerged from a study on preschoolers, it can be expanded to related research involving tablets or other similar connected portable devices.

4.1 Multimodal Hyper-Intertextual Culture

Following the lines of a *multimodal hyper-intertextuality* phones and tablets are seen in movies, cartoons and advertising, they are used by people around us as well as by characters in TV series. As mobile devices feature in this fantasy universe, they also belong to households across countries and cultures. An observant child therefore learns by watching not only people, but also TV shows, movies and flipping through comic books. Some of these TV shows are broadcast across the western and eastern areas of the world through various channels, both television and online, shaping a common knowledge and expectation towards various devices. The pervasiveness of mobile platforms in society has afforded the interesting phenomenon of 'mobile playing' among a wide age group, from young children to older generations [5]. Some of the game apps have developed from a piece of software into a whole product industry. For example, *Angry Birds* [21], and *Minecraft* [22], both produced in Scandinavian countries (Finland and Sweden, respectively), have become known worldwide and have developed into assorted merchandise and products, such as cartoons, toys, and clothing, creating brand universes of their own. They evolved from digital toys to physical ones. This brand pervasiveness shapes a cross-cultural language, reinforcing a common culture as stated by Buckingham [23], "... *global brands provide an international language or 'common culture', particularly among young people.*"

In the case of the above-mentioned Angry Birds, there are 'good' characters (birds) and 'bad' characters (pigs). However, in this case, the birds' intention is to destroy the pigs and the structure protecting them. The birds are launched from a sling platform and the player has to find the right angle in order to maximize the destruction caused by each throw. Children who have played this game can identify the symbolic representation of the characters, hero and victim, or hero and villain (pigs steal birds' eggs). Both the characters (birds and pigs) and how one plays this game (dragging a digital elastic band on a sling to reach a certain angle) become recognizable and replicable in other games or toys sharing any of the similarities (sling, pigs, birds, etc.). The game design follows laws of physics and although young children do not necessarily know about angles and projectiles, they play with them on the app, eventually learning about some of these properties in an informal setting. Such specific knowledge and behavior shape a digital *common culture* and the child as an active consumer of this culture [23], developing specific physical dexterities and knowledge, as in the illustration of digital sling throwing. Some interesting questions emerge from this: How does this culture eventually shape physical interactions? How are distinct cultures appropriating digital aspects? Are there specific cultural facets that inform the choice of apps? How does a *multimodal hyper-intertextual* experience frame expectations of digital interactions?

5 Concluding Remarks

The current paper contributes to the field of multisensory interfaces by introducing two key points that emerged from the pilot study regarding children's playful interactions with tablets. Acknowledging the role of fun within modes of interaction informs and broadens the field of multisensory interfaces. The concepts of *playful literacy* and *multimodal hyper-intertextuality*, which emerged from the analysis of the observations, challenge existing definitions of digital and media literacy while covering the close interaction and interrelations between modes of use of portable devices, their associated apps and their actual praxis. The purpose of presenting these definitions is to spark further discussion regarding not only children's digital (and playful) literacy, but also to provide an incentive to reflect on roles and uses of tablets in education while pushing boundaries towards acknowledging further related themes for investigation. Both definitions incite future research on how the growth of playfulness on portable devices is affecting expectations of digital interactions, and how it is shaping upcoming digital designs.

While tablets are being adopted as school tools, their full scope of use and impact has yet to be mapped. Observing and understanding the multiple ways pre-school children are experiencing and shaping their own concept of mobility and tablet interaction is a valuable asset for professionals from diverse areas, especially those involved in design and education. Furthermore, as digital interfaces have entered the sphere of everyday work and play, investigating how they become intertwined in cultural perceptions and expectations can guide prospective developments of interactive platforms.

Acknowledgements. I would like to thank all the children, pedagogues and parents from the partnering kindergarten institution in Frederiksberg, for their time and commitment to this research. I would also like to thank colleagues and reviewers, who have given valuable feedback towards this paper.

References

1. Danmark Statistik: Elektronik i hjemmet. http://www.dst.dk/pukora/epub/Nyt/2014/NR227.pdf
2. Fróes, I.: Dead-Until-Touched: how digital icons can transform the way we interact with information. In: Universal Access in Human-Computer Interaction, pp. 611–619 (2013)

3. Müller, H., Gove, J.L., Webb, J.S.: Understanding tablet use: a multi-method exploration. In: Proceedings of the 14th Conference on Human-Computer Interaction with Mobile Devices and Services, Mobile HCI 2012 (2012)

4. Kline, S., Dyer-Witheford, N., De Peuter, G.: Digital Play: The Interaction of Technology. Culture and Marketing. McGill-Queen's University Press, Montréal (2003)

5. 2014 Mobile Behavior Report. http://www.exacttarget.com/sites/exacttarget/files/deliverables/etmc-2014mobilebehaviorreport.pdf

6. EMarketer: Tablets Most Likely to Grab Time from PCs in Japan. http://www.emarketer.com/Article/Tablets-Most-Likely-Grab-Time-PCs-Japan/1011696

7. Apple - Education - iPad - Apps, Books, and More. https://www.apple.com/education/ipad/apps-books-and-more/

8. Tablet and e-learning Initiatives Around the World | Tablets For Schools. http://www.tabletsforschools.org.uk/worldwide-research/

9. Tjek lige iPad'en. http://www.uvm.dk/Aktuelt/~/UVM-DK/Content/News/Udd/Folke/2011/Nov/111108-tjek-lige-ipaden

10. Fróes, I.C.G.: Toyblet: A Taxonomy to Children's Playful Interactions with Tablets (Forthcoming, 2015)

11. Chang, A., Nunez, D., Roberts, T., Sengeh, D., Breazeal, C.: Pre-pilot findings on developing a literacy tablet. In: Proceedings of 12th International Conference on Interaction Design and Children, IDC 2013, pp. 471–474 (2013)

12. Liestøl, G.: The dynamics of convergence and divergence in digital domains. In: Ambivalence Towards Convergence. Digitalization and Media Change, pp. 165–178. Nordicom (2007)

13. Shuler, C., Ed, M.: Industry Brief: Pockets of Potential: Using Mobile Technologies to Promote Children's Learning (2009)

14. Couse, L.J., Chen, D.W.: A tablet computer for young children? exploring its viability for early childhood education. J. Res. Technol. Educ. **43**, 75–96 (2010)

15. Gilster, P.: Digital literacy. Wiley, New York (1997)

16. Martin, A.: Digital literacy and the "digital society." In: Lankshear, C., Knobel, M. (eds.) Digital Literacies: Concepts, Policies and Practices, pp. 151–176 (2008)

17. Buckingham, D.: Defining digital literacy - What do young people need to know about digital media? Nord. J. Digit. Lit. 263–276 (2006)

18. Leu, D.J., Kinzer, C.K., Coiro, J.L., Cammack, D.W.: Toward a theory of new literacies emerging from the internet and other information and communication technologies. Read. Online. **5**, 43–79 (2004)

19. Lankshear, C., Knobel, M. (eds.): Digital Literacies Concepts, Policies and Practices. Peter Lang, New York (2008)

20. Spencer, M.: Emergent literacies: a site for analysis. Lang. Arts. **63**, 442–453 (1986)

21. Angry Birds – It's our 5th BirdDay!. https://www.angrybirds.com/

22. Minecraft. https://minecraft.net/

23. Buckingham, D.: Beyond Technology. Polity Press, Cambridge (2007)

24. Marsh, J.: Media, Popular Culture and Play. In: Edwards, S., Blaise, M., Brooker, L. (eds.) SAGE Handbook of Play and Learning in Early Childhood, pp. 403–414. SAGE Publications Ltd., London (2014)

25. Marshall, D.: The new intertextual commodity. In: Harries, D. (ed.) The new media book, pp. 69–82. British Film Institute, London (2002)

26. Fiske, J.: Television culture. Methuen & Co. Ltd., London (1987)

27. Kinder, M.: Playing with Power in Movies, Television, and Videogames: From Muppet Babies to Teenage Mutant Ninja Turtles. University of California Press, Berkeley (1993)

28. Nelson, T. H.: Complex information processing: a file structure for the complex, the changing and the indeterminate. In: Winner, L. (ed.) Proceedings of the 1965 20th National Conference (ACM 1965), pp. 84–100. ACM, New York (1965)
29. O'Beirne, R.: From Lending to Learning: The Development and Extension of Public Libraries. Chandos Information Professional Series. Chandos Publishing, Witney (2010)
30. Fox, R.F.: Mediaspeak: Three American Voices. Praeger Publishers, Westwood, CT (2000)

AfterNext: Decoding the Future of Higher Education in 2030

Myk Garn[✉]

University System of Georgia, Office of Educational Access and Success,
Atlanta, GA, USA
myk.garn@usg.edu

Abstract. In the world of academic innovation there are many experts; experienced entrepreneurs who know what needs to be done next to improve faculty and student success in the rapidly changing environment of academe. More bandwidth, more funding, more professional development, more attention to quality and to test security; all very important — and all very unhelpful when one is tasked with visioning not what should come next — but what will come AFTER next.

Higher education is in the midst of turbulent change. An academic culture steeped in reflection and teaching is being disrupted and reconstructed into a globally connected ecosystem of networked, 24X7X365 co-creators and co-learners. Roles and paradigms held dear and true are challenged. The rate of change, the unpredictable, unrelenting emergence of new, disruptive models makes planning and preparing for the future even more conflicted, confusing – and critical.

This was the challenge facing the University System of Georgia in 2013. A recently completed report on distance learning needs had surfaced many critical needs — but few visionary directions — for the System to consider or plan from. This need was clear to Chancellor "Hank" Huckaby in November of 2013 when he addressed a convening of the System's leading educational entrepreneurs at a symposium entitled "MOOCs and Beyond." Challenging the leaders to examine and explore the future fearlessly, he acknowledged, "…we don't know what lies beyond…and that's important." This observation framed and guided the System initiative, and Georgia's intent, to "Invent the Beyond."

1 What Lies Beyond?

The University System of Georgia, in partnership with the Technical College System of Georgia, intends to increase the percentage of Georgians holding a postsecondary certificates or degrees from just over 40 % in 2013 to 60 % by 2020 (an additional 250,000 graduates). Ensuring that the pace and scale of the transformation needed is within the tolerance and ability of the stakeholders to grasp, embrace or endure – is critical to the future of Georgia.

To continue its leadership role the System must identify future trends and opportunities that both inform its current plans and catalyze the development of new ones. Over the next fifteen years higher education will move from a culture of an 18th Century memory-based, industrial teaching model – to a 21st Century social model of networked learning and co-creation.

© Springer International Publishing Switzerland 2015
M. Antona and C. Stephanidis (Eds.): UAHCI 2015, Part III, LNCS 9177, pp. 54–65, 2015.
DOI: 10.1007/978-3-319-20684-4_6

To this end the System created, in September 2014, the New Learning Models 2030 Taskforce. With a membership of sixty-five, the Taskforce brought together a broad, representative swath of USG stakeholders. From presidents, provosts, faculty, students and staff every one of the System's thirty institutions was represented by at least one stakeholder. Again, an assembly of the System's 'best and brightest' were asked to envision and chart a future path for higher education in Georgia. This is a difficult challenge.

2   Co-Authoring the Future of Education

The charge to the NLM 2030 Taskforce was to catalyze and build a more informed framework of future possibilities and strategic options. Scenario planning begins with a focus: an issue or idea that is at the heart of the matter. The focus is important because it helps to narrow down the possible futures to those that will help lead us to better decisions. For its activities, the NLM 2030 Taskforce focused on the future of higher education in 2030 setting out to determine:

- What factors will be critical to the success of the University System and its stakeholders over the next 15 years?
- What new learning practices and business models will best guide and support learners, faculty and institutions in and to 2030?

Because predicting the future with any certainty is wholly unsatisfactory, the NLM 2030 Taskforce chose a scenario-based planning process—not to predict the future but—to visualize a range of possible futures and reflect on how prepared the USG was for them. Scenario planning helps to make the driving forces at play in a market sector visible and, by developing them into scenarios with multiple possibilities, planners can anticipate a wider range of challenges, opportunities and outcomes.

Scenario-based planning increases the ability of stakeholders to envision future possibilities and challenges volatile and unpredictable markets that are beyond the immediate, predictable horizon. These explorations build a shared approach and conceptualization of future needs and opportunities for the USG ensuring, encouraging and supporting more effective and cohesive transformations. The resulting frameworks are authentic, internally valid, communicating the challenges and opportunities facing the System and the critical success factors and strategic options the System might employ in planning for the future.

3   Inventing the Beyond: Crowdsourcing the Future

Because 'new models' means new methods of learning – the Taskforce used online tools and models to conduct and complete a scenario-based planning project. While NLM 2030 Taskforce comprised the core stakeholder group – access and participation in the planning activity will be expanded to the entire System and to academic systems, institutions and stakeholders across the United States through the "Invent the Beyond" and "Explore the Beyond" massive, online, open-stakeholder, collaborations (MOOCs) that will overlay the activities, experiences and deliberations of the Taskforce.

Utilization of the MOOC format (a fall 2014 and spring 2015 courses were offered via the Brightspace Open Courses) enabled the Taskforce to work collaboratively, communicate regularly without the need to convene as frequently as they might have and to dramatically increase the number (over 500 individuals participated in the ITB and 194 in the ETB MOOCs) and distribution of stakeholders contributing to and informing the scenario building and planning processes (see Fig. 1).

Stakeholder Community	New Learning Models 2030 Taskforce (n=65)	Invent/Explore the Beyond MOOCs (n=500+)
HEd Administrators	87 %	23 %
Faculty	8 %	42 %
Students	5 %	23 %
Other		12 %

Fig. 1. Comparison of stakeholder participant percentage between NLM 2030 Taskforce and Invent/Explore the beyond MOOCs

The "Invent/Explore the Beyond" online collaborations used crowdsourcing to develop future scenarios and to explore and describe the factors critical to the success of student, faculty and postsecondary institutions in 2030. During fall 2014, through three interactive and discursive sessions, participants identified and quantified the driving forces and critical uncertainties facing higher education over the next fifteen years, they used those critical uncertainties to establish candidate matrices for scenario development, wrote 'headlines for the future,' selected the final matrix, and then developed four robust scenarios for the future of learning in 2030.

During the spring 2015 'Explore the Beyond' MOOC the Taskforce and MOOC participants identified the critical success factors for student, faculty and institutional stakeholders; evaluated the pressure to change current instructional services institutions provide to students and teaching activities that faculty perform are undergoing; determined the implications that new learning models would put these institutional functions under — and how they would need to change — by 2030. The final, capstone, session for both MOOCs was a recap and consolidation of the learnings and implications of the complete process to Invent and Explore the Beyond resulting in a set of critical success factors and a framework for informing institutions and individuals as they build their future plans.

4   Driving Change

The USG scenario-based planning process (Fig. 2) began by identifying and prioritizing the primary drivers of change (economic, technological/instructional, social/cultural and policy/political) as perceived by three primary stakeholder groups:

students, faculty and institutions. Those issues with impact on the future whose trajectory is relatively certain e.g. rising operational costs become categorized as 'trends' and help undergird the development of the scenarios. Drivers that were highly uncertain — where the degree and type of impact is unpredictable e.g. legislative mandates — become the variables from which the differing narratives of the USG scenarios would be crafted.

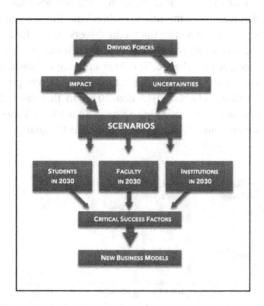

Fig. 2. The USG scenario-based planning process, adapted from Schoemaker, 1995

The Taskforce rated over 70 change drivers in terms of the potential impact each driver might have on the future and the degree of certainty or uncertainty of that impact on the System and its stakeholders. The resulting 30 most impactful and uncertain drivers were then presented to the 'Invent the Beyond' MOOC participants for their input. Thus over 500 individuals participated in determining the most impactful and uncertain drivers that were then combined and weighted using both implicit and tacit knowledge to combine them into what resulted in four general clusters of "key driving factors." The four clusters identified were:

(A) Sources of learning (open/co-created or closed/within the academy) vs. pace of change (rapid or managed/slow)
(B) Pace of change (rapid or managed/slow) vs. two complementary axes—national focus on education (strategic or self-reliant) and US competitive position (US leading or US waning)
(C) Sources of learning (open/co-created or closed/within the academy) vs three correlated axes—economic policy making (redistributive or pro-growth); cost of education (out of control or accessible); and the necessity of education (luxury or a necessary good.

(D) Sources of learning (open/co-created or closed/within the academy) vs funding sources (disciplined or opaque) and national focus on education (strategic or self-reliant)

The creation of the matrix is the most intellectually challenging analysis that takes place during a scenario-planning project. This work identifies and converges the top two key uncertainties into a matrix with a strong set of narrative characteristics. It is important that these matrices are plausible—that the stories that come out of this overlay are believable (without using magic or breaking the laws of physics).

By identifying the most impactful, uncertain drivers of the future from these four potential driver sets, determining the polarities of their trajectory e.g. a faster pace of change versus a slower pace of change, and then creating a matrix based on the two most informative drivers, the Taskforce constructed four different possible views of the future for higher education between 2015 and 2030. In this case, the NLM process identified the two key uncertainties (Fig. 3) as, "Sources of Learning," with polls labeled "Closed/Academy" and "Open/Open Source/Co-Created."

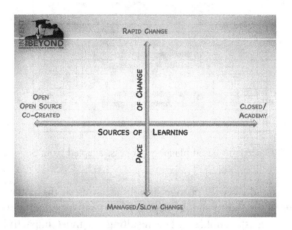

Fig. 3. Final candidate set presented as a matrix

5   From Critical Uncertainties to Scenarios

Moving forward, each quadrant of the matrix was filled out with its own story. The *divergence of poles* sets up the reasonable expectation that when the axes are crossed, the resulting quadrants will offer divergent narrative canvases. Using the critical uncertainties that form our matrix as reference points, the next step is to fill out the story of the future: how did it happen in this particular way? What had to happen first in order for us to get to this future? What else is going on in this future given the critical uncertainties?

During the narrative development process the "other" uncertainties—the 29 that did not end up in the matrix—were used to provide a much deeper sense of what the future would be like in a specific scenario. For example, in a future where the pace of change is rapid and most learning is from open, non-institutional sources, what would the public funding model be for higher education? What would the state of the national economy be? Answering these questions from the context of our critical uncertainties uncovers nuances in the futures that help to make them both distinct from other scenarios and sufficiently rich to serve as valuable planning tools.

Finally, each scenario (Fig. 4) was given a name to be used as a shorthand for what the conditions of that future are. The names should evoke the overall feel of the scenario and help someone who may not be familiar with the process or the steps taken to arrive at to this future understand the underlying pressures and conditions that define the scenario. For example, the "Find Your Own Path" scenario connotes learners (and faculty) who must chart their own course through an unruly world.

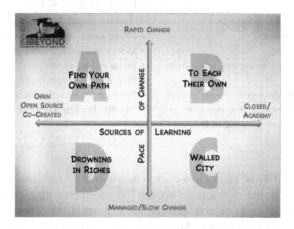

Fig. 4. Final Invent the Beyond matrix

6 Exploring the Scenarios

The four USG 2030 scenarios, co-developed by the NLM 2030 Taskforce and the Invent the Beyond MOOC participants provide four very different future narratives that higher education stakeholders can use to populate and plan for possible futures. By 'populating' each of these scenarios with avatars for the three stakeholder groups — the Taskforce would be able to identify the critical success factors necessary for each of these communities to thrive and succeed in 2030 — and the implications for new learning and new business models the System will need to invent and implement to support its students, faculty and institutions.

Presented next are tables showing the uncertainties driving each scenario (sorted into four change driver categories of social, technological, economic and political) and representative cameo content from each scenario narrative.

Find Your Own Path	
Rapid Change — Open Source/Co-Created	
Social	Technological
• US-Centric Global perspective • Education is inexpensive and accessible • All music is world music • Just-in-time skill learning augments life-long learning models (higher ed buys-in) • Well-respected content = credibility • Highly transparent social structure and behaviors	• Attention management systems help people organize information networks to meet needs • Technology displacement of labor • There are games for everything • Online portfolio systems replace transcripts and resumes/CVs • Rapid obsolesce and the need to relearn models and acquire new skills • Internet is free and fast
Economic	Political
• Vibrant world economy • Fewer trade barriers • International brands, many emerging from new markets • Situational results drive perceptions of value • Wide ranging employment issues arise as more and more labor is replaced by automation	• US-government actively reinventing itself • Movement toward more direct democracy • Weak public sector • Pragmatic decision making • Pressure for new definitions of "value" and "worth" become political issues

In the world of *Find Your Own Path*, change is the only constant, institutional prestige is devalued, the "wisdom of crowds" is interpreted through algorithms and predominates as the truth, data is destiny. In this world, analytics, algorithms and machine learning have triumphed. Apps now know how to make sense of the world well enough that most people don't care if a recommendation comes from a person or a program.

Information is everywhere, published by people and by programs. The world seems to seethe with change, and it is fast-paced – many people feel that the pace creates constant disruptions, if not on the grand scale, at least on the personal scale. There seems to always be something new to learn, something new to adapt to, something – from devices to skills – that has become obsolete.

In higher education, institutional prestige has been devalued. Value now resides in the ability to meet the needs of the individual, fueled by the collective "wisdom" of the crowd. The power of a degree is diminished as workplaces shift to micro-degrees and endorsements. The cost of "learning" plummets.

Leading-edge educators are working with learning apps to embed their own approach to learning and critical thinking within the recommendation and analysis engines. Educators who do this offer subscriptions to their "personal takes" on the world, which differentiates them from more generic, open-source analytics.

To Each Their Own
Rapid Change — Closed/Academy

Social	Technological
• Educators viewed as entrepreneurs • Education is expensive, but work programs make it reachable • Strong East Coast/West Coast bias • End of Inter-league sports leads to East/West Championship battles • Technology-driven isolation from standards fragmentation	• Rapid innovation and new technologies adopted within • Technologically savvy educational institutions "colonize" less tech savvy schools • Strong commercial space programs led by research programs
Economic	**Political**
• Higher education establishes strong position on patents, proprietary practices and intellectual property, often acting more like businesses than schools • Credentials are essential passports to opportunity • Only the biggest of businesses can keep up with pace of change • Poor management practices lead to greater organizational dysfunction	• Business and education carve up political clout leading to new battles and new gridlock • Courts and regulators fail to manage increasingly proprietary "standards"

The landscape of 'To Each Their Own' is one where higher education institutions have pushed back and closed ranks win the face of the unrelenting pace of of change. Higher education now competes directly with business, using its size, scope and position to block out external partners from trespassing on its patents, proprietary practices, and intellectual property. Educators, researchers in particular, who are now seen as intrapreneurs, take models of academic-economic cooperation to new heights.

Protecting the investment on research and development does not imply a slow transfer of technology, but rather a new competitive model where higher educational institutions share less among one another as they seek to convert their intellectual property into economic value.

The pace of change is fierce. Organizations that can't keep up, including many universities and colleges, get subsumed into larger structures. Embrace change or be eaten, is a common mantra. However, rapid mergers and acquisitions have led to increasingly dysfunctional management practices that often fail to find the right balance in the chaotic environment. Multiple cultures and multiple infrastructures slam into each other at light speed, but management has little time to weave a new, cohesive culture. When it comes to teaching nothing is sacred, because if it isn't relevant, then it doesn't count, and that means anything old that hasn't found a way to prove relevance has been swept away. Credentials and affiliations are the essential passports to opportunity. The economic gap between those with credentials and those without widens.

Walled City	
Slow Change — Closed/Academy	
Social	Technological
• People feel over managed and underachieved • Resurgence in book publishing • Education Institutions touted as the saviors for a world of underachievement • Traditional journalism returns (but not distributed in traditional ways) • Highly supplemented higher ed tuition	• Technology feels stale • Because technology isn't changing as fast, mastery of all forms of technology are at an all time high • Automation focuses on tracking negative political movements and other insurgencies
Economic	Political
• Stagnant global economy • Business is seeing long-term bets pay-off, albeit at subpar performance rates • Significant reductions in election costs as people have more time to actually engage in issues (advertising declines)	• Tight political control on change facilitated by industrial and social engineering • Reputation of government generally improves • Middle East continues to devolve as US pulls out to focus on domestic policy • Ideas about what "facts" should be versus actual facts predominate government decision making

In the 'Walled City,' stakeholders find comfort in a more 'livable' pace of change – but with anxiety over an environment somehow out of sync. Slow change means a slower economy with fewer opportunities for the ambitious. Tight restrictions and control on social, economic, and technological advances reinforce and extend social, cultural and political ossification. That said, the slow pace of change also means government promises get fulfilled before they get derailed or obsoleted by new technology. The Academy is seen as the arbiter of knowledge and skills, and institutions guard this power closely. Strategic alliances between institutions and private industries consolidate this power and encourage targeted innovation toward specific objectives. Educational institutions have found that for many classes, applying the industrial method is working well. They create cookie-cutter classes with clear, measureable outcomes and franchise them out.

The cost of education is high, but it has stabilized as the external sale of courses and the monetization of staff lead to new sources of income. With the costs of adopting to rapid change no longer a constant business cost, institutions and individuals can make other strategic investments, some to bolster their status (either as gatekeepers for institutions, or as individuals), others to extend their mission or interests.

Drowning in Riches	
Slow Change — Open Source/Co-Created	
Social	Technological
• Educational systems have lost control of their marketplace • People cobble together learning from a variety of sources • "Being Social" replaces "Being on Social Media" • Personal and local newsletters, blogs and other online media proliferate	• Technology adoption in academia is very slow • High distrust of automated solutions and "Big Data" • Bring-Your-Own-Device common • Ease of publishing and consumption • Technology is powerful but isolated as coordination and collaboration wanes • Social media falters
Economic	Political
• Lack of resources to transform information into value • "Information" labor jobs offer secure employment and upward mobility • Poor quality information increases accidents and leads to major industrial disasters	• Chaotic political system as new political movement emerge but most don't get broad traction • Business is equally disjointed in its leadership position as slow growth has left a vacuum of industrial leadership • Elected leaders have plenty of sources from with to choose their "facts"

The 'Drowning in Riches' scenario delivers what today's stakeholders thin they want; a controlled pace of change. There was a time when people trusted computers for everything, and they started to automate all manner of human endeavor from creating shopping lists to driving cars. The Great Attack stopped all of that. Over a period of a just few weeks hackers raided many major financial institutions. Billions of dollars simply disappeared.

Public funding for education is on the wane, along with tax dollars being taken in by the federal, state and local governments. The generally stagnant economy makes obtaining funds from other sources difficult. Some companies, however, are sitting on piles of pre-Great Attack cash hordes and offer funding to institutions that can offer specific research assistance or a particular hedge.

Now students can't turn to any single source to complete their education. Institutions remain stuck in a model that no longer meets the needs of their students or the workplace. They turn inward, reflecting on their lost stature, which further deteriorates their motivation for change.

7 What Success Looks Like in 2030

So, given these scenarios, what does success look like for higher education stakeholders such as students, faculty and institutions in 2030? When the NLM 2030 Taskforce was asked to populate each scenario and consider the critical success factors each of the stakeholder groups would need to survive and thrive in these very different futures they developed over 600 such factors. The analysis of these, by stakeholder group and by scenario resulted in a number of factors were common across multiple scenarios — making them 'super success' factors — and especially crucial to stakeholder success in the future. These super success factors were:

For higher education <u>students</u> in 2030 the critical success factors are the ability to:

1. Aware of their needs and able to pick the 'right' institution with resources, reputation and clout to help them achieve their educational and career goals.
2. Have or find access to alternative ways to fund educational programs & training
3. Predict what knowledge they will need and accumulate credentials and find quality mentors for support
4. Be independent, resilient, adaptive, versatile, prepared, self-directed and be prepared to confront shock, cynicism, and anxiety to prevent paralysis in acquiring an education
5. Have business savvy and the ability to market themselves
6. Continue their education to keep up with the pace of change

For higher education <u>faculty</u> in 2030 the critical success factors are the ability to:

1. Be a highly-specialized, recognized expert who is articulate and can communicate the value of their course & its outcomes to prospective students
2. Align themselves with institutional direction/efforts; focusing on teaching outcomes and the use of multiple delivery methods
3. Develop their 'brand' and market themselves as free agents
4. Give up autonomy and academic freedom for job security
5. Be content with an unfulfilling job

For the implications of new learning and business models for higher education <u>institutions</u> in 2030 the critical success factors are the ability to:

1. Reinvent their raison d'etre and clarify the mission likely by finding a niche and attracting buyers by demonstrating and marketing differentiation Have a highly visible valuation with the ability to articulate and communicate the value-added of working or learning through the institution and quality this may include looking for partners/acquisitions among other institutions.
2. Some institutions will get "back to basics" - deconstructing and reconstructing learning models in relevance to past (successful)
3. Other institutions will attempt to push back traditional forms of college, Aggressively focused on outcomes not process; emphasize flexibility quickly reacting to changing requirements where the learning is infinitely varied and free-form with no model but with clear learning outcomes and embracing new forms of measuring learning (e.g. self-directed learning, CBE, credentialing/badges, portfolios, experiential learning, service learning, internships, etc.)

So, what do these factors indicate about the future? Three observations seem evident. One, the degree of change expected across the three stakeholders varies. While the most dramatic (some would say tsunamic) changes are predicted for institutions, and faculty will have hard choices (balanced with a strong upside for an entrepreneurial few), students will see somewhat less disruption. Two, each stakeholder community will be expected to take greater individual responsibility for engaging and succeeding at their respective endeavors. Three, there will be an increased granularity, and atomization, of content, careers and credentials.

References

1. Rasmus, D.W.: Learning Insights Blog. http://www.seriousinsights.net/
2. Schoemaker, P.J.H.: Scenario planning: a tool for strategic thinking. Sloan Manag. Rev. **37**(2), 25–40 (1995)
3. Watts-Hull, J.: New Learning Models 2030 Taskforce updates, University System of Georgia (2014)

From Trebizond to Al-Andalus: Visualizing the Late Medieval Mediterranean

Eurydice S. Georganteli[(✉)] and Ioanna N. Koukouni

School of History and Cultures, University of Birmingham,
Edgbaston, Birmingham B15 2TS, UK
{e.georganteli,i.koukounis}@bham.ac.uk

Abstract. No place can better represent the meeting of cultures in late medieval Europe than the Mediterranean. Intellectual, artistic, and societal interactions during this time have impacted material culture on many levels. These interactions are yet visible in coins, monuments, cityscapes, languages, music, ideas, knowledge, and technologies. Byzantine, medieval Islamic, Norman, Italian, and Crusader coins have been the dominant evidence of cultural interactions between opposing Mediterranean shores. This paper presents aspects of cultural encounters in the late medieval Mediterranean, visualized in storylines and accompanying digitized datasets, and supported by computer technologies and related digital applications.

Keywords: Late medieval mediterranean · Cultural heritage · Coins · Intercultural dialogue · Digital cultural heritage · Mobile applications · Cloud-based platforms · Personalization

1 Introduction

This paper presents part of the work that the University of Birmingham has undertaken as one of the three pilot sites of the Tag Cloud Project – an ongoing European collaborative research project with contributors from a variety of academic disciplines. This project, beginning in 2013 and coming to a close in 2016, aims to enhance audiences' interactions with cultural heritage and engage them as lifelong learners. The case study "From Trebizond to Al-Andalus: Visualizing the Late Medieval Mediterranean" is a virtual itinerary and online exhibition exploring cultural encounters in the Mediterranean from the twelfth to the fifteenth centuries. The itinerary illuminates the history of the late medieval Mediterranean and is being incorporated into the mobile app COOLTURA, created by Tag Cloud for implementation on both iOS and Android mobile devices.

As a Tag Cloud partner, the University of Birmingham uses the numismatic resources of the Barber Institute of Fine Arts Coin Collection to showcase intercultural and interfaith dialogue in the late medieval Mediterranean. The Barber Institute of Fine Arts at the University of Birmingham, home to one of the finest medieval numismatic collections in the world, aims to use cutting-edge technologies to create new ways for its audience to engage with its considerable holdings. These include over 15,000 Byzantine, western medieval and Islamic coins.

© Springer International Publishing Switzerland 2015
M. Antona and C. Stephanidis (Eds.): UAHCI 2015, Part III, LNCS 9177, pp. 66–76, 2015.
DOI: 10.1007/978-3-319-20684-4_7

The itinerary covers coins that are associated with world heritage sites, historical landscapes, settlements, standing monuments, and architectural complexes. Geographically, it stretches over three continents, from the Black Sea and the Levant to Western Europe and the North African coast. Major ports and world heritage sites became points where different cultures and religions converged and exchanged raw materials, crafted goods, ideas, and art.

By means of the app COOLTURA developed by Tag Cloud, audiences of the virtual itinerary along the Late Mediterranean are able to virtually access cultural heritage sites and use mobile media to explore components placed into their geographical, historical, and archaeological settings. The aim is to create an enjoyable and memorable experience, offering a meaningful way to interpret cultural heritage.

2   Visualizing the Late Medieval Mediterranean: The Storyline

The Mediterranean Sea connects three continents, and throughout its history has witnessed the rise and fall of powers that confronted each other in their struggle for control of its waters. In the late middle ages the region was crossed and inhabited by a palimpsest of cultures and religions. Along and across its shores people travelled for commerce, war, piracy, pilgrimage, and diplomacy, encountering and blending with other cultures and religions. Navies under the banners of different kingdoms, empires, and maritime republics, patrolled the same waters.

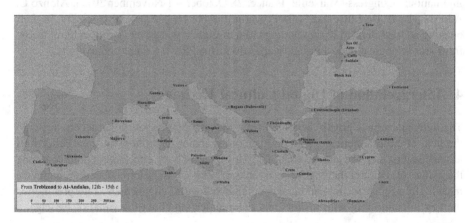

Intercultural and peaceful co-existence alternated with conflicts over control of sea-lanes and over acquisition of pillaged cargoes. Religious toleration was replaced by holy wars for propagation or defense of different religions. Religiously significant lands for Muslims, Jews, and Christians alike were alternately places of pilgrimage or arenas of war. Nevertheless, in peace and in war, trade between the Mediterranean coastlines never ceased to bring peoples into contact, with money as the common denominator. Gold, silver and copper coins with images of emperors and usurpers, kings, sultans, local rulers and doges circulated side by side. The many types of the circulating medium each declared political or economic authority, ideology or expressed faith. Commercial transactions, taxes and customs, expenditure related to warfare, diplomacy, pilgrimage, tribute, booty and ransom, have left their trace in stray and site coin finds, single finds and coin hoards. Spectacular discoveries such as the hoard of some 2,000 Fatimid gold coins recently discovered on the seabed of the ancient harbor in Caesarea National Park in Israel are a reminder of the importance of coins as a major primary source that continues to inform our understanding of the middle ages.

3 Digital Heritage

UNESCO established the concept of digital heritage in 2003 during its 32nd General Conference.[1] Offering "broadened opportunities for creation, communication, and sharing of knowledge among all peoples," digital heritage is of primary importance in preserving and protecting knowledge for the public benefit.[2] Acknowledging this need, the United Nations Educational, Scientific and Cultural Organization (UNESCO) adopted the Charter on the Preservation of Digital Heritage to ensure that Digital Heritage remains accessible to the public, "free of unreasonable restrictions" for current and future generations.

Expanding on that, UNESCO organized a conference in 2003 on digitization and preservation. The organization invited stakeholders to assess current policies in the heritage sector and raised awareness about the risk of loss of digital heritage.[3] Ten years later, the mission of digital heritage was reiterated at the Digital Heritage 2013 International Congress (Marseille, France, 28 October – 1 November 2013). Alonzo C. Addison, Livio De Luca and Sofia Pescarin, the congress's general co-chairs, in their opening address defined digital heritage as a discipline that covers every cultural theme from archaeological sites and landscapes, to virtual artworks and creative arts.[4]

4 Interpretation of Digital Cultural Heritage

The humanities have greatly benefited from the employment of digital technologies in the field of cultural heritage. The digitization by major institutions of their collections has been a first step towards accessibility. However, only by effectively communicating the value of cultural heritage can a cultural site or museum collection be made meaningful to their visitors and can encourage enhanced engagement. Interpretation is the key to connecting with visitors and communicating about the value of heritage.

---

[1] Charter on the Preservation of Digital Heritage, http://portal.unesco.org/en/ev.php-URL_ID= 17721&URL_DO=DO_TOPIC&URL_SECTION=201.html.

[2] *Op.cit.*, articles 8-9.

[3] UNESCO Conference on Digitization and Digital Preservation, https://www.prestocentre.org/ calendar/unesco-conference-digitization-and-digital-preservation.

[4] Addison, A.C. et al. (eds): Proceedings of the 2013 Digital Heritage International Congress, Marseilles, vol. 1, pp. xiii-xiv (2013).

Interpreting cultural heritage is "the art of helping people explore and appreciate our world. Interpretation enriches human life through engaging emotions, enhancing experiences and deepening understanding of places, people, events and objects from the past and present."[5] One of the action fields of the International Council on Monuments and Sites (ICOMOS) is to enhance public appreciation of humanity's material heritage in all its forms through interpretation.

In the twenty-first century, the implementation of information and communications technology (ICT) in the cultural sector offers new methods for interpreting heritage, as well as new challenges. Both ICOMOS and UNESCO have established policies to emphasize the importance of public communication and education in the preservation of heritage. The ICOMOS Charter for Interpretation and Presentation of Cultural Heritage Sites officially sets out the principles of employing ICT in the cultural heritage sector to both conserve and promote public appreciation of cultural heritage sites.[6]

Today, a range of methods and strategies have been investigated and implemented by museums and cultural heritage sites in order to engage with users and help them interpret monuments and works of art in a more inclusive manner. Hypermedia and cognitive tools have been especially successful in engaging younger generations of visitors/users.[7]

In the digital era, there has been increased demand by visitors and a growing market for developers for onsite digital interpretation of works of art both on display and in reserve collections of museums. Two factors have been limiting the scope and breadth of such digital interpretation. First, interpretation of digital heritage has been mainly through short-term pilot projects.[8] Although there are growing efforts by major cultural institutions to take into account digital interpretation, this approach is not yet universally employed. Second, most digital heritage projects do not take into account the end users' perspective. Yet end users are really the ones that need to relate to and take ownership of the cultural heritage that is being showcased to them in museum display cases, and in an array of apps and digital platforms.

Rahaman and Tan argue that understanding end users is the key to the interpretation of heritage.[9] At present, the prevailing trend in heritage interpretation is "descriptive interpretation", namely description of artefacts. This method presupposes that users/visitors experience and perceive time and the world around them the same way.

---

[5] Association for Heritage Interpretation, http://www.ahi.org.uk.

[6] The ICOMOS Charter for the Interpretation and Preservation of Cultural Heritage Sites, http://icip. icomos.org/downloads/ICOMOS_Interpretation_Charter_ENG_04_10_08.pdf.

[7] On hypermedia, that is an extension of hypertext, which includes graphics, audio, video, plain text and hypertext, see Lister, M., Dovey, J., Giddings, S., Grant, I., and Kelly, K., New Media: A critical introduction. Abingdon, Oxon & NYC (2009). See also Taylor, S.E., Thomson, S.C.: Stalking the elusive 'vividness' effect'. In: Psychological Review, vol. 89/2, pp. 155-181 (1982), Mayes, J.T.: Cognitive Tools: A suitable case for learning. In: Kommers, P., Jonassen, D. Mayes, J.T. (eds): Cognitive Tools for Learning. pp 7-18 Berlin Heidelberg (1992).

[8] Davies J.: On-site Digital Heritage Interpretation: Current Uses and Future Possibilities in World Heritage Sites. Unpublished MA Thesis, Department of Archaeology, Durham University (2014).

[9] Rahaman, H., Kiang Tan, B.: Interpreting Digital Heritage: A Conceptual Model with End-Users Perspective. In: International Journal of Architectural Computing, vol. 9, issue 1, pp. 99-113 (2011).

But "content that does not relate directly to how we perceive the world... causes heritage dissonance or 'disinheritance'",[10] making cultural integration and citizenship often quite challenging. As learning and identity are inextricably linked, the hetero-geneity of the end users' identities needs to be taken into account. Each end user's perspective about cultural heritage is different, and a single artefact can generate multiple interpretations. As a result, polyphony in interpretation should be encouraged to allow end users to tell their own stories.[11] This approach nurtures a more intimate engagement with museums and their collections, active participation, and crucially a sense of owning heritage.[12]

5 Methodology

The effectiveness of mobile technology for the delivery of cultural heritage content has been widely acknowledged. In our research area, we have employed a variety of tools to access cultural heritage sites and artefacts for Barber Institute visitors. These consist of the following:

5.1 Mobile Technology

We began with the simplest mobile technologies, QR codes (Quick Response), and NFC (Near Field Communications) tags. QR codes consist of small, black squares put on a white background and they are used to store data. Data can be read by mobile devices usually by means of a camera. In the case of cultural institutions, the codes are used to link to websites. QR codes are the most popular and widely-used mobile technology in UK cultural institutions because they are easy to download. NFC tags are a kind of wireless technology featuring in the majority of the latest technology mobile devices.[13] It is beneficial because it is interactive and contactless.[14]

5.2 Storytelling and Digital Storytelling

Conventional storytelling is one of the oldest methods of entertainment and compre-hending the past.[15] In our era, digital storytelling is an indispensable part of digital

---

[10] *Ibid.* See also Ardissono, L., Kuflik T., Petrelli D.: Personalisation in cultural heritage: the road travelled and the one ahead. In: User Modelled and User-Adapted Interaction. vol. 22, issue 1-2, pp. 73-99 (2012).

[11] Rahaman and Tan, 104.

[12] Museum Association 2012. http://www.museumsassociation.org/download?id=731198.

[13] Davies J.: On-site Digital Heritage Interpretation: Current Uses and Future Possibilities in World Heritage Sites. Unpublished MA Thesis, Department of Archaeology, Durham University (2014).

[14] http://www.museumsassociation.org/download?id=731198. Both codes were implemented in the first evaluation of Tag Cloud's 'Cooltura' app in November and December 2014. www.tagcloudproject.eu.

[15] Society for Storytelling. www.sfs.org.uk.

heritage; it is crucial to communicating the wealth of cultural heritage knowledge and helping audiences valorize and interpret it.

One of the most dynamic components of the Tag Cloud project is our approach to storytelling. Our storylines are not limited merely to historical facts; rather, they explain daily life in the Middle Ages in an entertaining way, *edutaining*[16] audiences by attracting their attention and by promoting intrinsic motivation. Places, coins, objects, and monuments are all real, each one with a story to tell. The storylines we have developed are based on the history and archaeology of select European cultural routes.[17] Further, the interface between users and cultural heritage takes place smoothly through the use of a virtual narrator, who is based on a 13th-century character.

5.3   The Storyteller

An essential element of storytelling is a story's teller. In our case, this teller is Benedetto Zaccaria, a wealthy Genoese entrepreneur. He takes visitors on a virtual journey where they have the chance to explore select Mediterranean ports, world heritage sites, monuments, coins and related works of art on three continents. Benedetto introduces himself at the beginning of the itinerary, providing a summary of what visitors are going to explore.

Benedetto Zaccaria is a historical figure who lived during the second half of the thirteenth century.[18] He was an admiral in the Republic of Genoa and a wealthy entrepreneur. A familial connection with the Byzantine Emperor, Michael VIII Palaiologos, granted him the right to rule over Phokaia (today's Foça in Turkey) and the nearby island of Chios. Benedetto thus held a monopoly in the trade of valuable regional products, such as alum from the mines of Phokaia and Karahissar and mastic from Chios.

Benedetto's virtual character has been developed in collaboration with Blind Mice Studio, UK.[19] His facial features pay homage to Anthony Bryer, OBE, Emeritus Professor of Byzantine Studies, founder of the Barber Institute Coin Collection, and one of the most engaging story-tellers of all things Byzantine. The specifications for Benedetto's attire, accessories, and coiffure were drawn from fourteenth to sixteenth century Italian and Dutch paintings. Thus, the features of the virtual narrator in combination with the artifacts, monuments, and other elements on display make the itinerary from Trebizond to al-Andalus both a dramatic and engaging experience for Benedetto's audience.

Select medieval Christian and Islamic coins from the Barber Institute's Coin Collection and its partner institutions entice visitors to embark on their virtual journey.

---

[16] Ioannidis, Y. et al.: One object, many stories: Introducing ICT in museums and collections through digital storytelling. First Digital Heritage International Congress, vol 1, pp. 421-424 (2013).

[17] Georganteli, E., Koukouni, I.: Designing personalised itineraries for Europe's cultural routes'. In: Stephanidis, C., Antona, M. (eds.) AHCI/HCII 2014, Part II, LNCS 8514, pp. 693–704 (2014)

[18] Lopez, R.S.: Benedetto Zaccaria, Ammiraglio e Mercante nella Genova del Duecento. Genoa (2004).

[19] Blind Mice Design, http://www.blindmicedesign.com.

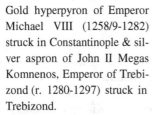
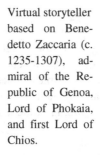

Gold hyperpyron of Emperor Michael VIII (1258/9-1282) struck in Constantinople & silver aspron of John II Megas Komnenos, Emperor of Trebizond (r. 1280-1297) struck in Trebizond. The Barber Institute Coin Collection, B6151 & ET37	Virtual storyteller based on Benedetto Zaccaria (c. 1235-1307), admiral of the Republic of Genoa, Lord of Phokaia, and first Lord of Chios.	Venetian silver ducat struck in Venice, in the name of Petro Zianni (r. 1220-1229) & Byzantine silver basilikon struck in the names of Emperors Andronikos II with Michael IX (r. 1294-1320) in Constantinople. The Barber Institute Coin Collection, IT1 & B6290

Information is displayed in the form of web pages with digital images of coins, artifacts, monuments, sites, audio, video, and geo-referenced maps.

5.4   Personalization

The focus of cultural experts has been drawn to methods of personalization in the cultural heritage sector that would attract and retain a wider audience.

The virtual character is an excellent platform for personalization, making human-computer interaction not only more appealing to a wider spectrum of users but also more responsive.[20] Visitors can interact with artifacts and monuments that were created and used in the middle ages and hear stories about peoples' lives. This combination of experiences offers users the opportunity to learn about tangible and intangible heritage simultaneously. Using the objects, artifacts, and monuments situated throughout the exhibit, visitors are able to learn stories about different peoples, places, and historical periods. The cross-cultural encounters this learning journey facilitates allow users/visitors to enhance their learning experience beyond the confines of a museum display, thus promoting social inclusion, a key issue for the UK Heritage Sector and EU cultural strategies.

Other mixed reality interfaces, such as geo-spatial maps and augmented reality, complement personalization to meet diverse users' needs.

---

[20] V. Lombardon & R. Damiano: Storytelling on Mobile devices for Cultural Heritage. In: New Review of Hypermedia and Multimedia. vol. 18, issues 1-2, pp. 11-35 (2012).

5.5 Omeka Platform: A Pool of Online Resources

We have collected selected digitized resources and stored them in an online pool at www.omeka.net. Omeka is a web-publishing platform that allows individuals or groups to create websites to display collections and build digital projects for entertainment or educational purposes. In Tag Cloud, we used it as a tool to create a digital exhibition with a variety of objects broken into distinct categories (jewelry, weapons, art, etc.). We also created a separate collection of digitized primary and secondary resources that are available in the public domain. These are useful tools because they allow users to access important resources all in one place.

Additional tools and functionalities have been used to create an environment in which users are encouraged to discover cultural heritage, to explore sites, and most importantly, to contribute their own content by commenting, editing, and publishing via social media.[21] Today, mobile phones are equipped with location-specific services. Selected tools that take advantage of location-specific content generation are:

5.6 Digital Fortalt

Digital Fortalt is a web portal developed in Norway with the two-fold aim to highlight the end-users role in cultural heritage and to help cultural institutions attract audiences by helping the latter become custodians of cultural heritage.[22] To do that, the platform encourages individuals and cultural institutions to create digital stories. The content it produces is accurate, clear, and concise, making it engaging and memorable for audiences.[23] The format of the stories may be an illustrated text (jpg, png), a video (mpeg, mp4, webm), an audio clip (mp3, ogg), an animation, a photograph, or even an online exhibition. Stories can be incorporated into a specific category according to a theme like archaeology, history, or visual arts. Digital Fortalt aims to encourage digital communication, social inclusion, and user interaction.

5.7 Stedr

Stedr is a mobile application prototype developed by fellow Tag Cloud partner SIN-TEF.[24] By emphasizing geo-location, the app helps users to discover digital stories related to places around them. Stories are retrieved from the Digital Fortalt platform, and then geo-location and the user's own generated content, like photographs and comments, allow one to add new places on the map. Stedr encourages users to contribute their own content (like stories, tags, and comments) and to share stories via their social media accounts. It also offers the option to create a digital collection by

---

[21] Findings from TAG CLOUD market survey conducted between Nov – Dec 2014 in the pilot sites. Tag Cloud, http://www.tagcloudproject.eu/.

[22] Digitalt Fortalt, http://digitaltfortalt.no; Tag Cloud, http://www.tagcloudproject.eu/.

[23] Digitalt Fortalt, http://digitaltfortalt.no.

[24] Stedr, http://www.stedr.blogspot.com.

organizing thematic stories. It enhances personalization in cultural interaction, thus inviting a wider audience to actively explore the wealth of cultural heritage.

Finally, we have included games, puzzles, augmented reality (AR, stories, and mixed reality as complementary and alternative solutions to enrich our virtual itinerary and make it more appealing to visitors.

6 COOLTURA Platform and App

As the main outcome of the Tag Cloud Project, COOLTURA is presented as a two-fold solution: COOLTURA Platform, a cloud-based platform that provides the intelligence to manage complex digital heritage, and COOLTURA App, an application which uses the COOLTURA platform to allow visitors to enjoy a unique, adaptive, and personalized cultural experience.

COOLTURA App is a single entry for a whole ecosystem of culture and ICT applications generated by and beyond Tag Cloud, including those for augmented reality, storytelling, and social media.

Thus COOLTURA App allows users to explore culture through sites and artifact dashboards that provide specific information in different ways, including through games, puzzles, and quizzes.

It is always a challenge to engage users beyond their physical visit to a museum and to provide them with a complete experience by means of a cultural route, making them "virtual travellers". With this in mind, COOLTURA aims to include a set of interactive interfaces to tell stories about the cultures of medieval Europe. This way users as virtual travelers may experience different steps along the route through a mobile device. Narratives are adapted and provided in a short and clear format that is easy to read and understand. The app's user interface is similarly simple and attractive, aiming to engage users in an immersive experience as travellers of a route, and to facilitate their learning experience.

COOLTURA's interactive off-site experience aims, firstly, to enhance the user experience with culture, second, to generate cultural engagement, and last, to make sure that the late medieval Mediterranean area comes alive for visitors.

7 Conclusion

This paper has presented the case study of the Late Mediterranean Cultural Route visualized with the aid of COOLTURA, a platform and app developed in the context of the Tag Cloud project. Advances in the digital heritage sector, accruing challenges, and the recent redefinition of the role of museums as cultural leaders in modern society (ICOM 2012)[25] have defined our objective, namely, to explore new and engaging ways to present and manage digital heritage content from the Barber Institute of Fine Arts and select European and North American museums and world heritage sites in an *edutaining* way. This initiative offers open access to cultural heritage assets for a global audience. Before deploying our methodology, we discussed how *edutation* could be achieved, and through research, thought and discussion, we were able to combine entertainment and learning in a constructive and attractive way, which, incidentally, has been a major challenge for museums in the 21st century. This paper also highlighted how valorization of cultural heritage and differentiation in its interpretation can be achieved by means of personalization and guided navigation through geo-location and an emphasis on individualized support of heterogeneous audiences.

Acknowledgments. With a contribution on COOLTURA by Silvia de los Rios (UPM), Maria Fernanda Cabrera-Umpierrez (UPM), Maria Teresa Arredondo (UPM).

References

1. Abulafia, D.: The Great Sea, A Human History of the Mediterranean. Oxford University Press, London (2011)
2. Addison, A.C. et al. (eds.) Proceedings of the 2013 Digital Heritage International Congress, vol. 1, pp. xiii-xiv, Marseilles (2013)
3. Ardissono, L., Kuflik, T., Petrelli, D.: Personalisation in cultural heritage: the road travelled and the one ahead. User Model. User-Adapt. Inter. **22**(1–2), 73–99 (2012)
4. Davies J.: On-site digital heritage interpretation: current uses and future possibilities in world heritage sites. Unpublished MA thesis, Department of Archaeology, Durham University (2014)
5. Georganteli, E., Cook, B.: Encounters. D. Giles, London (2006)
6. Georganteli, E.S., Koukouni, I.N.: Designing personalised itineraries for Europe's cultural routes. In: Stephanidis, C., Antona, M. (eds.) UAHCI 2014, Part II. LNCS, vol. 8514, pp. 693–704. Springer, Heidelberg (2014)
7. Goodale, P. et al.: Pathways to discovery: supporting exploration and information use in cultural heritage collections. In: Proctor, N., Cherry, R. (eds.) Museums and the Web Asia 2013, Silver Spring, MD, Museums and the Web (2013)
8. Ioannidis, Y., et al.: One object, many stories: Introducing ICT in museums and collections through digital storytelling. First Digit. Heritage Int. Congr. **1**, 421–424 (2013)
9. Kee, K. (ed.): Pastplay, Teaching and Learning History with Technology. The University of Michigan Press, Ann Arbor (2014)

---

[25] http://icom.museum/fileadmin/user_upload/pdf/ICOM_News/2004-2/ENG/p3_2004-2.pdf.

10. Lister, M., Dovey, J., Giddings, S., Grant, I., Kelly, K.: New Media: A critical introduction. Oxon & NYC, Abingdon (2009)
11. Lombardon, V., Damiano, R.: Storytelling on mobile devices for cultural heritage. New Review of Hypermedia and Multimedia. 18(1–2), 11–35 (2012)
12. Lopez, R.S.: Benedetto Zaccaria. Ammiraglio e Mercante nella Genova del Duecento, Genoa (2004)
13. Mayes, J.T.: Cognitive tools a suitable case for learning. In: Kommers, P., Jonassen, D., Mayes, J.T. (eds.) Cognitive Tools for Learning, pp. 7–18. Springer, Heidelberg (1992)
14. Miller, W.: The Zaccaria of Phocaea and Chios (1275-1329). J. Hellenic Stud. 31, 42–55 (1911)
15. Rahaman, H., Kiang, T.B.: Interpreting digital heritage: a conceptual model with end-users perspective. Int. J. Archit. Comput. 9(1), 99–113 (2011)
16. Smith, B.: Digital heritage and cultural content in Europe. Museum Int. 54(4), 41–51 (2002)
17. Spufford, P.: Power and Profit. The Merchant in Medieval Europe. Thames & Hudson Ltd, London (2002)
18. Taylor, S.E., Thomson, S.C.: Stalking the elusive 'vividness' effect. Psychol. Rev. 89(2), 155–181 (1982)
19. The ICOMOS Charter for the Interpretation and Preservation of Cultural Heritage Sites. http://icip.icomos.org/downloads/ICOMOS_Interpretation_Charter_ENG_04_10_08.pdf
20. Charter on the Preservation of Digital Heritage. http://portal.unesco.org/en/ev.php-URL_ID=17721&URL_DO=DO_TOPIC&URL_SECTION=201.html
21. Museums Association. http://www.museumsassociation.org
22. ICOM Definition of a Museum. http://uk.icom.museum/about-us/icom-definition-of-a-museum/
23. UNESCO 4th World Forum on Lifelong Learning. http://en.unesco.org/events/4th-world-forum-lifelong-learning
24. Association for Heritage Interpretation. http://www.ahi.org.uk
25. European Association for Heritage Interpretation. http://www.interpret-europe.net/top/heritage-interpretation.html
26. Stedr. http://www.stedr.blogspot.com
27. Digitalt Fortalt. http://digitaltfortalt.no
28. Tag Cloud. http://www.tagcloudproject.eu/
29. UNESCO Conference on Digitization and Digital Preservation. https://www.prestocentre.org/calendar/unesco-conference-digitization-and-digital-preservation
30. Blind Mice Design. http://www.blindmicedesign.com

STEM Scalable Model for Enhancing Secondary and Postsecondary Student On-Line Services

Noel Gregg[1](✉), April Galyardt[2], and Robert Todd[3]

[1] Institute for Interdisciplinary Research in Education and Human Development,
University of Georgia, Athens, GA, USA
ngregg@uga.edu
[2] Department of Educational Psychology (Quantitative Methods), University of Georgia,
Athens, GA, USA
galyardt@uga.edu
[3] Office of Educational Access and Success, University System of Georgia, Atlanta, GA, USA
robert.todd@usg.edu

Abstract. The purpose of this paper is to examine the BreakThru e-mentoring model for scalability purposes. Two aspects of this STEM e-mentoring program were examined: (1) the use of virtual environments and social media settings; and (2) the development of e-mentoring relationships (i.e., quality and engagement). Three secondary and three postsecondary institutions participated in the project. Mentors (n = 33) were recruited from postsecondary faculty, secondary teachers, graduate students, and business leaders. Of the BreakThru participants (n = 188), 57 % of the students continued in the program for multiple years. Specific design issues are described as essential for developing and measuring the outcomes of a similar student on-line resource.

Keywords: Scalable model · STEM · Disability · E-mentoring · On-Line services · Virtual world · Social media

1 Introduction

Science, technology, engineering, and mathematics (STEM) workers are no longer only bench scientists and engineers with bachelor's and graduate degrees, but also include engineering technicians, systems administrators, computer specialists, and others for whose skills can be obtained at the sub-baccalaureate level. Students who have a preexisting interest and ability in STEM, but who may not represent the traditional profile of STEM workers must be strongly encouraged to persistent in STEM careers. Electronic mentoring (e-mentoring) is one very effective practice for supporting secondary and postsecondary underrepresented students' persistence in STEM majors [1]. As more students use on-line learning for instruction, enhancing on-line support services such as e-mentoring has direct and indirect outcomes for student engagement and retention in STEM majors.

The Georgia STEM Access Alliance (GSAA) is a collaborative project between The University of Georgia (UGA) and Georgia Institute of Technology (Georgia Tech) to

© Springer International Publishing Switzerland 2015
M. Antona and C. Stephanidis (Eds.): UAHCI 2015, Part III, LNCS 9177, pp. 77–88, 2015.
DOI: 10.1007/978-3-319-20684-4_8

develop an e-mentoring student resource model that connects underrepresented students with mentors across distinct secondary and postsecondary institutions. The GSAA project, branded as BreakThru, was a five-year grant funded by the National Science Foundation. The purpose of this paper is to examine the BreakThru e-mentoring model for scalability purposes. Two aspects of a STEM e-mentoring program were examined: (1) the use of virtual environments and social media platforms; and (2) the development of e-mentoring relationships.

1.1 Participants

BreakThru student participants (n = 188) were enrolled in an e-mentoring program to increase the persistence of underrepresented secondary and postsecondary individuals in STEM majors. Student enrollment was restricted based on available grant resources. In addition, all mentors and mentees (students) were provided a financial incentive to participate in the program. Secondary mentees were selected from three distinct districts (i.e., rural, urban, suburb) with student enrollments of 500, 3,000, and 45,000 respectively. Postsecondary students were selected from three institutions including one open-enrollment two-year college with approximately 26,000 students, and two research universities with student enrollments of 35,000 and 21,000. Table 1 provides evidence that more males from the secondary schools and more females from the postsecondary institutions self-selected to participate in the BreakThru e-mentoring program. In addition, the race/ethnicity demographics (Table 1) illustrate that a larger number of minority students were represented in BreakThru.

Table 1. Student Gender by Race/Ethnicity across all years. *Majority = White or Asian; Minority = Black, Hawaiian, Hispanic, Other, Two or more races, Native American/Alaskan Native. ** Ethnicity data was not reported for 2 secondary females, 3 postsecondary males, and 3 postsecondary female so they are not included in the majority/minority data, but are included in the totals for gender data.

		Majority*		Minority*		Total**	
		n	%	n	%	n	%
Secondary	Male	17	61 %	34	56 %	**51**	**56 %**
	Female	11	39 %	27	44 %	**40**	**44 %**
	Total	**28**	**100 %**	**61**	**100 %**	**91**	**100 %**
Post-secondary	Male	20	54 %	17	31 %	**40**	**41 %**
	Female	17	46 %	37	69 %	**57**	**59 %**
	Total	**37**	**100 %**	**54**	**100 %**	**97**	**100 %**

Mentors (n = 33) were recruited from postsecondary faculty, graduate students, secondary teachers, and business leaders. The secondary mentors included 69 % females,

62 % majority racial/ethnic populations, and 4 % individuals with disabilities. The post-secondary mentors represented 53 % females, 62 % majority racial/ethnic populations, and 10 % individuals with disabilities.

1.2 BreakThru E-Mentoring Program

The key components to the BreakThru e-mentoring program included provision of online learning and training practices, access to virtual environments and use of social media platforms to promote networks of support, and virtual linkage to STEM resources. Essential to the mentor and student engagement was their collaborative use of the on-line STEM learning modules. During the development year of the grant, the project staff developed 12 discrete online learning modules. Four of the modules were identified as critical modules and were program requirements: accommodations, time management, introduction to STEM, and self-determination. In addition to these critical modules, early in the program mentors reported that they were encouraging their mentees to complete the math/science test anxiety module. All modules included universally-designed online, mobile device, and Second Life formats.

1.3 BreakThru Data Collection

Institutional descriptive data and monthly programmatic reports were collected over the five-year span. An on-line instrument was administered to all the students at the end of each of the semesters to provide detailed intervention data (i.e., engagement and quality of mentoring). All mentors were required to complete a survey to provide feedback about each of their assigned mentees. The primary purpose of the mentor survey was to inves-tigate the number of mentoring sessions, the communication platform mediums used for mentoring, and the length of mentoring sessions when certain mediums were used. Investigating the usage patterns of different communication platforms during e-mentoring provides a means of understanding the specific resources critical for such a practice.

1.4 Institutional Demographics

The BreakThru student demographics in Table 1 should be interpreted in relation to the demographics of the various participating institutions. The secondary institutions varied greatly in minority student enrollment (rural = 86 %; urban = 80 %; suburban = 54 %), but have similar proportions of students with disabilities (SwD) (rural = 11 %; urban = 15 %; suburban = 11 %). The post-secondary institutions have more distinct profiles of minority enrollment (two-year = 68 %; research universities = 20 %) and populations with disabilities (two-year = 1.9 %; research = 3.0-3.6 %). The total SwD enrolled in STEM majors (two-year = 2.5 %; research = 3.0 %; 9.2 %) compared to the percentage of SwD STEM graduating (two-year = 1.1 %; research = 1.5 %; 6.5 %) illustrates a significant need for student on-line resource support for these underrepre-sented populations.

2   BreakThru Model

We investigated the BreakThru model specific to the incremental cost of the model over time (i.e., five years) and the specific resources (i.e., grant leadership; design; and program administration) critical for student retention in the mentoring process (See Fig. 1). Year one of the grant was devoted to the development of the virtual platforms, on-line resources, and recruitment. No students or mentors were enrolled during year one of the project. The relationship of the following model variables to student retention was investigated: (1) participant demographics: gender; disability, institution; and race/ethnicity; (2) virtual resources; and (3) mentorship intervention (i.e., engagement and quality).

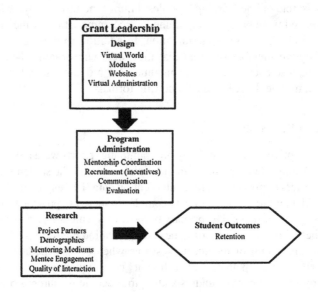

Fig. 1.   BreakThru model

2.1   Allocation of Resources

The resources allocated to support the BreakThru model are categorized as representing leadership, program management, and virtual design (see Fig. 2). The leadership resources were assigned to the grant administrative and research roles, the program management to the e-mentoring activities, and design to the development and management of the virtual world and social media platforms. The increase in leadership resources during years four and five was a function of grant research requirements. Design resources decreased over the five years of the project since platforms were created primarily during year one with iterative changes and maintenance being the focus over years two through five. The design products (i.e., virtual modules, on-line resources), are student support resources currently available on-line for use in replicating the model [2].

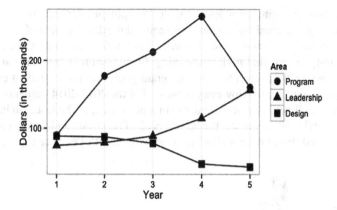

Fig. 2. Grant budget

The program management resources represent the scalable portion of the BreakThru e-mentoring program (see Fig. 3). Over the five years of the project, we tracked four essential components of developing and maintaining an e-mentoring program: communication activities; incentives; program evaluation; and staffing requirements. Some of the increase in program evaluation resources were a function of grant requirements and would not be essential for replicating this model.

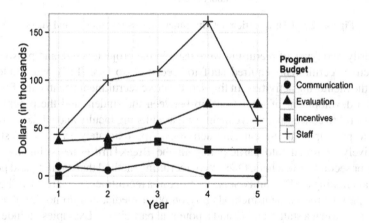

Fig. 3. Program budget for e-mentoring activities

2.2 Student Recruitment and Retention

BreakThru served 91 secondary students, 56 two-year postsecondary students, and 38 research institution post-secondary students. Fifty-seven percent of the BreakThru students continued in the program for multiple years. Enrollment in the BreakThru secondary and postsecondary institutions is provided in Fig. 4. The recruitment for secondary, and postsecondary students required very different communication strategies related to the unique institutional demographics and policies. Overall, we found one of the best recruiting communication strategies required the development of a short, visual (e.g., YouTube, video) message stressing virtual mentoring, avoiding the use of terms such as disability or remedial in the messaging. More resources were allocated during year one and two of the project to meet our grant goals specific to student enrollment (see Fig. 2, communication). However, at the end of the 2013-2014 academic year, the grant goal for enrollment of postsecondary students at each of the research institutions was approximately 30 % under the grant goal. Therefore, additional recruitment resources (i.e., staff time) were reallocated during the fourth year (see Fig. 2).

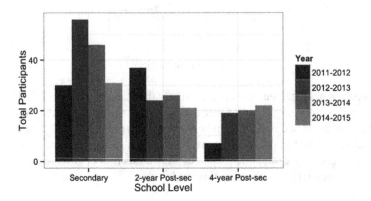

Fig. 4. BreakThru participant enrollment across institutions and years

Primarily two types of recruiting were used in the project, active and passive strategies. Active recruitment required staff to meet face-to-face (FtF) with students to describe the mentoring activities. In this sense, active recruitment became the first stage toward the development of a relationship between the student and the program. We found it useful to conceptual active mentoring as enlisting faculty and advisors to invite students to participate in e-mentoring activities. Approximately 75 % of the students were actively recruited into participating in the BreakThru e-mentoring by faculty members or secondary teachers. One active recruiting method that did not yield positive results was eliciting the Disability Service Office as a recruitment resource. Unlike active methods, passive recruitment methods rely on other media, and do not involve direct interaction between a staff member and a potential participant. Examples include flyers, social media messages, or blanket emails sent to a group of students. One drawback is that passive recruiting requires a student to be in the right place at the right time in order to see a message on a plasma screen, social media platform, or a flyer. We found the passive strategy of using social media platforms (e.g., website, Facebook, Skype) not very effective for recruitment.

Patterns in retention vary across the different types of institutions (see Fig. 5). Of the secondary schools, the suburban school system, the largest district population, had more student involvement and retained these individuals consistently across all years of the project. It is important to note that both the urban and rural secondary school districts demonstrated greater difficulty accessing virtual and social media platforms essential for the mentoring process as a result of school district broadband restrictions and home resources (e.g., internet access). Of the postsecondary institutions, the two-year institution was the most active in recruitment and retention of students for the program during year one as result of institutional program support. The two-year college students who continued in the program past year one remained active during the other three years of the program. While the research institutions did not have high initial recruitment figures, they recruited more students each year, and the majority of the students did stay throughout the four years with plans for graduate degrees. Therefore, the BreakThru model was effective for both two-year and research institutions.

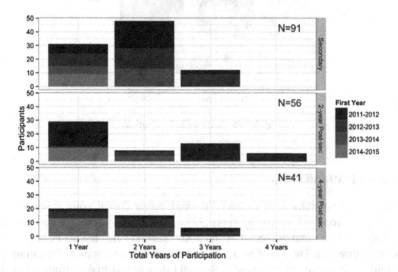

Fig. 5. Student retention in BreakThru e-mentoring across institutions and years. Note: this visualization shows total number of students and does not distinguish between students who graduated and students who chose to continue

2.3 Diversity of Population

Race, gender, and disability have different relationships with individual interest and retention in the BreakThru e-mentoring program. The majority of students at both the secondary and postsecondary levels interested in and remaining active throughout the four years of BreakThru were minority students, and of this population the African American students represented the largest group at both the secondary and postsecondary institutions (see Table 1). As noted earlier, males participated more in the secondary schools and females at the postsecondary institutions (see Table 1). The population of students with learning disabilities, attention deficit/hyperactivity disorder (ADHD), and autism spectrum disorder (ASD) represented the largest numbers of individuals at both the secondary and postsecondary levels who self-selected to participate and remain active in e-mentoring activities (Fig. 6).

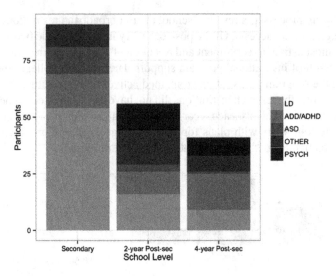

Fig. 6. Students with disabilities

2.4   Virtual Platform Usage

The e-mentoring sessions were provided through either digital voice communication platforms (e.g., Second Life voice, smart phone, video calls) or text-based communication platforms (e.g., emails, social media posts, Second Life chat posts, text message conversation threads). The use of Second Life was encouraged as part of the grant goals and activities. The e-mentoring island in Second Life was a virtual platform where individuals interacted with each other through avatars. Avatars communicated through voice (sue of a microphone) or by chat threads (written communication). To ensure that mentors and mentees had access to communication platforms other than the e-mentoring island, participants were provided options for social network sites such as Facebook, Google, Skype, Twitter, YouTube and/or a virtual learning environment on the program website, including virtual learning modules, a blog, and other support resources. Mentoring pairs were encouraged to find a platform that was beneficial to their mentoring activities. We examined the reflections of the secondary and postsecondary participants across these different communication platforms as reported by mentors through a monthly survey tool collected at the end of each academic semester (see Table 2). The percentages represent the total number of responses received for a given item out of the total number of responses received for that survey. These totals are aggregated across all data collection time points and are disaggregated by mentor/mentee responses and secondary/post-secondary responses.

The majority of the participants chose digital tools that were easily accessed on their smart phone. For instance, the chat feature on social media sites such as Facebook, were often used as a way to type quick messages between participants. Those messages, whether real-time or asynchronous, allowed the participants to engage in unscheduled, quick-response, and private one-on-one mentoring with little to no fiscal resources required by the program. No significant differences were noted across gender or race/ ethnicity.

Second Life was the only social media platform that incurred a cost to the project in either design or management. In addition, the learning curve for using Second Life was steep, and it was not a tool preferred by the students. The cost of developing and managing Second Life resources was disproportionate to student or mentor usage. We do not support Second Life as a communication platform for e-mentoring at either the secondary or postsecondary levels. Second-Life is just one example of why platform-dependent resources may not be a wise investment.

Table 2. Survey Responses to "Select all the ways you communicate with your mentor/mentee." Note: time points represent multiple time points not unique participants.

	Text			Voice			In Person
	Email	Facebook	Texting	Second Life	Skype	Smart Phone	
Mentees							
Secondary (n = 36)	81 %	8 %	75 %	47 %	11 %	69 %	61 %
Post-Secondary (n = 61)	97 %	31 %	57 %	52 %	20 %	69 %	15 %
Mentors							
Secondary (n = 43)	84 %	5 %	67 %	44 %	16 %	70 %	44 %
Post-Secondary (n = 72)	82 %	28 %	49 %	32 %	22 %	57 %	7 %

2.5 Student Engagement

Student engagement was measured by the number of modules completed across the four years of the project (see Fig. 7). We chose module usage since a metric such as the number of meeting times across virtual platforms did not appear to provide a reliable or valid index of program engagement. Figure 7 represents the module completion as reported by the mentor surveys, and as can be seen in the figure, there was a low response rate on the surveys. This low response rate speaks to the need for automatic real-time data collection methods rather than relying on self-report in surveys at the end of each semester.

Interestingly, we did find that of the participants reporting module completion, there appeared to be two very different ways that mentee and mentors engaged with the modules. One group of participants completed more than the required critical modules, but this group of students primarily remained in the program for only one year. The second group of students completed only the four critical modules, but this group of students remained in the program longer, many for all four years. The two different groups of students appear to be focused on different e-mentoring goals. As we noted in

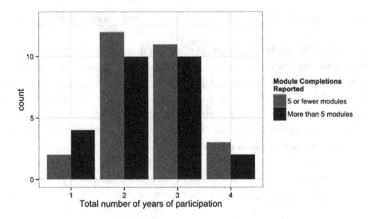

Fig. 7. Module completion reported across 2012-2014

a previous study, many of the BreakThru participants reported a number of positive benefits in addition to persisting in STEM majors. For instance, many of the participants reported the development of trusting and supportive relationships [3].

2.6 Quality of E-Mentoring

The quality of the BreakThru e-mentoring program was measured on the mentee survey by the question, "I am satisfied with my mentoring experience". Mentees active in the program were requested to complete the mentee survey each semester. Out of the 188 mentees who participated across the four years of the program, only 33 % completed at least one mentee survey. However, the vast majority (85 %) of those mentees completing a survey either strongly agreed (53 %) or agreed (33 %) that they were satisfied with their mentoring experience. The mentees most recent survey was used in the analyses. The low response rate for evaluating the quality of the program again speaks more to the need for automatic data collection methods rather than relying on self-report in surveys at the end of each semester.

3   Findings

The scalability of the BreakThru model was investigated specific to the incremental cost over time (i.e., five years) and the specific resources (i.e., grant leadership; design; and program administration) critical for student retention in the mentoring process. Results indicate that such an e-mentoring model is effective in the recruitment and retention of students in STEM majors and provides implications for the use of virtual student support resources for faculty and graduate students providing online instruction. The student retention rate (57 % over five years) suggests that the model was effective in recruiting and retaining students at both the secondary and postsecondary levels. As noted earlier, those students who did not continue in Break-Thru seemed to treat the e-mentoring program as a short-term training exercise rather than an opportunity to develop a long-term relationship. Underrepresented populations (i.e., minority, students with cognitive disabilities) were the largest group of individuals self-selecting to participate in the program.

Two aspects of a STEM e-mentoring program were specifically examined: (1) the use of virtual environments and social media platforms; and (2) the development of e-mentoring relationships (i.e., quality, engagement). The mentors' monthly surveys provided the evidence that text-based tools were often the most frequently used e-mentoring tools. It appears that one of the main reasons for using text-based tools was the practicality, user friendliness, and familiarity with the platforms. Email and chat platforms offered instant access to the participants, and their monthly surveys revealed that mentors and mentees spoke regularly though these mediums. Ease of use, availability, and disability accommodation needs all played a role in the determination of what type of communication tool to use and when to use it. Age, race/ethnicity, or gender did not appear to factor into the choice of a specific communication platform.

Race, gender, and disability often have different effects on the ability of individuals to engage with on-line student support services. While differences were noted across gender self-selection across secondary and postsecondary institutions, more underrepresented students, particularly African-American individuals, self-selected to participate in BreakThru regardless of type or level of institution. The largest number of postsecondary students self-selecting the program attended the two-year college. However, the retention rates were highest for the students attending research institutions.

Data collection within the BreakThru project has been one of the primary ongoing challenges for the project. As indicated previously, mentors and mentees communicated through multiple on-line and off-line platforms, thus collecting log-files through a single platform was infeasible. This led us to rely on surveys as the primary method for collecting data on the mentoring relationship. Unfortunately, asking students to complete long surveys at the end of the semester, near the finals period, resulted in low response rates.

We believe that streamlined, real-time, automatic data collection will be critical for both future research, and evaluating the implementation of BreakThru in other institutions. The learning modules now contain a survey at the end of each module with two questions which can be paraphrased as: (1) Was this helpful? (2) Please comment. This is a more convenient method for obtaining feedback than waiting months until the end of the semester to administer a survey. However, there is still the problem that if a student finds the module unhelpful, they may be more likely to quit in the middle, than finish the module and answer the survey question. When we examined the unique IP accesses to different modules, we found patterns that indicated students may not be completing all of the modules that they start. Also, we noted that if a student began the module on one computer and finished it on another computer, the hit count was affected. Thus page hits are a very limited measure of engagement. Nonetheless, it is useful to notice that some modules had a very high drop-off between first and last pages, while other modules have a higher percentage of visitors reaching the last page. For example, twenty-one students completed the end-of module survey for Classroom Accommodations during 2013-2014, and all of them either agreed or strongly agreed that the module was helpful; however, there are 3237 hits on the first page of the module, and

1335 hits on the last page. In contrast, Time-Management for High School Students had stronger retention between the first page (1339) and last page (1109), but only 10 students completed the end-of-module survey. Incorporating modules into a smartphone app, or an institution's learning management system will provide e-mentoring programs more accurate matching of students to learning module activities.

Collecting data on mentor-mentee virtual meetings is even more difficult. Initially, some mentors tended to report a pair of text messages as a meeting, while others reported a 30- minute phone conversation as a meeting. This confusion was resolved by the second year of the project as we defined a meeting using a digital voice communication platform (e.g., Second Life, video chat, smart phone) for a length of time. However, training mentors in the proper definition of a "meeting" so they can answer survey questions consistently, is not a good use of time. Mentor training time would be better spent learning how to help students. A more convenient method might be to incorporate a question into the welcome page of a smartphone app: "Have you had contact with your mentor in the last week?" We are designing new applications and procedures for data collection that capture real-time responses.

Acknowledgements. This research has been funded by the National Science Foundation, Research in Disabilities Education (RDE) award numbers 1027635 (UGA) and 1027655 (Georgia Tech).

References

1. Sowers, J., Powers, L., Shpigelman, C.: Science, Technology, Engineering and Math (STEM): Mentoring for Youth and Young Adults with Disabilities: A Review of the Research, Arlington, VA: National Science Foundation (2012). http://www.rri.pdx.edu/files/39/stem_mentor_monograph5_may2012.pdf
2. www.georgiabreakthru.org
3. Gregg, N., Wolfe, G., Todd, R., Moon, N., Langston, C.: STEM E-Mentoring and Community College Students with Disabilities. J. Postsecondary Educ. Disabil. (in press).

A TUI-Based Storytelling for Promoting Inclusion in the Preschool Classroom

Preliminary Results on Acceptance

Julián Esteban Gutiérrez Posada[✉], Heiko H. Hornung, Maria Cecília Martins, and Maria Cecília Calani Baranauskas

Institute of Computing and NIED, University of Campinas (UNICAMP), Av. Albert Einstein, 1251, Campinas, SP 13083-970, Brazil
{jugutier,heiko,cecilia}@ic.unicamp.br, cmartins@unicamp.br

Abstract. Technologies such as Tangible User Interfaces (TUIs) take advantage of the natural ability of children to tell stories, play and explain their personal and social behavior. TUI technologies can be designed to constitute scenarios of technology use for all and thus benefit inclusive schools. Challenges of designing such scenarios in the classroom include distraction of students, acceptance by teachers, and inclusion of students with disabilities. In this paper we focus on investigating the acceptance of a TUI environment, designed for the educational context of creating, sharing and telling stories collaboratively. We present a system as background for an evaluation of acceptance based on the Self Assessment Manikin model. Two groups of subjects participated in the evaluation: a group of HCI specialists, and a group of teachers working in an inclusive educational context. The pilot study with HCI specialists established a baseline showing that the system potentially has a high acceptance rate. The teachers reported in a subsequent study high levels of Pleasure and Arousal while we detected greater variance in the Dominance dimension. Although we do not see this variance as critical, it requires attention for the more complex modes of the system.

Keywords: TUI · Storytelling · Narrative · SAM

1 Introduction

Using Information and Communication Technology (ICT) in the classroom can be beneficial for education due to motivational factors [5]. Tangible User Interfaces (TUIs), which "augment the real physical world by coupling digital information to everyday physical objects and environments" [8], have shown an even stronger effect on engagement and motivation than traditional GUI-based systems, and thus have the potential to promote learning [11].

Challenges of using ICT in the classroom include distraction of students, acceptance by teachers, and inclusion of students with special needs. Regarding distraction, an advantage of a special-purpose TUI over general purpose ICT such as laptops, tablets or

© Springer International Publishing Switzerland 2015
M. Antona and C. Stephanidis (Eds.): UAHCI 2015, Part III, LNCS 9177, pp. 89–100, 2015.
DOI: 10.1007/978-3-319-20684-4_9

smartphones is that special-purpose TUIs seems to have a lower potential to distract students from classroom activities due to a lack of applications for browsing, chatting, etc.

Regarding teacher acceptance, when teachers feel that they do not dominate the technology or that their students are more proficient than themselves, teachers are often reluctant to incorporate technology into teaching activities [4]. As to inclusive education, students with certain special needs require assistive technology to be able to use many types of software and hardware.

In this paper we present and describe a storytelling application that uses the TUI paradigm and that can be used in different school subjects. Our application has been designed using a socially aware approach [1, 2], and addresses the challenges of distraction, acceptance and inclusion. Regarding distraction and acceptance, storytelling is seen as favorable to learning by theories such as constructionism [6]. Mediating storytelling with TUI has been described as "a powerful way to supply the storytelling process with affordances and intuition", promoting engagement and minimizing preliminary training and learning [10]. Inclusive aspects are treated by the universal design paradigm we considered in the design solution.

In this work, results of the acceptance for the designed storytelling application are discussed based on pilot and actual case studies; acceptance is investigated using as instrument the Self-Assessment Manikin (SAM) form [3]. The paper is structured as follows: Sect. 2 describes the context and method used in the pilot and in the case study, Sect. 3 presents the results of the two studies, Sect. 4 discusses the results, Sect. 5 concludes.

2   The Pilot and Case Studies – Context and Method

The work reported in this paper is based on one pilot study and one case study. The pilot study was conducted with seven Human-computer Interaction (HCI) specialists from our research team called Human-Digital Artifact Interaction Group[1] – InterHAD, and the case study involved eighteen teachers and twenty students of the Children Living Center[2] – CECI, a day care center for children from six months to six years of age, responsible for children's care and education during the workday or study day of their parents at the University of Campinas (UNICAMP) in São Paulo, Brazil.

2.1 The TUI Scenario

Figure 1 shows an outline of the system. The main input components are the RFID reader (Selection Controls) and the webcam with microphone (Creation Devices). Output components are the projector/screen and the speakers (Output Devices). The computer/laptop stays visually "hidden" in order to reduce the perceived complexity of the system. The use of RFID technology is related to accessibility considerations similarly to the way considered by Pastel [9].

---

[1] http://www.nied.unicamp.br/interhad

[2] http://www.dgrh.unicamp.br/dedic/ceci

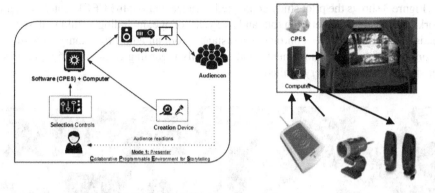

Fig. 1. Components of the system – Interaction mode 1: Presenter

This system configuration is called "Interaction mode 1: Presenter" and is one of four interaction modes proposed in the system. The four modes comprise "simple presentation with/without sound" (Interaction mode 1: Presenter), "multimedia presentation with animations and audio" (Interaction mode 2: Storytelling), "scripted multimedia presentation" (Interaction mode 3: Scriptwriter), and a mode that uses scripted multimedia presentation with audience-sensor feedback (Interaction mode 4: Scriptwriter Plus). The four interaction modes are intended to be used by people of different age groups, e.g. children and teachers. In this paper we focus on the presentation mode which has been designed especially for users with low technical skills such as young children from 4 years of age.

Regarding inclusion, the application uses an RFID reader and a webcam as input and a projector as output. Physical objects of interaction include RFID cards that can be customized and labeled by the students as well as any object (sketches, drawings, toys, etc.) that can be captured by the webcam. RFID cards might be beneficial to accessibility by enabling a more tangible and less abstract interface [9].

2.2 Participants

Figure 2 shows the pilot study with two master students and five doctoral students in computer science, all with thesis projects in the area of HCI and all with intermediate to advanced knowledge regarding accessibility, usability and related topics.

Fig. 2. Research team from Human-Digital Artifact Interaction Group (InterHAD)

Figure 3 shows the pilot study conducted with teachers of the CECI center, who are working with children between four and five years of age, including a child with special needs. This child requires continuous assistance from an adult, for example regarding locomotion, fine motor movements, and especially regarding communication, because her speaking ability is very limited.

Fig. 3. Teachers in activities at the Children Living Center – CECI of UNICAMP

The proposed system was used by some of these students (20 in total), including students with special needs sharing the same environment and activities. Although detailed analysis of the activity with the students is out of the scope of this paper, the activities conducted by the teachers presuppose their prospective use with the children; thus, the scope of this article is limited to the InterHAD group evaluation regarding the proposed system and the teachers activities in their preparation for the system use in the CECI center.

Just to illustrate what has happened with the students, we want to share two situations: the first is related to a little girl (almost 4 years) who, according to their teachers, is shy. However, she discussed the part of the story she wanted to create with her classmates and her teacher, designed the image that represent the part of the story using crayons, used the system to insert her drawing (as will be described later), and, most importantly, told her part of the story to the whole group. The second situation happened with a girl who has cerebral palsy which impedes speech and body movement. In order to tell her part of the story, she accepted help from her teacher for making her own drawing and using the system. When it came to telling her story, she made a great effort to do it. During the activity, she expressed happiness and desire for communication. According to her teachers, the final storytelling part was very difficult for her, especially in the presence of a group of strangers as we were at that moment.

2.3   Method

In both studies, the participants were divided into small groups of three or four and given the task to tell a story through a sequence of scenes (three or four) created by them using different physical resources (markers, colored pencils, clay, paper sheets...) (Fig. 4a), and capturing them through the system (Fig. 4b).

a) Example of a created scene

b) Capturing a scene

Fig. 4. Example of a created scene and the system capture process

To complete the task, the participants were asked to execute four sequential activities (Fig. 5): define the general topic to be presented with their respective subtopics; create, with different physical resources, each subtopic as if it were a slide; transfer these slides to RFID cards through the system; and finally tell the story for the whole group.

1) Define the topic and subtopics

2) Create slides for each subtopic

3) Transfer these slides to RFID cards

4) Tell the story for the whole group

Fig. 5. Activities executed by the InterHAD group

Finally, after completing all activities, we asked the participants to fill in a form for measuring the pleasure, arousal, and dominance dimensions of their experience for each sequential activity. The form is a non-verbal pictorial assessment technique, called Self-Assessment Manikin (SAM; Bradley and Peter, 1994).

Figure 6 shows some participants completing the SAM form and the options that the form offers for measuring pleasure, arousal, and dominance.

1) Filling the SAM form

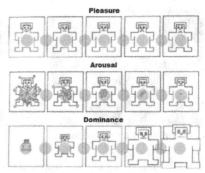

2) Self-Assessment Manikin (SAM)
(Adapted from Bradley and Peter (1994))

Fig. 6. Measuring the pleasure, arousal, and dominance dimensions of their experience

2.4 Materials and Procedure

The technology involved in the designed scenario occupies several different layouts, maintaining the principle of invisibility in terms of not being intrusive to the process of storytelling.

In some installations, the computer is physically close to the reader and therefore visible to users Fig. 7(a), however, the interaction is done through the RFID reader and the webcam, and not with the keyboard or the mouse, so the user is not distracted by the presence of the computer. In other installations, the computer is literally invisible, i.e. hidden for example under a table or in a grocery bag (Fig. 7b). In still other installations, we made an effort to hide other devices such as a monitor (Fig. 7c), or the camera within a lamp shade, (Figs. 7a and b). The intention behind these efforts is to make story and storytelling the focus, placing the technology in the backstage.

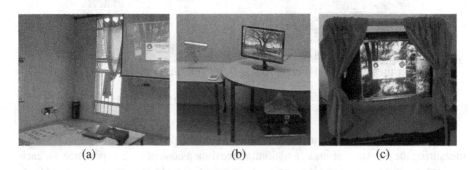

(a)   (b)   (c)

Fig. 7. Different system installations

Figure 8 shows how to interact with the system in mode 1. The user has a set of RFID cards with associated commands, such as: create a new slide; assign a narration or sound effect to a slide; delete the contents of a card. An example of creating a new slide can be seen in Fig. 8. In the first step (Fig. 8a), the user brings the card with the command to create a slide close to the reader. This action causes the system to turn on the webcam. Then the user places previously created content (e.g. a drawing or small figurines) under the camera (Fig. 8b). Subsequently (Fig. 8c), the user brings a card without an associated content close to the reader, and the system takes a picture and assigns the image to the card. Finally (Fig. 8d), when the user brings this new card close to the reader, the system displays the picture taken and plays an associated sound, if it has one.

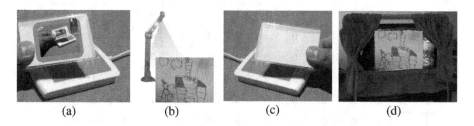

| (a) | (b) | (c) | (d) |

Fig. 8. Interaction with the system (Interaction mode 1)

To tell a story in interaction mode 1, it is required to assign different RFID cards to different moments of the history (for example to scenes for the beginning, the middle, and the end of the story) and to use these cards to actually tell the story. The narration can be performed at the same moment of telling the story, or recorded and associated to each card of the scenes.

3 Results

In this section we present the results of the participants' emotional self-assessment according to the SAM. Figure 9 shows the numerical values we assigned to the possible values of the SAM scales.

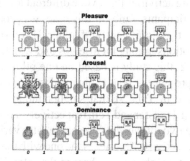

Fig. 9. Self-Assessment Manikin (SAM)

For each activity (Define, Create, Transfer, Tell) we determined the frequencies and the mode for each SAM dimension ((P)leasure, (A)rousal, (D)ominance). In this step, we noticed that not all participants completed the SAM form. Tables 1 and 2 show the result of this step.

Table 1. Frequency table of the InterHAD group.

Scale	Define			Create			Transfer			Tell		
	(P)	(A)	(D)	(P)	(A)	(D)	(P)	(A)	(D)	(P)	(A)	(D)
8	1	1	1	4	5	2	1	1	0	2	1	3
7	1	0	3	1	0	2	2	1	0	2	3	1
6	3	3	2	2	1	1	2	1	4	0	0	2
5	0	1	1	0	1	2	1	1	0	1	1	0
4	2	0	0	0	0	0	1	1	2	2	1	0
3	0	0	0	0	0	0	0	0	0	0	1	1
2	0	2	0	0	0	0	0	2	1	0	0	0
1	0	0	0	0	0	0	0	0	0	0	0	0
0	0	0	0	0	0	0	0	0	0	0	0	0
MODE	6	6	7	8	8	7	6	2	6	4	7	8

The question that we wanted to answer is or not here is a statistically significant difference among the four activities (Define, Create, Transfer, and Tell) regarding each of the three dimensions measured with SAM, that is, whether the (P)leasure, (A)rousal and (D)ominance remain similar or change during the four activities previously mentioned.

To answer this question, knowing that not all participants completed the form, we applied a variance analysis that supports different sample sizes and that does not assume restrictions on the data, e.g. normality. Specifically, we used the Kruskal–Wallis Test on the original data set for each dimension resulting in three tests.

If applying the Kruskal–Wallis Test on a certain dimension yields a p-value less than 5 %, then there is one or more activities that evoke different level of (P)leasure, (A)rousal or (D)ominance in the participants. Only in this case, we proceed to apply a multiple range test (Tukey's Honestly Significant Difference HSD Test) to determine which activities elicit similar emotions among themselves and which not.

As mentioned in Sect. 2, this study is based on one pilot study and one case study. In the following, we will present the results obtained in the interHAD group.

It is possible to observe in Table 1 that smaller modes occur for (A)rousal and (P)leasure in the activities of Transfer and Tell, respectively. However, looking at Fig. 10, we can see that justly these two dimensions present greater variability (larger box).

The (D)ominance of the activity "Define" is the one with the least variability (smaller box), i.e., this is the point at which the members of the InterHAD group agreed more.

Based on the Kruskal–Wallis Test, it is possible to conclude that for the InterHAD group there was no statistically significant difference between the four activities for each of the three SAM dimensions (p-values are presented in the Fig. 10, all of them are greater than 0.05). That is, there is no significant difference in the level of emotion that each of the four activities of the SAM dimensions evoked.

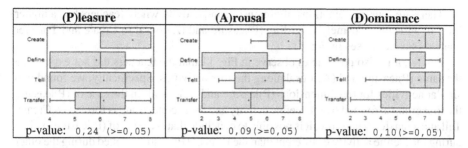

Fig. 10. InterHAD – Box-Whisker plot and p-value of Kruskal–Wallis test

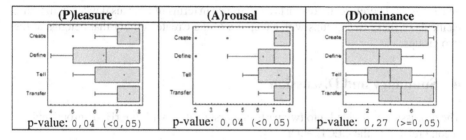

Fig. 11. CECI – Box-Whisker plot and p-value of Kruskal–Wallis test

The results obtained in the CECI center are presented following the following. In Table 2, it is possible to observe that smaller modes occur for (D)ominance in the activities Define and Create. Again, the two dimensions with smaller modes have the greatest variability (smaller box in Fig. 11).

Table 2. Frequency table of the CECI teachers

Scale	Define			Create			Transfer			Tell		
	(P)	(A)	(D)	(P)	(A)	(D)	(P)	(A)	(D)	(P)	(A)	(D)
8	7	5	0	13	10	4	11	10	5	11	11	2
7	2	4	2	3	4	1	1	4	2	1	1	1
6	4	4	2	1	0	2	3	1	0	4	4	4
5	1	1	1	1	0	0	0	0	2	1	1	0
4	4	2	3	0	1	3	0	0	3	0	0	3
3	0	0	1	0	0	0	0	0	0	0	0	2
2	0	1	3	0	1	0	0	0	1	0	0	1
1	0	0	0	0	0	1	0	0	1	0	0	1
0	0	0	5	0	0	5	0	0	2	0	0	3
MODE	8	8	0	8	8	0	8	8	8	8	8	6

There are four combinations of dimension and activity where teachers had a higher level of agreement, namely regarding (P)leasure and (A)rousal to Create and Transfer content (smaller boxes in Fig. 11).

Finally, it is also possible to observe in Fig. 11 that the teachers did not experience the same (P)leasure and (A)rousal along the four activities. Specifically, we found two similar activities for the dimensions (P)leasure and (A)rousal. In the case of (P)leasure, the first group is formed by the Define activity and the second group is formed by Create, Tell and Transfer. Therefore, it is possible to conclude that the level of (P)leasure evoked during the Define activity is different than the level of (P)leasure evoked during the other activities. Similarly, in terms of (A)rousal, it is possible to observe two groups. The first is formed by the Create and Define activities and the second is formed by Create, Tell and Transfer. Therefore, there exists a difference in terms of (A)rousal when comparing elements of these two groups with exception of the Create activity that belongs to the two groups.

4   Summary and Discussion

The discussion is divided into two parts, the first dealing with InterHAD group and the second related to the CECI center.

For all four activities in the InterHAD group (Fig. 10), we see a greater variability in the dimension (P)leasure and (A)rousal, and a greater degree of agreement in relation to (D)ominance. When analyzing the activities separately, we can see that variability in the response increases with respect to each of the activities in the following order: Create, Define, Tell and Transfer.

One possible explanation for the (D)ominance dimension may be related to the fact that this group of participants are expert users of technology. Regarding the other two dimensions, the explanation may be related to the fact that we presented all possible interaction modes to this group before conducting the activities. This a priori knowledge could have affected (A)rousal and (P)leasure since interaction modes two to four are more advanced and interactive.

With the group of teachers in the CECI center (Fig. 11), we have a slightly different behavior. The greatest variability is in (D)ominance and (P)leasure, leaving (A)rousal as the dimension where the teachers have higher level of agreement. Analyzing the activities separately, we observed that the variability increased in the activities following the order Transfer, Create, Tell and Define.

A similar explanation can be given for the teachers, i.e. assuming more heterogeneous skill levels regarding technology use compared to InterHAD group, the dimension of (D)ominance has greater variability. The interaction mode 1 was a novelty for teachers, and they did not know the most advanced interaction modes of the system, which could explain the results obtained in the (P)leasure and (A)rousal dimensions. The Define activity might evoke different levels of (P)leasure and (A)rousal among teachers, due to the challenge of selecting a unique idea among several proposals. Some people might experience different degrees of pleasure and arousal when working on their own ideas than when working on the ideas of others.

Besides all this, we observed a real desire among the teachers to use the system permanently in the institution with their students. They explicitly expressed the potential of the tool for activities in the context of an inclusive school, and highlighted some elements such as: allow to combine different types of designs and storytelling by the students with varying degrees of skill and physical needs; the use of technology selected for reasons of inclusion, for example the RFID reader that does not require fine motor skills; the "invisibility" of technology, leaving the focus on the story and not the devices; and allow combining of images and sounds created by the students themselves, thus creating a greater degree of motivation among students, and freedom to work all kinds of themes in the stories.

5 Conclusion

In this paper we presented a storytelling system that is based on the TUI paradigm and that targets the promotion of inclusion of preschool children in the classroom. The system supports different storytelling interaction modes that enable various levels of complexity of the storytelling process. An important aspect of such a system is teacher's acceptance.

As a preliminary approach to acceptance, we presented the results of a pilot study and a case study and analyzed the results of the study participants' self-reported levels of pleasure, arousal and dominance, using the SAM instrument. The pilot study among graduate students with an HCI research focus established a baseline and showed that the system potentially has a high acceptance rate. Although not explicitly investigated, this study also showed the system's potential for inclusion, since we received positive comments from the (universal) accessibility specialists among the participants.

The actual case study was conducted with 18 teachers of a day care center who teach children between four and five years, including children with special needs. Results provided evidence of a high acceptance rate among these teachers. The participants reported high levels of pleasure and arousal. We detected greater variance in the Dominance dimension. Although we do not see this variance as critical, the Dominance dimension will require more attention during future activities using the more complex interaction modes of the system. We detected differences in Pleasure and Arousal levels along the four activities within the system (Define, Create, Transfer and Tell). Future work includes establishing and testing hypotheses for these differences, as well as their quantification, relating them to the system design elements.

Other future work includes the use of the additional interaction modes and case studies involving preschool children in order to evaluate the acceptance of the more complex modes of storytelling, the acceptance by preschool children (detailed analysis of the activity with the students will be reported in a future article), and more aspects related to inclusion. We will furthermore perform an analysis using different data sources and instruments such as the principles of Design for Affectability [7].

Acknowledgements. This work was partially funded by CNPq (#162025/2014-9) and CAPES (01-P-1965/2012). We also thank the undergraduate students of the Human Factors in Computing

Systems lecture of the first academic semester in 2014 at the University of Campinas (UNICAMP), the students and teachers of the Division of Infantile and Complementary Education (DEdIC) of Unicamp, the research group on Human-Digital Artifact Interaction (InterHAD) at UNICAMP, and the University of Quindío.

References

1. Baranauskas, M.C.C., Martins, M.C., de Assis, R.: XO na escola e fora dela: uma proposta semio-participativa para tecnologia, educação e sociedade. Unicamp (2012)
2. Baranauskas, M.C.C.: Social Awareness in HCI. Interactions, July–August, pp. 66–69 (2014)
3. Bradley, M.M., Peter, J.L.: Measuring emotion: the self-assessment manikin and the semantic differential. J. Behav. Ther. Exp. Psychiatry 25(1), 49–59 (1994)
4. Buabeng-Andoh, C.: Factors influencing teachers' adoption and integration of information and communication technology into teaching: A review of the literature. Int. J. Educ. Dev. Using Inf. Commun. Technol. (IJEDICT) 8(1), 136–155 (2012)
5. Condie, R., and Munro, B.: The impact of ICT in schools: Landscape review. In: British Educational Communications and Technology Agency (BECTA) (2007)
6. Di Blas, N., and Bianca B.: Interactive storytelling in pre-school: a case-study. In: Proceedings of the 8th International Conference on Interaction Design and Children, pp. 44–51. ACM (2009)
7. Hayashi, E., Gutiérrez, J.E., Baranauskas, M.C.C.: Explorando princípios de Afetibilidade no redesign de aplicações para contextos educacionais. In: Anais do Simpósio Brasileiro de Informática na Educação, vol. 24(1) (2013)
8. Ishii, H., Ullmer, B.: Tangible bits: towards seamless interfaces between people, bits and atoms. In: Proceedings of the ACM SIGCHI Conference on Human Factors in Computing Systems, pp. 234–241. ACM (1997)
9. Pastel, R., Wallace, C., Heines, J.: RFID cards: a new deal for elderly accessibility. In: Stephanidis, C. (ed.) HCI 2007. LNCS, vol. 4554, pp. 990–999. Springer, Heidelberg (2007)
10. Shen, Y.T., Mazalek, A.: PuzzleTale: A tangible puzzle game for interactive storytelling. Comput. Entertainment (CIE) 8(2), 11–15 (2010)
11. Sylla, C., Branco, P., Coutinho, C., Coquet, E.: TUIs vs. GUIs: comparing the learning potential with preschoolers. Pers. Ubiquit. Comput. 16(4), 421–432 (2012). Springer, London

Delivering User-Centered Content on an Inclusive Mobile Platform: How to Produce It and Use It!

Valerie C. Haven[✉]

Ross Center for Disability Services, University of Massachusetts, Boston, MA, USA
Valerie.Haven@umb.edu

Abstract. The adoption of mobile learning in higher education is facilitating new avenues for inclusive and accessible learning. The bedrock for these learning environments is the accessible software/hardware included in newer smart devices. Non-traditional learners such as those from diverse racial, cultural, and linguistic backgrounds as well as learners with disabilities are gaining access to higher education using these technologies.

Even though inclusive technology is opening doors to the non-traditional learner, reliance on the access features within technology is still causing barriers to education. One barrier is that technology continues to evolve rapidly and with each upgrade new interface issues arise. The second barrier is that the dependence on smart devices to provide access to education does not address inaccessible course design and delivery of educational content.

Keywords: Mobile learning · Inclusive learning · Accessibility · Inclusive content · Productivity tools · Synergistic Learning Theory (S.L.T.)

1 Introduction

Mobile Learning is re-shaping education today. Using mobile technology to participate in educational environments not only offers new options for flexible learning it also promotes educational opportunities to non-traditional learners. The Pew Research Institute stated that smart devices offer affordable access to the internet and other mobile applications to non-traditional users from various cultures and economic backgrounds.[1]

Another component of mobile learning is the use of smart technology by learners with disabilities. A great deal of positive attention has been centered on the smart devices that have accessible technologies and applications embedded within them. The accessibility hardware in smart phones and tablets is changing how users with disabilities interact with co-workers and social peers.

The problem is that access to higher education still relies heavily on the capacity of assistive technology and other devices to support learning. Pedagogy and content delivery is often not being taken into account when evaluating the accessibility of

---

[1] Smartphone Ownership 2013. (2013, June 4). Retrieved March 1, 2015, from http://www.pewinternet.org/2013/06/05/smartphone-ownership-2013/.

© Springer International Publishing Switzerland 2015
M. Antona and C. Stephanidis (Eds.): UAHCI 2015, Part III, LNCS 9177, pp. 101–108, 2015.
DOI: 10.1007/978-3-319-20684-4_10

learning environments. Technology changes so rapidly that expecting the smart devices alone to promote educational inclusion is becoming a barrier to learning. Initial efforts to promote academic accessibility in the mobile learning realm were addressed by designing accessibility based on the assistive capabilities of a specific device.[2] Further research has shown that learners with disabilities prefer to use their own device since they are more comfortable with them and discover their own work-around to deal with access barriers.[3]

The primary focus of this paper will be on how content can be developed and presented in ways that can support diverse learners in a mobile environment. A theoretical framework for inclusive learning will be discussed along with showcasing some practical tools for creating inclusive content.

This paper will be divided into three parts. The first section will discuss how to design an inclusive mobile learning platform. The second part will describe how to incorporate Synergistic Learning Theory into pedagogy and how to develop accessible/inclusive content. The final section will showcase learner productivity tools that can be applied to a learning environment in order to support learner engagement.

1.1 Developing an Inclusive Mobile Learning Platform

In her investigation toward developing an inclusive definition of mobile learning Rebecca J. Hogue asserts there needs to be a balance between device-centric and learner-centric learning in the mobile –environment (Fig. 1):

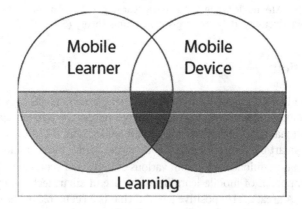

Fig. 1. Two-circles indicating the intersection of learner-centric and device-centric learning

"The first aspect of mobile learning, represented by the left circle, is the mobility of the learner. A mobile learner is a learner that is not in a classroom or in front of a desktop computer (home office, lab, etc.). The learner need not physically be moving, but they

---

[2] (n.d.). Retrieved March 6, 2015, from http://www.irrodl.org/index.php/irrodl/article/view/965/167.

[3] (n.d.). Retrieved March 2, 2015, from https://mobilelearninginfokit.pbworks.com/w/page/.../Accessibility.

are learning in a situation that is not considered a traditional learning environment. I call this type of mobile learning, learner-centric mobile learning…The second aspect of mobile learning, represented on by the circle on the right, is learning that takes place using mobile devices. This includes learning that takes place in the classroom or other traditional learning locations. It is the use of the mobile device that makes it mobile." [4]

Hogue's definition points to the need for developing a framework for evaluating balance between the device-centric and learner-centric aspects of mobile learning. Developing an inclusive mobile platform incorporating her definition could emphasize flexible use of technology and pedagogy that supports personalized learning.

Developing an Inclusive Mobile Learning Platform. The JISC TechDis organization developed criteria for evaluating the accessibility of mobile platforms. The four areas of consideration are the interface,

The cultural capital (is this way of learning culturally appropriate), accessibility of both tasks and content. "Accessibility needs to be seen in relation to:

- The whole learner experience – what they do and how they do it.
- The alternative learner experiences – what they would otherwise do to achieve the same learning objectives.
- The alternative resources – whether m-learning offers more flexibility than traditional resources or pedagogies e.g. handouts."[5]

For our purposes the "interface" could be any on-ground or on-line platform that qualifies as accessible under the terms of U.S. 508 compliance. Creating an inclusive learning environment is much more involved with the accessibility/usability of the course design and content. Designing a course delivery system using a simple web site can be just as effective as building a course in one of the nationally recognized learning management systems (LMS).

Once the overall accessibility for the LMS is established the first recommendation for building an inclusive m-learning platform is to Store content in a cloud-based storage vehicle. Uploading materials to a cloud-based storage repository such as Drop Box provides learners with more flexibility in retrieving materials. Cloud-based repositories can be utilized by both mobile devices and hard drives. Cloud-based repositories are also often simpler to access than an LMS shell and therefore can reduce the time and complexity of reviewing content.

The second recommendation is to push out course information in small increments. This can be done effectively using either an instant messaging system or using email. There are also applications that allow for a multi-modal presentation of information using both visual and auditory components. Sending a text message with a voice recording attached supports diverse learning styles as well as promotes fuller comprehension.

---

[4] An inclusive definition of mobile learning. (2011, July 17). Retrieved March 6, 2015, from http://rjh.goingeast.ca/2011/07/17/an-inclusive-definition-of-mobile-learning-edumooc/.

[5] A Model of Accessible m-Learning. (n.d.). Retrieved March 2, 2015, from http://www.jisc-techdis.ac.uk/techdis/technologymatters/mobilemodel.

The third recommendation is adding scaffold support to the course. This can be done in several ways. This author uses an avatar named, "The Tour Guide." The tour guide provides supplementary information on things ranging from due date reminders for assignments, recommendations for research, and techniques for studying more effectively. Another option is to establish learning pods among the learners. These are groups that can work together on course activities, provide learning assistance to one another or simply be a source of personal connection.

Nicole Krueger suggests that faculty teaching in a mobile learning environment also form support collaborates. Connecting with other teaching faculty can help address the technological shifts within the learning environment and provide resources for effective practice.[6]

Incorporating the above recommendations will set the stage for further discussion on what constitutes inclusive learning. By reducing the technical barriers present in m-learning and incorporating tools and techniques that foster personalized learning not only will learners with disabilities learn more easily many barriers that other learners experience will also be resolved (mobile learning access).

1.2 Synergistic Learning Theory (S.L.T.) as a Possible Starting Place for Learner-Centric Engagement

Synergistic Learning Theory (S.L.T.) applies the engineering principle of "synergy" to the use of technology in higher education. It acknowledges the constant evolution of technology and its effect on social engagement. The main premise is that technology needs to be taken into account as an active participant in a given learning environment. The authors assert there are three categories of participant in any given learning environment. The facilitator, the learner and the technology is being used within the course. The authors further develop S.L.T. into a framework using the principle that the three individual participants merge into the gestalt of the learning event where the technology emerges as an active participant. The advantage of this is that that both the facilitator and the participants can select the technology that would assist their participation the most and through this action social engagement is maximized resulting in personalized learning.

According to Boundless.com, personalized learning is defined as, "Personalized learning is the tailoring of pedagogy, curriculum and learning environments by learners or for learners in order to meet their different learning needs and aspirations. Typically technology is used to facilitate personalized learning environments."[7] Personalized learning allows the individual learner to choose for him or herself what resources and tools will accomplish their educational goals. Productivity tools may be added to a learning platform from which individuals can choose to support their learning or to help minimize barriers.

---

[6] (n.d.). Retrieved March 2, 2015, from https://www.iste.org/explore/articleDetail?articleid=167.

[7] Personalized Learning - Boundless Open Textbook. (n.d.). Retrieved March 6, 2015, from https://www.boundless.com/education/textbooks/boundless-education-textbook/working-with-students-4/teaching-strategies-21/personalized-learning-66-12996/.

Personalized learning also helps course facilitators and administrators provide the foundation for inclusion without having to understand the individual learning needs of each participant. It can also decrease the need for a learner with a disability to have to self-identify their disability in order to engage fully in a course.

Many learners with disabilities prefer the on-line environment because the parameters of social engagement shift. Learners who are uncomfortable self-identifying or want the chance to engage with their co-learners in a different way can do so. Many learners with disabilities are also comfortable using technology and find they can be successful in an on-line academic role.

Developing Inclusive Content for the Mobile Environment. We have arrived at the crux of this article. As stated earlier, educational inclusion is less about designing an LMS in an accessible format than it is in creating and delivering content that can be apprehended and comprehended easily. Some formats on how to deliver content were presented in section one of this paper.

There are two aspects to creating inclusive content. One is to prepare materials in ways that can be read and understood easily. The second aspect is to format materials ways that can be downloaded and managed on mobile devices. The first aspect relates to Hogues's learner-centric feature of her definition and the second relates to the device-centric feature.

Neuro-Science Research on How Storytelling Affects our Brains. Telling a story not only creates synchronicity between the teller and the hearer of the story, a well-crafted narrative lights up multiple areas of the brain resulting in greater comprehension of the narrative.[8] Describing something that tastes good lights up our sensory cortex and telling an exciting moment of a football game activates our motor cortex. Storytelling is not limited to conveying information in an auditory format. Writing narrative in ways that activate different areas of the brain is also effective.

Obviously using a narrative format will not work for all content presentation, but inserting active descriptive language where possible will enhance the comprehension of mobile content.

Now, let's discuss the second aspect of creating various reading formats. Converting the materials into various formats so that, they can be utilized in a personalized learning environment. In the past converting content into multiple formats has been time-consuming and expensive. Recently new technology and techniques to support content conversion have become available that make presenting materials in an inclusive format much easier.

The first step is to prepare written text so they can be converted into formats for diverse learning styles. The best way to begin preparing printed text is by making an electronic copy of it. There is software like Adobe Professional that can create electronic files such as a PDF (portable document file), but the software has to be purchased and

---

[8] What Storytelling Does to Our Brains. (2012, November 29). Retrieved March 6, 2015, from https://blog.bufferapp.com/science-of-storytelling-why-telling-a-story-is-the-most-powerful-way-to-activate-our-brains.

the learning curve can be time-consuming. Later version of Microsoft Word can also convert a Word document into a PDF.

One very efficient way to make a PDF file is by scanning a text file on a copy machine that has the capability to send a PDF as an attachment to an email. Many of the newer copy machines have optical Character Reader (O.C.R.) software in it. If this is available the file can be tagged for accessibility before it is sent as an attachment. If the copy machine does not have OCR software in it there is another resource academics can use to produce multiple formats of content.

SensusAccess is an organization in Denmark that produces cloud-based accessible documents in multiple formats. Once text has been saved as a PDF file it can be uploaded to the SensusAccess web site for further conversion. If the file was not tagged for accessibility by the copy machine adding the tags can be selected as an option.

There are other formats one can select for conversion. Electronic documents can be converted into MP3 audio files, Rich text Format, E-books, electronic braille as well as a number of other options. The web Site detects what type of file is uploaded and a dropdown list appears with the available conversion choices for the type of document.

After the file is uploaded and the format conversion choice is selected the file is sent to SensusAccess's server and the conversion is done. The converted file is then sent back to the person who uploaded the file via his or her email address. If the server was not able to convert the file for some reason an explanation of the problem will be sent back as a message so the problem can be corrected and re-submit it.

SensusAccess offers free use of its service to individuals with disabilities and other print limitations. It also offers a fee-based yearly subscription for educational institutions and other organizations that could benefit from the service. The URL for the free service is http://www.robobraille.org.

By offering documents in multiple formats learners can choose which format will support his or her learning style. It also permits selection of the type of file that will interface smoothly with the mobile device the learner is using.

Converting materials into multiple formats also has an advantage for the facilitator. Some materials have pictures and graphs in them which make downloading to a smart device a problem. Using SensusAccess or another conversion program would allow a facilitator to retain the photos and tables in documents while still offering a version of the document without the visual content for ease of download and comprehension.

The University of Massachusetts, Boston purchased a subscription two years ago and is using it with great success. UMass made the service available to the students, faculty, and staff on the campus. Registration with the disability services office is not required to use the service. The only requirement is that the person uploading documents use a dedicated campus email address.

Exploring Pedagogy Using S.L.T. By providing tools and software applications to support learning as well as social engagement learners can craft their own self-directed learning. This can be supported further by creating various activities and assignments from which learners can choose to demonstrate competency. Using audio/video and the other applications inherent within smart devices and other mobile hardware can also be very useful.

Group work is highly recommended to accomplish learning objectives. Group assignments allow for flexibility among the group members to assume learning tasks according to their individual skills and interests.

S.L.T. implies that the professor is also a learning participant within the learning environment. Communicating personal responses while assigning grades can foster greater communication with learners and can spark continued discussion on a more personal level.

1.3 Embedding Productivity Tools in the Mobile Environment

The term, "productivity tools" is being used intentionally by this author to make the addition of resources originally designed for people with disabilities more inclusive in the learning environment. Many of the open source and freeware available for diverse learners with disabilities are not utilized by other groups of learners because of the perception that they are meant for only one group. Some learners also feel that they are labelling themselves if they take advantage of these tools and that may cause discomfort.

The tools designed for learners with disabilities can be presented in the course as productivity tools to support different learning tasks. Instead of indicating that a tool such as Natural Reader assists people with learning disabilities that cannot read easily without support this excellent tool can be posted in the course shell as a resource to support reading on-line.

The one drawback to some open source and freeware tools is that they tend not to have any technical support. Before uploading a tool it is recommended that the facilitator try using it to be sure it is working properly and that he or she has some understanding of how it works. If the facilitator has a teaching assistant or other support staff that individual may be able to provide basic assistance.

Here are Some Examples of Productivity Tools. Note Pad in the Cloud is a single blank web page that can be used for taking notes or sharing work assignments among participants. It can be password-protected and it generates its own URL. The most valuable aspect of these resources is that any text added to the web page is automatically saved when the web page is closed. Learners can open the page from any computer or mobile device: http://notepad.cc.

Natural Reader Natural Reader is web-based reading software that is cross-platform. There is both a free and for purchase option of the application. Learners can read visually and listen to text at the same time. http://www.naturalreaders.com.

View Pure is a web site that supports viewing YouTube videos on a blank screen. Videos can be watched in either black or white without distraction. this saves bandwidth making the images sharper. Just paste in the video URL and begin watching.[9]

The Zen Productivity Guide: Tools and Tips for Distraction-free Work. This web site has a number of resources for reducing distraction while studying or working.

---

[9] ViewPure/ videos without clutter. (n.d.). Retrieved March 6, 2015, from http://www.view-pure.com.

Resources include ways to use white noise to minimize sound to web site blockers that prohibit surfing on the internet.[10]

There are numerous resources of this type available on the internet. Other kinds of resources include writing applications, information organizers, and screen enlargement programs, and virtual keyboards.

2   Conclusion

Higher education in the mobile environment is going to continue to evolve. The technology will also continue to move forward in development. Establishing flexible open-personalized education resources which support an individual's pursuit of knowledge will support all learners in the most inclusive way possible. By pre-purposing the tools developed specifically for learners with disabilities the sense of separation will diminish between learners with disabilities and other diverse learners.

Creating content that is accessible and usable in the mobile format will allow the facilitator to communicate his or her learning objectives more effectively with greater ease since learner comprehension will increase significantly.

References

1. Zhu, Z., Wang, Y., Luo, H.: Synergistic learning for knowledge age: theoretical model, enabling technology and analytical framework. In: Leung, H., Li, F., Lau, R., Li, Q. (eds.) ICWL 2007. LNCS, vol. 4823, pp. 207–217. Springer, Heidelberg (2008)
2. Mobile learning for quality education and social inclusion. (n.d.). http://iite.unesco.org/pics/publications/en/files/3214679.pdf. Accessed 6 Mar 2015

---

[10] The Zen productivity guide: Tools and tips for distraction-free work. (n.d.). Retrieved March 3, 2015, from http://www.pcworld.com/article/2099744/the-zen-productivity-guide-tools-and-tips-for-distraction-free-work.html.

Preparing All Students for 21st Century College and Careers

Margo Izzo$^{(\boxtimes)}$, Alexa Murray, Andrew Buck, Victor Johnson, and Eliseo Jimenez

The Ohio State University, Columbus, OH, USA
{margo.izzo,alexa.murray,andrew.buck,victor.johnson,
eliseo.jimenez}@osumc.edu

Abstract. Preparing all students for lifelong success in a rapidly changing global economy requires schools to reconsider both what and how educators teach and students learn in the 21st century. This paper presents examples of curricula, programs, and delivery methods that promote increased learning in core academics, technology, and life and career skills for students with disabilities at the secondary and postsecondary levels. Three initiatives, EnvisionIT (EIT), Ohio's STEM Ability Alliance (OSAA), and Transition Options in Postsecondary Settings (TOPS), provide models of engendering 21st century skills utilizing 21st century tools that support all students' transition from high school to college and careers.

Keywords: 21st century skills · College and career readiness · Employment · Students with disabilities · Self-advocacy · STEM · Technology · Transition

1 Introduction

Despite the emphasis of higher academic standards and mandated transition services, many students with and without disabilities are leaving school without the knowledge, skills, and abilities needed to succeed in postsecondary education and employment environments. In fact, students with disabilities from low-achieving high schools experience higher rates of school dropout, unemployment, and substance abuse, as compared to their non-disabled peers [1]. According to a 2009 report from the National Longitudinal Transition Study (NLTS-2), 45 percent of youth with disabilities enrolled in some type of postsecondary program in 2009, as compared to 53 percent of youth in the general population [24]. Regarding employment, 53 percent of out of school youth with disabilities were employed, as compared to 66 percent of youth in the general population [24]. For adults with disabilities ages 18 to 64 years living in the community, the employment rate is only 33.9 percent, as compared with a rate of 74.2 percent for individuals without disabilities ages 18 to 64 living in the community [14]. Clearly, many youth and adults are not receiving the support or skills needed to transition to postsecondary education programs and employment opportunities. Preparing individuals for lifelong success in a rapidly changing global economy requires schools to reconsider both what and how educators teach and students learn in the 21st century.

© Springer International Publishing Switzerland 2015
M. Antona and C. Stephanidis (Eds.): UAHCI 2015, Part III, LNCS 9177, pp. 109–119, 2015.
DOI: 10.1007/978-3-319-20684-4_11

2   Educating All Students in the 21st Century

2.1   Defining 21st Century Skills

The Partnership for 21st Century Skills (P21) identifies the knowledge and skills necessary to support successful student outcomes in the emerging global economy as: (1) a
foundation of core academic subject knowledge (e.g., reading, writing, and arithmetic);
(2) essential learning and innovation skills (e.g., critical thinking, communication,
collaboration, and creativity); (3) life and career skills (e.g., adaptability, self-direction,
accountability, and leadership); and, (4) information, media, and technology skills.
Positive outcomes are reinforced through 21st century learning environments, professional development, curriculum and instruction, standards, and assessments [26]. A 21st
century education encourages educators to: (a) emphasize core subjects while incorporating 21st century themes, tools, and innovation skills; (b) use 21st century tools to
develop learning skills in current curricula aligned to current standards; (c) use 21st
century assessments to measure 21st century skills; and (d) teach in a 21st century
context, using relevant examples and real-world applications to promote learning,
comprehension, and student growth. By integrating core subject knowledge with essential learning and innovation skills in a relevant and applied manner, and in coordination
with current international, national and state standards, students will graduate better
prepared to succeed in college, career pathways, and life [26].

2.2   The Need to Develop 21st Century Skills

The need to develop 21st century skills is critical given the national statistics on educational and employment outcomes of transition-age youth with and without disabilities.
The U.S. Department of Education reports that 80 percent of all students and 61 percent
of students with disabilities graduate from public high school on time with a regular
diploma while 3.3 percent of students in public high schools dropout annually [33]. In
postsecondary settings, only 59 percent of first-time, full-time students seeking undergraduate degrees at 4-year institutions in 2006 graduated with a bachelor's degree within
6 years from that institution, and only 31 percent of first-time, full-time undergraduate
students seeking a certificate or associate's degree at 2-year institutions in 2009 obtained
it within 150 percent of the normal time required to do so [21]. Moreover, students with
disabilities are far less likely than their nondisabled peers to complete a bachelor's
degree [37], and in 2007-08, only 10.9 percent of students enrolled in postsecondary
institutions reported having disability status [22].

In regard to employment, the 2012 Disability Status Report indicates that only 33.5
percent of persons with disabilities were employed as compared to 76.3 percent of
persons without disabilities [9]. More recently, the 2013 employment-population ratio
for persons with a disability was reported at 17.6 percent while the employment-population ratio for those without a disability was reported at 64 percent [35]. In fact, a
substantial disparity may be found for individuals with disabilities pursuing 21st century
careers within the emerging STEM fields and industries (i.e., Science, Technology,
Engineering, and Mathematics). According to the National Center for Science and

Engineering Statistics (NCSES), "scientists and engineers with disabilities are more likely than those without disabilities to be unemployed or out of the labor force" [23]. The current data purports that 11 % of the nation's scientists and engineers 75 years old or younger has a disability [23]. Furthermore, the majority of scientists and engineers in the nation's workforce were between ages 50 and 75 at the onset of their disability, while less than 30 percent were 19 years or younger at the onset of their disability, and less than 7 % had been disabled at birth [23]. These facts highlight the significance of supporting youth and young adults with disabilities in their pursuit of postsecondary degrees and careers, especially in STEM fields.

3   Policies to Support Positive Transition Outcomes

Mandates set forth in recent disability legislation are encouraging professionals to increase successful transition outcomes for young adults with disabilities. For example, the Individuals with Disabilities Act (IDEA) requires school districts to develop postsecondary goals based on the results of individual transition assessments [31]. The Council for Exceptional Children defines transition assessments as an ongoing process for collecting data on an individual's needs, preferences, and interests as they relate to the demands of current and future working, educational, living, and personal and social environments [29]. For transition assessments to be effective, a variety of tools must be used to gain knowledge of an individual's strengths, skills and abilities, goals, and needs [28].

The Workforce Innovation and Opportunity Act (WIOA) of 2014 improves the services provided to job seekers with disabilities and requires states to deliver supported employment services leading to employment for youth with the most significant disabilities. The law is a renewed commitment to prepare and educate a skilled workforce by strengthening a connection between education and career preparation, including partnerships with community and technical colleges [34]. Through WIOA, youth with disabilities will receive extensive pre-employment transition services (e.g., job exploration counseling, work-based learning experiences, job shadowing, internships, and apprenticeships) to obtain and retain competitive, integrated employment [34, 36]. Although policies have been established by the federal government, key stakeholders must practice strategies and interventions to ultimately improve positive transition outcomes for persons with disabilities.

4   Strategies to Support Positive Transition Outcomes

4.1   Technology

Persons with disabilities are less than half as likely to own computers and are about one-quarter as likely to use the Internet when compared with persons without disabilities [3]. Furthermore, technology that was not designed to be accessible to persons with disabilities can create an additional usability barrier. Access to information technology helps individuals improve their technical skills, which supports additional training and preparation for careers within the emerging technology fields. Several studies have used video prompting as a tool to increase functional daily living skills for people with disabilities [30]. One example includes a study conducted by Mechling, Gast & Seid (2009), where students with ASD were taught valuable cooking skills through the usage of a hand-held personal digital assistant (PDA) to provide various prompts to increase independence.

In order to promote positive academic and employment outcomes, students with disabilities must: (1) have access to information technology; (2) be able to use the technology; and (3) encounter a seamless transition in the availability of technologies from K-12 to postsecondary and employment settings [4]. Meeting these conditions would help equip persons with disabilities with essential 21st century skills–skills that not only include information and communications technology (ICT) literacy, but also career, life, and self-determination skills [13]. To promote these student outcomes, institutional structures that support the effective utilization of technology must be integrated into different levels of the educational system.

4.2 Supported Employment

Supported employment can promote opportunities to earn competitive wages, develop meaningful career goals, make social connections with peers, develop relevant problem solving and choice-making skills, and ultimately participate in society [12]. Through employment, youth with significant disabilities can gain increased ability to make choices, solve problems, make decisions, manage self-regulation, and self-advocate [25]. Without self-determination skills, many persons with significant disabilities do not effectively advocate for what they need in the community or the workplace [16]. Ultimately, when individuals with significant disabilities are successfully employed, they become more fully integrated into their communities [20].

Vocational rehabilitation service providers typically champion supported employment as a preferred option for persons with significant disabilities, because it is associated with more sustainable employment at less cost to society [8]. Supported employment models have greater potential to be cost efficient because work supports are faded, or decreased, through time, thereby creating a more independent worker. Using national averages, Cimera (2008) found that supported employment services cost $6,618 annually, whereas sheltered workshop (i.e., facility-based) services cost $19,388—a significant difference of $12,770. Corroborating this finding, Rogan and Rinne (2011) found that sheltered employment services cost the federal government 4 times as much as integrated community employment. Additionally, the ratio of taxpayer investment to outcome makes supported employment more cost-efficient.

4.3 Self-Determination

Numerous researchers have identified indicators that lead to improved post-school outcomes and independence for students with disabilities. For example, students with functional cognitive skills [38], high levels of self-determination [25], and strong academic skills [2] were more likely to experience post-school success. To increase self-determination, persons with disabilities must be able to perform tasks with as much independence as possible; therefore, the assessment process is critical when determining the best transition plan [32]. However, many of the traditional assessment batteries used to create transition plans purport to measure these skills, but it is unclear how these measures are used to inform the transition planning process and which components lead to the most successful outcomes.

To address strategies that improve the delivery of 21st century skills leading to positive transition outcomes for students with disabilities, The Ohio State University Nisonger Center, a University Center for Excellence in Developmental Disabilities (UCEDD), together with national experts, technology specialists, parents, students with disabilities, administrators, and teachers, have developed and tested intervention programs, including a web-based curriculum called EnvisionIT (EIT), an undergraduate and graduate program called Ohio's STEM Ability Alliance (OSAA), and a college program for students with intellectual disabilities called Transition Options in Postsecondary Settings (TOPS).[1]

5 Effective Interventions for Students with Disabilities

5.1 EnvisionIT

Scaling-Up EnvisionIT: A Model for Teaching 21st Century Skills to Students with Disabilities is a five-year program funded by the United States Department of Education, Office of Special Education Programs to disseminate and sustain the EnvisionIT curriculum nationwide. EnvisionIT is an innovative, online, high school transition curriculum that teaches 21st century skills and is aligned to current state, national, and international standards across four key competency areas: (1) English Language Arts; (2) Information and Communications Technology literacy; transition planning and self-determination; and, financial literacy. In prior projects, students with disabilities who completed EnvisionIT scored significantly higher in Information and Communications Technology literacy and transition knowledge as compared to students in control classrooms [17]. Using a knowledge utilization framework, the evidence-based practices obtained through these prior projects are now being applied to the current project. The curriculum has also been subject to national review processes by experts in the field, and the feedback gathered from these reviews has been used to refine and updated the curriculum.

EnvisionIT is designed as a teacher-directed online curriculum that supports the postsecondary transition of students with mild to moderate disabilities, as well as students without disabilities. Currently, the curriculum is being delivered to students in Ohio, Connecticut, New York, and Montana through the Schoology Learning Management System (LMS). Across 12 units, students acquire basic and advanced ICT literacy skills to: (a) utilize the Web for effective research; (b) edit, save, and organize digital documents and presentations; and, (c) complete computer based assessments.

---

[1] Scaling-Up EnvisionIT is funded by the US Department of Education, Award Number H327S120022. Ohio's STEM Ability Alliance was sponsored by the National Science Foundation, Award Number HRD-0833561. Transition Options in Postsecondary Settings is funded by the US Department of Education, Award Number P407A100039-14.

For instance, students complete age-appropriate transition assessments online, such as the O*NET Interest Profiler (IP), as well as pre-and post-unit quizzes within the LMS. By analyzing the results of a career inventory (e.g., IP), students are able to select careers that align with their preferences and interests. In order to develop a realistic plan, students then determine what type of postsecondary training or education is necessary, as well as possible jobs and related employment opportunities that may help them develop the knowledge, skills, and abilities that are required to pursue their preferred career options. Ultimately, each student develops a cumulative product called a Transition Portfolio, which contains measurable, postsecondary goals for training, education, and employment. The Transition Portfolio also includes a career essay, résumé, cover letter, sample job and college applications, an interview with a professional, and a digital presentation to share their research and transition plan with peers, parents, and service providers.

The curriculum also follows Universal Design for Learning practices to support differentiated instruction and alternate assessment design. Digital assessments, though, are built into the LMS, which allows students to practice skills necessary to complete 21st century assessments. Moreover, struggling readers and auditory learners may utilize free screen reader applications offered through Web browsers to support and enhance their learning experience. Group activities in the curriculum also allow students to build their "soft-skills" for interaction, discussion, and problem-solving. At the end of the course, one student stated:

> "When this class first started, I thought I wanted to be a school psychologist after college, or at least major in psychology. After researching careers and comparing colleges, my career path has completely changed. After high school, I want to go to Ohio State and major in education with a minor in creative writing. My next steps are visiting more colleges, taking the ACT and the SAT, and applying to colleges. I feel that the goals I have set are going to be very good preparation for my future."

Students who complete the curriculum have significantly higher levels of academic achievement, goal setting, and career knowledge [17]. Through the Scaling-Up EnvisionIT model, we provide an important and innovative opportunity for schools to teach—and for students to learn—the essential skills and competencies needed to navigate and succeed in the 21st century.

5.2   Ohio's STEM Ability Alliance

The *Increasing Achievement and Transition Outcomes in STEM Professions of Postsecondary Students with Disabilities* project was a six-year initiative funded by the National Science Foundation (NSF) to research and develop strategies to increase academic and employment outcomes for college students with disabilities in STEM fields at partnering institutions in central Ohio. The initiative, Ohio's STEM Ability Alliance (OSAA) was made up of two quads anchored by The Ohio State University in Columbus, and Wright State University in Dayton. Each quad consisted of the university, a community college, local secondary schools, and business/industry and community partners. Supports and interventions for the students were either delivered or facilitated by Ability Advisors (see Fig. 1), who were the liaison to connect students to the resources needed while simultaneously mentoring the student in self-advocacy and self-determination skills. The supports and interventions developed to enable the students to persist in their STEM major, graduate, and transition to graduate school and/ or STEM employment included: (1) Ability Advising; (2) Student Learning Communities (SLC); (3) Mentoring; and, (4) Internships.

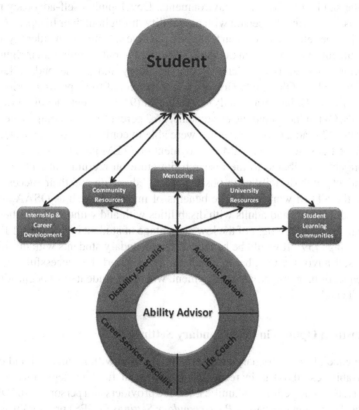

Fig. 1. Ability advising model of interactions between advisor, student, and resources (Source: The Ohio State University Nisonger Center. Diversifying the STEM pipeline from college to careers: A replication guide for supporting the transition of postsecondary STEM Students with disabilities, p. 20. Columbus quad replication guide prepared for the Ohio's STEM Ability Alliance (OSAA) project funded by the National Science Foundation, Award Number HRD-0833561. Available online at http://go.osu.edu/osaa)

A commonality for all students despite disability, age, gender, race, or even STEM major, was revealed in Ability Advising and the SLC when students developed a self-advocacy plan. The self-advocacy plan, supported by meetings with the Ability Advisor, proved to be a critical factor for each student in his/her ability to persist to graduation and employment. Multiple strategies for delivery were employed in the SLC, including online modules hosted within a private social media website. Students unable to attend face-to-face sessions were enabled to use technology to interact with their peers and the facilitator. Activities in the SLC for developing the self-advocacy plan included problem solving, collaboration, communication, and innovation, to enrich the student's 21st century skills. Ability Advising sessions supported the work done in the SLC and guided each student to assess, reflect upon and determine his/her: (a) strengths; (b) learning preferences; (c) understanding of their disability; (d) needs for assistive technology and accommodations; (e) identity; (f) future goals; (g) personal and career interests; and, (h) rights in the academic and career environments. Developing a self-advocacy plan has implications for serving the person with a disability throughout their lifespan. Activities in developing the self-advocacy plan fostered a positive self-image and identity, empowering the student to overcome anxiety and self-doubt about claiming their rights.

The project served 163 students at the secondary and postsecondary level; 112 students attended the Ohio State University. At the end of the reporting period (2008–2014), 46 of the 112 had graduated; 42 graduates (91.3 percent) acquired degrees in STEM fields. Out of the remaining 66 students, 86.3 percent are persisting in their STEM major. Of the 27 graduates on whom we were able to confirm follow-up data, 23 (85.2 percent) have transitioned to STEM employment or STEM graduate school.

The project contributed to the research literature on recruitment and retention of STEM students with disabilities in postsecondary education and their successful transition into the STEM workforce. The benefits of initiatives such as OSAA and EnvisionIT for adolescents and adults with disabilities with and without disabilities should be apparent, especially in light of the low percentage of student input in the IEP process in urban settings [39]. It would be beneficial for secondary students with disabilities to develop a self-advocacy plan before graduation to support the successful transition to training, education, or immediate employment, where the student must begin advocating for him or herself.

5.3   Transition Options in Postsecondary Settings

The emergence of postsecondary programs for students with intellectual and developmental disabilities (IDD) is increasing due to federal funding, legislation and most importantly, advocacy efforts of families, service providers and persons with IDD themselves. The *Transition Options in Postsecondary Settings* (TOPS) program was created at The Ohio State University in order to maximize adult life outcomes for individuals with IDD and those with other developmental disabilities (DD), including individuals with multiple disabilities. This is accomplished by providing college-aged students with IDD the opportunity to participate in college courses, residential living, internships and employment. The TOPS program includes a 2-year and a 4-year option, both designed to blend academics and employment opportunities that match students' desired employment goals. This comprehensive program provides technology training so students gain 21st century skills including: (a) the use of learning management systems; (b) video modeling and prompting programs delivered through tablets, iPads or iPod Touches as a support for job tasks; and, (c) Google calendar apps to manage work, class and social schedules.

In customized employment models, access to technology as an accommodation or support facilitates employment success [15] and potentially reduces the cost of job coaching. Though supported employment is more economical to sustain than sheltered workshops, it still can be costly to provide. Yet, persons with IDD need comprehensive supports to succeed in the workplace. Job coaches in supported employment settings can and do provide these supports; however, the cost of a consistently present job coach is significant, and full-time job coaching is not a sustainable model in long-term employment [8].

In this digital age, one alternative showing promise is the use of technology, specifically mobile and multimedia tools to help youth with IDD communicate and perform tasks [15]. Researchers have shown the potential benefit of video prompting [18], video modeling [5], picture prompting [6], visual/auditory schedules [10], and video instruction [11] to train, reinforce, and guide individuals with IDD to successfully complete work tasks. However, more research on this topic is needed to meet that need.

6 Conclusion

Legislators, educators, and business leaders recognize the importance of preparing all students with 21st century skills that enable an increasingly diverse student population to transition from school to college and into career settings. The costs of supporting persons with disabilities who want to work but are not provided the skills and supports needed to successfully engage in the labor market are rising and must be curbed. Providing education and workforce preparation so students with and without disabilities have the opportunity to become productive members of the workforce is a more cost-effective solution and must continue to be a priority for our nation. Leaders across governmental agencies and business enterprises must continue to invest in innovative programs to develop, disseminate, and sustain effective models to deliver 21st century skills to students today and in the future. Together, we must assure that all of our citizens have access to the technological tools and online curricula to develop the 21st century skills needed to gain and maintain employment in this increasingly global and high-tech world.

References

1. Annie E. Casey Foundation. Counting what counts: Taking results seriously for vulnerable children and families. Author, Baltimore (2009)
2. Benz, M., Yovanoff, P., Doren, B.: School-to-work components that predict postschool success for students with and without disabilities. Except. Child. 63(2), 155–165 (1997)
3. Burgstahler, S.: The role of technology in preparing youth with disabilities for postsecondary education and employment. J. Spec. Educ. Technol. 18(4) (2003)
4. Burgstahler, S., Comden, D., Lee, S.-M., Arnold, A., Brown, K.: Computer and cell phone access for individuals with mobility impairments: An overview and case studies. NeuroRehabilitation 28, 183–197 (2011)
5. Cannella-Malone, H.I., Sigafoos, J., O'Reilly, M., de la Cruz, B., Edrisinha, C., Lancioni, G.E.: Comparing video prompting to video modeling for teaching daily living skills to six adults with developmental disabilities. Educat. Training Dev. Disabil. 41, 344–356 (2006)

6. Cihak, D., Alberto, P.A., Taber-Doughty, T., Gama, R.I.: A comparison of static picture prompting and video prompting simulations strategies using group instructional procedures. Focus Autism Other Dev. Disabil. **21**, 89–99 (2006)
7. Cimera, R.: The cost-trends of supported employment versus sheltered employment. J. Vocat. Rehabil. **28**, 15–20 (2008)
8. Cimera, R.: Supported employment's cost-efficiency to taxpayers: 2002 to 2007. Res. Pract. Persons Severe Disabil. **34**, 13–20 (2009)
9. Erickson, W., Lee, C., von Schrader, S.: 2012 Disability Status Report: United States. Ithaca, NY: Cornell University Employment and Disability Institute (EDI) (2014)
10. Furniss, F., Lancioni, G., Rocha, N., Cunha, B., Seedhouse, P., Morato, P., O'Reilly, M.F.: VICAID: Development and evaluation of a palmtop-based job aid for workers with severe developmental disabilities. Brit. J. Educ. Technol. **32**, 277–287 (2001)
11. Goodson, J., Sigafoos, J., O-Reilly, M., Canella, H., Lancioni, G.E.: Evaluation of a video-based error correction procedure for teaching a domestic skill to individuals with developmental disabilities. Research Dev. Disabil. **28**, 458–467 (2007)
12. Grigal, M., Hart, D.: Think College!. Paul H. Brookes, Baltimore (2010)
13. Grunwald and Associates: Educators, Technology and 21st Century Skills: Dispelling Five Myths. Walden University, Richard W. Riley College of Education, Minneapolis (2010). www.WaldenU.edu/fivemyths
14. Institute on Disability, University of New Hampshire. 2014 Annual Disability Statistics Compendium (2014). http://www.disabilitycompendium.org/docs/default-source/2014-compendium/2014_compendium.pdf. Accessed 11 March 2015
15. Isaakson, C., Burgstahler, S.: AAC, employment, and independent living: A success story. Assistive Technol. Outcomes Benefits **3**(1), 67–78 (2006)
16. Izzo, M.V., Lamb, P.: Self-determination and career development: Skills for successful transition to postsecondary education and employment (White Paper) (2002)
17. Izzo, M.V., Yurick, A., Nagaraja, H.N., Novak, J.A.: Effects of a 21st-century curriculum on students' information technology and transition skills. Career Dev. Except. Individuals 33, 95–105 (2010). http://cde.sagepub.com/content/33/2/95
18. Van Laarhoven, T., Johnson, J.W., Van Laarhoven-Myers, T., Grider, K.L., Grider, K.M.: The effectiveness of using a video iPod as a prompting device in employment settings. J. Behav. Educat. **18**, 119–141 (2009)
19. Mechling, L., Gast, D., Seid, N.: Using a Personal Digital Assistant to Increase Independent Task Completion by Students with Autism Spectrum Disorder. J. Autism Dev. Disord. **39**(10), 1420–1434 (2009)
20. Miller, S.M., Chan, F.: Predictors of life satisfaction in individuals with intellectual disabilities. J. Intellect. Disabil. Res. **52**(12), 1039–1047 (2008)
21. National Center for Education Statistics. Institutional retention and graduation rates for undergraduate students (2014). http://nces.ed.gov/programs/coe/indicator_cva.asp. Accessed 9 March 2015
22. National Center for Education Statistics. Fast facts: students with disabilities (2013). http://nces.ed.gov/fastfacts/display.asp?id=60. Accessed 9 March 2015
23. National Science Foundation. Women, Minorities, and Persons with Disabilities in Science and Engineering, National Center for Science and Engineering Statistics (2015). http://www.nsf.gov/statistics/2015/nsf15311/digest/theme6.cfm. Accessed February 12 2015
24. Newman, L., Wagner, M., Cameto, R., Knokey, A.-M.: The Post-High School Outcomes of Youth with Disabilities up to 4 Years after High School. A Report of Findings from the National Longitudinal Transition Study-2 (NLTS2) (NCSER 2009-3017). SRI International, Menlo Park (2009). www.nlts2.org/reports/2009_04/nlts2_report_2009_04_complete.pdf

25. Palmer, S.B., Wehmeyer, M.L.: Promoting self-determination in early elementary school: Teaching self-regulated problem-solving and goal-setting skills. Remedial Spec. Educat. **24**, 115–126 (2003)

26. Partnership for 21st Century Skills. P21 common core toolkit: A guide to aligning the common core standards with the framework for 21st century skills, Washington, DC (2011). www.p21.org/images/p21/toolkit_final.pdf. Accessed 9 August 2011, February 22

27. Rogan, P., Rinne, S.: National call for organizational change from sheltered to integrated employment. Intellect. Dev. Disabil. **49**(4), 248–260 (2011)

28. Shaw, S.F., Madaus, J.W., Dukes, L.L.: Preparing students with disabilities for college success: A practical guide for transition planning. Brookes, Baltimore (2010)

29. Sitlington, P.L., Neubert, D.A., Begun, W., Lombard, R., Leconte, P.: Assess for success: A Practitioner's Handbook on Transition assessment, 2nd edn. Corwin Press, Thousand Oaks (2007)

30. Tereshko, L., MacDonald, R., Ahearn, W.H.: Strategies for teaching children with autism to imitate response chains using video modeling. Research Autism Spectrum Disord. **4**(3), 479–489 (2010)

31. Test, D.W., Aspel, N.P., Everson, J.M.: Transition methods for Youth with Disabilities. Merrill Prentice Hall, Columbus (2006)

32. Test, D.W., Fowler, C.H., Richter, S., White, J.A., Mazzotti, V.L., Walker, A.R., Kortering, L.: Evidence-based practices in secondary transition. Career Dev. Except. Individuals **32**, 115–128 (2009)

33. U.S. Department of Education. Public high school four-year on-time graduation rates and event dropout rates: school years 2010–11 and 2011–12 (2014). http://nces.ed.gov/pubs2014/2014391.pdf. Accessed March 11 2015

34. U.S. Department of Education. Rehabilitation act as amended by WIOA (2014). http://www2.ed.gov/policy/speced/leg/rehab-act-as-amended-by-wioa.pdf. Accessed 9 March 2015

35. U.S. Department of Labor. Persons with a disability: labor force characteristics – 2013 (2014). http://www.bls.gov/news.release/pdf/disabl.pdf. Accessed 9 March 2015

36. U.S. Department of Labor. The workforce innovation and opportunity act – July 22 2014 (2014). http://www.doleta.gov/wioa/pdf/WIOA-Factsheet.pdf. Accessed 9 March 2015

37. U.S. Government Accountability Office. College completion: Additional efforts could help education with its completion goals (GAO-03-568). U.S. Government Printing Office, Washington, DC (2003)

38. Wagner, M., Newman, L., Cameto, R., Garza, N., Levine, P.: After high school: A first look at the postschool experiences of youth with disabilities. A report from the National Longitudinal Transition Study-2 (NLTS2). SRI International, Menlo Park (2005)

39. Williams-Diehm, K.L., Brandes, J.A., Chesnut, P.W., Haring, K.A.: Student and Parent IEP Collaboration: A Comparison across School Settings. Rural Spec. Educat. Q. **33**(1), 3–11 (2014)

Universal Access to Media and the California Community Colleges Online Education Initiative

Michael James Jayme Johnson[✉]

California Community Colleges Online Education Initiative,
Foothill-DeAnza Community College District, 12345 El Monte Rd,
Los Altos Hills, CA 94022, USA
johnsonjayme@fhda.edu

Abstract. The California Community College system launched the Online Education Initiative in 2014 to address the needs of students and to more effectively leverage the collective resources of the 113 campuses to provide the services needed for degree completion and transfer to university. Providing a common base of instructional technology resources, student services, and a statewide exchange of courses, and with all of this being universally accessible, the Online Education Initiative is one of the most ambitious efforts to address the needs of online students and educators in the history of California.

Keywords: Online education · Accessibility · Adaptable computing · OEI · California · Digital ecosystem

1 Introduction

It has been observed that the evaluation of accessibility efforts in higher education have typically focused on the end products of instructional materials and resources rather than the processes that create these materials [1]. It has also been observed within the California Community College system that this approach inevitably results in sporadic efforts and inconsistent results. In order to address the accessibility issues with online education, we need to truly understand the needs of teachers and students, and support the processes that increase the accessibility of our online programs. The California Community Colleges Online Education Initiative is dedicated to increasing the success of all students and faculty by providing the supports and services needed to excel in their mutual roles.

The processes of an online learning community include a wide variety of behaviors, technologies, and attitudes. Oftentimes, inspiration and unforeseen circumstances can coincide in ways that result in inaccessible materials being used despite having access to the required tools, knowledge, and training for creating accessible instructional materials. This problem is not just an accessibility problem, it is an issue of baseline standards for acceptable quality.

The wide-ranging quality of instructional materials can be observed in any active learning management system, as information inevitably exists in a wide range of formats,

© Springer International Publishing Switzerland 2015
M. Antona and C. Stephanidis (Eds.): UAHCI 2015, Part III, LNCS 9177, pp. 120–126, 2015.
DOI: 10.1007/978-3-319-20684-4_12

gathered from a wide range of sources. By the end of any online class, teachers and students alike will possess a collection of digital information that includes drafts, notes, correspondence, final papers and manuscripts, as well as a variety of third party instructional materials, reports, and manuscripts. Broken into categories of digital media, we have a range of digital text, audio, video, and interactive constructs being used for instruction, much of which is typically inaccessible. We need a means to provide universal access to all of this digital media being used within online learning.

This paper is an investigation of the potential for accessible online education to become a sustainable reality in California, and as such, define a fundamental threshold for effective human computer interactions that are capable of supporting automated and adaptable computing for learning and teaching.

2   An Overview of the California Community Colleges Online Education Initiative

When the Online Education Initiative originated, California was dealing with budget shortfalls that had resulted in the widespread cancelling of classes across the 112 Community Colleges, wherein over a half million students were turned away. [4] Much attention had been given to the use of Massively Open Online Courses, and the idea of leveraging online technology to address localized shortages drove the concept of what would become the California Community Colleges Online Education Initiative (OEI), an effort to increase the overall capacity of degree transfer pathways while providing system-wide support for students and faculty with a deliberate emphasis on increasing the success of traditionally under-represented student populations [5]. As part of this emphasis on traditionally under-represented students in online education, accessibility for students with disabilities is a primary focus and concern.

The following information represents the current vision for ensuring accessibility within the OEI, and represents the viewpoint of the author, as Director of Accessibility and User Experience for the California Community College system. It is offered as a testimonial of the process for designing and implementing what history shall show as the official policy and procedural base that defines and organizes the OEI. It represents the educated opinion of an instructional designer and accessibility specialist who has spent most of the last decade working with faculty and staff from across the state of California, in order to help students with disabilities leverage technology for their academic success.

Finally, the following plan comprises a vision based on a technology base that has yet to be designed and implemented, but which has been agreed upon in terms of a common need and vision of how to meet the needs of supporting the students and faculty of the California Community College system. As of this writing, vendors have been selected for several key components of the technology base that will comprise the OEI, contract negotiations are under way, and expectations are high.

2.1 Primary Objectives of the OEI

Two of the primary concerns of the OEI will be to deliver a Common Course Management System for the entire 113 campus system, and to establish an exchange method for online courses to be shared between the different colleges in order to address the specific needs of ADT students in completing degree and transfer requirements. Surrounding the provision of these two components will be a range of services to address the needs of professional development, basic skills, accessibility, and the entire range of student and faculty services required to address the performance gaps between online education and face to face education.

2.2 The Common Course Management System and Digital Ecosystem

One of the most frequently asked questions thus far regards the Common Course Management System (CCMS) component, which is perhaps one of the best understood specific deliverables of the project.

The impact of the LMS can not be overstated, although it remains just one element of a larger system for delivering learning via online technology. This system will include a student services portal, common assessment and placement, education planning tools, degree audit tools, and a range of specific student services such as online tutoring, counseling, and basic skills remediation. Consider this larger system technology base as a digital ecosystem for learning, and you have an analogy for the complex interactions and data exchange of online education. The CCMS is expected to be one of the primary aspects of the digital ecosystem.

The technology of online education is used to mediate the separation between students and teachers through time and space. It is the power of digital media that conveys and communicates the concepts, principles, facts, procedures, affectation, and attitudes of communication between individual learners and with their instructors. When everything works optimally, technology and media support these fundamental aspects of education in the online context while simultaneously shaping and sustaining the critical interactions of a community of online learners in a way that can transcend the sum of the parts of technology, individual students, teachers, and support staff.

Collectively these different groups of individuals need to be able to interact with each other and exchange information in a variety of formats, from all over the world. All of these interactions and communication are controlled by the capabilities of the digital ecosystem. As the architects and administrators of this ecosystem, it is important to recognize the potential for environmental factors of the digital ecosystem to drive, influence, or even pre-determine certain behaviors and outcomes of the educational process. The analytic potential is exciting to consider, but the questions to drive the data gathering are still being defined.

In addition to the CCMS, the OEI will rely on a series of extendable modules from a common Student Services Portal (SSP) project, which is part of another statewide initiative of the California Community College system, the Educational Planning Initiative [6]. Intended to provide a framework that will help satisfy the needs of the entire spectrum of student services provided to California Community College students. In providing online resources and the capability to complete the various transactions and services that are a part of attending college, the SSP will allow different aspects of the educational process to be informed by student preferences and needs, while simultaneously helping satisfy the institutional needs for reporting and analytics gathering. The analytic data enables an adaptive capability that can be extended throughout the digital ecosystem so that the different processes and various supports provided to online students can be better monitored, understood, and enhanced.

Beyond the services and functionality of the SSP, the state of California has a Common Assessment Initiative (CAI) [7]. The purpose of the CAI is to provide consistency in the assessment instruments used to place incoming students by establishing a common statewide technology platform for administering assessment (placement) tests. In addition, the faculty of the CCC are working together with subject matter experts to define custom banks of questions for writing, mathematics, and English as a Second Language (ESL).

Collectively, the three initiatives of the OEI, EPI, and CAI are expected to help address the needs of CCC students across the entire timeline of their community college experience, while also leveraging the collective size and wealth of resources that comprises the CCC System to alleviate pressures for local campuses and communities.

3 Universal Access to Instructional Materials and Rich Media Communication

Working within the digital ecosystem of the OEI will be an assortment of students, faculty, and staff who will utilize, organize, maintain, and facilitate the creation, storage, and distribution of a wide range of rich digital media. While there is a never ending need for professional development and support in keeping pace with the tools and evolving world of rich digital media creation, there is an equal need for leveraging technology to better support the human processes that inevitably drive the use of these tools. The belief is that if technology can be integrated comfortably into your daily life, it is more likely to be used and not distract from other experiences and activities. We need to enable faculty and students to create universally accessible information without requiring excessive additional effort. The technology used for managing and facilitating online education should not provide additional cognitive load and difficulty to the process of achieving the original educational goal. The technology for communication needs to be an enabling influence rather than a distraction.

3.1 Supporting Faculty in Creating Accessible Instructional Materials

Faculty of the California Community College system are encouraged to utilize a wide range of digital materials and methodologies to enhance the interest and engagement of students, and maximize the potential for digital rich media to enhance the educational process. The focus is on finding ways to enable the use of the best media objects available for instruction and building online learning communities. We need to avoid the situation where a faculty member decides to not use rich media materials because the work required to make the media accessible is too burdensome for the faculty member.

3.2   Ensuring Accessibility of Rich Media Communications

In the California Community College system, there is a recognized need to provide training for the individuals who create digital media so they can create accessible documents. There is also recognition that leveraging technology to reduce the effort required by content creators is a powerful way to encourage certain behaviors in that process.

Providing effective tools for media authoring is a necessary component of ensuring accessible instructional materials, but even so, there are likely to be limitations in the number of digital file formats you can expect a faculty member to be able to create themselves. Fortunately there are technologies available for media conversion, which enable a well structured digital document to be automatically converted to a variety of different digital file formats, while retaining the accessibility of the document, and sometimes enhancing the accessibility of the information [8].

Beyond the need for supporting accessible document authoring and conversion, there is a need to capitalize on other potential efficiencies offered by technology. With a digital ecosystem that is adaptable and responsive to individual needs and preferences comes a certain capability for tracking user activities and engaging different processes based on the needs of the user. Establishing business rules that center around access strategies for certain media types enables automated processing and reporting that reduces the workload of faculty and staff, and helps ensure accessibility of digital media. For example, whenever a faculty member uploads a video file, that file can be recognized as a digital video file and automatically sent to a captioning service and then the captions can be automatically integrated into the video. The priority for processing the captioning job can be adjusted automatically in response to the needs of students enrolled in the class. If there are no students with hearing impairment, the video can be captioned for a lower cost and longer turn around time, while if there was a student with hearing impairment enrolled in the class, the job could be prioritized as a rush job so that captions could be in place for the student ASAP. In this way, students can customize their preferences and receive digital media that best matches their needs.

3.3   Determining Accessibility of Third Party Resources

In addition to creating instructional materials, many faculty find instructional materials on the Internet and integrate them into their learning activities. Problems arise when these third party instructional resources are not accessible for students with disabilities. Recognizing the potential difficulties that can arise in trying to provide accommodations for these situations in the midst of an online course, it is important to help faculty assess the accessibility of third party websites and digital media before they integrate the content into their courses.

Automated web testing technologies can be useful in this effort but they do not replace the need for human interpretation of the results. There are still things that computers can not do, such as recognizing the content of a digital image so as to provide a textual description, or determining if color is being used as the exclusive means of conveying information. Therefor it is important to address this need for human attention within professional development efforts and institutional policy and procedures.

4   A Plan for Accessible Online Learning Communities

Utilizing the Community of Inquiry model [2] to engage a group of instructional designers, the author is engaging a plan of instruction and training for course reviewers, online teaching faculty, staff who create online materials, and staff who support faculty and students. Integrating a social component to the professional development is an attempt to provide sustainability and invoke a sense of ownership and pride of authorship for faculty working within the OEI. By appealing to the best interests of faculty and supporting their needs to create exemplary online instruction, the hope is that the culture of the California Community College will evolve into one where the inherent standard of quality is based on universal access to education.

The challenge of fostering an online learning community will be balanced through the provision of technology and training based on standards for course design that encapsulate the best practices for online education as well as the legally mandated standards for electronic information and information technology [9], as well as for world wide web content [10]. Training will be conducted by a combination of online webinars, an online training course for online teaching, one on one consultations between faculty and instructional designers via web-conference, and a combination of online and in-person clinics and workshops for hands-on activities and remediation.

The ultimate test of any online community is the amount of traffic and interaction that occurs. Within the raw numbers of community members there is a wealth of data that can inform the process of building and sustaining the community. The value that community members find within the community is the main factor that drives participation and membership within the community, so the OEI must deliver services that are easy to use and provide obvious benefits for both students and faculty.

4.1   Designing a Technological Ecosystem for Online Learning Communities

The basic premise of the OEI digital ecosystem is to facilitate an ease of use that doesn't add complexity or tedium to the process of facilitating online educational processes. The first concern for enhancing ease of use centers around the concept of a single sign on capability to unify the many different systems already in use, and facilitate the creation and use of a central user profile across these technology platforms. Extending the functionality and communications capabilities between student information systems, course management systems, enterprise resource management tools, student scheduling systems, etc., is no small task, but it is essential to provide the user experience being sought by today's students and faculty. The OEI is expecting to push the boundaries of capability for facilitating the needs of online learning, in order to better support the success of online students while keeping the focus on education and not the supporting technology.

5   Delivering on the Promise of the OEI

One of the most exciting prospects of the OEI is the idea of harnessing the analytics capabilities of the digital ecosystem to drive an adaptable computing framework for learning. It is easy to imagine many different scenarios where computer power enables richer human interactions with information, but we need to engage the community of educators and technologists to collaborate and conceive of the methods that are best suited for our current capabilities and culture. There will be plenty of time to engage the more interesting and ambitious aspects of building online learning platforms and communities once the digital ecosystem is in place.

One of the first general challenges will be assisting faculty with the effort of knowing and understanding the student, monitoring academic progress, and enhancing the timeliness and effectiveness of communication. It is important to maintain appropriate transparency while also preserving privacy of information. Responsible communication about the benefits of data analytics and the assurances in place to protect privacy of end users can help faculty and students accept these potentially threatening concerns, as long as the ease of use and proposed benefits are delivered.

Ultimately, with analytics feeding adaptable computing technology, there is great potential to redefine the way we assess learning, place incoming students, and ensure faculty are properly trained. There are many exciting opportunities for further research in a wide range of subjects, and across many different industries. However exciting the opportunities for further research may be, it is critical that we show respect for the people that comprise the academic institutions, and honor the premise of student-centric policy and practices. This effort has to be about the success of students, first and foremost.

References

1. E-learning and Disability in Higher Education: Accessibility Research and Practice. Routledge, Jane K. Seale (2013)
2. Community Of Inquiry Model. https://coi.athabascau.ca/coi-model/
3. Pozzi, F., et al.: A general framework for tracking and analysing learning processes In Computer-Supported Collaborative Learning Environments. Innovations In Education & Teaching International 44.2 (2007): 169–179. Academic Search Premier. Web. 28 Feb. 2015
4. http://californiacommunitycolleges.cccco.edu/Portals/0/KeyFacts/California_Community_Colleges_Key_Facts_Updated_11_6_14.doc
5. California Community Colleges Online Education Initiative press release. https://www.insidehighered.com/sites/default/server_files/files/OEIPressReleaseFinal.pdf
6. California Community Colleges Educational Planning Initiative. http://cccedplan.org/
7. California Community Colleges Common Assessment Initiative. http://cccassess.org/
8. Automated document conversion system. http://www.sensusaccess.com/
9. http://www.section508.gov/
10. http://www.w3.org/WAI/guid-tech.html

How Competency-Based Education Can Fulfill the Promise of Educational Technology

Sally M. Johnstone[✉] and David E. Leasure

Western Governors University, Salt Lake City, UT, USA
{sally.johnstone,david.leasure}@wgu.edu

Abstract. Even with today's sophisticated technologies, we usually are still exporting the classroom as if that is the ideal learning environment. Learning science has advanced a great deal in the past several centuries since the lecture became the most common form of 'teaching' at colleges and universities. There is a lot we know about how people learn, yet very few faculty members are learning experts. There is good evidence that adaptive or personalized learning environments help more students be successful, but these are hard to implement in traditional settings. The use of a competency-based education model can facilitate the use of these new learning environments to benefit students.

Keywords: Competency-based education · CBE · Personalized learning · Adaptive learning · Student success · WGU

1 Introduction

In the late 1980's Johnstone and her team designed the first distance learning system to enable students in very rural communities of Maryland to take college classes in real-time with faculty teaching in College Park. The system required two telephone lines into each location. One was for voice, the other for a modem connected to computers. While the instructor lectured he/she could share slides, pictures, diagrams, text, and illustrations with the students in the rural areas. To make it more personal, the faculty member shared a picture of the local classroom-based students, and the remote students shared their pictures with all participants. The remote students could ask and answer questions during class and the instructor could hold virtual office hours using this rather low cost technology. A wide variety of classes were taught via this method. The students (and their employers) were grateful to be able to participate in college classes without driving five or six hours to a campus [1].

Today, we have much more sophisticated technologies. Students can watch a lecture in real-time regardless of where they are in the world. Even though the time zones may be inconvenient, the quality of the visuals and audio over the internet are quite good. The costs of the transmission are also much better than it was when paying for long distance phone calls. However, in most cases we are still just exporting a classroom as if that is the ideal learning environment.

© Springer International Publishing Switzerland 2015
M. Antona and C. Stephanidis (Eds.): UAHCI 2015, Part III, LNCS 9177, pp. 127–136, 2015.
DOI: 10.1007/978-3-319-20684-4_13

Learning science has advanced a great deal in the past several centuries since the lecture became the most common form of 'teaching' at colleges and universities. There is a lot we know about how people learn, yet very few faculty members are learning experts. By and large we still hold up the lecture (designed and delivered by a subject matter expert in their field to a group of students who as individuals are likely to be at varying levels of expertise) to be the pinnacle of best practices to which we will compare other types of learning environments. The federal financial requirements specify that for students to be eligible for grants or loans, there must be 'regular and substantive inter-action between faculty and students' or the experience is considered a correspondence course [2].

What do we know about how people learn – processing, active engagement, and motivation? As Richard Clark, a cognitive psychologist at the University of Southern California puts it, 'mental architecture' has limits on how much we can think about at a time. For most people it is about four ideas ($\pm$ 2) [3]. If we overload it with too much information, the system 'crashes.' This crashing actually protects us, so it is pleasurable. However it drives students to tune out completely or just shift over to checking Facebook to see what their friends are doing while they sit in the lecture hall.

To put this into perspective, consider a typical large lecture section of an introductory statistics class. The instructor is an expert in the field and has created a lecture based on his/her perspective. To the instructor the notion of 'central tendency' is a single idea that may be expressed as a mean, median, or mode and can be used to describe aspects of a group of scores. Some of the students will remember that from high school classes. For these students when the faculty member mentions these, it is one idea. Other students listening to the lecture do not recall any of this and they are trying to think about three different ideas plus the notion of a distribution of scores. They are overloading their cognitive architecture or coming close to doing so. When we add to this the reality that individuals process new information at different rates, we get to the impossible dilemma inherent to a lecture-based classed. The lecturer cannot individualize the information for each student based on his/her prior knowledge of pace of learning.

As the next section will make clear, the advances in personalized learning technol-ogies enable students to work within learning environments that meet an individual student where he/she actually is regarding their knowledge of the field of study, his/her learning style and the speed with which he/she is able to learn. As will become clear, in personalized learning systems the role of the faculty member is not to lecture, but rather to design the learning environment and the methods for determining how students can demonstrate what they have learned, as well as guiding/coaching students in the appro-priate application of their new knowledge.

2   Personalized or Adapted Learning

Adaptive Learning technology at its core combines competencies to be learned, assess-ments of those competencies, and instructional content into a system of learning that adapts or personalizes learning by repeatedly assessing the current state of learning of an individual learner against the desired competencies, and uses scaffolding of knowledge to determine what learning activities to present next to help the learner best progress to full competency. In more elaborate systems, individual learners may be presented with formative feedback and given prioritized options for study, and may be presented with reinforcement on learned competencies based on learning and forgetting curves. Faculty can be presented with dashboards on the progress of all students and presented with a prioritized list of the most troublesome concepts.

The New Media Consortium [4] identifies Adaptive Learning Technologies as an important development in educational technology for higher education with an implementation horizon of four to five years. In a recent report for the Bill and Melinda Gates Foundation, Adam Newman and his colleagues argue for the accelerated adoption of adaptive learning in higher education "…promises to make a significant contribution to improving retention, measuring student learning, aiding the achievement of better outcomes, and improving pedagogy" [5]. Decades ago we had promising intelligent tutoring systems research that was never seemed to be fully implemented. What is causing this optimism for adaptive learning technology?

A growing body of evidence for adaptive learning shows benefits in learning, completion time, completion rate, and better use of instructional time. The settings for these studies vary from hybrid courses to fully online courses, at both public and private universities as well as community colleges. The level of the learning in the studies is primarily college-level general education, but also includes graduate preparatory concepts. The subject matter to be learned in these studies included pre-algebra, algebra, statistics, logic & proof, business, and anatomy & physiology. The types of studies were implemented on a variety of platforms, and ranged from case studies to rigorous formal evaluation. The platforms involved in the studies and sharing the features described above are supported by the following organizations (selected from a wide field of systems):

- Open Learning Initiative (oli.cmu.edu) and its commercial descendant Acrobatiq (acrobatiq.com)
- ALEKS (aleks.com) is supported by McGraw-Hill Higher Education
- Knewton (knewton.com)
- RealizeIt (realizeitlearning.com)

The OLI platform is an outgrowth of research conducted at Carnegie Mellon University that began in 2002 and has grown to support over twenty open courses in foreign language, math, and science [6] The approach has evolved into a commercial initiative of called Acrobatiq that is associated with Carnegie Melon University. The original OLI research project remains at Carnegie Melon University and has now spread to Stanford University.

An overview article using OLI research [7] summarized a number of studies that variously showed reduced learning time by less than half the time of equivalent concepts with no significant difference in learning retention after one semester. These effects are not restricted to university-level students. In a proof and logic OLI course offers at a community college, there was 33 % more learning in the equivalent time of the lecture session. The same review reported completion rate improvement from 41 % to 99 % in a 300 student study at a large public university [8]. A separate effort involving six public institutions, documented a randomized study of an OLI statistics course that showed students using adaptive learning learned equivalent concepts a statistically significant 25 % faster over the control group that participated in the traditional lecture section [9].

These impressive results do not happen without faculty involvement. The importance of faculty experience, preparation, and use of the OLI system features, such as grade book to help trigger interventions, for successful learning by students is critical [10].

In a study encompassing 37 faculty members at 24 community colleges teaching primarily the OLI anatomy and physiology, biology, psychology, and statistics courses to over 1600 students, the learning results in OLI versus traditional courses were not significantly different overall. However deeper analysis showed that the more faculty used the grade book and the more experience they had in general, and with OLI in particular, the better their students performed in OLI versions of the course [11]. These findings on OLI, coupled with earlier results show the promise of adaptive learning, and the importance of training, experience, and commitment on the part of faculty.

ALEKS, which stands for "Assessment and Learning in Knowledge Spaces" grew out of a research project on Knowledge Space Theory with support from the National Science Foundation [12]. The ALEKS platform includes all the elements of adaptive learning technology and has been used most prominently for mathematics and also to support math, business, science, and behavioral science courses [13]. In a federally funded accelerated learning preparation program using ALEKS for minority students in New Mexico called Accelerate New Mexico across six college campuses. Fifty-five students of all backgrounds and ages participated in the study. Math instruction supplemented robotics instruction. Average scores on the pre-test for content mastery examinations were 22 % while average scores on the post-test were 42 points higher at 64 %, and were statistically extremely significant [14].

Other results on the efficacy of various platforms come directly from the vendors. Knewton is a well-known adaptive learning technology platform used by Pearson, Cengage, Elsevier, Wiley, and other publishers. Knewton reports on case studies from Arizona State University, the University of Alabama, and the University of Nevada Las Vegas [15]. The Arizona State University case study [16] is the most extensive and reports on a two semester study of over 2000 students in developmental mathematics. They report withdrawal rates drop from 16 % to 7 % and pass rates increase from 64 % to 75 % with an accelerated completion of four weeks for 50 % of the students. Case studies provided by Knewton showed improvement in remedial math by 17 points in pass rates at the University of Alabama and 19 point improvements at UNLV [17].

The adaptive learning platform created by RealizIt is used by University of Central Florida, Indiana University, the University of Texas System, Colorado Technical University, and others. The platform contains all the key elements defined above [18]. RealizeIt (operating under its old name, CCKF) has been used to implement 300 sections serving 11,000 general education students at Colorado Technical University and American Intercontinental University, which it's parent, Career Education Corporation refers to as Intellipath(™). The results for American Intercontinental University saw a 13.6 percent decline in withdrawals in a pilot group taking English composition and mathematics courses and slightly better final course improvements of 6.8 % [19]. The application of RealizeIt's adaptive learning platform to the MBA preparatory program at

Colorado Technical University, demonstrated a usage of the technology to content above the remedial and general education levels and won a WCET Outstanding Work, [20] though no score improvement is noted, the system ensures students have mastered prerequisite competencies [21].

These results shed some light on why higher education analysts are so optimistic for the adaptive/personalized learning approach to make contributions to student achievement for a wide array of students. While the studies are not completely uniform in their findings, they do point to very promising approaches for advancing the promises of technology to improve and open up learning.

3 Competency-Based Education

It is tough to incorporate personalized learning resources into current practices in higher education. Professors are comfortable lecturing. It is how they learned. They were the ones for whom it worked. If it worked for all their students just as well, there would be fewer poor grades in courses. Different students may need different amounts of time to master course content. If we try to allow students to progress through learning materials at their own rates, we get trapped by our semester or quarter requirements. In addition the technological systems we have in place to track students and their grades operate with strict start and ends dates. To complicate things further, the grade itself is just a means of differentiating the level of mastery among students within the fixed time period defined by the term. At most colleges and universities individual faculty members design and administer their assessments. So two students taking different sections of a course with the same name/course number are likely to be assessed quite differently by their instructors, which renders a grade fairly worthless in any absolute sense as a measure of what each individual mastered.

This brings us to competency-based education (CBE) as a means to allow the integration of what we know about how people learn and how to help them master a body of knowledge. As has been noted previously, we know different people learn at different rates. Some people can master the vocabulary of a new language very quickly, while others may have to practice for a much longer time to achieve mastery of the same material. In addition the same individual may take more time to understand an algebraic formula and apply it, than to learn a new tune on a familiar instrument. People bring different skills, background, and ability to each new learning opportunity, yet as mentioned above, our gold-standard of teaching, the lecture, delivers the same material to everyone in a class at the same pace. All students start their term at the same time and are expected to master a sufficient amount of the material by the end of a fixed period at which all will be graded. If a student demonstrates he/she has mastered 60 % to 100 % of the course material, he/she passes the course. If the student only masters 50 % of the course material, he/she fails and is left with two options: repeat the whole course again or just give up. If he/she chooses to repeat the course, it means paying another fee and sitting through a course half of which he/she knows and then trying to master the parts he/she does not know at the same pace at which it was covered the first time. Many students do just give up.

In the CBE model, the relationship between time and mastery is flipped. Students can learn at their own paces and get personalized support as they progress. They can accelerate based what they already know and slow down with novel material. Well-designed learning resources can easily be incorporated into a student's program of study and each student must demonstrate mastery in order to progress. The faculty still control the curriculum but it is now defined as 'what a student needs to know' and 'how we will determine if he/she knows it.'

The more traditional roles of faculty are typically disaggregated in CBE models so qualified experts can serve in appropriate roles, such as, defining learning objectives, creating or identifying appropriate learning resources, evaluating student learning demonstrations, and working directly with students on their learning plans. That means we are not asking faculty to adapt personalized learning tools to their usual practices. Instead we are creating learning environments into which we can plug tools like OLI, Knewton, ALEKS, or RealizIt as the learning resources. The faculty members are not creating lectures and delivering them to large groups of students in lock step each term nor grading tests or papers, but rather are freed to act as designers of the curriculum and able to offer individualized support to students as they need it. The personalized learning resources can be readily shifted as new, superior products emerge thus enabling students to get the benefit of the latest developments in learning science.

The best proof of concept for CBE is Western Governors University, a private, not-for-profit university. At this writing, it has over 53,000 students, is fully recognized by regional and specialized accreditors, and produces the largest number of secondary STEM teachers in the country [22]. WGU is among the top five producers of bachelor's degrees in nursing for minorities. In addition to Health Professions and the Teachers College, WGU offers degrees in Business and Information Technology that all include general education courses. Employers think highly of WGU graduates and it continues to change the learning resources it offers to students as learning science develops. In addition students pay less than $6,000 a year for tuition for as many courses as they are chose to take.

At WGU faculty members offer direct and personal support to students. Faculty members are called *mentors* and all are full-time employees who may be located anywhere throughout the United States. When a student enrolls at WGU, he/she is assigned a *student mentor* who stays in weekly or bi-weekly electronic contact with that student throughout his/her matriculation with the university. If a student needs tutorial support in a particular course, a *course mentor*, works with that student either one-on-one or in small group webinars. Students' work products are 'graded' by part-time evaluators who have been trained on grading rubrics created by faculty, instructional designers and psychometricians. Students are scored as either 'pass' or 'not pass' on an assignment and get feedback on their skill and knowledge deficits. This allows them to work with their faculty to learn what they did not know. By separating the evaluation component of a course and the direct support to the students, the nature of the relationship between the student and his/her faculty is different than in a traditional course where the role of the faculty member is both to instruct and evaluate.

Even though WGU's students and *mentors* do not meet face-to-face until commencement, students report high levels of engagement. In 2014, the National Survey of Student

Engagement (NSSE) polled more than 350,000 students from more than 600 institutions. Students gave WGU the highest scores possible at significantly higher levels than the national average in the follow key areas [23]:

- Quality of interactions with faculty – 20 % higher
- Quality of academic support – 23 % higher
- Would attend same institution again – 25 % higher
- Rating of entire educational experience – 16 % higher
- Time spent per week on studies – 13 % higher
- Acquisition of job-related knowledge and skills – 13 % higher

4 Design Principles of CBE [24]

There are quite a few higher education institutions now developing CBE programs. A January 2015 article in the Atlantic Magazine reported at least 50 [25]. Western Governors University is working with almost a dozen community colleges across the United States as they each develop their own CBE programs. To make the realities of CBE programs less mysterious, we created a set of design principles that our partner colleges are using. These five principles are guiding the development of high quality CBE programs.

1. Degree Reflects Robust and Valid Competencies. Competencies are core to the CBE curriculum. In professional programs, they should align with both industry and academic standards. The process by which they are developed should be explicit and transparent. Program-level competencies should reflect the skills and knowledge that students will need at the next stages of their development, whether it is for further education or employment.

2. Students are able to Learn at a Variable Pace and are Supported in Their Learning. A CBE program should allow students to attain mastery by progressing through the curriculum at an individualized pace. Student success when progressing at differential rates requires a strong support system to keep them motivated and on track. Just-in-time academic assistance must be provided to students as well.

3. Effective Learning Resources are Available Anytime and are Reusable. In order for students to accelerate in a CBE program, they need to be able to work through the learning resources at their own pace. The materials (e.g., e-texts, recorded lectures, simulations) need to be available anytime the student is ready to study and paced to the student's requirements, not the institution's schedule. This suggests asynchronous learning resources coupled with academic assistance available in a just-in-time manner.

4. The Process for Mapping Competencies to Courses/Learning Outcomes/Assessments is Explicit. Once the competencies are established at the program-level, academic teams need to translate them into topics that can then be formulated into courses of appropriate length and complexity. The courses are then broken into learning objectives, which will drive the selection of learning resources and the assessments.

5. Assessments are Secure and Reliable. Assessments are built using the expertise of academic subject matter experts and employers (for professional programs), thus ensuring content validity. Scoring rubrics can provide a shared understanding for students and evaluators and also contribute to the reliability of the assessments.

5   Different Types of CBE Implementations

As the whole arena of competency-based education develops, there are a number of different implementation strategies that stick to the principles noted above, but result in different looking programs. The institutions creating CBE programs are doing so in a variety of ways to fit with the structure and practices they have in place. WGU was created as a stand-alone institution and has over the last 18 years created policies and practices that allow students to be successful in self-paced but highly supported CBE programs.

Our partner community colleges are integrating the CBE programs into their already existing campus structures and practices. As they do so, they have chosen approaches that fit within their own cultures. For example, at Sinclair Community College (Ohio) they are using a centrally managed approached with their distance learning personnel supporting faculty and other units across the whole college as they develop CBE programs. At Austin Community College District (TX) they developed all the CBE support functions within a single academic department. As other academic areas are considering their own CBE programs, the support unit will need to shift. In the state of Washington, four colleges developed their own CBE programs (Bellevue College, Columbia Basin College, Edmonds Community College, and the Community Colleges of Spokane's Spokane Falls campus). As these programs have successfully launched, other colleges in the state created a consortium to develop and offer a transferable business management CBE degree that will share academic and support services [26]. Other partner colleges, Broward College (FL), Ivy Tech (IN), Lone Star College District (TX), and Valencia College (FL) are all using different strategies for integrating CBE programs into their existing institutions. The lessons they are learning are being shared publically (www.CBEinfo.org), but generally students are flocking to these programs that offer them flexible learning options with consistent, high quality learning outcomes.

6   Conclusion

In conclusion, competency-based education is a different but effective means of awarding credentials that is enabled by 21st century learning technologies. In a CBE program, students progress based on demonstrations of skills and knowledge unrelated to time. Time is only an administrative variable that can be used to measure the length of a term for financial aid disbursement but is not a proxy for learning. Qualified faculty and subject matter experts define the learning objectives, and qualified faculty and psychometricians determine how learning is measured. In a CBE model, the more traditional roles of faculty are typically disaggregated so qualified experts can serve in appropriate roles, such as, defining learning objectives, creating or identifying appropriate learning resources, evaluating student learning demonstrations, and working directly with students on their learning plans. Graduates of these programs will have demonstrated consistent learning outcomes with the skills and knowledge they need to be successful in either the workplace or further education. CBE can help us fulfill the promise of educational technology.

As researchers at Carnie Melon University were beginning the work that developed into the Open Learning Initiative, one of those researchers and a Nobel Laureate, Herbert Simon, put it, "Improvement in post-secondary education will require converting teaching from a 'solo sport' to a community-based research activity" [27].

References

1. Gilcher, K.W., Johnstone, S.M.: A Critical Review of the Use of Audio graphic Conferencing Systems by Selected Educational Institutions. International University Consortium College Park, MD (1988)
2. http://www.ecfr.gov/cgi-bin/text-idx?SID=f75dc5ef3be21a8e24d78975fa31eae4&node=pt34.3.600&rgn=div5#se34.3.600_12 Accessed 15 January 2015
3. Clark, R.E., Kirschner, P.A., Sweller, J.: Putting students on the path to learning. Am. Edu. **36**, 1–11 (2012)
4. New Media Consortium. Horizon Report 2015 Higher Education Edition, 1 January 2015 http://cdn.nmc.org/media/2015-nmc-horizon-report-HE-EN.pdf Accessed 14 February 2015
5. Newman, A., Stokes, P., Bryant, G.: Learning to adapt: a case for accelerating adaptive learning in higher education, p. 4 15 April 2013. http://tytonpartners.com/library/accelerating-adaptive-learning-in-higher-education/ Accessed 14 February 2015
6. http://oli.cmu.edu Accessed 14 February 2015
7. Lovett, M., Meyer, O., Thille, C.: The open learning initiative: measuring the effectiveness of the OLI statistics course in accelerating student learning. J. Interact. Media in Edu. (2008)
8. Schunn, C.D., Patchan, M.: An evaluation of accelerated learning in the CMU open learning initiative course logic proofs. Technical report. Learning Research and Development Center, University of Pittsburgh. https://oli.cmu.edu/wp-oli/wp-content/uploads/2012/10/Schunn_2009_Evaluation_OLI_Logic_Proofs.pdf Accessed 13 February 2015
9. Bowen, W.G., Chingos, M.M., Lack, K.L., Nygren, T.I.: Interactive Learning Online at Public Universities: Evidence from Randomized Trials. ITHAKA (2012)
10. Kaufman, J., Ryan, S., Thille, C., Bier, N.: Open learning initiative courses in community colleges: evidence on use and effectiveness (2013). http://www.hewlett.org/sites/default/files/CCOLI_Report_Final_1.pdf Accessed 14 February 2015
11. Ibid
12. www.aleks.com Accessed 14 February 2015
13. Falmagne, J., Cosyn, E., Doignon, J., Thi´ery, N. (n.d.).: The Assessment of Knowledge, in Theory and in. Practice. http://www.aleks.com/about_aleks/Science_Behind_ALEKS.pdf Accessed 14 February 2015
14. Rivera, M., Davis, M.H., Feldman, A., Rachkowski, C.: An outcome evaluation of an adult education and postsecondary alignment program: the accelerate New Mexico experience. Prob. Perspect. Manage. 11:4, 105–120 (2013)
15. www.knewton.com Accessed 14 February 2015
16. www.knewton.com/assets-v2/downloads/asu-case-study.pdf Accessed 14 February 2015
17. www.knewton.com/platform/efficacy Accessed 14 February 2015

18. Howlin, C., Lynch, D.: A Framework for the Delivery of Personalized Adaptive Content. In: Proceedings of the ICWOAL Conference (2014). http://realizeitlearning.com/papers/ FrameworkPersonalizedAdaptiveContent.pdf Accessed 14 February 2015
19. Fain, P.: New Player in Adaptive Learning, 29 July 2013. http://insidehighered.com/news/ 2013/07/29/career-education-corp-expands-major-adaptive-learning-experiment Accessed 14 February 2015
20. WCET.: WCET Outstanding Work Awards Announced (2014). wcet.wiche.edu/advance/ wow-media-release-2014 Accessed 14 February 2015
21. Johnson, C., Kleisch, E., Troyka, T. (n.d.).: Learning gets personal: transforming the one-size-fits-all approach to higher education. http://www.coloradotech.edu/~/media/CTU/Files/ ThoughtLeadership/ctu-adaptive-learning-whitepaper.ashx Accessed 14 February 2015
22. www.wgu.edu Accessed 22 January 2015
23. www.wgu.edu Annual Report 2014 Accessed 15 February 2015
24. These principles were first published in Johnstone, S.M., Soares, L.: Principles for Developing Competency-Based Education Programs Change The Magazine of Higher Learning, vol. 46:2 (2014). doi:10.1080/00091383.2014.896705 (link: http://dx.doi.org/10.1080/00091383. 2014.896705)
25. http://www.theatlantic.com/education/archive/2015/01/getting-credit-for-what-you-know/ 384919/?single_page=true&print Accessed 29 January 2015
26. Fain, P. (2015) Moving Ahead with Competency. Inside Higher Ed, 17 February 2015. https:// www.insidehighered.com/news/2015/02/17/two-year-colleges-washington-state-expand-competency-based-project-business-degree Accessed 17 January 2015
27. Simon, H.: A Need teaching be a loner's sport? Distinguished Lecture presented at Carnegie Mellon University, Pittsburgh, April 1996

Leveraging Virtual Worlds
for Electronic Mentoring

Christopher Langston[1](✉), Nathan Moon[2], Robert Todd[1],
Noel Gregg[3], and Gerri Wolfe[3]

[1] Center for Assistive Technology & Environmental Access,
Georgia Institute of Technology, Atlanta, USA
{chris.langston,Robert.todd}@coa.gatech.edu
[2] Center for Advanced Communications Policy,
Georgia Institute of Technology, Atlanta, USA
Nathan.moon@cacp.gatech.edu
[3] Regents Center for Learning Disorders, University of Georgia,
Georgia, USA
{ngregg,gwolfe}@uga.edu

Abstract. The Georgia STEM Accessibility Alliance's *BreakThru* electronic mentoring program responds to a National Science Foundation request for research on virtual worlds to support outcomes for students with disabilities. It also addresses student advancement through critical junctures to STEM careers, particularly from secondary to post-secondary education, and from the undergraduate to graduate level. *BreakThru* has developed from an exploration of technology platforms into a full-fledged mentoring program that currently enrolls 85 students and 38 mentors. The overall aim of *BreakThru* is to increase the persistence in STEM of students with disabilities who are enrolled in the program. Toward this end, efficacy is measured in part through enrollment and retention of secondary and postsecondary students with disabilities into virtual mentoring. *BreakThru* is unique among mentoring programs due to its use of the virtual world Second Life to support or implement most project activities.

Keywords: Second life · Electronic mentoring · Students with disabilities · Persistence · Retention · STEM

1 Introduction

The Georgia STEM Accessibility Alliance's (GSAA) *BreakThru* electronic mentoring program responds to a National Science Foundation request for research on virtual worlds to support outcomes for students with disabilities (SwD). Reports issued by the National Science Foundation (NSF 1996, 2000, and 2004) emphasize the need for increased persistence among students with disabilities in STEM professions. Given the significant barriers to accessing higher education STEM programs (Burgstahler, 1994; NSF, 2000) experienced by SwDs, the need for solutions is clear. Electronic mentorship provides students with necessary support while overcoming many of the restrictions of the traditional, face-to-face mentoring model.

© Springer International Publishing Switzerland 2015
M. Antona and C. Stephanidis (Eds.): UAHCI 2015, Part III, LNCS 9177, pp. 137–148, 2015.
DOI: 10.1007/978-3-319-20684-4_14

Inexperience with the software and interface metaphors of virtual worlds each present a number of challenges to new users. In some instances, the unfamiliarity of the platform makes it less appealing than more traditional communication methods. GSAA has attempted to meet the challenges of virtual world e-mentoring through a strategy focused on both accessibility and the use of gamification concepts to encourage use of the tools. This paper will explore the ways in which *BreakThru* has leveraged the affordances of virtual worlds to further enhance the e-mentoring model and discuss some of the findings regarding platform adoption that remain.

2   Virtual World Selection Process

Upon its inception in 2010, GSAA was confronted with an array of choices for virtual world platforms around which to develop *BreakThru*. GSAA had four major platform criteria: (1) It needed to enable very rapid prototyping and delivery of a functional product; (2) Computer hardware requirements needed to be minimal; (3) Costs of development and maintenance needed to be affordable; and, (4) It had to be as accessible as possible. Three virtual world platforms were selected as the most promising and compared according to these factors to select the best fit for *BreakThru*.

Second Life. Second Life is an online virtual world that is privately developed, owned and maintained by Linden Lab (http://www.lindenlab.com) which went live in 2003. While in many ways the most restricted virtual world platform in competition for hosting *BreakThru,* Second Life had a number of advantages which other platforms lacked. As of 2010, it was by far the most widely recognized and utilized virtual world platform (Meisenberger et al., 2008) among the options available. Second Life is a product, and the backing of an experienced developer with a financial investment in the software also meant that updates and new features could be relied upon with no additional resources needed from GSAA. In addition, Second Life also has a thriving economy supporting user created content both by individuals and specialized design groups offering development services. GSAA was able to leverage this third-party economy to provide its participants with a wide variety of virtual world resources and rewards for project activities.

GSAA conducted an assessment of three major platforms:, Forterra OLIVE, Second Life (http://www.secondlife.com), and OpenSim (http://opensimulator.org). GSAA selected Second Life as its primary virtual world platform based upon its adherence to the four criteria described previously (White and Todd, 2011; Todd, Todd, 2012). Second Life was the most mature platform with an extensive history of updates and active development by Linden Labs. The community of Second Life users and content authors enabled GSAA to prototype a functional virtual world for students enrolled in *BreakThru* mentoring within the first year of the project. Computer hardware requirements were minimal both as a result of the maturity of the Second Life software and extensive options to scale the visual fidelity of the virtual world according to end user hardware. Linden Labs also hosted the virtual world on their own servers, allowing GSAA to subscribe to Second Life as a service and minimize administrative overhead. Altogether, these advantages made Second Life both the fastest and most affordable platform option.

Accessibility of Second Life. Accessibility remained a major concern, and numerous accessibility barriers were reported with Second Life (Hickey-Moody and Wood, 2008). Second Life was mostly inaccessible to visually impaired users and the default client-side software, called a viewer, was incompatible with screen readers (Peters and Bell, Peters and Bell 2007; Verhoeven, 2007). The viewer worked better for hearing impaired users since a text chat option was available, but the advent of voice integration actually made the playing field more uneven (Peters and Bell, Peters and Bell 2007). However, the text chat would not necessarily align with spoken voice unless a transcriber was present within the virtual world. Users with mobility or dexterity limitations had the most success using the viewer, though more complex controls could potentially be difficult when using alternative input devices.

The accessibility issues highlighted as presented within Second Life also existed to a similar degree in other potential platforms. However, the much larger community of frequent Second Life users meant that there was also a larger focus on making Second Life accessible to those users. A number of open-source projects were available to GSAA that held potential to alleviate these barriers. Linden Labs allows for alternative viewers to connect to the virtual worlds hosted on their servers. One such alternative viewer Radegast (http://radegast.org/wp/), a Second Life viewer built for improved accessibility. Radegast eschews the traditionally 3-D graphics heavy approach to virtual worlds while maintain full functionality and interactivity. It also added features such as improved audio cues, automated text responses, and text-to-speech output. The existence of Radegast and other free accessibility tools such as Virtual Guidedog (http://www.virtualguidedog.com) made a strong argument that if no virtual world platform could be relied upon for native accessibility, then the presence of a strong user community held potential to alleviate at least some of the existing barriers (Kelly, 2008).

3 BreakThru Virtual World Development Process

GSAA partnered with the Vesuvius Group, LLC to rapidly prototype a Second Life virtual world suitable for use in electronic mentoring. Linden Labs sells parcels of 3-D virtual space on their server, called the Grid, as individual islands. Each of these parcels carries an associated annual maintenance cost and provides the owner and designated content managers with free reign over the aesthetics and functionality present in that space. In conjunction with Vesuvius, GSAA purchased two adjacent spaces on the Grid: one for secondary students and one for post-secondary students.

Training. Roughly 20 % of the space within the VLR is dedicated to a training obstacle course with detailed guideposts that explain how to use the Second Life client. Participants also undertake a 1-hour, mandatory training administered by GSAA staff that teaches the basic skills necessary to navigate, communicate, and interact with objects and other avatars in Second Life. The need for this training became apparent when early participants began encountering difficulties with the Second Life client. Initial plans for the obstacle course were for participants to undertake a self-guided training. However, many participants elected not to complete the course or simply failed to realize that it existed.

4 Methods of Communication Among BreakThru Dyads

Mentor and mentee participants connect with one another using a wide range of technologies. Participants are introduced to the range of communication methods supported by GSAA and then allowed to shape their mentoring relationship using whichever tools are most appropriate to their individual needs. GSAA monitors each dyad and collects data on the chosen method of communication.

Beginning in 2012, students were surveyed twice during each academic year of participation in *BreakThru*, once in the fall and once in the spring. Data collection took place five times: Fall 2012, Spring 2013, Fall 2013, Spring 2014, and Fall 2014. Students were asked to "Select all the ways you communicate with your mentor/mentee." The aggregate results of this question across all five data collection periods is shown below Table 1.

Table 1. Communications Methods Utilized Across 5 Reporting Periods

Survey Responses	Text			Voice			In Person
	Email	Facebook	SMS	Second Life	Skype	Phone	
Secondary Mentees Total (= 36)	81 %	8 %	75 %	47 %	11 %	69 %	61 %
Post-Secondary Mentees Total (n = 61)	97 %	31 %	57 %	52 %	20 %	69 %	15 %
Secondary Mentors Total (n = 43)	84 %	5 %	67 %	44 %	16 %	70 %	44 %
Post-Secondary Mentors Total (n = 61)	97 %	31 %	57 %	32 %	20 %	69 %	15 %

Participants generally reported a higher frequency of usage with communication platforms with which they were already acquainted. Email and phone, unsurprisingly, were reported as the most commonly used communication methods. Interestingly, SMS was reported as a more frequent method of communication than traditional telephone among secondary mentees. Regarding Second Life specifically, adoption was slightly higher among post-secondary mentors and mentees.

Anonymous usage statistics are collected within the VLR that record total logins and peak user concurrency each day. Aggregating this data month by month provides a clear picture of how usage ebbs and flows throughout the academic calendar. Discounting the summer months, students tend to be most active during September and October, and least active during March and November. March correlated with spring break for both secondary and post-secondary *BreakThru* participants, and that gap in instructional time may account for a portion of the consistently poor participation evident in March (Fig. 1).

Annual usage patterns begin to emerge when multiple years of project data are compared. Usage is generally highest at or near the beginning of each semester. This also coincides with the time period during which new participants are enrolled in the program. Fall semester usage drops sharply in November and December each year,

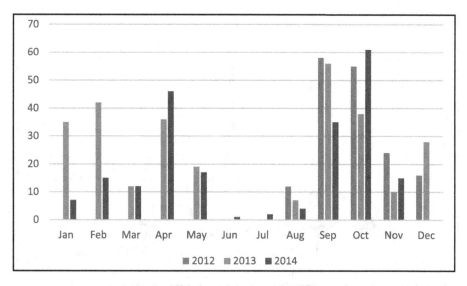

Fig. 1. Fall 2012– Fall 2014 Total VLR Users per Month

providing a narrow window of time during which users are logging in to the VLR. Spring Semester usage remains slightly more stable and time period during which students are logging in ranges from January until May with a peak in April. Both Fall and Spring semesters show peaks that are concurrent with the scheduling of guest speaker presentations or project-sponsored events taking place within the VLR. Project activities do not take place officially during the summer academic break, but a few users continue to log in periodically.

Overall use of the VLR peaked during September and October 2012 and tapered off dramatically as the semester continued. These months coincided with a series of mandatory training events which account for a significant amount of total monthly activity. August and December were each months during which participants were inactive owing to the start and end of fall semester.

September 2012 was the first month in which a significant number of participants had access to the island. However, peak concurrency never rose above 2 or 3 participants at a time (i.e., 1 dyad) except during the Fall Kick-off event hosted by GSAA in the VLR. The Kick-off was the first significant experience that many participants had with Second Life, and based on login records many students did log in subsequently until required to do so. Smaller peaks in October 2012 are associated with mandatory training events designed to acclimate participants to the interface of Second Life.

5   Interactivity and Gamification

Early data from 2012 strongly suggested that additional incentives would be necessary in order to entice participants into regular use of the VLR. Participation in e-mentoring activities remained high, but participants were relying on other communications

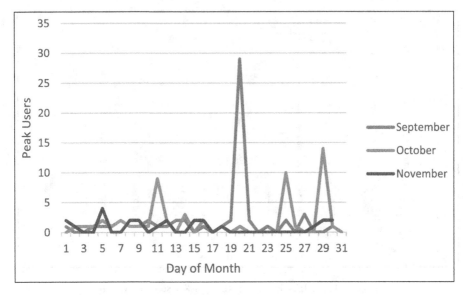

Fig. 2. Sep– Nov 2012 Peak Concurrency by Day

platforms to connect with one another. During winter 2012, efforts were made to increase the range of activities available to *BreakThru* participants within the VLR. Early research suggested that gamification was an effective means of increasing engagement among partciipants (Chrons and Sundell, 2011). The inclusion of game-like activities also showed promise for faciliating experiential learning (Duncan, Miller & Jiang, Duncan et al. 2012; Inman et al., Inman et al. 2010). Gamification applies game design concepts to other contexts such as education, and GSAA began a review of potential areas where gamification could be utilized to increase the degree of interest in Second Life as a mentoring platform.

Gamification shows potential for enhancing engagement and motivation among students, and for improving the interactivity of online media (Weber, 2004; Pursel & Bailey, 2005; Hamari et al., 2014). Universities are experimenting with the application of badging as a method of recognizing student achievment (Johnson et al., 2013). Badges, or visible rewards for completion of specific activities and goals, have been shown to positively influence behavior in certain situations (Grant and Betts, 2013). Due to the individualized nature of e-mentoring dyads in the program, *BreakThru* cannot uniformly apply badges for completion of specific activities related to mentoring. Instead, activities were developed with the intention of increasing the frequency and duration of logins to the VLR. It was expected that participants would have differing levels of interest in certain activity types, and the intent was that badging activities would serve as an enticement to log in to the VLR more frequently and for greater duration.

Badge Activities. GSAA leadership in collaboration with Vesuvius Group, LLC developed a series of activities intended to provide greater immersion to students using the VLR during mentoring. These activities are not tied directly to mentoring. Instead, they provide a sense of accomplishment and encourage collaboration between participants. A mixture of individual and group activities were developed, and certain activities can only be accomplished cooperatively Table 2.

Table 2. Badge Rewards Available to *BreakThru* Participants in the VLR

Symposium Attendee	Basic Training	Lake Angler	Clean Water
Kick-Off Attendee	Build 101	Coral Reef Angler	Wildlife
	Traveler	Sea Angler	Botany
	Scavenger Hunt	Master Angler	Light in a Bottle

Activities were selected to encourage exploration of the entire island and provide a connection to STEM education. *BreakThru* participants who spent longer in the VLR and took time to explore areas of the island that were not introduced during mandatory training were the most likely to encounter badge completion activities. For example, the Botany badge requires participants to find and interact with 10 different species of plant life represented within the VLR. Finding and clicking on each provides the participant with accurate details about that plant's biology. Other badges provide hidden training to participants about how to engage with one another in the VLR, such as the Traveler badge that requires participants to play with the various vehicles and mobility devices on the island (e.g., boats, bicycles, wheelchairs, etc.). Certain badge activities can only be completed cooperatively with another *BreakThru* participant (Image 1).

Image 1. Image of badge tracking UI element in the *BreakThru* VLR

Badge completion is tracked through a custom interface element available in the VLR. This interface provides participants with instructions on how to complete each activity along with a progress indicator showing how close they are to finishing. Activities also have an associated graphical badge which is presented to students who complete them. Badge completion data is aggregated on a leaderboard so that participants can compare their progress to one another. Once a participant completes the activites associated with a given badge, they are rewarded with a graphical signifier on their UI as well as a visual token (hats, clothing, pets or other digital goods) that represents to other users that the badge activity has been completed. Additional rewards are available for participants who complete multiple badges Table 3.

Table 3. Monthly Badge Statistics by Distinct User and Total Interactions

Month	Distinct Users	Total Interactions	Event
Feb 2013	10	154	Badge Launch
Mar 2013	1	1	
Apr 2013	4	53	
May 2013	4	20	End of Semester
Sep 2013	21	156	Kick-Off Event
Oct 2013	23	99	Grad Symposium
Nov 2013	6	24	
Dec 2013	5	15	
Jan 2014	1	2	
Feb 2014	3	3	
Mar 2014	1	17	
Apr 2014	9	37	End of Semester
May 2014	3	5	
Sep 2014	23	31	Kick-Off Event
Oct 2014	7	24	Grad Symposium
Nov 2014	3	7	
Dec 2014	0	0	
Jan 2015	4	5	
Feb 2015	1	1	

The badge implemtation in *BreakThru* shows significant spikes in usage that correlate with other events taking place within the VLR. While a high volume of usage was found among a small number of users during the initial launch event announcing the badge feature, the highest overall usage was recorded early in the Fall 2013 semester. Mentoring activities typically begin regularly taking place in September once new participants have finished enrollment both in classes and in the *BreakThru* program. The Fall 2013 Semester Kick-Off event both introduced new participants to the VLR and welcomed back returning participants from previous semesters. The Graduate Symposium in October 2013 enticed a significant number of participants to log in and attend a presentation by a special guest speaker. In each case, the badge system was not specifically addressed or referenced as part of the event, but the increased number of logged in users led to a much higher degree of interaction with the system.

Figure 3 shows the effect of badging on overall use of the VLR. Periods of elevated activity in the VLR correspond to an increased number of interactions with badge objects. Students returning from the holidays jumped back into the program quickly in January. However, overall logins for Jan-May 2013 drops 12.7 % as compared to Fall 2012 and owing to a significant drop in logins for March 2013. Aug-Dec 2013 rates dropped a further 3.5 % from spring, or 15.8 % compared to Aug-Dec 2012.

GSAA also tracks total Badge Interactions, or times a VLR participant clicked on a badge-related object, in an attempt to correlate overall badge activity more closely with Total Logins. Though not every student participated in badge activities, Fig. 3 depicts what might be expected for activities that a user completes over multiple logins. Distinct Badge Users records individual accounts that undertook an activity within the

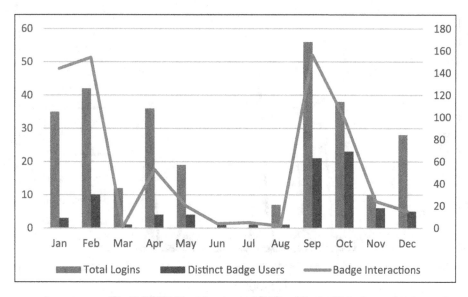

Fig. 3. 2013 Total Logins and Distinct Badge Users

VLR related to at least one badging activity during each monthly reporting period. Since each user is counted once at most, the total possible number of Distinct Badge Users is much lower than the aggregate of anonymous Total Logins during the same time period. Anonymous login totals cannot be compared to distinct badge users. Instead, peak concurrency must be compared in a more general way with overall interactions with badge activities.

Figure 4 shows that during both spring and fall data collection periods, the levels of highest activity were recorded on days where project training or events were already scheduled to take place in the VLR. Fall 2012 data (see Fig. 2) prior to the introduction of gamification elements showed a similar pattern, suggesting that participants were not enticed to log in with any greater degree of frequency as a result of badging activities being made available.

Overall, the data describing both interactions with badging activities and peak user concurrency suggest that gamification as implemented within the *BreakThru* VLR did not increase the frequency of visits by participants. However, the badges themselves were sought after by a minority of participants who already had a reason to log in. Guest speakers and special events were of much greater significance in predicting a higher peak concurrency among VLR users. Once logged in, badge activities saw a significant uptick in overall usage. This may suggest that badges were seen more as fun distractions than opportunities for STEM engagement in spite of the STEM focus of each activity (Fig 5).

Peak usage during Fall 2012 predates the inclusion of gamification concepts. Yearly trends show a gradual decline in usage from 2012 to 2014 despite an expanded range of activities available within the VLR. A number of additional factors may conribute to the reduced participation in the VLR over time, including the specific mixture of student and mentor participants, level of participation, events scheduled by project staff.

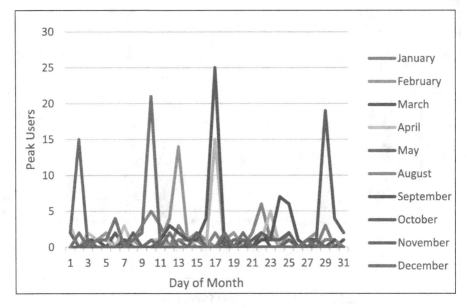

Fig. 4. 2013 Monthly Peak Concurrency by Day

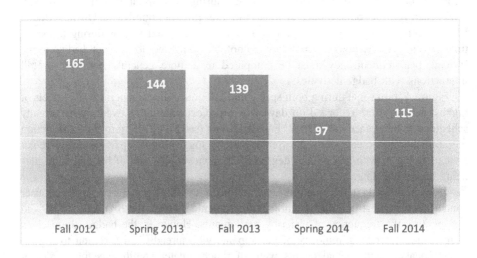

Fig. 5. Total VLR Logins 2012–2014

6 Conclusion

Virtual worlds such as the *BreakThru* VLR provide an interactive, graphically rich experience to participants seeking that level of immersion. While the available technology does present several barriers to accessibility, appropriate training and use of open-source accommodations can alleviate those barriers and allow for a unique e-mentoring experience not available through more traditional methods. However, virtual worlds must be supported through communication via other methods.

Students will generally default to using methods of communication that are faster and more familiar. Participants overwhelmingly reported using the telephone and email. Secondary participants also reported significant use of short-messaging service (a.k.a. texting). These three options are each available from mobile devices with full functionality, whereas Second Life mobile clients sacrifice graphical fidelity and several features in order to adapt to mobile platforms. This strips away several of the advantages virtual worlds might have over other mobile communications methods.

The results of *BreakThru* suggest that virtual worlds are most useful to students as a supplementary platform with a high level of specialized content available. Students are most likely to utilize the VLR when provided with incentives such as guest speakers or special event. Within the mentoring model explored via *BreakThru*, gamification concepts are not a successful driver of virtual world platform adoption. Badging is interesting to some users, but does not function as a means of increasing usage of VLR features on its own.

References

Burgstahler, S.: Increasing the representation of people with disabilities in science, engineering and mathematics. J. Inf. Technol. Dev. **4**(9), 1–8 (1994)

Chrons, O., Sundell, S.: Digitalkoot: Making old archives accessible using crowdsourcing. Workshop at HCOMP 2011, San Fransisco (2011)

Duncan, I., Miller, A., Jiang, S.: A taxonomy of virtual worlds usage in education. Br. J. Educ. Technol. **43**(6), 949–964 (2012)

Grant, S., Betts, B.: Encouraging user behavior with achievments: an empirical study. In: Proceedings of the 10th Working Conference on Mining Software Repositories, pp. 65–68, San Francisco (2013)

Hamari, J., Koivisto, J., Sarsa, H.: Does Gamification Work? – A Literature Review of Empirical Studies on Gamification. In: Proceedings of the 47th Hawaii International Conference on System Sciences, Hawaii (2014)

Hickey-Moody, A.C., Wood, D.: Imagining otherwise: Deleuze & desiring differenciation in Second Life. Proceedings of ANZCA Conference, Wellington, New Zealand (2008)

Inman, C., et al.: Use of Second Life in K-12 and Higher Education: A Review of Research. J. Interact. Online Learn. **9**(1), 44–63 (2010)

Johnson, L., Adams Becker, S., Cummins, M., Estrada, V., Freeman, A., Ludgate, H.: NMC Horizon report: 2013 Higher Education Edition (2013)

Kelly, B. Is Second Life accessible? (2008). https://ukwebfocus.wordpress.com/2008/01/14/is-second-life-accessible/Accessed Feb 2015

Miesenberger, K., Ossmann, R., Archambault, D., Searle, G., Holzinger, A.: More Than Just a Game: Accessibility in Computer Games. In: HCI and Usability for Education and Work, pp. 247–260 (2008)

National Science Foundation (NSF): Shaping the future: New expectations for undergraduate education in science, mathematics, engineering, and technology (NSF 96–139) (1996)

National Science Foundation (NSF): Land of plenty: Diversity as America's competitive edge in science, engineering and technology. Author, Arlington (2000)

National Science Foundation: In: Women, minorities, and persons with disabilities in science and engineering. (NSF 04–317) (2004)

Peters, T., Bell, L.: Otherworldly Accessibility. Comput. Libr. **27**(9), 38 (2007)

Pursell, B.K., Bailey, K.D.: Establishing virtual worlds: The impact of virtual worlds and online gaming on education and training (2005)

Todd, R.: BreakThru Research Data. Georgia Institute of Technology, Center for Assistive Technology & Environmental Access (2012). http://www.georgiabreakthru.org. Accessed Feb 2015

Verhoeven, P.: No second life for visually impaired (2007). http://www.magnifiers.org/news.php?action=fullnews&id=249. Accessed Feb 2015

Weber, K., Patterson, B.R.: Student interest, empowerment and motivation. Commun. Res. Rep. **17**(1), 22–29 (2000)

White, J.D., Todd, R.L.: Whitepaper on suitability and accessibility of selected virtual world platforms and communities. Georgia Institute of Technology, Office of Provost, Atlanta, GA (2011)

Integrating Motion-Capture Augmented Reality Technology as an Interactive Program for Children

Chien-Yu Lin[1(✉)], Chien-Jung Chen[2], Yu-Hung Liu[2], Hua-Chen Chai[3],
Cheng-Wei Lin[1], Yu-Mei Huang[1], Ching-Wen Chen[4], and Chien-Chi Lin[5]

[1] Department of Special Education, National University of Tainan, Tainan, Taiwan
linchienyu@mail.nutn.edu.tw
[2] National Pei-Men Senior Agricultural and Industrial Vocational School, Tainan, Taiwan
[3] Tainan City Da Chen Elementary, Tainan, Taiwan
[4] Tainan Municipal Syuejia Junior High School, Tainan, Taiwan
[5] Department of Leisure and Recreation Management, Da-Yeh University, Changhua, Taiwan

Abstract. The purpose of this study is to investigate the effects of free interactive games invention program on jumping performance. This study design interactive games using motion capture technology that enable participant to interact using body motion in augmented environment. Scratch 2.0, using an augmented-reality function via webcam, creates real world and virtual reality merge at the same screen. Scratch-based motion capture system which uses physical activities as the input stimulate. This study uses a webcam integration that tracks movements and allows participants to interact physically with the project, to enhance the motivation of children in elementary. Participants are 7 children in elementary school; the independent variable was some interactive games arranged by the authors, the dependent variable was the immediate effect by the intervention program on jumping performance. The experimental location was in a classroom of elementary school. The results show the Scratch-base free support system could be allowed the participants some clues, so they could have the motivation to do physical activities by themselves. The participants have a significant achievement via free Scratch-base augmented reality instead of traditional activities.

Keywords: Physical activity · Scratch 2.0 · Augmented-reality · Webcam · Motion capture

1 Introduction

Real-time interactive game is more popular [1], thus, allowing for the use of technology for physical activities [2]. Augmented reality (AR), as an interactive technology, has increasingly attracted public interest during the last few years [3, 4]. AR technology means the merging of virtual objects with real objects, resulting in augmented reality environments [5]. The output could be display such as sound or graphics [6]. Hardware components for augmented reality are: processor, display, sensors and input devices, in this study, computing devices used tablet computers with web-camera. Various

© Springer International Publishing Switzerland 2015
M. Antona and C. Stephanidis (Eds.): UAHCI 2015, Part III, LNCS 9177, pp. 149–156, 2015.
DOI: 10.1007/978-3-319-20684-4_15

technologies are used in AR rendering just as optical projection systems, monitors, portable devices, in this study, we used the same tablet computers. In augmented reality environments both virtual and real world could co-exist at the same time, the augmented reality applications are applied in many different fields [7], such as in education [8], textiles [9], surgical interventions [10], games [11], home-training system, online teaching [12], and learning disabilities [13].

Interactive games such as the Microsoft Xbox, Nintendo Wii or Sony PlayStation are not only for the play function, but have also been used in physical activities [14]. But Xbox, Nintendo Wii or Sony PlayStationare business product, there are not enough resource to arrange these interactive game tools in classroom. Recently, many open source could be applied, with their share their program, the users could design customers' interface, Recently, many open source or free platform have become available, which share their ideas and technology, so users can via this support to create their specific interfaces. This study via Scratch 2.0, which is a visual programming environment designed at the MIT Media Lab [15, 16]. Scratch Web site (http://scratch.mit.edu) support a free online interactive community, with people sharing, discussing their pro-grams, It also support offline system, designers could be designing, creating, and remixing one another's projects [17]. It's a collaboratively written system for free that provides information about the Scratch programming language and its website, and it continues to support designers use their open source of information. Via the free platform, designers could build, share, and participant their projects together.

The advantage of this study is that is it used laptop, via scratch 2.0 platform, the content easy to redesign or remix, thus for children to execute their activities.

2   Materials and Methods

2.1   Participants

There were 7 participants in this study, all of the children from resource classes in elementary school. This method allows the participants from resource class or study in normal class but need resource class extra support, with different disabilities from resource class, 5 boys and 2 girls. This study designed individual physical activities for the different needs of the participants to enhance their body motion motivation; we used "jump" physical activities.

2.2   Apparatus, Material and Setting

The author and co-authors are 8 teachers from university, elementary schools, junior high school and senior high school and graduate student; they all work in the field of special education, assistive technology and industrial design. We design the interactive program via Scratch 2.0 platform, then install the offline system, when the experimental process, we used the offline system to make sure in a stable environment.

They design the interactive teaching materials. The original design was a video pop balloon game, from an original program by Christine Garrity. With the Scratch 2.0 support webcam function, she designed an augmented reality interactive game.

Through webcam, user could see himself/herself and the balloons on the screen at the same time. When the balloon show on the screen, the user could use his/her hand (or any part of their body) to touch the balloon, just as Xbox-Based around a webcam-style, it enables users to control and interact with gestures instead of game controller. In this study, all the children know when they jump up to the red line; he/she could get the real time feedback including audio and visual feedback. The concept of the study is shown in Fig. 1. In the study, we focus not only on the result, but also consider the promotion in the future, from the experience, the hardware only used laptop, the less equipment and easy setup could attract teachers and parents want to participant the relative activities.

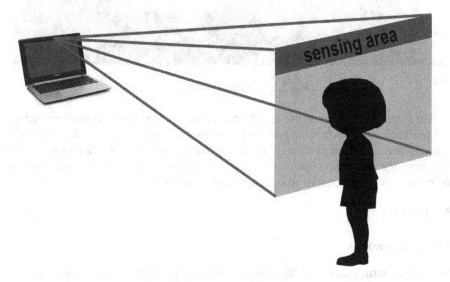

Fig. 1. The concept of this study

We used the webcam to detect the body movement on the screen. The goals for each participant were adjusted for each of their different disabilities.

2.3   General Procedure

This study focused on how the interactive audio and visual feedback can enhance the motivation of physical activities to assist children with disabilities. The laptop was arranged in front of the participants, when the participants jump up and touch the virtual red line; the participants received the visual and audio feedback dynamic pictures and sounds as feedback. Figure 2 shows the experimental setup.

The experimental process used Scratch 2.0 platform from the Media Laboratory at MIT, which allows for the development of collaborate and remix [18].

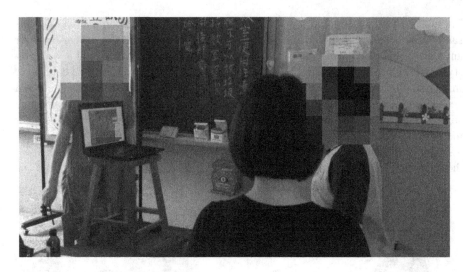

Fig. 2. The experimental process

The experimental process use laptop and internal webcam to detect jump movement and feedback effect. When the participant jumps; the webcam detects the movement when the participant jumps up into the sensor area. Because our participants were children from resource class, their response maybe not as quick as normal, and consider their ability, so the operating processing time was set to 30 s.

3   Results

3.1   Data Analysis

Because the participants were children with different disabilities from resource class, so this study focus on achievement instead of challenge, via Scratch 2.0, they have an opportunities to receive audio and visual feedback.

The record was just as from the analysis; we record the pre-test and experimental test. In the analysis, the study used t-test; this and all sub-sequent tests are two tailed.

From interactive physical activities, participants finish the jump up process. There are significant progress that used Scratch 2.0, $p = .002776 < .05$; So, Scratch 2.0 with webcam shows via augmented reality significant better than traditional physical training.

In the test trials of data analysis of physical activity, the participants have a significant achievement via free Scratch platform instead of only via traditional training.

4   Discussion

In this study, the concept via laptop and Scratch 2.0 to make a flexible free interactive game program.

The results indicated a significant result on the jump up physical activity. This study used Augmented reality (AR) could used in physical activity for children with special needs, this relative activities not only execute in elementary, we also promote the free platform in junior high school and senior high school.

Because this study applied free platform, its concept belongs to free, share, cooperate environment, teachers could be use the relative materials as reinforce. After the experimental process, we also supply related augmented reality games for them play together, just as Fig. 3. It also used the same concept and modified the original game, children tried their best to touch the balloons and enjoy get the visual and audio feedback.

Fig. 3. The modified concept for a group

While the Xbox, Wii, or Kinect may be suitable for normal people, but in resource classroom, they maybe not have the abundant resource to arrange this kind equipment, from Scratch 2.0, this problem could be getting a good resolve. In this study, we used open source and free platform to do the experiment; this is an example to promote interactive physical activity in class. We also share our experience with special education teachers in different conferences, also got positive feedback, Fig. 3 shows the process. Because the free platform interface easy to use, and the platform focus on share and rebuilt, so they can search our team and used our remix projects, so it support the interactive game design a special field for children with disabilities.

We also used the same concept, but just a little modify for young children in kindergarten and adolescents in senior high school. Fortunately, Scratch 2.0 added webcam detect motion function, that integration that can track body movements when apply on physical activities.

In kindergarten, we setup an external webcam against the wall in a kindergarten, through the projector, big pictures show on the screen and accompany with relative sounds, we took a stick pretend to hit the screen, then in the specific area, the webcam will detect body motion and give the real-time feedback - show another picture. Because they are too young and not the relative experience about AR, they are interested in touch real objects and receive feedback, via this method, they also enjoy the AR effect and Fig. 4 shows the interactive activity in kindergarten.

Fig. 4. The modified concept in kindergarten

Fig. 5. The modified concept in senior high school

In senior high school, we arrange step test to train adolescents' fitness level. The procedure of step test is step up with one foot and then the other. Step down with one foot followed by the other foot; we setup an external webcam beside the bench to detect the body movement to create an interactive feedback. So, in this case, through the laptop, the participant can receive audio and visual feedback when they do the step test, as show in Fig. 5.

Acknowledgements. This work was financially supported by the National Science Council, Taiwan, under the Grant No. 100-2410-H-024-028-MY2. Special thanks for Yu-Cheng Chen, who improve some of our programming skill.

References

1. Hwang, T.H.T.: Exploring real-time video interactivity with Scratch (Doctoral dissertation, Massachusetts Institute of Technology) (2012)
2. Kagohara, D.M., Sigafoos, J., Achmadi, D., O'Reilly, M., Lancioni, G.: Teaching children with autism spectrum disorders to check the spelling of words. Res. Autism Spectrum Disord. **6**, 304–310 (2012)
3. Olsson, T., Kärkkäinen, T., Lagerstam, E., Ventä-Olkkonen, L.: User evaluation of mobile augmented reality scenarios. J. Ambient Intell. Smart Environ. **4**(1), 29–47 (2012)
4. Radu, I., MacIntyre, B.: Augmented-reality scratch: a children's authoring environment for augmented-reality experiences. In: 8th International Conference on Interaction Design and Children, pp. 210–213. ACM Press, New York (2009)
5. Lin, C.Y., Chang, Y.M.: Increase in physical activities in kindergarten children with cerebral palsy by employing MaKey–MaKey-based task systems. Res. Dev. Disabil. **35**(9), 1963–1969 (2014)
6. Chang, Y.J., Kang, Y.S., Huang, P.C.: An augmented reality (AR)-based vocational task prompting system for people with cognitive impairments. Res. Dev. Disabil. **34**(10), 3049–3056 (2013)
7. Solari, F., Chessa, M., Garibotti, M., Sabatini, S.P.: Natural perception in dynamic stereoscopic augmented reality environments. Displays **34**(2), 142–152 (2013)
8. Wojciechowski, R., Cellary, W.: Evaluation of learners attitude toward learning in ARIES augmented reality environments. Comput. Educ. **68**, 570–585 (2013)
9. Harris, J.: Digital skin: how developments in digital imaging techniques and culture are informing the design of futuristic surface and fabrication concepts. Text. J. Cloth Cult. **11**(3), 242–261 (2013)
10. Volonté, F., Pugin, F., Bucher, P., Sugimoto, M., Ratib, O., Morel, P.: Augmented reality and image overlay navigation with OsiriX in laparoscopic and robotic surgery: not only a matter of fashion. J. Hepato-Biliary-Pancreat. Sci. **18**(4), 506–509 (2011)
11. Piekarski, W., Thomas, B.: ARQuake: the outdoor augmented reality gaming system. Commun. ACM **45**(1), 36–38 (2002)
12. Andujar, J.M., Mejías, A., Marquez, M.A.: Augmented reality for the improvement of remote laboratories: an augmented re-mote laboratory. IEEE Trans. Educ. **54**(3), 492–500 (2011)
13. Chang, Y.J., Kang, Y.S., Huang, P.C.: An augmented reality (AR)-based vocational task prompting system for people with cognitive impairments. Res. Dev. Disabil. **34**(10), 3049–3056 (2013)
14. Ding, Q., Stevenson, I.H., Wang, N., Li, W., Sun, Y., Wang, Q., Kording, K., Wei, K.: Motion games improve balance control in stroke survivors: a preliminary study based on the principle of constraint-induced movement therapy. Displays **34**, 125–131 (2013)

15. Resnick, M.: Mother's Day, warrior cats, and digital fluency: stories from the scratch online community. In: Proceedings of the Constructionism 2012 Conference: Theory, Practice and Impact, pp. 52–58 (2012)
16. Resnick, M., Maloney, J., Monroy-Hernández, A., Rusk, N., Eastmond, E., Brennan, K., Kafai, Y.: Scratch: programming for all. Commun. ACM **52**(11), 60–67 (2009)
17. Resnick, M., Rosenbaum, E.: Designing for Tinkerability. In: Solari, F., Chessa, M., Garibotti, M., Sabatini, S.P.(eds.) Natural Perception in Dynamic Stereoscopic Augmented Reality Environments. (2012) Displays, **34**(2), 142-152 (2013)
18. Brennan, K., Resnick, M.: Stories from the scratch community: connecting with ideas, interests, and people. In: 44th ACM Technical Symposium on Computer Science Education, pp. 463–464. ACM Press, New York (2013)

A JBrick: Accessible Robotics Programming for Visually Impaired Users

Stephanie Ludi[✉] and Scott Jordan

Department of Software Engineering, Department of Computer Science,
Rochester Institute of Technology, Rochester, USA
{salvse,saj1832}@rit.edu

Abstract. Despite advances in assistive technology, challenges remain in pre-college computer science outreach and university programs for visually impaired students. The use of robotics has been popular in pre-college classrooms and outreach programs, including those that serve underrepresented groups. This paper describes the specific accessibility features implemented in software that provides an accessible Lego Mindstorms NXT programming environment for teenage students who are visually impaired. JBrick is designed to support students with diverse visual acuity and who use needed assistive technology. Field tests over several days showed that JBrick has the potential to accommodate students who are visually impaired as they work together to program Lego Mindstorms NXT robots.

Keywords: Accessibility · Robotics · Visual impairment

1 Introduction

As robotics has become popular as a means for engaging pre-college students in computing and engineering [2, 15, 20], the need for accessibility persists. Robotics, such as Lego Mindstorms, are as appealing to students who are visually impaired as they are to sighted students [3, 12]. The default programming software available from Lego uses icons to represent commands. This software is not accessible, most notably in terms of screen reader compatibility. Whether for in-class activities or extracurricular outreach, the software needs to maximize accessibility in order to promote interest in computer science and related disciplines.

The underrepresented students of concern are those who are visually impaired, where the threshold is legally blind. The American Federation of the Blind defines the term "legally blind" as defined through federal law, with "central visual acuity of 20/200 or less in the better eye with the best possible correction, as measured on a Snellen vision chart, or a visual field of 20 degrees or less" [1].

The goal of the JBrick project is to devise accessible Lego Mindstorms programming software that can be used by those with or without sight. In the case of the Imagine IT workshops and future outreach, the target users are teens who are visually impaired. These teens are often novice programmers, as the focus of the outreach is to enable the

© Springer International Publishing Switzerland 2015
M. Antona and C. Stephanidis (Eds.): UAHCI 2015, Part III, LNCS 9177, pp. 157–168, 2015.
DOI: 10.1007/978-3-319-20684-4_16

participants to explore Computer Science via robotics, a common vehicle for engaging pre-college students [2, 13, 16, 20].

In this paper, we will explore the issues with making robotics programming accessible to individual with visual impairments, especially those who have little to no experience in programming. Prior work has discussed issues with using existing development software [11, 13], which at best has incomplete features and at worst is completely inaccessible due to the heavy use of graphics to depict commands and constructs. Participation in STEM (Science, Technology, Engineering, and Math) fields by the visually impaired is low in part due to inaccessible tool support, in particular at the initial, critical junctures that can encourage and captivate young people. Given that independent tool use and activity participation is needed (as opposed to reliance on a sighted person) this paper will focus on the features and design decisions that can be leveraged in other programming tools.

2   Background and Related Work

The need for JBrick is derived after evaluating exiting Lego Mind storms NXT robotics programming environments in order to ascertain at least one that was free/low-cost, accessible to the visually impaired, and was conducive to facilitating outreach/instruction for novice programmers of pre-college age.

In terms of general programming, contemporary environments such as Microsoft Visual Studio, Apple XCode and Eclipse can be made generally accessible though gaps remain. For the purposes of audience and outreach timeframe, these tools were ruled out as being irrelevant for the robotics programming or potentially daunting to young novices (Eclipse can be used for LeJOS). Many programmers who are visually impaired use text editors and command line compilers along with their assistive technology, while others also use tools such as emacspeak to help convey the nuances of code [4, 17].

In terms of programming environments developed for visually impaired programmers, the focus is on audio depiction [19]. The Java Speak project target user is a novice programmer, in particular someone who is entering the Computer Science major at the university level. The goal of Java Speak as presented in [5] was to use audio to help depict the structure of a Java program in a manner akin to the use of color in many development environments. As of this writing, JavaSpeak evolved into a set of Eclipse plug-ins that when used with JAWS provides audio feedback for compilation, runtime status, and the program tree as well as to aid with the focus of commonly used windows [9]. JBrick plans to use audio cues to aid in code orientation and navigation in a future release. Rather than focus exclusively on the blind, JBrick seeks to serve visually impaired programmers in addition to blind programmers.

Popular robotics programming environments designed for young, novice users are often graphical in nature. Lego's own NXT-G software (often used in schools and in the FIRST Lego League competition) consists of icons that are linked together and assigned attributes. At the time of this writing, the new version is the same, as shown in Fig. 1.

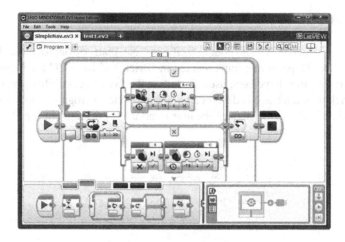

Fig. 1. Screenshot of lego NXT-G software [10]

Other visual programming environments can be found in the Microsoft Robotics Developer Studio as well as one based on Scratch [18]. As such traditional, text-based programming environments and technologies were assessed:

- LeJOS: buggy, not novice-friendly and required changing the Lego Mindstorms "brick" firmware (undesired)
- Microsoft Robotics Developer Studio's .net option: learning curve too high for the outreach, has accessibility issues
- RobotC: the IDE, which is tightly coupled to the language, has significant accessibility issues

The best solution at the time was BricxCC, developed by Hansen, and the NXC (Not eXactly C) language [7]. The evaluation for BricxCC is covered in [11, 13], and at the time the most critical need was for screen reader (JAWS) compatibility. The BricxCC software is not entirely compatible with JAWS. Assistance by a sighted person is needed at times. For example, code navigation requires assistance when the program is large as displayed code line numbers are not read. The alternative is for the user to count the lines, which can be frustrating and time consuming in a large program (at least 30 lines in this case).

In addition to the authors' ongoing work, BricxCC has subsequently been used with visually impaired students in another outreach project [3, 8] from researchers at Georgia Tech. The Georgia Tech team continues to use BricxCC though they compensate with the use of a wiimote to provide haptic feedback about the robot's status (e.g. distance to an object, distance travelled, whether the robot has bumped into something). We have taken the direction of improving the software itself in order to address accessibility gaps with BricxCC and to focus on programing rather than on the interface with the robot itself. After using BricxCC in several outreach workshops, the JBrick lead decided to design a fully accessible robotics programming environment that would also be cross-platform (Mac and Windows). Use of the NXC language remains though helper libraries are used to simplify working with the motors and sensors.

3   Software Design

JBrick is implemented in Java in order to facilitate cross-platform deployment. The NXC compiler is used, so programs implemented in JBrick and BricxCC are interoperable. Standard Java libraries have been used, including the Java Accessibility libraries.

The JBrick user interface is designed to be accessible to programmers with various degrees of vision. The screenshot of the user interface is presented in Fig. 2.

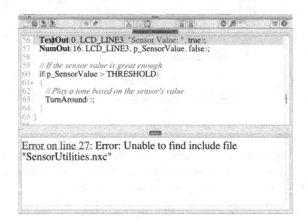

Fig. 2. Screenshot of JBrick showing larger font size and color changes

In addition to compatibility with screen readers, refreshable braille displays, and magnification software, the user interface itself was designed to accommodate both sighted and low vision users.

3.1   Code Display (Visual and Audio)

Accurate and legible depiction of the user's source code are critical to a programming environment. In the case of JBrick such depiction must be visually and audibly (when screen readers are used).

Reading code accurately means conveying the alphanumeric text and the punctuation since the NXC language uses punctuation in the same manner as the C language. Using JAWS for testing, code is read completely when the screen reader option to read punctuation is selected. As such any issue is that of the screen reader and is out of scope for JBrick directly. In addition to the code itself, line numbers are also read (see Sect. 3.3 for more details).

Programmers who are visually impaired have diverse needs and so a spectrum of accommodations are available for display customization. While some individuals may use magnification software (e.g. ZoomText), others have needs that preclude such software. For example, some programmers use accessibility options from with the operating system (e.g. screen resolution adjustment or selecting a larger pointer). Others may need enlarged text but may be frustrated by having to continuously move the magnified screen around when reading. JBrick provides enlarged icons for those who use the toolbar, but the ability to change the font and its size as well the coloration of text and the background was designed to aid both visually impaired and sighted programmers. These features are shown in Fig. 2. To further aid the programmer the current line of code that the cursor is on is highlighted so that it stands out.

3.2   Keyboard and Mouse Feature Execution

Drop down menus and a toolbar containing large icons exists in JBrick for use by those who wish to use them. Both the menus and icons are accessible by mouse and keyboard. Both the number of menus and icons are fewer than those in the BricxCC software, which streamlines the graphical user interface and aids users who need to listen to those features names.

Navigation can also be accomplished with the keyboard as the sole input device. Keyboard support for UI navigation is present for JAWS users. Commands such as compile, download, save, and tab navigation can be accessed through keyboard short-cuts. Before user testing, these shortcuts were tested to ensure that they do not interfere with the myriad of JAWS keyboard shortcuts. While conventions for tasks such as Open and Save follow the platform conventions (Windows, Mac), domain specific tasks such as compile and download to robot are simple, single key commands (function keys).

3.3   Line Numbering

The presence of on-screen line numbering has existed in programming environments for years. Line numbers facilitates locating the line of code that corresponds to a compiler error or to simply aid in locating to a line of code. In BricxCC line numbering can be activated but a screen reader does not read them.

In JBrick, line numbering is not only visible but as the font size is changed by the user the corresponding size of the line number also changes. The line numbers are displayed in a visually separated column just of the left of the code so that the numbers are not confused with source code content. JBrick manages line numbering so that they can be displayed, read by a screen reader, and displayed on a printout. When read by a screen reader, the line number is read as "line n" rather than merely the number so that the user understands that the number is to signify the line and not just a value that may be in the code itself.

3.4   System Feedback (Visual and Audio)

Feedback informs the user of the current state of a task/process or if action is needed to move a process forward. In robotics programming, interaction with the external hard-ware necessitates such feedback. During the programming workflow, the user must be informed of the status of the following:

• Is the robot (Lego Mindstorms) hardware connected to and recognized by the computer?

- Was the compilation successful or not? If not successful, then what are the errors and what line(s) do the errors correspond to?
- Has the program been downloaded to the robot successfully?

The feedback for thee areas must be provided both visually and with audio. The audio (and some visual) feedback was lacking in BricxCC for these aspects of the workflow. In order to run a program, the program must be successfully compiled and then downloaded to the robot. JBrick must recognize the robot before a program can be downloaded onto the robot. Upon starting JBrick the robot is selected, but given that the robot generally needs to be disconnected and moved elsewhere to run the program, it is possible to forget to reconnect the robot or the robot may have shut down during programming in order to save battery. Such occurrences require the programmer to know that the robot is not on or connected to the computer. JBrick will alert the programmer if the robot is not detected and alerts them to this whereupon the user can then go and correct the issue. In this Find Brick feature, the programmer can clearly see or hear what the status is and when the status changes (to being detected).

A successful compilation generates a text message that is read by the screen reader, as well as a tone. In JBrick, compiler errors are displayed in their own pane and these errors are read by the screen reader. When a compiler error is displayed or read, the corresponding line in the code is highlighted and the programmer can initiate the line being read to them. This feature expedites the need to find the line that the error corresponds to.

Once a program compiles successfully and the robot is detected, it is critical that the programmer knows when the program has downloaded successfully. If there is ambiguity, then when the programmer tries to run the program there will be confusion as to whether the error was in downloading the program or in the program itself (especially when a new version of a program is being tested). When the program is downloaded successfully, the user is notified with a tone. If the program is not successful, then an error alert is provided to indicate a problem (such as a brick detection issue).

4   Evaluation

Initial evaluation with JBrick is outlined in [11]. Long-term JBrick field tests were conducted during Summer 2013. Ten participants with visual impairments ranging from moderate vision impairments to completely blind used JBrick between 3-4 h per day over the course of 4 days. The participants were teens participating in a Computer Science exploration program. The participants were self-selected and their programming experience varied with only 3 having any experience (1 of the 2 had enough functional vision to use the graphical Lego NXT-G software). For the purposes of the exploration workshop novice programmers were encouraged to participate.

Participants worked in teams of 2-3 for the duration of the activity. Groupings were random within gender. The overview of the field test consisted of assistive technology setup, training in the NXC language and JBrick via a tutorial, and applying NXC via JBrick to solve a challenge for the duration of the activity.

Experiments. Before the tutorial started, any assistive technology was configured for the participants. 2 participants used refreshable Braille displays, 6 participants used screen readers, and 3 used screen magnification software and 1 adjusted screen resolution and appearance in the Windows Display preferences. All teams had at least one monitor so that the team could see the their work and headphones were used by participants who used screen readers.

During the first day, the participants were asked to go through the NXC programming tutorial with a provided Lego robot for each team that required each participant team to add sensors as needed. The tutorial has been used in prior workshops [11]. Display options were modified for those who need customized views. The adjustments included: *Increase font size, Change colors (for text, background, current line highlight), and Change cursor size.*

Participant groups worked at their own pace with members of the project team floating to answer questions and offer guidance as needed (e.g. how to use the robot, add sensors). The tutorial walked the participants through the NXC language in small chunks, integrating the programming workflow into the lessons. Practice with using compiler – working with error messages, finding line with errors.

Participants entered commands, constructs, expressions, and variables throughout the tutorial, which consists of 3 sections. The programming workflow of design, implementation (including compilation and downloading), testing, and evaluation was practiced many times during the tutorial and subsequent activities. All teams completed the tutorial within 4 h. If teams finished early, mini challenges were added in order for the team to apply their skills and experiment with the NXC language and the Lego Mindstorms robot.

Each session (day) lasted for 4 h and within each team each participant used JBrick directly for at least an hour, with the remaining time being used to accomplish tasks such as solve a problem, design/revise/test a programming solution or design/revise the robot itself. Participants who were particularly confidant with typing tended spend more time in JBrick so that the team could test a solution faster. Time to complete a task was not measured as typing speeds and the complexity of programs disallowed any comparison. Assistance was provided if the participants had difficulty with JBrick, programming, or robot building at any point during the activity. In addition, the team floated between the groups to see how they were doing from an instructional standpoint, as well as to observe the use of JBrick.

From the second day onward, the teams worked at their own pace to design and program their robot to complete a challenge. The challenge was devised to encourage collaboration and creativity so each team's solution was different. The challenge was for the robot to aid in a search and rescue mission to locate and guide people (designated by small cubes of foam) out of an area that was impacted by a natural disaster. Incremental design was used as the environment was made more complex (e.g. line following, a more complex route with obstacles) to maintain spectrum of challenge for the participants. To devise a solution, each team had to examine the environment, design their robot and then their programmatic solution. Each team needed to use at least one sensor and at least two motors in the robot design. Program design required the use of constants, motor and sensor commands, variables, expressions, audio, and at least one if or while construct. More advanced students used subroutines.

In order to construct the program, each team used the following JBrick features multiple times: file management, cut/copy and paste text within and between files, Undo, navigate the program file to enter or revise code including the use of line numbers (enlarged or read by the screen reader), compile and download code onto the robot, locate compiler errors (line numbering, also the cursor is placed and the line highlighted for the first error), revise desired screen display preferences (font, size, text and background color, highlight color, cursor), and use of keyboard shortcuts to access JBrick features and navigation.

The research team provided guidance when needed (in all aspects of the challenge and in use of JBrick), and teams could help each other as well. On the fifth day of the event, the teams showed their solutions to the overall group, the research team and to students who were participating in other discipline activities.

After Day 4, we conducted a semi-structured interview with each team using questions that were designed to capture the participant's preferences, as well as open-ended questions to capture their likes and dislikes about the JBrick software and the programming activity. The JBrick-related questions will be presented in this paper. Those questions included:

1. What did you like about using JBrick to program the robot?
2. What would you change about using JBrick?
3. How well were you able to customize JBrick so that you could use it (e.g. screen reader, font size, etc.)?

The participants were also asked to respond to five statements on a 5-point Likert scale (1 is strongly disagree, 5 is strongly agree) in the form of a short online survey. The statements were:

S1. The line numbering enabled me to locate the line of code with the error *faster* than if I did not have the line numbering displayed/read to me.
S2. The line highlighting/focus and cursor positioning enabled me to locate the line of code with the error *faster* than if I did not have this feature.
S3. I was *confidant* in being able to follow the structure of the programs I created.
S4. I am *satisfied* with using JBrick to program the Lego Mindtorms robot.
S5. I would *recommend* using JBrick to a visually impaired friend who was interested in programming a Lego Mindstorms robot.

In addition to the written responses for the above questions and statements, observation notes were taken during the activity. The participants' programs were also saved.

5   Results and Discussion

All participants used JBrick to complete the tutorial and activities. Post activity feedback will be divided between participants who read large print and those who read Braille or electronic files (and thus used the screen reader). In addition the data was also examined by the level of programming experience. The data is summarized in Table 1.

The participants were asked their level of agreement that line numbering helped them locate code faster when locating compiler errors, as well as their level of agreement that the line highlighting and cursor placement had in locating code when fixing compiler errors. In terms of line numbering, the mean for blind participants is 4.4 while the mean for the visually impaired participants is 5. When looking at the responses by programming experience, the mean for the four experienced programmers is 5 while the mean for the six novice programmers is 3.67. In terms of the line highlighting/focus and cursor placement, the mean for blind participants is 3.6 while the mean for visually impaired participants is 4.2. The means for experience programmers and novice programmers are 4.5 and 3.5 respectively.

Observations noted that blind participants had different levels of skill with using screen readers and the keyboard layout. As such familiarity with JAWS shortcut commands had an effect in the number of attempts needed to activate the desired command (e.g. read the current line). Familiarity with the keyboard had a more significant impact as there were many times when the novice programmers who are blind would add extraneous characters, thus adding to the defect correction task. The addition of the extra characters required more of a need to use the line numbering feature than the participants who were visually impaired. The visually impaired participants immediately were able to see the relationship between line numbering and the compiler errors, and when larger programs were created late in the activity. The visually

Table 1. Overview of participant feedback for the 5 Likert-scaled statements

ID	Degree of Vision	Programming Experience	S1	S2	S3	S4	S5
1	Blind	No	4	2	3	3	3
2	Blind	No	4	3	3	4	4
3	Blind	No	4	4	4	4	4
4	Visually Impaired	Yes	5	4	5	5	5
5	Visually Impaired	Yes	5	5	5	5	5
6	Blind	Yes	5	5	5	5	5
7	Visually Impaired	No	5	4	4	4	5
8	Visually Impaired	No	5	4	4	4	5
9	Visually Impaired	No	5	4	5	5	5
10	Blind	Yes	5	4	4	4	4
		Mean (Blind)	4.4	3.6	3.8	4	4
		Mean (Visually Impaired)	5	4.2	4.6	4.6	5
		Mean (Experience)	5	4.5	4.75	4.75	4.75
		Mean (No Experience)	3.67	3.5	3.83	4	4.33

impaired participants adjusted the font size during the tutorial to ensure that the line numbers were clearly discernable. The participants with programming experience were already familiar with line numbering; a participant mentioned having the line high-lighted as a positive feature (in addition to being able to change the colors of text, background).

When asked the degree of confidence in following the structure of their code, blind participants have a mean of 3.8 while visually impaired participants have a mean of 4.6. In terms of programming experience, novice programmers have a mean of 3.83 while experience programmers have a mean of 4.75. The means between both pairings are similar, indicating that there are issues with navigating the code that will need further study such as using audio differences (e.g. pitch, earcons) to aid in code orientation and navigation.

Observations of the blind participants, having sped up the reading of text sometimes became lost during code orientation in terms of constructs such as if/then and repeat blocks especially during when trying to fix errors. Of particular issue was nested if/then statements. Part of the issue was that some participants were not as familiar with the use of punctuation such as braces and brackets where locating them on the keyboard was an additional issue. Participants with vision were able to see the code layout (e.g. spacing, blank lines for clarity), however there was sometimes confusion between the curly braces and the brackets by some participants (on screen and on the keyboard). Both groups of students needed occasional assistance from the instructors though, the novice blind programmers needed extra assistance from the team or from teammates when confusion arose over how to find or fix a bug in code.

Participants were then asked to rate their level of agreement in terms of how satisfied there were in using JBrick to program their robot. The mean for blind participants is 4.0 while the mean for visually impaired participants is 4.6. The mean for novice programmers is 4.0 while the mean for experienced programmers is 4.75. For the final statement, participants were asked to what degree they would recommend JBrick to a visually impaired friend who was interested in programming a Lego Mindstorms robot. Blind participants had a mean of 4.0 while visually impaired participants had a mean of 5. In terms of programming experience, novice programmers have a mean of 4.33 while experience programmers have a mean of 4.75. Overall the experience was positive for both novice and experienced programmers, as well as both blind and visually impaired participants. This is partly due to the generally open-ended nature of the activity where participants get to decide on the robot design and the program designs along the way, including learning from mistakes and redesigning aspects as needed. In addition, for 8 out of 10 participants the opportunity to work with a robot was completely new. Thus the overall experience may have influenced the results. Regardless, the challenges that the blind participants had using JBrick did not severely impact their impressions of the software to the extent of recommending it to a peer. Some students either copied their programs to a flash drive or asked for copies of their programs to take with them even though they did not have access to a robot of their own.

6 Conclusions and Future Work

JBrick has been successful in terms of providing an accessible foundation in Lego Mindstorms NXT programming for pre-college students with visual impairments. In the context of outreach, the software allows students to collaborate with one another as well as with sighted peers during robotics activities that build technology skills.

Moving forward, further study is needed in order to improve the user experience for novice programmers who are blind. Some issues such as screen reader skill is outside the scope of JBrick. However additional features will be explored and added in order to provide students the ability to navigate code using audio cues, as well as debugging (a tool to help work through coding and logic defects). Remaining work will be completed in order to provide Mac OSX support. In addition, JBrick will be revised to accommodate the new version of Lego Mindstorms (EV3), as changes to the compiler are likely.

Acknowledgements. JBrick is supported by the National Science Foundation (#1240809). Thanks to students who have contributed to this project, as well as the participants who have provided feedback.

References

1. American Foundation for the Blind: Statistics and Sources for Professionals. (2006). from American Federation for the Blind: http://www.afb.org/section.asp?SectionID=15&DocumentID=1367Fröhlich Accessed March 1 2008
2. Cannon, K., Panciera, K., Papanikolopoulos, N.: Second annual robotics camp for underrepresented students. In: Proceedings of the 12th Annual SIGCSE Conference on Innovation and Technology in Computer Science Education, pp. 14–18, Scotland (2007)
3. Dorsey, R., Park, C.H., Howard, A.: Developing the capabilities of blind and visually impaired youth to build and program robots. J. Technol. Persons Disabil. 1(1), 55–67 (2014)
4. Emacspeak Homepage. from Emacspeak Homepage: http://emacspeak.sourceforge.net/ Accessed April 15 2014
5. Francioni, J., Smith, A.: Computer science accessibility for students with visual disabilities. In: Proceedings of the 33rd SIGCSE Technical Symposium on Computer Science Education, pp. 91–95, USA (2002)
6. Georgia Tech. Technology, Engineering, and Computing Camp. 2010. from Georgia Tech: http://www.coe.gatech.edu/diversity/wietec.php Accessed January 15 2010
7. Hansen, J.: BricxCC Command Center Homepage. 2007 from BrixcCC: http://bricxcc.sourceforge.net/ Accessed January 20 2010
8. Howard, A., Park, C.H., Remy, S.: Using haptic and auditory interaction tools to engage students with visual impairments in robot programming activities. IEEE Trans. Learn. Technol. 5(1), 87–95 (2012). doi:10.1109/TLT.2011.28
9. JavaSpeak Project Homepage. from: http://cs.winona.edu/cscap/javaspeak.html Accessed April 30 2014
10. Lego NXT-G EV3 screenshot. from Curious-on-Hudson Homepage: http://curiouson hudson.com/class-details.php?id=223 Accessed April 20 2014
11. Ludi, S.: Robotics Programming Tools for Blind Students. J. Technol. Persons Disabil. 1(1), 77–89 (2014)

12. Ludi, S., Reichlmayr, T.: Developing inclusive outreach activities for students with visual impairments. In: Proceedings of the 39th SIGCSE Technical Symposium on Computer Science Education, pp. 439–443, USA (2008)
13. Ludi, S., Reichlmayr, T.: The use of robotics to promote computing to pre-college students with visual impairments. ACM Trans. Comput. Educ. **11**(3), 1–20 (2011)
14. Marghitu, D.: Computer Literacy Academy for Children Homepage. from Auburn University 2008. https://fp.auburn.edu/comp1000/SummerOutreach/index.html Accesed January 22 2010
15. National Federation of the Blind. 2009. Youth Slam 2009 Homepage. from National Federation of the Blind: http://nfbyouthslam.org/ Accesed January 17 2010
16. National Science Foundation. 2010. Recent Awards for the Broadening Participation in Computing Program from National Science Foundation: http://www.nsf.gov/awardsearch/ Accessed January 22 2010
17. Rarnan, T.V.: Emacspeak - Direct Speech Access. In: Proceedings of Assets 1996, pp. 32–36, Vancouver April 11–12 (1996) http://cs.cornell.edu/home/raman/emacspeak/publications/assets-96.htrnl
18. Scratch Modification for NXT (Enchanting). Scratch Wiki from Scratch Wiki: http://wiki.scratch.mit.edu/wiki/Enchanting Accessed March 25 2014
19. Smith, A., Francioni, J., Matzek, S.: A java programming tool for students with visual disabilities. In: Proceedings of Assets 2000, USA (2000)
20. USFIRST.org. FIRST Homepage. from USFIRST: http://www.usfirst.org Accessed July 12 2009

Effects of Superimposing Salient Graphics on Learning Material

Shu Matsuura$^{(\boxtimes)}$ and Takumi Shigihara

Faculty of Education, Tokyo Gakugei University, 4-1-1 Nukuikita, Koganei,
184-8501 Tokyo, Japan
shumats0@gmail.com

Abstract. We investigate the effects of superimposing animated graphics of a
virtual character (VC) on physics simulation learning material. Eye-tracking
experiments revealed that the VC drew attention to the animated simulation
display in a tutorial mode in which the user remained passive to instruction. No
similar effect of superimposing was found when the user was engaged in the
interface of waiting for key-in mode. Visual incongruity together with contextual congruity is believed to work as a stimulus to raise interest in the intuitive
elements of the material. As one application, we describe the development of a
visual annotation system based on augmented reality technology. The annotations were visualized in stereoscopic three-dimensional graphics using a
see-through wearable binocular-type display. This system is useful for users to
obtain in-depth knowledge individually from a large projected image shared
with an entire class. This is expected to enable learners to retrieve knowledge at
their own paces, while raising interest in the entire view.

Keywords: Learning materials · See-through wearable display · Augmented
reality · Stereoscopic 3D

1 Introduction

Blackboard displays, projection screens, or large-format televisions are popular devices
for beginning a lecture or sharing ideas among many participants. In addition to providing these popular methods of presentation, a projection mapping technology can
afford an impressive visual experience [1]. In addition, augmented reality (AR) technology can annotate real objects or phenomena with virtual objects.

Santos et al. classified the learning use of AR into three categories [2]:

1. Real-world annotation.
2. Contextual visualization.
3. Vision-haptic visualization.

As an example of real-world annotation, AR technology was applied in web
content to annotate the image of a real apparatus [3]. AR graphics of balloons and
arrows located on images of buttons and switches provided explanations of their
functions. As an example of visual-haptic teaching material, images of calculated force
vectors were projected on a real experimental set in which three weights were

© Springer International Publishing Switzerland 2015
M. Antona and C. Stephanidis (Eds.): UAHCI 2015, Part III, LNCS 9177, pp. 169–178, 2015.
DOI: 10.1007/978-3-319-20684-4_17

connected at a node and hanged with strings. In this learning material of force balance, one could sense the change of the reaction force by pulling a string connected to the node. The haptic sensing was expected to be reinforced by the AR vector images.

In many cases of AR presentation, viewers feel incongruity between virtual AR graphics and real objects. This incongruity may be attributable to an inconsistency in their contexts or visual perspectives [4]. Further, if such incongruity stimulates the human perception of images, virtual objects are expected to superimpose on real objects in order to raise the interestingness of a real scene.

For interactive material, a tutorial is often required to enable users perform a complete function of the material; particularly for self-learning, a tutorial must explain virtual experiments using various parameters. To stimulate user's curiosity regarding the content, a tutorial with a graphic that has paired conditions of visual incongruity and contextual congruity might be effective when superimposed on the content.

A virtual tutor has been reported to enhance interactivities between learners and online contents [5]. In this study, we consider a virtual character (VC) as a tutor and superimpose it on the material. The VC explains the parameter setting step by step, and users follow the steps by clicking at the indicated buttons. We compare the dwell times of participants' eye movements on various parts of the simulation content in a VC-led tutorial using a simple letter-prompting tutorial.

The flow of our tutorial is one way, with the user just following each instruction step. Similarly, the presentation of learning contents in the classroom is generally conducted with an instructor showing a scene and pointing out specific locations in the scene step by step.

In this study, a pilot system for a wearable see-through head mount display (HMD) is set up to obtain images that describe knowledge associated with the parts of a projected large image. AR is used to display the related image contents that are superimposed on the large image through the HMD. A superimposed AR image annotating the parts of a large image is expected to raise the interestingness of the entire scene as an effect of moderate incongruity. In addition, a stereoscopic three-dimensional (S3D) display is beneficial for educational purposes because of an enhancement of the recognition of three-dimensional (3D) structures [6]. In this study, the binocular-type see-through HMD enables the superimposition of S3D images on the main scene.

2   Method

2.1   Eye-Tracking Measurement

Learning Material. To detect the effect of a VC, we created learning material with a simple scenario of a virtual experiment on free-falling objects. In the experiment, the falling time of an object from a fixed height to the ground was measured. The purpose is to learn that the falling time is the same for objects of any mass, but the falling time itself depends on the mass of the planet. This material was developed using Unity [7], a 3D game development environment, with the free-fall motion of spherical objects simulated based on Unity's built-in physics calculation engine.

The three-dimensional VC selected for this study was "unity-chan!," with digital image data provided and licensed for game developers by Unity Technologies Japan [8]. Voices of the character were composed using speech synthesis software, "Voiceroid + Yuzuki Yukari EX" [9]. The character's waiting and jumping motions were built-in motions of the character's package. The composition of additional motions for tutorial gestures was performed using the three-dimensional computer graphics animation software "MikuMikuDance" [10].

This VC behaves as a tutor in our material, by talking and responding with gestures to the user. Superimposing this VC on the free-fall simulation appears somehow incongruous, but the tutorial exhibits a contextual congruity with the simulation.

The material consists of two modes: "tutorial mode" and "waiting for key-in mode (or waiting mode, briefly)." In the tutorial mode, the aim and process of the virtual experiment are explained using text prompts and the VC's speech and gestures. The tutorial tells the user to click buttons to set parameters and perform experiments. The participants act passively in the tutorial mode to the direction of the tutorial.

In the waiting for key-in mode, the application waits for users' input. Users select buttons to click and perform the virtual experiment. The VC responds to the user's button clicking, repeating the parameter values.

Eye Tracking. To detect the effect of displaying a VC, eye-tracking measurement was performed using "ViewTracker" (DITECT corporation), a head-mounted-type eye tracker. Images were shown to a participant in a 27-inch liquid crystal display; the participant was sitting approximately 60 cm from the display.

Depending on the presence or absence of the VC, viewing types were classified as follows.

(vt1) tutorial mode without VC.
(vt2) tutorial mode with VC.
(vw1) waiting for key-in mode without VC.
(vw2) waiting for key-in mode with VC.

Table 1 summarizes the viewing classification.

Table 1. Classification of four viewing types

Mode	View	Character display	Leading element	Feedback to user input
Tutorial	vt1	None	Prompt	Prompt & parameter display
	vt2	Tutor & response	Prompt &VC	Prompt, parameter, character
Waiting for key-in mode	vw1	None	None	Parameter display
	vw2	Response	None	Parameter, character action

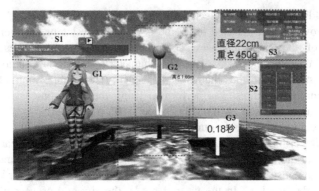

Fig. 1. Tutorial-mode image of the learning material. Broken lines show graphics and symbol component areas G1–S3, explained in Table 2.

In the eye-tracking experiments, we measure dwell times inside the component group areas. We define the dwell time as the time spent in a specific area of the interface. The interface of the material consists of graphic and symbolic component groups. The graphic component is intuitive, including the virtual tutor, free-fall animation, and display of the falling time. The latter two components are essential parts of this material. The symbolic component is comparatively logical, including the text prompt with a "next and back" button, buttons for selecting parameters, and display of parameter values. The component classification and the corresponding symbols of eye movement dwell time are summarized in Table 2.

Table 2. Interfacial components and the symbols of corresponding dwell times

Interface	Characteristics	Area of components	Symbol of dwell time	Symbol of area (Fig. 1)
Graphic	Intuitive, empirical, experimental	VC	T_{chr}	G1
		Free-fall animation	T_s	G2
		Display of time to fall	T_t	G3
Symbolic	Logical, procedural	Text prompt & next button	T_{pr}	S1
		Buttons for parameter selection	T_{bt}	S2
		Display of parameter value	T_p	S3
Outside		No component, outside the display	T'	

We compare the dwell time in the graphic interface with that in the symbolic interface, excluding from analysis the dwell time on the VC T_{chr}; that is, the total time of observation T is calculated as $T = T_s + T_t + T_{pr} + T_{bt} + T_p + T'$. The ratio of the dwell time in the graphic interface to the total time of observation σ_{gr} is defined as

$$\sigma_{gr} = (T_s + T_t)/T \tag{1}$$

In addition, the ratio of the dwell time in the symbolic interface σ_{sb} is defined as

$$\sigma_{sb} = (T_{pr} + T_{bt} + T_p)/T \tag{2}$$

Because T includes the tracking time for looking outside the functional interfacial areas, the sum of the values σ_{gr} and σ_{sb} is $\sigma_{gr} + \sigma_{sb} \leqq 1$.

Figure 2 shows examples of the four view types, indicating the interfacial areas from G1 to S3 in Table 2 for each view type. The free-falling objects are not shown in G2 in these figures. The boundary lines were drawn manually after each session, considering the measured eye movement trajectories.

S3D AR with HMD. To examine the superimposition of the S3D AR display through the see-through HMD, stereoscopic simulation material of molecular motions with Lennard-Jones and Coulomb potentials was created and presented using a dual projector with linear polarizers and projected on a polarization-preserving screen. A side-by-side S3D molecular motion graphic was created using Adobe Flash with Papervision3D and was made accessible on the web. AR markers were shown at the corners of the image.

An EPSON T-200 see-through HMD was used to present the graphics associated with the simulation content. A laptop equipped with a web camera was used to capture the AR markers and render the AR graphics, and the display was mirrored to the HMD. AR was created using Unity with a Vuforia [11] AR package. Only the AR graphics were rendered on the black background, without rendering a background video of the environment, enabling the user to superimpose the AR graphics at an arbitrary position in the projected image. The HMD eyeglasses were covered with polarization filters for viewing the S3D image on the screen.

3 Results and Discussion

3.1 Effect of VC on a User's View

Fifteen university students of the faculty of education participated in the eye-tracking measurements for the tutorial mode, and twelve or thirteen of them attempted it twice. Ten of the students participated also in the measurements for wait for key-in mode. The number of data and mean viewing time are summarized in Table 3. The viewing time of tutorial mode with VC was slightly longer than that without VC. This partially reflects the fact that participants looked at VC in addition to the text prompt from time to time. On the other hand, there was no significant difference between with and without VC in the waiting mode.

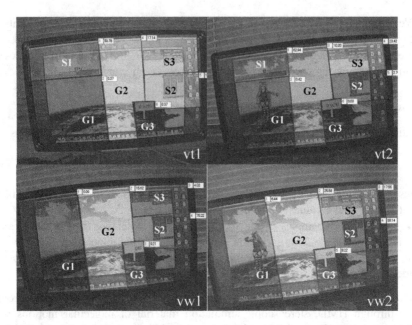

Fig. 2. Views of the learning material and the colored rectangular areas for detecting participant dwell time. Left top (vt1)-tutorial mode without VC, Right top (vt2)-tutorial mode with VC, Left bottom (vw1)-waiting mode without VC, and Right bottom (vw2)-waiting mode with VC.

Figure 3 shows the results of the mean dwell time of each component area for the tutorial mode. Total dwell times spent in the text prompt were 44 % (with VC) and 59 % (without VC). Total dwell times spent in the free-fall animation area were 22 % (with VC) and 15 % (without VC). The dwell time in the animation area was $T_s = 18.4 \pm 11.5$ s with VC and $T_s = 10.8 \pm 5.6$ s without VC. The equality of these mean values was rejected at a significance level of 0.05 (*) using the Welch t test. These results suggest that attention to the animation increased with animated VC.

Figure 4 shows the dwell times of wait for key-in mode with and without VC. Total dwell times spent at the control button area were 39 % (with VC) and 46 % (without VC). At the simulated animation area, total dwell time spent was 21 % (both with and without VC).

The display of falling time and parameters were regarded as feedback components. Attention to these feedback components increased from tutoring to wait mode. In

Table 3. Viewing time of eye-tracking measurements

Mode	View	Character display	Viewing time [s]	No. of samples
Tutorial	vt1	None	71.7 ± 20.1	27
	vt2	Tutor & response	82.6 ± 10.6	28
Waiting for key-in mode	vw1	None	72.4 ± 8.6	10
	vw2	Response	74.2 ± 4.4	10

particular, raised attention to the time display implies that interest in the quantitative results of this simulation increased more in the wait mode than in the tutorial mode. This suggests a change in participants' intention from passively following the tutoring to actively experimenting to see the results of falling time.

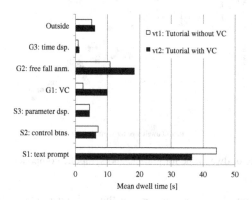

Fig. 3. Mean dwell times for graphic and symbolic components in the tutorial mode

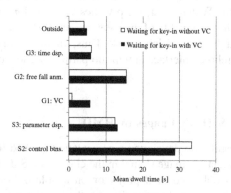

Fig. 4. Mean dwell times for graphic and symbolic components in the waiting mode

Figure 5 shows the plots of σ_{gr} and σ_{sb} of the tutorial mode with and without VC. As an overall tendency, participants paid more attention to the symbolic components than the graphic components. However, relatively higher values of σ_{gr} were found with the presence of VC. Specifically, mean values of σ_{gr} were $\sigma_{gr} = 0.26 \pm 0.16$ and $\sigma_{gr} = 0.18 \pm 0.10$ with and without VC, respectively. The Welch t test showed that the p value of mean σ_{gr} was 0.055, indicating a rejection of equality of σ_{gr} at a significance level slightly greater than 0.05 (*). Mean values of σ_{sb} were $\sigma_{sb} = 0.65 \pm 0.19$ and $\sigma_{sb} = 0.72 \pm 0.14$ with and without VC, respectively. The equality of these values was not rejected at the same significance level. Although the text prompt had a strong attention-drawing effect, the results suggest that the presence of VC induces attention to the other graphical components, even when the user is in a reactive state.

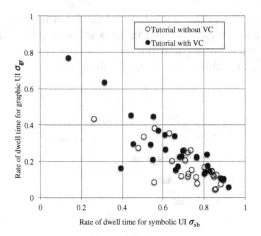

Fig. 5. Plots of the rate of dwell time for graphic and symbolic components in the tutorial mode.

Figure 6 shows the plots of σ_{gr} and σ_{sb} of the waiting mode with and without VC. Mean values of σ_{gr} and σ_{sb} were $\sigma_{gr} = 0.32 \pm 0.12$ and $\sigma_{gr} = 0.30 \pm 0.08$ with and without VC, respectively, and $\sigma_{sb} = 0.61 \pm 0.32$ and $\sigma_{sb} = 0.64 \pm 0.30$ with and without VC, respectively. By the Welch t test, the p values of σ_{gr} and σ_{sb} were 0.67 and 0.72, respectively. As a result, the equality of the mean values of σ_{gr} and σ_{sb} with and without VC were not rejected by the Welch t test. Thus, in the waiting mode, in which participants use the symbolic interface at will, no particular effect of VC on dwell time was detected.

3.2   Presentation of S3D AR Images by HMD

Based on the above results, we developed a presentation method for providing images to be superimposed on a large image shared in the classroom. Side-by-side S3D images were projected from a polarized dual projector on a polarization-preserving screen. Participants viewed this projected image through the see-through HMD in which left and right eyeglasses were covered with polarizers.

The projected image included AR markers, as shown in Fig. 7 left. Positions of AR markers in the left and right images of the side-by-side display were equivalent, resulting in the superimposed marker images having no positional displacement. Consequently, the AR marker depth positions in the S3D display were on the plane of the screen.

The AR application for detecting markers and generating side-by-side stereoscopic AR images was run using a laptop with a web camera. The user obtained the images of AR markers using the web camera. AirPlay mirrored the generated AR images to the see-through HMD in side-by-side 3D mode. In the AR display, a created image targeted by the marker was rendered with a black background, as shown in Fig. 7 right. The exclusion of environmental video enabled the superimposition of a single AR image on the projected image on the screen.

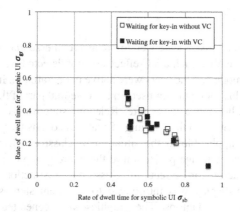

Fig. 6. Plots of the rate of dwell time for graphic and symbolic components in the wait for key-in mode.

Because the web camera was connected to a laptop, users could adjust the position of the AR image in two ways. First, by moving the web camera, one could change the position of the AR image in the HMD-view frame. Second, the user's head motion could change the position of the AR image in relation to the screen image.

In this method, the user uses the see-through HMD as a viewer of the laptop. PC operation wearing the HMD is possible if the HMD-vision background color is sufficiently dark. In our method, obtaining an AR image from the screen image is one of the activities enabled by combining HMD and PC. The web camera is used for AR image switching.

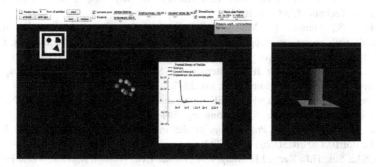

Fig. 7. Screenshot of molecular motion content. Left image: Interacting particles in the central area are displayed stereoscopically on the screen. The graph inside shows the Lennard-Jones potential energy curve. The AR marker is in the left up position. Right image: A 3D graphic of the Lennard-Jones potential superimposed as an S3D image on the screen projection of the left image through the see-through HMD view.

4 Conclusion

We found that users in a passive state were more aware of essential graphic components with the presence of the VC. Such a VC effect was not detected when the interface was in waiting for key-in mode and the users were active in operating it. It was suggested that a VC acted as a stimulus for engaging users in the essential part of the learning material, rather than simply following a procedure. Relevant superimposition of such salient graphics as a visual stimulus to the learning of materials opens the possibility for a user to be active. This is applicable to the situation of classroom learning, in which an instructor explains a large image projection to the entire group of participants.

To apply this activation effect in classroom instruction, a binocular-type see-through wearable display was introduced to represent stereoscopic 3D graphics mirrored from individuals' laptops. The graphics were generated as AR images by detecting markers attached to the large image. The AR technology played a role in annotating the shared image, while it provided stimuli to activate personal learning. Using this method, we expect to enable learners to retrieve knowledge at their own paces, while raising interest in the entire view.

Acknowledgments. A part of this study has been funded by a Grant-in-Aid for Scientific Research (C) 21500842 from the Ministry of Education, Culture, Sports, Science and Technology, Japan. The authors would like to thank Enago (www.enago.jp) for the English language review.

References

1. Kanazawa, A., Asai, T., Minazuki, A., Hayashi, H.: IIAI 3rd International Conference on Advanced Applied Informatics, pp. 247–252 (2014)
2. Santos, M.E.C., Chen, A., Taketomi, T., Yamamoto, G., Miyazaki, J., Kato, H.: IEEE Trans. on Learn. Technol. **7**, 38–56 (2014)
3. Tsuchida, S., Yumoto, N., Matsuura, S.: Development of augmented reality teaching materials with projection mapping on real experimental settings. In: Stephanidis, C. (ed.) HCI 2014, Part II. CCIS, vol. 435, pp. 177–182. Springer, Heidelberg (2014)
4. Liestøl, G., Morrison, A.: IEEE International Symposium on Mixed and Augmented Reality–Arts, Media, and Humanities, pp. 23–28 (2013)
5. Yamamoto, T., Miyashita, R.: IEEE International Conference on Sensor Networks, Ubiquitous, and Trustworthy Computing, pp. 564–568 (2008)
6. Yoshii, T., Matsuura, S.: Proceedings of the International Conference on 3D Imaging (2011). doi:10.1109/IC3D.2011.6584372
7. Kim, S.L., Suk, H.J., Kang, J.H., Jung, J.M., Laine, T.H., Westlin, J.: IEEE World Forum on Internet of Things, pp. 21-26 (2014)
8. Unity-chan. http://unity-chan.com. Accessed 20 February 2015
9. Kenmochi, H.: IEEE International Conference on Acoustics, Speech and Signal Processing, pp. 5385–5388 (2012)
10. Xu, J., Takagi, K., Sakazawa, S.: Proceeding of SIGGRAPH Asia (2011). doi:10.1145/2073304.2073332
11. Qualcomm, Vuforia. https://www.qualcomm.com/products/vuforia. Accessed 20 February 2015

Determining the Efficacy of Communications Technologies and Practices to Broaden Participation in Education: Insights from a Theory of Change

Nathan W. Moon[1(✉)], Robert L. Todd[2], Noel Gregg[3],
Christopher L. Langston[2], and Gerri Wolfe[3]

[1] Center for Advanced Communications Policy (CACP),
Georgia Institute of Technology, 500 10th Street NW, Atlanta
GA 30332-0620, USA
nathan.moon@cacp.gatech.edu
[2] Center for Assistive Technology and Environmental Access (CATEA),
Georgia Institute of Technology, 490 10th Street NW, Atlanta
GA 30332-0156, USA
[3] University of Georgia, Athens, GA, USA

Abstract. BreakThru is the core project of the Georgia STEM Accessibility Alliance (GSAA), which is supported by the Research in Disabilities Education (RDE) program of the National Science Foundation (NSF). Launched in 2010, GSAA is one of 10 RDE Alliances throughout the United States designed to broaden the participation and achievement of people with disabilities in STEM education and careers. The most distinctive feature of GSAA has been its use of virtual worlds and online communications platforms to support or implement most project activities. Empirical findings have informed the creation of a theory of change to explain how characteristics of technologically mediated mentoring practices may positively impact students' internal characteristics across five indicators (intention to persist, increased self-advocacy, increased self-determination, decreased math anxiety, and decreased science anxiety). Successful internalization of these characteristics may be expected to increase students' intention to persist in STEM education and support concrete steps to persist. This project seeks to fill a critical research gap and inform the field about the potential efficacy of e-mentoring programs and how they might be evaluated. It also seeks to determine appropriate methodologies and approaches for doing so.

Keywords: STEM education · Disability · Accessibility · Electronic mentoring · Evaluation · Theory of change

1 Introduction

Policymakers and scientific leaders in the United States (US) have prioritized the cultivation of a diverse science, technology, engineering, and mathematics (STEM) workforce in the US [1–3]. In its 2010 report *Preparing the Next Generation of STEM*

© Springer International Publishing Switzerland 2015
M. Antona and C. Stephanidis (Eds.): UAHCI 2015, Part III, LNCS 9177, pp. 179–188, 2015.
DOI: 10.1007/978-3-319-20684-4_18

Innovators, the National Science Board offered two mutually reinforcing observations. First, the US's long-term prosperity is dependent upon "talented and motivated individuals who will comprise the vanguard of scientific and technological innovation." Second, every student in the US "deserves the opportunity to achieve his or her full potential" [4]. In short, excellence and equity in STEM education are interrelated.

This goal can be realized only if underrepresented groups receive a larger proportion of the nation's STEM degrees. Educators and policymakers long have empha-sized the need to overcome disparities of race, ethnicity, gender, and socio-economic status in realizing equality and diversity in STEM fields, and rightfully so. However, Americans with disabilities historically have been excluded from postsecondary STEM education and remain underrepresented in the STEM workforce.

2 Broadening Participation in STEM

The National Science Foundation's (NSF) Research in Disabilities Education (RDE) program has sponsored research and development projects to broaden participation and increase achievement of people with disabilities in STEM education and the STEM workforce. At the heart of these efforts has been RDE's "Alliances for Stu-dents with Disabilities in STEM" (Alliances) project track. Intended to serve a specific geographic region, Alliances involve multiple institutions of higher education and secondary school systems working as a team "to employ evidenced-based practices and promising interventions to advance students across critical academic junctures, to degree completion, and into the workforce or graduate STEM degree programs." Taken together, Alliances create a unified program of change extending beyond academia to include industry and government research experiences for students with disabilities. In addition, Alliances typically go beyond matters of STEM content knowledge to focus on underlying issues affecting the differential learning, participation, retention and graduation rates of postsecondary students with disabilities in STEM.

NSF has funded 10 RDE Alliances to across the US, each of which is tasked with serving its specific region or state. The primary mission of the Alliances is to support the advancement of students with disabilities from high school into college (including transfer from two-year to four-year colleges), from undergraduate STEM degree programs into graduate STEM education, and from postsecondary education into the STEM workforce. Emphasis is placed upon successful navigation of the critical transition points between secondary education, undergraduate education, graduate education, and employment [5]. Stated Alliance goals typically focus on recruitment to, retention within, and progression through project activities, as well as graduation of students with disabilities from secondary and two-year and four-year postsecondary education.

At the same time, Alliances are also charged with establishing scalable and replicable models to demonstrate how comprehensive, multidisciplinary networks of high schools, 2- and 4-year undergraduate institutions, and graduate programs may broaden participation of students with disabilities within STEM education and the STEM workforce. Alliances also may pilot novel interventions to serve as promising practices.

3   Establishing a Theory of Change

Researchers concerned about the evaluation of higher education have argued that the basic availability of data should not dictate the approach for undertaking such evaluations [6]. If evaluation is to determine educational efficacy, then it must be considered from the beginning through the development of meaningful indicators and the provision of data collection and analysis for such ends. There exists a voluminous and robust scholarship around the selection of indicators for the evaluation of education, especially at the more complex, system level [7–11] (Fig. 1).

To determine the efficacy of BreakThru, lead investigators have worked closely with project evaluators to identify a theory of change underlying the project, including its interventions and activities and progress toward stated goals. Based on the framework for theory-driven evaluations [12], the evaluation questions have driven the development of BreakThru's Theory of Change, which is informed primarily by the project's emphasis on e-mentoring.

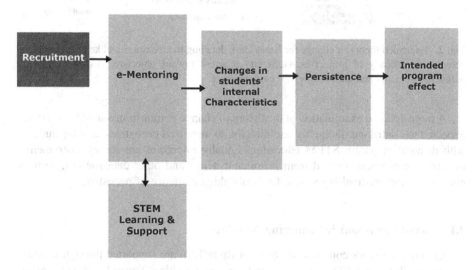

Fig. 1. Overall theory of change for BreakThru

Most broadly, BreakThru holds that successful recruitment into the project will lead to participation in e-mentoring activities at the heart of BreakThru as well as broader increases in STEM learning and support received by students with disabilities. Participation in these activities will result in positive changes in student's internal characteristics and enable them to persist through STEM education, thereby accomplishing BreakThru's intended effect of increased graduation among students with disabilities. (Fig. 2).

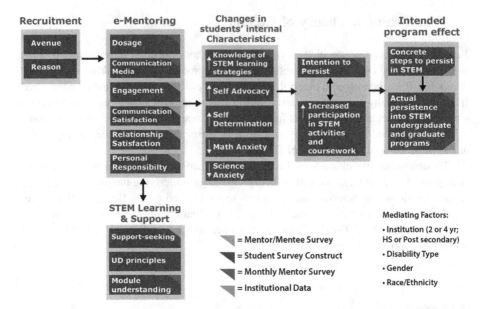

Fig. 2. Expanded theory of change for BreakThru, detailing the measures and key constructs for determining efficacy of project activities and progress toward objectives. Color-coded tabs outline instruments and data sources for each measure.

A more detailed examination of the theory of change demonstrates specific activities expected to contribute, indirectly and directly, to increased persistence among students with disabilities within STEM education. Equally important are survey instruments, as well as constructs derived from instrument items, and other data sources, such as enrollment and graduation records, for establishing evidence of persistence.

3.1   Recruitment and E-Mentoring Activities

E-mentoring activities comprise the heart of BreakThru are supported through targeted recruiting efforts and STEM learning and support activities. Toward this end, project evaluation and its theory of change are informed by the manner in which students are recruited and their reasons for joining the project.

The purpose of BreakThru's e-mentoring is to foster a relationship through which experienced persons share knowledge and perspective, as mentors work to achieve the personal and educational growth of students through digital communication, including a variety of social media and online platforms to support mentoring relationships. This type of mentoring is known as electronic mentoring or, simply, "e-mentoring" to distinguish it from traditional face-to-face mentoring. As e-mentoring can occur asynchronously and remotely, it offers benefits not associated with conventional mentoring. A growing literature has described the usefulness of e-mentoring in educational, business, human resources, and social environments. Unfortunately, while conceptual models have been developed to describe the e-mentoring relationship, there is limited empirical evidence for their overall effectiveness. For students with disabilities interested in STEM careers, the use of e-mentoring allows for more access to mentors representing a variety of disciplines and locations. Project evaluation takes into account and measures, to the extent possible, dosage (i.e. frequency and duration) of e-mentoring activities, communication media used within the project (e.g., SecondLife, e-mail, telephone), as well as key evaluation measures of communication satisfaction, relationship satisfaction, and participants' perceptions of student personal responsibility.

In addition to e-mentoring activities, the theory of change also takes into account STEM learning strategies such as time management, study strategies, reading skills, and dealing with text anxiety through completion of 25 student learning modules created as part of the project and frequently completed by project mentors and mentees together.

3.2   Changes in Internal Characteristics

Participation in e-mentoring activities and complementary STEM learning and sup-port activities such as the learning modules are expected to result in positive changes as mentees internalize the support they have received from e-mentoring relationship and knowledge received through module completion, among other project activities. Changes in internal characteristics may be assessed by six measures:

Self-advocacy. – In response to concerns that overprotection of people with disabilities by authority figures and professionals resulted in dependency and undermined autonomy, self-advocacy emerged as a key concept within disability and educational research for the successful transition of students with disabilities toward independent adulthood [13–15]. Toward this end, Test et al. [16] offered a conceptual framework specifically for students with disabilities. In their conception, self-advocacy is composed of four overarching components: knowledge of self, knowledge of rights, communication, and leadership, each of which is guiding by a series of subcomponents. In addition, the measurement of self-advocacy among students with disabilities has been informed by instruments such as the General Self-Efficacy (GSE) Scale [17, 18], which query individuals' perceptions about their ability to solve problems, achieve goals, cope with difficulties, and overcome challenges.

BreakThru accepts self-advocacy as "the ability to effectively communicate, con-vey, negotiate or assert one's interests, desires, needs, and rights" [19]. Self-advocacy is measured by a 12-item scale within the Student Survey, drawn primarily from the Self Determination Student Advocacy Skills (SDSAS) Questionnaire [20].

Self-determination. – The ability of people with disabilities to make decisions and attain goals underlie the principles of self-determination. Self-determination is closely related to self-advocacy, but whereas self-advocacy stresses speaking and acting on one's behalf, self-determination emphasizes actual decision-making processes and control of one's life. Algozzine et al. [21] defined self-determination as "the combination of skills, knowledge, and beliefs that enable a person to engage in goal-directed, self-regulated, autonomous behavior" (219) and identified the requisite skills associated with effective self-determination, such as decision making, goal setting, and problem solving.

This initial work was elaborated by Cobb et al. [22] and others, and a number of scales have been offered to measure self-determination [20, 23].

BreakThru accepts self-determination as "the ability to act as the primary causal agent in one's life and set goals and make decisions that are unrestricted from undue external influence or interference." This also involves making informed decisions and taking responsibility for those decisions [15]. Self-determination is measured by a 17-item scale within the Student Survey drawn from the AIR Self Determination Scale [24] and the Self-Determination Student Scale [25].

Science and Math Anxiety. – Science affect may be defined as perceptions or emotions associated with science. Previous research has found that science affect is significantly correlated with reported high school preparation in science and college science GPA [26]. There are two measurable aspects of science affect: Negative science affect involves anxiety about performing well on science exams and uneasiness when doing a science experiment. Positive science affect involves perceiving science as interesting and enjoyable and useful for one's career. Science affect is measured by a 16-item scale within the Student Survey.

Math affect similarly may be understood as perceptions or attitudes associated with mathematics. Math affect has been shown to involve complex factors such as feelings of pressure, performance inadequacy and test anxiety that interfere with the ability to solve math problems [27]. There are two measurable aspects of math affect: Negative math affect involves anxiety about solving problems, general confusion, and uneasiness when solving problems. Positive math affect entails perceiving math as interesting and useful for one's future. Math affect is measured by a 14-item scale in the Student Survey.

Intention to Persist. - the likelihood to persist by pursuing more education or a career in STEM. This 8-item scale is adapted from Toker's (2010) scale that measures short-term commitments and long-term commitments as they apply to education, as well as degree attainment intentions. The scale is also informed by Williams, Wiebe, Yang, Ferzli, & Miller (2002).

3.3   Intended Program Effect

Increased intention to persist is expected to result in concrete steps to persist, such as applying to and enrolling in graduate school, participating in a STEM-related internship, or obtaining a STEM-related job. Open-ended responses are collected from project mentors and mentees as part of monthly reporting and qualitatively analyzed for evidence of concrete steps to persist. In addition, actual persistence is measured by educational attainment and successful navigation of critical transition points for STEM careers.

4   Results

The Student Survey to assess changes in students' internal characteristics and intention to persist has been administered over the lifespan of the BreakThru since Fall 2011 to present. The following tables summarize changes from "pre," when the student first completed the survey upon induction into the project, to "post," when the student last completed the survey. As of Spring 2014, 29 postsecondary participants had completed the student surveys for "pre" and "post" analysis. (Table 1).

Table 1. Internal characteristics constructs for postsecondary students enrolled in BreakThru between Fall 2011 and Fall 2014, with change over time and statistical significance.

Constructs		Pre- Mean	Post- Mean	Change	Paired Samples t-test
	Intent to Persist	3.90	3.94	+0.04	p = 0.90
	Self-Determination	3.74	3.91	+.0.17	p < 0.01*
	Self-Advocacy	2.99	3.66	+0.67	p < 0.001**
Science Affect	Negative Science Affect	2.96	3.76	+0.80	p < 0.01*
	Positive Science Affect	3.72	3.68	-0.04	p < 0.01*
Math Affect	Negative Math Affect	3.09	3.45	+0.36	p < 0.01*
	Positive Math Affect	3.71	3.47	-0.24	p < 0.001**

The construct scores are presented using 5-point Likert scale (1, Strongly Disagree to 5, Strongly Agree) based upon the Student Survey items. The higher the score, the greater the indication of progress for that construct. For assessment purposes, negatively worded construct items were reverse-coded.

5 Discussion

Over the duration of the project, secondary and postsecondary students participating in BreakThru have experienced improvements in internal characteristics related to persistence in STEM education, as measured by the project's evaluation instruments. Among postsecondary students, all constructs except intention to persist were statistically significant. Of these, gains in self-advocacy were highest, suggesting that e-mentoring activities and targeted modules on improving self-advocacy and putting it into practice have resulted in positive changes in students' internal characteristics. While not as great of a change, self-determination similarly increased over the duration of the project. A more nuanced examination of responses to individual items reveals that students feel more capable of determining their own strengths and weaknesses, even if do not necessarily feel comfort with the material overall. They show the largest increase when evaluating their ability to check over their work.

Regarding science and math anxiety, results have been somewhat more mixed. Decreases in negative affect have been offset somewhat by decreases in positive affect, making it necessary to examine individual items for a more nuanced interpretation of results. For scale items related to science affect, for example, increases in positive affect were seen on many items, with the notable exceptions of students' enjoyment in learning and their desire to do better than classmates. Of particular concern for negative affect are student anxiety levels and concern about failing tests. Regarding math affect, improvements were seen in a number of areas, including students' interest in taking more classes in the future and their enjoyment in learning mathematics.

Despite these somewhat mixed findings regarding affect, longitudinal findings from the Student Survey that informs the Theory of Change suggests the efficacy for e-mentoring in improving persistence in STEM education. It also is worth noting that both "pre" and "post" scores are above average in terms of the Likert-type scale being utilized. Most constructs were close to a score of 4.00, which constitute general agreement with construct items.

6   Conclusions

E-mentoring activities at the heart of BreakThru may represent a promising approach for improving student persistence through STEM education and for navigating critical transition points to STEM employment. The purpose of the theory of change presented in this paper is to establish a promising means for documenting the efficacy of these activities and their effect on student intention to persist and concrete steps to persist. We hope to inform the field at large about ways to assess and evaluate the efficacy of these technologically mediated activities.

Acknowledgements. BreakThru is a project of the Georgia STEM Accessibility Alliance, which is supported by the National Science Foundation (NSF), Research in Disabilities Education (RDE) Awards # 1027635 and 1027655. Any opinions, findings, and conclusions or recommendations expressed in this material are those of the authors and do not necessarily reflect the views of the National Science Foundation.

The authors wish to acknowledge the contribution of Dr. Tom McKlin and Dr. Shelly Engelman of SageFox Consulting Group for their external evaluation services. The authors also acknowledge Ms. Jana Thompson and Mr. Scott Pollack at the University of Georgia and Dr. Meltem Alemdar at the Georgia Institute of Technology for their internal evaluation support.

References

1. National Science Foundation, Advisory Committee to the NSF Directorate for Education and Human Resources. Shaping the future: New expectations for undergraduate education in science, mathematics, engineering, and technology. National Science Foundation. Washington (1996)
2. National Science Foundation, Congressional Commission on the Advancement of Women and Minorities in Science, Engineering and Technology Development. Land of plenty: Diversity as America's competitive edge in science, engineering and technology. National Science Foundation. Washington (2000)
3. National Science Foundation, Division of Science Resources Statistics. Women, minorities, and persons with disabilities in science and engineering (No. NSF-04–317). National Science Foundation. Arlington (2004)
4. National Science Board. (2010). Preparing the Next Generation of STEM Innovators: Identifying and Developing Our Nation's Human Capital. Arlington, National Science Foundation from http://www.nsf.gov/nsb/publications/2010/nsb1033.pdf Accessed 29 December 2011

5. AccessSTEM and DO-IT. (2011). Alliances to promote the participation of students with disabilities in science, technology, engineering, and mathematics. Seattle, WA: RDE Collaborative Dissemination, University of Washington from https://www.washington.edu/doit/sites/default/files/atoms/files/rde-alliance.pdf Accessed 27 January 2015

6. Coates, H.: Excellent measures precede measures of excellence. J. High. Educ. Policy Manage. **29**(1), 87–94 (2007)

7. McDaniel, O.: The theoretical and practical use of performance indicators. High. Educ. Manage. **8**(3), 125–139 (1996)

8. Kells, H. (ed.): The Development of Performance Indicators in Higher Education: A Compendium of Twelve Countries. OECD, Paris (1993)

9. Taylor, J.: Improving performance indicators in higher education: the academics perspective. J. Further High. Educ. **25**(3), 379–393 (2001)

10. Shin, J.C.: Impacts of performance-based accountability on institutional performance in the U.S. High. Educ. **60**(1), 47–68 (2010)

11. Harvey, L., Williams, J.: Fifteen years of quality in higher education. Qual. High. Educ. **16**(1), 3–36 (2010)

12. Donaldson, S.I., Lipsey, M.W.: Roles for theory in contemporary evaluation practice developing practical knowledge. In: Shaw, I., Greene, J.C., Mark, M.M. (eds.) The Handbook of Evaluation Policies, Programs, and Practices, pp. 56–75. Sage, Washington (2006)

13. Aune, E.: A transitional model for postsecondary-bound students with learning disabilities. Learn. Disabil. Res. Pract. **6**(3), 177–187 (1991)

14. Izzo, M.V., Lamb, P.: Developing self-determination through career development activities: Implications for vocational rehabilitation counselors. J. Vocat. Rehabil. **19**(2), 71–78 (2003)

15. Wehmeyer, M.: Self-determination: critical skills for outcome-oriented transition services. J. Vocat. Spec. Needs Educ. **15**(1), 3–7 (1992)

16. Test, D.W., Fowler, C.H., Wood, W.M., Brewer, D.M., Eddy, S.: A conceptual framework of self-advocacy for students with disabilities. Remedial Spec. Educ. **26**(1), 43–54 (2005)

17. Jerusalem, M., Schwarzer, R.: Self-efficacy as a resource factor in stress appraisal processes. In: Schwarzer, R. (ed.) Self-Efficacy: Thought Control of Action, pp. 195–213. Routledge, New York (2014)

18. Schwarzer, R., Jerusalem, M.: Generalized self-efficacy scale. In: Weinman, J., Wright, S., Johnston, M. (eds.) Measures in Health Psychology A user's portfolio Causal and Control Beliefs, pp. 35–37. NFER-Nelson, Windsor (1995)

19. VanReusen, A.K., Bos, C.S., Schumaker, J.B., Deshler, D.D.: Facilitating student participation in individualized education programs through strategy instruction. Except. Child. **60**, 466–475 (1994)

20. Miller, R.J., Lombard, R.C., Corbey, S.A.: Transition Assessment: Planning Transition and IEP Development for Youth with Mild Disabilities. Pearson Education, Boston (2007)

21. Algozzine, B., Browder, D., Karvonen, M., Test, D.W., Wood, W.M.: Effects of interventions to promote self-determination for individuals with disabilities. Rev. Educ. Res. **71**(1), 219–277 (2001)

22. Cobb, B., Lehmann, J., Newman-Gonchar, R., Alwell, M.: Self-determination for students with disabilities a narrative metasynthesis. Career Dev. Except. Individuals **32**(2), 108–114 (2009)

23. Hoffman, A., Field, S., Sawilowsky, S.: Self-determination assessment battery user's guide. Wayne State University College of Education. Detroit (2004). https://rugby.ou.edu/content/dam/Education/documents/Users%20Guide%20Third%20Edition_1.doc

24. Wolman, J., Campeau, P., Dubois, P., Mithaug, D., Stolarski, V.: AIR Self-Determination Scale and User Guide, p. 26. American Institute for Research, Palo Alto (1994)

25. Field, S., Hoffman, A.: Development of a model for self-determination. Career Dev. Except. Individuals **17**(2), 159–169 (1994)
26. Glynn, S.M., Koballa Jr, T.R.: Motivation to learn college science. In: Mintzes, J.J., Leonard, W.H. (eds.) Handbook of College Science Teaching, pp. 25–32. National Science Teachers Association Press, Arlington (2006)

Enhancing Students' Motivation to Learn Software Engineering Programming Techniques: A Collaborative and Social Interaction Approach

Ricardo Rodrigues Nunes[1,2(✉)], Daniela Pedrosa[1,3],
Benjamim Fonseca[1,2], Hugo Paredes[1,2], José Cravino[1,3],
Leonel Morgado[2,4], and Paulo Martins[1,2]

[1] Universidade de Trás-os-Montes e Alto Douro (UTAD),
Vila Real, Portugal
{rrnunes,dpedrosa,benjaf,hparedes,
jcravino,pmartin}@utad.pt
[2] INESC TEC, Porto, Portugal
[3] Research Centre Didactics and Technology in Education of Trainers
(CIDTFF), Aveiro, Portugal
[4] Universidade Aberta, Lisbon, Portugal
leonel.morgado@uab.pt

Abstract. To motivate students to study advanced programming techniques, including the use of architectural styles such as the model–view–controller pattern, we have conducted action research upon a project based-learning approach. In addition to collaboration, the approach includes students' searching and analysis of scientific documents and their involvement in communities of practice outside academia. In this paper, we report the findings of second action research cycle, which took place throughout the fourth semester of a six-semester program. As with the previous cycle during the previous academic year, students did not satisfactorily achieve expected learning out-comes. More groups completed the assigned activities, but results continue to reflect poor engagement in the communities of practice and very low performance in other learning tasks. From the collected data we have identified new approaches and recommendations for subsequent research.

Keywords: Motivation · Learning programming · Collaboration · Social interaction · Communities of practice · Project-based learning · Problem-based learning

1 Introduction

For students following a software engineering study program, learning object-oriented programming approaches for system development with well-structured coding is a complex challenge [1, 2]. During introductory programming courses, typically students become able to develop small programs, as well as adapt and combine pieces of existing

M. Antona and C. Stephanidis (Eds.): UAHCI 2015, Part III, LNCS 9177, pp. 189–201, 2015.
DOI: 10.1007/978-3-319-20684-4_19

code, but they do not clearly understand the importance of writing well-structured code from pre-existing structures such as frameworks, libraries, and application programming interfaces (API) [3]. In more advanced programming situations - for example, involving the use of architectural styles such as model–view–controller (MVC) [4, 5] - students need to develop a set of complex skills [3]. Furthermore, besides the programming skills required to apply such best practices during system development, students also need to develop social skills in order to collaborate with other developers as part of the teamwork-based process for developing large, complex software systems.

Literature addressing engineering education has reported that current learning approaches do not align with the professional practice required by the labor market [6, 7]. These approaches are narrowly focused upon the acquisition of technical knowledge supported by heavy workloads and promote a meritocracy of difficulty-based belief system instead of prioritizing active learning and integrating knowledge, skills more aligned with professional realities [8–11].

The pedagogical context in which students learn influences their engagement and resolve to achieve learning outcomes [12, 13], and much research has examined approaches to the above described problem employing project-based learning (PBL) and teamwork environments [14–16]. While engineering problems are designed so that multiple solutions of varying mathematical and scientific sophistication are possible, teamwork skills and both oral and written communication skills used to model these problems are essential to the success of future engineers [8].

2   Background

The PBL context may impact students' motivation regarding their development of feelings of autonomy, competence, and relatedness. Teachers who use PBL methodologies assist students to overcome difficulties that can negatively influence their motivation such as team composition or task difficulty [16]. PBL and its derivatives have been reported in literature addressing engineering education to constitute a methodological approach that can promote and maintain students' motivation [17–19], as well as develop their situational interests [20].

Pascual [21] has described an extension of project-oriented learning to in-crease the social development of knowledge and learning. His approach aims to maximize students' opportunities for sharing knowledge with professionals in order to unite academia and communities of practice. Such proposals are based on theories of motivation focused on enhancing students' intrinsic motivation by creating conditions that can meet their needs of relatedness. Several activities were developed during Pascual's study, including meetings between communities of students and maintenance engineers, scholastic and recreational activities both on and beyond campus, and the development of a web-based decision support system. The author hypothesized that this multimodal approach increases active learning and social relations, and results identified that enhanced intrinsic motivation, thereby confirming that communities of practice and relatedness needs are relevant factors for learning outcomes. For instance, students and professionals can meet in online environments (e.g., virtual worlds) and, therefore, students can receive constructive feedback that helps them to clarify their doubts [22]. Other psychological needs such as autonomy and competence are also related to PBL and other approaches, as well as favor social interaction to promote active learning and self-study with engineering coursework [23, 24].

In this study, we posit that learning environments based on communities of practice can allow students to become motivated and take advantage of the expertise of experienced (professional) programmers in order to recognize the value of better code organization. From this perspective, personal, behavioral, and environmental factors are related in a dynamic way that influences students' feelings regarding the skills necessary to overcoming challenges that arise during their learning [25, 26]. In this process, we thus took into account students' social and cognitive factors.

3 The Course Context, Approach, and Assignments

3.1 Course Context

The present action research effort was developed in the course Programming Methodologies III (PM3) which is part of the fourth semester of the undergraduate program in Informatics Engineering at Portugal's Universidade de Trás-os-Montes e Alto Douro (UTAD). Before reaching this stage of the undergraduate program, students participated in other courses, with coursework addressing programming techniques and concepts, including computational logic, basic procedural programming, structured procedural programming, object-oriented programming, assembly programming, and introductory concurrent programming. They also participated in two semester-long "laboratory" projects (i.e., tutored development of a project), based on structured programming and object-oriented programming techniques, respectively. Alongside PM3, students are attended a course concerning algorithms and developed a semester-long laboratory project where they should apply the concepts being learned in PM3 [27].

The goal of PM3 is to introduce large-scale programming concepts, which is a learning objective of the ACM /IEEE CSC [28]. In PM3, students progress toward working with the MVC architectural style, which essentially proposes a structural division of programs among three blocks: the model (i.e., program state), the view (i.e., output), and the controller (i.e., program flow). In PM3, the original proposal of the MVC style [4] which handles input in the controller, is contrasted with a more recent one [5], which handles input in the view.

When students arrive at this mid-program level, they are not entirely motivated to attain the long-term benefits of a more structured and manageable code organization [29]. This reality, if not tackled until graduation, would leave them unprepared for the labor market, for which such skills are essential [30]. Our research goal is to address this problem. We thus hypothesize that students are not motivated and do not recognize the importance of better code organization due to their inexperience with team-based approaches involved in long-term software development.

3.2   Approach

We conducted a blended-learning approach during the second semester of the 2010–2011 academic year within the PM3 course, in which students confronted problems they would have to solve in groups over 8 weeks. The first approach has been described in detail in an earlier paper [29]. In the first action research cycle, a course assignment on software architecture styles was used. Students had to study a problem, develop an approach, and discuss it online with programmers in communities of practice and /or social networks. The expectation was that students would find motivation for their studies, both because of their contact with the developer communities, and because of having to study and reflect on their problems well enough to be able to discuss them with the members of these communities. Most students failed to achieve successful outcomes. Only 7 groups out of the 19 groups that participated showed some output during the various phases of the project, and only 4 groups had positive feedback from their involvement with professional developers and online communities of practice. The students indicated that their main difficulties were in understanding what was being asked and in finding professionals and communities in the field. In relation to the assignment, lack of motivation, lack of feedback on the development of the work and lack of time were identified as the main problems. Finally, most students considered the current assignment appropriate. We was changed based on the analysis of learning outcomes and observational data. Here we describe the resulting second approach.

The new approach was implemented during the second semester of the 2011–2012 academic year. The project length was increased to 13 weeks (i.e., the full semester minus the entry week), and learning activities were more time-structured (i.e., weekly tasks and checkpoints). Two tutors became available to support students via email, instant messaging (MSN and GTalk), Facebook, and Moodle fora. We also scheduled face-to-face meetings with students, either individually or in groups, in the case that they had difficulty with the tasks. We additionally changed the online environment (PBworks wiki platform) chosen in the first approach by Moodle. Moodle allowed us to separate all of the activities into modules over several weeks. This arrangement allowed the teacher and the tutors to better monitor the development of the assignment.

3.3   Assignments

The assignments presented to students involved solving a specific problem using a software architecture in order to stimulate and foster advanced programming skills in students via their participation in communities of practice and their analysis of scientific and technical documents. The assignments required students to develop of a written document explaining in detail the coding approaches used to apply an MVC-related architectural style involving different frameworks, libraries, and/or specific APIs. Our approach entailed providing a generic assignment framework or meta-assignment to be instantiated differently for each group of students (Table 1). The aim was for students to render into concrete terms (i.e., the coding approaches with specific libraries) the abstract concepts of the MVC style.

Table 1. Sample assignment instantiations

Groups	Description
G1	Write a detailed document explaining how to use the MVC architectural style to develop applications using OpenSimulator and/or Second Life virtual worlds as a user interface employing the libOpenMetaverse library. The document should include specific examples of implementations to illustrate the explanation
G2	Write a detailed document explaining how to use the MVC architectural style to develop applications using the Windows Phone Application Platform employing the XNA framework. The document should include specific examples of implementations to illustrate the explanation
G3	Identical to Group 2, but with the Silverlight framework

With 95 students, 21 groups were formed, most of which consisted of five students, though two groups had four students, one group had three, and two groups had two. The assignment instantiations were made available via UTAD's Moodle e-learning platform. In addition to the assignments, set weekly tasks and documents to be completed by students were also available. To support students' development of the activities, we created and provided an online example as a guide for what was expected.

We created two Moodle fora: (1) questions and suggestions, including generic messages exchange; and (2) task-related notices. Students also had access to slides from classes with included audio explanations by the course professor.

Task submissions were made via the administrative teaching support information system, called SIDE [31]. Submissions were weekly for individual and group tasks, and activities were developed in three complementary phases (Table 2).

In P1, the objectives were to increase knowledge of the problem domain and encourage participation and discussion in communities of practice, albeit not yet discussions related to the assigned problem. P1 took place over 3 weeks (Weeks 1–3). During Week 1, two individual tasks were undertaken: taking reading notes about scientific and technical literature related to the assigned theme and getting in touch with professionals in communities of practice, in order to understand the communities'culture and present themselves. Week 2 also consisted of two individual tasks: summarizing other group members' notes and attempting to help on a generic problem

Table 2. The assignment phases

Phases	Tasks
P1	Search for literature addressing the assigned topic; take reading notes; contact professionals and communities of practice online related to the assigned theme; adapt knowledge gained from the context and professional styles
P2	Become involved with professionals and communities of practice online; debate the assigned topic, either asynchronously or synchronously; devise tentative approaches for developing and solving the assigned topic; present, debate, and further develop assigned topics
P3	Provide an online report of results and present them in class

posted by any member of the selected community of practice (not related to the assignment theme), in order to contribute to the community. Week 3 involved a group task and an individual task; while the former consisted of developing a summary of all scientific and technical literature found by the group about the assigned theme, the individual task involved each student's helping to solve another generic problem submitted by a member of the community of practice, primarily in order to strengthen his/her identity within the community.

In P2, students were expected to develop effective contact within communities of practice, now debating the assigned topic. This phase lasted for 5 weeks (Weeks 4–8). During Week 4, students as a group identified questions remaining after P1, after which each student posed his/her question to the community of practice in order to promote discussion about the assigned topic. During Week 5, it was suggested that groups should expand their discussions with new questions and ideas, after which during Week 6 they as a group discussed results obtained in the communities and drafted a report addressing the assigned theme. Week 7 consisted of an individual task in which each student published his or her reflection based on the group's drafted report in order to again generate feedback within communities of practice. Lastly, during Week 8, each student and then each group had to finalize a report with the reflections generated during the project that explained in detail the process of negotiating the assigned problem, preferably with practical examples.

Lastly, in P3, we asked students to prepare a final report and a slideshow on an assigned theme. This phase was executed over the course of 5 weeks (Weeks 9–13). During Week 9, each student was asked to prepare an individual final report describing in detail the entire project process and including their reflections on the assigned theme. Each student also had to complete a self-assessment form. During Week 10, each group produced its final report. Week 11 involved teams' refinement of their final reports based on the analysis and feedback of individual and group reports made by tutors. During Weeks 12 and 13, each group delivered a presentation of their slideshow.

4   Results and Discussion

In this section, we present reflections formed as a product of data analysis and the tutoring of students during the semester. Compared with the previous action research cycle [29], we found that more groups actively participated in the tasks throughout the semester. In fact, 9 of the 21 groups that started the project participated regularly and obtained feedback in communities of practice online (Table 3). Some factors have been reported to be relevant to the development of the project, including flexibility, task deadlines, and tutors' feedback.

Students did not satisfactorily achieve expected learning outcomes. Of all the groups that completed the project, only six students obtained satisfactory grades. We noted that even students involved in the community of practice and who per-formed all activities did not feel motivated. In addition, all students interviewed said that they did not study regularly but rather made intensive, last-minute efforts to meet task deadlines and study for tests. Their lack of motivation and time were considered to be the primary reasons for their lack of dedication to studying and performing tasks.

Table 3. Assignment development by each group

Group	Assignment development					
	N° members	Contacts with tutors		Contact on communits		Summary
		Email	Face to Face	N° topics	N° messages	
G1	4	2	1	40	107	Literature and reading notes; posts in several forums; brief contact with colleges and members of communities of practice
G2	5	3	1	14	44	Literature and reading notes; posts in a few forums and on Facebook; questions lacked focus and clarity; no significant results were generated
G3	5	–	–	28	55	List of literature and a few reading notes; posts in a few forums; questions lacked focus and clarity; no significant results were generated
G4	5	2	1	17	24	List of literature and a few reading notes; posts in a few forums; questions lacked focus and clarity; no significant results were generated
G5	5	–	–	3	12	Only worked during Week 1
G6	3	1	1	19	92	List of literature and a few reading notes; brief contact with colleges and members of communities of practice; questions lacked focus and clarity, particularly during contact via Facebook; no significant results were generated; the solution was unoriginal
G7	5	1	–	16	91	List of literature and a few reading notes; posts in a few forums and use of Google groups; brief

(Continued)

Table 3. (*Continued*)

Group	Assignment development				
	N° members	Contacts with tutors		Contact on communits		Summary
		Email	Face to Face	N° topics	N° messages	
						contact with colleges and members of communities of practice
G8	5	3	1	9	28	Only one student completed all activities; questions lacked focus and clarity; no significant results were generated
G9	5	–	–	13	78	List of literature and a few reading notes; brief contact with colleges and members of communities of practice; questions lacked focus and clarity; no significant results were generated
G10	5	–	–	2	19	Only worked by 4 weeks
G11	5	2	–	12	53	Only worked by 6 week
G12	5	2	1	6	14	Did not work during the final weeks
G13	4	1	–	4	169	List of literature and a few reading notes; brief contact with colleges and members of communities of practice; questions lacked focus and clarity; no significant results were generated
G14	5	1	–	14	54	List of literature and a few reading notes; posts in a few forums; questions lacked focus and clarity; no significant results were generated
G15	5	–	–	0	0	Only worked during Week 1
G16	5	1	1	2	18	Only one student completed the activities yet did not work during the final weeks

(*Continued*)

Table 3. (*Continued*)

Group	Assignment development				
	N° members	Contacts with tutors		Contact on communits		Summary
		Email	Face to Face	N° topics	N° messages	
G17	5	–	–	9	43	The most of the group did not work during the final weeks; two students worked individually; without any significant results; use of an unoriginal solution
G18	5	1	1	9	0	Did not work during the final weeks
G19	5	–	–	2	11	Only one student completed the activities yet did not work during the final weeks
G20	2	–	–	1	6	Did not work during the final weeks
G21	2	–	1	2	13	Only one student completed the activities yet did not work during the final weeks

This lack of motivation was also reflected in the collaboration of peers in each group. In only two groups did all members actively participate throughout the project; in another seven groups, not all students took part in all tasks, which significantly compromised the quality of the project. Still in other groups, only one or two students participated in the tasks, and most students gave up between the second and third phase of the project. From this, it is clear that rigor and the requirement of deadlines may not always be positive, meaning that the negotiation and flexibility of task deadlines can be decisive factors for the success of learning outcomes.

Concerning the participation of students in online communities of practice, "Portugal a Programar"[1] and "MSDN"[2] were the communities that experienced the most interaction. Though students declared that they did not know how to address the assigned themes with professional developers in these communities, when students received constructive feedback that helped them to clarify their doubts, their interaction with such professionals was considered to be a primary factor of the appropriateness of the task in the course. Another positive indicator was the participation in these communities of PM3

---

[1] http://www.portugal-a-programar.pt/.

[2] https://msdn.microsoft.com/pt-pt/default.aspx.

alumni who collaborated in students' discussions of assigned topics. There were also situations in which students collaborated with group members in these communities.

Some students were reprimanded by communities' members for using the same introduction text in communities and for inserting too many topics for the same subject. Most students simply reused the introduction text model given by the teaching staff instead of customizing it. Yet, even though the topics of questions included by students addressed the same subjects, the staff of the communities guided students in correcting them, which shows that students did not clearly know the social protocols developed by these communities. We will doubtlessly keep these factors in mind for future activities. We conclude that it is necessary to provide better guidance for students' interactions in communities of practice. In this sense, in subsequent research iterations we intend to create a community of practice with students, alumni, and programmer experts to improve interaction and student motivation.

Though we asked students to become involved by discussing concepts and ideas, most students viewed the communities as a simple source of information. The factors that influenced this result occurred largely due to the students' inexperience with participation in communities of practice. Students tended to state that they often did not know how to discuss their questions with more experienced developers, partly due to their difficulty in the theoretical domain (e.g., understanding the problem and the development of its resolution). Most students sought an exact answer or a "magic solution" to the assigned problem, and there was generally poor involvement and application of their knowledge; for example, no group developed a basic coding for discussing its ideas in the communities.

Regarding tutoring, subjects ranged from problems with group composition and task delivery, as well as with the activity itself. Due to problems with group composition, some students started their tasks two or three weeks late and were thus affected by not having started the literature search early enough and not initiating contact with communities of practice. Meanwhile, problems with delayed task delivery affected students' reading notes, for one assessment criterion was to not assign grades to delayed work. The quality of work was another concern of tutoring; many students claimed to have difficulty developing strategies for solving their problems, even with feedback from face-to-face meetings and class discussions.

At the end of P1, some students who had difficulty with executing tasks could not report the possible causes of their difficulty. In response, we developed a series of dynamic groups in subsequent classes. To discuss barriers identified during the learning process, and attempt to generate more informal participation, we conducted a talk show with students during class. One of the tutors took the presenter–interviewer role and asked some students to be interviewed, while the other students formed the audience and were encouraged to contribute during the interviews. From our analysis of data obtained through the talk show, we identified that students did not know how to address the professional communities about their assigned problems. We conclude that this circumstance occurred be-cause the students had little knowledge of the problem domain, as also reflected in their search of technical papers. Another problem identified was students' difficulty with understanding how theoretical knowledge covered in the course related to the practice of programming. In this sense, the dynamic also served to meet students' weekly study routines. Two factors that caught our attention were that students did not continually meet to work on tasks and devoted little time for group meetings; instead, they preferred to exert great effort on the eve of dead-lines.

For the subsequent class, we invited an alumnus of the course in order to motivate students by offering them a personal view about the assignments given by the guest. The presentation addressed aspects of their academic routine, their leisure activities (e.g., video games), the difficulties encountered during the course, and how to overcome them. Students also presented an illustrative schematic of how to address the assigned problems and define steps toward solving the problem. As a result, we expected that students would adapt these ideas to their realities.

The third and last group dynamic developed aimed to examine the difficulties with working in a group. During the dynamic called "complete the music," students were asked to form groups, and different colors were assigned to each group. While the music was played, the lyrics of the parts were displayed in different colors, and each group had to stand up and sing the part written in its as-signed color. The dynamic occurred in a gradual, interwoven process toward the end of the song, at which point all groups sang together. The students stated that this activity was fun and allowed reflection on the difficulties with working in groups. Activities like this have a long history in management and business [32, 33].

At the end of the project, we considered adopting other tutoring strategies and feedback so that students could achieve the learning outcomes in terms of motivation and engagement. Tutoring students is a process that requires a heavy workload for one teacher and two tutors in which the role of team leaders becomes essential to assisting the teaching staff, both in forming teams and motivating students.

At the end of the action research cycle, students were asked to complete an online survey addressing their personal information, opinions of the adequacy of the tools, and difficulties with developing the project. However, only nine of the 95 students fully responded to the survey. Given this low response rate, which fails to take into account data collected, we list it among the limitations of the investigation.

5   Conclusions and Future Work

In this paper, we have reported the outcomes of the second cycle of action re-search. As in the previous cycle, students did not satisfactorily achieve expected learning outcomes. However, more groups completed the assigned activities. Results nevertheless reflect their poor engagement in the communities of practice and dismal performance with the other learning tasks. From these results, we have identified several ideas and recommendations that we intend to apply in subsequent versions of the coursework. For example, creating a community of practice with students, alumni, and invited programmer experts, rather than asking students to participate in external communities right away, might improve interaction and student motivation. Also, selecting better project-management practices in order to identify problems at an earlier stage may enable better guidance from the teaching staff to support students' needs and hence help them achieve better results. Consequently, we propose that interaction and pedagogic assessment strategies are reshaped to simulate a business-like environment, including project management methods, e.g., SCRUM [34]. It should also include other aspects of a professional environment, such as teamwork, coaching, continual feedback and/or self-assessment strategies. We can consider this proposal to be a simulation of programming in a business context, and plan to refer to it in the future as the SimProgramming approach.

Acknowledgments. Nunes, R. R. & Pedrosa D. Thank the Fundação para a Ciência e Tecnologia (FCT), Portugal, for Ph.D. Grants SFRH/BD/91309/2012 and SFRH/BD/87815/2012.

References

1. Tappan, D.: A holistic multidisciplinary approach to teaching software engineering through air traffic control. J. Comput. Sci. Coll. **30**(1), 199–205 (2014)
2. Zschaler, S., Demuth, B., Schmitz, L.: Salespoint: a Java framework for teaching object-oriented software development. Sci. Comput. Program. **79**, 189–203 (2014)
3. Jenkins, T.: On the difficulty of learning to program. In: Proceedings of 3rd Annual Conference of the LTSN-ICS, 27–29 August 2002, Loughborough (University of Ulster, LTSN Centre for Information and Computer Sciences) (2002)
4. Krasner, G.E., Pope, S.T.: A description of the model view controller paradigm in the Smalltalk-80 system. J. Object-Oriented Program. **1**(3), 26–49 (1988)
5. Curry, E., Grace, P.: Flexible self-management using the model-view-controller pattern. IEEE Softw. **25**(3), 84–90 (2008)
6. Duderstadt, J.J.: Engineering for a changing world. In: Grasso, D., Burkins, M.B. (eds.) Holistic Engineering Education, pp. 17–35. Springer, New York (2010)
7. Sheppard, S.D., Macatangay, K., Colby, A., Sullivan, W.M.: Educating engineers: Designing for the future of the field, vol. 2. Jossey-Bass, San Francisco (2008)
8. Adams, R., Evangelou, D., English, L., De Figueiredo, A.D., Mousoulides, N., Pawley, A. L., Schiefellite, C., Stevens, R., Svinicki, M., Trenor, J.M., Wilson, D.M.: Multiple perspectives on engaging future engineers. J. Eng. Educ. **100**, 48–88 (2011). doi:10.1002/j. 2168-9830.2011.tb00004.x
9. Litzinger, T., Lattuca, L.R., Hadgraft, R., Newstetter, W.: Engineering education and the development of expertise. J. Eng. Educ. **100**(1), 123–150 (2011). doi:10.1002/j.2168-9830. 2011.tb00006.x
10. Stevens, R., Amos, D., Jocuns, A., Garrison, L.: Engineering as lifestyle and a meritocracy of difficulty: Two pervasive beliefs among engineering students and their possible effects. Paper presented at the American Society for Engineering Education Annual Conference, Honolulu, Hawaii (2007)
11. Stevens, R., O'Connor, K., Garrison, L., Jocuns, A., Amos, D.M.: Becoming an engineer: Toward a three dimensional view of engineering learning. J. Eng. Educ. **97**(3), 355–368 (2008)
12. Johri, A., Olds, B.M.: Situated engineering learning: Bridging engineering education research and the learning sciences. J. Eng. Educ. **100**(1), 151–185 (2011)
13. Patterson, E.A., Campbell, P.B., Busch-Vishniac, I., Guillaume, D.W.: The effect of context on student engagement in engineering. Eur. J. Eng. Educ. **36**(3), 211–224 (2011)
14. Sancho-Thomas, P., Fuentes-Fernández, R., Fernández-Manjón, B.: Learning teamwork skills in university programming courses. Comput. Educ. **53**(2), 517–531 (2009)
15. Esteves, M., Fonseca, B., Morgado, L., Martins, P.: Improving teaching and learning of computer programming through the use of the Second Life virtual world. Br. J. Educ. Technol. **42**(4), 624–637 (2011)

16. Schaffer, S.P., Chen, X., Zhu, X., Oakes, W.C.: Self-efficacy for cross-disciplinary learning in project-based teams. J. Eng. Educ. **101**(1), 82–94 (2012)
17. Bédard, D., Lison, C., Dalle, D., Côté, D., Boutin, N.: Problem-based and project-based learning in engineering and medicine: determinants of students' engagement and persistance. Interdisc. J. Probl. Based Learn. **6**(2), 8 (2012)
18. Yadav, A., Subedi, D., Lundeberg, M.A., Bunting, C.F.: Problem-based learning: influence on students' learning in an electrical engineering course. J. Eng. Educ. **100**(2), 253–280 (2011)
19. Zhou, C., Kolmos, A., Nielsen, J.F.D.: A problem and project-based learning (PBL) approach to motivate group creativity in engineering education. Int. J. Eng. Educ. **28**(1), 3–16 (2012)
20. Rotgans, J.I., Schmidt, H.G.: Problem-based learning and student motivation: The role of interest in learning and achievement. In: O'Grady, G., Yew, E.H.J., Goh, K.P.L., Schmidt, H.G. (eds.) One-Day, One-Problem, pp. 85–101. Springer, New York (2012)
21. Pascual, R.: Enhancing project-oriented learning by joining communities of practice and opening spaces for relatedness. Eur. J. Eng. Educ. **35**(1), 3–16 (2010)
22. Morgado, Leonel, Varajão, João, Coelho, Dalila, Rodrigues, Clara, Sancín, Chiara, Castello, Valentina: The attributes and advantages of virtual worlds for real world training. J. Virtual Worlds Educ. **1**(1), 15–35 (2010)
23. Stolk, J., Harari, J.: Student motivations as predictors of high-level cognitions in project-based classrooms. Act. Learn. High Educ. **15**(3), 231–247 (2014)
24. Vanasupa, L., Stolk, J., Harding, T.: Application of self-determination and self-regulation theories to course design: Planting the seeds for adaptive expertise. Int. J. Eng. Educ. **26**(4), 914 (2010)
25. Slavich, G.M., Zimbardo, P.G.: Transformational teaching: Theoretical underpinnings, basic principles, and core methods. Educ. Psychol. Rev. **24**(4), 569–608 (2012)
26. Pritchard, A., Woollard, J.: A Psychology for the Classroom: Constructivism and Social Learning, p. 112. Routledge/David Fulton Education, Oxford (2010)
27. Universidade de Trás-os-Montes e Alto Douro, "Despacho nº 14253/2011 - Regulamento do curso de Licenciatura em Engenharia Informática", Diário da República, 2ª série, nº. 202, 20 October 2011
28. Joint Task Force on Computing Curricula. Computer Science Curricula 2013: Curriculum Guidelines for Undergraduate Degree Programs in Computer Science. ACM, New York
29. Morgado, L., Fonseca, B., Martins, P., Paredes, H., Cruz, G., Maia, A.M., Nunes, R.R., Santos, A.: Social networks, microblogging, virtual worlds, and Web 2.0 in the teaching of programing techniques for software engineering: a trial combining collaboration and social interaction beyond college. In: IEEE Engineering Education 2012 - Collaborative Learning & New Pedagogic Approaches in Engineering Education - Proceedings, Marrakesh (2012). doi:10.1109/EDUCON.2012.6201129
30. Brandel, M.: 8 hot IT skills for 2014 (2013). http://www.computerworld.com/article/2484858/it-management/8-hot-it-skills-for-2014.html. Accessed 29 September 2014
31. Barbosa, L.F., Alves, P., Barroso, J.: SIDE - teaching support information system. In: 2011 6th Iberian Conference on Information Systems and Technologies (CISTI), pp. 1–6. IEEE, June 2011
32. Nilson, Carolyn: Team games for trainers. McGraw-Hill, New York (1993)
33. Pike, Robert W., Solem, Lynn: 50 creative training openers and energizers: innovative ways to start your training with a bang. Jossey-Bass/Pfeiffer & Creative Training Techniques Press, San Francisco (2000)
34. Schwaber, K.: Agile Project Management with Scrum. Microsoft Press, Redmond (2004)

Guidelines for Designing Accessible Digital (Text) Books: The Italian Case

Eliseo Sciarretta[1(✉)], Andrea Ingrosso[1], and Alessandra Carriero[2]

[1] DASIC - Link Campus University, Via Nomentana 335, 00162 Rome, Italy
{e.sciarretta,a.ingrosso}@unilink.it
[2] Università Degli Studi Della Basilicata, Via Nazario Sauro 85,
85100 Potenza, Italy
alecarriero1509@gmail.com

Abstract. In this paper, the authors analyze the state of the art of digital publishing, with particular attention towards what is going on in Italy, and investigate eBooks' accessibility features, in order to understand whether this growing phenomenon may represent a resource and a possibility of inclusion for all individuals, regardless of their (dis)abilities, their needs and their interests, and how to make this possible. Given the recent turmoil around the so-called School 2.0 and the subsequent need to guarantee every student the right to a profitable and successful school career, the discussion will focus on issues related to digital textbooks, aiming at elaborating a proposal of guidelines and editorial techniques which can assist the process of preparation of works all learners can access, discarding the "one-size-fits-all" logic, but rather adapting to individual needs.

Keywords: Accessibility · Learning · School · Ebook · Guideline · Universal access

1 Introduction

School 2.0 is a school that uses the possibilities offered by new technologies to innovate the teaching processes trying to keep pace with a changing world [1].

School 2.0 is a much spoken of concept but it is little used, at least in Italy.

Above all, School 2.0 is an unmissable opportunity to promote the inclusion of all [2], because the digital tools can be adaptable to as many people as possible, complying to reading preferences, ways of use, levels of language proficiency.

Technologies can constitute a great opportunity to achieve social integration but it is necessary to plan the change and the gradual transit from one model to another, taking into account the accessibility needs of all [3, 4].

Given the centrality of the accessibility issue, the first part of the work will serve to frame this concept in various perspectives [5]. Accessibility will be considered as a discipline, placed in relation to similar concepts such as the Design For All [6], scenarios in which accessibility can be crucial will be described and "who" is addressed will be clarified [7].

© Springer International Publishing Switzerland 2015
M. Antona and C. Stephanidis (Eds.): UAHCI 2015, Part III, LNCS 9177, pp. 202–213, 2015.
DOI: 10.1007/978-3-319-20684-4_20

A brief overview on web accessibility will follow: it can't be forgotten this is the area where the greatest efforts have been done to ensure equal access to anyone [8].

The accessibility issue is not limited, however, to the web: technologies need to be accessible too, above all devices that can be used to read a digital book, as eReaders.

Then, a specific section will be devoted to the accessibility of digital documents [9], where the discussion will contextualize the problems that the publishing sector has to face to offer digital products. The focus will be on the features of digital publishing and how to make them accessible [10, 11].

The authors, then, will shift on digital textbooks, as they are considered the main tool in the school "revolution".

The analysis will focus on the major structural and educational changes that are affecting the (Italian) school in recent years, and on the contentious debate that has emerged and the problems that have been highlighted [12, 13].

Great attention will be paid to the so-called Universal Design for Learning [14], an approach that builds on Universal Design to apply its principles in the education field.

The data emerging from the deepening of the major themes mentioned above will be elaborated in the last section of the work, in order to formulate a proposal for a set of guidelines for the creation of digital (text)books that comply with accessibility criteria and meet the needs of the readers.

Two different sets of guidelines will be provided, one for the production of accessible digital books and documents, and one for the design of eReader devices that can be enjoyed by all.

2 Accessibility

2.1 Definitions in Different Contexts

Accessibility is the feature of a device, a service, a resource or an environment of being easily usable by any type of user.

The term is commonly associated with the possibility for people with reduced or impaired capabilities to access physical environments (therefore called physical accessibility), to independently enjoy cultural content (cultural accessibility) or to use information systems through the use of Assistive Technologies or through compliance with accessibility requirements of products.

There are several definitions of accessibility according to the different contexts in which it is applied.

The "discipline" of accessibility, as the set of rules, procedures and regulations designed to allow easy access to something, is born in the urban design context, especially for public utilities [15].

The urban accessibility is the set of spatial characteristics, distribution and organization of the built environment that can allow easier use of places and equipment in the city, in conditions of adequate security and autonomy, even by persons with reduced or impaired motor skills.

Still, accessibility of spaces alone, in the era of the "information society", may not be enough. In fact, the concept of accessibility does not apply only to the physical environment, but also to information and communication.

So, accessibility is also meant to be the possible use of information, tools and environments (also through appropriate aids) without limitations.

2.2   Techniques for Web Accessibility

The Web, since its creation, has been seen as a system that can help people, as long as it is designed for everyone, and this led to the development of the culture of accessibility. Still, this culture has not always evolved properly.

In the early days, especially in the 90 s of last century, the idea has established that an accessible site needed to be added to the original one, as an alternative.

This approach is now strongly deprecated, as contrary to the cardinal principle that inspires accessibility, namely the inclusion. Far from obtaining this objective, in fact, a site thus produced constitutes a new "segregation" for who are in the need to use it.

An accessible website, has to be fully usable by all: both by those who have a physical disability that requires the use of Assistive Technologies, and by those who have difficulties accessing the Web due to technical limitations (old computers, slow connections) or unfamiliarity with the Internet.

The content of a Web site is accessible "when it can be used by someone who has a disability" [16]; more specifically Web accessibility means that people with disabilities can perceive, understand, explore and interact with the Web.

But already in 1999, in his book "Weaving the Web" [17], Tim Berners-Lee said the Web should allow equal access to those who are in a different economic or political situation, to those who have physical or cognitive disabilities, to who belongs to a different culture and to those who use different languages with different characters that are read in different directions on the page.

Web accessibility can be achieved only if all of its components are accessible: content, user agents and authoring tools.

Standards play a key role in the definition of accessibility requirements for each of these components. Involving users early on and throughout the course of the design is essential to make it easier.

2.3   Devices and Documents Accessibility

Information accessibility can not be limited only to the content, but it has to be extended to hardware and software used to access it.

W3C's Web Accessibility Initiative (WAI) has been operating on multiple fronts, and one of their groups focuses on the development of guidelines, techniques and other documentation to promote the accessibility of so-called User Agents (browsers and plug-ins): the User Agent Accessibility Guidelines (UAAG 2.0) [18].

Browsers and User Agents, however, are only a small part of the tools used every day, for which it is necessary to ensure accessibility: technological gadgets used for a variety of functions.

In this paper the authors deal with a specific device, it is to say the eReader (or eBook Reader), a portable electronic device that allows users to upload a large number of texts in digital format and read them as analogous to a paper book.

The relationship between eBook and eReader is very profound: electronic text isn't equal in itself to electronic book; eBooks must be enjoyed through appropriate interfaces, an evolution of paper books ones, with similar features: portable, light, little tiring for the eyes, free of cables and wires, not too expensive nor "fragile" [19].

As for accessibility, text-to-speech software can be installed on eReaders, transforming electronic texts into audio books: an essential opportunity for the blind and visually impaired persons, but also a possibility to explore new strategies that can lead to re-discover the pleasure of reading through the combination of text and voice.

Still, if technology becomes accessible, the problem shifts to document formats.

A document is a text, written in a certain language, that has some content, a structure and semantics, that can be related to other documents.

An electronic document is a document made of bits within a computer system.

An accessible electronic document is available for use by anyone, including people with disabilities. An electronic document, to be accessible, needs to comply with specific rules and guidelines.

There is no real standard format to be used for the distribution of electronic documents. The DOC format is used only because it is very widespread, being the native format of Microsoft Word.

The formats that mostly contend the market are, for different reasons, the PDF, the MOBI and especially the ePub, which picked up the heritage of the predecessor OEB.

The key feature of PDF format, developed by Adobe, is to be independent of the various output devices. This format has become a "de facto" standard, but its use as a format for digital books has some limitations. The PDF file has to be created taking into account the device that will display it: the pages of the document can only be enlarged or shrunk to fit the screen on which it will be displayed.

An ISO standard, PDF /UA-1, sets the accessibility features for PDF: it can be made completely adherent to WCAG 2.0 [20].

The MOBI format is based on the Open eBook standard and it is rather frequently updated, which can create compatibility problems with older or inferior devices.

The ePub format is an open standard specifically designed for digital books and it is gradually emerging as one of the reference points for publishing.

Its third version, ePub3, was published in October of 2011, and, being based on HTML5 and CSS3, integrates the specifications on accessibility.

3   Digital Publishing

Traditional publishing industry is in crisis: the number of books, magazines and newspapers sold has been declining for some time.

Year 2013 was simply dramatic in terms of revenues in Italy, as the annual report of AGCOM certifies [21]. The turnover of the newspapers was down by 7 % year on year, while for magazines there was a real collapse with a scary -17 %.

But Italians do not read less (always little when compared with the rest of the Europeans, but not less than before), they are only changing habits.

The new frontier is in fact digital publishing.

According to forecasts of PWC E&M Outlook 13-17 [22], revenues from sales of digital copies of publications in Italy will grow by about 40 % in 2017.

eBooks are a cultural phenomenon still difficult to decipher but certainly of great significance. Initially the debate on these "objects" have focused almost exclusively on the potential conflicting relationship between eBooks and books. Indeed, it is a false issue. eBooks are not a technological alternative to books or a variant, but represent the evolution, and consequently the survival, of the book itself.

The meaning of the book, its role and value are still the same, while the "format", which determines the intrinsic characteristics and mode of production, distribution and use, is changing. eBooks are the books of the future and the future of the books.

In the paper book there's never been anything natural: it is a technology. No stage of its production, with the sole exception of the conception of the idea by the author, lives far from technology. The paper it is written on, the pen, the typewriter once, the computer today, all these objects are technologies.

Some authors see in the eBook a solution to the problem of preservation and dissemination of content [23], rather than an opportunity to redefine the relationship between authors, readers and publishers [24] or even a chance to renew the utopian idea of universal access to knowledge.

Digital reading will not replace the one on paper. A strong reader won't stop buying printed books: if anything he will buy also digital ones. The two things don't overlap, because they have different functions. Some kind of content isn't suitable for digital publication: for example photo books.

Readers who first may recognize the benefits of digital books are the students, who need more than others to frequently consult a large number of books, to perform searches inside them, to take notes, to insert bookmarks, to re-read several times a particular step and to put it in relation to other parts of the book, and so on.

4   School 2.0

4.1   Underway Changes

Textbook has always been, in the school, the ultimate learning tool, over time its reassuring form has never really changed, nor its role has been seriously questioned. At least so far. School "digital revolution" is imminent.

In Italy, as well as throughout the Western world, a process of analysis for the creation of models of schools 2.0 is undergoing. Within the "National Plan for Digital School" (Piano Nazionale per la Scuola Digitale - PNSD), there is a specific action, called School 2.0, aimed at a significant modification of the learning environments.

However, if in traditional schools scheme and structural characteristics are established and recognizable, schools 2.0 lack a characterization and prototypes.

The legislation that guides the transition from paper to digital proceeds between acceleration and braking. One reason for this slowness is the refusal to adhere by the publishers, who rather together ask for a continuous postponement of the procedures. What are the reasons for this hostile attitude?

Not everyone is convinced that the School 2.0 is really a solution to the problem of education, or at least that it can be so in the short term.

First, the introduction of new technologies could produce a short circuit between the traditional and "new" concept of teaching. The current teaching staff may not be able to grasp the essential differences of this transition.

Someone argues that behind all the pressure to switch to digital school there are the interests of software multinationals, which could get their hands on public schools.

There's a further fear for the future of teachers figure, which is likely to be reduced to the role of "facilitator of learning processes" in totally computerized classrooms.

In response to these criticisms, there are reasons pushing for adoption of digital technology, even if the benefits will be seen more medium-term than short-term.

Benefits would be numerous: from paper saving to the use of multimedia content.

Many of the advantages (but also limitations) of the electronic book lie in its "digital existence" as an object composed of bits: immateriality, transmissibility, storage, reproducibility, ductility and especially accessibility.

Technology in school should be "pervasive" and "invisible": it should be in the everyday environment of learning, so that its presence looks natural.

Teachers don't see their role undermined; far from that, they are called to cultivate the "digital wisdom" [25], that is both wisdom that comes from the use of digital tools which enhance cognitive skills, and the necessary wisdom to a conscious use of tools.

The transition to digital, like everything else, must be subject to a project, especially if the result to achieve is not only the digital as an instrument (and already this would be a noble and ambitious goal), but as a lever for the renewal of the methods of teaching.

The practices of reading and study are also modifying: text is enjoyed on a screen, but often not on a desk anymore, in "lean forward" mode, rather in "lean back" mode, thanks to the recent spread of eReaders and tablets; tools traditionally used to intervene on the text, such as pencils and markers, have taken a different form (for example, highlights and notes are always changeable and removable); new features have expanded the possible actions when reading (e.g. word search inside the text, activation of links and multimedia objects, sharing of notes to the text).

Without wishing to alter life of classes, it seems necessary to make paper coexist with digital, finding a good balance between the protection of traditional knowledge and forms of modernization in progress, so that children can learn to use the tools that are the basis of their daily life with more awareness. A school open to the 2.0 can further stimulate pupils and provide them with the intellectual tools needed to manage new technologies and resources at their disposal.

Actually, the biggest fear of publishers is to lose control of the market, with the severe crisis of the copyright, that limits the property of the buyer. Who buys a printed book becomes the owner of the physical object, which can be given or lent. However, in the case of digital book, this border is more subtle: both because an eBook loses the physicality to become "pure" content, and because the reproducibility of a file is much simpler.

Digital Rights Managements (DRM) were created to respond to new requirements regarding the copyright in the digital environment. Digital files are encoded and encrypted by DRM, so their spread con be controlled. Born with the main objective to combat piracy, the "closed" concept of DRM has disappointed especially those who legally buys content, because of its extreme rigidity.

Publishers are turning to alternative forms such as Social DRM (or watermarks), through which files aren't blocked in any way, but they are marked with the personal data of the purchasers in order to trace potential abuses.

Digital books, and especially textbooks, should comply with the accessibility requirements, but often they don't.

ICT can be a great opportunity to achieve social integration but in Italy, on many fronts, including public administration, even the established rules are disrespected.

4.2   Universal Design for Learning

Textbooks represent a barrier to learning if the support isn't accessible and if content isn't understandable: they can be inadequate due to the difficulty of used language, the excessive articulation of content and bad choices of typography, to the point that inaccessibility of texts is even counted among the causes of school dropouts [26].

As the literature shows, the book in digital format can result, for flexibility of tools and languages, in a technology adaptable to the greatest possible number of readers [27], complying with reading preferences, ways of use, language proficiency.

To expand learning opportunities, by providing alternative access through the use of technology, is the main goal of the Center for Applied Special Technology (CAST) that has developed studies on the application of the Universal Design philosophy to the educational context: the Universal Design for Learning (UDL).

Traditionally, the approach of the interventions to ensure accessibility has been to adapt the equipment designed for the general market for use by people with disabilities, through products such as the Assistive Technologies.

This methodology has two main limitations: adjustments are normally made available when a technology is mature and require a constant updating; furthermore systems are designed using interaction metaphors optimized for certain skills and therefore any adjustment for disabled persons is not optimal.

Universal Design (or Design For All), affirms, instead, that the design of products and services needs to take into account the abilities and preferences of all potential users, in a proactive approach.

The basic idea is that what is designed from the beginning for users who have some difficulties, will inevitably be also suitable for those who have no special needs.

A "project for all" doesn't have to realize all the possible workarounds for the various users, but it has to make possible for users to use alternative configurations, with different hardware and software modules according to their needs.

In the definition of CAST, the Universal Design for Learning "is a set of Principles for curriculum development that give all individuals equal opportunities to learn."

The goal is to overcome the logic of Assistive Technologies to design training programs that should be flexible, equitable in access to information and, above all, to learning processes [14].

UDL, acting on the forms of production, communication and use of the content, invites everyone to re-think education so as to make it suitable for all people, to the greatest extent possible, without the need for adaptation or specialized design, according to the Universal Design model that the UN Convention on the Rights of Persons with Disabilities calls for taking in the design of environments, products, programs and services [28, 29].

5 Accessible Digital Publishing

5.1 Guidelines for Accessible Books

Requirements for eBook accessibility vary depending on the individual skills, abilities or preferences. In general, it is a valid strategy to allow readers to customize the stylistic elements and graphics to optimize the reading experience.

To make a eBook accessible it is necessary to combine various factors, such as the technical features of the product, the skills of the readers and their familiarity in the use of Assistive Technologies.

Users, particularly students with disabilities, interested in having accessible eBooks, have different needs depending on their impairment:

- blind: files accessible by screen readers, transferable for Braille printing;
- visually impaired: files with possibility to enlarge the characters, recognizable by speech synthesis associated with magnification software;
- motor impairments of the upper limbs: possibility to "browse" the text in an alternative way using assistive technologies replacing keyboard and mouse;
- dyslexic: visual reading supported by speech synthesis to facilitate the under-standing of the text;
- cognitive or linguistic-lexical difficulties: possibility of adaptation that requires manipulation of the document, both in content and formatting;
- Hearing impaired: subtitling.

These characteristics, can be achieved by following the following guidelines, the result of the evaluation and selection process made by the authors during research.

Content vs. Graphics. It is essential to separate form from content, that is not to assume that the visual appearance alone can convey a certain meaning to readers.

Structure. An effective navigational structure should include:

- metadata: they make the book more easily available;
- a hierarchy of titles, parts, chapters, sections and subsections: this allows the various Assistive Technologies to provide quick navigation in the document;

- notes, footnotes and references: they should be provided with hyperlinks to the corresponding element in the main text;
- a logical reading order of the content: this should be preserved even when text divided into blocks or columns is linearized;
- titles and page numbers that allow readers with visual disabilities to compare their position in the document with that of conventional book readers;
- index and table of contents with active links and return links to the index at the end of each section;
- semantic tagging: accessible content must be logically structured and subjected to semantic markup.

Text to Speech. A digital text can easily be converted into a spoken text using appropriate software. Screen readers are used to navigate through the page, they announce bullet lists and tables, can spell the words and can be set to read at different speeds and to change the voice and tone depending on the content. All this provided that the content is structured in an accessible way.

Images. Dealing with images is one of the greatest challenges in eBook accessibility. The most important thing is the correct use of alternative texts, which allow to describe the illustrations for readers with reduced access to graphic information. Alt texts should provide equivalent information, commensurate to the function performed by the original object they are replacing.

Color. Although the color is an effective visual method to attract the reader's attention, it should never be the only way to transmit information. The choice of color plays an important role in facilitating interpretation of content. Adequate contrast between background colors and foreground colors should be ensured.

DRM. It's necessary to check that DRM doesn't inhibit the accessibility of books.

Language. The primary language of the document should always be indicated.

Multimedia Elements. Audio or video elements must be accessible too.

Modules. Since paper forms require handwriting are by nature totally inaccessible. Electronic forms are therefore preferable, provided that an accessible format is used.

Scientific Symbols. Accessible mathematical symbols are a difficult challenge, since there isn't a technological solution that fits all. It is necessary to refer to ePub3 specifications.

Measures for vision problems. Some factors affect the readability of all documents:

- font size of the text should be 12-14 points;
- font should be clear and open;
- body of the text should be aligned to the left;
- text layout should be clear, simple and consistent;
- italics and bold should be moderately used;
- space between columns of text must be large enough to be clearly perceived.

ePub3 is the most appropriate standard for achieving accessible eBooks, since it has incorporated the specifications of the DAISY (Digital Accessible Information System) format, making possible the creation of accessible files. Matt Garrish [10] argues that, in the economic perspective, accessible publishing means to reach new community of readers and cover new market segments. The accessibility is therefore not a philanthropic consideration, but a logical and commercially profitable choice.

5.2   Guidelines for Accessible eReaders

eReader devices need to be accessible too, because, as already said, the accessible content alone is not enough, if devices can't allow an easy reading.

These guidelines are the result of the research carried out, which led to their selection from existing good practices and previous studies.

The guidelines are divided according to the functional limitation, and thus the type of problem that aim to solve.

Total blindness or severe low vision:

- all the functionalities of the device, should be mapped to be available for interaction via screen reader;
- speed of the voice, pitch, and volume should be easily adjustable, preferably without leaving the book;
- physical keyboards should have tactile markers for orientation and screen keyboards should provide the knowledge of the selected key before its activation; ideally, there should be some form of feedback that the user can feel (i.e., haptic feedback);
- devices should have controls easily identifiable by touch;
- it should be easy to disable, and pause the audio on the player;
- devices should offer the possibility to set personal keyboard shortcuts.

Low vision:

- devices should have controls clearly marked and large enough to be highly visible and distinguishable or easily identifiable by touch;
- eBook software should ensure the user full control over typography of the content, including the ability to set the color of the text in the foreground, background and highlights, choose the font, increasing the size of the text, set the line length and the column width, and set the spacing between words, lines, characters.

Motor disabilities to the upper body:

- devices should be lightweight, durable (possibly should not suffer damage in case of a fall), and able to be mounted on a wheelchair or on a support;
- touch screen devices should allow interaction via non-human touch (e.g., alternative conductive pointing devices);
- touch screen devices should have onscreen controls that allow a certain aim inaccuracy or they should ensure that the controls can be presented cyclically through simple movements, such as the swipe;
- hardware controls should be large enough to be operated with alternative pointing devices.

Cognitive disabilities that affect understanding, including reading problems:

- text-to-speech should provide an option for synchronized highlighting word by word and sentence by sentence;
- controls of the device should be simple and intuitive;
- eReaders should allow users set bookmarks, take notes, and highlight text;
- eReaders should provide options for word prediction while typing and options for spell checking and errors correction.

Deafness or hearing difficulties:

- any audio signal or warning should have a evident visual equivalent;
- devices should be able to provide synchronized subtitles for videos;
- a "mono" audio output option should be available so that users with hearing problems in one ear can direct both audio channels to the other ear.

Finally, there are a couple of global criteria that can not be included in the above lists: first, people with disabilities should be able to set up the devices by theirself, without the need for further assistance. Furthermore, eBook stores should also meet accessibility standards.

6 Conclusions

The transition to digital, if well planned, can have considerable benefits, not only in terms of saving resources, but also to give a boost to Italian school system which for too long is stagnating and resting on its laurels of ancient glories.

The adoption of technological tools can indeed break the inertia and finally kick off the long-awaited revolution.

From the analysis, several guidelines have been identified, to be applied in the production of accessible digital (text) books.

These guidelines consider the technical characteristics that accessible documents must have and the features that the tools have to provide to be usable by all people.

As a book that is accessible for a person not necessarily is so for another, guidelines are not equally applicable to all, but they must be grouped according to abilities.

For eReaders, guidelines have been divided according to the functional limitation, too. The most important recommendation is to make sure that they are designed to support integration with Assistive Technologies.

The guidelines can be transformed in measurable testing criteria, that aim to become a checklist to be used to conduct assessments on the accessibility of digital documents.

In order to facilitate this verification process, a support tool can be conceived to guide the human evaluator; this may be useful to publishers and authors to make sure that their books comply with the criteria. The next step of the research aims at the creation of this evaluation tool.

Through this greater impetus to the transition from paper to digital book can be given, ensuring that no one is excluded, thanks to accessibility.

References

1. Novella, C., Lembo, D., Mecella, M., Vacca, M.: Note sulla scuola del 21°secolo: il concetto di scuola 2.0 e una proposta di classificazione. Technical Report. Department of Computer, Control, and Management Engineering Antonio Ruberti (2012). http://eprints.bice.rm.cnr.it/ 4397/1/Note_sulla_scuola.pdf
2. Medeghini, R., Fornasa, W.: L'educazione inclusiva. Franco Angeli, Milano (2011)
3. Benyon, D.: Designing Interactive Systems. Pearson Education, Harlow (2010)
4. Preiser, W., Ostroff, E.: Universal Design Handbook. McGraw-Hill, New York (2001)
5. Diodati, M.: Accessibilità. Guida completa. Apogeo, Milano (2007)
6. Accolla, A.: Design for all. Franco Angeli, Milano (2009)
7. Pavone, M.: Dall'esclusione all'inclusione. Mondadori, Milano (2010)
8. Artifoni, R.: Una legge nata Stanca. In: DM, n. 155, 2005 (2005). http://www.uildm.org/ archivio_dm/155/rubriche/20stancaweb.shtml
9. Brivio, F., Trezzi, G.: ePub. Apogeo, Milano (2011)
10. Garrish, M.: Accessible epub3. O'Reilly Media, Cambridge (2012)
11. Sechi, L.: Editoria digitale. Apogeo, Milano (2010)
12. Fiore, M.G.: Le nuove adozioni dei libri di testo e l'accessibilità dimenticata: scenari normativi. In: Atti del Convegno Didamatica 2012, Bari, 14-16 Maggio 2012 (2012)
13. Celentano, M.G., Colazzo, S.: L'apprendimento digitale. Prospettive tecnologiche e pedagogiche dell'e-learning. Carocci, Roma (2008)
14. CAST (Center for Applied Special Technology): Universal Design for Learning Guidelines version 2.0. CAST, Wakefield (2011)
15. Bennett, T.: Planning and People with Disabilities. In: Montgomery, J., Thornley, A. (eds.) Radical Planning Initiatives: New Directions for Planning in the 1990s. Gower, Aldershot (1990)
16. W3C – Web Accessibility Initiative: Introduction to Web Accessibility (2005). http://www. w3.org/WAI/intro/accessibility.php
17. Berners-Lee, T.: Weaving the Web: The Original Design and Ultimate Destiny of the World Wide Web by its Inventor. Harper (1999)
18. W3C: User Agent Accessibility Guidelines (2014). http://www.w3.org/TR/UAAG20/
19. Roncaglia, G.: Libri elettronici: problemi e prospettive. "Bollettino AIB", 4 (2001)
20. ISO: ISO 14289-1. Document management applications – Electronic document file format enhancement for accessibility – Part 1: Use of ISO 32000-1 (PDF/UA-1) (2012)
21. AGCOM: Relazione annuale 2013, sull'attività svolta e sui programmi di lavoro (2013). http://www.agcom.it/documents/10179/16292/Rel_2013_completo/e7fe680a-81de-47d7-b135-4b27b834b4e1
22. PWC: Entertainment and Media Outlook in Italy 2013–2017 (2013). http://youmark.it/wp-content/uploads/2013/09/Executive-Summary.pdf
23. Liu, Z.: Paper to digital: documents in the information age. Libraries Unlimited, Westport (2008)
24. Jenkins, H.: Convergence Culture: Where Old and New Media Collide. New York University Press, New York (2006)
25. Prensky, M.: From digital natives to digital wisdom. Corwin, Thousand Oaks (2012)
26. Gallina, M.A.: (a cura di): Scegliere e usare il libro di testo. Franco Angeli, Milano (2009)
27. Rotta, M.: La rete tradita. In mrxKnowledge, 9 luglio 2010 (2010). http://www.mariorotta. com/knowledge/2010/07/la-rete-tradita/
28. CUD (Center for Universal Design): The principles of Universal Design (1997). http://www. ncsu.edu/www/ncsu/design/sod5/cud/about_ud/udprinciplestext.htm
29. UN General Assembly: Convention on the Rights of Persons with Disabilities (2007). http:// www.refworld.org/docid/45f973632.html

The Evolution of an Online Approach to Preparing Young Students with Disabilities for College and Careers

Clark A. Shingledecker[✉] and Jennifer Barga

Wright State University, Dayton, OH, USA
clark.shingledecker@wright.edu

Abstract. This paper describes an initiative to address the underrepresentation of persons with disabilities (PwD) in science, technology, engineering and mathematics (STEM) fields using online educational methods. The objectives of the program are to build motivation for pursuing STEM careers among students with disabilities in middle school and early high school and to improve their preparation for postsecondary education. We first outline the problem of underrepresentation of PwD in STEM and present the underlying reasoning for targeting younger students and addressing the objectives using online methods. Next, we describe the development of online content designed to increase STEM career motivation and college readiness and the initial implementation of the program using a series of informal educational webcasts aimed at students with disabilities and their parents. In the final section of the paper, we identify some of the lessons-learned about online educational approaches from the original implementation, and describe a subsequent evolution of the program using multilevel web-based content designed to reach a wider range of problem stakeholders including teachers and rehabilitation counselors.

Keywords: Students with disabilities · STEM careers · Online education · College preparation

1 Introduction

Increasing the participation of individuals from underrepresented groups in science technology engineering and mathematics (STEM) careers is key element of the national strategy to maintain U.S. global economic competitiveness by growing a larger and more competent science and engineering workforce. While much attention has been focused on women and racial minorities, persons with disabilities (PwD), who constitute over twelve percent of the population of working age Americans, remain disproportionately underrepresented in the STEM enterprise. Efforts aimed at reducing this disparity have primarily targeted students with disabilities (SwDs) in high school [1] or already in college [2] to prevent or remediate shortfalls in academic knowledge or metacognitive and psychosocial skills that often are the proximal causes of college failure.

However, many educational researchers have emphasized the importance of introducing career development and college preparation activities in young students, with and

M. Antona and C. Stephanidis (Eds.): UAHCI 2015, Part III, LNCS 9177, pp. 214–223, 2015.
DOI: 10.1007/978-3-319-20684-4_21

without disabilities, even before high school. Kerka [3] examined research on early college and career preparation and found that middle school students are at a critical age during which career aspirations and powerful beliefs about self-efficacy are formed and where implicit choices are made that strongly determine future educational and career pathways. Overall, the findings suggest that activities aimed at exploring career goals and understanding the postsecondary course requirements that must be met to achieve them benefit students from the general population both vocationally and in their pre-college academic performance [4]. Some examples of results relevant to the importance of preparation include the early crystallization of sex-role and gender-appropriate occupation stereotypes [5], the lack of realistic career plans among middle schoolers [6], and (significantly for this paper) data showing that students at risk, girls, and those who are members of minority groups often limit their career choices early [7].

The rarity of early interventions focusing on college and career readiness is reflected in the fact that many high school seniors are not prepared academically or psychosocially for success at college, although over 90 % say they intend to go on to postsecondary education [8]. Comparable levels of interest in attending college are seen in high school SwDs, however, their level of readiness for success is typically even lower than that observed in the general population [9].

In an analysis of factors contributing to the underrepresentation of PwD in STEM fields, Shingledecker [2] presented a model identifying five barriers that limit the numbers of SwDs that enter college to obtain STEM degrees and who persist to earn these degrees when they do enroll. While the factors described below are not unique to any single group of students, the probability that these barriers will limit the achievement of SwDs is likely to be much higher because of the unique ways in which both visible and non-visible disabilities can adversely impact a student's educational history and personal experiences, habits, and attitudes. Some of these negative influences can be attributed directly to the effects of a disability, but others are caused by prior experiences in the home and school that are affected by lingering misconceptions and erroneous beliefs held by STEM educational and employment gatekeepers, or even by the students themselves.

Interest and Motivation: Inaccurate beliefs about personal potential and ability, lack of role models, limited hands-on experience with STEM, and insufficient knowledge of careers in science and engineering contribute to lower rates of enrolling in college to pursue STEM majors. As noted earlier, career interests are strongly shaped by academic and personal experiences during elementary and secondary education, and SwDs may fail to consider STEM careers because of early failures in related coursework. Others may have been subtly steered away from these subjects by parents, teachers, and advisors because of their concerns about providing special physical accommodations in STEM classes or about viable career choices for SwDs.

Opportunity: Traditional, but persistent, factors affecting the opportunity to succeed in STEM studies include lack of physical access to laboratory and classroom spaces or of specialized laboratory equipment adapted for use by PwDs. However, possibly more common restrictions are created by flawed attitudes and beliefs of stakeholders in the student's education. These opportunity limitations may be externally or internally (self) imposed. Powerful internal limiters to opportunity are created by distorted beliefs of

SwDs about their own abilities and potential. Such beliefs, often created by past negative academic experiences and the lack of interaction with disabled role models in STEM professions of interest, can deter the SwD from even exploring education and careers in science or engineering fields.

Academic Preparation: SwDs often fail to receive adequate high school academic preparation in subjects key to STEM success at college [10]. Specific learning disabilities and some neurological disorders clearly play a contributing role and may require early attention before and during high school to develop reading, mathematical, and executive control skills to make the student capable of success in college. However, problems also arise because high school course requirements and success criteria may be relaxed under current disability education laws, and because parents and high school counselors sometimes fail to encourage capable SwDs to follow a rigorous college preparation course of study. In addition, intensive physical and/or academic support given to some SwDs in high school can result in poorly developed general study skills, note taking, and time management abilities that impair academic performance in the college environment.

Psychosocial Skills: In addition to academic skills and knowledge, there is a growing awareness that many SwDs face problems in college that are associated with what are commonly referred to as psychosocial, meta-cognitive, or life success skills [11]. SwDs often leave high school with underdeveloped skills for acting independently, problem solving, advocating for themselves with instructors and others, and communicating clearly and effectively. Low self-confidence, lack of persistence in difficult tasks following set-backs and failures, and ineffective time management strategies can be additional problems that directly impact academic success.

Some of these deficiencies are directly related to a student's disability (e.g., autism spectrum disorder). However, they are also created or exacerbated by exposure to protective parenting as well as teaching and student support practices that limit the development and exercise of critical personal skills. As suggested by Wehmeyer [12], these restrictive social contexts detract from the critical levels of competence and autonomy that SwDs need to succeed in the unrestricted college environment and challenging requirements of STEM studies.

Higher-Level Cognitive Skills Needed for STEM: Because of the academic and psychosocial factors cited above, some SwDs arrive at college with poorly developed abstract thinking, reasoning, problem-solving, and critical-thinking skills that are essential to high academic achievement in STEM fields. Ideally, these skills are developed in high school science and mathematics coursework, and are central to modern curricula that employ inquiry-based methods. Unfortunately, such open-ended pedagogical methods calling for students to exercise advanced cognitive skills in ad hoc research activities are the most difficult to support using specific accommodations for SWDs [13].

2   The Starting Wright Program

The need for career and college preparation prior to the final years of secondary schooling discussed above, as well as an understanding of the barriers to postsecondary education in STEM fields faced by PwD were the motivations for developing an informal educational program aimed at increasing STEM college and career readiness. Dubbed *Starting Wright,* the program was given its name to connect it not only to our institution (Wright State University), but also to the historical legacy of its namesakes, the Wright brothers, who were pioneers in American scientific and technological innovation, and whose accomplishments exemplify the qualities of starting early to ensure success, perseverance, and self-reliance that we hoped to instill in our young participants as they plan for their careers.

The overarching goal of Starting Wright has been to increase the success of disabled youth in transitioning to college education, earning degrees, and achieving inclusion in STEM career fields. The program was designed primarily to deliver information to middle school and early high school-aged youth with disabilities, along with their parents, in order to increase motivation toward careers in STEM (including medical fields), and to provide educational guidance, practical information about college, and approaches to developing attitudes and personal skills that are associated with success.

2.1   Why Online?

Since its inception, Starting Wright has focused on the use of the internet to reach students with disabilities preparing for transition after high school as well as other stakeholders in their educational and career success. This approach is founded on our conviction that online methods show particular promise for improving transition outcomes of students with disabilities by influencing their career motivations, academic preparations and personal development.

While the online tools and stakeholder targets of the program have expanded over the life of the program (see Sect. 3 of this paper), the webcast format was chosen as the original vehicle for providing content for two primary reasons. First, the information that Starting Wright was designed to provide cannot be easily offered to young SwDs within the school environment. As a whole, students with disabilities form a significant, but widely-distributed segment of the population. Because these students are geographically dispersed as individuals or small clusters in schools across the country, it is extremely difficult to provide them with tailored support for postsecondary transition in a particular field such as STEM through traditional classroom instruction or intensive counseling. The internet provided a way to reach these scattered students in a single forum outside of school.

The second reason for using an online approach was that available research suggests that Starting Wright would be more effective if students and their parents could experience the content together as a family. Parents of middle schoolers typically have a strong influence on students' early career considerations. Moreover, the data indicate that there is a mismatch between the expectations of young adolescent SwDs for college attendance and those held by their parents. Although SwDs share a high degree of confidence for transitioning to postsecondary education with their non-disabled peers, the parents of SwDs are much less confident that their students will be able to successfully attend college than parents of students who do not have a disability [14]. Because Starting Wright is intended to promote planning for setting and reaching educational goals, these disparate findings suggest that providing content in the home using online webcasts presented at a time that students and parents could participate together would be beneficial.

2.2 Overview of the Initial Webcast Project

Starting Wright was originally conceived and produced as a series of 40-minute web broadcasts containing audio and visual content that address topics surrounding the issues of career choices and possibilities for persons with disabilities, academic and personal preparation for college, and practical advice for achieving inclusion and succeeding in college and beyond. To accommodate the widest range of participants, the web conferencing tools used for the programs were compatible with screen readers and permitted adjustment of the visual features of the display. Closed captioning was also provided for participants with hearing impairments. The web format enabled direct interaction between live presenters and the audience of students and parents partici-pating at home using text chatting features. Recruitment of families to participate in the Starting Wright webcasts was limited largely to the state of Ohio, with the largest effort limited to the southwest quadrant of the state surrounding Wright State University. Brochures were distributed by mail throughout the state to high school counselors, STEM teachers and special education /transition specialists for passing on to students and parents. These were supplemented by presentations to regional transition stake-holder organizations that included teachers, school administrators, state rehabilitation services representatives, and parent advocates as members.

2.3 Webcast Content and Structure

To define critical content for the Starting Wright programs we used the findings of previous postsecondary transition research, lessons-learned from college disability service professionals, and accounts of personal experiences from college students with disabilities to gain an understanding of the factors that limit enrollment in STEM postsecondary majors or interfere with persistence in these areas. Based on a these resources, we identified four key areas for developing content which closely map onto the barrier model described by Shingledecker [2]:

- Raising awareness, motivation and Interest in pursuing science and technology-based careers
- Building psychosocial and metacognitive skills needed for college and career success
- Connecting high school and college coursework, knowledge and skill attainment to success in college and career entry.
- Encouraging development of cognitive skills critical to STEM success.

Guided by these objectives, a series of twelve Starting Wright programs were progressively developed, produced, broadcasted and refined over a period of three academic years. Three of these programs provided an introduction to the goals and subject matter of Stating Wright. *Getting Started in Starting Wright* emphasized the importance of early preparation and planning for college and a career, defined STEM and gave an overview of the rest of the series. *STEM Careers* introduced the concept of a career, provided a multimedia tour of STEM fields, and included an interview with a SwD who was graduating from college with science degree. *Planning for College* presented basic information on requirements for college entry, support that SwD can expect at college and how it differs from that provided in high school, paying for college, and academic and student life. It also introduced personal skills and that would be needed for college success including independence, resourcefulness, and communication.

The next six programs in the series used the context of a specific STEM career field to reinforce the broader aims of the project including a focus on STEM motivation, early academic planning, using appropriate role models, developing independence, and sharpening personal skills. The STEM fields and careers presented in these individual programs included basic sciences (biology and life sciences, chemistry and physics, geology and earth science), engineering, computer science, and derivative STEM fields (allied health professions, animal science).

The introductory live segment of each program included a welcome by the host, a review of "homework" contest submissions from the last program and prize awards, and a brief lead-in to the featured STEM field. A corresponding live wrap-up segment was included at the end of each broadcast to answer questions submitted by the audience during the prerecorded content, present of a new set of student-parent homework questions based on the core segment, Starting Wright announcements, and closing remarks.

Following the introduction, the themed episodes began with an extended video survey of the focus STEM field and related careers which was hosted by *Dr. STEMM*, a cartoon character who added humor to the programs. In addition, each included recurring feature segments designed to appear as episodes over multiple programs. These new prerecorded segments featured unique host personalities and a general topic area that the audience could anticipate each week. Some of these were introduced to create a transition between major program elements, while others were designed to stand alone as primary components. The recurring features were:

"Great Minds in STEMM" was a 2 -m segment that introduced well-known contemporary and historical figures in STEM fields who had disabilities and overcame any limitations to succeed in their careers. These spots included synchronized background music, sound effects and even audio clips of the featured STEM professional's own voice. Some great minds covered included Thomas Edison, Alexander Graham Bell, Albert Einstein, Jack Horner, Alan Turing, Temple Grandin and John Wesley Powell.

"Hints from Miss Hannah" was written and presented by an experienced middle school teacher and administrator who offered ideas and methods for improving academic performance in preparatory middle and high school classes, usually with a nod to the focal STEM field of the program. Examples of topics included "insider hints" on how students can do better at figuring out what material an instructor views as most

important to learn, the steps to "engineering" an essay, the importance of diversity in ecosystems AND in the classroom, finding places to learn about STEM outside of school, and knowing what information to trust when using the internet for research.

"*Katherine's Tech Tips*" addressed Starting Wright's goal of providing students with information on assistive technologies that are available to help them learn in science, mathematics and other academic areas. Equipment and software demonstrated in these segments included calculators available in Windows software, adaptive microscopes, and laboratory containers and measuring devices that can be safely used by persons with limited manual dexterity.

"*STEMM – Up Front and Up Close*" presented interviews with the experts in the program's focal STEM area. Each of the career-themed webcasts included an interview segment in which a STEM professional described their work, and career in the area. Guests included a science and mathematics college dean, a field biologist, a geologist, a marine biologist, an electrical engineer, a computer scientist working in robotics, a blind chemist, an animal trainer and a medical technologist.

A final set of two special programs were created to address college readiness issues not fully covered in the introductory or career themed episodes. A program on *Problem Solving* was designed to help teach this skill that is so crucial to scientific reasoning and to effective interpersonal relationships and communication. The program portrayed problem solving as the fundamental cognitive skill underlying both scientific research and the engineering design process with illustrations from both global STEM fields. Corresponding examples of personal problem solving used videos of college SwDs discussing their use of problem solving skills in dealing with issues that arise in the pursuit of higher education. The episode on *Early College Transition Planning* delved into the details of what students and parents can do during middle school and the first two years of high school to improve their readiness for college. The focus areas for this program were career path goal setting, academic preparation, "understanding my disability," communication, time management and study skills, and knowing the services and agencies available to assist in the transition to college.

3 Evolution of *Starting Wright*

The focus of the Starting Wright webcasts was to improve college and career preparation by communicating to students and parents together in the home environment. As experience with this format increased and we began to receive evaluative inputs from participants, it became apparent that content could be disseminated even more effectively by using additional channels for reaching the target students and other stakeholders.

Surveys of students, parents and educator/observers were conducted during each of three program years to gather feedback on the content and quality of the webcasts and on the perceived value of Starting Wright. Overall, survey responses showed that the programs had increased participant interest in planning for college and STEM careers and that they had improved students' confidence in their ability to attend and succeed in college and their willingness to work at high school classes that will prepare them for college. Additionally, based on exposure to the most refined version of the series of programming, most students and parents felt that Starting Wright had reduced their worries and uncertainties about attending college.

Despite these positive findings, other feedback indicated that changes were needed to improve the program's effectiveness. Comments from parents and educators suggested that difficulties experienced in recruiting and maintaining participation in the biweekly, fixed-schedule evening webcasts were likely a result of competing school, sports and other obligations experienced by most young families. Accordingly, we began to explore more efficient ways to connect with students and parents. Subsequent meetings with educators and vocational rehabilitation counselors made it apparent that, in addition to scheduled webcasts, online content should be added to the portfolio that is individually tailored for use by students and other stakeholders and is available for on-demand access.

Guided On-Demand Content: Our approach to providing open access to online content was influenced by recent research regarding the "NetGen" or "Google Generation" that describes contemporary adolescents as a unique group of technology and digital content consumers. While they are confident in their ability to use technology, they typically are not equally skilled in the areas of information gathering and properly vetting content for accuracy and relevance. These students are accustomed to having information available instantly, but they lack a clear understanding of how information systems and search engines function, how to appropriately search for relevant information, and how to evaluate the information they do find [15]. Given these characteristics, we elected to evolve the online program to one which provided guided exploration of STEM careers and of the multifaceted process of preparing academically and personally to enter these fields. At the same time, we chose to expand our focus by targeting other stakeholders in the future of SwDs with Starting Wright content that they had indicated would be useful in their work with adolescent SwDs.

Accordingly, we expanded the Starting Wright website, which was originally used only as a portal to the biweekly webcasts, to an online resource. The website was constructed around a set of "tracks" designed to provide accurate and appropriate information for target audiences. By offering well-researched, synthesized, and accurate content in one place we could provide information to students that addressed the concerns they had regarding career exploration and college planning. Likewise, parents could focus on their current concerns such as how disability accommodations change when students enter postsecondary education. In addition, the website served as a way to house all of the programming in podcast form so that students, parents, and educators could access as desired.

Online Lesson Plans for Educators: In part as a result of the new website, local educators began asking if they might be able to use portions of the programs in their own classrooms. They still recommended that some students watch programs outside of class or as part of personal career exploration journeys. However, most felt that the academic and personal skills taught in the programs would be beneficial in the classroom environment. In response, we worked with six local educators to develop a set of sixteen comprehensive lesson plans that utilized the media created through the Starting Wright program. The lessons incorporated academic content woven together with personal skills lessons and career exploration. All of the lessons were aligned with the State of Ohio Academic Content Standards and specifically addressed the need to reach students in more than one way by adding in-class lessons and assignments to encourage and reinforce student access to online content.

Online Assistance for Vocational Rehabilitation Counselors: In addition to making the Starting Wright Teacher's Manual available online, we chose to create a path to the use of Starting Wright for our state Bureau of Vocational Rehabilitation counselors who work intensively with students ages 14 and up during the transition process to prepare them for further education and the workforce. Because they focus their efforts on encouraging career exploration and personal skills development with younger transition age SwDs. We created he Starting Wright Counselor's Manual which provides individualized prescriptive guidance to counselors for the use of our online content based to address the specific career interests of the student and on the non-cognitive personal skills that the student needs to improve. In addition, the manual provides discussion questions for counselors and students, and follow-up assignments and projects that would allow the student to delve deeper into the skills and concepts presented in the podcasts.

4   Conclusions and Future Directions

The experience of producing and evolving the Starting Wright program provides useful insights for the design of online approaches for presenting career exploration opportunities and college preparation guidance to adolescent students. In the initial stage of the effort, we were able to successfully identify factors that have led to low college enrollment and participation in STEM careers, and to develop informational and instructional content to address these problems in the context of online webcasts aimed at SwDs and parents in the home environment. We clearly demonstrated that this form of online education can be a valuable tool for reaching the target audience. However, these webcasts did not provide the expected level of "market penetration" that we had hoped to achieve. Feedback from stakeholders led us to broaden the scope of the effort to include a website offering students and parents guided open access to descriptive career content and targeted information for college preparation. It also led to the development of online materials specifically focused on the needs of educators and counselors that work with these students in person on a daily basis. By collaborating with parents, teachers and counselors who are able to assist the student in processing the information provided online and to participate directly in the college planning process, we found that the impact of Starting Wright could be greatly increased. In fact, as we expanded the website and began work with other stakeholders, we saw increases in the number of people accessing the information online. During the first years of the webcast program, monthly participation topped out at 35 students. In contrast, with the expanded program the number of visits to the website increased dramatically and monthly downloads of content grew from 3 to 5 times the original number of students participating in the scheduled webcasts.

References

1. Burgstahler, S.: DO-IT: Helping students with disabilities transition to college and careers. National Center on Secondary Education and Transition Research to Practice Brief 2(3) (2003)
2. Shingledecker, C.A., Todd, R., Weibl, R., Auld, S.: Interventions with college students to increase the representation of persons with disabilities in STEM careers. In: Stem, B.S., Duerstock, C.A., Shingledecker (eds.) From College to Careers: Fostering Inclusion of Persons with Disabilities. pp. 31–47. Science/AAAS, Washington, DC (2014)
3. Kerka, S.: Middle School Career Education and Development. Clearinghouse on Adult, Career, and Vocational Education (2000). http://www.calpro-online.org/
4. Hughes, K., Karp, M.: School-Based Career Development: A Synthesis of the Literature. Teachers College, Columbia University, p. 1 (2004). http://www.tc.columbia.edu/iee/PAPERS/CareerDevelopment02_04.pdf
5. Guss, T.O., Adams, L.: Gender orientation and career maturation among rural elementary school students. (ERIC Document Reproduction Service No. ED417364) (1998)
6. Finch, C.R., Mooney, M.: School-to-Work Opportunities in Middle School: Concepts and Issues. National Center for Research in Vocational Education, University of California, Berkeley (1997)
7. O'Brien, K.M., Dukstein, R.D., Jackson, S.L., Tomlinson, M.J., Kamatuka, N.A.: Broadening career horizons for students in at-risk environments. Career Dev. Q. 47(3), 215–229 (1999)
8. Kuh, G.D.: What student engagement data tell us about college readiness. Peer Rev. 9(1), 1 (2007)
9. Horn, L., Bobbitt, L.: Students with disabilities in postsecondary education: a profile of preparation, participation and outcomes U.S. Department of Education (1999)
10. O'Brien, K.J.: An Investigation of the Academic Preparation of Students with Disabilities Planning to Attend a Four Year College or University. Doctoral Dissertation, University of Maryland, College Park, MD (2011). http://hdl.handle.net/1903/11998
11. Getzel, E.E., Thoma, C.A.: Experiences of college students with disabilities and the importance of self-determination in higher education settings. Career Dev. Except. Individuals 31(2), 77–84 (2008)
12. Wehmeyer, L.: Self Determination. International Encyclopedia of Rehabilitation. Center for International Rehabilitation Research Information and Exchange (2013). http://cirrie.buffalo.edu/encyclopedia/en/article/34/
13. Moon, N.W., Todd, R.T., Morton, D.L., Ivey, E.: Accommodating students with disabilities in science, technology, engineering, and mathematics (STEM). National Science Foundation, Washington, DC (2012)
14. Doren, B., Gau, J.M., Lindstrom, L.: The relationship between parent expectations and post-school out comes of adolescents with disabilities. Except. Child. 79, 7–23 (2012)
15. Tenopir, C.: Reaching the Net Gen. Library Journal. 134, 21–22 (2009)

The Promise and Pitfalls of Virtual Worlds to Enhance STEM Education Success: Summary of the GSAA BreakThru Model

Robert L. Todd[✉]

Center for Assistive Technology and Environmental Access (CATEA), Georgia Institute of Technology, 490 10th Street NW, Atlanta, GA 30332-0156, USA
robert.todd@coa.gatech.edu

Abstract. The Georgia STEM Accessibility Alliance (GSAA) is a research project funded by the U.S. National Science Foundation (NSF) Research in Disabilities Education (RDE) program, grants 1027635 and 1027655. A collaborative RDE Alliance, it combines the expertise of the University of Georgia and the Georgia Institute of Technology. Launched in 2010 and projected for completion in 2016, GSAA is one of 10 RDE Alliances throughout the United States designed to broaden the participation and achievement of people with disabilities in STEM education and careers. Although the GSAA encompasses many innovative features to achieve its goals, its core features are the use of virtual worlds (Second Life) and online and smartphone technologies to enhance student success through mediated mentoring, collectively referred to as the BreakThru project. This paper will provide provide a brief summary of the status of the use of virtual worlds in STEM education, as well as an overview of the GSAA BreakThru goals, theory of change, demographics, and subject participation. It will posit conclusions that can be advantageous in future research on online, mediated approaches to enhanced education, to ensure the maximum potential for all students to complete educational goals.

Keywords: STEM education · Disability · Accessibility · Electronic mentoring · Virtual worlds · Online education

1 Introduction

The influence of digital media has changed the way students learn, play and socialize. As a result, researchers at University of Georgia (UGA) and the Georgia Institute of Technology (GT) have partnered to develop a virtual learning environment that combines creative avatars and social networking tools to assist secondary school and college students with disabilities to succeed in science, technology, engineering, and math (STEM) programs. The universities work alongside Georgia Perimeter College and the secondary school systems of Georgia's Greene, Clarke and Gwinnett counties to serve targeted students.

The GSAA BreakThru project provides Second Life Mentoring Islands where students meet and interact with mentors to address their STEM education needs. Students have the option to create avatars that simulate their disability realities (e.g., wheelchairs

© Springer International Publishing Switzerland 2015
M. Antona and C. Stephanidis (Eds.): UAHCI 2015, Part III, LNCS 9177, pp. 224–235, 2015.
DOI: 10.1007/978-3-319-20684-4_22

for mobility, orientation tools for blindness, etc.) or create a personal avatar that is entirely different from their physical self. BreakThru has constructed a virtual environment in Second Life that exemplifies the best of accessible and universal design, with special care taken to accommodate assistive technologies and non-standard browsers. The Mentoring Islands are the primary meeting space for mentoring and teaching, social networking, academic support, transition assistance, and research participation for the initiative, but the project makes extensive use of common social networking tools (SMS, Skype, audio calls, etc.) to supplement the virtual interaction. BreakThru teachers and faculty can also virtually access custom training modules on universal design and evidence-based teaching strategies for their classrooms and labs.

The project serves as a pipeline between secondary and postsecondary institutions to strengthen students with disabilities' capacities to access and succeed in STEM programs across critical junctures: high school | two-year college | four-year college | graduate school. The overall project goals are to increase the retention of students with disabilities who are enrolled in STEM classes and majors and the number of students participating in BreakThru mentoring activities.

Ongoing efforts are focused on Georgia pipeline schools and students with disabilities, but outreach and dissemination efforts can potentially extend beyond to all students who need assistance in STEM, with or without disabilities. BreakThru has been created to provide broad impact through its applicability to students and faculty who are separated geographically and through its potential to gather a national/international network of STEM stakeholders. The digital media model is scalable to secondary and postsecondary institutions broadly. Its foci on universal design for learning and inclusion of accessible materials are aimed at assisting all students in need.

The United States National Science Foundation and National Science board have recognized the need for a larger and more diverse STEM workforce [1–4]. To date, various minority groups, chief among them students with disabilities, have not been properly included in attempts to promote a more successful STEM workforce. The GSAA BreakThru project, in cooperation with colleagues from related NSF efforts, seeks to address that imbalance.

2 Need for Increased Participation in STEM

The National Science Foundation's (NSF) Research in Disabilities Education (RDE) program has sponsored research and development projects to broaden participation and increase achievement of people with disabilities in STEM education and the STEM workforce. At the heart of these efforts has been RDE's "Alliances for Stu-dents with Disabilities in STEM" (Alliances) project track. Intended to serve a specific geographic region, Alliances involve multiple institutions of higher education and secondary school systems working as a team "to employ evidenced-based practices and promising interventions to advance students across critical academic junctures, to degree completion, and into the workforce or graduate STEM degree programs." Taken together, Alliances create a unified program of change extending beyond academia to include industry and government research experiences for students with disabilities.

In addition, Alliances typically go beyond matters of STEM content knowledge to focus on underlying issues affecting the differential learning, participation, retention and graduation rates of postsecondary students with disabilities in STEM.

Considerable attention has been given to the need for educating a diverse workforce in STEM in the U.S. National Science Foundation reports [1–4] stress the critical importance of strengthening efforts to recruit and retain students chronically under-represented in STEM fields. Government and educational entities consistently emphasize broad participation and inclusion as critical factors in achieving excellence in STEM fields [5]. Individuals with disabilities are among the most marginalized of these groups [6] and face significant obstacles and barriers to accessing higher education STEM programs [2, 4, 7].

As one of the RDE's Alliance projects, the GSAA BreakThru initiative has focused on researching the use of online, especially virtual, mentoring, to retain students in STEM education and in mentoring programs. In particular, the GSAA has sought to investigate the uses of online mentoring to assist students in persistence in degrees and across critical educational junctures. The GSAA BreakThru project has also been designed as a scalable model to be replicated by other institutions to broaden participation and increase retention for secondary and post-secondary students in a variety of setting and conditions.

3 BreakThru Focus on Virtual Tools

Virtual worlds, or simulated 2-D and 3-D online environments (e.g. Second Life), have become an increasingly common software platform for education and training applications during the last decade [8–15]. They hold the promise of opening new horizons for students and educators, but can also present unexpected barriers to access, especially for students who have disabilities [16–19]. For purposes of this discussion, "virtual world" is defined as "a synchronous, persistent network of people, represented as avatars, facilitated by networked computers [20]. The GSAA BreakThru virtual Mentoring Islands have used the platform of Second Life, with appropriate instructions, modifications and use of third-party tools, where necessary, to maximize accessibility. Applying the definition of online accessibility from the World Wide Web (W3C) Web Accessibility Initiative [21] "accessibility" refers to the degree to which **people with disabilities can use the virtual world**. More specifically, accessibility means that people with disabilities can perceive, understand, navigate, and interact with the virtual world, and that they can contribute to it. "Disability" in this context can be defined as any functional limitation (physical, sensory, cognitive) that impedes a student's ability to fully engage in the educational process, as compared to similar-age norms.

Given issues of complexity, accessibility and adoption, it would be fair to question the uses of virtual worlds in educational settings. However, one common assumption about the educational uses of virtual worlds is that *immersion,* or "the subjective impression that one is participating in a comprehensive, realistic experience" [22] can enhance the learning experience. Researchers have also observed that virtual worlds offer possibilities for experiential learning; an approach that encourages students to engage in problem solving activities within a flexible environment that facilitates collaborative and constructivist learning [9]. Educators have also been drawn to the potential that virtual worlds offer for distance learning, social interaction, and learner engagement [8]. In these applications, the presence of avatars can enhance "engagement and learning beyond computer-mediated communication without such agents" [23]. Researchers have also noted the capacity of virtual worlds to facilitate experiential learning [24] via simulations, role-playing, and group work. Outputs like user created content are also of particular interest. In many virtual world environments, such as Second Life, the students themselves become the creators of content, and mediate their own interaction and learning [23]. Instructors and researchers continue to explore the potential of virtual worlds to enhance education on many levels.

While these affordances can contribute to the effectiveness of virtual mentoring and support systems in education, it must be noted that researchers have also discussed disenchantment with the limitations and complexities of using virtual world environments [10]. Concerns that must be addressed include a reluctance to accept virtual environments as an effective educational tool [9, 25], potential technical and information technology issues [9, 25], privacy and distraction issues, intellectual property and legal issues, and not least, concerns that virtual environments will not be accessible to all students with disabilities without considerable knowledge and effort by developers and instructors [9, 25].

All of these factors play a role in the implementation of BreakThru, since the project focuses on digitally mediated e-mentoring and STEM learning support. The Second Life Mentoring Islands provide the backbone of project intervention with students, with other digital tools (SMS, Skype, audio calls, etc.) used to supplement the virtual world interactions, as needed. Of particular concern has been the provision of full accessibility to students with a broad range of disability issues. BreakThru has emphasized the need for advance planning and development, use of Universal Design for Learning principles [27] in all project tools, and training for all users to address the specific access needs of each student, mentor and instructor.

4 Theory of Change

The GSAA BreakThru Theory of Change guides the project's efforts to improve student success in STEM. The Change model demonstrates the project's core efforts to recruit students into the program and deliver e-mentoring and STEM learning/support activities that lead to changes in students' internal characteristics pertinent to STEM. These changes are intended to increase the students' intention to persist in STEM and increase participation in relevant activities. Finally, the model posits program effects and concrete steps taken by students to persist in STEM that lead to actual persistence and completion of undergraduate and graduate degree programs (see Fig. 1, below).

As expressed in the Figure, BreakThru relies upon multiple points of information to assess progress toward goals, including survey instruments, evaluation constructs, and enrollment and graduation records.

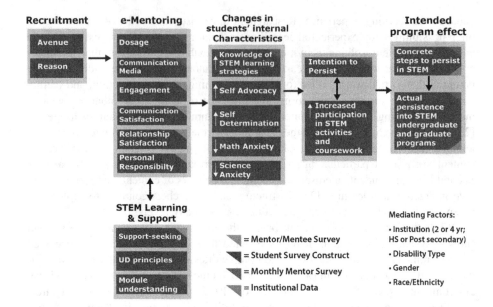

Fig. 1. Theory of change for GSAA BreakThru, with data input sources and core measures for determining efficacy of project activities and progress toward objectives. Color tabs indicate instruments and data sources for each measure.

5 Project Goals

The GSAA BreakThru program seeks to put students with disabilities on the path to post-secondary STEM education that otherwise would not have entered or persisted in STEM education programs. It serves three cohorts of students over a five year period from 2010 to 2015: 105 unduplicated high school students; 65 unduplicated 2-year students; and 55 unduplicated 4-year students. Its primary goals include:

1. **Retain Students in Virtual Mentoring and STEM Majors**: Retain high school, 2-year, and 4-year students with disabilities participating in the GSAA Virtual Mentoring Program at a year-to-year persistence rate of at least 50 %.
2. **Enroll to Virtual Mentoring:**

   - Enroll (assign to a mentor) 105 unduplicated high school students with disabilities to the GSAA STEM Virtual Mentoring Program by the end of the project award period.
   - Enroll (assign to a mentor) 65 unduplicated two-year students with disabilities to the GSAA STEM Virtual Mentoring Program in STEM majors at one 2-year college partner institution (Georgia Perimeter College) by the end of the project award period.
   - Enroll (assign to a mentor) 55 unduplicated four-year students with disabilities to the GSAA STEM Virtual Mentoring Program in STEM majors at two alliance universities (UGA and GT) by the end of the project award period.

An overview of the results of **Goal 1: Retain Students in Virtual Mentoring and STEM Majors** for 2011–2014 for all three cadres of students follows (Figs. 2, 3, 4 and 5):

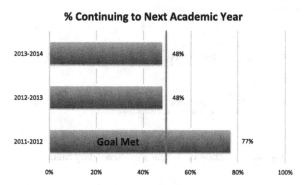

Fig. 2. Retention of Secondary Students

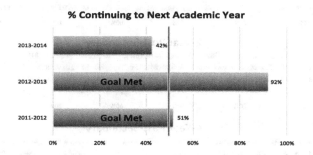

Fig. 3. Retention of 2-Year Post-Secondary Students

Retention results varied by academic year and by student cadre. In each year, the target was exceeded in one or two of the cadres, with other student cadres close to goal percentages.

The results of **Goal 2: Enroll to Virtual Mentoring**, are summarized in the figure following (Fig. 6):

4-Year Post-Secondary Students
Retain 50% in Virtual Mentoring and STEM Majors

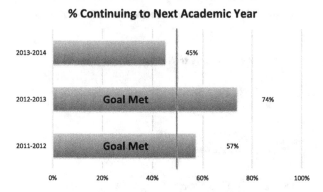

Fig. 4. Retention of 4-Year Post-Secondary Students

% Continuation during Academic Year[1]

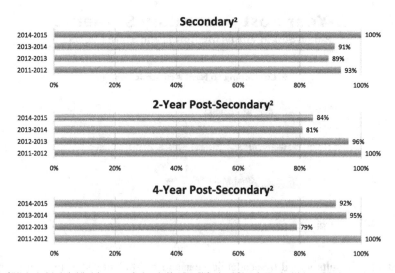

Note. [1] % Continuation during Academic Year is the percentage of students who did not disenroll before the end of the academic year for which they enrolled; % determined using enrollment and disenrollment dates. [2] 2014-2015 percentages are based on continuation from Fall 2014 to Spring 2015. These numbers may change at the end of the Spring 2015 semester.

Fig. 5. Summary of Retention/Continuation Data

In academic years 2011–2014, targets for Goal 2, as measured by number of students enrolled, were not met, but in each student cadre approached the goal by 78 % to 87 %.

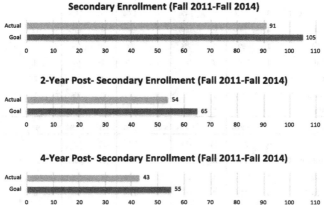

Fig. 6. Goal 2 - Enroll to Virtual Mentoring

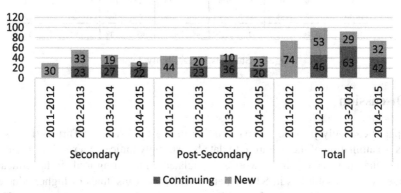

Fig. 7. Continuing Versus New Students

As noted in Goal 2, it is important for project staff to distinguish between students continuing in the program and those newly enrolled in each year. The following figure summarizes that information (Fig. 7):

6 Students by Disability Type

The GSAA BreakThru initiative welcomes students of all abilities. The following chart summarizes the distribution of students by disability type. Note that students with learning disabilities comprise a high percentage of the total enrolled, but this reflects, to a large extent, the percentage of students with disabilities as a whole across institutions (Fig. 8).

		2011-2012		2012-2013		2013-2014		2014-2015		Total (across all years)	
		n	%	n	%	n	%	n	%	n	%
Secondary	LD	14	47%	30	54%	23	50%	18	58%	54	59%
	ADD/ADHD	8	27%	8	14%	8	17%	5	16%	15	17%
	ASD	4	13%	10	18%	9	20%	4	13%	12	13%
	HEALTH	1	3%	1	2%	1	2%	0	0%	1	1%
	EBD	1	3%	3	5%	2	4%	2	6%	4	4%
	VI	0	0%	1	2%	2	4%	1	3%	2	2%
	MOBILITY	1	3%	1	2%	0	0%	0	0%	1	1%
	SPEECH	1	3%	2	4%	1	2%	1	3%	2	2%
	Total	30	100%	56	100%	46	100%	31	100%	91	100%
Post-secondary	LD	12	27%	14	33%	13	28%	13	30%	25	26%
	ADD/ADHD	8	18%	10	23%	9	20%	11	26%	26	27%
	ASD	1	2%	1	2%	1	2%	2	5%	4	4%
	HEALTH	5	11%	4	9%	5	11%	4	9%	8	8%
	PSYCH	10	23%	6	14%	10	22%	7	16%	20	21%
	HEARING	2	5%	3	7%	2	4%	1	2%	3	3%
	VI	2	5%	2	5%	3	7%	3	7%	5	5%
	MOBILITY	2	5%	1	2%	1	2%	1	2%	3	3%
	DIS	0	0%	1	2%	1	2%	1	2%	1	1%
	NONE	2	5%	1	2%	1	2%	0	0%	2	2%
	Total	44	100%	43	100%	46	100%	43	100%	97	100%

Fig. 8. Students by Disability Type

7 Discussion

This paper can only provide a broad outline of the GSAA BreakThru activities and results. Examination of the literature to date has strongly indicated a need for more data to determine the place of virtual worlds and related e-mentoring tools in the education of students with disabilities in STEM fields. While most institutes of higher education and government agencies in the United States agree that broader participation in STEM fields is a desirable goal, consensus of opinion on the efficacy of virtual world platforms to address this goal will remain unattainable until sufficient data has been evaluated. In its efforts to provide a scalable model for virtual e-mentoring, its focus on Universal Design for Learning principles, accessibility for all students and enrollment of students with diverse abilities, the GSAA BreakThru project seeks to provide data to move researchers closer to answering these questions.

8 Conclusions

The GSAA BreakThru data from 2011-2014 indicate trends of interest to the field at large. Points of note include:

- Creation and implementation of a scalable model and theory of change to guide the replication of the project across institutions internationally.
- Potential viability of a virtual e-mentoring program through data that indicate a high percentage of "continuing" students across academic years as well as relatively high retention rates of students with disabilities in STEM programs.
- The ability of a virtual world environment to accommodate students with a wide range of disabilities through careful development and education.

While GSAA BreakThru data contribute to the overall field of knowledge, it must be admitted that the project results to date raise many questions. For example: Precisely why do some students continue with the project across academic years while others do not? Are the low rates of participation of students with visual disabilities simply a reflection of institution demographics, or do these students "opt out" for specific reasons? While retention of students in STEM programs may appear to be relatively high, does this reflect on completion of educational programs and entry into STEM-related careers?

Data from the current academic year will contribute to the knowledge base, but it must be state that the GSAA BreakThru project will provide perhaps its most important information when it is applied to create and scale a program in replication.

Acknowledgements. BreakThru is a project of the Georgia STEM Accessibility Alliance, which is supported by the National Science Foundation (NSF), Research in Disabilities Education (RDE) Awards # 1027635 and #1027655. Any opinions, findings, and conclusions or recommendations expressed in this material are those of the authors and do not necessarily reflect the views of the National Science Foundation.

References

1. National Science Foundation, Advisory Committee to the NSF Directorate for Education and Human Resources. Shaping the future: New expectations for undergraduate education in science, mathematics, engineering, and technology. National Science Foundation, Washington, DC (1996)
2. National Science Foundation, Congressional Commission on the Advancement of Women and Minorities in Science, Engineering and Technology Development. Land of plenty: Diversity as America's competitive edge in science, engineering and technology. National Science Foundation, Washington, DC (2000)
3. National Science Foundation, Division of Science Resources Statistics. Women, minorities, and persons with disabilities in science and engineering (No. NSF-04-317). National Science Foundation, Arlington (2004)
4. National Science Board. (2010). Preparing the Next Generation of STEM Innovators: Identifying and Developing Our Nation's Human Capital. National Science Foundation, Arlington. http://www.nsf.gov/nsb/publications/2010/nsb1033.pdf. Accessed 29 December 2011
5. Access STEM and DO-IT. Alliances to promote the participation of students with disabilities in science, technology, engineering, and mathematics. RDE Collaborative Dissemination, University of Washington, Seattle (2011). https://www.washington.edu/doit/sites/default/files/atoms/files/rde-alliance.pdf. Accessed 27 January 2015

6. Wolanin, T., Steele, P.: Higher Education Opportunities for Students with Disabilities: A primer for policy Makers. The Institute for Higher Education Policy. Washington, D.C. http://www.ihep.org/Publications/publications-detail.cfm?id=59

7. Burgstahler, S.: Increasing the representation of people with disabilities in science, engineering, and mathematics. Inf. Technol, Disabil. 1(4) (1994)

8. Chou, C.C., Hart, R.K.: The pedagogical considerations in the design of virtual worlds for organization learning. In: Yang, H., Yuen, S. (eds.) Handbook of Research on Practices and Outcomes in Virtual Worlds and Environment, pp. 561–569. Information Science Reference/IGI Global, Hershey (2012)

9. Cremorne, L.: Interview—Denise Wood, University of South Australia. Metaverse Journal—Virtual World News, November 2 2009

10. de Noyelles, A., Kyeong-Ju Seo, K.: Inspiring equal contribution and opportunity in a 3D multi-user virtual environment: Bringing together men gamers and women non-gamers in Second Life. Comput. Educ. 58(1), 21–29 (2012)

11. Kingston, L.: Virtual world, real education: A descriptive study of instructional design in Second Life. Capella University (2011)

12. Taylor, T.L.: Living Digitally: Embodiment in Virtual Worlds. In: Schroeder, R. (ed.) The Social Life of Avatars: Presence and Interaction in Shared Virtual Environments. Springer, London (2002)

13. Jones, D.E.: I, Avatar: constructions of self and place in second life and the technological imagination. Gnovis, the peer-reviewed J. Commun. Cult. Technol. 6 (2007)

14. Brown, B., Bell, M.: CSCW at play: 'There' as a collaborative virtual environment. In: CSCW 2004, Proceedings of the 2004 ACM Conference on Computer Supported Cooperative Work ,pp. 350–359. Association for Computing Machinery, New York (2004)

15. Gerald, S., Antonacci, D.M.: . Virtual World Learning Spaces: Developing a Second Life Operating Room Simulation. Edu. Q. 32(1) (2009). http://www.educause.edu/EDUCAUSE +Quarterly/EDUCAUSEQuarterlyMagazineVolum/VirtualWorldLearningSpacesDeve/ 163851. Accessed 10 February 2015

16. Folmer, E., Yuan, B., Carr, D., and Sapre, M.: TextSL: a command-based virtual world interface for the visually impaired. Assets 2009, Proceedings of the 11th International ACM SIGACCESS Conference on Computers and Accessibility, pp. 59–66. Association for Computing Machinery, New York (2009)

17. Forman, A.E., Baker, P.M.A., Pater, J., Smith, K.: The not so level playing field: disability identity and gender representation in second life. In: Livermore, C. (ed.) Gender and Social Computing: Interactions, Differences, and Relationships. IGI Global, Hershey (2012)

18. Mancuso, D.S., Chlup, D.T., McWhorter, R.R.: A study of adult learning in a virtual environment. Adv. Dev. Hum. Res. 12(6), 681–699 (2010)

19. Stendal, K., Molka-Danielsen, J., Munkvold, B.E., Balandin, S.: Initial Experience with Virtual Worlds for People with Lifelong Disability: Preliminary Findings, Nokobit, pp. 105–118. The University of Nordland (2011)

20. Bell, M.: Toward a Definition of "Virtual Worlds". J. Virtual Worlds Res. 1(1), 2–5 (2008)

21. W3C Web Accessibility Standards. http://www.w3.org/standards/webdesign/accessibility. Accessed 12 February 2015

22. Dede, C.: Immersive Interfaces for Engagement and Learning. Sci. 323(5910), 66–69 (2009)

23. Jarmon, L.: Pedagogy and learning in the virtual world of second life. In: Rogers, P., Berg, G., Boettcher, J., Howard, C., Justice, L., Schenk, K. (eds.) Encyclopedia of Distance and Online Learning (2008)

24. Jarmon, L., Traphagan, T., Mayrath, M., Trivedi, A.: Virtual world teaching, experiential learning, and assessment: an interdisciplinary communication course in second life. Comput. Educ. 53(1), 169–182 (2009)

25. Inman, C. et al.: Use of Second Life in K-12 and Higher Education: A Review of Research. J. Interact. Online Learn. 9(1) (2010)
26. Ellis, K., Kent, M.: iTunes is pretty (Useless) when you're blind: digital design is triggering disability when it could be a solution. Med. Cult. J. 11(3) (2010)
27. CAST, Universal Design for Learning. http://www.cast.org/our-work/about-udl.html#. VRsXUzvF8z0. Accessed 12 February 2015

Quality Analysis of Polish Universities Based on POE Method - Description of Research Experiences

Dorota Winnicka-Jasłowska[✉]

Faculty of Architecture, Department of the Theory, Design and History of Architecture,
The Silesian University of Technology, Akademicka 2a, 44-100 Gliwice, Poland
Dorota.Winnicka-Jaslowska@polsl.pl

Abstract. The paper summarizes the research experiences of the author, related to the pilot quality assessment studies of university buildings and campuses in Poland. The studies are linked by the method Post Occupancy Evaluation (POE). The scope of the quality analyses conducted by the author in University of Silesia in Katowice was the general efficiency assessed from the point of view of organizational and behavioral needs of users. The main research tools of the pilot quality assessment studies carried out by the author was focused on the selected buildings and university campus space. The discussed University of Silesia is currently undergoing changes in its campus. In the beginning of the 21st until nowadays some important buildings of University were erected and opened up. The University authorities are planning new facilities and extension of the campus site. The author's analyses were used for pre-design studies. The analyses gave grounds for students' conceptual designs concerning further growth of the University.

Keywords: University building · Campus · Post Occupancy Evaluation (POE) · Users needs · Higher education · HE

1 Introduction

Poland has been a member of the European Union for ten years. This period has been significant in terms of changes in the school and higher education systems. As a member state, since 2004 university education has been subjected to transformations and university facilities and academic sites modernized to comply with the UE standards. Older buildings have been gradually technically improved, and new facilities constructed-including head offices of faculties and modern libraries. Currently many university campuses are modified. Until recently, university sites were isolated from other urban quarters with an invisible boundary. Research and teaching activities took place mainly in the interiors of university structures and spaces.

Nowadays, this pattern is changing. To develop properly, universities must cooperate with the city, region, industry and foreign partners. The European Union model is based on the assumption of unification, that is the intertwining of the functions that comprise one system.

M. Antona and C. Stephanidis (Eds.): UAHCI 2015, Part III, LNCS 9177, pp. 236–242, 2015.
DOI: 10.1007/978-3-319-20684-4_23

In Poland the past form of dividing universities into colleges and faculties is still functioning, but in the face of new challenges and tasks the boundaries between separate organizational units are beginning to blur. The most common model of a Polish campus is the site that accommodates the buildings and facilities of one state university. Each building houses the head office of one faculty. The campus area should contain all essential functions that support effective operation of a university (including commercial functions, shops, cafeterias, etc. Leased by private owners). Another, less frequent model is represented by subsidiary divisions of universities located on one area and comprising a campus for several different universities.

2   State of the Research and Substantiation of the Research Theme

The model of universities in Western Europe is an outcome of multitudes of studies and research methods. All activities are supported by specialized institutions or consortia that are commissioned to conduct studies on the strategies of university development [9, 10][1].

In Poland there are no research projects devoted to this issue, for several reasons, including: insufficient funds for a wide strategic range of such studies, or even local needs analyses of universities, poor awareness of decision-makers about the necessary changes in higher education and the infrastructure (campuses, buildings, equipment), absence of the knowledge of the tools required for such studies and lack of interest in "universities research" on the part of the Polish Ministry of Science and Higher Education. There are only few publications discussing the current needs and problems that Polish universities are facing, for example [5–8] published in English by the author of this paper, Tymkiewicz J. [4], Złowodzki M. [11] and others.

The changes initiated at Polish universities are rather more intuitive than supported by results of analyses. Also, it is difficult to assess their suitability and efficiency. To be effectively transformed, the existing campuses must be analyzed not in terms of their supporting functions (traffic, parking lots, greenery) but in terms of their academic qualities (informal contacts, places for meetings and dialogues) and ergonomically organized space (including the conditions of the internal environment, for example: lighting of the interiors), in compliance with the aesthetic and way-finding needs of their users. The manners in which university space is currently utilized should be examined in order to find the optimal, most effective solutions. Under the conditions prevailing in Poland, the costs of maintenance are especially important. Therefore, the studies on university space should engage building administrators, facility managers and main users: students and university staff. The programming and design of modern functional and spatial solutions

---

[1] One of such institutions is DEGW, which runs research into the future development of universities and the most efficient models of academic space. www.degw.com.

OECD - Organization for Economic Cooperation and Development, incorporates 34 highly developed democratic countries. Founded Upon the Economic Cooperation and Development Convention signed by 20 states on Dec 14th 1960. Poland has been a member of OECD since 1996. www.oecd.com.

for university facilities should be preceded by in-depth analyses of their functional needs in relation to the organization of the academic processes.

Unfortunately, in Poland such analyses are not conducted. In the absence of "universities research" the author has been making quality analyses of university facilities and sites for many years. The scope of the paper is a recapitulation of the author's research experiences and results.

3   Scope of the Analyses

The analyses conducted by author at the campus of the University of Silesia in Katowice were focused on evaluating if the examined academic sites support the efficiency and development of the university, and, at the same time, have a positive impact on the working conditions for students and teaching staff, to provide high-quality of the work environment organization. The organizational quality of the facilities and sites of universities are the features of their design and other amenities that support the operations of a given institution or organizational unit. The elements of the organizational quality, including the design solutions in buildings, the infrastructure and equipment, supplemented by other labour resources, should satisfy the organizational needs of the institution,[2] which is also applicable to the functional and spatial organization of university sites.

The discussed University of Silesia is currently undergoing changes in its campus. In the beginning of the 21st century two new university buildings were erected. In 2012 the Centre for Scientific Information and Academic Libraries at the University of Silesia and University of Economics in Katowice was opened up. The University authorities are planning new facilities and extension of the campus site. The author's analyses were used for pre-design studies. The analyses gave grounds for students' conceptual designs concerning further growth of the University.

4   Description of Research Methods and Procedures

The method of analyses used by the author was based on worldwide trends in quality assessment in architecture. POE - Post Occupancy Evaluation [3] is the method of assessing quality criteria of architectural objects (technical, functional, economic, organizational and behavioral quality). The analyses were also based on the author's experience gained over years of conducting case studies of buildings and university sites in selected scopes.

Despite different ranges of the undertaken studies and types of facilities (buildings and campuses), some research steps were the same. In the case of each of the analyzed building or campus, the research was divided into two stages. The first stage involved the theoretical and organizational preparation of the research team, including:

- Studies on literature concerning the HE issues,
- Collection of the information about the campus or analysed university building,

---

[2] The author's own definition (D.Winncka –Jasłowska).

- Examination of the architectural and construction documentation,
- preparation of drawings and functional analyses, measurements of class rooms and lecture rooms to determine the actual space floor standards per one student;
- Obtaining permission for conducting studies in the building and at the campus and appointing the time of in situ visits;
- Selection of students – surveyors for direct participation in the research, discussion of the methods and scenarios of the surveys, assignment of particular tasks to specific persons.

Stage two involved the performance of the analyses, in the following order:

- Walkthrough with the facility manager to detect the main problems,
- Compilation of the assessment criteria list, the functional, organizational, behavioural and technical quality – in view of the organizational efficiency of the university site/campus;
- Interviews with users (students) conducted, in proportion, in all the buildings of the faculties located at a given campus- focused on the efficiency of the use of space, its functionality, aesthetics and safety;
- The second in situ visit – interviews and questionnaires and further observations (including the ergonomic analysis of class room and lecture rooms, in view of the efficiency of the use of space, its functionality, aesthetics and safety- as subjectively perceived by its users;
- Summary of the results of the interviews.

For a more detailed description of the analyses - see [5–8] and other publications of the author in Polish. A synthesis of the conclusions from the case studies is presented below.

5   Analyses of University Facilities and Campuses Elaborated by the Author

Case study: Campus of the University of Silesia. The University of Silesia in Katowice is one of the two biggest universities in the region (the other one is the Silesian University of Technology in Gliwice). It was founded in 1968 and it grew dynamically in the 1970s. Upper Silesia is the most important industrial region in Poland. The summary of the results of the questionnaires and of the expert's evaluation enabled the formulation of the conclusions that could be used as guidelines for future development of the campus of the University of Silesia (Fig. 1).

At present; however, the collected and elaborated material was only used as the own scientific documentation and as introductory to the project of the development of the campus of a purely academic nature, completed by students as their semester project. The observation of the changes that occurred at the sites of the University of Silesia in Katowice led to the decision about conducting check-up studies on their impact on the functional and organizational quality. The studies were divided into stages corresponding to specific functional, technical, behavioural and aesthetic quality. During stage I the transport and traffic connections between the University and the region were analyzed, and, in addition, a general inventory of the sites was taken. All objects belonging to the University were identified. The sites were described in a graphic manner and the neighbouring housing quarters that in future could be incorporated to the campus identified. The analysis of the complexity of the functional offer was conducted. The conclusions were formulated on the grounds of the surveys and questionnaires addressed to students of all disciplines.

Stage II concerned technical quality. Technical quality does not only involve the technical condition of the buildings and the infrastructure, but also engineering, technical and technological amenities that should provide safety and ease of use. The first criteria subjected to the analysis were the safety of people and property. The expert evaluation of the fire safety around the buildings was made, with special focus on fire exit routes and evacuation manners. Furthermore, the campus was checked in terms of the compliance with "design out crime" conditions. In addition, the maintenance of the buildings and their surroundings was checked.

Stage III concerned behavioural and aesthetic quality. The assessment criteria were, among others: way-finding, aesthetic perceptions of users, and social integration at the campus.

In the case of university buildings, the analyses were, first and foremost, focused on spaces associated with the teaching and learning processes and social integration. The IT revolution resulted in the emergence of new methods of teaching and learning. In comparison with the past, university space, mainly inside the buildings is nowadays used in a different way. The modes of worked have changed due to the advancement of the internet and mobile equipment. Students need new workplaces for individual studies, and mobile aids, for example notebooks, enable learning to take place anywhere. Hence, public and generally accessible space should be adjusted to support the process. The author's analyses conducted in university buildings involved the assessments to what extent old type facilities "manage" the functions associated with these new modes of work and how new buildings address "self- learning".

Fig. 1. Centre for Scientific Information and Academic Library at the University of Silesia in Katowice (Poland). Photo by D. Winnicka-Jasłowska.

Another important issue is the integration of the academic environment. There is a growing awareness of the need for shaping the space of HE buildings to support integration, meetings, team work, formal and informal contacts. The author's analyses entailed both old and new generation university buildings in view of their fulfillment of students' needs and new forms of student activity. Likewise at campus sites, the analyses involved expert methods evaluating the quality criteria and participative method engaging the users of the analyzed buildings.

6 Conclusions

The conclusions give grounds for further, in-depth studies that may lead to the introduction of favourable spatial changes in university facilities and campus sites. The analyses run in the university buildings and at campuses showed that a university must be unified in terms of its buildings and sites. The sites supplement the functions of the buildings and constitute connections, not only in terms of traffic and movement (routes) but, first and foremost, in terms of the functions that supplement the university structure. Apart from many detectable problems and the fact that Polish universities are still in the period of transition, it should be stated that as far as research is concerned, Polish university staff are often leaders in this field. There are many drawbacks of Polish university facilities, yet, they are not obstacles to the development of the research and teaching staff. Polish university graduates have no problems in finding work in Western European countries and overseas. This is a sort of verification of the Polish level of science and higher education, which in the last 25 years has undergone a tremendous scientific, economic, social and technological advancement, followed by changes in university campuses that provide better studying, working and living conditions.

References

1. Fross, K.: Ergonomics in the practice of project architect on selected examples. In: Kurosu, M. (ed.) HCI 2014, Part I. LNCS, vol. 8510, pp. 77–85. Springer, Heidelberg (2014)
2. Masły, D., Sitek, M.: Analysis of natural lighting with regard to design of sustainable office buildings in Poland. In: Stephanidis, C., Antona, M. (eds.) UAHCI 2014, Part IV. LNCS, vol. 8516, pp. 227–236. Springer, Heidelberg (2014)
3. Preiser, W.F.E,. Rabinowitz H.Z., White E.T.: Post-Occupancy Evaluation. Van Nostrand Reinhold, NY (1988)
4. Tymkiewicz, J.: The advanced construction of facades. the relations between the quality of facades and the quality of buildings. In: 2nd International Conference on Advanced Construction. Advanced Construction, Kaunas Univ. Technol., Kaunas, Lithuania, 11–12 November 2010, pp. 274–281 (2010). http://alephfiles.rtu.lv/TUA01/000030265_e.pdf
5. Winnicka-Jasłowska, D.: Internet based - study on users' needs. students' functional and spatial needs in facilities of architecture faculties at technical universities in Poland In: Ajdukiewicz, A. (eds.) ACEE Architecture, Civil Engineering, Environment, vol. 1. The Silesian University of Technology, Gaudeo, January 2008

6. Winnicka-Jasłowska, D.: New outlook on higher education facilities. modifications of the assumptions for programming and designing university buildings and campuses under the influence of changing organizational and behavioral needs. In: Ajdukiewicz, A. (eds.) ACEE Architecture, Civil Engineering, Environment, vol. 5, The Silesian University of Technology, Gaudeo, February 2012

7. Winnicka-Jasłowska, D.: Creating a functional and space program for new building of the faculty of the biomedical engineering building. silesian university of technology In: Ajdukiewicz, A. (eds.) ACEE Architecture, Civil Engineering, Environment, vol. 5. The Silesian University of Technology, Gaudeo, March 2012

8. Winnicka-Jasłowska, D.: Ergonomic solutions of facilities and laboratory work-stands at universities. In: Stephanidis, C., Antona, M. (eds.) UAHCI 2014, Part IV. LNCS, vol. 8516, pp. 314–321. Springer, Heidelberg (2014)

9. www.degw.com

10. www.oecd.com

11. Złowodzki, M.: Science and higher education in the era of globalization. their place in work structures and influence on urban architecture. In: Czasopismo Techniczne (Technical Transaction) 3-A(13), 106 (2009). https://suw.biblos.pk.edu.pl/resources/i1/i8/i6/i7/r1867/ZlowodzkiM_NaukaSzkolnictwo

E-mentoring Supports for Improving the Persistence of Underrepresented Students in On-line and Traditional Courses

Gerri Wolfe[1(✉)] and Noel Gregg[2]

[1] Regents' Center for Learning Disorders,
University of Georgia, Athens, GA, USA
gwolfe@uga.edu
[2] Institute for Interdisciplinary Research in Education and Human Development,
University of Georgia, Athens, GA, USA
ngregg@uga.edu

Abstract. On-line education has broadened access to college allowing the same educational opportunities as students enrolled at a traditional campus. The increase in on-line enrollment is over shadowed by course drop out and failure rates which are higher than campus-based rates. With many underrepresented students facing barriers to campus-based education, on-line courses hold great appeal. However, the on-line environment has posed challenges due to the limited availability of support services which can lead to frustration and subsequent withdrawal from courses. The purpose of this paper is to explore e-mentoring using the BreakThru e-mentoring model as a back drop. Three aspects of the e-mentoring program will be examined: (1) factors associated with how underrepresented students use social media tools, including virtual platforms, while participating in an e-mentoring program; (2) factors contributing to the development of mentee/mentor relationships; and (3) factors which affect a mentee's increased persistence in a STEM major.

Keywords: E-mentoring · On-line courses · Underrepresented college students · Disability · Virtual platforms social media · Persistence · STEM

1 Introduction

On-line education has broadened access to higher education for many students including non-traditional and underrepresented students allowing the same educational opportunities as students enrolled full-time at a campus. The growth of on-line education is reflected in recent data that shows greater enrollment rates than for campus-based matriculation [1]. Underrepresented students have turned to on-line coursework due to family obligations, work responsibilities, and travel/geographic restrictions that make a commitment to campus-based education difficult [2]. Additionally, advances in technology offer students the ability to participate in higher education while juggling personal and work demands. Unfortunately, the increase in on-line enrollment is over shadowed by course drop out and failure rates which are higher than campus-based rates [3]. With many underrepresented students facing

© Springer International Publishing Switzerland 2015
M. Antona and C. Stephanidis (Eds.): UAHCI 2015, Part III, LNCS 9177, pp. 243–251, 2015.
DOI: 10.1007/978-3-319-20684-4_24

barriers to traditional campus-based education, on-line courses hold great appeal. However, the on-line environment has posed new challenges due to the limited availability of support services which can lead to frustration and subsequent withdrawal from courses [4]. The need for student engagement opportunities and collaboration (mentoring) to positively influence on-line student retention is apparent [5]. As more and more students use on-line learning, understanding the effectiveness of e-learning supports is critical to retention and degree completion. Face-to-face mentoring has been found to be effective for increasing student retention [6] and improving achievement [7]. However, few studies have examined whether electronic mentoring (e-mentoring) and the related platforms is an effective practice for supporting students' persistence with coursework.

Social networking is hugely popular among postsecondary students. The Joint Information Systems Committee [8] reported postsecondary students regularly access social networking sites. Many spend a great deal of time posting messages to social media networks, chatting via internet messaging (IM), and communicating by text messages, but our understanding of the strategies that effectively help them manage these technologies in academic settings is limited. Since many students are already using social media tools, it makes sense to reimagine how social networking can be used to support students' academic pursuits.

Consistent with the growing popularity of on-line learning, there is an increasing interest in the potential of virtual worlds to create a learning environment that enables social and experiential learning. Virtual worlds allow users to create avatars that can interact with each other in a three-dimensional digital environment. One popular example is Second Life created by Linden Labs in 2003. Virtual spaces provide opportunities for users to form a community that promotes social and collaborative learning [9]. The belief that Second Life can offer a virtual e-mentoring experience that simulates face-to-face mentoring is compelling in light of postsecondary students' time and geographic limitations, yet little attention has been given to this potential student support resource.

The Georgia STEM Accessibility Alliance (BreakThru), an e-mentoring project funded by the National Science Foundation, explores factors influencing science, technology, engineering, and math (STEM) participation of underrepresented college students with disabilities. BreakThru provides social media and virtual tools so students can connect with mentors whose expertise is in a STEM field. BreakThru investigated students' use of social media tools and Second Life for developing mentoring relationships and identifying the supports critical for them to persist in STEM majors.

Identifying successful practices to support retention and enhance the persistence of underrepresented postsecondary students in on-line courses is a critical need. A growing literature base is available describing the effectiveness of e-mentoring practices in educational, business, human resources, and social environments [10]. A limited amount of this research has focused on enhancing educational success of underrepresented students [11]. The purpose of this paper is to explore e-mentoring using the BreakThru e-mentoring model as a back drop. Three aspects of the e-mentoring program will be examined: (1) factors associated with how underrepresented students use social media tools, including virtual platforms, while participating in an e-mentoring program; (2) factors contributing to the development of mentee/mentor relationships; and (3) factors which affect a mentee's increased persistence in a STEM major.

1.1 Social Media Tools and E-mentoring

E-mentoring as compared to face-to-face (FtF) mentoring can occur across asynchronous time and place, providing benefits not found with FtF programs. The use of e-mentoring allows for more access to mentors representing a variety of disciplines and locations. The type of communication platforms (e.g., Second Life, email, Facebook, Twitter, Skype, texting, mobile phone) most effective during e-mentoring has not been fully explored in the literature.

1.2 Mentoring

The literature suggests that mentoring programs provide students increased discipline knowledge, higher achievement, greater self-efficacy [11], increased aspirations, stronger program engagement [12], and a reduction of negative learning behaviors [13]. E-mentoring specific to underrepresented students using virtual/social media tools (i.e., Second Life, text, e-mail) remains largely unstudied.

1.3 Persistence in STEM

The importance of better understanding the multiple dimensions surrounding persistence is critical for improving educational and employment outcomes for college students. Persistence is a continuous learning process that influences the educational and career goal aspirations of an individual [14]. Level of persistence is highly correlated with adult learners' academic performance [15]. Many adults with disabilities are less motivated to engage in academic tasks as a result of their difficulties with the demands of academic learning and social stereotyping. It is important that researchers have a better idea of the factors influencing e-mentoring to provide effective resources to underrepresented adults in postsecondary settings that will affect their motivation to persist.

2 BreakThru E-mentoring Review

This review used survey data from participants enrolled in the Georgia STEM Accessibility Alliance project. The e-mentoring component of the project is referred to as BreakThru. BreakThru is an innovative and inclusive learning world that combines elements of social networking and virtual communities for adolescents and adults with disabilities interested in pursuing STEM careers. BreakThru integrates e-mentoring, virtual training, social networking, and personalized virtual learning communities. One of BreakThru's distinctive features is the use of virtual islands to support or implement e-mentoring activities. The BreakThru e-Mentoring Islands are located in the world of

Second Life (SL); it is a core resource for BreakThru activities. The BreakThru participants engage in a virtual world using avatars to access e-mentoring, social networking, academic support, transition assistance, and research. BreakThru mentors, and students are able to virtually access an inclusive learning environment using a variety of social networking tools (Twitter, Facebook, Skype, text, e-mail, Second Life).

BreakThru mentors are recruited from postsecondary faculty/staff, graduate students, business leaders, and project staff. All have expertise in a STEM field and have previous experience as a mentor or a mentee. The BreakThru staff matches mentors to students based on a set of criteria: STEM interest; experiences of mentor with diverse learning styles (disability consideration); expertise of mentor in STEM academic coursework; mentor preference for secondary or postsecondary.

2.1 Participants

This study centered on post-secondary students participating in the BreakThru e-mentoring program during 2011-2014. The criteria for mentee selection requires that a student be enrolled in one of the project schools, have a disability, and demonstrate an interest in pursuing a STEM major.

2.2 Survey Instruments

All mentees were administered the *BreakThru Persistence Survey*. This survey addressed five persistence constructs identified in the literature as critical for the intent to persist in STEM majors and careers [16]. The constructs included: intent to persist; self-determination; self-advocacy; science affect; and math affect. In addition, all mentees filled out the *BreakThru Mentee Semester Survey*, an on-line five point Likert scale instrument. The purpose of this survey was to evaluate the mentees' interactions with the e-mentoring experience across the following; satisfaction; support seeking; personal responsibility; communication; and engagement. All the mentors were required to complete the *BreakThru Mentor Monthly Survey*. Data collected through the survey included the number of sessions, the communication mediums, and the length of mentoring sessions.

3   BreakThru Findings

3.1   Associated Factors with How Postsecondary Students Use Social Media Tools During E-mentoring

The BreakThru e-mentoring sessions were provided through either digital voice communication platforms (e.g., Second Life voice, smart phone, video calls) or text-based communication platforms (e.g., emails, social media posts, Second Life chat posts, text message conversation threads). Text-based mentoring is a progressive written communication interchange addressing a relevant mentoring subject.

Table 1. Number of E-mentoring sessions by medium. data analyzed from the monthly mentor surveys 2012-2014.

	Digital voice tools			Text-based tools		
	Second life	Skype	Phone	Facebook	Texting	Email
2012-2013	35	36	122	25	131	229
2013-2014	24	5	64	44	87	142
Total	59	41	186	69	218	371

The mentoring pairs often used email, chat posts, and text messaging as it is conveniently accessed via smart phone and/or computer and is very user friendly to implement. Table 1 shows the media tools used for mentoring sessions.

As seen in Table 1, participants integrated a variety of social media platforms into their e-mentoring sessions. The selection of a communication platform for e-mentoring was a decision made by each mentoring pair, and the platform often changed depending on personal preference, availability, ease of use, and convenience (*Break-Thru Mentee Semester Survey* and the *BreakThru Mentor Monthly Survey*). The *BreakThru Mentor Monthly Surveys* indicated participants most frequently used text-based (email, chat, etc.) e-mentoring tools that were effective across both social and academic activities. It appears that one of the main reasons for using text-based tools was the practicality, user friendliness, and availability of the platforms. Email and chat platforms offered instant access to the participants and their monthly surveys revealed that mentors and mentees spoke regularly though these mediums.

3.2   Associated Factors that Affect Development of Mentor/Mentee Relationship

The mentoring roles described by the participants appear complex and multifaceted, contributing to a dynamic rather than static mentoring model. The participants were clear that the presence of a mentor greatly impacted their personal and academic lives. Survey comments reflect different aspects of e-mentoring such as developing better study skills, living successfully with a disability, and continuing to persist in their major. However, most mention the importance of having a close mentoring relationship while enrolled in their major. This was corroborated by the mentees feedback on the Mentee Survey. Table 2 illustrates the participants' perceptions of the mentoring relationship.

As seen in Table 2, mentees perceive the mentors served in the capacities identified as important to their academic and/or developmental needs. Whether it was support within or to continue in STEM courses or to teach study skills and resourcing, the mentors were able to assist their mentees with advice that served their academic and personal mentees needs.

Table 2. Support seeking items 2012-2014. [1]n represents the number of survey responses received for a given item; n does not represent unique individuals. [2] Scale: 1, *strongly disagree* to 5, *strongly agree*. [3]An independent samples t-test was conducted to determine if there was a statistically significant difference between mentees' and mentors' average construct rating. **p < .001, * p < .01.

Construct item		n[1]	Mean[2]	t-test[3]
My mentoring experience has increased my confidence that I can be successful in STEM courses.	Mentees	98	4.24	P = 0.002*
The mentee seems to have more confidence in his/her ability to be successful in STEM courses than when we first began working together.	Mentors	114	3.89	
I am more interested in STEM classes because of my mentoring experience.	Mentees	98	4.0	P = 0.006*
Over the time we have worked together, my mentee has become more interested in STEM classes.	Mentors	114	3.89	
Through mentoring, I have been able to get the information and resources I need (such as how to find resources I need, developing study skills, etc.).	Mentees	98	4.37	p < 0.001**
I have been able to help my mentee get the information and resources he/she needs.	Mentors	114	3.97	
My mentoring experience has encouraged me to push beyond what is comfortable or easy for me.	Mentees	98	4.20	P = 0.001*
The mentoring experience has enabled the mentee to push beyond what is comfortable or easy.	Mentors	114	3.79	

3.3   Factors that Increase a Mentee's Persistence in STEM

The five persistence constructs we explored included: intent to persist; self-determination; self-advocacy; science affect; and math affect. Figure 1 shows the significant persistence factors and the students' intentions to persist in STEM.

As shown in Fig. 1, e-mentoring lead to gains in self-advocacy and self-determination which influenced the mentees intention to persist in a STEM major. According to survey results, the participants feel more capable of determining their own strengths and weaknesses and report an increase in their ability to self-advocate. Findings from the Mentee Survey mirror the persistence data and indicate that e-mentoring has significantly increased decision making and problem solving skills. Moving towards advocacy is one way that these students are persisting in their studies. According to the survey data, the participants are persistent and consistent in their pursuit of their specific majors.

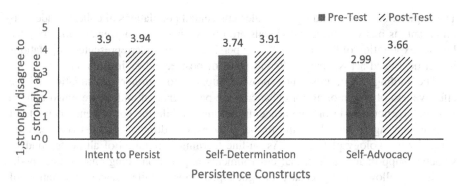

Fig. 1. Mean responses to persistence constructs on the Student Pre/Post Survey

4 Discussion

In exploring the research on e-mentoring as a support for college students enrolled in on-line courses, we reviewed the findings from the BreakThru e-mentoring project. Although BreakThru did not single out on-line students, it did examine e-mentoring with underrepresented college students and the factors associated with educational persistence. Historically, several factions of this population have been under-served by policy-makers, service providers, researchers, and agencies. These groups include, but are not limited to, individuals with disabilities, non-traditional age adults (i.e., > 30), females, and ethnic/racial minorities [14]. Historically underrepresented students, often delay postsecondary enrollment one or two years past high school graduation, enroll part time, and remain fully employed [17]. It is critical for professionals to identify effective practices, such as e-mentoring, for enhancing the persistence of underrepresented populations of students in majors.

The communication platforms that we were most interested in exploring focused on a variety of digital voice and text tools effective during e-mentoring activities. Our findings suggest that a variety of social media tools should be utilized during e-mentoring. However, a missing resource for many underrepresented college students is the availability of e-mentoring relationships. In this review, the e-mentoring relationship provided the opportunities to learn additional virtual communication tools, practice with academic and social strategies, and develop supports (trust) essential to long-term success in careers. It is also critical to note that the technology challenges faced by participants in using BreakThru's virtual e-mentoring island, served to build the e-mentoring relationship as the pair worked to overcome the technology learning curve.

The five STEM persistence constructs (i.e., intent; self-determination; self-advocacy; and anxiety) investigated in BreakThru require further exploration with underrepresented college students. The participants reported the greatest pre-to-post gains on the self-advocacy and self-determination constructs, indicating the e-mentoring experience did influence their growth as a student. There is a significant amount of research documenting that promoting self-determination and self-advocacy has positive postsecondary school and career benefits for students with disabilities [18].

The implications of our findings for underrepresented populations of college students is important, as many of these individuals are not persisting in courses and majors [19]. Further exploration of factors influencing persistence for underrepresented populations is a critical need across many different types of postsecondary institutions.

The findings from this study provide support for further investigation of the effectiveness of e-mentoring for enhancing the persistence of underrepresented college students, particularly in on-line academic settings. While the convenience benefits of on-line learning is appealing, the format may expose different barriers (i.e. learning curve for technology platforms). As on-line learning is required of all postsecondary students, support for such virtual environments requires on-going change and modification to allow for universally designed platforms. While greater exploration of e-mentoring for students in on-line classes is needed, results from the BreakThru study indicate that underrepresented populations of college students receiving STEM e-mentoring opportunities have a greater change for successful academic outcomes.

Acknowledgements. The research reported here was supported by the National Science Foundation (NSF) through Grant 1027635 to the University of Georgia and 1027655 to the Georgia Institute of Technology. The opinions expressed are those of the authors and do not represent the view of NSF.

References

1. Allen, L., Seaman, J.: Going the Distance: Online Education in the USA 2011. Babson Survey Research Group, Wellesley MA (2011)
2. Levy, Y.: Comparing Dropouts and Persistence in E-learning Courses. Comput. Educ. **48**(2), 185–204 (2013)
3. Perez, E.: Online Community College Students More Likely to Fail, Withdraw (2011). http://californiawatch.org/dailyreport/online-community-college-students-more-likely-fail-withdraw-11581
4. Heyman, E.: Overcoming Student retention issues in higher education online programs. Online Journal of Distance Learning Administration 8(4) (2010)
5. Kinghorn, J. The New Digital Divide: Peer Collaboration as a Bridge. Association for University Regional Campuses of Ohio Journal **20** (2014)
6. Ashwin, P.: Peer Facilitation and How it Contributes to the Development of a More Social View of Learning. Res. Post-Compulsory Educ. **8**, 5–7 (2003)
7. Muldoon, R.: Recognizing and Rewarding the contribution and personal Development of Peer Supporters at University. J. Further High. Educ. **32**(3), 207–219 (2008)
8. Joint Information Systems Committee. Great Expectations of ICT, How Higher Education Institutions are Measuring Up. http://www.jisc.ac.uk/publications/publications/greatexpectations.aspx
9. Kirriemuir, J.A.: A Spring 2008 'snapshot' of UK Higher and Further Education Developments in Second Life. http://www.eduserv.org.uk/~/media/foundation/sl/uksnapshot052008/final%20pdf.ashx
10. Single, P.B., Single, R.M.: E-mentoring for social equity: review of research to inform program development. Mentoring and Tutoring **13**(2), 45–60 (forthcoming)

11. Sowers, J., Powers, L., Shpigelman, C.: Science, Technology, Engineering and Math (STEM): Mentoring for Youth and Young Adults with Disabilities: A Review of the Research, Arlington, VA: National Science Foundation (2012). http://www.rri.pdx.edu/files/39/stem_mentor_monograph5_may2012.pdf

12. Ensher, E.A., Murphy, S.E.: E-mentoring: next generation research strategies and suggestions. In: Ragins, B.R., Kram, K.E. (eds.) The Handbook of Mentoring at Work: Theory, Research and Practice, pp. 299–322. Sage Publications, Los Angeles (2007)

13. DuBois, D.L., Holloway, B.E., Valentine, J.C., Cooper, H.: Effectiveness of mentoring programs for youth: a meta-analytic review. Am. J. Community Psychol. 30(2), 157–197 (2002)

14. National Research Council. Improving Adult Literacy Instruction: Options for Practice and Research. Washington, DC (2012). http://www.nap.edu/download.php?record_id=13242

15. Kahn, J.H., Nauta, M.M.: Social-cognitive predictors of first-year college persistence: the importance of proximal assessment. Res. High. Educ. 42(6), 633–652 (2001)

16. Toker, Y., Ackerman, P.L.: Utilizing occupational complexity levels in vocational interest assessments: assessing interests for STEM areas. J. Vocat. Behav. 80(2), 524–544 (2012)

17. Compton, J.I., Cox, E., Laanan, F.S.: Adult learners in transition. In: Laanan, F.S. (ed.) Understanding Students in Transition Trends and Issues, 73–80. Jossey-Bass, San Francisco (2006)

18. Wehmeyer, M.L.: Framing for the Future: self-determination. Remedial and Special Education, 1–4 (2014)

19. National Science Foundation. Women, Minorities, and Persons with Disabilities in Science and Engineering: 2011. Arlington: VA (2011). http://www.nsf.gov/statistics/wmpd/pdf/nsf11309.pdf

Comparison Research Between ICT-Based Design and Traditional Design for Hearing Impaired Children

A Case Study on Speech Training Tool

Ying Yang, Junnan Yu, Wenyi Cai, and Ting Han[✉]

School of Media and Design, Shanghai Jiao Tong University, Shanghai, China
hanting@sjtu.edu.cn

Abstract. There are about 27.8 million hearing impaired people in China, and among them 137 thousand are children under six. Traditional approaches of hearing and speech rehabilitation for children are using medical treatments at first and subsequently following a speech training in professional institutes, to make up the delayed speech development. It has been found that there are some weaknesses in traditional approaches.

Since the emergence of ICTs (Information and Communication Technologies), they have been applied in many different fields, especially in the education field. ICTs have an obvious advantage in education. In this paper, the application of ICTs in speech training has been proposed, and a comparison with traditional speech training approaches has been made. Based on these research findings, a speech training prototype, New Voice was developed.

Keywords: Design for pleasure of use · Human Factors / System Integration · Training design and analysis · ICT-based design

1 Introduction

1.1 Speech Training Condition in China

There are about 27.8 million hearing impaired people in China, and among them 137 thousand are children under six. This number is increasing at an annual rate of 23 thousand. At present, more than 80% hearing and speech impaired children in developed countries can recover, while the proportion is only 29.7% in China. Hearing impairment usually hinders the development of children's speech competence and greatly impacts on their education level and social involvement [1].

Some researchers claimed that most families with hearing impaired children are in a low income. Some families in poor areas pay little attention to the rehabilitation and education of hearing impaired children due to the low level of culture, long distance to schools and poor economic conditions [2].

In addition, the number of hearing impaired children varies from different areas. The conditions of hearing impaired children in developed areas are generally better than those in less developed areas. In Shanxi Province (a less developed area in China),

© Springer International Publishing Switzerland 2015
M. Antona and C. Stephanidis (Eds.): UAHCI 2015, Part III, LNCS 9177, pp. 252–263, 2015.
DOI: 10.1007/978-3-319-20684-4_25

only 40% hearing impaired children are able to enter normal school, while the percentage in more developed provinces can reach 80% [2].

Security and service systems for hearing impaired children in China are in great challenge. According to WHO global Fangrong Cooperation Center, there are still 5 provinces without hospitals that can do cochlear operation; 68 cities without rehabilitation institutions for hearing impaired children. In all the Chinese hearing rehabilitation institutions, 57% lack conditions to test hearing and 68% lack conditions to fit audiphones [3].

Currently, some hearing impaired children are diagnosed and assessed in medical institutions in preschool age, and then have speech training there. However, in school age, most of them enter special education schools, where speech training is beyond the abilities and duties of medical institutions. As a result, special education teachers have to be responsible for education and rehabilitation of hearing impaired children. It is quite a heavy task for special education teachers [4].

1.2   The Development of ICTs

Since the emergence of ICTs (Information and Communication Technologies), they have been applied in many different fields, especially in the education field. ICTs are formed by information technology and communication technology.

ICTs have an obvious advantage in education. For example, it is found that ICTs are of vital significance in preschool educational process [5]. Furthermore, in music education, ICTs successfully contribute to young children's musical learning, music creativity and cognitive development [6]. In recent decades, more and more studies about ICTs focus on the needs of disadvantaged groups, for instance, the rehabilitation and training for hearing impaired children [7].

One type of information technologies, speech signal digital processing technology has been applied to the diagnosis and rehabilitation in speech therapy [8]. Other ICTs, Real-time feedback control technology and multimedia means have been applied to the speech training to improve the efficiency and intuition [4]. In countries with large geographical space or limited resources, ICTs also offer a method of reaching families who may otherwise have missed out on services altogether [9]. For instance, VidKids®, used a video conferencing approach to provide services to families in remote areas [10]. One type of ICTs, Online technology is a viable alternative to face-to-face sessions. For example, Constantinescu examined both therapist and parent satisfaction with the online delivery of auditory verbal therapy and overall satisfaction was high with the majority of therapists and parents [11]. An e-training tool was designed to help hearing impaired children learn and practice words in Thai language more correctly [12]. The tool used speech recognition technology, to overcome the limitations of the traditional face-to-face speech therapy.

2   Methodology Description

2.1   Study Framework

The study framework is as follows (Fig. 1):

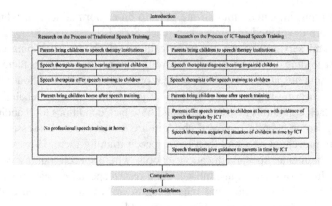

Fig. 1. Study framework

2.2   Traditional Speech Training in China

In China, traditional approaches of hearing and speech rehabilitation for children are using medical treatments at first and subsequently following a speech training in professional institutes, to make up the delayed speech development.

Parents usually choose special school for their own hearing impaired children to receive speech training, since there are professional speech therapists.

Usually, the traditional speech training process in China is as follows:

1. Parents bring children to speech therapy institutions.
2. Speech therapists diagnose hearing impaired children according to subjective audition and other medical equipment.
3. Speech therapists offer speech training to children. They often use cards, toys, games and other interesting forms, leading children to speak and then correcting their wrong pronunciation. Children learn to speak by repeated exercise.
4. Parents bring children home after speech training. Since parents are lack of professional skills, children cannot have professional speech training at home.
5. Parents bring children back to speech therapists the next day. In fact, parents have to take children to speech therapy institutions every day, aiming for good training effects.

It has been found that there are some shortcomings in traditional approaches as follows.

1. Best time for speech training is likely to be delayed due to expensive medical fees and defective health care system. The best ages for speech development are 2 ~ 7 years old [7]. Receiving speech training earlier is more beneficial to the rehabilitation. According to the survey of China Disabled Persons Federation, only 50% hearing impaired children can be admitted to rehabilitation institutions and then only half of them can enter the normal kindergartens or primary schools, whereas the rate in developed countries is 90%.
2. Parents have no chance and condition to participate in the speech training. Children spend most time with their parents, thus parents play an important role in training

[14]. However, there is a lack of speech training professionals in China. According to the developed countries level, 55000 audiology staff and 490000 speech therapy professionals are demanded in China, while in fact there are only 7775 and 100, respectively. One speech training teacher has to take charge of several children. As a result, each child receives less training [15].

3. Monotonous training models result in the loss of children's learning interest. Existing speech training tools are simple and mainly focus on the mechanical training of vocal organs. Experts state that interesting training models and effective feedbacks contribute to children active participation in training [16].

2.3 ICT-Based Speech Training

The speech therapy profession has expanded rapidly with complex clinical education and practices over the past 30 years, while recently making use of available ICTs [17].

ICTs are mainly used for assessment and intervention purposes of speech and language disorders both in children and adults. As speech training is sometimes time-consuming and laborious for both therapists and patients, intelligent diagnosis and therapy systems have been created as a way to enhance speech therapy efficiency [18]. A study in Greek introduced an internet-based Speech Pathology Diagnostic Expert System, which is used for assessing the oral language abilities of children aged between 4 and 7 [19].

It is also found that ICTs impact on intervention in people with hearing impairment. ICTs in intervention should be designed in accordance to the disability, in an easy and understandable manner for the user, in order to allow speakers to achieve the highest speech, language and cognitive performances possible [20, 21]. A software system was developed for Persian hearing impaired children, which promotes the interaction of language learning activities both at home and in clinic [22].

Based on the brief overview of ICTs in speech training, most ICT-based speech training tools are designed for a certain language and for therapists, in order to raise training efficiency. However, there are no tools designed for home use and improving the user experience of patients. Therefore, based on the national conditional in China, an ICT-based speech training progress for Chinese hearing impaired children are designed as follows:

1. Parents bring children to speech therapy institutions.
2. Speech therapists diagnose hearing impaired children.
3. Children have speech training.
4. Parents bring children home after speech training.
5. Parents offer speech training to children at home with guidance of speech therapists by ICT. Thanks to ICTs, parents are more accessible to professional speech training knowledge. Multimedia offer a variety of training modes, which are more attractive to children.
6. Speech therapists acquire the situation of children in time by ICTs. Speech therapists can communicate with parents through ICT-based speech training tools.
7. Speech therapists give guidance to parents in time by ICTs.

8. Parents bring children back to speech therapists institutions after a period of time. Speech training from both parents and speech therapists can accelerate this learning process of children.

2.4   Design Guidelines

Based on the shortcomings of traditional speech training and previous researches on ICTs in the field of speech therapy, the needs of parents and hearing impaired children in speech therapy should be given attention. Their needs are concluded as follows:

- Hearing impaired children should have speech training as early as possible.
- Parents should be professionally trained with speech training skills and offer speech training to their children by themselves.
- Hearing impaired children prefer interesting speech training.
- Speech training has remarkable effects for hearing impaired children.

In accordance to the needs of parents and hearing impaired children, four design guidelines for ICT-based speech training tool are concluded as follows:

- The speech training tool is more accessible.
- Parents can participate in speech training more.
- The speech training tool is more attractive to hearing impaired children.

3   Case Study of Speech Training Tool

3.1   Design Framework

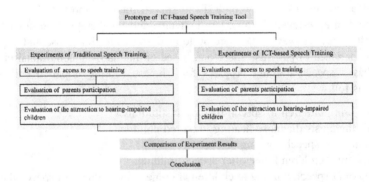

Fig. 2. Design framework

3.2   Prototype

Based on above research findings, a prototype of an ICT-based speech training tool, named New Voice, was developed. The prototype includes a speech training app for iPad and a smart toy. It is an auxiliary speech training tool for parents and hearing impaired children to easily use at home. It is recommended for hearing impaired children with residual hearing by means of hearing aid devices or operations, since it is more effective for them to use than for totally deaf children (Fig. 2).

The Speech Training App for iPad. The app is designed for both parents and hearing impaired children to use. It has three main functions: speech training, training records, course recommendation.

- **Speech training.** A series of speech training courses is designed for users. There are 21 consonants and 6 vowels in Chinese pinyin. It is more systematic for children to learn Chinese beginning with pinyin. Therefore, every course is aimed that children learn one consonant or one vowel of Chinese pinyin through three different two-character Chinese words. Parents can choose proper courses for children with guidance of speech therapists at homepage (Fig. 3). Subsequently, parents are guided to record teaching videos for chosen courses. The video can teach children to speak Chinese in case that parents do not stay with children. Besides videos, children can also learn to speak Chinese by game at the study page (Fig. 3). The game, whack-a-mole, is designed to offer visual learning feedbacks to children. The voice of children can be captured through speech recognition technologies and parsed to Chinese pinyin. The parse results will be compared with the correct pinyin and it shows corresponding animations to children at the study page. If children speak the right Chinese word of this course, a mole will be whacked, otherwise it will not be whacked. Children win the game when wracking moles for a certain times. That also means children have mastered this course for a certain degree.

Fig. 3. From left to right: login Page, homepage, recording page; study page

- **Training records.** The app can record game results, which reflects training effect of a certain course. *Accuracy* is used to describe the training situation. Higher *Accuracy* indicates better training effects.

$$Accuracy = \frac{\text{Right times in the game}}{\text{Total times in the game}} \qquad (1)$$

Accuracy is showed at the homepage of the app (Fig. 3), in shape of circle around the course name. A grey circle means unlearned; a red circle means $0 \sim 25\%$ *accuracy*; a yellow circle means $25 \sim 75\%$ *accuracy*; a green circle means $75 \sim 100\%$ *accuracy*.

- **Course recommendation.** According to the training records, the app can automatically recommend those courses with low *Accuracy* to parents. At the homepage (Fig. 3), those courses will be marked with an orange icon.

The Smart Toy. Tongue movement is one of the essential factors for speech. Hence, New Voice also includes a speech training toy for children (Fig. 4), which can display the tongue movement as a real man speak Chinese. The toy is a tumbler, in case children drop and break it. The shape of the toy is like a bird. Children can observe and touch its mouth and tongue when having speech training. In that way, they can understand the right way to pronounce and imitate the tongue and mouth movement from the toy.

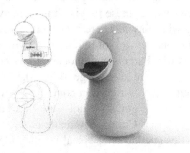

Fig. 4. Smart toy

The tongue and mouth movement is under the control of the app. When the video in the app is playing, the tongue and the mouth of the toy move according to the content of video.

3.3   Experiments

The experiments were designed based on the design guidelines, aiming to compare ICT-based speech training with traditional speech training. The comparison experiments were divided to 3 parts: access to speech training, parent participation and attraction to children.

Comparing Access to Speech Training. Three experts (two doctors and a speech therapist from Shanghai Children's hospital) were invited to compare the two approaches in the aspect of access to speech training. They assessed and graded the two speech training approaches on the aspect of access.

Comparing Parent Participation. Eight families with hearing impaired children and one therapist were invited to the experiments. All the hearing impaired children had regain part hearing by operation,but still needed to have speech training. The eight children were divided into two groups. Four children needed to learn a Chinese word by traditional way first and then another similar Chinese word by ICT-based way. These two words were of an equivalent level of difficulty. The other four children learned in reverse order. The traditional training was offered by a therapist and the ICT-based one was offered by a parent with New Voice. Each process lasted for half an hour and were divided into 4 parts:

- Review: children were led to review last course and required to answer questions about last course.
- Study: children learned the assigned words.
- Practice: children practiced the assigned words constantly.
- Reinforce: children were led to practice the less skilled words.

The experiments were both recorded by camera. Two experimenters observed and took notes. The duration of parent participation were recorded by experimenters. Parents finished questionnaires and graded the participation degree of themselves after the experiments.

Comparing Attraction to Children. This comparison experiment was the same with the above one. The parents finished questionnaires and graded the attraction degree to children after the experiment. The emotion performance of children in the two processes was recorded by experimenters with emotion scores. The scores ranged from -2 to 2. -2 means very unhappy; -1 means a little unhappy; 0 means no obvious emotion; 1 means a little happy; 2 means very happy. Experimenters took notes of what happened when emotion varied.

3.4   Results

Access to Speech Training. Experts graded traditional speech training approach and ICT-based approach in the aspect of access (full mark is 10). The scores are shown in Table 1. The score of ICT-based approach is higher than the traditional one.

Table 1. Scores of two approaches in the aspect of access

Expert No.		1	2	3	Average
Score	Traditional	4.5	3	5	4.17
	ICT-based	7	6.5	8	7.17

Experts affirmed that portable autonomous household medical supplies is trend of the development. Due to lack and misallocation of professional resources, it is hard to access to professional speech training in some remote areas of China. Traditional speech training is based on the direct interaction between children and therapist via a set of activities developed by the therapist. This direct interaction is essential and effective in giving a personal feedback to each child, but this approach requires a high number of therapists to help all the hearing impaired children in case of slowing down the maximum progress in speech, that, unfortunately, is not feasible now in most of the cases. New Voice is a good ICT-based household medical supply. With it, doctors and speech therapists can guide parents to participate in speech training in the distance. In a degree, ICT-based speech training makes up of professional resources shortage, for professional knowledge is popularized among ordinary families through ICTs and more children can have speech training in time.

Table 2. Participation duration of eight parents in two training processes

Parent No.		1	2	3	4	5	6	7	8	Average
Participation Duration (min)	Traditional	5	8	4.5	8.5	10	5	7	7	6.875
	ICT-based	22	23	24	30	28	21.5	22	26	24.5625

Parent Participation. Participation duration of parents in two training processes was recorded in Table 2.

According to the experimental data, all the eight parents participated much longer in ICT-based process than in the traditional one. It proves that parent participation is improved in speech training process by ICT.

In the traditional process, the speech therapist was mainly responsible for the whole training process, while parents dominantly participated in the review part to inform the therapist of the practice performance of children at home and consulted corresponding questions.

However, in the ICT-based process, parents offered speech training by themselves. They received professional training knowledge by app. When they needed to leave temporarily, children practiced with the video in the app.

Attraction to Children. Emotion performance of the eight children in the two training processes was marked by emotion scores by each minute. For example, the emotion performance of one child was recorded in Table 3 and Fig. 5, according to which average emotion score of the two processes was calculated and displayed in Table 4 and Fig. 6.

Table 3. Emotion performance of one child in two training processes

Time(min)		0	1	2	3	4	5	6	7	8	9	10	11	12	13	14	15	16	17
Emotion Score	Traditional	0	-1	-1	0	1	1	0	0	0	0	0	0	0	0	0	2	2	2
	ICT-based	0	-1	-1	0	1	1	1	1	1	2	2	2	2	2	2	2	2	0

Time(min)		18	19	20	21	22	23	24	25	26	27	28	29	30	Average
Emotion Score	Traditional	2	1	0	-2	1	1	-1	-2	-2	-2	-2	-2	-2	**-0.13**
	ICT-based	2	0	-1	-2	1	1	1	1	1	1	2	2	2	**0.97**

According to the experimental data, seven children were happier in ICT-based process than in the traditional one and only one child was on the contrary. It proves that ICT-based speech training process is more attractive to children.

In the traditional training process, children learned words by repeating what the speech therapist said. The speech therapists corrected pronunciation mistakes of children again and again. In that way, children were easy to be tired of monotonous and repeating training modes. They were forced to have training. On the contrary, parents taught children words and demonstrated how to pronounce with the smart toy in the ICT-based training process. Children were guided to practice with the toy and reinforce words in games on their own. Children were happy naturally and the fun of speech training was significantly increased through games and toys.

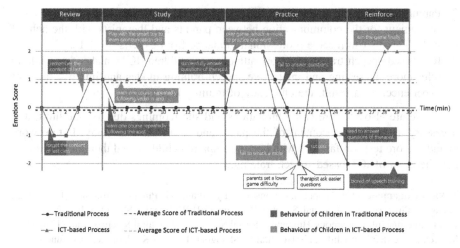

Fig. 5. Emotion performance of one child in two training processes

Table 4. Average emotion scores of each child in two training processes

Child No.		1	2	3	4	5	6	7	8
Average Emotion Score	**Traditional**	-0.13	0.3	-0.26	0.56	1.34	-1.21	1.27	0.13
	ICT-based	0.97	0.47	1.03	0.73	1.57	-0.75	1.02	1.16

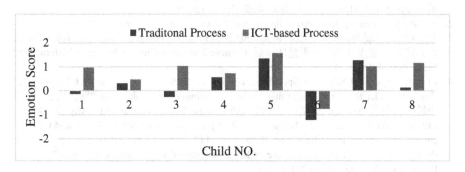

Fig. 6. Average emotion scores of each child in two training processes

4   Conclusion

In this paper, the application of ICTs in speech training has been proposed, and a comparison with traditional speech training process has been made. The comparison results are as follows:

1. ICT-based speech training are more accessible. In result, families with hearing impaired children can have access to speech training in time.

2. Parents can participate more in ICT-based speech training. Besides, it is more convenient for the communication between parents and therapists with the help of ICTs. Parents can receive professional guidance from experts by ICTs.
3. ICT-based speech training is more attractive to children. ICTs make it possible to offer more interesting and interactive speech training modes and improve the user experience. As a result, the efficiency of training is improved.

There are also some research limitations and shortcomings due to time limit, it is necessary to further the content of the paper and to add further study. Future work includes more tests on families with hearing-impaired children and then there will be a next iteration of ICT-based speech training.

Acknowledgement. This paper is sponsored by Shanghai Pujiang Program (13PJC072), Shanghai Philosophy and Social Science Program (2012BCK001), Shanghai Jiao Tong University Interdisciplinary among Humanity, Social Science and Natural Science Fund (13JCY02). Moreover, we thank to Children's Hospital of Shanghai, Lanxilu Kindergarten, Co-funding TV Program-the Makers and the students of Shanghai Jiao Tong University who have contributed to this research.

References

1. Sun, X., Yu, L., Qu, C.: An epidemiological study on the hearing impaired population identified in China and proposed intervention strategies 中国听力残疾构成特点及康复对策. Chin. Sci. J. Hear. Speech Rehabil. **2**, 21–24 (2008)
2. Summary of hearing impaired children. http://www.infzm.com/content/104975
3. The whole rehabilitation service for hearing impairment children in China lags behind 中国听力障碍儿童康复服务水平整体落后. Chinese Journal of Clinical Medicine Maternal and Child 9(3), 419(2013)
4. Zhu, Q.: Special Children's Speech Rehabilitation Status Investigation and Performance Research under the Background that Medical Combined with Education "医教结合" 背景下特殊儿童言语康复的现状调查及绩效研究. East China Normal University (2014)
5. Liu, X., Toki, E.I., Pange, J.: The use of ICT in preschool education in Greece and China: a comparative study. Procedia – Soc. Behav. Sci. **112**, 1167–1176 (2014)
6. Panagiotakou, C., Pange, J.: The use of ICT in preschool music education. Procedia – Soc. Behav. Sci. **2**, 3055–3059 (2010)
7. Drigas, A., Petrova, A.: ICTs in speech and language therapy. Int. J. Eng. Pedagogy (iJEP) **4**(1), 49–54 (2014)
8. Huang, Z., Du, X.,: Speech therapy 言语障碍的评估与矫治 29 (2006)
9. Leigh, G.: Changing parameters in deafness and deaf education: greater opportunity but continuing diversity. In: Marschark, M., Hauser, P.C. (eds.) Deaf Cognition Foundations and Outcomes, pp. 24–51. Oxford University Press, New York (2008)
10. VidKids (2014). http://www.vidkids.org
11. Constantinescu, G.: Satisfaction with telemedicine for teaching listening and spoken language to children with hearing loss. J. Telemedicine & Telecare **18**(5), 267–272 (2012)
12. Witsawakiti, N., Suchato, A., Punyabukkana, P.: Thai language e-training for the hard of hearing. Spec. Issue Int. J Comput. Internet and Management **14**(1), 41.1–41.6 (2006)
13. Meng, Z.: Baby Psychology 婴儿心理学. Beijing University Press, Cambridge (1997)

14. Li, S.: Discuss the role of parents in rehabilitation education of hearing impaired children 浅谈家长在听障儿童康复教育中的作用. Educ. Chin. After-sch. **2**, 26 (2011)
15. Wang, X., Tao, Y.: Recommendations for the hearing impaired infants family early intervention 关于听障婴幼儿家庭早期干预的建议. Sci. Innov. **16**, 131–132 (2014)
16. Yan, Q.: How to arouse hearing impaired children's interest in speech learning 寓教于乐寓学于趣_如何在语言训练中激发聋童的学习兴趣. The New Course **10**, 419 (2012)
17. Hoben, K., Morris, J.: PATSy: Innovations in Learning for Speech and Language Therapy. Bulletin of the Royal College of Speech and Language Therapists (2005)
18. Popovici, D.V., Buică-Belciu, C.: Professional challenges in computer-assisted speech therapy. Procedia-Soc. Behav. Sci. **33**, 518–522 (2012)
19. Toki, E.I., Pange, J., Mikropoulos, T.A.: An online expert system for diagnostic assessment procedures on young children's oral speech and language. Procedia Comput. Sci. **14**, 428–437 (2012)
20. Paniagua Martín, F., Colomo Palacios, R., García-Crespo, Á.: MAS: Learning support software platform for people with disabilities. In: Proceedings of the 1st ACM SIGMM International Workshop on Media Studies and Implementations that Help Improving Access to Disabled Users, pp. 47-52 October (2009)
21. Öster, A.M., House, D., Protopapas, A., Hatzis: A presentation of a new EU project for speech therapy: OLP (Ortho-Logo-Paedia). In: Proceedings of the XV Swedish Phonetics Conference (Fonetik 2002), pp. 29-31 May 2002
22. Bastanfard, A., Rezaei, N.A., Mottaghizadeh, M., Fazel, M.: A novel multimedia educational speech therapy system for hearing impaired children. In: Qiu, G., Lam, K.M., Kiya, H., Xue, X.-Y., Kuo, C.-C., Lew, M.S. (eds.) PCM 2010, Part II. LNCS, vol. 6298, pp. 705–715. Springer, Heidelberg (2010)

Universal Access to Health Applications and Services

Haptics-Enabled Surgical Training System with Guidance Using Deep Learning

Ehren Biglari[1,2], Marie Feng[1], John Quarles[1,2], Edward Sako[3], John Calhoon[3], Ronald Rodriguez[4], and Yusheng Feng[1,5(✉)]

[1] Center for Simulation, Visualization and Real-Time Prediction, San Antonio, TX, USA
{ebiglari,marie.feng}@gmail.com
[2] Department of Computer Science, The University of Texas at San Antonio, San Antonio, TX, USA
jpq@cs.utsa.edu
[3] Department of Cardiothoracic Surgery, The University of Texas Health Science Center at San Antonio, San Antonio, TX, USA
{sako,calhoon}@uthscsa.edu
[4] Department of Urology, The University of Texas Health Science Center at San Antonio, San Antonio, TX, USA
rodriguezr32@uthscsa.edu
[5] Department of Mechanical Engineering, The University of Texas at San Antonio, San Antonio, TX, USA
yusheng.feng@utsa.edu

Abstract. In this paper, we present a haptics-enabled surgical training system integrated with deep learning for characterization of particular procedures of experienced surgeons to guide medical residents-in-training with quantifiable patterns. The prototype of virtual reality surgical system is built for open-heart surgery with specific steps and biopsy operation. Two abstract surgical scenarios are designed to emulate incision and biopsy surgical procedures. Using deep learning algorithm (autoencoder), the two surgical procedures were trained and characterized. Results show that a vector with 30 real-valued components can quantify both surgical patterns. These values can be used to compare how a resident-in-training performs differently as opposed to an experienced surgeon so that quantifiable corrective training guidance can be provided.

Keywords: Virtual surgical training system · Haptic device · Machine learning · Deep learning algorithm · Autoencoder · Motion tracking and quantification

1   Introduction

Patient safety is a fundamental issue in medical and health care. It was estimated by The Office of Inspector General for Health and Human Services that approximately 440,000 patients suffer some types of preventable harm due to medical errors in hospitals every year, which becomes the third leading cause of deaths in U.S. Behind heart disease and cancer [1]. The surgical skill of a surgeon is one of the important attributes to patient

© Springer International Publishing Switzerland 2015
M. Antona and C. Stephanidis (Eds.): UAHCI 2015, Part III, LNCS 9177, pp. 267–278, 2015.
DOI: 10.1007/978-3-319-20684-4_26

safety. The current master-apprentice style of training in operation room seems not to fully prepare medical students since they do not have enough time to practice within the period of their training. Also, it is recognized that residents-in-training need to be exposed to various surgical emergency situations to be prepared psychologically and skill-wise. One of the important questions is: how are medical students expected to be well trained and not make costly mistakes given the limited amount of practice time on patients? To resolve this dilemma, one approach is to design a realistic surgical simulator system, which may provide a training platform for basic skill practices as well as emergency response. The advantages to use surgical simulator include (1) motion tracking and quantification of hand motion, (2) integration of haptic device to quantify force feedback, and (3) use of machine learning algorithm to compare hand motion between experienced surgeons and medical residents-in-training.

Although the concept of using visualization for skill training may be traced back to the 1970s and 1980s with videogames and primitive flight simulators [2, 3], only in the 1990s (with 3D graphics) and the 2000s (with the use of motion sensors for motion control) has visualization become a tool to construct incredibly realistic virtual reality (VR) based training. One of the successful VR applications is training pilots using flight simulators [4–6]. Similar to a flight simulator, VR simulators also play an important role in medical education [7–9]. A VR surgical training simulator is a computer system with certain human/machine interface to simulate surgical procedures in a virtual world for the purpose of training medical professionals, without the need of a real patient, cadaver or animal. A surgical training simulator can provide the capability to learn and practice specific techniques in a controlled setting allowing emphasis on specific aspects of these techniques. Reported evidence shows that VR-based training leads to faster adaptation of novel psychomotor skills and improved surgical performance [10]. It can also save time to be trained in the operating room that may reduce training cost and improve the risk to the patient.

In spite of surgical simulators emergence more than twenty years ago, the quest for their effectiveness has continued up to recently [11]. The challenge to teach a set of complicated surgical skills involves translating a heuristic experience from a skillful surgeon to a trainee who needs to comprehend the given oral instructions and convert to hand motions.

In this paper, we present a haptics-enabled surgical training system integrated with deep learning algorithm for characterization of particular procedures of experienced surgeons to guide medical residents-in-training with quantifiable patterns. We have developed a realistic prototype of VR surgical system for open-heart surgery with specific steps and biopsy operation. Two abstract surgical scenarios are designed to emulate incision and biopsy operational patterns. Using a version of deep learning algorithm [12] proposed by Hinton et al., we demonstrate that a vector with 30 real-valued components can quantify both surgical patterns. These values can be further used to compare how a resident-in-training performs differently as opposed to an experienced surgeon so that more quantifiable corrective training guidance can be provided.

2   Haptics-Enabled Virtual Surgery Training System

In the process of learning, visualization as a cognitive skill plays a central role in navigating different modes of representation. Visualization allows one to make cognitive connections between imaged and observed reality and acts as a bridge for disseminating and accepting knowledge between theory and reality [13]. The same principles also apply to medical education [14]. With enhancement of haptic devices, the virtual surgery training system can be designed to be more realistic by providing "touch-and-feel" when performing on the virtual system.

Our ultimate goal is to develop a comprehensive VR surgical training system with multiple features and human-machine interfaces including 3D immersive visualization, haptic devices with three and six degree of freedoms, free-hand haptic device and motion tracking backed controllers. We have chosen to train for the surgical scenarios of cardiac surgery and the common cancer operation of a biopsy. We have designed the system with the following considerations: (1) setting difficulty levels for each surgical task, (2) incorporating rationale for each difficulty setting, (3) designing assessment methodology based on learning proficiency, and (4) providing feedback based on performance criteria of expert proficiency. By using advanced visualization to recreate the immersive surgical environment and realistic human-computer interface, a surgical simulator can provide virtual training environment for medical students as what a flight simulator offers to train pilots.

One of the benefits to use a realistic simulator for surgical training is, to certain extent, that it could take the place of "cadaver labs," and make it much easier for surgeons to have access to high fidelity training on "virtual live tissues" that could be made to bleed excessively and provide various anatomical variations that complicate the procedures. It is tremendously advantageous to use a surgical simulator with digital patient over "dead tissue" simulation with a cadaver. This would also allow us to teach not just the procedure, but how to deal with complications of the procedure that require immediate decisions and changes in management. To offer realistic training simulation, it requires both a virtual environment and a realistic haptic interface. This interface needs to be able to track hand movements and allows the user to "grab and use" surgical tools in a virtual environment to actually perform the procedure.

Our design of surgical simulator consists of three major components: (1) integrated immersive virtual patient/environment visualization module, (2) haptic interface module, and (3) motion tracking and machine learning feedback module. The integrated immersive virtual patient/environment visualization provides a realistic environment for the trainee. Also, given that surgical rooms can vary within hospitals as well as between hospitals, the virtual surgical rooms can be customized to mirror a specific room in order to better prepare the trainee on where screens, certain tools, and lights may be oriented. Haptic interface provides trainees with "touch and feel," which is necessary for their skill training and transfer to real surgical. The motion tracking records their hand motion and quantify each surgical step to be analyzed and categorized by machine learning algorithms to distinguish the level of skillfulness for certain tasks. The comparative analysis will show the difference of a resident-in-training and an experienced surgeon. Using machine learning algorithms (e.g., [15]), the feedback will be provided for

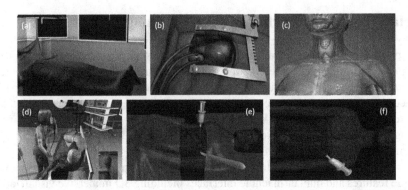

Fig. 1. Prototype of surgical simulator with organ removal function on a digital patient in a virtual surgical room: (a) Virtual surgical room environment with a covered digital patient laying on the surgical table and surgical lighting fixtures (not shown). (b) The digital patient with clamped open heart and connected to the tubes of a perfusion pump. (c) A realistic digital patient with detailed muscle group and bone structures. (d) A digital patient laying down on his side along with a digital nurse checking his vital signs, (e) a digital patient on tan operation table. A user can use two-hand haptic control for virtual operation. Both biopsy needle and scalp are shown in the figure. (f) A digital patient with exposed internal organ for virtual biopsy operation.

designing the next practice set. Figure 1 shows a preliminary model of a digital patient, a typical section procedure with haptic interface and associated surgical environment.

We have developed a 3D modular virtual system that can be visualized by immersive visualization devices such as Oculus Rift [16] that allows a user to perform incision and organ removal operation (see Fig. 1e). The visualization framework we developed is based on the open source *Processing programming language*. Processing is a set of libraries (http://processing.org) that can be considered as an extension of Java language. The Processing language offers capability of rapid development of visualizations while providing an environment that is easy to learn. We chose this environment to make the development of custom scientific visualizations easy for researchers, to minimize the time spent on visualization development. In addition, the platform also has the added benefit of being suitable for real-time rendering to any platform running Java. In addition to Processing language and the MPE library, we have added our own framework for programmable data-driven visualizations, integration with the Oculus Rift Virtual Reality headset, and integration with the motion and orientation controller the Sixense Razer Hydra, OMNI/Phantom, and Quanser/HD2 haptic devices.

The developed programmable data-driven visualization framework - Immersive Data Visualizer (IDV), consists of eight components: (1) a Wavefront.obj file loader, (2) an XML data file loader, (3) a 3D force-directed graph algorithm, (4) a rendering module, (5) an animation module for time series visualization, (6) a Oculus Rift VR headset integration module, (7) a Sixense Hydra Razor controller integration, and (8) a VizWall (large tiled screen) integration module. The IDV can also be used for finite-element simulation and visualization in engineering applications. In fact, real-time finite element simulations can be programmed in Processing and displayed on the VizWall and Oculus Rift. Alternatively, MATLAB can be used to generate finite-element simulations and the data can be saved as.csv point cloud file, and an optional.csv link file. The visualization can then, optionally, be programmatically manipulated and combined with other external data loaded by the XML file. To achieve visual realism, both professional version of 3ds Max (http://www.autodesk.com/products/3ds-max/overview) and UNITY (http://unity3d.com/unity) software are used to create digital patients and surgical room environment.

3 Surgery Training and Pattern Quantification by Deep Learning Algorithm

3.1 Abstraction of Surgical Procedures

As discussed previously, the challenge to train medical students to be a future surgeon is how to effectively transfer knowledge and experience from a skillful surgeon to a resident-in-training. The current practice heavily relies on oral instructions with heuristic commends. If typical surgical procedures can be quantitatively described, it would be much easier to teach surgical steps and correct mistakes with precise instructions and commands. To that end, we took two surgical procedures and made two abstract scenarios so that machine learning can be applied. The first scenario is chosen to be incision procedure, which is usually performed by cutting through tissues by following marked line segments. We designed a template with six letters that represent various curves and sharp turns (Fig. 2). The participants were asked to trace the letter accurately with a time limit in mind. Also, the elbow of the drawing hand cannot touch the desk for support while tracing the letters.

C D Δ H P S

Fig. 2. First abstract surgical procedure for machine learning: tracing six letters *C, S, Δ, H, P, S*.

The second surgical abstraction emulates biopsy operation. In Fig. 3, three circles represent an organ with embedded tumor (top), a nerve bundle (bottom left) and a blood vessel (bottom right), respectively. To increase the level of difficulty of emulated surgical procedure, various sizes and distances are designed so that different biopsy path needs to be chosen in order not to damage either the nerve bundle or the blood vessel. The participants were asked to draw a straight line from the bottom of the square to the black spot representing the tumor. It is required that the line has to be drawn as straight

Fig. 3. Second abstract surgical procedure for biopsy tumor tissue embedded in a normal organ (top circle with black spot). The biopsy path cannot penetrate either the nerve bundle (the circle to the bottom left) or the nearby major blood vessel (the circle to the bottom right).

as possible with a time limit in mind. Also, the elbow of the drawing hand cannot touch the desk for support while drawing.

3.2 Data Generation and Imaging Processing

The imaging data for the first abstract surgical scenario are generated by tracing the letters to mimic the incision procedure. One set of images are treated as the master patterns and used as references for comparison (Figs. 2 and 3). Fifteen sets of images that constitute 7,200 letter-tracing images were made. The imaging data for the second abstract are generated by drawing 6,000 biopsy line images. There were fourteen participants who represent fourteen inexperienced residents. The original template is treated as work from the experienced surgeon. Six letters are chosen to represents both smooth and sharp turns. Five biopsy images are designed to represent various sizes and distances for tumor, nerve bundle, and blood vessel. As instructed, the biopsy line needs to be drawn from the bottom and reach to the tumor (black spot in the middle) without touching the nerve bundle (circle on the bottom left filled in with small dots) and the blood vessel (circle on the bottom right filled with big dots). Otherwise, the image will be considered as surgical accident. All images are scanned and processed for machine learning (see detailed processing steps in Sect. 4.2).

3.3 Deep Learning Algorithms for Pattern Comparison and Feature Extraction

Machine learning algorithms are a set of methodology that automatically detects features and patterns in the data, which can be used either for classification and decision-making. Machine learning, as a scientific discipline, is widely used in many areas [17]. It is even more so after Hinton et al. demonstrated that training process can be accelerated by using deep belief network and efficient gradient calculation by contractive divergence [12]. In this paper, we are interested in exploring applications of deep learning algorithm to quantify features and patterns of surgical procedure illustrated by two abstract scenarios so that surgical outcomes between an experienced surgeon and a resident-in-training so that identified patterns can be objectively compared.

The classical deep learning algorithm is built on neural network by stacking single-layer Restricted Boltzmann Machine (RBM) onto each other to form so-called Deep Belief Network (DBN) [12]. By recognizing difficulty in training a densely-connected, directed belief net with many hidden layers, Hinton et al. pointed out that poor approximation of true conditional distribution due to either presumptuous independency or scalability as number of parameters increases. To overcome this challenge, they presented the deep belief network (DBN) model in which the two hidden layers form an undirected associative memory and the remaining hidden layers form a directed acyclic graph that converts the representations in the associative memory into observable variables such as the pixels of an image. This algorithm extracts features and patterns to form of bit vectors. By comparing these vectors, it is possible to adjust model parameters to produce predicted data closer to the given training data. Thus, this algorithm can be used as a form of unsupervised learning. Considering the learning process by a resident-in-training, it seems that the learning style is very similar - medical students learn how to perform surgery through a show-and-tell apprenticeship. However, it is very difficult for a resident-in-training to translate what he/she hear and see into hand motions precisely. With machine learning to quantify the difference, it is possible to make this translation in a more precise manner so that the medical training can be more efficient.

Deep learning perhaps is one of the most rapid growing fields in the areas of machine learning (see a collection of review papers in [18] and latest review [19]). In this paper, we have adopted Hinton's deep learning MATLAB code (http://www.cs.toronto.edu/~hinton/) with modifications so that it will be applicable to images we obtained from two abstract surgical scenarios. We used both DBN classifier and autoencoder to process the image data and seek for features and patterns between the reference images as the surgical outcome of an experienced surgeon and images generated by fourteen participants. The learning rate and other parameters in the code are adjusted for optimal learning.

4   Results and Discussion

4.1   Virtual Surgical Simulation Environment

To ensure training effectiveness, our Virtual Surgical Training (VST) System is designed with built-in advanced features of monitoring, alarming, engineering changes based on increased knowledge of biomechanical interactions during surgeries. To make the VST System more useful for medical education, adverse events are designed with built-in results of unexpected emergency scenarios, which are based on human error or operational patient risk factors documented in the literature or real surgical cases. In VST System, when the emergency scenarios do arise, it is expected for a resident-in-training to take the first step is to recognize the problem, then make assessment of the extent of the problem, and finally formulate a solution and proceed to perform the surgery with formulated solution in a systematic step-wise methodical manner. In almost all the emergency cases, time is a critical factor. All the steps mentioned above have to be accomplished in a few minutes with or without availability of additional consultation and assistance from more experienced surgeons.

Our current prototype system (Fig. 1, also [20]) uses the Oculus Rift Virtual Reality headset provides an immersive 3D visualization environment for guiding and controlling simulations. Other viewers are able to watch on the large tiled screen called VizWall as an effective education tool. In addition, the MPE environment (provided by TACC at the University of Texas at Austin) makes loading data, models, and animations from a variety of sources easy and intuitive. The data can contain reference to 3D models, animations, CSV point clouds, CSV link clouds, and CSV/XML topological data. Point clouds can contain additional metadata such as vectors, colors, scales, rotation, and OBJ model name or number. Also, data-driven visualization can be expanded with Fruchterman-Rheingold force-directed graph algorithm, and parameters of that expansion can be changed in the data-driven XML file. Furthermore, in addition to data-driven visualization, after the data is loaded, the user can easily program visualizations that dynamically modify point locations and links based.

4.2   Training Results and Applications

To emulate incision procedure, we have participants write on templates to trace the letters as quickly as possible to introduce some variation in the lines so that they resemble scalpel cutting on marked traces. For the biopsy procedure, we have participants start at the bottom edge of each figure and draw a straight line up towards the black dot (tumor region), which signifies the presence of some cancer that needs a biopsy or other surgical intervention. After scanning all marked images, we obtain a dataset of images we number and group by participant.

Each of our fourteen participants marked on 80 rows similar to those shown in Fig. 4. The template rows of letters are evenly distributed across 20 sheets of papers with 4 rows per sheet. Similarly, the biopsy lines were drawn by each of our participants with 4 rows per sheet and 20 sheets per participant (Fig. 5). The participants used a colored pen that makes image-processing techniques for marking line extraction process much simpler.

Fig. 4. One row of images from letters image dataset

Fig. 5. One row of surgical lines obtained from image dataset

The extraction process of marked images is straightforward. First we use a SnapScan S510 M to scan in all of the sheets. Each of the participant markings for both letters and surgical lines is scanned into one PDF file. We use a GIMP 2 plugin to quickly convert PDFs into PNG images and save them to separate directories numbered 1 to 14 for each participant. In addition, some of the template sheets were scanned in upside down. Rather than flipping them manually, the Matlab *flipud()* function makes the process simple to program and the end result is the same. Given images of letter markings each containing four rows of C, D, Δ, H, P, and S, we isolate the bounds of each letter on the page and extract the colored marking. In the process of images of marking extraction, the marking image is downsampled and converted to a 63 pixel by 70 grayscale image consisting of double floating point value between 0.0 and 1.0. The purpose of downsampling is to reduce the total amount of data per image, and thereby reduce the total dataset size. Each of the isolated grayscale images is added to a MATLAB matrix named "letters". Similarly, given images containing four rows of surgical line markings, we isolate the bounds of each box containing a surgical scenario with line markings, and perform a similar colored pen extraction tailored for extraction from white backgrounds. For both of these extractions, we wrote a MATLAB script for preprocessing to obtain the data set. Each of the isolated grayscale images is added to a MATLAB matrix named "surglines".

Next, the "letters" matrix was converted to batches of 96 letters and processed with a Deep Belief Network (DBN). First, we isolate the extent of each letter or surgical line marking and produce 4 random shifts that keep each marking within the bounds of the image. We use an autoencoder DBN and pre-train a series of stacked Restricted Boltzmann Machines (RBM) with layer sizes 4410-2100-1050-525-30. To train the RBMs we employ the wake-sleep algorithm with one step of the Contrastive Divergence algorithm per epoch (CD1). Then, we unroll the neural network into a neural network with layer sizes 4410-2100-1050-525-30-525-1050-2100-4410 and train by applying conjugate gradient with 4 lines. On an 8 core Intel machine at 3.5 GHz and 32 GB of RAM this training process takes approximately 18 h to reach a batch test set MSE of 39.28 after 131 epochs (Fig. 6). However, we expect that the code will run significantly faster on a GPU based computer. We apply a similar technique with the "surglines" matrix. However, we instead use a batch size of 100 and a input/reconstruction layer of size of 7007, due to the larger image size of 91 by 77 pixels. After training we obtain a batch test set MSE of 8.59 after 101 epochs of conjugate gradient.

Fig. 6. The letters during different phases of training using the deep learning algorithm

At the end of training, we obtained the results (Figs. 7 and 8) that letters and surgical lines can be represented by a series of 30 floating-point values that are strongly correlated with characteristics of the shapes of the letters involved and the individual characteristics of the participants.

Fig. 7. Original letters (top) reconstructed (bottom) from 30 floating point values on test MSE of 39.28 after 131 epochs.

Fig. 8. Original surgical (top) reconstructed (bottom) from 30 floating-point values on test set with MSE of 8.59 after 101 epochs.

Fig. 9. Typical plots of the mean of the 30 floating point values for each participant and each of the six letters as a grayscale bar plot. Each participant has his or her own unique characteristics and mean pattern that is generally consistent for their tracing patterns (only Participant 1, 2, 3, 4 and 6 shown here).

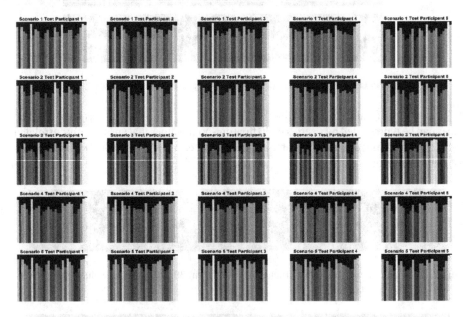

Fig. 10. Typical plots of the mean of the 30 floating point values for each participant and each of the five surgical scenarios as a grayscale bar plot. Each participant has their own unique mean pattern that is generally consistent for their surgical lines.

The plots below (Figs. 9 and 10) show characteristic vectors of 30 floating point numbers that can be used to determine unique characteristic of surgical lines that can be used to quantitatively assess the characteristics of surgical techniques. Further study may allow the choice of an optimal surgical line for a surgical scenario based on the association of characteristic vectors with outcomes by applying a classification based Deep Belief Network.

5   Conclusions and Future Work

We have demonstrated that the prototype of a virtual reality surgical system is built for open-heart surgery with specific steps and biopsy operation. We analyzed two abstract surgical scenarios designed to emulate incision and biopsy surgical patterns using deep learning algorithm. It is found that two surgical patterns generated by each participant can be uniquely characterized by a vector with 30 real-valued (floating-point) components. These vectors can be used to compare how a resident-in-training performs differently as opposed to an experienced surgeon. We plan to further investigate the correlation of these characteristic vectors with the patterns generated by various hand motions. We will also study the relationship between these vectors with cutting force, surgical path, duration of each cut, and other surgical factors of interest.

Acknowledgement. This project is sponsored by San Antonio Life Science Institute (SALSI) as part of the Medical Data Analytics and Visualization Cluster grant. We also appreciate the assistance of Sam Newman from Multi-media Lab at University of Texas Health Science Center at San Antonio, who generated digital representation of the virtual surgical room and the patient.

References

1. http://www.propublica.org/article/how-many-die-from-medical-mistakes-in-us-hospitals
2. Valverde, H.H.: A review of flight simulator transfer of training studies. Hum. Factors: J. Hum. Factors Ergon. Soc. **15**(6), 510–522 (1973)
3. Yan, J.K.: Advances in computer-generated imagery for flight simulation. Comput. Graph. and Appl.w IEEE **5**(8), 37–51 (1985)
4. R. N. Haber, "Flight Simulation," Scientific American, 255(1), 1986
5. Hays, R.T., Jacobs, J.W., Prince, C., Salas, E.: Flight simulator training effectiveness: A meta-analysis. Mil. Psychol. **4**(2), 63–74 (1992)
6. Hays, R.T., Jacobs, J.W., Prince, C., Salas, E.: Requirements for future research in flight simulation training: Guidance based on a meta-analytic review. Int. J. Aviat. Psychol. **2**(2), 143–158 (1992)
7. Satava, R.M.: Virtual reality surgical simulator. Surg. Endosc. **7**(3), 203–205 (1993)
8. Tekkis, P.P., et al.: Evaluation of the learning curve in laparoscopic colorectal surgery: comparison of right-sided and left-sided resections. Ann. Surg. **242**(1), 83–91 (2005)
9. Liu, A., Tendick, F., Cleary, K., Kaufmann, C.: A survey of surgical simulation: applications, technology, and education. Presence: Teleoperators Virtual Environ. **12**(6), 599–614 (2003)
10. Aggarwal, R., Grantcharov, T.P., Eriksen, J.R., Blirup, D., Kristiansen, V.B., Funch-Jensen, P., Darzi, A.: An evidence-based virtual reality training program for novice laparoscopic surgeons. Ann. Surg. **244**(2), 310 (2006)
11. Grantcharov, T.P.: Is virtual reality simulation an effective training method in surgery? Nat. Clin. Pract. Gastroenterol. Hepatol. **5**(5), 232–233 (2008)

12. Hinton, G.E., Osindero, S., The, Y.-W.: A fast learning algorithm for deep belief nets. J. Neural Comput. **18**(7), 1527–1534 (2006)
13. Seymour, N.E.: VR to OR: a review of the evidence that virtual reality simulation improves operating room performance. World J. Surg. **32**(2), 182–188 (2008)
14. Larsen, C. R., Soerensen, J. L., Grantcharov, T. P., Dalsgaard, T., Schouenborg, L., Ottosen, C., Schroeder, T. V., Ottesen, B. S.: Effect of virtual reality training on laparoscopic surgery: randomised controlled trial, BMJ: British Medical Journal, 338, 2009
15. Entwistle, N.: Promoting deep learning through teaching and assessment: conceptual frameworks and educational contexts. In: Proceeding of TLRP Conference, Leicester, November 2000
16. Biglari, E., Feng, Y.: Interactive virtual reality driven learning framework for engineering and science education. In: Proceedings of American Society for Engineering Education Gulf-Southwest Conference, New Orleans, LA 2014
17. Murphy, K.P.: Machine Learning: A Probabilistic Perspective. MIT Press, Cambridge (2012)
18. Bengio, Y.: Learning deep architectures for AI. Found. Trends Mach. Learn. **2**(1), 1–127 (2009)
19. Schmidhuber, J.: deep learning in neural networks: an overview. Neural Networks **61**, 85–117 (2015)
20. Yasmin, S., Du, N., Chen, J., Feng, Y.: A Haptic-enabled novel approach to cardiovascular visualization. Comput. Animation and Virtual Worlds **25**(3–4), 255–269 (2014)

A Goal- and Context-Driven Approach in Mobile Period Tracking Applications

Richard A. Bretschneider[✉]

TOMORROW FOCUS News+ GmbH, Cologne, Germany
richard.bretschneider@netmoms.de

Abstract. Over the past few years the interest in period tracking apps increased, which represent a sub-genre of quantified self apps in women health. They are available in a variety of complexity levels ranging from simple menstruation diaries up to applications with complex fertility calculation algorithms. The goal of this paper is to propose an approach for a period tracking app with an adaptive user interface that takes the users goal and context into account. Our research focusses on the motivations to use a period tracker, the questions that users have regarding their cycle data and how a quantified self app could help in answering these questions.

Keywords: Self-tracking · Period tracking · Context · User experience · Personalization · User monitoring · Quantified self

1 Introduction

Period tracking originates from the medical field and has its roots long before the age of quantified self apps. Beginning of the early 1930s period tracking became important for calendar based contraceptive methods called Knaus-Ogino or rhythm method [12]. These kind of methods are based on the biological facts that most menstrual cycles can be divided into fertile and infertile phases. These phases can be roughly calculated from the average cycle length, but today this approach considered to be unreliable [4]. From the late 1930s until the early 1970s a couple of methods have been developed that take changes in one or more of the primary fertility signs basal body temperature, cervical mucus or cervical position of women into account. Usually women who were using one of those methods documented their symptoms with pen and paper on template sheets. With the rise of mobile technology and new personal informatics tools [6] it is possible to track symptoms and moods on mobile devices. Period tracking habits more and more shift towards using apps instead of pen-and-paper [5]. For the ongoing development of the NetMoms Cycle Calendar app for iOS and Android smartphones we are continuously researching in the field of HCI to meet the requirements and overcome common pitfalls in this special genre of self-tracking apps.

M. Antona and C. Stephanidis (Eds.): UAHCI 2015, Part III, LNCS 9177, pp. 279–287, 2015.
DOI: 10.1007/978-3-319-20684-4_27

2 Research

The NetMoms UX team conducted a competitive research of app reviews, an online survey and usability tests with pre-existing period tracking apps in a lab (5 participants) to gain insights and requirements for the first implementation of our own app. Based on these insights we built our first prototypes and the first implementation of the app which has been released in June 2014.

2.1 Competitive Research of App Reviews

In order to identify common pitfalls in period tracking we analysed comments on app ratings of 13 period tracking apps. Ratings of 7 apps were analysed in the Android Play Store, the ratings of 6 apps in the Apple iTunes Store. We don't see these comments as a reliable source for definite conclusions about the quality in HCI, but they were a useful indicator to develop the hypothesis for our first usability lab studies and the online survey. Frequently mentioned problems were the following:

– List of possible symptoms / moods is too confusing
– GUI lacks clarity
– Too few gradations to enter menstruation
– No option to set a reminder for the pill
– App is missing pregnancy mode

2.2 Online Survey

As an additional indicator for common problems in period tracking we set up an online survey that has been publicised on our website netmoms.de. The goal was to get more insight in typical behaviour of women using period trackers or substitute products. 90 % of the 196 women that participated, were using Smartphones on a daily basis, 61,60 % already used at least one period tracking app within the last year. 43 % of the participants mentioned they were tracking their period with an app for more than one year, 49,60 % were using such an app for less than a year, the remaining participants didn't answer this question. 22 % stated they already switched from one period tracking app to another. An interesting insight was that more than 50 % of the reasons, which can be seen in Fig. 1 mentioned for switching the app could directly be related to HCI; In 28,6 % the reason was "Too complex" and also in 28,6 % the participants mentioned that the app was "too confusing".

55 % of the participants said that they would use period tracking apps to get pregnant, while only 10 % would use it as contraception method. 63 % stated that they would use such an app just to observe their menstrual cycle without having birth control purposes in mind.

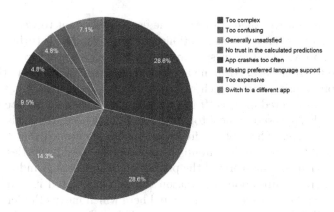

Fig. 1. Reasons to uninstall a period tracking app

2.3 Usability Tests with Pre-existing Apps

In order to gain understandings about typical problems and desires that users have when using period trackers, we tested pre-existing apps of competitors. This lab-based usability study consisted of five sessions with one user at a time. Besides the participant and the test-leader one note-taker was attending the test. Period tracking is a very personal topic, which may make the participants feel uncomfortable to talk about in a lab-situation. To reduce this effect we also strictly made sure that at least one person, either the test-leader or the note-taker was female. The session consisted of a screening questionnaire, a Concurrent Think Aloud Test (CTA) and a semi-structured retrospective interview. The CTA was recorded on audio and documented by the note-taker. One of the participants was using a period tracker on a daily basis, three were not using such an app at the moment, but used period tracker apps before and one participant never used one before. All participants were familiar in using smartphones and apps while three of the participants were iPhone users and two were using Android smartphones. For the test we used the respective device the user was familiar with. Per session one app has been tested. As the aim of the study was to gain insights about period trackers in general, but not on the usability of a certain app we decided to use different apps for the test sessions. The test itself was structured as a scripted set of tasks given to the participants. We prepared the app with a set of entries to simulate a long-term usage. The script was loosely based on a typical daily routine of a fictive woman using a period tracker in order to increase the chances to get pregnant. Summarized in short the tasks were the following:

1. Enter your basal body temperature
2. Enter that you had stomach aches and that you felt tired
3. Interpret the temperature chart of the current cycle. Based on that: Can you make a statement about your fertility?
4. Does the app tell you when your next fertile window is predicted?

As a general insight we could state that the users don't want to waste time with the process to enter data. It was mentioned to be extremely disturbing by three users, if the app was loading or synchronizing data for several seconds before it was possible to enter data. Also one app was displaying ads or alerts that stood in the way on entering data, which was mentioned to be distracting. One of the participants commented on this 'If it's early in the morning, I'm late to go out for work and this app shows me a ton of things I don't need, then this really can make me aggressive.' Three of the five participants mentioned that they would appreciate it, if the app would remind them of making specific entries. While all of the five participants interpreted the prediction of the fertile window correctly, all of them were unsure about the reason the app calculated it that way. E.g. one tester asked 'Okay, I see a flower symbol here which means I'm fertile at this day, I think. But I would have thought that, if I click on the symbol, I would get some kind of explanation.'

An interesting side-note is that three of the five participants mentioned their preference towards period trackers with an unobtrusive appearance and name. 'I don't want anybody using my phone to see that I have such an app.' one participant stated.

2.4   Critical Evaluation of the Test Methods

The outcome of the tests gave us valuable insights into common challenges and problems in mobile period tracking apps. For the special case of period tracking we determined some weaknesses of the specific methods:

Competitive Research of App Reviews. While the feedback comes directly from real life usage a typical problem regarding app store reviews is that most of the detailed feedback is negative. The majority of positive feedback is accompanied with short descriptions like 'Very good' or 'Helped me getting pregnant', but rarely detailed feedback about what exactly this user likes about the app. Another problem is that usually it's not clear in which context the app is being used (device type, knowledge about device and period tracking). Therefore the outcome of this kind of research only serves as indicator towards possible fields of problems.

Online Survey. Our survey gave us insights in the user's experiences with period tracking apps in the past. As this survey was de-contextualized from the current usage of any concrete product it was mostly helpful to learn about the users motivations and attitudes to use such apps.

Usability Tests. The CTAs conducted were an important source for behavioural data. As it is known that lab-situations can bias the participant's behaviour, [11] we encounter additional problems in the case of period tracking: At first the topic 'period tracking' may make the participants feel uncomfortable in talking about this very intimate topic. This leads to the second problem that real data of the users is too intimate and private to be used in an usability test.

3   User Goals in Period Tracking

The research we conducted led us to the conclusion that the user's motivations to track their cycle data could be classified in the two higher-level goals 'trying to conceive' and 'not trying to conceive'. While users of the first category are mainly tracking their data to find the most fertile days in their cycle (as close as possible to the ovulation), the motivations of the latter are more heterogeneous. Users not trying to conceive using this kind of apps for birth control, medical reasons (e.g. while they are under medical treatment against endometriosis) and/or to get to know their body and to learn about individual patterns of their cycle. Typical goals mentioned were the estimation of the beginning of the next menstruation or to see, if particular symptoms appear regularly in a certain phase of the cycle. The accuracy for the predictions and calculations about the fertile days and upcoming menstruation depends highly on what data the users track and how accurate and how regularly they measure this data. While tracking 'menstruation', 'basal body temperature' and 'cervical mucus' evolves from the medical origin of period trackers we now see a trend that modern period trackers are being perceived in a broader sense as 'all-purpose life tracker' instead of just a medical purpose (e.g. New York Times article written by Jenna Wortham [13]). The participants of our survey verified this observation: 83,8 % mentioned that tracking symptoms (like headache, skin problems or stomach ache) is an important feature, followed by 66,7 %, who said that tracking their mood is important. Tracking basal temperature (41 %) and cervical mucus (43,6 %) was valued as less important. While tracking all these different parameters could be seen as an all-in-one solution, current research in quantified self clearly points out the downsides of such a diversity of options: tracking too many parameters might cause tracking fatigue [3] and the users are often unclear about what tracking options count as use [9]. Users of period trackers usually are curious about how their entered data and the predicted fertility or predicted cycle beginning are related. Entering a bleeding or a temperature might have important consequences according to the fertility prediction, while entering stomach ache or any moods doesn't affect the predictions at all. So one important challenge is to make it clear and visible, if entering a certain value will lead to an update of any prediction.

4   Functionality of the NetMoms Cycle Calendar App

The core of the app is the possibility to track cycle related data for each calendar day. We implemented the following categories:

- Bleeding / Menstruation
- Basal body temperature
- Consistency of cervical mucus
- Symptoms (stomach ache, skin problems, ...)
- Influences (alcohol, timezone change,...)
- Moods (Happiness, desire to eat salty food, ...)

- Notes
- Tests (pregnancy test, ovulation test)
- Sexual intercourse

By entering a menstruation a new cycle gets started, so the first calendar day where a bleeding has been entered until the last day before the next bleeding (typically 26 - 30 days) is being interpreted as one cycle. Three methods were implemented to help the users to get insights about their fertility [8,10]: Knaus-Ogino method (rough fertility predictions based on average cycle length), temperature method (retrospective calculation of the fertile days based on daily measurements of the basal temperature) and symptothermal method (temperature method enhanced by daily measurements of the quality of the cervical mucus). The more complex the chosen method is, the more accurate predictions and evaluations can be calculated.

The app consists of four main screens: graphical chart, overview, calendar and entry menu. The graphical chart displays all temperature and cervical mucus values that have been entered for one cycle. If enough data has been entered so that the fertility of one cycle can be calculated, the fertile window is being highlighted through icons and background color in the chart. Also the charts of all cycles that have been entered in the past can be accessed on this page. The overview page aims to give the users a quick and easy insight about the current status of their cycles. On the top of the page a carousel has been placed in which it is possible to slide through different calendar days. The color coding of the different calendar days and a text below the carousel indicate if this day is predicted to be part of the fertile window or the next menstruation. As the primary action users want to reach quick and easy is to enter data, we put a plus-button at the center of the page. This button opens the main entry menu for the day currently selected in the carousel. At the bottom of the overview page there are two displays, one giving information about the current cycle day and the predicted cycle length and another counting the number of days until the next menstruation. On the calendar page it is possible to see all fertile windows and cycle beginnings (predicted and actually entered by the users) in a more global context. Also there is the option to click on a certain day to edit the respective data. Users who are using either the temperature- or symptothermal method are able to compare their fertile window that has been calculated by the method chosen and the fertile window that has been predicted at the beginning of the cycle. The main entry menu consists of nine buttons which correlate with the nine categories mentioned above. On click a popup window appears, which shows more details that can be tracked in this category (Fig. 2).

5   A proposal for a Goal- and Context-Driven Approach

The first implementation of our period tracker is a basic version, which will continuously be improved through ongoing research as described in the previous chapter. To support users in period tracking we propose a goal- and context-driven approach. Our next implementations will be gradually enhanced by the following features:

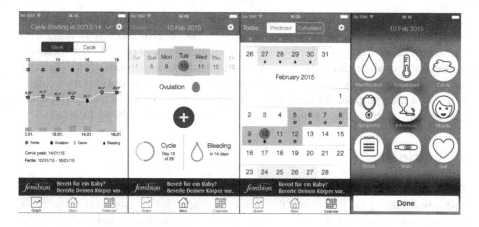

Fig. 2. Main screens: graphical chart, overview, calendar, entry menu

- In order to be able to reveal patterns and trends it is important that the tracked data can be assigned to a certain cycle phase
- Users easily can compare data of different cycles and cycle phases
- The app supports the user by taking the current cycle phase and the user's goal into account

As pointed out the user needs can be put on the three dimensions 'goal', 'preferred method' and 'current cycle phase'. In line with the results of Li et al.'s research about tracking in general [7] as well our tests showed that users have different questions about their data in different phases of their cycle in the case of period tracking. We treat the cycle phase in which a specific entry has been made, as the main context indicator in our period tracker. This is essential as the tracked data may lose it's sense when being removed from it's context [9] (Fig. 3).

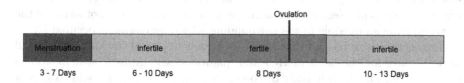

Fig. 3. Overview of the cycle phases

Especially the data the users enter during and right before their menstrual and fertile days are of high relevance to them as these cycle phases typically correlate with a higher emergence of body symptoms. The main goal of period tracking is long-term reflection as users want to compare their data of different cycles. The user's goals (in this case: trying to conceive or not trying to conceive) fundamentally influence their reflection- and action stage [7] of the tracking process. Therefore it should affect, which information should be high-lighted in the app. Also the app should be able to give intelligent hints and reminders in case the user forgets to enter enough data. The different methods to predict/calculate the fertility vary dramatically in how much effort the user needs to make. Highly engaged users need to be given more options and coher-ently need more supported navigation within the app. On the contrary the users who are not using a more complex method prefer a more reduced interface.

6 Outlook

The behavioural research we conducted so far was only lab-based and therefore de-contextualized from the real life usage. But as a lot of users are using their period tracking apps at least once a day we can only explore a small slice of the pitfalls and problems in this topic. We expect deeper insights from long-term ethnographic field studies, which are planned to be conducted with a set of 3 to 5 users over a time period of 6 to 12 months. This way we expect to learn more about typical problems users have in using period trackers to achieve their higher-level goals as 'trying to get pregnant' or 'get to know the body'. In other words: With long-term studies we hope to learn more about how period trackers can be enhanced and optimized in order to improve the user's life. Nonetheless we continuously invite users for CTAs to improve existing and new features. Our latest, but yet not completed studies show that especially features that help the users to examine their data and compare different cycles or cycle phases are meaningful test-cases for lab-based CTAs.

Actually the users get reminders to enter certain data like e.g. temperature. These kinds of reminders work for values like basal body temperature that can be measured at a defined time. Reminders to enter data like moods or symptoms are way more difficult to implement as the system doesn't know, if any of them occured. If the user doesn't enter moods or symptoms directly when they're occuring, it's difficult to reconstruct the perceptions as memories become more schematic or stereotypical the more time has passed [1]. As Cena et al. point out this especially is problematic in tracking emotions, if the user is not aware of the location, time and people in the surrounding when the emotions occured [2].

In general it can be said that the latest trends in period tracking are a broad area of study for the fields of HCI and quantified self. Apps that help women to learn more about their body or to get pregnant can truly be said to have a strong impact on them. Optimizing the collection and reflection of cycle data in mobile applications will definitely remain an interesting area of research.

References

1. Bartlett, F.C.: Remembering : A Study in Experimental and Social Psychology. Cambridge University Press, Cambridge (1995). Originally published: London: Cambridge U.P. (1967)

2. Cena, F., Lombardi, I., Rapp, A., Sarzotti, F.: Self-monitoring of emotions: a novel personal informatics solution for an enhanced self-reporting. In: UMAP Workshops (2014)
3. Choe, E.K., Lee, N.B., Lee, B., Pratt, W., Kientz, J.A.: Understanding quantified-selfers' practices in collecting and exploring personal data. In: Proceedings of the SIGCHI Conference on Human Factors in Computing Systems (CHI 2014), pp. 1143–1152. ACM, New York (2014)
4. Bundeszentrale fuer gesundheitliche Aufklaerung. Unsicher: Knaus-ogino-methode, koitus interruptus und stillen, February 2015. http://www.familienplanung.de/verhuetung/verhuetungsmethoden/unsichere-methoden/. Accessed 5 Feb 2015
5. Laird, S.: How smartphones are changing health care, September 2012. http://mashable.com/2012/09/26/smartphones-health-care-infographic/. Accessed 5 Feb 2015
6. Li, I., Dey, A., Forlizzi, J.: A stage-based model of personal informatics systems. In: Proceedings of the SIGCHI Conference on Human Factors in Computing Systems, (CHI 2010), pp. 557–566. ACM, New York (2010)
7. Li, I., Dey, A., Forlizzi, J.: Understanding my data, myself: Supporting self-reflection with ubicomp technologies. In: Proceedings of the 13th International Conference on Ubiquitous Computing(UbiComp 2011), pp. 405–414. ACM, New York (2011)
8. Raith-Paula, E., et al.: Natürliche Familienplanung heute: Modernes Zykluswissen für Beratung und Anwendung. Springer, Berlin Heidelberg (2013)
9. Rooksby, J., Rost, M., Morrison, A., Chalmers, M.C.: Personal tracking as lived informatics. In: Proceedings of the 32nd Annual ACM Conference on Human Factors in Computing Systems (CHI 2014), pp. 1163–1172. ACM, New York (2014)
10. Rötzer, J.: Natürliche Empfängnisregelung: der partnerschaftliche Weg - die sympto-thermale Methode. Herder, New York (1996)
11. Schnell, R., Hill, P.B., Esser, E.: Methoden der empirischen Sozialforschung. Oldenbourg Wissenschaftsverlag, Munich (2011)
12. Singer, K.: The Garden of Fertility. Penguin Group, New York (2004)
13. Wortham, J.: Our bodies, our apps: For the love of period-trackers, January 2014. http://bits.blogs.nytimes.com/2014/01/23/our-bodies-our-apps-for-the-love-of-period-trackers/. Accessed 5 Feb 2015

Unforeseen Challenges

Adopting Wearable Health Data Tracking Devices to Reduce Health Insurance Costs in Organizations

Mads Christophersen, Peter Mørck, Tue Odd Langhoff[✉], and Pernille Bjørn

IT-University of Copenhagen, Copenhagen, Denmark
{madc,pemo,tuol,pbra}@itu.dk

Abstract. Wearable health-tracking devices are being adopted by American self-insured companies to combat rising health insurance costs. The key motivation is to discourage employees' unhealthy behavior through monitoring their data. While wearable health-tracking devices might improve users awareness about personal health, we argue that the introduction of such devices in organizational settings also risk introducing unforeseen challenges. In this paper we unpack the unforeseen challenges and argue that wearable health-tracking devices in organizational settings risk disciplining employees, by tempting or penalizing them financially. Further, health concerns are reduced to numbers through wearable health-tracking devices providing surveillance of bodies, impacting people's lives. We stress how important it is that designers and researchers find ways to address these challenges in order to avoid future abuse of personal health data collected from wearable health-data tracking devices.

Keywords: Wearable Health-Tracking devices · Health data · Health insurance · Differentiated pricing · Wellness programs · Personal healthcare records · Privacy · Surveillance · Disciplining · Health as numbers

1 Introduction

In this paper, we explore the unforeseen challenges, which the introduction of wearable health-tracking devices might cause. In particular, we investigate how the introduction of such devices in an organizational setting shapes the relationship between the employee, the organization, and health conditions in certain unforeseen ways. Self-insured companies in the USA have started to adopt wearable health-tracking devices into their organizational setting through corporate wellness programs [26, 30]. This was a response to part of the Patient Protection and Affordable Care Act (PPACA), which made it possible, under federal law, for employers to vary health insurance premiums by up to 30 % based on employee's health factors [31]. In 2011, the national US healthcare expenditures reached $2,700 billion [10] and wearable health-tracking devices holds promises to decrease healthcare spending by differentiating insurance premiums and motivating people to get healthier. More than half of all Americans receive health insurance through their employers [10], thus the introduction of wearable

M. Antona and C. Stephanidis (Eds.): UAHCI 2015, Part III, LNCS 9177, pp. 288–299, 2015.
DOI: 10.1007/978-3-319-20684-4_28

health-tracking devices in organizational settings have huge potential impact on the American society. However, the nature of the impact might take different forms. We found that the introduction of wearable health-tracking devices within organizations have created the risk of disciplining human behaviors; reducing health concerns in measurable numbers, thus neglecting important aspects of health; and finally bring health surveillance into the everyday lives of people jeopardizing privacy. We argue that there is a need to further investigate the intentions and effects derived from adopting wearable health-tracking devices to contend rising health insurance costs. The financial incentives to reduce costs or generate profits on health insurance seem to benefit the few and not the many who are dependent or left without health insurance. Thus, it seems important to pause and debate wearable health-tracking technology before it is fully embedded into organizational settings and societies.

The paper is structured as follows: First we present our method and data sources which is comprised of a variety of written sources on wearable health-tracking devices in the USA. We then move into the section *Data, Technologies and Personal Health Data* in which we present external literature on the subject of health data and personal healthcare records, for then to present the theoretical approach of our work. The result section has three subsections, each unpacking the challenges we have identified by pointing to the data we investigated. This is followed by discussions of *The Wearable Dream, Newborn Artifacts, and Unfit Cyborgs*, ending with final remarks.

2   Method

Healthcare is not universal in the USA, and the majority of Americans with healthcare insurance have it organized through their employer [10]. This alongside the PPACA has created an environment for adopting wearable health-tracking devices by self-insured companies. Thus, to study the possible unforeseen challenges that emerge when wearable health-tracking devices are introduced into organizations we decided to focus on the USA. To gain a comprehensive overview and insights into the possible challenges of wearable health-tracking devices we collected and analyzed data from several diverse sets of sources including academic papers, consultant reports, corporate web-sites, government reports, government web-sites, and other online articles. Analyzing our data, we took a grounded theory approach [16], and thus identified categories capturing the diverse set of challenges emerging in these documents. Our coding made us able to conceptualize and structure the identified actors as well as the unanticipated challenges. Our classification provided us the opportunity to compare data from several sources, thus, allowing us to identify key actors and challenges in relation to health data gathered by wearable health-tracking devices.

In total, we analyzed 28 different data sources identifying potential challenges, merging challenges across sources with similarities. This process made us question each challenge seeking further empirical confirmations. Our data began to reveal corresponding challenges, formed by a collective of abstractions and events throughout our material, such as; the context and manipulation of data; data ownership, security and anonymity; minimizing insurance risk by incentives to get healthy; dictating behavior;

differentiated pricing; and no opt out options toward using wearable health-tracking devices. Then, by studying the emerging groupings of data, we reframed the key challenges worth pursuing and abandoned the ones having diffused or random content. Hence, our categories lead us to three central challenges, namely; how wearable health-tracking devices risk being used to discipline; how health-tracking devices risk reducing health into numbers; and finally, how health-tracking devices risk surveil and compromise privacy.

3   Data, Technologies, and Personal Health Data

Designing technologies to collect data about health is not something new, but have been pursued in research on personal healthcare records and medical records [13]. Most research in this area has been done within hospital organizations and findings point to the challenges in terms of: standardization and reconfiguration across healthcare institutions [5]; that difficulties in adaptation and reconfiguration is part of design [29]; and that patchwork is extra work required to make the multiple healthcare systems within hospital work together [14]. Various myths exist concerning healthcare systems [3], and clearly it is difficult to design systems which support healthcare practices rather than constrain them. One of the major challenges in the design of healthcare systems is the issues concerning categories and classifications [1, 17]. How we develop the categorization, which becomes embedded within healthcare technologies, clearly impact the way in which healthcare personnel are able to do their work by surveillance of practices rather than supporting work [4]. However, while the above research have been critical in terms of driving research on health information systems forward, they do not pay attention to the situation where we move out of the hospital and into people's work and lives.

In this paper, our interest is not the professional setting of healthcare practitioners, but instead the practices by which technologies collecting health data move into the workplace or the homes of people [6]. We study how wearable health-tracking devices have been brought into an organizational setting of self-insured companies and the challenges that have emerged. We apply the socio-technical perspective as a lens to uncover the challenge of how wearable health-tracking devices risk being used to discipline. This perspective makes us pay attention to the design of the technology and how it enacts power to discriminate against certain groups and favor others [22, 33]. There are currently a large variety of wearable health-tracking devices available, and it is unclear if they follow the same standards and classifications, even though we know that such classification strictly impact peoples' practices [8]. Numbers has in healthcare been seen as the most reliable and objective way of presenting facts [11], thus we must investigate what it means when health is monitored and presented in terms of numbers. Classifying health is difficult and complex as it is more situated and subjective [8]. Individuals agreeing to use wearable health-tracking devices can be viewed as a form for participatory surveillance [7], where bodies are producing numbers. By initially agreeing to terms of agreements before using the technology, it can be argued that users begin to self-regulate their behavior toward becoming healthier, allowing other parties to discipline and punish from afar [15]. The interconnection in between health-tracking devices and their users can be viewed as a form for cybernetic information system [2], in which individuals will not only be concerned about their physical health but also become self-conscious about their digital health and financial stature. In this merge, between human and technology, they become cyborgs [19]. To understand the incentives to implement wearable health-tracking technology there is a need to pry into the dynamics of capitalism, whose logic is somehow separate from the physical world we all live in [23].

4   Disciplining, Reducing Health to Numbers, Surveillance, and Privacy

In investigating how wearable health-tracking devices risk being used to discipline employees, we will dig into the possible challenges employees experiences when tracking devices are introduced in an organizational setting. We found different types of disciplining to emerge when wearable health-tracking devices are introduced. Several self-insured companies have started to use these tracking devices to financially tempt or penalize their employees through wellness programs. Employees at one of these companies are offered a chance to win $10,000 if they walk more steps than the top executives, thus financially tempting them to use these devices [30]. Another company tempts employees financially to share their health data, but in this case by awarding them with a $25 bi-weekly discount if they fill out a health questionnaire. However, in order to qualify for this $25 reduction a health screening, showing acceptable levels regarding waistline, blood pressure, glucose, HDL and triglyceride, is required [18]. More wide reaching initiatives was found in wellness programs at other companies, namely that of penalizing through fines. A company requires employees to submit health data which included weight, body fat, glucose levels, and other vitals. Employees refusing to comply with this requirement receive a monthly fine of $50, thus penalizing the employees through fines to share their health data [28]. A similar practice also existed at another company where an employee was charged $40 extra a month for health insurance because of a refusal to provide health data with said company [28]. The challenge of how wearable health-tracking devices risk being used to discipline employees may have greater implications for certain types of individuals. Healthy individuals will have few drawbacks besides privacy concerns from sharing their health data, whereas individuals who are worse off health wise or are on a tight budget may face other challenges on top of that. People on a tight budget can potentially not afford to either pass on rewards for sharing health data or receive fines for refusing to do so, even if they so wished [18]. Hence, penniless employees risk ending up in a situation where they are disciplined into sharing their health data. Unhealthy individuals potentially end up being caught between a rock and a hard place as they have to choose whether or not to share their health data. By sharing health data they can collect rewards and avoid fines, but the health data could potentially lead to higher insurance premiums if the individual becomes classified as unhealthy. On the other hand by refusing to share health data they face fines and no rewards, meaning their financial situation risk changing to a worse state than what has previously been the case [18]. A situation where unhealthy individuals are disciplined into paying more for health insurance, face fines, or lose out on financial rewards is at risk here.

The second major risk area concerns how wearable health-tracking devices reduce health into numbers and why it could turn out to be problematic. Wearable health-tracking devices contain sensors which measure a person's health data such as number of steps taken, glucose levels, blood pressure, amount of sleep [26, 30]. Based on these readings an individual's insurance premium could be differentiated, increasing or decreasing in price, depending on whether the data is classified as healthy or unhealthy. By reducing health to numbers individuals risk facing a number of consequences. The readings made by wearable health-tracking devices fail to factor in social, psychological, environmental and physical circumstances [32], which can all influence the readings and the state of a person's health. By reducing health to numbers there is a risk that blind spots are created within the data because the circumstances, which are not accounted for digitally, are lost and the context of how the data came to be is missing [12]. The actions of the individual are not enough to explain how or why insurance premiums are differentiated; the actions of the multitude are needed to understand the premise [12]. The health data of the multitude is within the organizational setting compared and assessed, which is accommodated by reducing health to numbers, and health insurance premiums can thus be differentiated in between individuals. However, wearable health-tracking devices on today's market lack common standards and practices as they have not gone through any validation process [9]. Thus, each device or sensor could potentially collect different data even when measuring the exact same situation [9]. Other medical devices used for research and professional use have to be meticulously tested before being approved by the U.S. Food and Drug Administration [9]. This is not the case with wearable health-tracking devices as they have not been validated, further they do not follow common standards [9] and it can thus be questioned whether or not they should be used for differentiating insurance premiums. When health data is analyzed there is a possibility for manipulation, and the algorithms used can potentially be modified by an organization wishing to change the analytical outcome [24]. This could particularly become a problem when there are financial incentives to manipulate the data, for instance if healthier looking data means lower health insurance cost [27]. Self-insured companies could save large amounts of money when bargaining with an insurance provider if their employee's health data is manipulated to look healthier. The employees could also have incentives to manipulate their own health data. For example, step count could be manipulated by attaching the wearable health-tracking device to an animal, co-worker or perhaps a machine thereby fooling the wearable health-tracking device to record fake steps [24]. Reducing health into numbers through the use of wearable health-tracking devices is followed by a number of consequences that could impact individuals and how the price of their health insurance premium is determined.

The third risk area is that of surveillance and privacy. In wellness programs health data is collected by wearable health-tracking devices, stored in personal health data sets, while being administered by a heterogeneous host of intermediaries [27]. Employees are being prompted to participate in wellness programs, driven by their employers wish to keep health insurance costs low, which in turn invade the privacy of employees as the wearable health-tracking devices are being used as a form for surveillance tools [9]. As wearable health-tracking technologies evolve they begin to be able to track more sensitive data such as heart rates, glucose levels and body temperatures revealing a more intimate picture of a person's health [25]. Thus, in order to preserve the privacy of individuals from their insurance provider, neutral third parties are brought in to manage the data. In the slipstream of wearable health-tracking technology lays privacy concerns on how wearable health-tracking provider's access and use individual's health data. The privacy concern is embedded in how terms of use agreements are accepted before using wearable health-tracking technologies [20]. Terms of use agreements typically state that the organization providing the wearable health-tracking technology either fully owns or has full and complete rights to the health data, including rights to repackage and sell datasets to other parties as long as it has been anonymized [9]. Further, while some people are aware of these privacy issues, others are indifferent or oblivious, thus personal health data can be used for other purposes than what the users expected [9]. Subsequently, there is a risk that anonymized personal health data can become de-anonymized when two or more data sources are combined [9]. Finally, there is a security risk in guarding the stored personal health data as repositories of data are characteristically unstable. Data has a tendency to escape in unexpected ways, be it through errors, leaks or hacks [12]. Wearable health-tracking devices, operating as a form for surveillance tools, endanger individual's privacy. The collected health data may be used for other purposes than what was originally intended.

5   The Wearable Dream, Newborn Artifacts and Unfit Cyborgs

A new dream is forming in America - the wearable dream. As a result of the PPACA employers have been permitted to differentiate the prices of health insurance premiums with the help of wearable health-tracking devices. It is for example cheaper to eat unhealthy than healthy [21], but instead of trying to regulate the market to make it more financially attractive to eat healthy, the individual is disciplined in an attempt to make them healthier [18, 28, 30]. Whether or not that is the right choice, we still see that the responsibility of reducing the vast health related expenses in the USA is placed on the individual through wellness programs and not on the industries that lead people to unhealthy lifestyles. A vital actor in these wellness programs is wearable health-tracking technology which can be used to enhance the privilege of some over others [33]. Healthy individuals will potentially be able to benefit from sharing their health data beyond that of receiving rewards or avoid fines. By sharing their health data they can prove their healthiness, becoming less risky to insure and therefore be entitled to lower health insurance premiums. On the other side individuals unwilling to share their health data, possibly because they are unhealthy or have privacy concerns [9, 18], will not be able to prove their healthiness and could thus be deemed more risky to ensure and face a higher health insurance premium. These wearable health-tracking devices are because of their prescriptions discriminating against people who are unhealthy or have privacy concerns, as it prevents them from getting the same financial benefits as healthy persons [22, 33]. Whether or not the challenges health-tracking devices bring are intended or not by the designers are uncertain. Nevertheless, it is clear that tracking devices can be used to execute political power in certain ways, which benefit some on the cost of others [33].

The PPACA created by the US government has made it possible for the wearable health-tracking device to be used as a mean by which employers can reduce health insurance costs [31]. The tracking technology provides both the government and the employers a way to act at a distance [22], which gives them a certain power over the individuals who use these wearable health-tracking devices. The government exerts its power through the wearable health-tracking devices by making the individuals perform the action of becoming healthier and in a sense they have delegated the work to the wearable health-tracking device. However, the tracking device is not capable of transforming an unhealthy human to a healthy human on its own, it requires the humans to be motivated or forced into making the transformation. In the case of wellness programs the motivating or forcing driver is money exemplified by financial temptations and fines [18, 28, 30]. When health data collected from wearable health-tracking devices becomes part of the personal health data set it has the potential to structure the US society in a different way. If the healthy are getting cheaper health insurance and the unhealthy more expensive health insurance, then a situation possibly arise where the only ones able to afford health insurance are the ones who are healthy or wealthy and need it the least. What should also be considered problematic is that people with low incomes are more prone to being unhealthy [10] and as a result of being unhealthy they could risk facing higher health insurance premiums. In a potential scenario the health insurance premiums for unhealthy persons could rise to such high levels that low-income individuals cannot afford health insurance at all. However, if unhealthy people cannot afford health insurance and all the healthy people are getting cheaper health insurance, then it seems like some money is going to be missing if the insurance industry is to be profitable. If that is the case the insurance industry could again turn to the health data wearable health-tracking devices collect and re-categorize what is considered healthy and unhealthy. This would mean that people who were once considered healthy could suddenly become classified as less healthy without any changes in their health data. This could potentially have great implications on the US society as it could end up in a situation where only the most healthy or wealthy people can afford health insurance.

New artifacts have been born: wearable health-tracking technologies. Since their birth they have not undergone any official tests and do not have to comply with a specific rule set [9]. Companies providing wearable health-tracking technologies can, to some extent, make up their own rules in relation to how their specific device is measuring and collecting health data. Presently, there is a risk that the lack of standards for wearable health-tracking devices could mean that a person's health data set might vary depending on which tracking device is used to measure and collect it [9]. Individuals could very well face a situation where they have to seek out an employer at which their health data set is within a health range that would not present them with a large insurance bill, a seemingly impossible task for individuals with long term illnesses or other chronic diseases. By adopting wearable health-tracking technologies the determination of an individual's health status could, instead of visiting a doctor for a diagnosis, be based on the numbers produced by the health-tracking devices. However, the collected health data could prove problematic since health is more situated and subjective [8]. The integrity and validity of the health data is compromised especially when considering how the tracking devices fail to factor in psychological, environmental and physical circumstances [32]. This should create concerns for employees whose insurance premiums might be unfairly changed based on their health data.

Companies are treating numbers from the wearable health-tracking devices as a representation of people's health which is justifiable since numbers for a long time have represented an objective way of presenting facts [11]. However, employees might quickly find themselves in a variety of situations, which could compromise this truth and objectivity. For example, a high pulse rate measurement might be due to an obese employee walking a lot of stairs but it could also be due to a normal weight person having an office romance. Wearable health-tracking devices cannot account for such external factors and contexts, they only collect the numbers, which could mean that a perfectly healthy employee find their health insurance priced unjustly. An intriguing point is that health could prove to be much more complex than the numbers wearable health-tracking devices reduce them to [9, 12, 32]. Self-insured companies are creating health profiles on their employees based on these numbers, which is concerning if it turns out that they are not valid or true in the first place, in fact it might be the opposite and provide a completely distorted picture of the state of a person's health.

Disturbingly, employees who are constantly being tracked and monitored might seek any means possible in order to create a healthy data set and not lose out financially for example by manipulating the data [24]. More desperate employees who cannot afford a more expensive health insurance could try to find ways to inflate their data to look healthier. A scenario made possible by the lack of control, since it, for example, is difficult to check if an employee gets a friend or coworker to wear their device for a period of time. However, for some employees inflating their data might become a necessity in order to keep their economy afloat. It is a scary thought but employees might in the future need to be concerned about how healthy they are, not out of common sense, but because health has become a currency with which they can bargain lower insurance premiums. Chronically ill individuals also risk having to bargain their insurance premiums and will thus most likely have to pay more regardless due to circumstances out of their control. In a sense it could be considered fair that obese individuals would have to pay a higher premium until they get healthier, but they have the possibility to change and improve whereas the chronically ill do not. The gap between healthy and unhealthy individuals will only get bigger as will the gap between rich and poor, which could be a consequence of a market where it is cheaper to eat unhealthy than healthy [21].

In the disciplining of fit as unfit individuals, different parties may have different incentives to collect personal health data through wearable health-tracking devices [28]. Further, these actors may also differ on how they use, store and manipulate the data [12, 24]. These predicaments are specified in terms of agreements usually written in large bodies of legal texts, in small fonts, and in a foreign language to most laymen. Very few people actually read these terms of agreements [20], by just clicking 'agree' whenever opted to make the choice. Thereby, blindly agreeing to an array of complex laws, interests, warnings and disclaims from a multitude of actors which may have direct consequences on individual's daily lives [20]. In doing so, people adhere to a form for participatory surveillance [7], where administrators of the technology may manifest a desire to realize a system with only healthy people in it. What at first glance seemed like a harmless pulse rate tracker could soon come to dictate human behavior and insurance choices to an unforeseen extent. A panoptic grid may be realized by the multitude of worn wearable health-tracking technologies, serving different purposes, but collectively granting a productive increase of power to lessen costs on healthcare ever so subtly [15]. A cybernetic information system [2], where wearable health-tracking technologies work to replace human function, such as the ability to reason what is healthy. If a person is at risk of becoming obese a wearable artifact will cry out through the information system, calling for assistance to discipline the individual to behave healthy, and if not be penalized until showing a change of attitude [18, 28]. By clicking 'agree' people may enter this cybernetic realm of surveillance, often free of charge but with far reaching consequences into time and space. By agreeing to one's health data being collected by wearable health-tracking devices it may affect future insurance options and prices, even if annulled, because the data has already become part of the digital health sets immortal memory. Furthermore, the irony is not lost if a person by chance should not agree to participate, evidently he or she would still be penalized for showing lacking health data and thereby risky to insure [18, 28]. Wearable health-tracking technology's ability to read, process and communicate bodily signals enhance people to evaluate their health, and potential financial risk, thus becoming cybernetic creatures in the merge of human and machine. They become cyborgs [19] reborn with a hybrid consciousness surrounding their physical, financial and digital well-being, between physical heart rates, insurance premiums and personal health records.

Not so long ago in the 'Western World' it would be viewed as heresy to question religious belief, the divine was an unquestionable second nature to the first nature of man [23]. In modern times a new entity has taken residence in this second nature, namely capitalism [23]. Few laymen fully grasp the dynamics of capitalism and are reluctant to question its logic. In this second nature we find something other in the mind of the cyborg, an ambiguous player known as unregulated capitalism. Wearable health-tracking technologies tend to gamify their use and intent, inviting people to play a casual game with high stakes [18, 26, 30]. Thus, resistance is hopeless in the eye of the cyborg, you play along or you do not, either way we look at a possible soon-to-be scenario where both choices hold consequences. People may pay more or less for their insurance premiums by wearing or not wearing health-tracking devices [18, 28, 30]. The personal health data sets will either show plentiful or lacking data, consequently producing differentiated health risk profiles. While this is not a rant against capitalism, we argue that unregulated capitalism have found an abnormal shortcut, by the cyborg, in entering its logic directly into human flesh. The amount of money at stake when playing with healthcare is huge [10], and this bait big fish to enter its waters. Big fish usually eat smaller fish, and this logic also seems to follow through when differentiating individual health by using wearable health-tracking technology. Instead of regulating the healthcare market as a whole it seems to befall the individual [18, 31]. Unrestrained capitalism will always hunt for new prey yielding profits. Thus, if all cyborgs were to become fit, the health boundaries defining what is natural could quickly be remade to be unnatural, thereby creating an everlasting and profitable herd of unfit cyborgs.

The purpose of the paper has not been to provide a solution on how to accommodate the emerging challenges from the use of wearable health-tracking technology. Instead, we strive to describe the challenges and possible consequences for society when adopting wearable health-tracking devices into organizational settings. If we are not careful the wearable dream could very well turn into a nightmare. Health insurance premiums of individuals are differentiated in price based on whether or not healthy looking data can be provided. This can create a situation where only the most healthy or wealthy can afford health insurance. A new artifact has been born alongside the wearable dream. Wearable health-tracking devices are constantly tracking, measuring and collecting personal health data. The health of individuals is reduced to numbers by the mercy of this newborn artifact. However, the integrity and validity of this health data can be compromised through the lack of standards, context and manipulation leading to wrongly determined insurance premiums. The wearable health-tracking technologies are invading the privacy of individuals by constantly monitoring and surveil them. By participating, willingly or unwillingly, in this endeavour individuals become something else, cyborgs. In this hybrid creature, an ongoing battle, in between unregulated capitalism and human behavior, is taking place. A far reaching point, perhaps, but we have to wake up from the wearable dream and face reality. We need to debate, research and rethink how wearable health-tracking technologies are embedded into societies in order to prevent the potential abuse of personal health data.

References

1. Balka, E., Bjørn, P., Wagner, I.: Steps towards a typology for health informatics. In: Computer Supported Cooperative Work (CSCW), pp. 515–524. ACM, San Diego (2008)
2. Balsamo, A.: Reading cyborgs writing feminism. In: Hovenden, F., Janes, L., Kirkup, G., Woodward, K. (eds.) The Gendered Cyborg: A Reader, pp. 148–158. Routledge, London (2000)
3. Berg, M.: Implementing information systems in healthcare organizations: myths and challenges. Int. J. Med. Inform. **64**, 143–156 (2001)
4. Bjørn, P., Balka, E.: Health care categories have politics too: unpacking the managerial agendas of electronic triage systems. In: ECSCW 2007: Proceedings of the Tenth European Conference on Computer Supported Cooperative Work, pp. 371–390. Springer, Limerick (2007)
5. Bjørn, P., Burgoyne, S., Crompton, V., MacDonald, T., Pickering, B., Munro, S.: Boundary factors and contextual contingencies: Configuring electronic templates for health care professionals. Eur. J. Inf. Syst. **18**, 428–441 (2009)
6. Bjørn, P., Markussen, R.: Cyborg heart: the affective apparatus of bodily production of ICD patients. Sci. Technol. Stud. **26**(2), 14–28 (2013)
7. Bloomfield, B.: In the right place at the right time: Electronic tagging and problems of social order/disorder. Sociol. Rev. **49**, 174–201 (2001)
8. Bowker, G.C., Star, L.S.: Introduction: to classify is human and some tricks of the trade in analyzing classification. In: Sorting Things Out: Classification and Its Consequences, pp. 1–51. MIT Press, Cambridge (2000)

9. California Institute for Telecommunications and Information Technology Personal data for the public good (2014). http://www.calit2.net/hdexplore/images/hdx_final_report.pdf. Accessed 11 November 2014

10. Centers for Disease Control and Prevention. Health, United States, 2013: With special feature on prescription drugs (2014). http://www.cdc.gov/nchs/data/hus/hus13.pdf#112. Accessed 11 November 2014

11. Cohen, P.C.: A calculating people: The spread of numeracy in early America, pp. 205–227. University of Chicago Press, Chicago (1982)

12. Crawford, K., Miltner, K., Gray, M.L.: Critiquing big data: politics, ethics, epistemology. Int. J. Commun. **8**, 1663–1672 (2014)

13. Ellingsen, G., Fitzpatrick, G.: A review of 25 years of cscw research in healthcare: contributions, challenges and future agendas. Comput. Support. Coop. Work **22**, 609–665 (2013)

14. Ellingsen, G., Monteiro, E.: A patchwork planet integration and cooperation in hospitals. Comput. Support. Coop. Work (CSCW) Int. J. **12**(1), 71–95 (2003)

15. Foucault, M.: Panopticism. In: Discipline & Punish: The Birth of the Prison (A. Sheridan, Trans., pp. 195–228). Vintage Books, New York (1975)

16. Glaser, B.G., Strauss, A.M.: The credibility of grounded theory. The Discovery of Grounded Theory: Strategies for Qualitative Research, pp. 228–233. Aldine Publishing Company, Chicago (1967)

17. Grisot, M., Vassilakopoulou, P.: Infrastructures in healthcare: the interplay between generativity and standardization. Int. J. Med. Inform. **82**, 170–179 (2013)

18. Goldberg, C.: Can my company's wellness program really ask me to do that? (2012). http://commonhealth.wbur.org/2012/09/wellness-program-legal-limits. Accessed 11 November 2014

19. Haraway, D.: A Cyborg Manifesto: Science, Technology, and Socialist-Feminism in the Late Twentieth Century. In: Haraway, D. (ed.) Simians, Cyborgs and Women: The Reinvention of Nature, pp. 149–181. Routledge, New York, US (1991)

20. Hoback, C.: Terms and conditions may apply [Motion Picture] (2013)

21. Houle, B.: How obesity relates to socioeconomic status (2013). http://www.prb.org/Publications/Articles/2013/obesity-socioeconomic-status.aspx. Accessed 11 November 2014

22. Latour, B.: Where are the missing masses: sociology of a few mundane artefacts. In: Bijker, W., Law, J. (eds.) Shaping Technology/Building Society - Studies in Sociotechnical Change, pp. 225–259. MIT Press, Cambridge (1992)

23. Latour, B.: On Some of the Affects of Capitalism. At The Royal Academy, Copenhagen, 26 February 2014

24. Lazer, D., Kennedy, R., King, G., Vespignani, A.: The parable of Google Flu:Traps in Big Data analysis (2014). http://scholar.harvard.edu/files/gking/files/0314policyforumff.pdf. Accessed 11 November 2014

25. Martin, J.A.: Pros and cons of using fitness trackers for employee wellness (2014). http://www.cio.com/article/2377723/it-strategy/pros-and-cons-of-using-fitness-trackers-for-employee-wellness.html. Accessed 11 November 2014

26. Olson, P.: Wearable tech is plugging into health insurance (2014). http://www.forbes.com/sites/parmyolson/2014/06/19/wearable-tech-health-insurance/. Accessed 11 November 2014

27. Olson, P., Tilley, A.: The quantified other: Nest and Fitbit chase a lucrative side business (2014). http://www.forbes.com/sites/parmyolson/2014/04/17/the-quantified-other-nest-and-fitbit-chase-a-lucrative-side-business/. Accessed 11 November 2014

28. Osunsami, S.: CVS Pharmacy wants workers' health information, or they'll pay a fine (2013). http://abcnews.go.com/blogs/health/2013/03/20/cvs-pharmacy-wants-workers-health-information-or-theyll-pay-a-fine. Accessed 11 November 2014

29. Park, S.Y., Chen, Y.: Adaptation as design: learning from an EMR deployment study. In: Computer Human Interaction, pp. 2097–2106. ACM, Austin (2012)

30. Satariano, A.: Wear this device so the boss knows you're losing weight (2014). http://www.bloomberg.com/news/articles/2014-08-21/wear-this-device-so-the-boss-knows-you-re-losing-weight. Accessed 11 November 2014

31. U.S. Department of Labor: The Affordable Care Act and wellness programs (n.d.). http://www.dol.gov/ebsa/newsroom/fswellnessprogram.html. Accessed 11 November 2014

32. WebMD: 5 heart rate myths debunked (2013). http://www.webmd.com/heart-disease/features/5-heart-rate-myths-debunked. Accessed 11 November 2014

33. Winner, L.: The Whale and the Reactor: A Search for Limits in an Age of High Technology. In: Winner, L. (ed.) Do Artifacts Have Politics, pp. 19–40. University of Chicago Press, Chicago (1986)

Rehabilitation of Balance-Impaired Stroke Patients Through Audio-Visual Biofeedback

Cristina Gheorghe, Thomas Nissen, Daniel Christensen, Paula Epure[✉],
Anthony Brooks, and Eva Petersson Brooks

Department for Media Technology, Aalborg University, Niels Bohrs Vej 8, Esbjerg, Denmark
{cgheor12,tniss12,djrc12,pepure12}@student.aau.dk,
{tb,ep}@create.aau.dk

Abstract. This study explored how audio-visual biofeedback influences physical balance of seven balance-impaired stroke patients, between 33–70 years-of-age. The setup included a bespoke balance board and a music rhythm game. The procedure was designed as follows: (1) a control group who performed a balance training exercise without any technological input, (2) a visual biofeedback group, performing via visual input, and (3) an audio-visual biofeedback group, performing via audio and visual input. Results retrieved from comparisons between the data sets (2) and (3) suggested superior postural stability between test sessions for (2). Regarding the data set (1), the testers were less motivated to perform training exercises although their performance was superior to (2) and (3). Conclusions are that the audio component motivated patients to train although the physical performance was decreased.

Keywords: Audio-visual biofeedback · Stroke rehabilitation · Postural stability

1 Introduction

Biofeedback is increasingly used within treatment programs for various health conditions and disorders. Data sourced from different bodily functions is, more than ever, readily available to map to media feedback through recent technical system advances. In line with this, audio-biofeedback systems have been investigated in respect of benefit for regaining postural control [1, 2]. The objective of this study was to investigate to what extent audio-visual biofeedback affected physical balance. Patients were provided with audio and visual cues to perform certain physical exercises as part of their rehabilitation process. It was argued that the main challenge when designing a multimodal system is being aware of feedback relationships [3]. Using multiple biofeedback parameters may result in a perceptive and cognitive overload, which also might influence testers at a psychological level. Different studies compared biofeedback-induced therapy with regular therapy and discovered there was no significant difference in the improvement rate [4, 5]. However, biofeedback may add more variability to the training sessions.

For this study a comparison between two different exposure situations: visual biofeedback and audio-visual biofeedback - indicated that the type of biofeedback used represented a difference for stroke patients. In order to investigate the objective of the

© Springer International Publishing Switzerland 2015
M. Antona and C. Stephanidis (Eds.): UAHCI 2015, Part III, LNCS 9177, pp. 300–311, 2015.
DOI: 10.1007/978-3-319-20684-4_29

study a bespoke balance board and a music rhythm game, named "Balance Hero" were utilized. The balance board functioned as a controller for the game by measuring the pressure exerted on it. Test subjects were stroke patients, five males and two females, between 33–70 years-of-age, involved in a local rehabilitation program in Denmark. Patients sat on the balance board and shifted their weight by leaning to each side in order to control a music rhythm game. The aim of the game was to simulate guitar playing by controlling a 3D virtual fret using visual or/and audio cues. The cues were 3D note objects that scrolled on screen according to the rhythm of the song selected.

1.1   Balance Impairment, Sensory Systems and the Auditory Impact on Human Motor Behavior

1.1.1   Balance Impairment in Stroke Patients

Physical balance is defined as a harmonic arrangement that uses all the information sent by the sensory systems to place the body in connection with the gravity and earth. A balance disorder is a condition which increases the risk of falling by making an individual physically unstable. It can be caused by certain health conditions, medications, and a dysfunction of the inner ear or brain damage [6].

Research indicated that there are several medical conditions associated with gait and balance disorders: affective disorders and psychiatric conditions, cardiovascular disease, infectious and metabolic disease, musculoskeletal disorders, neurological disorders, sensory abnormalities and others. One of the neurological disorders that cause balance impairment is stroke [7]. This study focused on stroke patients with balance impairment. In order to determine how stroke affects postural stability it is necessary to investigate the implication of stroke; it is defined as a disturbance of cerebral function with apparently no other cause than vascular origins [8]. Commonly, it results from the blockage of a major artery in the brain and it leads to the death of all cells in the affected area [9]. Stroke causes symptoms such as loss of strength, sensation, vision or other neurological functions [10]. As an effect of a stroke, patients may need to adjust to the new functionality of the sensory system. In consequence, physical therapy has rehabilitation purposes, to restore movement, balance and coordination [11]. In order to regain postural stability certain physical exercises are practiced by patients on a daily basis. The system used to test our hypothesis simulated a training session.

1.1.2   Sensory System

To determine the functionality of physical balance it is essential to explore the mechanisms of sensory systems. Maintaining postural control is a multisensory process that uses the information received from different sensory systems.

There are three major sensory systems involved in balance and posture: visual, vestibular and somatosensory [12]. Balance generally decreases in the absence of any visual input or in experimental conditions that affect the quality of visual input [13].

Spatial hearing cues provide moderately accurate abilities to localize sound sources. A connection can be established between spatial hearing and postural control [14]. Moreover, a single fixed sound source can provide sufficient spatial cues for the central nervous system to an improved control of postural stability [14]. It has also been outlined that the compensation effect received in the vestibular system from the auditory cues is more reduced compared to the one from visual cues. In our study the veracity of the aforementioned idea would be further observed through the design of the testing sessions.

1.1.3   Auditory Impact on Human Motor Behavior

Concerning the psychological reaction to audio input, in relation with physical movements, studies established that rhythm enhanced human motor behavior [15]. Moreover, by synchronizing movements to the rhythm, individuals indicated gratification, as it replicated natural movement forms.

The idea was further supported in a similar study, confirming that young adults endured longer periods of physical exercise training when their body movement was synchronized to the rhythm of music, compared to moving asynchronously [16]. Additionally, the increase in endurance is caused by an emotional response from music [15]. Moreover, in research with acquired brain injured patients (stroke) and audio and multimedia feedback of near-range and far-range balance and proprioception, positive outcomes were indicated in [17].

2   Methods

In order to investigate how the audio component in audio-visual biofeedback affects postural control, a system was developed, to observe, measure, and analyze physical balance. The system consists of: (a) a self-created balance board and (b) a music rhythm game. The bespoke components are detailed below.

Three stages of a user centered design were approached to satisfy the necessities of patients and stakeholders; early focus on users and tasks, empirical measurement and iterative design [18]. Different aspects of the system were discussed and further implemented in order to achieve an efficient and suitable system: (a) balance board – functionality and synchronization and (b) the music rhythm game: speed, music, appearance and functionality.

2.1   Balance Board

A balance board was created to measure and record the pressure exerted on it. It consisted of: a Spider 8 data logger, 4 S-type load cells, 3 connection cables for the load cells, 8 bolts to secure the load cells, 2 wood countertops, and 4 wood support blocks (Fig. 1). The load cells register the variables made by the bending of metal foil inside the cell, transforming the mechanical deformation into an electrical output signal. To mount the load cells, two pieces of wood countertop were used. The Spider 8 data logger was connected to a PC through a USB/RS232 converter cable in order to communicate with the PC. The load cells were calibrated before each test, to register and control the game.

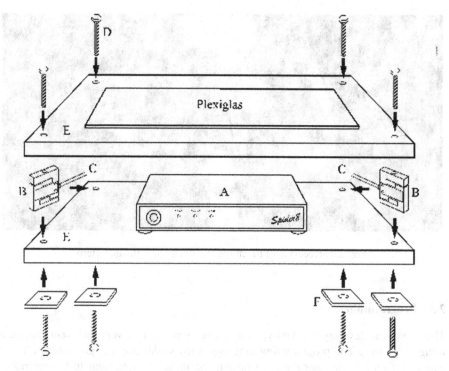

Fig. 1. Setup of the balance board (Width: 60 cm/Length: 70 cm/Height: 13 cm)

For this study, a program was created in Visual Basic 6 to receive the data from the four load cells and send it through a local User Datagram Protocol (UDP) connection. Lastly, this was mapped to the Unity game engine within which the graphical music rhythm game was programmed.

2.2 Graphics and Sound

A music rhythm game was developed to stimulate transitions in postural position and immerse the patients in a fun and engaging interactive environment. The aim was to simulate guitar playing by controlling a 3D virtual fret using visual or/and audio cues. The cues were 3D note objects that scroll on screen according to the rhythm of the song selected (Fig. 1). The player had to control a diamond-shaped object to hit colored note objects by leaning left or right. Unity was the main development platform, with imported models from Google SketchUp Pro 8.

The audio stimuli was represented by the song "Viva la Vida" by Coldplay (2008) which was suggested by the physiotherapist as preferred for the target group. The physiotherapist argued that the patients were familiar with the song and that it was appropriate for the age range. Different aspects were considered, such as musical style, tempo and rhythm. Additionally, extra-musical associations evoked by the music were examined in line with that they are considered as primary factors in stimulating emotional responses in aiding motor activity [19].

Fig. 2. Screenshot of the music rhythm game – Balance Hero

2.3 Programming

The game was developed in Unity, a game engine utilizing several different programming languages. The programming language used to develop the game was C#. An essential factor in the game was to design the in-game movement to be controlled through the readings of the balance board. The 3D virtual fret board was programmed to have five lanes where the user controlled the diamond-shaped object, each corresponding to a certain pressure value on the balance board. This value was calculated as the difference between the two left sensor values and two right sensor values on the balance board. In consequence, when the participant distributes their weight evenly on both sides of the board, the in-game character will remain in the middle lane.

In order to gain an overview of the patients' balance distribution while playing the game, the values gained from the balance board were written to a comma separated value (CSV) file every 20th of a second.

The synchronization between the note objects and the rhythm of the song playing were programmed to correspond during the entire gameplay. The beats per minute (BPM) of the song were used in the formula below to calculate note intervals:

$$\frac{\frac{60}{BPM}}{N_{value}} = N_{interval}; \text{ where } N_{value} \in \{0.25, 0.5, 1, 2, 4\}$$

Here N_{value} is equivalent to the different note values from a whole note to a sixteenth part note. The result, $N_{interval}$ is the note interval in seconds used to synchronize the note objects to the rhythm of the song. Moreover the speed at which the note objects are moving is proportional to the BPM. This formula allows a change of pitch with a speed modifier by utilizing the modified BPM value.

The adjustment of the music was necessary in order to obtain coordination between the physical exercise proposed by the physiotherapist and the song. The notes were placed according to the training exercise suggested. In accordance, the music was changed for a better quality of sound that fitted the requirements mentioned above.

2.4 Data Analysis

The study was conducted on seven balance-impaired stroke patients between 33–70 years-of-age. The unit of analysis was group-based; therefore the procedure was grouped into: (1) a control group with two testers who performed a balance training exercise without any technological input, (2) a visual biofeedback group, with two testers playing the game via visual input, and (3) an audio-visual biofeedback group, with three testers playing the game via audio and visual input.

Following each test, an evaluation session consisting of semi-structured interviews was conducted and supervised by a physiotherapist, to collect user data and feedback. The physiotherapist suggested what type of physical exercise will improve the rehabilitation process, to be implemented in the game. Furthermore, the physiotherapist tried the system and indicated a possible usefulness for the rehabilitation process.

2.4.1   Control Group

Two balance-impaired stroke patients performed a balance training exercise, by sitting on the balance board. The exercise was developed to simulate the game without technological input. The patients had to perform a physical exercise by following post-it notes numbered from one to five, to simulate the game without technological input. The lanes in the game were represented by numbers. The first lane (numbered one) suggested a full leaning to the left and the last lane (numbered five) a full leaning to the right.

2.4.2   Visual and Audio-Visual Biofeedback Group

The visual group was formed of two balance-impaired stroke patients, who played the game with visual input. The audio-visual group was represented by three patients performing the full system test, which included both visual and audio biofeedback.

To analyze the data, graphs were created from CSV files and had two points of reference: the x-axis, representing the time interval for each participant, and the y-axis, showing the pressure exerted on the balance board. A computer-generated line was added to the existing graph, representing the flawless game-play. The aspects evaluated were values and line fluctuations.

The points obtained by the patients playing the game were calculated into a mean value and an improvement rate (%) for each patient and subsequently for both groups. The formula utilized for the improvement rate was the following:

$$I_{rate} = \frac{V_1 + V_2}{2}$$

$$V_{1,2} = \left(S_n - S_{n-1}\right) * \frac{100}{S_{n-1}}$$

Where V = Value, I_{rate} = Improvement Rate and S_n = Score corresponding to a test session (e.g. S_2 – score obtained in the second session of the test). In order for the formula to be applicable, it is necessary to mention that the "$_n$" in "S_n" can be equal only to 2 or 3, representing the second, respectively third test session. The individual mean and improvement rate indicated the progress of each patient throughout the testing session. The groups' mean and improvement rates facilitated a comparison between the visual and audio-visual biofeedback groups. The patients' feedback was collected via semi-structured interviews with a focus on gameplay, sound and motivational aspects. In order to validate the study, a physiotherapist specialized in rehabilitating stroke patients supported the experiment by providing feedback throughout the entire process. The procedure was recorded with a video camera, in order to validate the results and enable the possibility of a post-analysis of the sessions for further assessment.

3   Results

The data collected during the test sessions, based on the semi-structured interviews revealed that five of the users were males and two were females, between 33–70 years-of-age. Five of them suffered from stroke in the left side of the brain, one from stroke in the right side and one from stroke in the brain stem.

Table 1. Visual representation of Patients' scores, mean values and improvement rates

User	S1	S2	S3	Mean	Improvement rate
Visual Group					
K.	626	647	664	645	2.98 %
V.	611	693	717	673	8.44 %
Group Mean:				659	5.71 %
Audio-Visual Group					
Ki.	609	626	653	629	3.55 %
L.	605	616	655	625	4.07 %
Ka.	620	539	573	577	−3.38 %
Group Mean:				610	1.41 %

3.1   Balance Board Data Readings

3.1.1   Control Group

The fluctuations of the graph lines decreased for both patients from the first to the second test.

3.1.2 Visual Biofeedback Group

The fluctuations of the graph lines decreased for both patients, throughout testing sessions. In consequence, the points obtained in the game by both participants increased, indicating an improvement rate of 2.98 % and 8.44 %. The individual scores, group scores and improvement rates can be seen in Table 1.

3.1.3 Audio-Visual Biofeedback Group

The fluctuations of the graph lines presented a minor decrease from the first to the third test for two patients, while for the third patient the fluctuations increased. In consequence, the improvement rates for the first two patients were 3.55 % and 4.07 %, while the third patient presented an improvement rate of -3.38 %. The individual scores, group scores and improvement rates can be seen in Table 1.

Figures 1, 2 and 3 illustrate the graphs for one of the patients (Ki.) through all three tests. The improvement is visible, as the fluctuations decrease throughout the test sessions (Fig. 4).

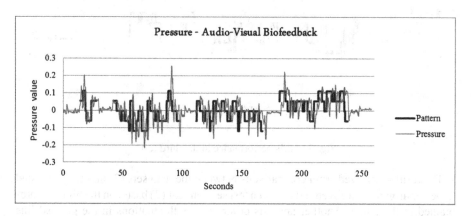

Fig. 3. Ki.'s performance in the first test

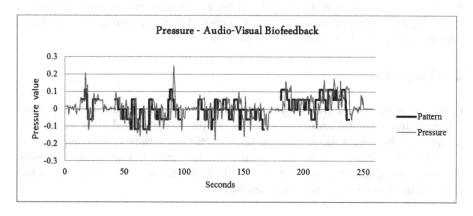

Fig. 4. Ki.'s performance in the second test

3.2 Semi-structured Interviews

The results from the first interview indicated that three out of five patients considered the game easy to understand, while the other two experienced difficulties in under- standing and playing the game. Three out of five patients stated that the speed of the game was too fast. Regarding motivation, two patients affirmed that they would use the setup at home. The second interview indicated that four out of five patients considered the game easy to understand. Concerning the speed, all patients considered it suitable. Four patients indicated that they considered the game motivating and would use it for further training. In relation with the in-game music, the patients indicated enjoyment and recognition when hearing the song selected (Fig. 5).

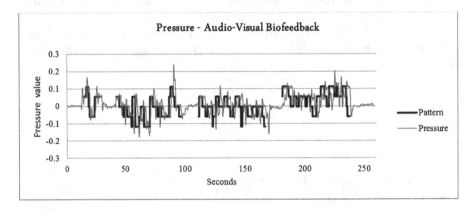

Fig. 5. Ki.'s performance in the third test

The results retrieved from comparisons between the data sets (2) and (3) suggested a superior in-game improvement between test sessions for (2) based on the higher scores obtained in the game. Another analysis criterion was fluctuations in the graphs' line (Fig. 3). The data set (3) indicated an inferior in-game improvement compared to (2). Moreover, one of the testers from (3) had the lowest score in the entire procedure. Regarding the data set (1) testers were less motivated to perform the training exercises although their performance was superior to (2) and (3).

4   Discussion

Results from the control group test revealed that the performance level of the patients increased throughout the testing session. The two patients presented fewer fluctuations of the graph lines than the patients in the other groups; however, the comparison is invalid as the conditions are different. The patients performed the training exercise using the post-it notes, numbered from one to five; therefore they had no clear point of refer- ence to indicate the correct amount of leaning.

The results retrieved from comparisons between (2) and (3) suggested a superior in-game improvement between test sessions for (2). A better in-game improvement rate, higher scores and less fluctuations of the graph lines were observed in (2). This indicates that the patients (2) had better postural stability than (3). The better in-game performance by (2) can be a consequence of several factors, including: cognitive overload, individual level of balance and sample size.

4.1 Cognitive Overload

Using multiple biofeedback parameters may influence users on a psychological level, according to [3]. However, a related study suggests that sensory overloading might not be of great concern when designing for augmentation [20]. As a consequence, users had smoother movements when provided with both audio and visual information. This argument is supported by additional research stating that rhythm positively influences motor behavior [15].

4.2 Individual Level of Balance

The testing sessions were conducted over a period of only two weeks, and each patient played the game for approximately 25 min in total. Since the amount of training with the setup was limited, it cannot be established how their individual balance level affected the result.

4.3 Sample Size

The number of available patients was limited, thus the result cannot be generalized. Based on the semi-structured interviews and the feedback from the physiotherapist, the patients from the Visual and Audio-Visual biofeedback groups considered the game motivating, as it follows the concept of "Gameflow" [21]. Along with this, it was discovered that music improves motivation for exercising [19]. In [22] certain users were more receptive to audio stimuli while others to visual stimuli, however when exposed to both types of stimuli simultaneously the degree of immersion increased significantly. The feedback from the physiotherapist who supervised the testing session corresponds with these points.

5   Conclusion

The main objective of this study was to investigate how the audio component in audio-visual biofeedback affects the rehabilitation process of balance-impaired stroke patients. It can be concluded that the Audio-Visual biofeedback group indicated less postural stability when compared to the Visual biofeedback group. However, the Audio-Visual biofeedback group performed smoother moves during the test sessions, which according to the physiotherapist are beneficial for the rehabilitation process. Both groups considered the game motivating.

A limitation of the study was the size of the sample and the testing time. A larger sample should be tested over a longer time period to achieve more conclusive results. Moreover, there is a need to establish a baseline level of balance for each patient at initiation to draw an accurate comparison of intervention. Nonetheless, whilst there is a need for extra validation of the system, the physiotherapist concluded that it could still be useful as an additional and recreational training tool for regaining postural stability.

References

1. Mirelman, A., Herman, T., Nicolai, S., Zijlstra, A., Zijlstra, W., Becker, C., Chiari, L., Hausdorff, J.: Audio-Biofeedback training for posture and balance in Patients with Parkinson's disease. J. Neuroeng. Rehabil. **8**, 1–7 (2011)
2. Hurkmans, H.L., Bussmann, J.B., Benda, E., Verhaar, J.A., Stam, H.J.: Effectiveness of audio feedback for partial weight-bearing in and outside the hospital: a randomized controlled trial. Arch. Phys. Med. Rehabil. **93**, 565–570 (2012)
3. Chen, Y., Huang, H., Xu, W., Wallis, R.I., Sundaram, H., Rikakis, T., Ingalls, T., Olson, L., He, J.: The design of a real-time, multimodal biofeedback system for stroke patient rehabilitation. In: 14th Annual ACM International Conference on Multimedia, pp. 763–772. ACM, New York (2006)
4. Geiger, R.A.: Balance and mobility following stroke: effects of physical therapy interventions with and without biofeedback/forceplate training. Phys. Ther. **81**, 995–1005 (2001)
5. Walker, C., Brouwer, B.J.: Use of visual feedback in retraining balance following acute stroke. Phys. Ther. **80**, 886–895 (2000)
6. National Institute on Deafness and Other Communication Disorders. http://www.medicinenet.com/vestibular_balance_disorders/article.htm#what_is_a_balance_disorder
7. Salzman, B.: Gait and balance disorders in older adults. Am. Fam. Physician **82**, 61–68 (2010)
8. Thorvaldsen, P., Davidsen, M., Bronnum-Hansen, H., Schroll, M.: Stable stroke occurrence despite incidence reduction in an aging population: stroke trends in the danish monitoring trends and determinants in cardiovascular disease (MONICA) population. Stroke **30**, 2529–2534 (1999)
9. Sims, N.R., Muyderman, H.: Mitochondria, oxidative metabolism and cell death in stroke. Biochim. Biophys. Acta **1802**, 80–91 (2010)
10. Eckerle, B.J., Southerland, A.M.: Bedside Evaluation of the Acute Stroke Patient. Wiley, Oxford (2013)
11. U.S. Department of Health and Human Services. http://womenshealth.gov/publications/our-publications/fact-sheet/stroke.html
12. Winter, D.A.: Human balance and posture control during standing and walking. Gait Posture **3**, 193–214 (1995)
13. Hunter, M.C., Hoffman, M.A.: Postural control: visual and cognitive manipulations. Gait Posture **13**, 41–48 (2001)
14. Zhong, X., Yost, W.A.: Relationship between postural stability and spatial hearing. J. Am. Acad. Audiol. **24**, 782–788 (2013)
15. Macdougall, R.: The relation of auditory rhythm to nervous discharge. Am. Psychol. Assoc. **9**, 460–480 (1902)
16. Anshel, M.H., Marisi, D.Q.: Effect of music and rhythm on physical performance. Res. Q. Exerc. Sport **49**, 109–113 (1978)

17. Brooks, T.: HUMANICS 1. a feasibility study to create a home internet-based telehealth product to supplement acquired brain injury therapy. Int. J. Disabil Hum. Dev. **4**, 277–282 (2005)
18. Rogers, Y., Sharp, H., Preece, J.: Interaction Design: Beyond Human-Computer Interaction. Wiley, Hoboken (2011)
19. Gfeller, K.: Musical components and styles preferred by young adults for aerobic fitness activities. J. Music Ther. **25**, 28–43 (1988)
20. He, H., Ingalls, T., Olson, L., Ganley, K., Rikakis, T., Jiping, H.: Interactive multimodal biofeedback for task-oriented neural rehabilitation. In: 27th IEEE Engineering in Medicine and Biology, pp. 2547–2550. IEEE Press, New York (2005)
21. Sweetser, P., Wyeth, P.: GameFlow: a model for evaluating player enjoyment in games. CIE ACM. **3**, 1–24 (2005)
22. Brooks, T., Camurri, A., Canagarajah, N., Hasselblad, S.: Interaction with shapes and sounds as a therapy for special needs and rehabilitation. In: 4th International Conference on Disability, Virtual Reality and Associated Technologies, pp. 205–212. ICDVRAT and The University of Reading (2002)

Speech Driven by Artificial Larynx: Potential Advancement Using Synthetic Pitch Contours

Hua-Li Jian$^{(\boxtimes)}$

Institute of Information Technology, Faculty of Technology, Art and Design
Oslo and Akershus University College of Applied Sciences, Oslo, Norway
Hua-Li.Jian@hioa.no

Abstract. Despite a long history of development, the speech qualities achieved with artificial larynx devices are limited. This paper explores recent advances in prosodic speech processing and technology and assesses their potentials in improving the quality of speech with an artificial larynx – in particular, tone and intonation through pitch variation. Three approaches are discussed: manual pitch control, automatic pitch control and re-synthesized speech.

Keywords: Artificial larynx · Fundamental frequency · Assistive technology

1 Introduction

Some individuals lose their ability to produce vowels after having their larynx surgically removed, for instance, after cancer in the throat. The larynx, or voice-box, produces the sound in the throat that drives speech. Individuals who have had their larynx removed can learn to produce esophageal speech, that is, the oscillation of the esophagus. Esophageal speech requires training and is strenuous and has a limited volume. Another approach is to surgically implant voice prosthetics. This paper focuses on the non-surgical approaches based on the electrolarynx. The advantages of eletrolarynxes are that very long sentences can be produced. There is no need for surgical procedures, and the device can be operated with virtually no skill and no maintenance.

There are various types of artificial larynxes or electrolarynxes. Most artificial larynxes are handheld devices held towards the throat. The device generates a vibration that is directed towards the throat that the speaker can use as basis for generating vowels in addition to consonants, in particular, plosives which are generated without the larynx.

Artificial larynxes have a push-to-talk button, and some designs have also a pitch control. An issue with artificial larynxes is the lack of naturalness and research has thus gone into assessing their naturalness [1, 2]. The interaction of a speaker and the chosen artificial larynx may also affect the intelligibility of the speech realized. Factors including gender, physiological states, and user proficiency may all impact such realization. Formalized tests concerning speech intelligibility and acceptability were thus advised for individual users prior to settling the most suited artificial device [1].

Artificial larynx speech can be stigmatizing for its users due to the highly noticeable monotone speech. Such speech has been used as characteristics in popular culture such

© Springer International Publishing Switzerland 2015
M. Antona and C. Stephanidis (Eds.): UAHCI 2015, Part III, LNCS 9177, pp. 312–321, 2015.
DOI: 10.1007/978-3-319-20684-4_30

as Ned Gerblansky in the South Park TV-series or Charlie in the Mad Max movie. An individual with an artificial larynx may not be taken seriously on the phone if the talker at the other end does not know that the speaker uses an artificial larynx. Moreover, as the speech is harder for untrained listeners to understand, miscommunication can occur, especially in a noisy environment such as a public space. By striving towards more natural sounding speech, it is likely that both the stigma can be reduced and the communication with others improved.

Although some development has been made over the course of nearly 120 years, the amount of research into artificial larynxes is limited. One possible explanation for the lack of attention could be that the proportion of individuals dependent on artificial larynxes are relatively limited with perhaps less than 100 per million people. The objective of this paper is to explore the possible use of recent technological developments and off-the-shelf third party technology intended for other purposes to improve the quality of speech by individuals without a natural voice box.

2 Background

Surgery of the larynx can lead to partial or full disability to produce vowels [3]. This study focuses on individuals who are reliant on artificial larynxes to produce speech. The waveform produced by the human larynx is complex and some research has gone into understanding the underlying mechanisms leading to the rich timbre produced by the larynx [4]. Some researchers have also attempted to improve the spectrum produced by the electronic larynx by the means of piezoeletronic ceramics as the source of the vibrations [5].

The artificial larynxes are also known to produce harsh background noises that reduce the speech quality, and measures to reduce the noise have been made using adaptive noise cancellation. The processes also helped preserve the voice's acoustic characteristics and hence speech acceptability was improved [6].

Recent technology allows researchers to focus even more on the naturalness of the actual vibrations through accurate observation of the larynx using high speed video [7]. With such objectively quantified information, further rehabilitation of the substitute voice may be achieved.

Without a larynx, individuals are able to whisper without the aid of an artificial larynx. However, whispering is usually too weak in volume to be practical in everyday conversation. To overcome these problems, researchers have also attempted to capture whispered speech and re-synthesize normal speech externally [8]. However, this approach is sensitive to background noise in the environment.

Alternative means of controlling the artificial larynx have also been used, such as employing the myoelectric signals that can be measured around the neck [9, 10] to control both push-to-talk and pitch at low, medium and high frequencies. Experiments with wireless connections between the neck sensors and the vibrator have also been explored [11].

Pitch has been identified as a key characteristic of speech. In one approach, air pressure through breathing was used to control the pitch of an artificial larynx [12].

This setup required training and users' training needs might vary. The intonation of a short sentence thus produced was reported to be similar to that of a normal subject.

3 Pitch Control by Manual Adjustments

The idea of manual pitch control for artificial larynxes is not new. Initially, some artificial larynx devices were designed with a pitch control. Recent studies have explored hands-free approaches to pitch control using breathing pressure [12] and myoelectric signals [9].

The monotonic voice of synthetic speech for disabled users has troubled researchers. One strategy proposed allows typically non-technical users to transcribe prosodic features of speech for artistic performances off-line in configuration files [13]. However, this is more suitable for users relying on synthetic speech and not users relying on artificial larynxes.

With current mobile technology enabling real world gestures, a specialized hand-held mobile device or a general one such as a smartphone could be used to express gestures that again would control the pitch of the device. For instance, a rising pitch could be achieved by lifting the device, while a falling pitch could be achieved by lowering the device (see Fig. 1).

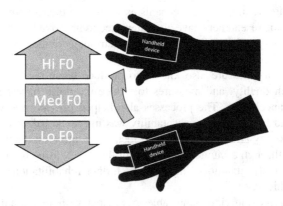

Fig. 1. Lowering and lifting the device to control pitch (f0) height

Most smartphones are equipped with accelerometers that are able to accurately detect such gestures [14]. Wireless communication, such as Bluetooth, could be used to send the pitch information from the handheld device to the artificial larynx. Such gesticulation control would not be subject to the gesture segmentation problem that is present in other application areas where gestures are used [15].

This approach would be relatively simple to implement from a technical standpoint. It would give the speaker complete control over the pitch, although some hand-pitch coordination training might be needed. The approach would be particularly effective in performance settings, e.g., during public speaking where gesticulations and exaggerated prosody often are used to emphasize the message. On the other hand, this approach may not be as effective, and even disturbing, during more calm settings such as when conversing in a small group. It may also be strenuous to physically articulate pitch with the hands for long periods of time. Automatic pitch enhancements are thus explored in the subsequent sections.

4 Pitch Control by Intelligent Systems

An alternative to manual pitch control is automatic pitch control. One may hypothesize that imposing randomly selected natural pitch curves to the speech would improve its naturalness by breaking the monotony. By employing an even more intelligent strategy, that is, choosing a more fitting pitch curve than random is likely to yield better results. We can draw inspiration from text-to-speech systems.

Speech quality is found to be most sensitive to pitch in text-to-speech systems [16, 17]. The addition of pitch accents to synthetic speech has long been a research topic with many innovative approaches. For instance, Hidden Markov models are applied to estimate the prosodic features of synthetic speech [18]. Researchers have also examined the detailed assignment of pitch marks at waveform level [19].

Simple rules have also been used to set the pitch accent of synthetic speech. Hirschberg [20] proposed the following rules: cue phrases (e.g., *now, we,* and *by the way*) are key accented, closed classed words are de-accented, words with their root in local or global focus are de-accented, compound stress assignments suggesting de-accenting are de-accented, and all other cases are accented. Algorithms may also be created to infer topic structure from paragraphing, punctuation, and lexical cues [21]. For achieving speech naturalness and successful listeners' interpretation, accent assignment denoting which words to emphasize or de-emphasize intonationally is important. Recent experiments on recorded read speech and elicited speech have demonstrated considerable success (over 80 % correctness) in modeling speakers' accenting strategies by merely using automated text analysis [22].

Most of the work on prosody for text-to-speech systems is based on pitch measurements for various transcribed speech corpora, that is, pitch extracted from authentic speech. The pitch contours can be associated with single vowels, words or phrases, and sometimes combined with sentence templates. It is likely that a prosodic module from a text-to-speech system could be adopted to the automatic pitch control of artificial larynxes with relatively moderate effort.

4.1 Acquiring Speech Information

A key difference between a text-to-speech system versus an artificial larynx is the lack of information available. With a text-to-speech system, the text to be uttered is known a priori. With an artificial larynx. there is no basic information available. However, the following information could be solicited.

Segment durations: the user of the artificial larynx controls the device with the on/off switch. The state of the on/off switch provides useful information in terms of when speech is uttered and when it is not. Moreover, the timing of the speech segments, that is, the speech duration, and the durations of the pauses, could provide useful cues.

Audio: the resulting speech produced with the artificial larynx could be recorded in real time and subjected to speech recognition technology. This could be achieved by attaching a microphone to the artificial larynx device. For the system to work in real time, the recognition would have to be at the level of phonetic units. The feasibility and accuracy of acquiring phonetic information from speech driven by an artificial larynx would need to be investigated. However, there is potential to specially train a speech recognition engine for such speech.

Neck muscle signals: by attaching sensors at the neck, valuable information about the throat muscle activity could be measured to help classify the uttered sound. Such signals could be used together with audio signals to improve the recognition rates.

Image data: to further help the real time recognition of the uttered signals, visual cues could be acquired using a video camera. Research into video analysis has successfully managed to lip-read utterances simply from visual cues in color videos [23–25]. By combining several channels such as audio, video and muscle information, a more accurate phonetic classification may be achieved. One challenge is where and how to fit the camera to obtain high recognition rates while ensuring sufficient pervasiveness in the setup.

4.2   Speech Prediction

As the pitch has to be adjusted in real time, partially uttered speech needs to be used to predict the intended utterances. For this purpose, text prediction algorithms [26] such as trie structures can be employed. Text prediction algorithms in the simple form can be composed using di-grams, where pairs of phonetic elements comprise each di-gram key and the di-gram entry is assigned a pitch contour. Table 1 shows an extract of such a di-gram. Next, imagine that the first syllable of an utterance is A and the second is D, with the corresponding pitch contour being LEVEL. The trie approach involves a linguistic model using a dictionary with all forms of the words organized into a tree-like structure [27].

Table 1. Example syllable di-gram extract with pitch contours

1st syllable	2nd syllable	Pitch contour
A	B	FALL
A	D	LEVEL
A	E	RISE
...	...	...

For the approach to work, the data structure needs to be based on phonetic elements rather than spelling. One benefit of pitch prediction over spelling prediction is that the number of unique pitch patterns is smaller than the set of possible spellings. Examples include using the simple SOUNDEX or more sophisticated metaphone strategy [28];

the latter is commonly employed for phonetic matching in spelling correction applications. Instead of mapping the partial utterance with a particular word, it is associated with a given frequency contour. Interpolation of pitch contours can be used to make a smooth switch from an incorrectly predicted contour to the intended contour in erroneous cases. As predictions are based on partial utterances, the prediction accuracy will be lower in the beginning of an utterance compared to when the utterance is complete. If there is a tie between several pitch contours, the most probable contour can be selected.

Table 2 shows an example of pitch prediction where the first syllable of the utterance is Y and thus assigned a mid-level pitch contour with a low confidence of 10 %. The second syllable is E giving the prefix YE, which means that the pitch contour prediction is altered to a rising contour with 25 % confidence.

Table 2. Example of observation window, prediction and confidence

Observation	Prediction	Confidence
Y*********	mid-level	10 %
Ye********	Rise	25 %
Yes*******	Rise	50 %
Yes *******	Rise + pause	100 %

Next, the third syllable is S giving the prefix YES, which also is assigned to a rising pitch contour with a confidence of 50 %. Finally, a pause is detected and the uttered word is detected as YES with a rising pitch contour.

A simple selection scheme was also proposed to reduce mismatch of pitch and thus increase pitch prediction rate [17]. By means of annotations employing linguistic foot structure, local pitch contours of syllables could be predicted more accurately.

4.3 Speech Correction

Misrecognition for any spoken system is to be avoided or corrected. Strategies for correcting, rejecting, or changing misrecognized hypotheses have been proposed [29–31]. Prosodic features such as F0 perturbation, duration, and loudness were shown to significantly characterize failed recognition runs in terms of word-accuracy and conception-accuracy [32]. Machine learning experiments also indicated that use of prosodic differences may greatly improve prediction of misrecognition in terms of word-accuracy and obtain even greater predication rate when combining prosodic features with other automatically available features of speech recognition systems.

Variation of speaking rate may have a negative impact for automatic recognition systems [33]. Possibly longer utterances, varied or irregular pausing, and slow articulation combined with disfluency may all cause recognition errors [32]. Understandably, such chances of error may be even higher for individuals using artificial larynxes.

It may, however, be possible to make users aware of recognition errors [34] and also correct them [35]. Efforts into examining prosodic variations have been made to account for why some voices are more poorly recognized than others [36, 37]. Failure identification and reaction strategies in speech recognition systems may be enhanced by integrating prosodic-related information [32].

Correcting misrecognitions by users have also been predicted and analyzed. User corrections were more poorly recognized than non-corrections, but they were not more frequently rejected by the recognition systems. Corrections paraphrasing the original information were found to be less recognized than those omitting it [38]. However, user corrections were found to be better identified by means of a combined feature set of prosody and specific system-derived features. Future techniques to improve correction prediction and to further execute modifications for automatic correction identification would also add to positive development of speech recognition for artificial-larynx-driven speech.

5 Total Synthetic Speech

One could imagine going one step further by synthesizing the speech in real time based on the successfully recognized utterances. In this case the artificial larynx would be replaced by an artificial voice altogether using synthetic speech. In this way it may be possible to somehow restore the original voice of someone who has undergone surgery on the larynx. Some research has also gone into synthesizing speech with arbitrary voices [39].

However, such an approach raises new issues such as where the sound should come from. An advantage of the artificial larynx is that the sound still originates from the throat of the speaker. With synthetic speech, it is important that the speaker is as close as possible to the speaker's mouth to give the impression that the sound actually originates from the speaker. Otherwise, if the speech comes from a different location, the listeners may get confused in conversational settings. Moreover, this scheme would require highly accurate speech recognition. The impact of misrecognition consequently resulting in erroneous speech synthesis is more severe than an incorrect pitch contour, which in the worst case will only sound odd.

One major issue with synthetic speech systems is potential lags caused by processing delays as the detection and synthesis involved are in essence complex operations.

6 Summary and Future Work

This paper has explored the problem of lacking prosody in speech produced with artificial larynx devices. Three approaches to improving the expression pitch for such speech using recent technological advances and off-the-shelf hardware are discussed, namely, the simplest strategy of manual control of pitch through gestures via a handheld device, the automatic control of pitch via speech recognition, and finally the most challenging idea of total real-time synthesis of speech based on real-time speech recognition.

The simple approach such as the manual control would probably be associated with an unperceivable delay. With efficient algorithms and high performance hardware, it may be possible to reduce processing lags to a minimum. Future work will focus on (a) exploring the perception effects of altering the pitch and (b) developing a robust pitch-contour prediction algorithm.

References

1. Stalker, J.L., Hawk, A.M., Smaldino, J.J.: The intelligibility and acceptability of speech produced by five different electronic artificial larynx devices. J. Commun. Disord. 1(5), 299–301 (1982)
2. Pindzola, R.H., Moffet, B.: Comparison of ratings of four artificial larynxes. J. Commun. Disord. 21, 459–467 (1988)
3. Modrzejewski, M., Olszewski, E., Wszol, W., Rerona, E., Strek, P.: Acoustic assessment of voice signal deformation after partial surgery of the larynx. Auris Nasus Larynx 26, 183–190 (1999)
4. Alipour, F., Scherer, R.C., Finnegan, E.: Measures of spectral slope using an excised larynx model. J. Voice 26(4), 403–411 (2012)
5. Ooe, K., Fukuda, T., Arai, F.: A new type of artificial larynx using a PZT ceramics vibrator as a sound source. IEEE/ASME Trans. Mechantronics 5(2), 221–225 (2000)
6. Niu, H.J., Won, M.X. Waq, S.P.: Enhancement of electronic artificial larynx speech by denoising. In: IEEE International Conference on Neural Networks & Signal Processing, pp. 908–911. IEEE Press (2003)
7. Schwarz, R., Huttner, B., Dollinger, M., Luegmair, G., Eysholdt, U., Schuster, M., Lohscheller, J., Gurlek, E.: Substitute voice production: quantification of PE segment vibrations using a biomechanical model. IEEE Trans. Biomed. Eng. 58(10), 2767–2776 (2011)
8. Sharifzadeh, H.R., McLoughlin, I.V., Ahmadi, F.: Reconstruction of normal sounding speech for laryngectomy patients through a modified CELP codec. IEEE Trans. Biomed. Eng. 57(10), 2448–2458 (2010)
9. Ooe, K.: Development of controllable artificial larynx by neck myoelectric signal. Procedia Eng. 47, 869–872 (2012)
10. Stepp, C.A., Heaton, J.T., Rolland, R.G., Hillman, R.E.: Neck and face surface electromyography for prosthetic voice control after total laryngectomy. IEEE Trans. Neural Syst. Rehabil. Eng. 17(2), 146–155 (2009)
11. Heaton, J.T., Robertson, M., Griffin, C.: Development of a wireless electromyographically controlled electrolarynx voice prosthesis. In: 33rd Annual International Conference of the IEEE EMBS, pp. 5352–5355. IEEE Press (2011)
12. Uemi, N., Ifukube, T., Tamashi, T., Matsushima, J.: Design of a new electrolarynx having a pitch control function. In: IEEE International Workshop on Robot and Human Communication, pp. 198–203. IEEE Press (1994)
13. Blankinship, E., Beckwith, R.: Tools for expressive text-to-speech markup. In: Proceedings of the 14th Annual ACM Symposium on User Interface Software and Technology, pp. 159–160. ACM press (2001)
14. Győrbíró, N., Fábián, A., Hományi, G.: An activity recognition system for mobile phones. Mobile Netw. Appl. 14(1), 82–91 (2009)

15. Carrino, F., Ridi, A., Ingold, R., Abou Khaled, O., Mugellini, E.: Gesture vs. gesticulation: a test protocol. In: Kurosu, M. (ed.) HCII/HCI 2013, Part IV. LNCS, vol. 8007, pp. 157–166. Springer, Heidelberg (2013)
16. Plumpe, M., Meredith, S.: Which is more important in a concatenative text to speech system - pitch, duration or spectral discontinuity? In: Proceedings of the Third ESCA/COCOSDA Workshop on Speech Synthesis, Jenolan, Australia (1998)
17. Klabbers, E., van Santen, J.P.H.: Control and prediction of the impact of pitch modification on synthetic speech quality. In: Eurospeech 2003 (2003)
18. Gu, H.Y., Yang, C.C.: An HMM based pitch-contour generation method for mandarin speech synthesis. J. Inf. Sci. Eng. 27, 1561–1580 (2011)
19. Chen, J.H., Kao, Y.A.: Pitch marking based on an adaptable filter and a peak-valley estimation method. Comput. Linguist. Chin. Lang. Process. 6(2), 1–12 (2012)
20. Hirschberg, J.: Accent and discourse context: assigning pitch accent in synthetic speech. In: AAAI 1990 Proceedings (1990)
21. Hirschberg, J., Litman, D.: Disambiguating cue phrases in text and speech. In: Proceedings of COLING 1990, Helsinki, August (1990)
22. Hirschberg, J.: Pitch accent in context predicting intonational prominence from text. Artif. Intell. 63(1), 305–340 (1993)
23. Chiou, G.I., Hwang, J.N.: Lipreading from color video. IEEE Trans. Image Process. 6(8), 1192–1195 (1997)
24. Zhou, Z.H., Zhao, G.Y., Pietikainen, M.: Towards a practical lip-reading system. In: IEEE Conference on Computer Vision and Pattern Recognition (CVPR), pp. 137–144 (2011)
25. Li, M., Cheung, Y.M.: A novel motion based lip feature extraction for lip-reading. In: International Conference on Computational Intelligence and Security, CIS 2008, vol. 1, pp. 361–365 (2008)
26. Garay-Vitoria, N., Abascal, J.: Text prediction systems: a survey. Univers. Access. Inf. Soc. 4(3), 188–203 (2006)
27. Fredkin, E.: Trie Memory. Commun. ACM 3(9), 490–499 (1960)
28. Philips, L.: Hanging on the metaphone. Comput. Lang. 7(12), 38–43 (1990)
29. Litman, D., Walker, M., Kearns, M.: Automatic detection of poor speech recognition at the dialogue level. In: Proceedings of the 37th Annual Meeting of the Association of Computational Linguistics, ACL 1999, College Park, pp. 309–316 (1999)
30. Litman, D., Pan, S.: Empirically evaluating an adaptable spoken dialogue system. In: Proceedings of the 7th International Conference on User Modeling (UM), Banff, pp. 55–64 (1999)
31. Walker, M., Kamm, C., Litman, D.: Towards developing general models of usability with PARADISE. Nat. Lang. Eng. Special Issue on Best Practice Spoken Language Dialogue System Engineering 6, 363–377 (2000)
32. Hirschberg, J., Litman, D., Swerts, M.: Prosodic and other cues to speech recognition failures. Speech Commun. 43(1), 155–175 (2004)
33. Ostendorf, M., Byrne, B., Bacchiani, M., Finke, M., Gunawardana, A., Ross, K., Roweis, S., Shriberg, E., Talkin, D.,Waibel, A., Wheatley, B., Zeppenfeld, T.: Modeling systematic variations in pronunciation via a language-dependent hidden speaking mode. In: Report on 1996 CLSP/JHU Workshop on Innovative Techniques for Large Vocabulary Continuous Speech Recognition (1997)
34. Litman, D., Hirschberg, J., Swerts, M.: Predicting user reactions to system error. In: Proceedings of the ACL-2001, Toulouse, pp. 329–369 (2001)
35. Hirschberg, J., Litman, D., Swerts, M.: Identifying user corrections automatically in spoken dialogue systems. In: Procedings of the NAACL 2001, Pittsburgh, pp. 208–215 (2001)

36. Doddington, G., Liggett, W., Martin, A., Przybocki, M., Reynolds, D.: Sheep, goats, lambs and wolves: a statistical analysis of speaker performance in the NIST 1998 speaker recognition evaluation. In: Proceedings of the International Conference on Spoken Language Processing-98, Sydney, pp. 608–611 (1998)
37. Hirschberg, J., Litman, D., Swerts, M.: Prosodic cues to recognition errors. In: Proceedings of the Automatic Speech Recognition and Understanding Workshop (ASRU 1999), Keystone, pp. 349–352 (1999)
38. Litman, D., Hirschberg, J., Swerts, M.: Characterizing and predicting corrections in spoken dialogue systems. Comput. Linguist. **32**(3), 417–438 (2006)
39. Tamura, M., Masuko, T., Tokuda, K., Kobayashi, T.: Text-to-speech synthesis with arbitrary speaker's voice from average voice. In: Proceedings of Eurospeech 2001, pp. 345–348 (2001)

Multimodal Feedback for Balance Rehabilitation

Bruce J.P. Mortimer[✉], Braden J. McGrath, Greg R. Mort, and Gary A. Zets

Engineering Acoustics, Inc., Casselberry, USA
{Bmort,McGrath,Mort,Zets}@eaiinfo.com

Abstract. This paper describes development of an activity based, multimodal balance rehabilitation training device. Various sensors can be used, including a force plate, inertial sensors, and depth sensing cameras, and various combinations of visual, auditory and tactile feedback can be configured depending on the rehabilitation task and activity. Tactile feedback is presented via a lightweight belt that is worn on the torso. Generally, visual feedback is only needed at the start of rehabilitation training (task orientation) while tactile feedback may be used to augment balance control. Tactile feedback can be configured as a cue that certain movement targets or limits have been reached or as an immediate indicator of the variance in postural sway. Tactile feedback allows the subject to naturally concentrate on the functional rehabilitation task, and is less reliant on visual or verbal cues.

Keywords: Balance · Rehabilitation · Tactile feedback

1 Introduction

Balance dysfunction is often associated with aging, stroke, mild traumatic brain injury (mTBI), neurological disorders and disease [1]. For patients who have balance deficit, a physical therapy (PT) program can be used to "habituate" sensory and motor systems through exercise, and "compensate" the systems through sensor reweighting and learnt skill sets [2]. Clinical studies have shown that vestibular rehabilitation training (VRT) programs resulted in significant improvement in patients with unilateral peripheral vestibular dysfunction [3]. However, these rehabilitation programs require specialist therapists and multiple intensive customized clinical sessions that are presented over the course of several weeks [4].

Real time postural feedback from external sensors can also be used to augment or replace normal internal (vestibular, visual and proprioceptive) sensory information [5]. For example, body sway information can be measured using an inertial sensor and displayed using visual, auditory or tactile means, and previous research efforts have reported improvements in balance control during standing and gait with sensory feedback [6–10]. While an ambulatory sensory feedback prosthesis is a meaningful goal for the treatment of balance disorders, that approach currently presents significant technical challenges as natural movement can be complex and stability limits are based on intent. An alternate paradigm is to consider postural sensory feedback as an instructional tool

© Springer International Publishing Switzerland 2015
M. Antona and C. Stephanidis (Eds.): UAHCI 2015, Part III, LNCS 9177, pp. 322–330, 2015.
DOI: 10.1007/978-3-319-20684-4_31

during rehabilitation physical therapy. This paper describes our development of an activity based, multimodal balance rehabilitation training device.

2 Design of a Sensory Feedback System for Rehabilitation

The primary goals for postural stance and control are equilibrium and orientation [11]. We often take the postural control system for granted because it usually operates primarily at a non-cognitive level. However it actually depends on a complex and active interaction among the sensory, muscular, and nervous systems [12]. This central-nervous-system (CNS) process is known as sensory integration.

It is well known that the human sensory system is capable of adaptation. For example, if a fixed reference (such as a fingertip on a surface) is provided to a patient who has been blindfolded, body sway has been shown to reduce [13]. Thus, the sensory system has compensated for the loss of the visual reference system and adapted to use the force feedback from the fingertip to provide the body with a spatial reference. Moreover, the brain has a built-in mechanism that allows change according to experience [14].

2.1 Multisensory Feedback Displays

Providing postural sensory feedback or context data to a patient during rehabilitation physical therapy presents a human-machine interface design problem for the rehabilitation training system. There are typically two users of the rehabilitation training system: the therapist and the patient. The rehabilitation training system user interface must track with the work flow and expectations of the physical therapist and any postural sensory feedback presented to the user (or patient) must be immediate and effective. Specifically, the feedback information to the patient must be natural and intuitive, and ideally should not increase cognitive workload.

Postural control using visual or audio displays typically requires significant cognition (i.e. concentration) as the feedback information must be recognized before deciding on an appropriate motor response reaction. Tactile events, in contrast, may be processed preattentively [15, 16]. Furthermore, proprioceptive and tactile sensory information is naturally used in postural control. Therefore, the tactile modality can potentially offer significant advantages as a feedback display during balance therapy.

The sense of touch is arranged somatotopically so location based tactile cues are a highly effective method for providing orientation. An array of vibrotactile actuators (or tactors) that are spaced over an area of the body that is implicitly aligned with the patient's local coordinate axis eliminates cognitive translation. Thus, the torso is preferred as it is usually aligned with the direction of intended motion.

We have previously reported on our work using an array of eight lightweight vibrotactile actuators (tactors) mounted in a lightweight, stretchable belt – this approach represents a useful compromise between localization accuracy and resolution [17]. Our current tactor belt design incorporates 8 EMR tactors as shown in Fig. 1.

Visual displays are highly effective user interfaces that are potentially capable of communicating large amounts of data to a user. However, the role of vision in postural control feedback is complex, and mostly limited to low frequency postural control [18].

Fig. 1. Tactor belt array containing 8 EMR tactors, a wearable controller (including Bluetooth wireless interface) and a rechargeable internal battery. The EMR tactor is a motor based design that operates at about 100 Hz.

Typically, vision provides information regarding reference to verticality, motion of the head, self motion and navigation. The role of vision in balance rehabilitation can change depending on the postural task, balance deficits, stage of recovery, and the environment. For example, vestibular-ocular (VO) deficits often accompany blast related balance dysfunction and in these cases the vision system requires compensation and habituation during rehabilitation [19, 20].

The visual display can be used for rehabilitation task orientation and also provide visual flow (disruptive stimuli) or tasks(for example cognitive or immersive) to assist VO rehabilitation. The visual display must be mounted at eye-level and preferably have a touch screen interface for the therapist to input patient specific data and parameters.

Auditory displays can potentially convey both direction and informational components and have been used as a feedback display for postural control [21]. However, wearable audio displays use binaural headphones and synthesize apparent sound source direction. Audio localization is also subject to well known front and back localization ambiguity [22], which usually requires head or body movement to resolve. Therefore headphones were not considered and our design approach has been to limit audio to pitch and rate, and use it only as a qualitative indicator of a feedback parameter or limit in a therapeutic task.

2.2 Postural Sensor Design and Selection

A real-time measurement of the patient's postural state is needed for the rehabilitation training system. Various sensors and biomechanical models of movement can be used depending on the chosen rehabilitation activity. Rehabilitation training tasks can be generally classified into stable (sitting and upright stance) and dynamic (gait, turns and sit-to-stand) movements.

Upright stance can be simply modeled as a single segment or as a more complex multi-segment inverted pendulum. Feedback stability during single segment upright stance is defined by the angle of lean and controlled by ankle torque [23]. In multi-link upright stance, the ankle torque and hip torque control the predominant movements. Feedback stability during multi-segment lean is then more accurately defined by the location of the center of mass with respect to the balance of support (feet).

Dynamic movements can be modeled using more complex multiple segment models, where the contact forces and movement kinematics are estimated or known. Capturing generalized dynamic movement usually requires sensors that are capable of tracking the kinematics of the multi-segment model. Rehabilitation systems require real-time measurement of multiple segment data which can usually only be implemented using a simplified model.

Feedback during dynamic activities is also more complex as the postural stability depends on previous and anticipated movements. Movements may also be relatively fast, leaving very little time to use any additional system feedback to compensate for any erroneous trajectories. In contrast, gait is cyclical and patients are usually relatively stable in the anterior/posterior axis. Therefore, gait feedback can be simplified to only the mediolateral axis, and the system stability can be approximated using an inverted pendulum model.

Our approach has been to consider multiple sensor components as modular and scalable to meet intended activity and therapeutic needs. A combination of sensors were selected for our system including: a light weight custom force plate, a wearable inertial sensor (Microstrain® 3DM-GX3®-25), and a depth sensing camera (Microsoft Kinect®). The available sensors are fused together to provide an estimate of a user's biomechanical state. A lightweight force plate is low cost, robust and measures location of the center of pressure (COP) of the patient standing on the plate. Our force plate design is easily scalable; multiple force plates can be attached together in order to construct a wider sensing area. Similarly, the depth sensing camera can measure the position of the patient and approximate the COG, or an inertial sensor mounted on the small of the back can provide a measure of the body tilt [24].

During static activities, any of the sensors (force plate, inertial and depth camera sensor) can be used individually, or in combination, to provide an adequate estimation of patient stability. During dynamic activities, the force plate data must be supplemented with measurements of body segment center of gravity (COG). Methods for measuring body segment COG include using one or more inertial sensors, and /or the depth sensing camera. The inertial sensor is lightweight and can be mounted on the patient's head to track head orientation – this is useful during functional gait tasks [25] and during vestibular ocular habituation exercises [26].

The complete multimodal balance rehabilitation training device comprises a stand, computer, touch screen display, speaker, force plate, depth sensing camera, wearable inertial sensor and tactile belt as shown in Fig. 2.

2.3 Design of Therapeutic Activities

The typical therapist workflow associated with a balance rehabilitation training protocol for the treatment and rehabilitation of subjects with balance dysfunction comprises the following components [1, 2]:

- Assessment: Clinical examination, history, classification, diagnosis and treatment planning
- PT Interventions:

Fig. 2. Multimodal balance rehabilitation training device showing the force plate, Microsoft Kinect camera and wearable inertial sensors, together with the touch screen and tactile belt.

- Adaptation /substitution exercises
- Postural and oculormotor control
- Steady stand concentrating on: sensory integration, core /strength exercises, vestibular ocular reflex (VOR) visual acuity training
- Dynamic tasks : turns /gait
- Movement sensitivity training
- Functional exercises
- Immersion /dual task exercising
- Home exercises

A range of activities is required for balance rehabilitation training, and the selection and configuration of each of the activities must be under the control of the therapists. The type and amount of feedback, as well as the task difficulty must also be selectable and individualized for a particular patient and the stage in their rehabilitation program.

Our design approach to a balance training rehabilitation system is shown in Fig. 3. The system recognizes the two users in the system; the therapist and patient. The patient forms part of a human-in-the-loop feedback system. Multiple sensors measure the patient's postural state and a computer controller combines the therapist selected activity configurations to provide multisensory feedback to the patient.

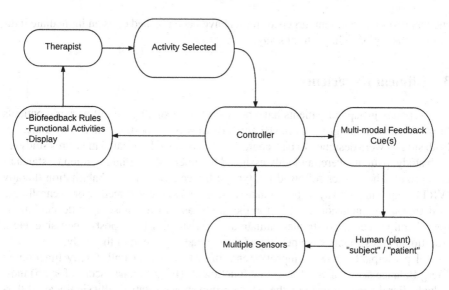

Fig. 3. Block diagram relationship between the human-in-the-loop and the multi-modal sensory feedback system. The predefined functional activity and feedback settings are determined by the therapist.

The addition of multi-modal feedback to the patient has several potential advantages: 1) feedback can be provided continuously and simultaneously along multiple channels which should increase system performance (and also bypass any possible bottle necks due to injury), 2) it should be easier to understand the feedback (cross verification of the feedback "message" leads to less confusion), and 3) the human ("plant") is itself a non-linear adaptive (neuro) controller that can internally optimize the loop. Each of the activities was designed to make optimum use of the multi-modal feedback and each feedback mode was selected by the therapist.

The functional activities designed for the system include: steady stand, sit-to-stand, limited gait, adaptive immersive activities including movement to goals, movements with visual flow distraction and various assessment tools. Some of the activities address specific deficits within patient population groups. For example, vestibular ocular disorders are especially important for the rehabilitation of blast related balance dysfunction. Our device implemented prototype activities where the patient had to follow a visual or auditory tracking task in combination with postural control. Other patient groups such as geriatric and stroke required other functional tasks; for example, the sit-to-stand movement sequence can be trained using tactile cues.

2.4 Design of Multisensory Feedback for Activities

Various combinations of visual, auditory and tactile feedback can be configured for each therapeutic activity. Generally, visual feedback is needed at the start of rehabilitation training to provide task orientation. After orientation, tactile feedback is then primarily used to augment balance control. Tactile feedback is versatile; it can be configured as a cue that certain movement targets or limits have been reached or as an immediate indicator of the variance in postural sway.

3 Clinical Experience

Two separate groups of patients have been studied; a small group of geriatric patients (n = 12) and a small group of mTBI and TBI (n = 30) reporting balance dysfunction. Both studies were designed to be a controlled, randomized, repeated measures study. In each study, patients were randomly assigned to either a device intervention or standard care group. The studies followed the typical 8 week vestibular rehabilitation therapy (VRT) treatment pathway. A preliminary assessment was performed prior to enrollment to demonstrate inclusion criteria for the study and to diagnose specific conditions (peripheral vs. central vestibular, unilateral vs. bilateral, BPPV, post-concussive, etc.). Additional assessments were performed during and at the end of the study.

All participants showed improvements in test scores for both highly functioning (Berg Balance score of > 50) and low functioning (Berg Balance score of < 35) individuals. For the geriatric study, the device group showed statistically significant differences to the control group by the second week of treatment. The results from the mTBI / TBI study group were more variable and although the device intervention group showed good results, there were not statistically significant differences between the two groups. Further detailed analysis of this data suggests that a subgroup with known vestibular issues potentially benefited more from the device intervention, but the study numbers are too small for statistical significance.

4 Conclusions

The device was very well received by patients and therapists, and clinical measures show that the device may be more effective, especially during the early stages of rehabilitation, than standard care. Results indicate that the system, in at least one study group, initially facilitates a more rapid rehabilitation and training than the conventional approach and then, with time, the conventional approach "catches up" and the overall outcome is similar.

Another observation from clinical testing was that the system appeared to offer an increase in the efficiency of the therapist. Subjective comments suggest that by using the system, a therapist could treat multiple patients without decreasing outcomes - this result has potentially significant economic value both for the military and civilian populations and needs further investigation.

References

1. Herdman, S.: Role of the Vestibular System in Postural Control. In: Herdman, S. (ed.) Vestibular Rehabilitation, 3rd edn. FA Davis Company, Philadelphia (2007)
2. Shumway-Cook, A., Woollacott, M.: Motor Learning and Recovery of Function. In: Motor Control, 2nd edn. Lippincott Williams and Wilkins, Philadelphia (2001)

3. Han, B.I., Song, H.S., Kim, J.S.: Vestibular rehabilitation therapy: review of indications, mechanisms, and key exercises. J. Clin. Neurol. (Seoul, Korea) 7(4), 184–196 (2011)
4. Hillier, S.L., McDonnell, M.: Vestibular rehabilitation for unilateral peripheral vestibular dysfunction. Clinical Otolaryngology : Journal of ENT-UK; Official Journal of Netherlands Society for Oto-Rhino-Laryngology & Cervico-Facial Surgery 36, 248–249 (2011)
5. Rupert, A.H., Mateczun, A., Guedry, F.E.: Maintaining spatial orientation awareness. Situation Awareness in Aerospace Operations. Copenhagen, Denmark. AGARD-CP-478, pp. 21-1–21-5 (1990)
6. Allum, J.H.J.: Method and apparatus for the diagnosis and rehabilitation of balance disorders, US patent 6,063,046
7. Hegeman, J., Honegger, F., Kupper, M., Allum, J.H.J.: The balance control of bilateralperipheral vestibular loss subjects and its improvement with auditory prosthetic feedback. J. Vest. Res. 15, 109–117 (2005)
8. Kentala, E., Vivas, J., Wall, C.: Reduction of postural sway by use of a vibrotactile balance prosthesis prototype in subjects with vestibular deficits. Ann. Otol. Rhinol. Laryngol. 112(5), 404–409 (2003)
9. Chiari, L., Dozza, M., Cappello, A., Horak, F.B., Macellari, V., Giansanti, D.: Audio-biofeedback for balance improvement: an accelerometry-based system. IEEE Trans. Biomed. Eng. 52(12), 2108–2111 (2005)
10. Bach-y-Rita, P.: Tactile sensory substitution studies. Ann. NY Acad. Sci. 1013, 83–91 (2004)
11. Horak, F.B., Macpherson, J.M.: Postural equilibrium and orientation. In: Rowell, R.B., Shepherd, J.T. (eds.) Handbook of Physiology, pp. 255–292. American Physiology Society, Oxford University Press, New York (1996)
12. Huxham, F., Goldie, P.A., Patla, A.E.: Theoretical considerations in balance assessment. Aust. J. Physiotherapy 47, 89–100 (2001)
13. Jeka, J., Olie, K., Schoner, G., Dijkstra, T., Henson, E.: Position and velocity coupling of postural sway to somatosensory drive. J. Neurol. 79, 1661–1674 (1998)
14. Kolb, B., Gibb, R., Robinson, T.: Brain plasticity and behavior. Curr. Dir. Psychol. Sci. 12, 1–5 (2003)
15. Hanson, J.V.M., Whitaker, D., Heron, J.: Preferential processing of tactile events under conditions of divided attention. NeuroReport 20(15), 1392–1396 (2012)
16. Van Erp, J.B.F.: Validation of Principles for Tactile Navigation Displays. In: Proceedings of the 50th annual meeting of the Human Factors and Ergonomics Society (2006)
17. Mortimer, B., Zets, G., Mort, G., Shovan, C.: Implementing effective tactile symbology for orientation and navigation. In: Jacko, J.A. (ed.) Human-Computer Interaction, Part III, HCII 2011. LNCS, vol. 6763, pp. 321–328. Springer, Heidelberg (2011)
18. Fukuoka, Y., Tanaka, K., Ishida, A., Minamitani, H.: Characteristics of visual feedback in postural control during standing. IEEE Trans. Rehabil. Eng. 7(4), 427–434 (1999)
19. Scherer, M.R., Burrows, H., Pinto, R., Littlefield, P., French, L.M., Tarbett, A.K., Schubert, M.C.: Evidence of central and peripheral vestibular pathology in blast-related traumatic brain injury. Otol Neurotol 32(4), 571–580 (2011)
20. Lawson, B.D., Rupert, A.H.: Vestibular aspects of head injury and recommendations for evaluation and rehabilitation following exposure to severe changes in head velocity or ambient pressure. In: Turan, O., Bos, J., Stark, J., Colwell, J. (eds.) Peer-Reviewed Proceedings of the International Conference on Human Performance at Sea (HPAS), University of Strathclyde, Glasgow, U.K., 16–18 June, pp. 367–380 (2010). ISBN: 978-0-947649-73-9
21. Dozza, M., Horak, F.B., Chiari, L.: Auditory biofeedback substitutes for loss of sensory information in maintaining stance. Exp. Brain Res. 178(1), 37–48 (2007)

22. Carlile, S., Leong, P., Hyams, S.: The nature and distribution of errors in sound localization by human listeners. Hearing Res. **114**, 179–196 (1997)
23. Winter, D.A.: Human balance and posture control during standing and walking. Gait and Posture **3**, 193–214 (1995)
24. Wall, C., Merfeld, D.M., Rauch, S.D., Black, F.O.: Vestibular prostheses: the engineering and biomedical issues. J. Vestib. Res. **12**(2–3), 95–113 (2002)
25. Wrisley, D.M., Marchetti, G.F., Kuharsky, D.K., Whitney, S.L.: Reliability, internal consistency, and validity of data obtained with the functional gait assessment. Phys. Ther. **84**(10), 906–918 (2004)
26. Cawthorne, T.: The Physiological Basis for Head Exercises. J. Chartered Soc. Physiotherapy **30**, 106 (1944)

A Virtual Reality System for Occupational Therapy with Hand Motion Capture and Force Feedback

A Pilot Study of System Configuration

Kouki Nagamune[1](✉), Yosuke Uozumi[1], and Yoshitada Sakai[2]

[1] Graduate School of Engineering, University of Fukui, Fukui, Japan
nagamune@u-fukui.ac.jp
[2] Graduate School of Medicine, Kobe University, Kobe, Japan

Abstract. This study proposes a virtual reality system for occupational therapy with hand motion capture and force feedback. Force feedback is realized by using a vibration motor. In the experiment, the proposed system was applied for three health males. The results with force feedback were close to the setting distance more than the results without force feedback. As a future work, actual working task used in clinical situation should be applied to this system.

Keywords: Virtual reality · Occupational therapy · Force feedback

1 Introduction

Japan is facing to high aged society. Japanese government estimates 4.7 million people who has dementia in 2025 [1]. On the other hand, the number of occupational therapist is only 57 thousands in 2011 [2]. This number cannot be rapidly increased due to the falling birth rate. Therefore, decreasing the task of occupational therapist is essential for the future. This problem is not limited to Japan. Other developed countries also have similar situation.

Occupational therapy is useful for treatment of patient with dementia which is derived from some diseases such as Parkinson's disease [3]. In occupational therapy, an examiner (occupational therapist) assigns a motion task based on standard procedure to a patient. The motion task aims to recover the motor function of the patient. Usually, the motion task requires that the examiner should explain the motion task and measure the operational time to finish the motion task. If this operation can be realized with a computer instead of the examiner, it can support to decrease the daily work of the occupational therapist. The difference between conventional and proposed occupational therapy is shown in Fig. 1.

In the past two decades, virtual reality technology has been researched to apply for rehabilitation [4]. Some studies [5, 6] have been reported that a virtual realty can be applied to the occupational therapy. The studies employed only motion capture device for virtual reality. Most of studies are focusing on motion of the body. However, it is difficult

M. Antona and C. Stephanidis (Eds.): UAHCI 2015, Part III, LNCS 9177, pp. 331–337, 2015.
DOI: 10.1007/978-3-319-20684-4_32

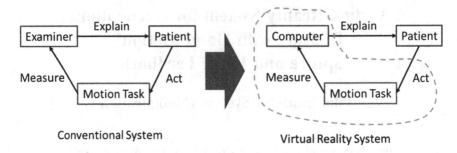

Fig. 1. Virtual reality system for occupational therapy

for patients to do actions such as taking objects, because visual feedback provides a little information for recognizing the condition relating the body and objects in the virtual space. Kelly et al. proposed a new system which employed a mechatronic-virtual system to train human motor control [7]. The mechatronic virtual system is realized by using air pressure to make a force. However, the air pressure system needs air pump which is comparatively large size. In addition, an air tube possibly interferes motion of the subjects due to the tension of the air tube, when the air fulfils in the air tube.

The purpose of this study is to develop a system which provides a force feedback such as touching feelings to subjects by using a vibration motor. The reasons to use the vibration motor are easy feasibility and light weight.

2   Method

The basic concept of the proposed system is shown in Fig. 2. In the general virtual reality, a subject acts to object. Then the change as the result is projected through visual sense. In this case, it is difficult to recognize the relationship between the body and objects where the a part of body is placed in front of the objects along visual line.

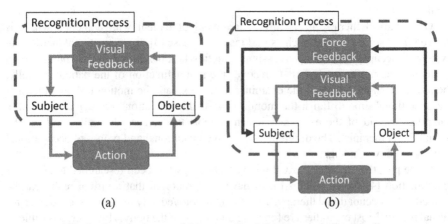

Fig. 2. Basic concepts of (a) general and (b) proposed virtual reality

Obstacles often exist in the field of view. To overcome this problem, the proposed system provides additionally force feedback to the fingers of the subject.

The proposed system consists of motion capture (LM-C01, Leap Motion), digital/analog convertor (USB-3114, Measurement Computing) and vibration motor (LBV10B-009, NIDEC COPAL Corporation). The specification of the motion capture is tabulated in Table 1. The motion capture has an image sensor, and can obtain information of points of each joints and endpoints of the fingers in real-time. The coordinate system of virtual space is determined by the motion capture (Fig. 3). This study focuses on only tips of the thumb and index finger.

Table 1. The specification of the motion capture

Precision	0.01 (mm)
Sampling rate	200 (frames per sec)
View angle	150 (degrees)
The number of detectable fingers	10 (fingers)
Connection	USB cable

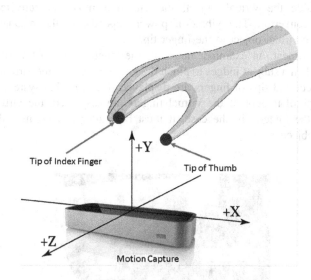

Fig. 3. Coordinate system

This study employed vibration motor to provide a force which can impress a virtual object on subjects (Fig. 4). In the virtual space, the vibration motor is activated when the finger touches the virtual object. The vibration power depends on the dent degree of the finger to the virtual object. When the finger pinches with large distortion of the virtual object, the vibration motor strongly shakes. The vibration motors attach to the fingers by thumbstall (Fig. 5). The thumbstall has three types (small, medium, large) for size, because the finger diameter has variation from person to person. The proper size was choosen by the subject.

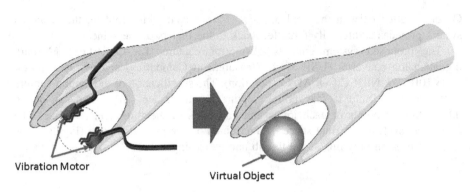

Vibration Motor

Virtual Object

Fig. 4. Virtual object with vibration motor

This study used a cubic shape with 30 mm edge and a spherical shape with 30 mm diameter as virtual objects. The virtual object is set to be directly above the motion capture. We developed a software to display the virtual space and control the vibration motors. The software is monitoring the position of the finger tip. When the finger tip is recognized inside the virtual object, the vibration motor is activated with the digital/analog convertor. The vibration power depends on the distance from the boundary of the virtual object to the finger tip.

In the experiment, an examiner measures the length between tips of thumb and index finger, when a subject judges to pinch the virtual object. In the virtual space, only the virtual object and tips of fingers are displayed (Fig. 6). This system consciously shows only tips of fingers. If the virtual fingers are displayed, the virtual object is hidden under the fingers. In the case, it must be harder to recognize the pinching condition to subjects.

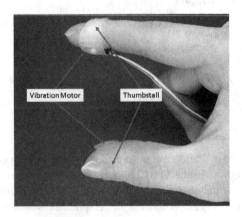

Vibration Motor   Thumbstall

Fig. 5. Setting of vibration motor

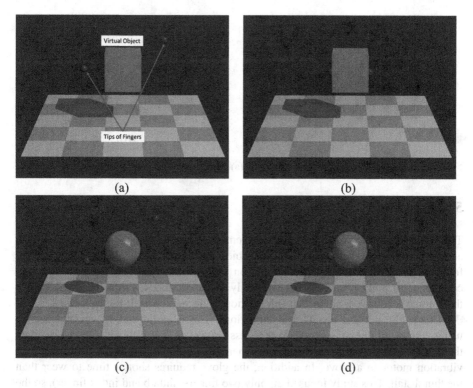

(a)   (b)

(c)   (d)

Fig. 6. Pinching conditions of (a) off and (b) on in case of cubic object and (c) off and (d) on in case of spherical object.

3 Experiments

Subjects are three healthy males (age: 22–38 years old) who has no injury about upper limbs. All subjects performed five trials with dominant hand (all subjects are right hand). The virtual target was cubic and spherical objects. First, they performed without force feedback. Second, they performed with force feedback. After each trial, the real distance between fingers was measured by a caliper.

4 Results

Results in case of cubic and spherical objects are shown in Fig. 7. The vertical axis indicates the pinching distance where the unit is mm. The results show that pinching distance with force feedback is close to the setting one (30 mm) more than without force feedback. The pinching errors with and without force feedback were 7.7 mm and 12.9 mm in case of cubic object, respectively. As same way, the pinching errors with and without feedback were 4.3 mm and 9.9 mm in case of spherical object, respectively. However, most results indicated higher distance than setting one.

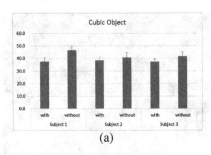
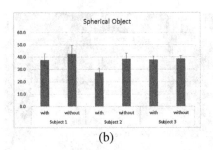

(a)   (b)

Fig. 7. Experimental results of (a) cubic and (b) shperical objects

5 Discussions

The result show the force feed back system is effective to pinch with accuracy. In addition, subjectives felt easily a virtual object from their finger. When they have no force feedback, the judgement depends on only visual feedback. Subjects have no confidence to pinch some objects with only visual feedback. From these results, we think force feedback is important information to do motion task for patients.

This study includes mechanical limitations. The vibration motor was attached by using thumbstall due to easy making process. However, it is difficult to be worn, even though the subject is healthy person. Therefore, it might be better to embed the vibration motor to a glove. In addition, the glove requires shorter time to wear than the thumbstall. This study focused on only two fingers (thumb and index finger), so the experiment was limited about pinch motion. To measure real pinching motion, the vibration motor should be attached to all the fingers.

As the other limitation, the distances between tips of the fingers were manually measured with a caliper. It possibly includes manual error due to the accuracy. This is reasonable approach to measure the distances. As previously mentioned, we think virtual system gives importance to have touching feeling for the subjects more than accuracy.

6 Conclusion

This study proposed a virtual reality system for occupational therapy with hand motion capture and force feedback. Force feedback was realized by using a vibration motor. In the experiment, the results with force feedback were close to the setting distance more than the results without force feedback. As a future work, actual working task used in clinical situation should be applied to this system.

Acknowledgements. This work was supported by JSPS Grant-in-Aid for Young Scientists (B) Grant Number 25870273.

References

1. Health, Labour and Welfare Ministry. http://www.mhlw.go.jp/stf/houdou/2r9852000002iau1-att/2r9852000002iavi.pdf
2. Health, Labour and Welfare Ministry. http://www.mhlw.go.jp/stf/shingi/2r98520000029a85-att/2r98520000029ad1.pdf
3. Sturkenboom, I.H.W.M., Graff, M.J.L., Hendriks, J.C.M., Veenhuizen, Y., Munneke, M., Bloem, B.R., van der Sanden, M.W.N.: Efficacy of occupational therapy for patients with Parkinson's disease: a randomised controlled trial. Lancet Neurol. 13(6), 557–566 (2014)
4. Proffitt, R., Lange, B.: Considerations in the efficacy and effectiveness of virtual reality interventions for stroke rehabilitation: moving the field forward. Phys. Ther. 95(3), 441–448 (2015)
5. Shin, J.-H., Ryu, H., Jang, S.H.: A task-specific interactive game-based virtual reality rehabilitation system for patients with stroke: a usability test and two clinical experiments. J. NeuroEng. Rehabil. 11(32) (2014)
6. Yin, C.W., Sien, N.Y., Ying, L.A., Chung, S.F.-C.M., Leng, D.T.M.: Virtual reality for upper extremity rehabilitation in early stroke: a pilot randomized controlled trial. Clin. Rehabil. 28(11), 1107–1114 (2014)
7. Thielbar, K.O., Lord, T.J., Fischer, H.C., Lazzaro, E.C., Barth, K.C., Stoykov, M.E., Triandafilou, K.M., Kamper, D.G.: Training finger individuation with a mechatronic-virtual reality system leads to improved fine motor control post-stroke. J. NeuroEng. Rehabil. 11(1), 171 (2014)

Methodology for Evaluating the Usability of Public Equipment for Physical Activity: An Approach to Interface with Blind and Low Vision Individuals

Sabrina Talita de Oliveira and Maria Lucia Leite Ribeiro Okimoto[⊠]

Design Department, Federal University of Paraná, Curitiba, Brazil
sabrina.talita@pucpr.br, lucia.demec@ufpr.br

Abstract. The objective of this study is to present a methodology for evaluation of public equipment, from usability issues, ergonomics and accessibility. We believe that products of common use can be used by normal people and by people with disabilities. Thus, we decided to develop a methodology for evaluate public exercise equipment in Brazil, as a group of blind and low vision users constantly use such products. The methodology aims to measure the User Experience using the products of outdoor gyms, showing criteria of satisfaction, effectiveness, efficiency, intuitiveness, pleasantness and perception of pain or discomfort.

Keywords: Public gyms · User experience · Usability · Blind people · Low vision

1 Introduction

The activities that promote the social inclusion of people with special needs by the public administration are still scarce. Constantly in Brazil increases the number of visually impaired people, including people with blindness and low vision.

In this context, the Brazilian public gyms for physical activity appliances consist of no possibility of load adjustments, i.e., using only your body weight for activities such as stretching, flexibility, muscle strength and movement. Currently, Brazil has various academies on the national territory. Only in the city of Curitiba, capital of Paraná State there are over one hundred equipment available for use in the community. This is an initiative of the government to promote recreation, health and quality of life. The equipment may be used by anyone, working as a fitness outdoors. For correct use, just follow the simple guidelines set out in the near panel (Fig. 1).

The equipment outdoor fitness are public. Thus, should be utilized to most people, or must meet the most different individual capacities. Given the above in theory should meet minimum requirements of Universal Design. However, this study proposes a methodology for evaluation of equipment capable of use by blind and low vision people, noting that the equipment must meet the basic criteria for use of normal users

M. Antona and C. Stephanidis (Eds.): UAHCI 2015, Part III, LNCS 9177, pp. 338–344, 2015.
DOI: 10.1007/978-3-319-20684-4_33

Fig. 1. The Brazilian public gyms for physical activity (Source: City of Curitiba, 2012)

and also for the use of individuals with visual constraints, seeking by a better physical condition. In this context, this research arises from the following question: How to evaluate the usability, user experience and emotion of blind and low vision individuals in the interface with public exercise equipment?

To answer the research question we present a methodology for measuring the user experience. The methodology was adapted for people with visual constraints and emphasizes the user interaction with the products. Assessment procedures of equipment that were adopted provide evaluation criteria from ergonomic, usability and emotional factors. This methodology serves as a support for evaluation in the context of real use of fitness equipment public.

The methodology for this study includes: familiarity test with products, perception of pain or discomfort, formal perception and intuitiveness of use, evaluation of the experience [1–3] emotional factors and evaluation with a focus group after context use by all members of the group.

The result include techniques for collecting data, relating to usability specifically adapted for blind and people with low vision. This paper also reaches a pilot experiment to validate the method. The experiment was conducted with a blind person the Paraná Institute for the Blind, located in the city of Curitiba, Brazil.

This research is a study of ergonomics and usability lab of the Federal University of Paraná (UFPR), is embedded in the research group of Ergonomics (UFPR) and it was a search of the Pos-Graduate Program in Design. The project has partnered with the government of Curitiba, which reviewed the project and issued an ethical opinion for testing the city's public spaces. Partner is still with the Paraná Institute of the Blind and the Center for Visual Support Area, located in the town of Araucaria, also in the state of Paraná, Brazil.

The resulting methodology of this research can contribute to ergonomists and designers evaluate the usability of products commonly used by individuals who are blind and low vision to find directions for design, improving user experience and to improve the configuration industrial products.

2   User Experience Evaluation

Tullis and Albert [3] present some usability metrics that reveal aspects about the user experience and interaction between the user and the object emphasizing: effectiveness, efficiency and satisfaction [4]. The authors note that the metrics are focused on users and assess behavioral aspects and attitudes, not the product alone.

Metrics are not final conclusions about the products, but means to assist the designer in decisions from data obtained through usability testing with users. Thus, the results serve during the product development process. The evaluation metrics widespread by Tullis and Albert [3] in the book "Measuring the User Experience" are:

- Performance: Evaluates aspects of specific tasks already planned in the use test. Evaluates aspects such as efficiency and effectiveness.
- Based Usability Issues: Assist the detection and identification of problems in usability. Expressed by users during testing products or systems.
- Self- Reports: Data collection occurs from reports of users.
- Behavioral and Physiological: The data collected depart from information not explicitly said or consciously planned.

Therefore, the user experience measurement metrics have been taken into account in the formulation of evaluation protocols for field-testing of this research.

2.1   Pain or Discomfort Perception

The Diagram Corlett [5, 6], adapted from Corlett and Manenica (1980), is an ergonomic assessment protocol of the user experience. It is divided into left and right body regions, each of which allows for five levels intensity of discomfort or pain: none (1); little discomfort (2); moderate (3); enough (4); excessive (5). It can be applied by the investigator or by the person, which will indicate which regions feel discomfort or pain during or after performing some activity and which side: right or left. Still, the people can report which feels discomfort level indicating some number. It is a technique for assessing postural discomfort (Fig. 2).

2.2   Circle of Emotions

The Circle of Emoticons [7] can be used to measure the emotions of users through self-reports or tag manifest their feelings about a product or system. It requests that the individuals to report any emotion, according to the circle (Fig. 3).

3   Proposed Method

The experiment aimed to measure the experience of the blind and low vision users in the interface with the products of Outdoor Fitness. Before the experiments with individuals, was the application of a "Statement of Consent". During the pilot experiment with a user were collected self-reports that expressed perceptions regarding the use of each device. During the execution of tasks on each product, questionnaires were

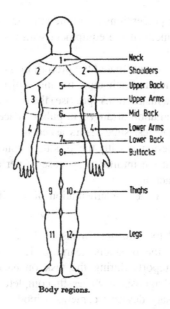

Body regions.

Fig. 2. Corlett Diagram (Source: Humanics Ergonomics, 2015)

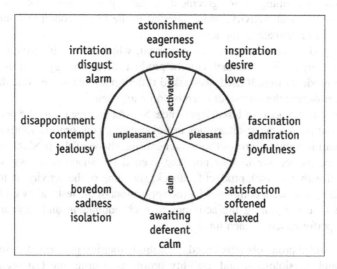

Fig. 3. Circle of Emotions by Desmet, 2007; adapted from Russel,1980 (Source: International Journal of Design, 2015).

applied on intuitiveness of use, satisfaction, comfort, pleasantness, accessibility and use of motivation. Also were collected behavioral and physiological manifestations through the audio and video recording.

The user's performance in each of the devices was performed using the diagnostic task completion of each product, and counting the number of errors. In the course of testing the user reported their perceptions about the interface of each device, suggesting usability trends for improvement of the equipment with respect to comfort, intuitiveness and communication task.

An expert (physical coach) coordinated the prescription of tasks; the explanation of the exercises repetitions series in each unit; training objectives of each device and orientation of rest breaks. The instructions (pre-use) the physical guiding allowance had the information signs of orientation arranged in public spaces.

During the experiment the test supervisors asked the participant verbalization of self-reports, about your experience with the products concerned. At this stage, we applied some protocols about the intuitiveness, ease of performing the task, comfort, motivation and use of satisfaction.

The processes involved for the implementation of usability testing the equipment were:

- Defining the objective of the pilot test: measure the comfort, intuitive use, attractiveness of the shape of the products, learning, feedback, satisfaction and user experience through self-reports during the task on each product. Also measure performance through the diagnosis of successful completion and error number count.
- Preparation of the necessary devices: cameras, tripods, video cameras for filming and audio recording, thus allowing registering behavioral manifestations.
- Application of Questionnaires Pre- test: consent form signed by the experiment participant, confirming their agreement to participate in the pilot test. Form of Fitness for Physical Activity, which attested to the health conditions and physical necessary to participate in the test.
- Familiarity Questionnaire with the equipment, which aimed to verify whether the person had any previous contact with the products of outdoor gyms or used at some point the product often. If used, was asked if the person felt some difficulty, pain or discomfort during the course of exercise on equipment.
- Measurement Protocols of User Experience: Self-reports regarding the perception of satisfaction; pleasantness; difficulties in tasks; pain or discomfort; motivation; ease of use, learning ability; product intuitiveness (the shape of the product induced the function performed the task or not, and even if the shape was easy recognition associated with exercise); product feedback; signaling of the activity on the product itself. Still, forms were completed by the applicators of the tests, allowed to note the presence of errors during the activities in each equipment and measuring timed exercise performance in each unit.

The assessment protocols were based on usability metrics: performance, self-reports, behavioral and physiological and usability problems. During the test scenario were recorded pictures, sound recording and video for the collection of non-verbal expressions and user behavior. There has also been the completion of the task successfully and the number of errors in performing the task on each physical activity equipment.

In the pilot test, the user is encouraged to report usability issues and put suggestions for improvements that could be applied to products. Thus, the tests aimed to verify if the equipment meets the usage requirements and meet the expectations of users and the Brazilian technical standards (Figs. 4 and 5).

Fig. 4. User using the walk simulator equipment during the pilot test (Source: The Authors, 2015).

Fig. 5. User using the extender equipment during the pilot test (Source: The Authors, 2015)

4 Conclusion

Observing apparatus for physical exercise of public spaces in Brazil, we found that many of them do not include accessibility requirements in the technical and current standards in law.

Still, from the observation that many blind and low- vision users a Brazilian city practice physical activities in the equipment, note that such products can meet both people without restrictions as visually impaired.

Thus, this work proposes a methodology that evaluates the user experience of public gyms equipment in order to identify whether the products meet basic principles of universal design, as they are objects of collective use, arranged in public places. This method can be replicated in other contexts, to assess common use of products that can be used both by normal people as by disabled people.

References

1. Bevan, N.: Classifying and selecting UX and usability measures. In: the Proceedings of Meaningful Measures: Valid Useful User Experience Measurement (VUUM), 5th COST294-MAUSE Open Workshop, 18th June, Reykjavik, Iceland 2008
2. Bevan, N., Petrie, H.: The evaluation of accessibility, usability and user experience. In: Stepanidis, C. (ed.) The Universal Access Handbook. CRC Press, New York (2009)
3. Tullis, T., Albert, B.: Measuring the user experience – Collecting, analyzing and presenting usability metrics. Morgan Kaufmann, Burlington (2008)
4. IIDA, Itiro. Ergonomia: projeto e produção. São Paulo, Edgard Blücher (2005)
5. Corlett, E.N., Manenica, I.: The effects and measurement of working postures. Appl. Ergonomics Trondheim **11**(1), 7–16 (1980)
6. HUMANICS ERGONOMICS. Corlett Diagram (2015). http://www.humanics-es.com/bodypartdiscomfortscale.htm#discomfort
7. INDUSTRIAL JOURNAL OF DESIGN. Circle of Emotions (2015). http://www.ijdesign.org/ojs/index.php/IJDesign/article/view/66/15

Virtual Liver Surgical Simulator by Using Z-Buffer for Object Deformation

Katsuhiko Onishi[1]([✉]), Hiroshi Noborio[1], Masanao Koeda[1],
Kaoru Watanabe[1], Kiminori Mizushino[2], Takahiro Kunii[3],
Masaki Kaibori[4], Kosuke Matsui[4], and Masanori Kon[4]

[1] Osaka Electro-Communication University, 1130-70 Kiyotaki, Shijonawate,
Osaka 5750063, Japan
{onishi,nobori,koeda,kaoru}@oecu.jp
[2] Embedded Wings Co. Ltd, Minoh, Japan
k_mizushino@ewings.biz
[3] Kashina System Co. Ltd., Minoh, Japan
kunii@tetera.jp
[4] Kansai Medical University, Moriguchi, Japan
{kaibori,matuik,kon}@hirakata.kmu.ac.jp

Abstract. Virtual surgical simulator which is using computer graphics is much popular system than before. It is generally used in the medical areas, such as medical hospital or medical university. The simulator uses virtual organ models like liver, brain and so on. These models are usually based on the scanning data from patients and are used as volume models. Fortunately, the volume model is familiar with its cutting or deforming operation in a surgical system. For this reason, there are many kinds of surgical simulation or navigation systems using the volume model. However, visual reality of the volume model is not sufficient for human being including doctors. This means that the doctors cannot identify shape or location of a target organ from volume objects. In order to overcome this, we should use the translating method, such as marching cubes method and so on, for getting precisely polygon models which is included normal vectors of volume object. However, the method is quite time consuming and consequently the doctors cannot operate the virtual model in real-time.

On these observations, we propose the virtual surgical simulator for operating the human liver in a virtual environment, which is based on the cooperation of polygon models and Z-buffer in GPU. By using parallel processing of GPU, the simulator allows uses to cut or deform a virtual liver model by using several kinds of medical tools like a scalpel in this system. In addition, visual reality of polygon model is wonderful for a doctor to identify its shape or location because this model maintains their precise normal vector.

Keywords: Z-buffer · Liver surgical simulator · GPU · Object deformation

1 Introduction

Surgical simulation is becoming popular theme in the medical operation. In these simulators, the system use organ models and allow user to cutting or deforming it for training of surgical method [1]. And in the field of computer graphics, hardware of

© Springer International Publishing Switzerland 2015
M. Antona and C. Stephanidis (Eds.): UAHCI 2015, Part III, LNCS 9177, pp. 345–351, 2015.
DOI: 10.1007/978-3-319-20684-4_34

graphics processing Unit (GPU) is becoming high efficiency and can carry out the parallel processing of 3D virtual space.

In this paper, we describe about our surgical simulator which is aimed at liver surgery. Our simulator uses virtual liver model which is included blood vessels. And it allows user to cutting or deforming these models by haptic devices. It is enable to display the any part of vessel such as that closed to a scalpel.

Virtual organ model such as liver and so on, is generated from patient scan data by MRI/CT. the model is typically generated as volume model. Volume model is included whole structured of the organ. It means that it is included inside blood vessels. Therefore, the volume model is used in such as surgical simulator. Some of the simulators use organ model generated from patient in real time by using MRI [2]. But these system is almost used in case of neurosurgery. Because the brain is surrounded by skull bones and it is almost not moving or deforming its shapes. Therefore, it is adequate to process by volume data. On the other hand, the liver is not same situation as the brain. It is in human body. And the liver surgery navigator or simulator is needed to measure some parameter for recognizing its posture which varies in real-time. Therefore it is adequate to use the virtual liver model as polygon model in the simulation system. For this reason, some system use Marching cubes algorithm [3] for translating into polygon models, which are surface models included position and normal vector data, from volume models in real-time. But it is difficult to show the detailed polygon model to users in real-time because of [4–6].

Therefore, our system uses only the virtual liver models constructed by polygon data for operating surgical tasks in real-time. Our system render the liver models by using Z-buffer included in GPU. By using parallel processing of GPU, the simulator allows uses to cut or deform a virtual liver model by using several kinds of medial tools like a scalpel in this system.

2   Deformation Algorithm

2.1   Overview

In our system, it is used a deformation algorithm for rendering a liver model to operating surgical tasks, cutting, deforming and so on. The liver model is created from volume image data (Fig. 1(a)). Figure 1(b) shows the liver model that our system have used. This polygon model has the body and blood vessels, the hepatic artery and vein. And our system use a scalpel model to operate surgical tasks (Fig. 1(c)). The deformation algorithm is based on that our previous study which is used for our dental surgical simulator [7]. In order to reduce the computation time to rendering it, this method uses a coordinate system organized the depth direction as an operation direction. And our system use Z-buffer that is stored depth map in the coordinate system. Figure 2 shows the image of our algorithm overview.

2.2   Procedure of Deformation

Z-buffer is used to rendering only the model showed from a viewpoint in 3D graphic scene. To use the Z-buffer, the system is enable to process many polygons

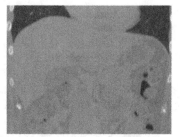

(a) A volume data image of a liver.

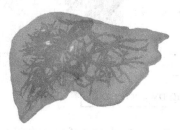

(b) A polygon liver model.

(c) A scalpel model.

Fig. 1. An image of virtual liver models.

simultaneously and reducing the rendering time. In our algorithm, it is used to measure the deforming volume by user's operation. At first, the region of manipulation is defined from view volume by a camera for operation. And the coordinate system is defined in this region and stored the depth map. Figure 3 shows summary of this process.

In order to generate the depth map after the deformation by operating with a virtual tool, it is stored amount of changing the depth map when the virtual scalpel slink to the liver model. This is used to change the shape of liver model and calculate parameters to generate tactile feedback. This depth map is a simple two-dimensional array.

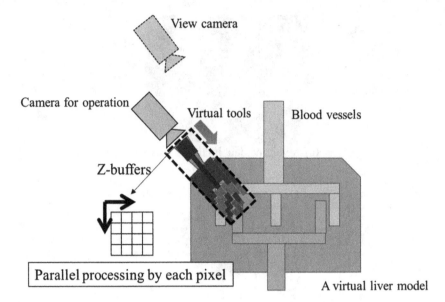

Fig. 2. The abstract of our algorithm.

The deformation of liver model is generated by the following process. In order to be assigned vertex of the liver model to Z-buffer, it uses a conversion method to change the vertex with world coordinate system, which constructs Z-buffer. And it acquires z value from the pixel, which contains the vertex in Z-buffer. The deformation volume is defined from this volume and it is reconverted to the vertex position in world coordinate system. All of this process is executed in the high-speed transaction by using the parallel processing in GPU.

Finally, to adapt this deformation process, it changes the vertex point of the liver model to deform it. In this process, some surfaces of the model is extended to a direction of deformed region and it is not enable to deform to other direction. To solve this problem, our system uses a subdivision surface algorithm to divide the extended surfaces. A summary of this method is that generates middle point to the edge between 2 vertexes with length more than a certain threshold.

3 Approach Notification Algorithm

Our simulator has been required to have a function of alert notification. It is that the system has some notification event, when a virtual scalpel model is come closed to blood vessels. In order to realize this function, it is using the Z-buffer to measure the distance between the scalpel and blood vessels. While the scalpel model is moved in world coordinate space, vertex point of the scalpel edge and blood vessels is converted to the depth value in the region of manipulation. And it is calculated the distance between the scalpel edge and the vertex of blood vessels in the depth map. This calculation is executed by using the parallel processing in GPU. Therefore it uses mutual exclusion by using the unit for distance.

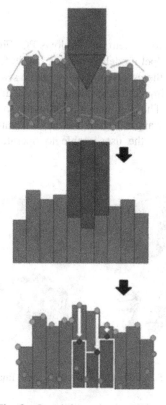

Fig. 3. Our deformation procedure.

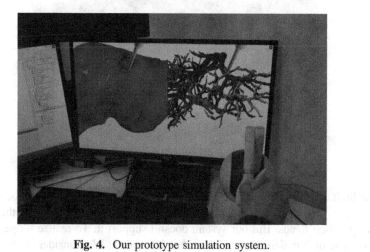

Fig. 4. Our prototype simulation system.

4 Implementation

We implemented this simulator system on Windows PC. Figure 4 shows our prototype system. The user operate scalpel model by using a haptic feedback device. It is enable to display force feedback to the user, while they operate scalpel model. Figure 5 shows an example of user's view image. Our system shows 4 different views And the user enable to select these views. The user enable to show the liver model and blood vessels included in the liver from any angle. Figure 6 shows an example scene of user's cutting operation. We confirmed that the user enable to operate the surgical tasks in our system.

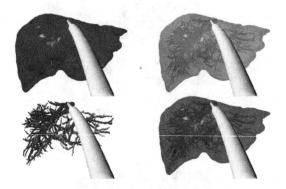

Fig. 5. An example of user's view image.

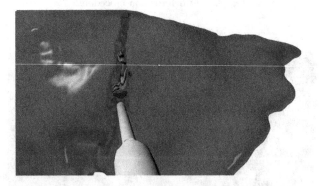

Fig. 6. An example of cutting operation.

The limitation of our system is that the user enable to treat the liver model through the scalpel model. In case of real surgery, the doctor have often changed the shape of the liver by their hands. But our system doesn't support it. To realize it operation, the improvement of our deformation algorithm is needed. We consider it as our future work.

5   Conclusion

We proposed a virtual liver surgical simulator system by using Z-buffer for object deformation. Our system uses the polygon liver model and uses the deformation algorithm based on parallel processing in GPU. We constructed a prototype system and confirmed the capability and the limitation of this system.

In future work, we will consider the improvement of our deformation algorithm which is able to show the liver model more precisely, and consider the evaluation of our system.

References

1. Jerabkova, L., Bousquet, G., Barbier, S., Faure, F., Allard, J.: Volumetric modeling and interactive cutting of deformable bodies. Prog. Biophys. Mol. Biol. **103**, 217–224 (2010)
2. Nimsky, C., et al.: Integration of functional magnetic resonance imaging supported by magnetoencephalography in functional neuronavigation. Neurosurgery **44**(6), 1249–1255 (1999)
3. Lorensen, W.E., Cline, H.E.: Marching cubes: a high resolution 3D surface construction algorithm. Comput. Graph. **21**(4), 163–169 (1987)
4. Chen Y.-W., Kaibori M., et al.: Computer-aided liver surgical planning system using CT volumes. In: Proceedings of International Conference of the IEEE Engineering in Medicine and Biology Society (EMBC 2013), pp. 2360–2363 (2013)
5. Yamaguchi, S., Yamada, Y., Yoshida, Y., Noborio, H., Imazato, S.: Development of three-dimensional patient face model that enables real-time collision detection and cutting operation for a dental simulator. Dent. Mater. J. **31**(6), 1047–1053 (2012)
6. Yoshida, Y., Yamaguchi, S., Kawamoto, Y., Noborio, H., Murakami, S., Sohmura, T.: Development of a multi-layered virtual tooth model for the haptic dental training system. Dent. Mater. J. **30**(1), 1–6 (2011)
7. Onishi, K., Mizushino, K., Noborio, H., Koeda, M.: Haptic AR dental simulator using z-buffer for object deformation. In: Stephanidis, C., Antona, M. (eds.) UAHCI 2014, Part III. LNCS, vol. 8515, pp. 342–348. Springer, Heidelberg (2014)

Fashion Design for Health:
A Multidisciplinary Approach

Mariana Rachel Roncoletta[✉]

Anhembi Morumbi University, São Paulo, Brazil
mariana@roncoletta.com

Abstract. The aim of this research is presenting intersections points concerned with health, fashion and design with the propose of allowing multidisciplinary studies to enter into a dialogue by employing the same language. Qualitative methodology was applied on the bias of epistemological Constructivism. It was analysed and compared secondary sources through a biographic review. It was concluded that the examples of *The Alternative Limb Project,* a hybrid project, are intended to embody fashion as a socio-cultural phenomenon can foster social-cultural inclusion for people with disability. It is possible to discern a feasible approximation of the outlook of the designer in the area of health with the outlook of the designer in the area of fashion, so that, in partnership, they can foster effective socio-cultural inclusion and improve physical health in a way that culminates in a better quality of life and state of well-being.

Keywords: Fashion design · Health · People with disability

1 Introduction: Society and Disabilities - New Conceptual Paradigms for Health in the 21st Century

According to Üstün *et al.* (2001), *disability* is a widely used and ambiguous term. In classifying health categories, these authors set out by adopting another term, *disablement,* which encompasses three different notions in the medical area: *impairment, disability* and *handicap.* However, it has been found difficult to translate the word *disablement* into other languages and so they have resorted again to the term *disability.* According to the authors, disabilities are found in the relationships between three notions of physical functionality or usefulness and include three contextual factors.

At the beginning of the 19th Century, with the advent of pathology in medicine and the social sciences, disabilities became an area that could now be studied. The word *pathology* can be understood as an area where any anatomical or physiological variance can be studied that constitutes or characterizes a particular disease. In light of this, disabilities were initially classified by their pathological features and divided into the following categories: mental, physical and sensory perceptual (auditory and visual), all of which allowed medical diagnosis and treatment. As a result, the disabled were seen as people who had some incapacity or handicap that stemmed from their physical condition.

As well as suffering on account of the functional and structural nature of their bodies, disabled people have experienced social alienation, according to Rocha (2006).

© Springer International Publishing Switzerland 2015
M. Antona and C. Stephanidis (Eds.): UAHCI 2015, Part III, LNCS 9177, pp. 352–363, 2015.
DOI: 10.1007/978-3-319-20684-4_35

Vash (1988: 22) draws attention to three tendencies that perhaps explain why a disabled person is socially disparaged: (a) human beings instinctively reject any organisms that have been damaged; (b) evident physical differences are treated with less tolerance in the psycho-social domain; (c) the victim is viewed as being unproductive from an economic standpoint and harms the dynamics of the normal operations of families, the community or society. At a psycho-social level, the authors, Correr (2003) and Rocha (2006), agree that this stigma is still deeply rooted in Brazilian society. The UN *Convention on the Rights of Persons with Disabilities* (CRPD), a global arena of which Brazil forms a part, seeks to *"encourage, protect and ensure the full and equal enjoyment of all human rights and fundamental freedom of people with disabilities"* (CRPD, 2006). However, its application depends on political and economic spheres (among other factors).

In 1980, the first *International Classification of Functioning and Disability* (ICIDH), was held by the *World Health Organization* (WHO). This was an attempt to standardize a single language about disabilities, incapacities and handicaps. According to Üstün *et al.* (2001), this classification, which is only based on diseases and their sequel, has been criticized on the grounds that it was only designed to give medical guidance. Its model traces a linear sequence:

Health - > disability - > incapacity - > handicap.

In 2001, the ICIDH-2 was published; according to the WHO search portal, it is more commonly known as the *International Classification of Functioning, Disability and Health* (ICF). It should be underlined that the ICF was set up for *everybody* and not just for people with disabilities.

It can be seen that the concept of health is implicit in both the title and definition of this new classification - *"Health is a state of complete physical, mental and social well-being and not merely the absence of disease or infirmity"* which was provided by WHO (1946: 01). A healthy human being is someone who feels well physically, mentally and socially. The concept was broadened in the definitions of health given by Stedman (2003: 569):

"Health; the state of the organism when it functions optimally without evidence of disease or abnormality.
Mental health – emotional, behavioral and social maturity or normality; the absence of a mental or behavioral disorder; a state of psychological well-being in which one has achieved a satisfactory integration of one's instinctual drives, acceptable to both oneself and one's social milieu.
Public health: the art and science of community health concerned with statistics, epidemiology, hygiene and the prevention and eradication of epidemic diseases"[1].

After 2001, socio-cultural issues in the health area became involved in the classification of every individual. This transition can be seen as a change from a medical model to a social model, *in which* the *World Report on Disability* (2011), adds *"people are seen to be disabled by society and not by their bodies"*. According to Rocha (2006), the main purpose of this new classification was to reduce the stigma of stereotypes and prejudices that can be found in the history of the concept of disability. The ICF recognizes the importance of personal factors such as motivation and self-esteem in the awareness of people with disabilities, although these factors have not been classified or conceptualized by the ICF itself.

Moreover, the proposed axis in the conceptual health model in Fig. 1, shows that the state of health can be understood both as an interaction between the functions and structures of the body (diagnosis) and as an activity that allows a kind of participation that is contextualized by environmental and personal factors. In this way, disability refers to the difficulties experienced in the physical structures and functions and in the constraints that limit the way some activities are carried out or on restrictions that prevent participation, as for example by discrimination. These are the difficulties experienced in some or all of the three areas of operation. Thus it can be observed that society, or the milieu, can also be disabled and not just the individual.

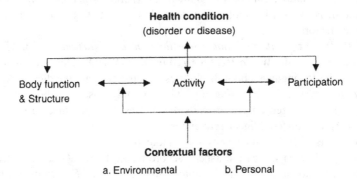

Fig. 1. Conceptual model of WHO – ICF, 2001. Source: Üstün *et al.* (2001)

This recent more complex research allows biological, psychological, social and environmental factors to be interwoven, since they all have an effect on each other, which means that the environment or other factors can lead to either a better or worse state of health. The concepts introduce a new paradigm that can be used when thinking about or working on disability and incapacity, which allows multidisciplinary studies to enter into a dialogue by employing the same language, as is pointed out by Farias and Buchalla (2005).

With regard to the quality of life in a psychological and socio-cultural context, the ICF related it to well-being, which was used as a construct for the quality of life. Seidl and Zannon (2004) make clear that the psychological dimension is the perception the individual has of his affective and cognitive condition. In other words, it is mental health – when someone has attained a state of psychological well-being and satisfactory integration both with himself and his socio-cultural milieu. For this reason, it is essential to map out his mode of being and psychological quality of life, so that the relations between self-esteem and stigma (positive and negative feelings) can be observed, together with the question of the physical image and appearance of people with disabilities.

2 Method and Methodology

Flick (2009), Richardson (2010) and Gray (2012) adopt an epistemological stance for research and the researcher that provides a philosophical background to the study. This means that when reflecting about the relations among fashion, design and health, it must be made clear that this research is embedded in an epistemological Constructivism where *"truth and meaning are created through the interactions of people with the world"* (Gray, 2012: 21). Schwandt *in* Denzin and Lincoln (2000: 197) point out that epistemologies are debated by researchers in various areas and adds *"we do not construct our interpretations in isolation but against a background of shared understandings, practices, languages, and so forth."* These authors clearly adopt a philosophic approach, as does Schwandt (2000) who distinguishes between Interpretivism and Constructivism. In this research, an epistemological stance of Constructivism is adopted to understand how three areas mention above can be important to a multidisciplinary research.

The choice of a theoretical perspective is also recommended by Denzin and Lincoln (2013) with propose of clarifying the research position as well as its methodological coherence. It should be noted that the study was undertaken from the perspective of an Interpretivist Theory.

According to Crotty (1998), Interpretivism seeks interpretations that are culturally derived and traditionally based in the world of social living. Schwandt *in* Denzin and Lincoln (2000) state that, from this standpoint, individual constructions of the social world are personal and can be legitimized and shared as a result of an interaction between the researcher and the field researched. For this reason, it is agreed that the *reflectiveness* that can be found in this research when viewed as a relationship, is not neutral and occurs between the researcher and the object of the research. (Gibbs, 2009).

Marconi and Lakatos (2010) draw a distinction between method and methods. The former is viewed as a broad approach at a level of heightened abstraction which discriminates between inductive, deductive, hypothetical-deductive and dialectical methods. The latter involve procedural methods: *"more concrete stages of investigation"* adds Marconi and Lakatos (2010: 88), which can be understood as being analytical techniques and procedures. As a result, this research employs the inductive method and a qualitative methodology.

With regard to the rigor of the methodology of data collection and analysis, this can be attributed both to the internal validity of the comparative technique itself and the reliability that results from employing specialist publications in different periods; however, it should be underlined that there are divergences of opinion.

3 Discussion: Intersections Among Fashion, Design and Health

There is no consensus among the authors about definitions of design (Cardoso, 2004 and 2012; Bürdek, 2006; Schneider, 2010; among others). The review of the bibliography, in this research, is something that makes the designer shoulder a range of social and cultural responsibilities which might have a direct bearing on the health and quality of life of the people involved.

The *International Council of Societies of Industrial Design* (ICSID) recommends that its design activities should take account of its production system and life-cycle, as well as the interaction between cultural, social and economic factors. Krippendorff (1969) adds that *"design is making sense of things"*, "a conveniently ambiguous phrase", the author comments, and he then goes on to broaden his own interpretation by stating that "*the products of design are to be understandable to their users*" (Krippendorff 2006). In other words, the design products must include meaningful semantics that can be understood by the users. For example, the old-fashioned children's orthopedic boots, that depend on pathology, are replaced by gym shoes (sneakers), which through the design of this product convey the idea of ordinary sneakers for ordinary children and do not impose any restrictions. According to Roncoletta and Preciosa (2009), orthopedic problems are camouflaged by the communicative aspects of ordinary sneakers for children.

Thus it can be argued that artifacts convey concepts by means of aesthetic and symbolic features, and these are often preplanned by the designers. Krippendorff (2006) argues that design products should be understandable for the users, not only in terms of aesthetic quality but also cultural quality. The author provides evidence that communication is a quality that is understandable for users and has close ties with emotions and culture.

Flüsser (2007) states that culture can be regarded as embracing the entire range of objects in use, or to put it in another way, the artifacts that surround us serve as materials for a diagnosis that can lead to an understanding of the world. Since designers are responsible for a wide range of products that are used in different areas (cars, domestic appliances, computers, clothing and so on), it must be admitted that everyday objects are, at least in part, responsible for the cultural composition of the world.

Fashion is a social-cultural phenomenon that allows understanding society. Etymologically, the Portuguese word for fashion "*moda*" derives from the Latin *modus,* which has several meanings including measurement, rhythm and also manner or knack. It can be understood as having a broad range of meanings which cover periodical changes in several social sectors, to such an extent that it is possible to speak about political, religious, scientific and aesthetic fashions and so on. It is as a result of this broad meaning that fashion is an intrinsic part of non-traditional societies and viewed as being a social phenomenon. (Souza (1987); Laver, 1989; Lipovetsky (1989); Baldini, 2005; Seeling, 2000 and 2011; Baudot, 2000; Crane, 2006, Boucher (2010); among others).

The second meaning, according to Souza 1987), which is more restricted and widely known, describes fashion in terms of its periodical changes in styles of clothing and in other aspects of personal adornment. The author refers to the creation and production of goods. Castilho and Martins (2005) pursue this idea further by stating that fashion is a system of language, a kind of discourse where ideas are turned into products and that these, in turn, reflect the values and socio-cultural concerns that are involved in the subjective interpretation of their creator - the designer. This concept is underlined by Preciosa (2004: 30), who states that:

"[fashion] as a unique blend of ideas and sensations, and is modeling the contemporary world by embodying them. In this sense, it can, to a certain extent, carry out a diagnosis of the world in which we live. In its various manifestations, it provides us with subjective modes that will be worn by us."[2].

Both in a broad and in a more restricted sense, it can be noted that fashion is not an isolated phenomenon in the world but forms a part of it and brings together the most wide-ranging and varied subjects that can be appropriated by material culture. Fashion can thus be viewed as a domain of dreams and fantasies which is playful, paradoxical, ephemeral, individualized and widely diversified. It is a socio-cultural phenomenon that is a mirror-image of society.

Fashion system has its origins in Western Europe in the 14th Century where it began to follow prescribed social rules concerning manners, which were characterized by their brief duration and entailed periodic changes of habits and styles, initially among the Western aristocracy. Researcher bellows attribute this rise to complex causes of which the following can be highlighted:

(a) The movement from a closed society to an open society that values the present. Open societies that value novelty and the present moment are one of the pillars of the *ephemerality* of the fashion system. The word *ephemeral*, in the sense of something transitory, is one of the concepts discussed. How ephemeral can a fashion or product be in contemporary society? Currently, there are two opposing views both of which are discussed in the sphere of production: *Fast-fashion* (Joy et al.2002) and *Slow-fashion* (Clark, 2008).

(b) Great technological advances in the textile industry. According to Lipovetsky (1989), Mesquita (2004) and Boucher (2010), when France and England recovered from the Hundred Years War (1337-1453), there was a demand for greater trade, both in the sense of an exchange of goods and also in *technological innovation*. It is in this sense that the authors link fashion with trade and technology. How technological innovation can be associated in contemporary society?

(c) Economic expansion strengthened by trade. Boucher (2010) argues that the textile industry (in terms of volume and range of products) became more important in the 16th Century in response to the widespread opening up of trade in the previous century. As a result, fashion was and is linked *to consumption, trade and business*.

(d) Class competition. The middle classes imitated the habits and customs of the aristocracy in a search for social recognition. The mimicry that is found in clothes and accessories allow psychological and social fantasies to be staged. According to Mesquita (2004), socio-economic distinctions based on appearance are no longer possible in societies that are fragmented like those of the contemporary world.

(e) The emergence and strengthening of anthropocentrism. The recognition of the value of the individual, or rather *individuality* is a pillar of fashion but one that leads to a paradoxical situation. At the same time that the individual is distinguished in aesthetic terms for example, he/she is also subjected to collective rules and standardization, whether in types of clothing or behavioral patterns. Mesquita (2004) states that since the 1990 s, the pillars of fashion – ephemerality, aestheticism, individuality and the paradox of standardization/differentiation, form a non-linear pattern that is more complex than the old framework.

This paradox is important to understand user's experiences. Coleman (1999) in his chapter *Inclusive Design – Design for All* argues that design for everybody must include socio-cultural factors, or in other words, the experiences of the customers/users should be taken into account when making products and those these, in turn, can provide users with pleasures. With regard to the socio-cultural context, there is a dilemma which is outlined by Üstün *et al.* (2001):

> "The experience of disability is unique to each individual, not only because the precise manifestation of a disease, disorder or injury, but also because the consequences of these health conditions will be influenced by a complex combination of factors, from personal differences in experience, background and basic emotional, psychological and intellectual make-up to differences in the physical, social and cultural context in which a person lives." Üstün *et al.* (2001: 09) [3].

In providing a flexible classification model for health which embodies the perceptions of each individual in the physical, psychological and socio-cultural context in which someone lives, the definition, or rather the experience of disability when only characterized in physical terms, is clearly influenced by different experiences. This perception is unique and individual, and depends on the socio-cultural context since it is bound up with socio-cultural and historical interpretations.

3.1 Design for Health that Embodies Fashion

Health design has close ties with inclusive design which, in turn, follows the principles of responsible design. Cooper (2005) argues that health design can be understood as a kind of design that seeks improvements in the provision of services and better experiences for the patients, and hence should be regarded as a design that allows an improvement in the quality of life, by concentrating on the perceptions of patients. The definition is open-ended and sets out a range of intermingled categories: (a) service, (b) architecture, (c) products and communications, this research focus in the last one.

Cardoso (2012) explains that they are immobile artifacts in the physical sense – that is, products built by man which *cannot be moved*, such as architectural projects. It should be pointed out that usually the artifact in itself cannot be altered structurally but its semantic meanings can, since these are related to changes undergone in space and time.

Hence, it can be understood that the design of products for health consists of mobile artifacts which can improve the quality of life of patients. It is necessary to separate product designs for health into two basic categories that take account of the world of the patients:

(a) *Products designed FOR the use of the patient:* artifacts required by various users such as surgical instruments, thermometers, and hospital stretcher beds. This category concerns products that affect a wide range of users such as doctors, nurses and patients. When the product is designed, account should be taken of the architectural environment as well as the way it will be handled by the patients themselves, and other users too, such a health personnel and cleaners.

The health products used by patients are very often included in the hospital surroundings. It is worth pointing out that there is a wide range of health products that can be transferred to the home (such as the stretcher beds themselves) or which can be designed for the socio-cultural world of the users.

(b) *Products designed for use BY the patient*: artifacts required by a single user such as prosthetics and clothing.

Design products for health are understood here as being *wearable*, whether removable or not, and worn on the body of the wearer-patients with a view to improving their quality of life.

The English language draws a clear distinction between a *user* and a *wearer*, the former being applied to *non-wearable* products such as chairs and stretcher beds for example and the latter for garments/articles that can be worn such as clothing and shoes. This semantic distinction is an aid to the development of hybrid products which can usually be employed in different environments and socio-cultural milieus. This means that designing a stretcher bed is very different from designing a *wearable* product. The bed is likely to form a part of the socio-cultural milieu of the user, either in his house or in hospital surroundings. Designing a *wearable* product means that the *wearer* will have it on his person at different times in his life and thus the designer must take into account other socio-cultural milieus of the individual and his surroundings.

Wearable items for health can be divided into two large subcategories – clothing and accessories. Garments are the main artifacts that drape the body while accessories are adornments or additional features of the body and/or clothing such as glasses, handbags, walking-sticks and footwear including upper limb prostheses. According to Vainshtein (2012: 140), *"in Western cultures accessories not only decorate, but also, magically protect the vulnerable body against evil forces and close imaginary gaps."* Moreover, in carrying out research in the area of fashion, the author has found evidence of the symbolic function of accessories.

Bonsiepe (1982: 19) was one of the first researchers of health design in Brazil. In his view, design products for health can be regarded as prosthetics or orthotics. The former are responsible for replacing the function of an organ or limb and the latter *"have the capacity to correct deformities and/or prevent them from deteriorating."* In this way, when considering clothing design for health, the design products are essential for ensuring that the pathological conditions of the wearers are prevented from getting worse.

Research into the question of clothing for the disabled in general, is centered on the basic requirements of comfort, usability, usefulness and durability. The study of human anatomy and pathology are drawn on for the development of products with ergonomic principles.

Many items produced for people with special needs – disabled people, the elderly and even children, still have a medical or clinical aesthetic condition that is easily recognized through their appearance, which conveys an idea of the restrictions imposed on those who use them and which leads to social exclusion rather than inclusion. Roncoletta and Martins (2011) point out that this can cause a social situation of dissatisfaction and discomfort for the wearer, if for example, the appearance of shoes worn by diabetes patients testify to the restrictions imposed on the wearers and confer a negative value on their *emotional benefit*. These kinds of products do not fashion products, just clothes. Why? Because they are just functional – the paradox of standardization/differentiation, ephemerality, aestheticism and specially individuality is too weak.

Roncoletta and Loschiavo (2012) also state that usability and usefulness are not only combined as practical design functions but are also aesthetic-symbolic features. By the former is understood the use of the object and by the latter, the relationship between an object of use and its communicative power, the context in which it is employed and the previous experiences of the wearer; these are often emotional subjective elements that are of crucial importance for personal symbology.

Vainshtein (2012: 143) states that prosthetics was usually designed to replace a limb and could also act as a *"fashionable* [accessory], *the distinctive additions to a person's identity and looks".*

The Alternative Limb Project[1] is an example of the development of prosthetics that can reflect the *"imagination, interests and personalities of the wearers".* In other words, the paradox of standardization/differentiation and individuality are preset in a deep level. This is carried out in a number of accompanying stages, the first of which involves finding something that is fitting between the organic body or artifacts and the discussion of ideas and concepts.

The criterion of fittingness is regarded by the person concerned as satisfactory when he/she feels physically comfortable. The appearance of the prosthetics is the outcome of discussions of ideas and concepts between planners and wearers. In this stage, the socio-cultural dimension of the wearer is investigated so that the aesthetic-symbolic features of the prosthetics can (according to the *website* of the project) reflect *"the imagination, interests and personality of the wearers".* As a result, the project expects the prosthetics to lead to the socio-cultural inclusion of a disabled person since its appearance is designed to reflect some of their socio-cultural dimensions.

The *website* provides information about two basic categories: realistic limbs (Fig. 2) – which imitate the human body –, and alternative limbs (Fig. 3) – where the aesthetic appeal is created in accordance with the wishes of the wearer. In both categories, the project encourages socio-cultural inclusion because the wearer can choose the prosthetic replacement.

The first, realist project, is a copy of human body, however is good emphasize the singularity of human body.

The second category which involves exploring the life-style of the wearers, can be related to fashion individuality. Figure 3 shows the singer Viktoria Modesta. In website *Alternative Limb Project,* she *adds "...it's important to take control of your own body and most importantly improve it or reflect your personality through altered body image".*

Can be observed the power of image communication through the hybrid wearable artifacts that could be at the same time a fashion accessory, a design project and a health prosthetic.

---

[1] The Alternative Limb Project by Shopie de Oliveira Barata, London, UK. According to website profile "Sophie comes from an art background at London Arts University where she studied Special Effects prosthetics for film and T.V. She then went on to work for 8 years, as a sculptor making realistic looking, bespoke prosthetics for amputees at one of the leading prosthetic providers". Available: http://www.thealternativelimbproject.com/. Accessed in January 2013.

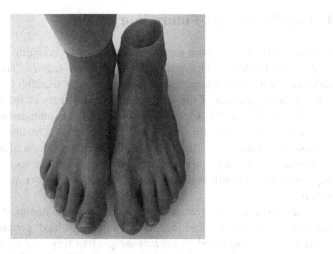

Fig. 2. Realist limbs. Undertaken by: The Alternative Limb Project. Available at: http://www. thealternativelimbproject.com/. Accessed in January 2013.

Fig. 3. Prosthetic that recognizes the value of the aesthetic-symbolic features of the artifact and lead to socio-cultural inclusion. Undertaken by: The Alternative Limb Project. Available at: http://www.thealternativelimbproject.com/. Accessed in January 2013.

4   Conclusions and Future Work

The process of changing the paradigm was begun by adopting the social model in ICF of the WHO when it incorporated socio-cultural factors. Thus it was possible to understand why most schemes for disabled people in the 20th Century were carried out without taking account of the socio-cultural dimensions of the wearer.

The examples of *The Alternative Limb Project* are intended to embody fashion as a socio-cultural phenomenon. It is possible to discern a feasible approximation of the outlook of the designer in the area of health with the outlook of the designer in the area of fashion, so that, in partnership, they can foster effective socio-cultural inclusion and improve physical health in a way that culminates in a better quality of life and state of well-being.

When fashion is viewed as a socio-cultural phenomenon, it is clear that from the moment when society first began including disabled people into society, some designers of orthoses and prostheses adapted to this new climate, albeit somewhat timidly, and developed designs that recognized the value of the socio-cultural dimension of the individual, or rather, a combination of their personal styles and practical purposes (or "functionality"), as for example, *The Alternative Limb Project*.

Thus, the two categories – realist and alternative limb - are hybrid wearable artifacts which pose a challenge to crossing the border among the organic/material body, fashion design (clothing or accessories) and health products.

References

Bonsiepe, G.: Desenho industrial para pessoas deficientes. CNPq – Coordenação Editorial, Brasília (1982)

Boucher, F.: História do vestuário no ocidente. Cosac & Naify, São Paulo (2010)

Bürdek, B.: Design: história, teoria e prática do design de produtos. Blucher,São Paulo (2006)

Castilho, K., Martins, M.: Discursos da moda: semiótica, design e corpo. Editora Anhembi Morumbi, São Paulo (2005)

Cardoso, R.: Design para um pensamento complexo. Cosac & Naify, São Paulo (2011)

C.R.P.D. - Convenção das Nações Unidas sobre os Direitos das Pessoas com Deficiências. http://www.un.org/disabilities/

Correr, R.: Deficiência e inclusão social – construindo uma comunidade. Coleção Saúde & Sociedade. Editorial EDUSC, Bauru (2003)

Crane, D.: A moda e seu papel social -classe, gênero e identidade das roupas. Editora SENAC, São Paulo (2006)

Denzin, N., Lincoln, Y.: Handbook of Qualitative Research. SAGE Publications, Los Angeles (2000)

Farias N., Buchalla C. A classificação internacional de funcionalidade, incapacidade e saúde da Organização Mundial da Saúde. In: Revista Brasileira de Epistemologia. http://www.scielo.br

Flick, U. Desenho da pesquisa qualitativa. Artmed, Porto Alegre (2009)

Flüsser, V.: O mundo codificado: por uma filosofia do design e comunicação. Cosac & Naify, São Paulo (2007)

Goffman, E.: Stigma. Simon & Schuster, New York (1963)

Gibbs, G.: Análise de dados qualitativos. Artmed, Porto Alegre (2009)

Gray, D.: Pesquisa no mundo real. Artmed, Porto Alegre (2012)

Joy et al. Fast Fashion, Sustainability, and the Ethical Appeal of Luxury Brands. In: Fashion Theory, volume 16, issue 3, pp. 237–296. Berg, London (2012)

Krippendorff, K.: The Semant Turn: a New Foundation for Design. Taylor & Francis, Boca Raton (2006)

Laver, J.: A roupa e a moda – uma história concisa. Companhia das Letras, São Paulo (1989)

Lipovetsky, G.: O Império do efêmero – a moda e seu destino nas sociedades modernas. Editora Schwarcz, São Paulo (1989)

Marconi, M., Lakatos, E.: Fundamentos da metodologia científica. Editora Atlas, São Paulo (2010)

Mesquita, C.: Moda contemporânea, quatro ou cinco conexões possíveis. Editora Anhembi Morumbi, São Paulo (2004)

Preciosa, R.: Produção Estética – notas sobre roupas, sujeitos e modos de vida. Anhembi Morumbi, São Paulo (2004)

Richardson, R.: Pesquisa social: métodos e técnicas. Editora Atlas, São Paulo (2010)

Rocha, E.: Eucenir Reabilitação de pessoas com deficiência. Roca, São Paulo (2006)

Roncoletta, M.R., Loschiavo, M.C.: Shoe design requirements for the physically disabled women. In: Design Research Society – DRS -2012. Chulalongkorn University, Bangkok (2012)

Roncoletta, M. R., Martins, S.: Usabilidad, placer y comodidad in calzado para mujeres com deficiencia física. In: Flores (org.) Diseño y ergonomía para poblaciones especiales. Designio, Cidade do Mexico (2011)

Roncoletta, M.R.: Preciosa, R. Reflexões sobre responsabilidade social e design de moda. In: Anais P&D. Editora SENAC, São Paulo (2009)

Santos, M.C.L.: Design e responsabilidade social: entrevista com Rachel Cooper. In: Revista Design em Foco, vol. II, number 02. Universidade do Estado da Bahia, Salvador (2005)

Schneider, B.: Design – Uma introdução: o design no contexto social, cultural e econômico. Blucher, São Paulo (2010)

Schwandt, T.A.: Constructivist, Interpretivist Approaches to Human Inquiry. In: Denzin, N.K., Lincoln,Y.S. (eds.) Handbook of Qualitative Research. Newbury Park, Sage (2000)

Seeling, C.: Moda – 150 anos. Posdam, Tandem Verlag GmbH (2011)

Seidl, E., Zannon, M.C.: Qualidade de vida e saúde: aspectos conceituais e metodológicos. In: Caderno de Saúde Pública (2004). http://www.scielo.br

Souza, G.: O espírito das roupas - a moda no século dezenove. Editora Schwarcz, São Paulo (1987)

Stedman, L.: Dicionário médico, Guanabara, Rio de Janeiro (2003)

Vash, C.: Enfrentando a deficiência – a manifestação, a psicologia, a reabilitação. Pioneira, São Paulo (1988)

Vainstein, O.I.: Have a suitcase just full of legs because i need options for different clothing. In: Fashion Theory, 18(2) pp. 139–170. Berg, London (2012)

Üstün, et al.: Disability and Culture: Universalism and Diversity. World Health Organization. Hogree & Huber Publishers, Gottingem (2001)

W.H.O. - Constitution of the World Health Organization. http://www.who.int/library/collections

Smart Mirror Where I Stand, Who Is the Leanest in the Sand?

Marianna Saba[1], Riccardo Scateni[1], Fabio Sorrentino[1],
Lucio Davide Spano[1(✉)], Sara Colantonio[2], Daniela Giorgi[2],
Massimo Magrini[2], Ovidio Salvetti[2], Novella Buonaccorsi[3], and Ilaria Vitali[3]

[1] Dipartimento di Matematica e Informatica, University of Cagliari,
Via Ospedale 72, 09124 Cagliari, Italy
{mariannasaba,riccardo,fabio.sorrentino,davide.spano}@unica.it
[2] ISTI-CNR, Via G. Moruzzi 1, 56125 Pisa, Italy
{sara.colantonio,daniela.giorgi,massimo.magrini,
ovidio.salvetti}@isti.cnr.it
[3] Intecs, Via Forti 5, 56121 Ospedaletto, Pisa, Italy
{novella.buonaccorsi,ilaria.vitali}@intecs.it

Abstract. In this paper we introduce the Virtuoso project, which aims at creating a seamless interactive support for fitness and wellness activities in touristic resorts. The overall idea is to evaluate the current physical state of the user through a technology-enhanced mirror. We describe the state of the art technologies for building a smart mirror prototype. In addition, we compare different parameters for evaluating the user's physical state, considering the user's impact, the contact requirements and their cost. Finally we depict the planned setup and evaluation setting for the Virtuoso project.

Keywords: Smart mirrors · Self-monitoring · Wellbeing monitoring · Design for quality of life technologies · Resort

1 Introduction

During our vacation time, especially in the summer, we would like to interrupt our daily routine and to regain the energies we lost during the whole year. At the beginning of the summer, many people do not like the image reflected in the mirror, and it is common to start the vacation with the intention of spending some time in physical activities. Mirrors do not lie... But what if mirrors were able to suggest solutions rather than complain?

This is the objective of the Virtuoso project: to create a seamless interactive support for fitness and wellness activities in touristic resorts. The overall idea is to evaluate the current physical state of a resort guest through a mirror metaphor. Then, the system will try to help her in enhancing it during the stay, suggesting different activities available in the resort. Both the analysis and the suggestions should be provided in a playful way. In this paper, we introduce

© Springer International Publishing Switzerland 2015
M. Antona and C. Stephanidis (Eds.): UAHCI 2015, Part III, LNCS 9177, pp. 364–373, 2015.
DOI: 10.1007/978-3-319-20684-4_36

the project requirements and we provide a survey on the existing enabling technologies for creating the mirror metaphor and to acquire data from the user. It can be helpful for researchers and practitioners interested in creating a similar environment.

From a technological point of view, creating such environment poses a set of challenges, both technical and related to the user experience. The first challenge is how to design and realize the smart mirror and its related apparels. Different companies provide off-the-shelf smart mirrors whose functions are related to controlling and supporting smart home environments, multimedia controllers and augmented reality (AR) devices. In this paper, we will provide a detailed review of the existing devices in all three categories, discussing their advantages and disadvantages in general, and in particular for the Virtuoso project.

The second challenge for our project is how to support the evaluation of the user's physical state. Such evaluation does not require the same precision if compared to a real diagnosis, which is out of our scope. In addition, since a resort is a relaxed environment where users expect to enjoy themselves, it is not feasible for Virtuoso to use intrusive equipments or methodologies for acquiring data. Therefore, in this paper we analyse different measurements that can be quickly performed on a user. For each of them, we detail the procedure for acquiring the data, assessing its cost both money-wise (i.e., the equipment to be used) and user-wise (i.e., how bothering it can be).

At the end of the vacation the mirror should profile our user again, if the activities had their effect, the resort guest can bring home a valuable souvenir: an improved physical shape. Or at least some good suggestions!

2 Virtuoso

The main aim of the Virtuoso project is to provide a set of tools, easy to use, that does not necessarily require to be used by specialized health personnel (medical or paramedical), to assist tourist operators. The typical user of the system will be the fitness and/or wellness coach. Such a kind of professional is a figure that is more and more diffused also in a contexts of vacation resort. The activity of the wellness coach is to identify the tourists' need and guide them in choosing and practicing fitness activities offered by the resort.

The main tool we want to develop will be a computer-based application for the general assessment of the psychological and physical conditions of the customer. We aim, in other words, to measure his or her well-being with some simple and compact indicators. The application used by the center will have a companion mobile app, for end users, that allows to browse the information produced in the initial evaluation session, to log the activities during the vacation, to socially share it, and to bring back home the lesson learnt and continue to practice the good customs.

To reach this goal we will study and develop methods and techniques for the analysis of the general health of an individual, based on heterogeneous data acquired from non-invasive and non-intrusive sensors like, for example, cameras and platforms with sensors, contactless or minimally contact, such as multifunction armbands.

The basic idea behind the whole project is the ability to assess the physical and psychological condition of an individual and give him or her good advices on how to improve, through an analysis of diagnostic signs collected using different techniques and technologies.

3   Smart Mirrors

In this section we review the existing technologies that may be used for building interactive mirrors. Recent introduction of new materials and the overall ICT proceedings make different solutions for building interactive mirrors possible, in order to transform it from a simple reflecting surface to a more interactive device. We can group them in three sets: (1) Multimedia players (e.g. music or videos), (2) Interactive home controllers and (3) Augmented reality devices. We discuss their advantages and disadvantages in general, and in particular for the Virtuoso project.

3.1   Multimedia Players

The multimedia players category contains devices equipped with a touch screen, or TV enhanced with external full body tracking devices (e.g. Microsoft Kinect). However, most of them support only entertainment tasks, like playing music or videos.

- **Mirror 2.0** [1] combines the advantages of a smartphone and a mirror. It contains an LCD display, positioned behind the glass. It provides news and weather information and it allows the playback of both videos and music. The user controls its functionalities through gestures and vocal commands.
- **Smart Washbasin** [2] displays different information on a washbasin mirror such as mails, weather forecast, the water temperature and pressure, the calendar and the user's weight measured through a built-in scale in the base portion. The device consists of an Android tablet that displays the widgets on the basin mirror, made with a semi-reflecting glass put on top of an LCD display. It is possible to control it without touching the screen surface, since it is equipped with proximity sensors able to track the hands position and motion.
- **NEOD Framed Mirror TV** [3] is a standard LCD screen (up to 50 in.), covered by a mirror, specifically designed for the screen. The screen provides only TV functionalities, and it does not provide more interactive features.

3.2   Interactive Home Controllers

Interactive home controllers allow to control different home appliances through the interface displayed on the mirror. The following is the list of the devices belonging to this category.

- The **Smart Mirror for home environment** [4] allows to control all the smart devices at home. It relays on face recognition for authenticating the user and displays personalised information (news, mail, messages etc.). The system exploits a touch screen monitor and two webcams, one for the face recognition and one for the home surveillance.
- The **Multi Display in Black Mirror** [5] by Toshiba is a prototype that combines the functionalities of a tablet together with the reflecting surface of a mirror. It provides two configurations taking into account two different home environments: the bathroom and the kitchen. Considering the bathroom, the prototype provides useful information for the beginning of the day such as the weather forecast and fitness information coming from personal devices. In the kitchen, the setting includes a camera allowing the user to interact through gestures while preparing recipes and controlling the appliances.

3.3 Augmented Reality Devices

Many mirror devices provide Augmented Reality (AR) features, which are useful especially for advertisement purposes in shop showcases. In addition, there are different attempts to use smart mirrors for supporting routine activities. In this category we can include, for instance, an application that monitors and guides a user while brushing teeth through the information displayed on the smart mirror. Finally, the so called "medical mirrors" are particularly interesting for the Virtuoso project, since they can measure different physical parameters such as heart and breath rate.

- The **Reveal** project [6], created in the New York Times research and development department, consists of an LCD Display covered by a mirror glass. The device exploits a Microsoft Kinect for tracking user's movements in real-time. It visualizes different information on its surface (calendar, mail, news, online shopping websites, instant messenger etc.). In addition, it responds to vocal commands. A peculiar feature is the medicine box scanner, which allows the user to buy medicines recognizing their packages.
- The **Cybertecture Mirror** [7] is a complete PC contained into a 37 in. mirror, equipped with a 32 in. LCD screen. Through a smartphone application, the user accesses different information overlaid on the reflected image. The interface allows to visualize instant messages, the calendar, the mailbox, and the weather forecast. In addition, it provides information on the user's physical state. Indeed, the device provides a set of external wireless sensors that allow to measure the user's weight, fat, muscle and bone mass.
- The **Interactive Mirror** [8] by Panasonic seems to be an ordinary mirror: neither camera nor other sensors suggest the features of a smart object. Once the user sits down in front of it, the mirror displays an enlarged frame for her face, together with menus for accessing different functionalities. The system analyses the face hydration, wrinkles and other details in order to recommend products and treatments to take care of her skin (e.g. to make it softer etc.),

to slow ageing and so on. The mirror supports the user in buying such products. In addition, it provides make-up style previews, simulating lighting and ambient conditions (e.g. at home, outdoor, shopping center etc.).

- The **Connected Store Demo** [9] by eBay and Rebecca Minkoff provides interactive experiences in both the store showcase and in the fitting room, equipped with a mirror surface overlaid by store user interface. In the showcase setting, the user explores the different items in the store. Once she finds something interesting, she requests to try it in the fitting room. Once finished, the shopper prepares the fitting room with all the items. Inside the fitting room, the user exploits the mirror for looking for other items and/or providing feedback. In addition, she may select some of them for buying.
- The **Brushing Teeth Mirror** [10] displays the information collected by a smart brush about inflammations or infections of the teeth and gums.
- The **Medical Mirror** [11] combines computer vision and signal processing techniques for measuring the heart rate from the optical signal reflected of the face. The prototype consists of an LCD display with built-in camera and a two way mirror fitted onto the frame. The smart mirror recognizes the presence of a user when she stands in front of it and, after about 15 seconds, it displays the heart rate below the user's reflected image.

4   Physical State Acquisition

In this section we report different physiological parameters that can be evaluated through different sensors. We summarize their definition and the measurement procedure. After that, we compare them in Table 1, according to three dimensions:

1. How much the procedure is annoying or requires uncommon actions for a user (*Impact*). We consider the project's audience: people monitoring their physical status for wellness purposes and not for a real diagnosis (they are spending their holidays in a resort). We consider three possible degrees: *High* if the procedure takes a long time or it requires difficult actions, *Low* if the procedure is short or very easy, and *Medium* for values in between.
2. Whether the sensors used for measuring the parameter require some *Contact* or not.
3. The *Cost* of the equipment for measuring the parameter. We considered three cost levels (*Low, Medium* and *High*).

For instance, acquiring user's weight through a pressure sensitive board (e.g., the Wii Balance Board) and her height through a laser tool, makes it possible to calculate the Body Mass Index (BMI). Combining such data with a volumetric representation of the user's body allows to analyse the body weight distribution without any direct contact with the user. So the BMI has a low cost in terms of intrusiveness and a reasonable cost in terms of hardware. Such measurement together with other information provide the evaluation data and could drive the activity during the stay. The following is the list of parameters we considered:

1. **Metabolic Balance of Fat and Glucose.** Breath acetone is a parameter for detecting the correct exploitation of all energetic substrates [12]. Indeed, some metabolic diseases cause a predominant use of the fat substrate instead of glucose. This increases the production of acetone which is expelled through the lungs. The presence of acetone in the breath may indicate infectious diseases or diabetes. It can be measured through colorimetric reactions on a disposable transparent support with a reactive substance. We can detect the colour change with a camera.

2. **Glucose metabolism.** There is a correlation between the saliva and the blood glucose level. A variation of the value from the reference levels reveals an altered glucose metabolism, caused by organ or hormonal diseases. It can be measured again through colorimetric reactions.

3. **Circulation of blood.** An irregular body heat distribution indicates blood circulation problems such as e.g. the venous stasis. Therefore, we can obtain such distribution through an infrared camera and analysing the thermal image [13].

4. The **Body Mass Index** (BMI) is the ratio of a person's weight and height squared. This biometric parameter indicates whether the weight correlates well with a height. In general, a person having a BMI greater than 25 is overweight, greater than 30 is obese, while below 18.5 is underweight. For calculating this index it is sufficient to measure the weight through a pressure board (e.g. the Wii Balance Board [14]) and the height with a laser sensor

5. **Fat distribution.** It is possible to use the ratio between waist and hips circumference for identifying an excessive visceral adipose tissue mass accumulation, which is strongly correlated with cardio vascular diseases. The circumferences can be measured through laser and infrared sensors [15].

6. Heart and breath functionalities can be evaluated through the **oxygen-haemoglobin saturation** levels (indicating a good lung ventilation and blood) and the heart rate. We can measure these parameters using a pulse oximeter, which requires a light pressure on a finger.

7. **Stress level.** Persons react to specific visual stimuli with different face movements, which can be evaluated for establishing the stress level. Therefore, it is possible to create a test where the user looks to a sequence of pictures and a software analyses the face movements [16].

8. **Muscular tone** evaluation. The muscular strength allows to evaluate the physiological condition of the active lean mass. We consider the strength of the quadriceps and of the dominant hand and forehand muscles, since they represent better the general condition of the entire muscle mass. We can measure the quadriceps strength with a dynamometer set in a fixed position while we measure the hand strength measuring the grip force [17].

9. **Body mass distribution.** The intracellular and extracellular water volume allows to evaluate the lean mass percentage (through a simple ratio). We can measure such volumes through the bioimpedance analysis: the user stands on impedance board and grabs two handles to allow the electricity flow from hands to feet [18].

10. **Hearing** can be evaluated with an audiometric curve: a device emits a sound scale, ranging from 15 to 20000 Hz. The volume is variable between 0 and 100 dB. The user listens to the sounds and signals at which pitch s/he starts hearing [19].
11. **Night vision.** We evaluate the functionality of the rods (the black/white and shape photoreceptors) testing the adaptability of the eye to night vision, asking the user to recognize the objects in a set of images in low light conditions. We evaluate the recognition and detail degree of their image descriptions.
12. **Blood pressure.** It provides information about the circulation of blood and also on the stress level. We can measure it with a sphygmomanometer applied at the user's wrist. The method is unintrusive and requires some contact.

Table 1. Physical state parameters summary.

Id	Parameter	Impact	Contact	Cost
1	Fat and Glucose Balance	High	Yes	Low
2	Glucose Metabolism	High	Yes	Low
3	Circulation of blood	Low	No	High
4	Body Mass Index	Low	No	Low
5	Fat distribution	Low	No	Low
6	Oxygen-haemoglobin saturation	Low	Yes	Medium
7	Stress level	Low	No	Low
8	Muscular tone	Medium	Yes	Medium
9	Body mass distribution	Low	No	High
10	Hearing	Medium	Yes	Low
11	Night Vision	Low	No	Low
12	Blood pressure	Low	Yes	Low

5 Setup Discussion

The ideal setup of the system developed in the Virtuoso project is as following.

Imagine a tourist arriving at his or her chosen resort, in summer, in Sardinia, to enjoy a relaxing week or fortnight of vacation. Most probably, he or she does not like to undergo a set of medical exams to figure out what is his or her state of health. But, what if, he or she will enter wearing a swimsuit, a funny room whit a board on ground, and a Microsoft Kinect mounted on a rotating arm capable of turning around the board, and a mirror interacting with him or her asking to answer simple questions just waiving a hand?

This will be a kind of fun, subtracting just, maybe, five or ten minutes to the beach, and will be the basic set of information to compute a profile containing age, height, weight, BMI, body volume, fat vs muscle ratio, and some more parameters that, put together in a model, will tell which kind of activity is best suit and, why not, the best restaurant you can find in the resort for your needs. This is the long term goal of the project, scheduled for the summer of 2016.

In order to put such objectives into practice, we plan to create our mirror device prototype, starting from existing consumer hardware (Kinect 2.0 and a wide LCD screen), similarly to those described in Sect. 3.3. Considering the physical state parameters, we plan to include those having a low or medium cost, without any contact and with a low user impact in the measurement.

With respect to the evaluation of the prototype, we plan to validate the Virtuoso results in a holiday resort scenario. Being this setting one of the most important for wellness in both research and industrial effort, we expect to collect important insights on the effectiveness and the acceptance of the approach. We plan to perform both technical test and evaluations with end users.

On the technical level, the evaluation should address two points. The first one is assessing the reliability of the physical insights collected through our prototype with ground-truth data. In order to do this, we will evaluate a group of people whose physical state has been already assessed with proper diagnosis techniques and we will compare the results. The second point is related to the deployment of the entire solution in a real resort setting, considering hardware, software and the staff training.

Last but not least, we plan to evaluate the user overall usability of the approach through a long-term study. We will deploy the system in a well-known resort in Sardinia, and we will collect both qualitative and quantitative data. In particular, we plan to apply the SUM model [20] for combining different usability metrics into a single score. In order to collect the data, considering that it would be annoying for resort guests to complete questionnaires, we plan to instrument the software for tracking task completion, time, and errors. With respect to the post-task satisfaction ratings, we will provide a playful interface for collecting the answer, e.g. punching the rating number as physical exercise. Such evaluation method is convenient since it would be possible to automatize the data collection and to perform analysis at both a global and a task level.

6   Conclusion and Future Work

In this paper, we reported on the state of the art technologies for building smart mirrors and for sensing the user's physical. We described smart mirrors devices and prototypes working as multimedia players, interactive home controllers and augmented reality devices. Moreover, we described and compared different parameters for evaluating the user's physical state, considering whether they require annoying or uncommon actions, the contact between the sensors and the user and the procedure cost.

Finally, we introduced the scope and the objectives of the Virtuoso project, which aims to create a seamless interactive support for fitness and wellness activities in touristic resorts. We explained how, in future work, we are planning to create the project setup and to evaluate its results.

Acknoledgments. The Virtuoso project is funded by Sardinia Regional Government (CUP code F78C13000530002) with the funds of Regional Law 7/07, year 2013, "Invito a presentare progetti di ricerca fondamentale o di base orientata a temi di carattere specifico di stretto interesse regionale". Lucio Davide Spano gratefully acknowledges Sardinia Regional Government for the financial support (P.O.R. Sardegna F.S.E. Operational Programme of the Autonomous Region of Sardinia, European Social Fund 2007–2013 - Axis IV Human Resources, Objective l.3, Line of Activity l.3.1 "Avviso di chiamata per il finanziamento di Assegni di Ricerca".

References

1. Grynkofi, R.: Mirror 2.0. http://bathroominnovation.com.au/finalists#Year2013 Accessed 23 January 2015
2. Seraku, C.: Smart Washbasin. http://smart-washbasin.seraku.co.jp/english/ Accessed 23 January 2015
3. NEOD: NEOD Framed Mirror TV. http://www.neod.org/ Accessed 23 January 2015
4. Hossain, M.A., Atrey, P.K., El Saddik, A.: Smart mirror for ambient home environment (2007)
5. Toshiba: Toshiba to unveil leading-edge technologies at CES 2014. http://www.toshiba.co.jp/about/press/2014_01/pr0702.htm Accessed 26 January 2015
6. House, B., Lloyd, A., Zimbalist, M.: Reveal project. http://brianhouse.net/works/reveal/ Accessed 23 January 2015
7. Law, J.: Cybertecture Mirror. http://www.jameslawcybertecture.com/index.php?section=Company Accessed 23 January 2015
8. Panasonic: The future mirror: a beautiful innovation. http://youtu.be/-2_kc9GQYIE Accessed 23 January 2015
9. Ebay: Rebecca Minkoff Connected Store Demo. https://www.youtube.com/watch?v=6G3JIyG_GeY#t=10 Accessed 26 January 2015
10. Mullins, T.: Brushing Teeth Mirror. http://www.designboom.com/contest/view.php?contest_pk=36&item_pk=44258&p=1 Accessed 23 January 2015
11. Poh, M.Z., McDuff, D., Picard, R.: A medical mirror for non-contact health monitoring. In: ACM SIGGRAPH 2011 Emerging Technologies, SIGGRAPH 2011, p. 2:1–2:1. ACM, New York (2011)
12. Galassetti, P.R., Novak, B., Nemet, D., Rose-Gottron, C., Cooper, D.M., Meinardi, S., Newcomb, R., Zaldivar, F., Blake, D.R.: Breath ethanol and acetone as indicators of serum glucose levels: an initial report. Diabetes Technol. Ther. **7**(1), 115–123 (2005)
13. Bagavathiappan, S., Saravanan, T., Philip, J., Jayakumar, T., Raj, B., Karunanithi, R., Panicker, T.M., Korath, P., Jagadeesan, K.: Investigation of peripheral vascular disorders using thermal imaging. Br. J. Diabetes Vasc. Dis. **8**(2), 102–104 (2008)

14. Clark, R.A., Bryant, A.L., Pua, Y., McCrory, P., Bennell, K., Hunt, M.: Validity and reliability of the nintendo wii balance board for assessment of standing balance. Gait Posture **31**(3), 307–310 (2010)
15. Anunciação, P., Ribeiro, R., Pereira, M., Comunian, M.: Different measurements of waist circumference and sagittal abdominal diameter and their relationship with cardiometabolic risk factors in elderly men. J. Hum. Nutr. Diet. **27**(2), 162–167 (2014)
16. Yong, C.Y., Sudirman, R., Chew, K.M.: Facial expression monitoring system using pca-bayes classifier. In: 2011 International Conference on Future Computer Sciences and Application (ICFCSA), pp. 187–191. IEEE (2011)
17. Agre, J., Magness, J., Hull, S., Wright, K., Baxter, T., Patterson, R., Stradel, L.: Strength testing with a portable dynamometer: reliability for upper and lower extremities. Arch. Phys. Med. Rehabhil. **68**(7), 454–458 (1987)
18. Jaffrin, M.Y.: Body composition determination by bioimpedance: an update. Curr. Opin. Clin. Nutr. Metab. Care **12**(5), 482–486 (2009)
19. 389, I.: Acoustics-standard reference zero for the calibration of pure-tone air conduction audiometers (1991)
20. Sauro, J., Kindlund, E.: A method to standardize usability metrics into a single score. In: Proceedings of the SIGCHI Conference on Human Factors in Computing Systems, CHI 2005, pp. 401–409. ACM, New York (2005)

A Virtual Reality Lower-Back Pain Rehabilitation Approach: System Design and User Acceptance Analysis

Wu-Chen Su[1](✉), Shih-Ching Yeh[2,3], Si-Huei Lee[4,5], and Hsiang-Chun Huang[3]

[1] Chang Gung University, Taoyuan, Taiwan
wuchen_sue@hotmail.com
[2] School of Mobile Information Engineering (SMIE), Sun Yat-Sen University,
Guangzhou 510275, People's Republic of China
[3] Department of Computer Science and Information Engineering, National Central University,
Taoyuan, Taiwan
yehshch@mail.sysu.edu.cn
[4] Department of Physical Medicine and Rehabilitation, Taipei Veterans General Hospital,
Taipei, Taiwan
[5] National Yang-Ming University, Taipei, Taiwan
leesihuei@gmail.com

Abstract. Low back pain (LBP) affects people of all ages and it is a very common health problem globally. Eighty percent of all people may have experienced LBP in their life. Furthermore, there is no perfect strategy which can be used to treat all kinds of LBP patients. Moreover, LBP rehabilitation takes a long period of time, while patients may lack motivation to finish the entire course of treatment. As a result, LBP poses substantial impact on individuals, organizations and society. Fortunately, the advancement of computing hardware and software offer us a virtual reality based solution in the rehabilitation field. For example, cheaper and highly accurate wearable devices can also be used to coordinate with analytical software packages in order to carry out motion tracking and measure a patient's movement promptly and effectively.

Therefore, in this study, a VR-based LBP rehabilitation system utilizing wireless sensor technologies to assist physiotherapists and patients in undertaking three stages of rehabilitation exercises for low back health is proposed. The major functions of this VR system are as follows: (1) Monitor and correct a patient's posture to establish basic movement patterns. (2) A physiotherapist can customize appropriate rehabilitation programs for an individual patient in order to enhance muscle strength and endurance. (3) Provide supports to a patient so as to establish whole body and joint stability.

A total of twenty LBP patients have been recruited for this study, and a user acceptance of technology questionnaire is used to investigate the effectiveness and efficiency of the system proposed. Participants are treated 2–3 times a week for 4–6 weeks and experimental results demonstrate that uses of this VR system for rehabilitation courses have a high degree of technology acceptance and patients are willing to continue to use this system for LBP rehabilitation in the future.

Keywords: Wireless sensor IMU · Virtual reality · Low back pain

© Springer International Publishing Switzerland 2015
M. Antona and C. Stephanidis (Eds.): UAHCI 2015, Part III, LNCS 9177, pp. 374–382, 2015.
DOI: 10.1007/978-3-319-20684-4_37

1 Introduction

Low Back Pain (LBP) poses an impact on any affected individual's muscle strength, flexibility and endurance and may be accompanied by many associated diseases such as depression, anxiety, and low self-efficacy [1, 2]. As a result, medication costs and other tangible burdens are increased and witnessed in our society [3]. The main LBP type is Non-Specific Low Back Pain (NSLBP) which is induced in the cases when individuals have poor posture, overburden the pertinent muscles or injure themselves in sports [4]. However, traditional programs of LBP rehabilitation usually are laborious and tedious for patients and require the full attention of physiotherapists to monitor, to record and to correct inappropriate motions of patients. This leads to a lack of objective assessments as well as unsatisfactory rehabilitation progress. In spite of this, those suffering LBP most numerously are middle-aged individuals who provide economic support to their families; they work industriously and need physical exercise in their daily activities to reduce recurrence of LBP [3]. Through understanding the limitations of current approaches and how and when such fail to meet the needs of LBP suffers, LBP prevention and administration have to align principles to achieve: (1) Reduction of pain, (2) Prevention of disability and (3) Maintenance of work capacity [5] as design guidelines and further use in the application of therapeutic development.

Recently, this VR-based therapy has been used to administer LBP intervention in various populations, for example, Kim et al. [6] assigned thirty middle-aged female patients to either a physical therapy program or a VR-based yoga program for a period of four weeks. The results indicate that the VR-based yoga program can be employed as a therapeutic medium to prevent and to cure LBP. Park et al. [2] investigated the effects of different exercise programs on chronic work-related LBP. They randomly assigned factory workers to either a lumbar stabilization exercise group or a Nintendo Wii exercise group. After an eight week intervention, they found that the Nintendo Wii exercise program demonstrated influences on mental health due to its gaming components. In sum, the need for a comprehensive and interdisciplinary rehabilitation program with a combination of treatments, education, strengthening exercises and fitness training are suggested in these studies.

In a LBP rehabilitation study, the researcher McGill points out that a fixed and unchangeable intervention program could not achieve expected treatment outcomes and also finds that the creation of spine stability should be a first priority. Once pain stability is established and the pain is resolved, many patients find that their mobility returns without further intervention [5]. Therefore, McGill develops the three training stages for back health and includes associated exercises found effective for the treatment of LBP sufferers. However, it can be readily observed that some individuals are not very "body aware" to successfully perform motion suggestions upon command. An example of this difficulty is for instance when a physiotherapist must place a straight bar along a patient's spine while asking the patient to maintain contact with it for separating hip rotation from lumbar motion in rehabilitation sessions [5]. Additionally, physiotherapists need to prepare various training tools and facilities, and that requires their physical presence all of the time. As a result, additional efforts at rehabilitation assistance and performance measurements are carried out by other medical staff. Additionally, the present VR system should offer the capacity for patients to blend learning patterns into daily activities due to the fact that the recurrence rate of LBP is more than sixty percent [7]. Consequently, people can easily relate to the circumstances targeted by LBP rehabilitation tasks with which they are familiar in their workplace or home to prevent a recurrence of LBP, e.g. rising from a chair and sitting, carrying heavy objects, etc. However, such familiar tasks are rarely found in current LBP intervention studies. Thus, these requirements enable us to develop and configure an interactive and flexible VR-based therapeutic approach alleviating deficit to provide immediate visual and auditory feedback to users, and allowing physiotherapists to monitor movements of patient and use statistical information tracked and analyzed for further treatment support and medical decision making. Through building the aforementioned mechanisms, the benefits to the mental and physical health of patients can be improved by this work.

The objective of this paper is two-fold: (1) present the design and development of a VR-based LBP rehabilitation system to measure joint flexion angle via a self-built wireless sensor modules and provide visual and auditory feedback to the user which is based on reestablishment and analysis of human postures in the training session; and (2) understand the technology acceptance of system users and summarize their feedback as per future work.

This essay is organized as follows: In Sect. 2, the system design requirements, IMU measurement system, strategies of rehabilitation and the methods used for analysis and evaluation are presented. Section 3 presents the experiment design, setup and analytical results obtained in this present study. Section 4 summarizes the contributions of this work and highlights future research directions.

2   Materials and Methods

2.1   System Design Requirements

The system requirements are collected and summarized from a research literature review and discussions with physiotherapists and attending hospital physicians via multiple interviews and meeting discussions. Subsequently, a VR system using Unity 3D engine as the development platform and accompanying with revised therapeutic guidance in [5, 8] is proposed. The three training stages for back health are: (1) Motion correction (2) Exercises for LBP (3) Increase muscle endurance and strength. In each stage, the rehabilitation tasks of a patient are measured by an inertial measurement unit (IMU) measurement system in real time and patients can see themselves as a projected avatar on the screen with information about training frequency, measuring angle, time remaining, etc. This offers consistent assistance to patients performing the exercises as defined by medical staff. Accordingly, if the result is correct then the system communicates this to the patient; if not, the system provides specific visual and auditory advice to encourage the patient to complete the rehabilitation tasks in the correct way. Furthermore, all patient training histories and outcomes are recorded in the system for further analysis of the patients' rehabilitation progress by physiotherapists.

2.2 IMU Measurement System

The primary hardware sensor for measuring the joint flexion angle and motion trail is a 9DOF Razor IMU (SparkFun Electronicstems Inc., USA), which includes a gyroscope, a magnetometer and an accelerometer for differentiating between when the subject is stationary versus walking. Furthermore, it integrates a Xbee wireless module (Digi International Inc., USA) to transmit the patient's rehabilitation information to a personal computer. We adopt it as a transmission medium due to its low cost designs, low energy consumption and support of reliable and short distance wireless transmission. In conclusion, the integration of these computing devices is very suitable for us to implement a highly flexible measuring mechanism and use it in various LBP rehabilitation scenarios (Fig. 1).

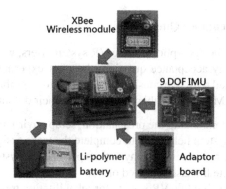

Fig. 1. Overview of own-built wireless IMU measurement system

2.3 Three Training Stages for Back Health

The used therapeutic guidance is amended from [5, 8] and a summary of three training stages is depicted in Fig. 2.

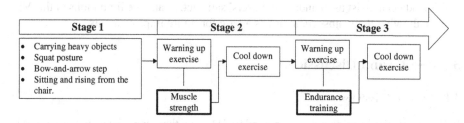

Fig. 2. Overview of three training stages for back health

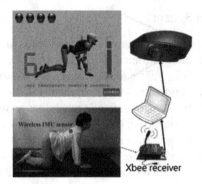

Fig. 3. Overview of VR-based LBP rehabilitation system

2.4 Technology Acceptance Questionnaire

In order to understand the perceptions of the VR system users, we invite all patients to complete the technology acceptance questionnaire after experiments. The content of questionnaire is designed with five constructs according to a combination of technology acceptance model (TAM) and flow theory [9, 10], and their definitions are:

1. Presence: Does understanding the presentation, setup environment and given information of the VR system help users to complete the tasks assigned or not.
2. Usefulness: Can the resources (i.e., physiotherapist and VR system) effectively guide the users to complete the task assigned or not.
3. Playfulness: While using this VR system for rehabilitation training, do patients will feel interested or not.
4. Intention to use: Would the patients recommend the proposed VR system to friends or use it themselves for LBP rehabilitation in the future.
5. Perspectives of flow theory: Do the patients feel that they can integrate use of the training scenarios and feel satisfied while using the VR system.

There are in total 31 questions designed and these can be scored with a Likert 7 point scale, for instance, 1 = "Strongly Disagree" and 7 = "Strongly Agree." The outcomes of this study can assist us to understand users' satisfaction and the limitations of this VR system allowing their subsequent use as a base for future improvements.

3   Results and Discussions

3.1 System Overview

In Fig. 3, recruited participants fasten wireless IMUs on their upper back and/or left thigh with elastic Velcro straps depending on different assigned tasks. Afterwards IMUs will transmit angle information from the affected side to personal computer and a mounted projector will project an avatar on a display screen with analyzed information immediately. Simultaneously, physiotherapists can work with patients to adjust training targets, provide customized support and reduce the burden incurred by traditional training sessions.

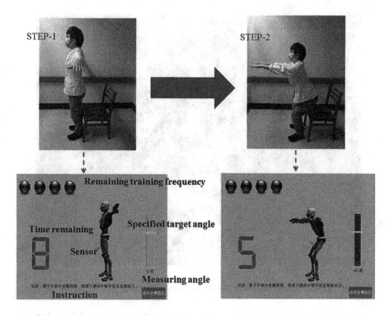

Fig. 4. Overview of rehabilitation information tracked and analyzed

3.2 System Functions

The patient has to maintain a specified angle for a particular target angle for a pre-defined period. Further, after completing one repetition, a virtual bomb will explode on the screen to reward the user for task completion. However, if the user fails to finish their assignments, the VR system will encourage them with auditory feedback, i.e., "You have almost done it!", "You can do it!" and "Keep trying!" The description of each item of information tracked is depicted in Fig. 4. In addition, the physiotherapist and patient can access rehabilitation performance and training histories stored in the system, for example, rehabilitation motion, completion date, training frequency, etc. A physiotherapist may utilize this information as a basis to define a new round of training if necessary. The essential concepts are demonstrated in Fig. 5.

3.3 Experiment Outcomes

In this interventional study, participants invited meet inclusion criteria and agree to sign consent forms. An understand has been sought as to whether this VR-based rehabilitation system is acceptable to LBP patients with regards to constructs of presence, usefulness, playfulness, intention to use and perspectives of flow theory. Therefore, in total twenty participants for experimental treatments are studied. Their average age is 65 years old and the average LBP period of duration is 14 months. An exit survey was distributed and collected from eighty percent of participants and indicates that most participants are satisfied with this VR system. Specifically, the feedback from visual, auditory responses by the system and information on the screen are a useful resource to guide the system users to complete their tasks. Furthermore, patients also feel that they are interested in

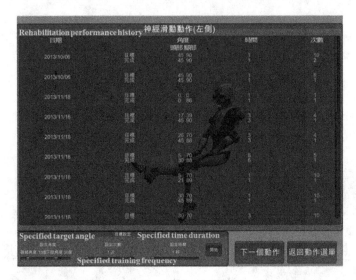

Fig. 5. Rehabilitation course setup and demonstrated performance record

the design of the avatar and projected information on the screen and this also encourages them to step into a new form of training. To that end, participants have readiness to recommend this system to their friends and relatives when these individuals do have similar rehabilitation requirements. In the meantime, participants also look forward to the addition of a serious game design to be added and implemented within these rehabilitation exercises. To sum up, it is creditable to conclude that the proposed VR-based system for assisting rehabilitation of LBP sufferers of this study has a potential to be accepted by the target LBP rehabilitations population (Table 1).

Table 1. Descriptive statistics and reliabiltiy analysis (N = 16)

Construct	Mean[†]	SD	Cronbach's α value
Presence	5.94	0.92	.933
Usefulness	5.97	0.81	.798
Playfulness	5.31	1.27	.836
Intention to use	5.63	1.36	.924
Perspectives of flow theory	5.84	1.04	.814

[†] Rating categories from (1) strongly disagree to (7) strongly agree.

3.4 Discussions

In this study, there are twenty male LBP patients effectively treated with the proposed VR-based LBP rehabilitation programs. The recent studies by Park et al. [2] and Kim et al. [6] also recruited LBP patients to participate in Wii-based rehabilitation programs. By comparison this innovative VR-based system considers varied LBP training exercises and attempts integration of the training into a patient's daily routines. Consequently, it offers a better, customized and individualized rehabilitation program which is not easily achieved by commercial exercise programs. The researchers in [3] found daily work will cause cumulative LBP, thus, physical therapy is insufficient for LBP rehabilitation. In the outcomes of this study, proposed learning patterns are fundamental to re-align living behaviors, posing an impact on different scenarios, i.e., general living activities and (vigorous) exercises to improve muscle strength and endurance. Therefore, in this work, a therapeutic and preventive approach is considered as an innovative point. In addition, this study uses technology acceptance questionnaires to understand the effectiveness and satisfaction of the proposed VR-based system and assists in taking advantage of the findings of the current study vis-à-vis future developments.

4 Conclusions and Future Works

This study integrates wearable wireless IMU sensors and virtual reality technologies to successfully develop and configure a VR-based LBP rehabilitation system. In addition, the questionnaire survey results also confirm the evidence that the system users recognize that this system will motivate them to engage in a therapy and further receive the benefits of muscle strength and endurance enhancements.

In the near future, the researchers plan to enhance this system with more precisely joint angle measurements. For instance, suggestions have been proposed and discussed in [11], whose researchers suggest two sensors can be deployed on the lumbar spine and thoracic spine and incorporate motion analysis algorithms to prompt the angle detection precision. In addition, in order to augment entertainment factors of this system, a serious game design with multiple interactive stories and functions is necessary. To that end, and thereby, the LBP population may likely be further encouraged to participate in rehabilitation programs through the use of this enhancement to the proposed system.

References

1. Licciardone, J.C., Gatchel, R.J., Kearns, C.M., Minotti, D.E.: Depression, somatization, and somatic dysfunction in patients with nonspecific chronic low back pain: results from the osteopathic trial. JAOA: J. Am. Osteopath. Assoc. **112**, 783–791 (2012)
2. Park, J.-H., Lee, S.-H., Ko, D.-S.: The effects of the Nintendo Wii exercise program on chronic work-related low back pain in industrial workers. J. Phys. Ther. Sci. **25**, 985 (2013)
3. Hoy, D., Bain, C., Williams, G., March, L., Brooks, P., Blyth, F., Woolf, A., Vos, T., Buchbinder, R.: A systematic review of the global prevalence of low back pain. Arthritis Rheum. **64**, 2028–2037 (2012)
4. Krismer, M., van Tulder, M.: Low back pain (non-specific). Best Pract. Res. Clin. Rheumatol. **21**, 77–91 (2007)
5. McGill, S.: Low Back Disorders: Evidence-Based Prevention and Rehabilitation. Human Kinetics, Champaign (2007)

6. Kim, S.-S., Min, W.-K., Kim, J.-H., Lee, B.-H.: The effects of vr-based wii fit yoga on physical function in middle-aged female lbp patients. J. Phys. Ther. Sci. **26**, 549 (2014)
7. Sterud, T., Tynes, T.: Work-related psychosocial and mechanical risk factors for low back pain: a 3-year follow-up study of the general working population in Norway. Occup. Environ. Med. **70**, 296–302 (2013)
8. McGill, S.M.: Low back exercises: evidence for improving exercise regimens. Phys. Ther. **78**, 754–765 (1998)
9. Davis, F.D., Bagozzi, R.P., Warshaw, P.R.: User acceptance of computer technology: a comparison of two theoretical models. Manage. Sci. **35**, 982–1003 (1989)
10. Koufaris, M.: Applying the technology acceptance model and flow theory to online consumer behavior. Inf. Syst. Res. **13**, 205–223 (2002)
11. Lee, J.K., Park, E.J.: 3D spinal motion analysis during staircase walking using an ambulatory inertial and magnetic sensing system. Med. Biol. Eng. Compu. **49**, 755–764 (2011)

'Weather' Wearable System: A Design Exploration to Facilitate the Collaboration and Communication with Chronic Pain Patients

Xin Tong[✉], Diane Gromala, Amber Choo, Mahsoo Salimi, and Jeewon Lee

Simon Fraser University, Surrey, Canada
{tongxint,gromala,achoo,salimi}@sfu.ca,
fleecy_cloud215@gmail.com

Abstract. Unpredictable spikes in pain intensity can easily interrupt the lives of chronic pain patients. The uncertainty of when these painful experiences will occur inhibits positive communications and collaborations with friends, families or co-workers in daily life. In this paper, the authors explore an affective design space for developing a wearable technology piece using real-time biofeedback monitoring capabilities. The intent of the device is to mitigate chronic pain patients' pain uncertainty in order to facilitate daily collaborations between the worker who lives with chronic pain and co-workers through social signaling. This exploratory design process, including the wearable system organization and presentation rationale, was developed in participatory design collaboration with target users: a chronic pain patient and people she works with in an academic workplace context. After three iterations, two prototypes were developed; each addresses the control of privacy and information sharing issues. In future work, appropriate evaluation methods will be explored and the iterative design prototype also will be improved based on user feedback. The long-term goal is to improve the wearable's applicability in a variety of social contexts, and applicability for other chronic conditions.

Keywords: Wearable computing system · Chronic pain · Collaboration and communication · Uncertainty mitigation

1 Introduction

Chronic Pain (CP) is a degenerative condition that can cause significant discomfort, constrain mobility and social interactions, and pose unpredictable disruptions in daily interactions [1]. Thus, living with CP often means that patients live with both "bad days and good days," [2] ranging from some days that are manageable to other days which are almost intolerable. Beyond possible negative effects on their general availability, ability and attitude toward social interactions, CP patients also experience related conditions that impede their ability to plan and take part in activities even when they do not deliberately withdraw [3]. In addition, CP patients also face considerable stigma

© Springer International Publishing Switzerland 2015
M. Antona and C. Stephanidis (Eds.): UAHCI 2015, Part III, LNCS 9177, pp. 383–393, 2015.
DOI: 10.1007/978-3-319-20684-4_38

from those who are unaware of the disease and its manifestations, which can cause negative and exclusionary attitudes among co-workers.

When such situations occur, CP patients need assistance to deal with communication and collaboration issues. CP patients need a tool that encourages non-patients to improve their understanding of pain uncertainties and to develop real-time approaches to coping with uncertainty, and a method that could present a patient's current condition without costing the patient too much effort to articulate.

As wearable technologies become a part of our embodied experiences as non-verbal communicators, clothing and accessories have begun to move away from an exclusive focus on style and convenience towards integrating health-related functions. It is important, however, to understand that such wearable technologies are not simply stand-alone devices devoid of context. In Susan Ryan's [4] examination of wearable technology, for example, she conceives of wearable technology as an evolving set of ideas and their contexts, always with an eye on wearable artifacts—on clothing, dresses, and the histories and social relations they represent. Current wearable systems are not specifically designed for CP patients and for collaborative purposes in the workplace, and since physical and social contexts decide how a wearable system could take effect, it is important that the needs specific to CP patients are accounted for.

Therefore, in this paper, the research question is how to design and explore a wearable system to facilitate collaboration based on a patient's experience. In this case, X (the name is coded as X), is a CP patient who heads a group of people, and experiences unpredictable pain spikes. Such increases in bodily pain, coupled with the unpredictability of when such pain spikes occur, effectively discourages collaboration with others on social and professional levels, particularly when coworkers are unaware of the CP condition.

We introduce a participatory and exploratory design of a wearable CP system. Next, three iterations are described, which led to design variations for a wearable piece titled Chronic Pain Patients' Weather System. We also present a critique on form factors and address the limitations of the system. In future work, to make this wearable system more universal and applied to generalized scenarios for chronic conditions, more patients need to be involved in the design process, diverse workplace contexts should be considered, as well as wider contexts.

2   Related Work

Although wearable technology has been widely used as a health-monitoring tool and is often applied to persons with chronic conditions, how to facilitate the communication of a long-term pain experience and to enhance efficacy of collaboration among CP patients with non-patient co-workers is still unexplored. Pain is difficult to communicate, and difficult to understand by people who do not experience it. Thus, CP patients' interaction experience during daily activities requires a longitudinal, team-based collaborative approach [5].

2.1 Communication and Collaboration Between Chronic Pain Patients and Non-patients in Daily Activities

The complex challenges of chronic pain and its effects on collaborations between CP patients and non-patient co-workers requires a multi-faceted approach, in contrast to verbal communication alone, in order to deal with uncontrolled pain [6]. One of the challenges is that chronic pain is "invisible" — that is, it typically lacks observable physiological responses, visible signals or absences of behaviors, making it difficult for co-workers or others to get a sense of the variability of the CP patient's general state in the ways in which, for instance, we assess someone's mood. Moreover, the ways in which CP patients cope with "bad days" and the disruptions they may create may vary considerably from patient to patient, or according to the tasks at hand. For example, as Benjamin et al.'s research discovered [3], a CP patient currently experiencing a really 'bad day' or spike in perceived pain may not want to be interrupted while conversely, another may really want a distraction. In Wells et al.'s study [6], they found that nonverbal methods of assessment provide useful information, and that self-reports of pain are the most accurate. Therefore, in health care contexts, it is recognized that certain interventions are essential to allow communication among patients, clinicians or others about the current status of the patient's pain and their responses to the plan of care [6]. Therefore, we adopted a similar approach: the goal of our intervention is to enhance communication, especially during disruptive spikes in pain, in a manner that takes into account a patient's self-reports in a non-verbal manner.

Because of widespread stigma, revealing that one has CP in a workplace context is a choice that may result in negative attitudes that worsen over time. Obviously, any technological intervention cannot in itself change widespread misinformation and social attitudes. However, it was determined that if a CP patient finds that information about their states may improve communication among co-workers, that information may potentially work best when it can remain in an ambient form, much like the weather. One may look out of the window to see that it is raining and respond by taking their umbrella, but much of the time, what is outside of the window is simply background information.

As previously described, a CP patient's "bad days" and spikes in pain introduce uncertainty both for the CP patient as well as for co-workers. In order for any proposed system to work, it must not only clearly communicate the state of the CP patient, but the patient's co-workers must also feel that they know how to respond appropriately. For example, certain collaborations in workplaces, such as informal meetings with coworkers or non-urgent questions from them, might bring unnecessary physical and mental fatigue for the CP patient during "bad days." As our initial participatory design meetings revealed, co-workers' responses to information about a CP patient's state varied because they were uncertain about how they should respond. Some interpreted indications of a "bad day" as a signal to avoid *any* social interaction with the CP patient at all. Others interpreted it to mean that more attention was desired, which the patient found inappropriate. Both responses are common responses that contribute to increasing social isolation that many CP patients experience. The CP patient simply wanted to mitigate uncertainty to better manage work and does not desire more attention, which was interpreted as pity. Therefore, we found that knowing what are and are not appropriate responses to the information were critical to the design of the system.

2.2   Wearable Systems as Communication and Collaboration Tools

In recent years, there has been increasing interest in wearable health monitoring devices that have been developed for sports conditioning and weight management areas, both in industrial and academic fields [14]. Despite medical and health monitoring uses, many wearable systems are also developed to foster social interaction and collaboration. As proposed by Ryan [4], wearable technologies comprise a pragmatics (being utilized and understood in certain circumstances or contexts) of enhanced communication in a social landscape. Wearable systems embedded into daily activities embody the wearers' information so that they inspire motivation and more collaborations and communication [11, 12]. The popularity of wearable bracelets like some forms of Fitbit and Nike FuelBand, are just two examples of how health monitoring (including heart rate, sleep patterns, activity levels and so on) has been adopted by non-medical users. They are worn like a watch, and data from them is uploaded to a personal computer or website where users can see visualizations of their data. Other examples, such as Nuria and Fernando's [7] Health-Gear, are real-time wearable systems for monitoring, visualizing and analyzing physiological signals that are wirelessly connected through Bluetooth to cell phones that monitor users' blood oxygen levels and pulse rates while sleeping.

Several researchers also demonstrated how wearable systems are used collaboratively, how they influenced interactions among users and how they could enrich the building of a collaborative network. Light Perfume [8], for instance, is an interactive wearable system designed to help wearers better communicate with each other by mirroring their partners. In this design, the output of Light Perfume is based on input from the user's environment, such as noise levels and body gestures; these synchronize the blinking speed and the color of LEDs. The user study showed that all participants enhanced their sociability dimension of impression towards their partners, and that they also felt closer and more familiar with each other. Kate Hartman's [9] idea about wearable systems is that the body per se can be designed as interfaces and platforms for promoting physically expressive engagement, which could process, transmit and receive data with outside world – including both people and environment. In her Inflatable Heart and Glacier Embracing Suit, she employed wearable electronics to explore how people communicate with self and the outside world, allowing new modes of expression and communication.

The use of wearable technology for monitoring health in clinical contexts has been addressed as well. Paolo Bonato [10] examined wearable technology and its medical applications on a theoretical level. He concluded that a great deal of progress in the field patient monitoring has benefited from the wearable sensors and systems which provide tools for the prevention of chronic conditions, and the ability to promptly respond to emergency situations. He also demonstrated that wearable technologies could work as informatics systems that promote improved care for medical purposes, especially in regards to chronic illnesses.

3 Methodologies and Design Principles

To better clarify users' needs and the contexts in which this wearable would be utilized, single-case exploratory design and participatory design were adopted. A focus group was set up, consisting of eight members, including X and seven of her coworkers.

3.1 First Interview: Analyzing Contexts in the Exploratory Design

Since few studies can be referred to, and few wearable technologies have been designed specifically for CP patients' collaboration purposes, the goal of this exploratory sequential design (also known as exploratory design) focused on gaining insights into and familiarity with the design problem for further investigation. Because the problem was in a preliminary stage of investigation, this exploratory design first utilized a focus group comprised of the stakeholders — X and her colleagues — which enabled us to gain background information. Two interviews were conducted, each lasting one hour. Questions that were asked concerned: (1) the seven coworkers' experience collaborating with X, and if, how and how often the uncertainty of her condition affected their ability to work effectively; (2) if they felt the information about X's pain state might enhance communication; (3) what kind of information would be most valuable; (4) how to display and present the information.

Although her CP condition is invisible, it can impact X's collaborations, particularly with those of her colleagues who were employed as her assistants. Table 1 is a summary of her self-reported regular pain level and its correspondent consequences on her collaborations from the interview. The pain scales were also provided by her to better illustrate where the boundary of pain influences over her daily collaborations seems to be. For example, she sometimes must miss meetings. While all can adapt by Skype or by rescheduling, the matter of uncertainty emerged as the primary concern. To conclude X's case, higher levels of pain distracts her because it takes additional effort to manage the pain, making concentration more challenging, especially when it involves communicating with others.

Table 1. A Use Case of X: pain weather and possible solutions to maintain a better collaboration

Weather	Pain Level (0-10)	Collaboration Condition with Others
Good Day & Fatigue Day	< 3	Pain is not too bad but fatigue becomes the problem – can work
Pain Day	3-5	Talk and action in the lab is welcome and energizing
Worse Pain Day & Bad Day	> 5	Moves more slowly, has intermittent cognition disruption from pain, finds interruptions difficult

In the interview with X, her opinion showed that this wearable design might help her to deal with pain distractions in the following way: for instance, when X is experiencing a 'Worse Pain Day,' the wearable will act as a display and will generate a sign of her current state. The needs of non-patient coworkers who are involved in the same activities are also significant: as the signal's receiver, they would respond by modulating their communication with her. Since these responses may significantly influence the collaboration process, we investigated the attitudes of non-patient coworkers as well.

During the interviews with the whole team, they all agreed that they would like to have such a wearable piece, not for inferring mood but for better understanding the pain condition so that they could arrange their work activities efficiently.

3.2   Second Interview: Analyzing Target Users, Tasks and Goals

After making sure that such a wearable has value and a design space in the first interview, the following, more concrete questions were answered in the second phase: (1) Who will be the targeted users, exactly, and what is the context? (2) What is the task of this wearable design? (3) What is the goal, or specifically what characteristics would you like to have in this wearable design? Specific scenarios were conducted to more specifically determine how visible the wearable should be, under what conditions, and how could privacy be maintained?

Here are some responses from the group. When asking about what this wearable could be like, one participant proposed this idea: *I think it could be a small simple thing that you could just take it off. So it is obtrusive enough that I could know, and unobtrusive enough so it doesn't bother you or me.* As for what special things will be taken into consideration when designing this wearable, here is the opinion we found regarding the privacy issues: *If I were you, I would like to have the control over my privacy. For example, I do not want to show it to the public. I want to show it inside the group members.*

Therefore we arrived at the following conclusions: (1) Targeted Users: The system was designed for CP patients who might constantly be interrupted by their uncertain CP and distracted from daily communication and collaboration with others, especially in workplace. The disruptive nature of CP can constrain availability for interaction [13] and introduce occasions where those with the illness have to take deliberate steps to avoid negative social consequences [1]. However, the unpredictable pain cannot easily be understood by their colleagues or communicated by the patient (2) Task: The task is to communicate hard to understand pain via a wearable system that falls into the category of clothing or an accessory. In reference to the wearable's real-time conditions, the audience (colleagues, friends or family) should be able to make quick decisions about appropriate strategies, plans or schedules upon changes detected by the system; (3) Goal: The goal of the design of this wearable system is to facilitate communication and collaboration between CP patients and non-patients in a workplace through nonverbal, unintrusive methods.

3.3   Privacy

An information sharing mechanism like the wearable weather system might give rise to potential concerns of privacy because it displays personal physical conditions.

Interview questions concerning privacy were asked of the patient during our exploratory design. Users responded that a human-control button should be added to this wearable so that the CP patients would be able to show their data in smaller, known contexts, like in the workplace. Also, they do not need to worry about their private information since the design outlook of the wearable itself has a context, and would only be used in this context. For instance, the LED's off and on status' indication would only be understood within the wearers' pre-determined context.

3.4 Chronic Pain Patients' Weather Framework

Presentation Rationale: As described in Table 1, the extent of pain varies from no pain at all to disabling pain. Five categories were offered by X to describe these pain states. Also, from the interviews with her coworkers, 3 levels (regular day, painful, and extreme pain) of pain displayed in the same wearable were considered enough for their collaboration and decision-making purposes. Therefore, a scaled measurement of pain level was used to better communicate the pain, allowing the coworkers to respond appropriately and to figure out efficient solutions according to different pain levels.

System Framework Design: The wearable was composed of three main parts: the input, which monitors the pain state and transmits the data to the wearable system; a control switch, that allows users to maintain their privacy and sustain information sharing in certain groups; output, to display pain data to coworkers for purposes of enhancing communication by changes in the displayed state of this wearable. Biofeedback sensors (GSR and heart rate variability will be investigated in future phases of development, as that data provides a way to make good inferences about anxiety, which accompanies periods of greater pain; for now, what is implemented is the pulse sensor) can capture CP patients' real-time physiological data, reflecting the user's comparative physiological stress level directly, and pain level indirectly. Under the control and wish of the user, certain contents can be displayed in this wearable weather system based on contexts. Like watching a 'weather' broadcast, both the patient and co-workers observe changes and develop feasible collaborative solutions. For one thing, it could facilitate communication and enhance collaboration efficacy. For another, CP patients may detect a positive change in coworkers' ability to ascertain and respond to the uncertainty of CP, which in turn may mitigate a patient's anxiety about the negative effect their uncertainty has on coworkers, and affording them to better manage times of greater pain.

Technical Implementation: During the implementation, we chose the pulse sensor to gather biofeedback data from patients, an Arduino LilyPad as the main electronic board to process and then present the display data, a switch for the user to control the device and the LEDs as the pain level indicators. In Fig. 1, we summarized the composition of the wearable system in terms of users, hardware and software. Based on the interviews with the CP patient and people she works with (described in the Method section), three signals will be displayed for communication purposes: the blinking of the LED stands for data from the biofeedback sensor (pulse sensor). White color means it is a normal day; red color means it is a painful day; and a constant red (because red is associated with the danger or failure in achievement contexts and evokes avoidance motivation [15]) represents the highly painful experience. What, when and where to show the signal depends on the patients and his/her control.

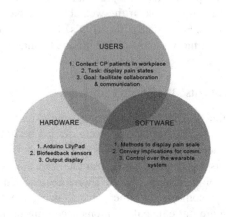

Fig. 1. Wearable weather system compositions

4   Design Exploration and Evolution

This wearable was named "weather" system because it could imply different conditions of CP patients' unpredictable pain. In this section, an overview of the system design is described. Design iterations and evolutions were demonstrated together with the patient in this participatory design, from the initial sketches to prototype design, and later, final implementations.

4.1   Evolutions and Iterations

As we sewed the electronic components into the fabric, we noticed that some cloth has patterns which can be fitted with electronic components (Fig. 2). This correlation inspired us to integrate electronics into the patterns, because such connection between displayed location and way and the cloth would enable the appearances of the wearable piece with more wearability and functionality.

Fig. 2. Initial implementation; First iteration

However, after the first implementation, when the patient wore the prototype, she reported that it was not flexible enough for her when the wearable is in her clothing. Since it would be expensive to fit every garment with the wearable system, she expressed the preference for a small accessories, such as brooches, jewelry or badges, which would be more easily attached or detached from her clothes. As for the material, the patient also mentioned that ligthtweight fabric might be too thin to hold the electronics when the wearable was designed as an accessory. So in the second iteration, felt was chosen since it was thicker than regular shirt fabric.

After the first iteration, we made a quick test with the patient and used the first prototype to check its functionality. Then the patient came up with critical design questions regarding the outfits and metaphors of this wearable system: (1) the electronic can be an identifiable factor for others to know it's a wearable in a more public context, but it will also bring out the electronic aesthetic beauty of the front of the design. For the electronic components, whether should we try to mirror it and visualize them in front of the wearable accessories instead of hiding it? (2) What will be the differences that outfits could generate?

Therefore, we put the electronics in front side of the wearable and then tested it with patient wearing it (Fig. 2). Then we designed a poppy flower that already has the metaphor of pain as well as an abstraction image, which use small size of medicine bottles to indicate pain data and the outfit cannot tell anything to other people (Fig. 3).

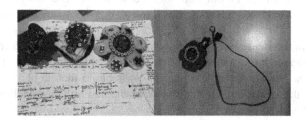

Fig. 3. Implementation of the first iteration (left); Implementation of the final design (right)

5 Discussion

5.1 Chronic Pain Patients' Weather Wearable System Design Critique

In the era of communication and device proliferation, it is important to think about how CP patients can improve their workplace collaborations even when they are in pain. Chronic Pain Patients' Weather System measures CP patients' physical index and returns biofeedback data real-time, then mapping the body condition into three types of presentation methods (regular day, painful day, and worst painful day). Based on the displayed information, coworkers can understand the pain information by observation when needed and they could make decisions of how to collaborate with the patient (for instance, either to leave her in a quite environment or to reschedule activities).

This wearable piece can affect decisions as how non-patients and CP patients' communication and collaboration with others from two sides. For one thing, it reflects

CP patients' temporal pain condition and allows others to make a judgment to better cope with uncertainties. For another, patients are able to focus more on managing their pain without worrying about misunderstanding, or social stigma due to the interruption from constantly uncontrolled pain during their work time. Their collaboration with colleagues is also taken care of by others. The responses from others towards the interaction process transmits the signal of careful interaction that could change CP patients experience about collaborating with others from a frustrated social process into an acceptably encouraging one.

5.2   Limitations and Future Work

In the design process, X is the only patient who got involved in the participatory design process. More CP patients from different backgrounds should join the design process to better evaluate the prototype. Second, in the current wearable system, it is a one-way projection from patients to coworkers, not a two-way interaction. Coworkers' response towards the patient are also valuable for communication and collaboration purposes. How to design the mechanism of presenting both of the patients' and non-patients' responsiveness to each other and how to encode it in a nature way under certain context still needs to be studied. However, the most significant issue is that we neither designed for nor considered remote conditions in our research. There is a large possibility that the patient could not even go out from their home, so we need to figure out how this wearable could work remotely (such as sync data with mobile devices and send messages).

Therefore, in the future work, we probably give a sample of each current design to patients from various backgrounds in different contexts. Besides, we will try to fix the remote condition problem by connecting the wearable to mobile phones and sending information to the coworkers so that the wearable can still be functional when the patients are too sick to work.

6   Conclusion

Living with chronic pain means that patients often need to deal with pain distractions, with uncertain occurrence. Such uncertainty inhibits positive communications and collaborations with friends, families or co-workers in daily life. Therefore, based on X's personal experience and needs to enhance efficacy of communication and collaboration in her daily life, Chronic Pain Patients' Weather System is designed and developed for CP patients to better collaborate and communicate with non-patients in their daily activities. This wearable contributed in exploring design space for CP patients' health care which is a new health realm besides information monitoring: (1) the design space was explored under the case of X and her research team; (2) it could imply different conditions of CP patients' unpredictable pain, since there is an uncertainty of 'good days' and 'bad days' for them, and this weather could bring distraction for them during collaboration and communication process.

References

1. Miles, A., Curran, H.V., Pearce, S., Allan, L.: Managing constraint: the experience of people with chronic pain. Soc. Sci. Med. **61**(2), 431–441 (2005)
2. Charmaz, K.: Good Days, Bad Days: The Self in Chronic Illness and Time. Rutgers University Press, New Jersey (1991)
3. Benjamin, A., Birnholtz, J., Baecker, R., Gromala, D., Furlan, A.: Impression management work: how seniors with chronic pain address disruptions in their interactions. In: Proceedings of the ACM 2012 Conference on Computer Supported Cooperative Work, New York, NY, USA, pp. 799–808 (2012)
4. Ryan, S.E.: Garments of paradise: wearable discourse in the digital age. MIT Press, New York (2014)
5. Dorr, D., Bonner, L.M., Cohen, A.N., Shoai, R.S., Perrin, R., Chaney, E., Young, A.S.: Informatics systems to promote improved care for chronic illness: a literature review. J. Am. Med. Inform. Assoc. JAMIA **14**(2), 156–163 (2007)
6. Wells, N., Pasero, C., McCaffery, M.: Improving the quality of care through pain assessment and management. In: Hughes, R.G. (ed.) Patient Safety and Quality An Evidence Based Handbook for Nurses. Agency for Healthcare Research and Quality (US), Rockville (2008)
7. Oliver, N., Flores-Mangas, F.: HealthGear: a real-time wearable system for monitoring and analyzing physiological signals. In: International Workshop on Wearable and Implantable Body Sensor Networks, 2006. BSN 2006, 2006 p. 4 pp.–64
8. Choi, Y., Parsani, R., Pandey, A.V., Roman, X., Cheok, A.D.: Light perfume: a fashion accessory for synchronization of nonverbal communication. Leonardo **46**(5), 439–444 (2013)
9. Hartman, K.: The art of wearable communication. TED. http://www.ted.com/talks/kate_hartman_the_art_of_wearable_communication. Accessed 08 February 2014
10. Bonato, P.: Advances in wearable technology and its medical applications. In: 2010 Annual International Conference of the IEEE Engineering in Medicine and Biology Society (EMBC), pp. 2021–2024 (2010)
11. Post, E.R., Orth, M., Russo, P.R., Gershenfeld, N.: E-broidery: design and fabrication of textile-based computing. IBM Syst. J. **39**(3–4), 840–860 (2000)
12. Rachel Pezzlo, E.P. Intelligent Clothing: Empowering the Mobile Worker by Wearable Computing (2009)
13. International Pain Summit Of The International Association For The Study Of Pain: Declaration of montréal: declaration that access to pain management is a fundamental human right. J. Pain Palliat. Care Pharmacother. **25**(1), 29–31 (2011)
14. Park, S., Jayaraman, S.: Enhancing the quality of life through wearable technology. IEEE Eng. Med. Biol. Mag. **22**(3), 41–48 (2003)
15. Elliot, A.J., Maier, M.A., Moller, A.C., Friedman, R., Meinhardt, J.: Color and psychological functioning: The effect of red on performance attainment. J. Exp. Psychol. Gen. **136**(1), 154–168 (2007)

The Benefits of Haptic Feedback in Telesurgery and Other Teleoperation Systems: A Meta-Analysis

Bernhard Weber[1(✉)] and Clara Eichberger[2]

[1] German Aerospace Center, Oberpfaffenhofen, Germany
Bernhard.Weber@dlr.de
[2] Ludwigs-Maximilians-Universität, Munich, Germany

Abstract. A quantitative review of empirical studies investigating the effects of haptic feedback in teleoperation or virtual reality systems is provided. Several meta-analyses were conducted based on results of 58 studies with 1104 subjects from the medical and other teleoperation domains, revealing positive, substantial effects of kinesthetic force feedback on task performance (Hedges' $g = 0.62$–0.75) and force regulation ($g = 0.64$–0.78) and positive, but small effects on task completion time ($g = 0.22$). Vibrotactile substitution of force feedback results in significantly lower effects on task performance ($g = .21$). Yet, exaggerated force production can be avoided effectively. Finally, we found evidence that the magnitude of the force feedback effects are moderated by task characteristics like force regulation demands and complexity.

Keywords: Haptics · Force feedback · Vibrotactile · Sensory substitution · Teleoperation · Telemanipulation · Telerobotics · Telesurgery · Virtual reality · Simulation

1 Introduction

In contrast to more conventional human-machine interfaces, which simply transfer operator commands to a technical system or provide visual or auditory information to the operator, haptic interfaces generate stimuli (like mechanical forces) allowing tactile or kinesthetic sensations. Haptic information is crucial when exploring or manipulating objects in remote or virtual environments. For environments which are difficult to access or too hazardous for humans (e.g. nuclear plants, deep sea), so-called teleoperation systems can be used in which a robot is acting as an "extended arm", remotely controlled by the human operator. The great advantage of teleoperation is that the human operates from a safe location while human skills, attention, problem solving capabilities etc. can be extended to the remote location [53, 64]. In a similar vein, instead of interacting with a physically remote environment, it is also possible to use haptic interfaces for virtual reality (VR) applications (like training simulators, virtual assembly verification etc.), with computer-generated sensory feedback.

© Springer International Publishing Switzerland 2015
M. Antona and C. Stephanidis (Eds.): UAHCI 2015, Part III, LNCS 9177, pp. 394–405, 2015.
DOI: 10.1007/978-3-319-20684-4_39

One major precondition to take full advantage of teleoperation or VR systems is a bidirectional exchange of haptic information between operator and the remote or virtual environment, enabling the operator to perceive collisions, contact forces, weight, object shapes, surfaces textures, etc.

The main benefits of providing haptic information in physically remote or virtual scenes are manifold [23]. Firstly, there is a natural interaction with the environment, similar to real-world experiences. This also allows for a higher degree of immersion and an improved sense of (tele)presence; i.e. the operator's subjective impression of being physically present in the remote or virtual environment [53]. Secondly, compared to systems with visual information only, providing additional haptic information improves spatial awareness of the remote or virtual scene. Constantly updated haptic information allows for a better understanding of the movement and positions of the end effector (e.g. robotic hand) or the manipulated objects (e.g. a tool) in the remote/ virtual environment. Force feedback even allows implementing physical constraints (like virtual fixtures) and avoids exaggerated force application. Also, the operator is better able to generate an egocentric frame of reference, i.e. position and orientation of the teleoperated end effectors or objects are specified in relation to the operator. Finally, using the haptic channel not only matches real world experiences, it also decreases the operator's cognitive load when visual resources are restricted.

In the last decades, numerous haptic devices for teleoperation and VR systems were developed and have been used successfully in a wide range of applications. In telesurgery, for instance, an operation is performed inside the patient's body with the instruments being controlled by the surgeon via remotely controlled robotic arms. Here, haptic feedback about forces acting on the instrument's tips (e.g. when palpating tissue or when pulling a thread during surgical knotting or suturing) is crucial. In a recent meta-analysis on 21 studies [62], the positive overall effect of providing (kinesthetic) force feedback for surgical applications was documented for task accuracy and force regulation.

Moreover, Nitsch and Färber [36] performed a meta-analysis on the effects of haptic feedback on teleoperation performance in general including 32 studies, mainly investigating telerobotic tasks like moving a mobile robot and basic manipulation tasks like pick-and-place, peg-in-hole, and grasping (except for five studies with surgical tasks). The authors reported significant positive effects of haptic feedback on task success and completion times compared to conditions without haptic feedback. Although both meta-analyses provide clear evidence for the benefits of haptic feedback in a broad variety of applications and experimental tasks, the influence of the specific task demands on the magnitude of these effects has not been investigated so far [36].

In the present paper, we report the results of different meta-analyses investigating the effect of force feedback on task performance in (tele-)surgical and other teleoperation systems controlling real robotic systems as well as VR simulators. The main objective is the assessment of the overall effect of haptic feedback when comparing telesurgical tasks (like suturing or knotting) with common teleoperation tasks (like assembly, peg-in-hole). Moreover the effect of substituting force feedback by other modalities (like vibrotactile information) during tele-manipulation tasks was explored.

2 Methods

Sample of Studies. We conducted a literature search using different library databases (PubMed, IEEE Xplore, ScienceDirect, Springer.com, Web of Science). Additionally, we used Google Scholar, to seek further references not identified in the formal scan procedure. Different combinations of keywords [*teleoperation* OR *telerobotics* OR *telesurgery* OR *virtual reality* OR *simulation*] AND [*haptics* OR *force feedback* OR *force* OR *tactile* OR *sensory substitution*] were used. Next, reference lists of the identified articles were checked to find additional related studies. Moreover, researchers were contacted and asked for unpublished papers, dissertations, diploma or master's theses on this topic. Altogether, 128 primary studies were collected.

Criteria for Study Inclusion. Next, the following inclusion criteria were applied: (1) direct empirical comparison of conditions with and without haptic feedback (or sensory substitutes) for the same experimental task and with the same input/ output devices, (2) no focus on haptic training effects, (3) sufficient information to determine effect size estimates, (4) telerobotic systems or virtual reality simulations, (5) methodological control of time effects (learning, fatigue) and, (6) original publication. After application of the inclusion criteria, a sample of 58 studies (27 journal articles, 24 conference papers, 6 doctoral or master's theses and one book article; 37 studies with general telemanipulation and 21 with telesurgical tasks) with a total of $N = 1104$ subjects remained. The studies included in the current meta-analysis are identified in the reference listing of the current paper by an asterisk.

Calculation of Effect Sizes. The effect of haptic feedback on performance was calculated comparing the mean difference between conditions with and without feedback in standardized by the pooled standard deviation s (i.e., Cohen's d [11], see Formula 1).

$$d = \frac{MNoFeedback - MFeedback}{s} \qquad (1)$$

For a more conservative estimation of the effect sizes in case of small sample sizes, we calculated Hedges' g by multiplying d with a correction factor J ($g = d * J$; see Formula 2, df is the degrees of freedom; $df = n_1 + n_{2-2}$ for two independent groups, for instance, see [6]).

$$J = 1 - \frac{3}{4df - 1} \qquad (2)$$

When the information required for effect size calculation was missing, effect sizes were estimated on basis of p or t statistics reported in the studies. Conventionally, effect sizes from 0.2 to 0.5 are considered as small, from 0.5 to 0.8 as medium and from 0.8 to infinity as large effects [11].

For a more fine-grained analysis and to obtain an adequate number of analysis units, we calculated effect sizes from different experimental conditions of each study and different outcome variables. As main measures for task performance, task-specific criteria for task success (like number of successful trials, avoided collisions), accuracy (like penetration depths, optimal path deviations) and detection rates (during surgical palpation tasks) were aggregated. In addition, the average and peak forces applied during task completion were analyzed. Finally, we explored whether the use of additional haptic feedback has an impact on task completion times. Most of the studies only reported a subset of these outcome variables or only one of them. In sum, $k = 171$ no haptics vs. haptics comparisons were available.

Effect Size Integration. As a preparation of effect size integration across studies, their reliability, i.e. the study's variance, was taken into account. Each effect size was weighted by the study's inverse-variance W ($W = 1/s^2$, [25]). After aggregation of a class of effect sizes, a mean weighted effect size was computed, and heterogeneity within the class of the k effect sizes was tested with the Q statistics. Q is defined as the sum of squared differences between each study (i) effect size (Y_i) and the mean effect size (M) weighted by the inverse-variance (W_i) of that study (see Formula 3). A significant difference indicates that the aggregated effect sizes do not share a common effect size, but that there are e.g. further moderating factors causing heterogeneity.

$$Q = \sum_{i=1}^{k} W_i (Y_i - M)^2 \tag{3}$$

After integration of a class of effect sizes, the impact of potential moderators (like task type) was tested by ANOVAs (fixed effect categorical model; [25]), resulting in between class effects Q_b and a within class effect Q_w (see [6]) All analyses were performed using the CMA$^{©}$ software package (version 2.2; Biostat).

Table 1. Overall effects of force feedback

Outcome variable	k	g	95 % CI (g)	Q
Task success	45	0.75***	0.64–0.85	200.4***
Task accuracy	26	0.69***	0.53–0.85	46.4**
Detection rates	5	0.62***	0.32–0.92	21.5***
Average force	19	0.78***	0.60–0.96	169.2***
Peak force	22	0.64***	0.46–0.82	132.9***
Completion time	79	0.22***	0.13–0.30	331.0***

Note. ** $p < .01$; *** $p < .001$; 95 % CI = upper and lower limit of the 95 % confidence interval.

3 Results

In a first step of analysis, the overall effects of (kinesthetic) force feedback (FF) were computed. Indeed, force feedback significantly improved task success ($g = .75$) and accuracy ($g = .69$), detection rates during palpation ($g = .62$), significantly reduced the average and the peak forces applied during the task ($g = .78$ or $g = .64$, respectively) and decreased the time to complete the task ($g = .22$; see Table 1). Yet, a significant amount of heterogeneity was found for all aggregation classes, indicating the potential influence of moderator variables.

In a subsequent analysis, we compared the effects of force feedback (FF) reported above with vibrotactile feedback (VT). Indeed, results indicated that task success significantly differed for both feedback modalities, with only a small mean effect size when substituting force feedback by vibrotactile feedback (gVT = .21 vs. gFF = .75, Qb = 34.2; p < .001; see Table 2). Moreover, moderation effects were evident for average force and completion times (Qb = 29.3; p < .001 and Qb = 4.8; p < .05): Providing vibrotactile feedback did not have any substantial positive effect. Yet, no evidence for a moderation effect was found for peak forces with similar moderate effect sizes for both modalities (gVT = .60 vs. gFF = .64). No moderation analysis was performed on the task accuracy variable, since only two primary studies using vibrotactile feedback could be identified.

Table 2. Moderating influence of feedback modality (Force vs. Vibrotactile Feedback)

Outcome Variable	Q_b	k	g	95% CI (g)	Q_w
Task Success					
FF	34.2***	45	0.75***	0.64- 0.85	200.4***
VT		19	0.21**	0.07- 0.36	33.6*
Average Force					
FF	29.3***	19	0.78***	0.60- 0.96	169.2***
VT		13	-0.13	-0.41- 0.15	105.3***
Peak Force					
FF	0.1	22	0.64***	0.46- 0.82	132.9***
VT		5	0.60***	0.31- 0.89	11.3**
Completion Time					
FF	4.8*	79	0.22***	0.13- 0.30	331.0***
VT		18	0.03	-0.11- 0.18	85.4***

Note. *p <.05; **p <.01; ***p < .001; CI = confidence interval.

Finally, we conducted a moderator analyses, comparing effects of force feedback for surgical tasks (like e.g. suturing) and simple teleoperation tasks (like e.g. peg-in-hole). Results show that the positive effects of FF on peak force reduction was only evident during surgical tasks ($g_{Surgical} = 1.06$ vs. $g_{Non-Surgical} = -0.40$; see Table 3). The negative value for non-surgical tasks indicates that peak forces were even higher with force feedback compared to conditions without. Furthermore, moderator analysis revealed that the positive effect of force feedback on completion times is restricted to non-surgical teleoperation tasks ($g_{\text{Surgical}} = -0.05$ vs. $g_{\text{Non-Surgical}} = 0.29$). Please note that no moderation analyses could be performed for task success and detection rates, because the former variable was only used for non-surgical tasks and the latter for surgical palpation tasks only.

Table 3. Moderating influence of task domain on the force feedback effects

Outcome Variable	Q_b	k	g	95% CI (g)	Q_w
Task Accuracy					
Surgical	1.5	18	0.61***	0.32– 0.93	33.2*
Non-Surg.		8	0.81***	0.57– 1.05	11.7
Average Force					
Surgical	0.5	12	0.82***	0.61– 1.04	35.2***
Non-Surg.		7	0.69***	0.37– 1.01	133.5***
Peak Force					
Surgical	52.1***	17	1.06***	0.85– 1.27	49.5***
Non-Surg.		5	-0.40*	-0.74– -0.07	31.3***
Completion Time					
Surgical	11.2***	24	-0.05	-0.23– 0.13	51.4**
Non-Surg.		55	0.29***	0.20– 0.39	268.5***

Note. $^*p <.05$; $^{**}p <.01$; $^{***}p < .001$; CI = confidence interval

One possible explanation for the significant moderation effects on peak force is that during surgical tasks critical force thresholds of course play a much more important role. All surgical studies reporting peak forces used tasks in which force regulation is important or with a critical force level (breaking threads, damaging tissue asf.), while this was not the case in any of the non-surgical studies. Re-analyzing data by classifying studies along the criterion whether there was a critical force level or not, we found a similar moderation effect for the peak force variable ($g_{\text{Threshold}} = 1.06***$ vs. $g_{\text{NoThreshold}} = 0.19$; $Q_b = 22.7***$).

Moreover, we further explored the moderation effect regarding the required completion times. As discussed in [62] the stronger effect of additional force feedback during basic telemanipulation tasks might be due to the less demanding task character compared to the surgical tasks. In the current sample of surgical studies, manipulation tasks like dissection, suturing, knotting and needle insertion were mainly performed (90 % of the studies). The non-surgical tasks also included simple target acquisition, selection or navigation/ tracing tasks, besides classical (tele-)manipulation tasks like peg-in-hole, pick-and-place and assembly (55 % of the studies). Interestingly, we found a significant moderation effect of task type ($Qb = 28.9***$), when categorizing studies reporting completion times into manipulation tasks ($g = .09$), navigation or tracing tasks ($g = .21$), selection tasks ($g = .47***$) and target acquisition tasks ($g = .74***$).

4   Discussion

Altogether, the quantitative review based on 58 studies with 1104 subjects investigating the impact of force feedback provides strong evidence for the benefits of haptics in a large variety of experimental tasks and different performance dimensions. There are substantial positive effects of additional force feedback on task performance, force regulation and a small positive effect on the task completion times. Evidently, providing force information is indispensable to maintain high performance levels during teleoperation or VR simulations. An alternative to displaying force feedback is vibrotactile feedback. In contrast to force feedback systems, vibrotactile devices are less expensive, lighter, and provide larger workspaces. Besides, tactile feedback provides passive responses (no forces are applied actively). Therefore, there is no conflict between feedback and the user's sense of position and less muscular fatigue [10]. However, no realistic contact forces are available and there are no kinesthetic constraints avoiding inadequate force production and supporting the operator by forcing her/him into the correct orientation or position e.g. during assembly tasks [32]. In line with this notion, the results of our meta-analysis revealed no reduction of the average force application and compared to force feedback a significantly lower – but still existent and significant – effect of vibrotactile feedback regarding task performance. Similar to force feedback, vibrotactile force information also helps avoiding exaggerated force levels.

Yet, substituting force feedback with vibrotactile stimuli is cognitively more demanding because the kinesthetic events have to be inferred from tactile signals. Consistently, we did not find a time saving effect when providing this kind of feedback. Altogether, vibrotactile devices could be a reasonable alternative if high resolution of haptic information is not critical or as a warning function (e.g. damage or collision avoidance). Still, force feedback is indispensable to improve task performance during tele-manipulative tasks (like assembly tasks or suturing), requiring multi-dimensional (e.g. three-dimensional force and torque information) and high-resolution haptic information.

Next, we explored the effects of different task characteristics on the force feedback effects. Integrating the findings of two meta-analyses, one with a focus on general teleoperation tasks [35], one on surgical application [62] and several additional studies, we compared findings for surgical vs. non-surgical tasks. During the more complex and delicate telesurgical tasks, force feedback is crucial to adjust the input forces adequately and to avoid exaggerated forces (e.g. damaging tissue, breaking threads). Meta-analytical moderation analysis showed that a large positive effect of force feedback occurs for the surgical tasks but even a negative effect for other teleoperation tasks, which is mainly due to the fact that there are usually no critical force thresholds for these tasks. Finally, we did not find a significant reduction of task completion times during surgical tasks, but for the other teleoperation tasks. Subsequent analyses provided evidence that this effect can be explained by the higher complexity of surgical tasks. During (tele-)manipulation tasks, additional force information might be used in an explorative manner, to better understand the spatial configuration. Also, more complex visual and haptic information has to be processed and integrated, resulting in higher cognitive requirements. Analogously, for simple one or two-dimensional selection or target acquisition tasks, significant time saving effects occur.

As one major limitation of the current meta-analysis (and the cited prior meta-analyses), is the remaining amount of heterogeneity in almost all moderation analyses.

Evidently, the numerous haptic devices, qualities of force feedback, different remote systems, visualizations [62], experimental tasks, task performance operationalizations, experience levels of subjects, and so forth are the main reason for the variability of results.

References

1. Adams, R.J., Klowden, D., Hannaford, B.: Virtual training for a manual assembly task. Haptics-e **2**(2), 1–7 (2001). (This study included in the meta-analysis)
2. Arata, J., Takahashi, H., Yasunaka, S., Onda, K., Tanaka, K., Sugita, N., Hashizume, M., et al.: Impact of network time-delay and force feedback on tele-surgery. Int. J. Comput. Assist. Radiol. Surg. **3**(3–4), 371–378 (2008). (This study included in the meta-analysis)
3. Arsenault, R., Ware, C.: Eye-hand co-ordination with force feedback. In: Proceedings of the Sigchi Conference on Human Factors in Computing Systems, pp. 408–414. ACM, April 2000. (This study included in the meta-analysis)
4. Bauernschmitt, R., Gaertner, C., Braun, E.U., Mayer, H., Knoll, A., Schreiber, U., Lange, R.: Improving the quality of robotic heart surgery: evaluation in a new experimental system. In: Proceedings of the 4th Russian-Bavarian Conference on Biomedical Engineering at Moscow Institute of Electronic Technology (Technical University), Zelenograd, Moscow, Russia, July 8/9 2008, p. 137–140 (2008). (This study included in the meta-analysis)
5. Blake, J., Gurocak, H.B.: Haptic glove with MR brakes for virtual reality. IEEE/ASME Trans. Mechatronics **14**(5), 606–615 (2009). (This study included in the meta-analysis)
6. Borenstein, M., Hedges, L.V., Higgins, J.P., Rothstein, H.R.: Introduction to Meta-Analysis. Wiley, New York (2011)
7. Braun, E.U., Mayer, H., Knoll, A., Lange, R., Bauernschmitt, R.: The must-have in robotic heart surgery: haptic feedback. In: Bozovic, V. (ed.) Medical Robotics, pp. 9–20. I-Tech Education and Publishing, Vienna (2008). (This study included in the meta-analysis)
8. Braun, E.U., Gaertner, C., Mayer, H., Knoll, A., Lange, R., Bauernschmitt, R.: Haptic aided roboting for heart surgeons. In: Proceedings of the 4th European Conference of the International Federation for Medical and Biological Engineering, pp. 1695–1696. Springer, Berlin (2009). (This study included in the meta-analysis)
9. Chamaret, D., Ullah, S., Richard, P., Naud, M.: Integration and evaluation of haptic feedbacks: from CAD models to virtual prototyping. Int. J. Interact. Design Manufact. (IJIDeM) **4**(2), 87–94 (2010). (This study included in the meta-analysis)
10. Cheng, L.T., Kazman, R., Robinson, J.: Vibrotactile feedback in delicate virtual reality operations. In: Proceedings of the Fourth ACM International Conference on Multimedia, pp. 243–251. ACM, February 1997. (This study included in the meta-analysis)
11. Cohen, J.: Statistical Power Analysis for the Behavioral Sciences. Psychology Press, Mountain View (1988)
12. Cutler, N., Balicki, M., Finkelstein, M., Wang, J., Gehlbach, P., McGready, J., Handa, J.T.: Auditory force feedback substitution improves surgical precision during simulated ophthalmic surgery. Invest. Ophthalmol. Vis. Sci. **54**(2), 1316–1324 (2013)
13. Debus, T., Becker, T., Dupont, P., Jang, T.J., Howe, R.: Multichannel vibrotactile display for sensory substitution during teleoperation. In: Proceedings of SPIE–The International Society for Optical Engineering, vol. 4570, pp. 42–49, October 2001. (This study included in the meta-analysis)

14. Deml, B.: Telepräsenzsysteme - Gestaltung der Mensch-System Schnittstelle, Dissertation thesis, University of the Armed Forces (2004). http://edok01.tib.uni-hannover.de/edoks/e01dd01/482342803l.pdf. Accessed 16 January 2014. (This study included in the meta-analysis)
15. Dennerlein, J.T., Yang, M.C.: Haptic force-feedback devices for the office computer: performance and musculoskeletal loading issues. Hum. Factors: J. Hum. Factors Ergon. Soc. **43**(2), 278–286 (2001). (This study included in the meta-analysis)
16. Edwards, G.W.: Performance and usability of force feedback and auditory substitutions in a virtual environment manipulation task (Master's thesis, Virginia Polytechnic Institute and State University, Virginia, USA) (2000). http://scholar.lib.vt.edu/theses/available/etd-12212000-094328/. (This study included in the meta-analysis)
17. Farkhatdinov, I., Ryu, J.-H.: A study on the role of force feedback for teleoperation of industrial overhead crane. In: Ferre, M. (ed.) EuroHaptics 2008. LNCS, vol. 5024, pp. 796–805. Springer, Heidelberg (2008). (This study included in the meta-analysis)
18. Garbaya, S., Zaldivar-Colado, U.: The affect of contact force sensations on user performance in virtual assembly tasks. Virtual Reality **11**(4), 287–299 (2007). (This study included in the meta-analysis)
19. Gerovich, O., Marayong, P., Okamura, A.M.: The effect of visual and haptic feedback on computer-assisted needle insertion. Comput. Aided Surg. **9**(6), 243–249 (2004). (This study included in the meta-analysis)
20. Gupta, R., Sheridan, T., Whitney, D.: Experiments using multimodal virtual environments in design for assembly analysis. Presence: Teleoperators Virtual Environ. **6**(3), 318–338 (1997). (This study included in the meta-analysis)
21. Gwilliam, J.C., Mahvash, M., Vagvolgyi, B., Vacharat, A., Yuh, D.D., Okamura, A.M.: Effects of haptic and graphical force feedback on teleoperated palpation. In: ICRA 2009, IEEE International Conference on Robotics and Automation, pp. 677–682. IEEE, May 2009. (This study included in the meta-analysis)
22. Hacinecipoglu, A., Konukseven, E.I., Koku, A.B.: Evaluation of haptic feedback cues on vehicle teleoperation performance in an obstacle avoidance scenario. In: World Haptics Conference (WHC), pp. 689–694. IEEE, April 2013. (This study included in the meta-analysis)
23. Hale, K.S., Stanney, K.M.: Deriving haptic design guidelines from human physiological, psychophysical, and neurological foundations. IEEE Comput. Graph. Appl. **24**(2), 33–39 (2004)
24. Hannaford, B., Wood, L., McAffee, D.A., Zak, H.: Performance evaluation of a six-axis generalized force-reflecting teleoperator. IEEE Trans. Syst. Man Cybern. **21**(3), 620–633 (1991). (This study included in the meta-analysis)
25. Hedges, L., Olkin, I.: Statistical Methods for Meta-Analysis. Academic Press, San Diego (1985)
26. Hurmuzlu, Y., Ephanov, A., Stoianovici, D.: Effect of a pneumatically driven haptic interface on the perceptional capabilities of human operators. Presence: Teleoperators Virtual Environ. **7**(3), 290–307 (1998). (This study included in the meta-analysis)
27. Kazi, A.: Operator performance in surgical telemanipulation. Presence: Teleoperators Virtual Environ. **10**(5), 495–510 (2001). (This study included in the meta-analysis)
28. Lee, S., Kim, G.J.: Effects of haptic feedback, stereoscopy, and image resolution on performance and presence in remote navigation. Int. J. Hum Comput. Stud. **66**(10), 701–717 (2008). (This study included in the meta-analysis)

29. Lee, S., Sukhatme, G., Kim, J., Park, C.M.: Haptic control of a mobile robot: a user study. In: IEEE/RSJ International Conference on Intelligent Robots and Systems, vol. 3, pp. 2867–2874. IEEE (2002). (This study included in the meta-analysis)

30. Lindeman, R.W., Sibert, J.L., Hahn, J.K.: Towards usable VR: an empirical study of user interfaces for immersive virtual environments. In: Proceedings of the SIGCHI conference on Human Factors in Computing Systems, pp. 64–71. ACM, May 1999. (This study included in the meta-analysis)

31. Mahvash, M., Gwilliam, J., Agarwal, R., Vagvolgyi, B., Su, L.M., Yuh, D.D., Okamura, A.M.: Force-feedback surgical teleoperator: controller design and palpation experiments. In: Symposium on Haptic Interfaces for Virtual Environment and Teleoperator Systems, Haptics 2008, pp. 465–471. IEEE, March 2008. (This study included in the meta-analysis)

32. Massimino, M.J.: Sensory substitution for force feedback in space teleoperation (Doctoral dissertation, Massachusetts Institute of Technology) (1992). http://dspace.mit.edu/bitstream/handle/1721.1/12033/31318142.pdf. (This study included in the meta-analysis)

33. Moody, L., Baber, C., Arvanitis, T.N.: Objective surgical performance evaluation based on haptic feedback. Stud. Health Technol. Inform. **85**, 304–310 (2002). (This study included in the meta-analysis)

34. Nam, C.S., Shu, J., Chung, D.: The roles of sensory modalities in collaborative virtual environments (CVEs). Comput. Hum. Behav. **24**(4), 1404–1417 (2008). (This study included in the meta-analysis)

35. Nitsch, V.: Haptic Human-Machine Interaction in Teleoperation Systems and its Implications for the Design and Effective Use of Haptic Interfaces (Doctoral dissertation, Universität der Bundeswehr München) (2012). (This study included in the meta-analysis)

36. Nitsch, V., Färber, B.: A meta-analysis of the effects of haptic interfaces on task performance with teleoperation systems. IEEE Transactions on Haptics, 1 (2012)

37. Oakley, I., McGee, M.R., Brewster, S., Gray, P.: Putting the feel in 'look and feel'. In: Proceedings of the SIGCHI conference on Human Factors in Computing Systems, pp. 415–422. ACM, April 2000. (This study included in the meta-analysis)

38. Panait, L., Akkary, E., Bell, R.L., Roberts, K.E., Dudrick, S.J., Duffy, A.J.: The role of haptic feedback in laparoscopic simulation training. J. Surg. Res. **156**(2), 312–316 (2009). (This study included in the meta-analysis)

39. Paul, L., Cartiaux, O., Docquier, P.L., Banse, X.: Ergonomic evaluation of 3D plane positioning using a mouse and a haptic device. Int. J. Med. Robot. Comput. Assist. Surg. **5**(4), 435–443 (2009). (This study included in the meta-analysis)

40. Pawar, V.M., Steed, A.: Evaluating the influence of haptic force-feedback on 3D selection tasks using natural egocentric gestures. In: IEEE Virtual Reality Conference, VR 2009, pp. 11–18. IEEE, March 2009. (This study included in the meta-analysis)

41. Peon, A.R., Prattichizzo, D.: Reaction times to constraint violation in haptics: comparing vibration, visual and audio stimuli. In: World Haptics Conference (WHC), pp. 657–661. IEEE, April 2013. (This study included in the meta-analysis)

42. Petzold, B., Zaeh, M., Faerber, B., Deml, B., Egermeier, H., Schilp, J., Clarke, S.: A study on visual, auditory, and haptic feedback for assembly tasks. Presence **13**(1), 16–21 (2004). (This study included in the meta-analysis)

43. Pillarisetti, A., Pekarev, M., Brooks, A.D., Desai, J.P.: Evaluating the role of force feedback for biomanipulation tasks. In: Haptic Interfaces for Virtual Environment and Teleoperator Systems, pp. 11–18. IEEE, March 2006. (This study included in the meta-analysis)

44. Radi, M., Nitsch, V.: Telepresence in industrial applications: implementation issues for assembly tasks. Presence **19**(5), 415–429 (2010). (This study included in the meta-analysis)

45. Reinhart, G., Reiter, A.: An investigation of haptic feedback effects in telepresent microassembly. Prod. Eng. Res. Devel. **5**(5), 581–586 (2011). (This study included in the meta-analysis)
46. Reiter, A., Nitsch, V., Reinhart, G., Färber, B.: Effects of visual and haptic feedback on telepresent micro assembly tasks. In: 3rd International Conference on Changeable, Agile, Reconfigurable and Virtual Production CARV 2009, Munich (2009). (This study included in the meta-analysis)
47. Richard, P., Coiffet, P., Kheddar, A., England, R.: Human performance evaluation of two handle haptic devices in a dextrous virtual telemanipulation task. In: 1999 IEEE/RSJ International Conference on Intelligent Robots and Systems, IROS 1999, Proceedings, vol. 3, pp. 1543–1548. IEEE (1999). (This study included in the meta-analysis)
48. Salkini, M.W., Doarn, C.R., Kiehl, N., Broderick, T.J., Donovan, J.F., Gaitonde, K.: The role of haptic feedback in laparoscopic training using the LapMentor II. J. Endourol. **24**(1), 99–102 (2010). (This study included in the meta-analysis)
49. Sallnäs, E.-L.: Improved precision in mediated collaborative manipulation of objects by haptic force feedback. In: Brewster, S., Murray-Smith, R. (eds.) Haptic HCI 2000. LNCS, vol. 2058, pp. 69–75. Springer, Heidelberg (2001). (This study included in the meta-analysis)
50. Sallnäs, E.L., Zhai, S.: Collaboration meets fitts' law: passing virtual objects with and without haptic force feedback. In: INTERACT (2003). (This study included in the meta-analysis)
51. Santos-Carreras, L., Beira, R., Sengül, A., Gassert, R., Bleuler, H.: Influence of force and torque feedback on operator performance in a VR-based suturing task. Appl. Bion. Biomech. **7**(3), 217–230 (2010). (This study included in the meta-analysis)
52. Seibold, U.: An Advanced Force Feedback Tool Design for Minimally Invasive Robotic Surgery. Dissertation thesis, Technical University Munich (2013). (This study included in the meta-analysis)
53. Sheridan, T.B.: Telerobotics, automation, and human supervisory control. MIT Press, Cambridge (1992)
54. Stepp, C.E.: Matsuoka, Y.: Relative to direct haptic feedback, remote vibrotactile feedback improves but slows object manipulation. In: 2010 Annual International Conference of the IEEE Engineering in Medicine and Biology Society (EMBC), pp. 2089–2092. IEEE, August 2010. (This study included in the meta-analysis)
55. Talasaz, A., Trejos, A.L., Patel, R.V.: Effect of force feedback on performance of robotics-assisted suturing. In: Proceedings of the 4th IEEE RAS & EMBS International Conference on Biomedical Robotics and Biomechatronics (BioRob), pp. 823–828. IEEE, June 2012. (This study included in the meta-analysis)
56. Tejeiro, C., Stepp, C.E., Malhotra, M., Rombokas, E., Matsuoka, Y.: Comparison of remote pressure and vibrotactile feedback for prosthetic hand control. In: 2012 4th IEEE RAS & EMBS International Conference on Biomedical Robotics and Biomechatronics (BioRob), pp. 521–525. IEEE, June 2012. (This study included in the meta-analysis)
57. Tholey, G.: A teleoperative haptic feedback framework for computer-aided minimally invasive surgery (Doctoral dissertation, Drexel University) (2007). (This study included in the meta-analysis)
58. Viciana-Abad, R., Reyes-Lecuona, A., Rosa-Pujazón, A., Pérez-Lorenzo, J.M.: The influence of different sensory cues as selection feedback and co-location in presence and task performance. Multimedia Tools Appl. **68**(3), 623–639 (2014). (This study included in the meta-analysis)

59. Vo, D.M., Vance, J.M., Marasinghe, M.G.: Assessment of haptics-based interaction for assembly tasks in virtual reality. In: EuroHaptics Conference, 2009 and Symposium on Haptic Interfaces for Virtual Environment and Teleoperator Systems, World Haptics 2009, Third Joint , pp. 494–499. IEEE, March 2009. (This study included in the meta-analysis)
60. Wagner, C.R., Howe, R.D.: Force feedback benefit depends on experience in multiple degree of freedom robotic surgery task. IEEE Trans. Rob. **23**(6), 1235–1240 (2007). (This study included in the meta-analysis)
61. Wagner, C.R., Stylopoulos, N., Howe, R.D.: The role of force feedback in surgery: analysis of blunt dissection. In: Symposium on Haptic Interfaces for Virtual Environment and Teleoperator Systems, pp. 73–79, March 2002. (This study included in the meta-analysis)
62. Weber, B., Schneider, S.: The effects of force feedback on surgical task performance: a meta-analytical integration. In: Auvray, M., Duriez, C. (eds.) EuroHaptics 2014, Part II. LNCS, vol. 8619, pp. 150–157. Springer, Heidelberg (2014)
63. Wiebe, E.N., Minogue, J., Jones, M.G., Cowley, J., Krebs, D.: Haptic feedback and students' learning about levers: Unraveling the effect of simulated touch. Comput. Educ. **53**(3), 667–676 (2009). (This study included in the meta-analysis)
64. Wildenbeest, J.G., Abbink, D.A., Heemskerk, C.J., van der Helm, F.C., Boessenkool, H.: The impact of haptic feedback quality on the performance of teleoperated assembly tasks. IEEE Trans. Haptics **6**(2), 242–252 (2013). (This study included in the meta-analysis)
65. Yiasemidou, M., Glassman, D., Vasas, P., Badiani, S., Patel, B.: Faster simulated laparoscopic cholecystectomy with haptic feedback technology. Open Access Surg. **4**, 39–44 (2011). (This study included in the meta-analysis)

Games for Learning and Therapy

An Evaluation Method of Educational Computer Games for Deaf Children Based on Design Guidelines

Rafael dos Passos Canteri[1(✉)], Laura Sánchez García[1],
Tanya Amara Felipe[2], Diego Roberto Antunes[1],
and Carlos Eduardo Iatskiu[1]

[1] Federal University of Paraná, Curitiba, PR, Brazil
{rpcanteri,laurag,ciatskiv}@inf.ufpr.br, drantunes@gmail.com
[2] National Institute of Deaf Education, Rio de Janeiro, RJ, Brazil
tanyafelipe@gmail.com

Abstract. Computer games have been used for a long time as a valuable tool in the teaching and learning of a variety of subjects. The Deaf communities and in particular the Deaf children have different learning needs compared to hearing children. For this reason, there have been, even timidly, some educational games that focusing on such children. However, as these games do not have a standard methology for development, they usually do not meet the needs of the target audience. Therefore, this paper proposes a method for evaluating the quality and suitability of existing educational games for Deaf children through a tested set of design guidelines for Deaf children games. Two computer educational games for Deaf are evaluated. In addition, after the evaluation, a case study is presented to demonstrate the redesign of a game based on the guidelines and the results obtained.

Keywords: Human-Computer Interaction · Deaf culture · Social inclusion · Computer games · Educational games · Education of deaf children

1 Introduction

Deaf communities live today a historical period of assurance for social rights, which were denied for them for at least a century [2]. One major right that has been recently granted is the use of Sign Language. The Sign Language is an important component of the Deaf culture, characterized by a visual-spatial form [1]. Sign languages are the natural languages for the Deaf, they are complete language system with lexicon, syntax, and ability to generate an infinite set of sentences [3].

Even with current advances, the need for computational tools to assist the Deaf in communication and access to information is clearly noticed [4,5]. One useful computational tool that is lacking for the Deaf is quality computer educational games. Adequate educational games for Deaf children are games that

M. Antona and C. Stephanidis (Eds.): UAHCI 2015, Part III, LNCS 9177, pp. 409–419, 2015.
DOI: 10.1007/978-3-319-20684-4_40

communicate mainly through sign languages with the user while also teaches some knowledge area to the player.

There are few specific games for Deaf children, and some of them do not have all the requirements/characteristics necessary for the target audience. This leads to the question: **"What is missing in these games for effective success?"**. If the answer to this question if found, the development of inappropriate educational games can be avoided, and also the improvement of existing games can be supported.

1.1 Motivation and Goals

The work [6] presents an exploratory study for guidelines that support the design (creation of new games) of educational computer games for Deaf children. Such work considers the gameplay, language and interface needs that the game must attend to. The guidelines creation is based on an effective methodology for teaching Deaf children, as well as reputable models for development of general educational games.

This paper's motivation is the evaluation of existing educational computer games, in order to improve their quality and suitability for Deaf children. Therefore, this article intends to use the guidelines of [6] as a quality inspection method of existing digital games.

As contributions, this study presents the adequacy of the guidelines as an inspection method, the evaluation results of two games, and a case study of the improvement of an educational game. In addition, self critical analysis of some guidelines are pointed out.

The remainder of this paper is as follows: Sect. 2 discusses the subject of digital games, from general video games to educative games for Deaf children. Section 3 presents the guidelines used in the process of games evaluation for Deaf children. Section 4 shows the evaluation process proposed. In Sect. 5 a case study with one game is performed. Finally, Sect. 6 concludes the paper and discusses future works.

2   Computer Games

Digital games have become a major entertainment area today. They have a way of immersing players into an epic challenge that consumes them physically, intellectually, and emotionally. There is no denying the fact that children and teenagers love computer games [7]. The development of computer games involves professionals from various areas however, an important part of its development lies with the Computer Science professionals.

Just as in the film industry, there are several genres in the industry of games currently [8]. These genres serve both to guide the consumer at the time of purchase, and to guide the team in a direction of development. One sub-genre of games are the educative games. These kind of games have the purpose to teach some field of knowledge in a playful manner.

2.1 Educational Games

Studies such as [9,10] show that digital games not only satisfy the entertainment needs of children, but also contributes to the cognitive, social, emotional and cultural development. Added to these benefits of general computer games, the educational game has the potential to teach relevant contents to the player.

Despite all the benefits the educational games can bring to children, the design and development of educational games with authentic learning content while also keeping the user entertained, can be quite challenging [11]. Not everything that is called 'game' is fun and motivating, the game design needs to be well prepared to ensure these qualities. The educational games should include good game design and good pedagogy in order to ensure the effectiveness of learning [11].

The educational game can not only be considered as a kind of educational media, but also as a learning environment to study, because the game itself contains the basic elements that are needed in learning activities [12]. Educational games are embedded within the concept called Educational Software, important concept of the field Education Informatics.

2.2 Games and the Deaf

There are works that address the development of digital games for the Deaf. The works [13–15] deal with the development of a game for American Sign Language (ASL). The work [16] shows the creation of a mobile game for Deaf children to learn Australian Sign Language (Auslan). The common problem found in these works is the fact that the developed applications are more interactive software than digital games. These applications lack many gameplay elements such as clear goals, score, completion of stage, to be fully characterized as games.

There have been attempts to make contact with the authors of the papers from the previous paragraph, in order to apply the guidelines for evaluating their games. However, the authors did not respond the contact attempts. Since there are few academic papers on games for Deaf children and the access to the executables of the games from the published papers [13–16] was not possible, a decision has been made to evaluate two educational games present on web sites for children educational games,[1] instead.

3 Guidelines

As previously pointed out, the study that serves as base for this one, created a set of guidelines in order to guide game designers and developers into making effective educational games for Deaf children. The design guidelines contain rules that should be followed in the development of a game to make it suitable for Deaf children education.

---

[1] http://www.educajogos.com.br/jogos-educativos/alfabetizacao/.
http://www.atividadeseducativas.com.br/index.php.

A new possibility that has been perceived in the set of guidelines is to asses the quality of a given educational game for Deaf children. Most likely, the educational games already developed for Deaf children did not follow the set of design guidelines, since they were created in a recent work. In this sense, it is possible to assess the suitability of educational games and point out possible improvements using these guidelines as tools.

3.1   Conception Methodology

The design guidelines used, as foundation, respectable educational game models and a methodology for education of Deaf children. The construction process of the guidelines was carried out as follows: When intersections between the guidelines in the most important studies of educational games were found, these were incorporated immediately. On the other hand, when the guidelines were not consensus among the main papers of the area, those guidelines that attended the Deaf education were followed. When there were guidelines that, although consensus among the models studied, did not fit in the situation of Deaf people (e.g. guidelines directing sound feedback or guidance on the game music), they were discarded and not included in the set.

3.2   Classification

There is a total of 31 guidelines. Each of them can be classified corresponding to the game element they relate to, that, is the Interface, the Educational Content and the Gameplay. Figure 1 summarizes this structure.

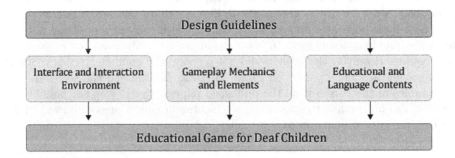

Fig. 1. Guidelines classification

Any educational game for Deaf children can be summarized in these three game components. Some of the guidelines have responsibilities that cross over those sections. Some examples of guidelines will be shown in the next subsection.

3.3   Pratical Examples

Next an example of each type of guideline is presented.

G6: The feedback for the players actions must always be as fastest and as understandable as possible. E.g. when an error is committed, the screen reaction must be fast and understandable.

G11: The game needs to offer levels of difficulty or have automatically adaptive difficulty according to the player's performance. E.g. usually the options of Easy, Medium and Hard difficulties are enough.

G20: Educational games for deaf children should be constructed from semantic triples (Portuguese, Libras and illustration), especially when the children's age is more than 4 years old. E.g. a space shooter that requires the player to destroy an asteroid which has the word in Portuguese, an asteroid which has the word in Libras and an asteroid with a picture of the corresponding object.

4   Games Suitability Evaluation

As mentioned in Sect. 2, two games from Brazilian educational games websites were used for the evaluation process.

The first one is a game that trains fingerspelling and word construction. The game shows a picture of a given concept and asks the child to construct the word, letter by letter, that names the concept. It teaches simultaneously Libras fingerspelling and the written alphabet. The game has two levels of difficulty: the easiest has a table containing the alphabet in Libras and the written alphabet, the second and more difficult mode does not have any auxiliary tool. Figure 2 shows a screenshot from the game play.

Fig. 2. Game 1 - Figure and fingerspelling match

The second game belongs to another website of games for Deaf children. This game asks the player to combine the figure of an animal (to the right of the screen) with the figure of a child signaling in Libras the animal's name (in the left side of the screen). Figure 3 shows the game in execution.

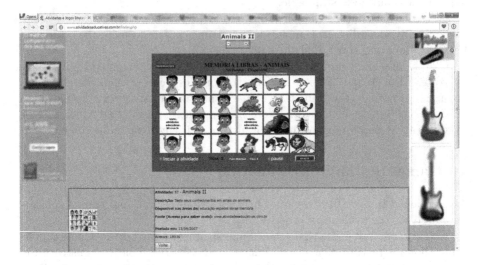

Fig. 3. Game 2 - Animals' names in libras

4.1   Process Methodology

The process of evaluation took place at the Human-Computer Interaction laboratory of Federal University of Paraná. The technique used was "heuristic" inspection by experts. Each game was played for 30 min. Then, every guideline from the set was checked, in order to see if the game fully meets, partially meets or does not meet the guideline, or yet if the guideline is not applicable in this kind of game.

Checklist Structure. The main tool used in the evaluation process was an organized checklist. It basically consists of a system that shows in order: a guideline, a guideline example of use and, finally, the question of game about the presence of the guideline in the game. The question checks whether the educational game meets, partially meets or does not meet the guideline or if the guideline does not apply to the game under evaluation.

Figure 4 shows an example of guideline verification. The complete checklist can be publicly accessed online[2], it can be used by anyone that intends to test an educational game for Deaf children.

---

[2] http://goo.gl/forms/N9H8tdhCuh.

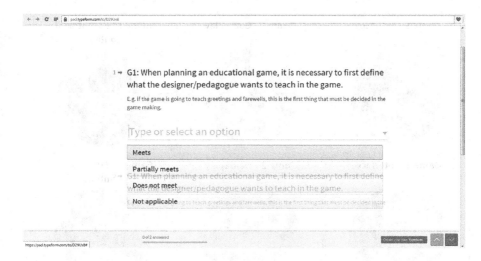

Fig. 4. Main evaluation tool - Checklist

4.2   Evaluation

In order to observe effective pratical results, the obtained data generated three graphs for each game. The graphics correspond to the quality of the graphical Interface, the Educational content and Gameplay of the game, based on the guidelines. Figure 5 comprises the graphics generated in the process.

The results are given according to the number of guidelines the games attended. In cases of non applicable guidelines, these were not counted in the final assessment of the game. The game's performance is fair according to the guidelines that fit to it, non applicable guidelines have no negative impact on the game.

Some problems encountered in the games can be easily perceived by any user. For example, the Guideline 29 states that "Objects from the sides of the screen need dynamic and shapes that do not distract the player from the main task", this guideline is missing on both games, since they are browser-based games from free websites and the sides of the screen are full with advertisements that distract the player's attention.

The analisys of the results shows that both games met the requirements regarding the educational contents. The major issues were with the interface environment, which showed poor results on both games. The gameplay is also a large problem in the second game, as well.

The interface problems can maximize the user learning curve and create difficulties for the user to achieve the game's objectives. In this context, the user may feel frustrated, may not understand the rules and forms of interaction, among other problems. For example, in Game 2, a major problem seen in the interface is the use of terms in English, it is already hard enough for a Deaf children to read in Portuguese, adding English to the interface makes it even worse. The main interface problem of Game 1 is an easily solvable one. The problem is the

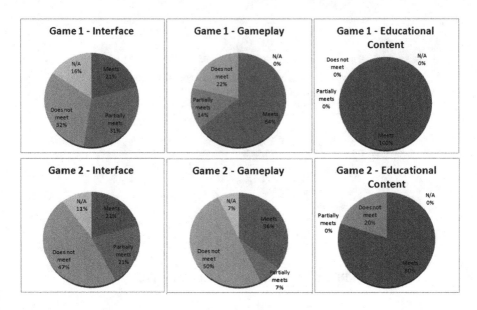

Fig. 5. Main evaluation tool - Checklist

inappropriate positioning of the playable part, which is not centralized, thus losing highlight and possibly diverting the attention of the user.

Gameplay problems tend to remove the potential for fun/motivation of the game. Furthermore, such problems may causa the player to lose interest and, in more severe cases, even irritate them. For all these reasons, it is very important to guarantee a good gameplay in educational computer games. For example, in Game 2, the player needs to choose some picture in the right side of the screen, before selection one in the left side, that is totally unnatural and can cause confusion to the player.

5   Case Study with Game

The previous section showed an evaluation analysis of educational games and the viability of the evaluation process based on design guidelines. However, these results should be used to adequate the game for the users, with the application of the guidelines. Thus, this section presents a case study to correct a educational game based on design guidelines and their new results when applied.

The game consists of a puzzle in which the player needs to fit the pieces referring to the figure of a concept, the signal in Libras and the word in Portuguese. The player fits pieces from geometrical figures on their edges, simulating the fittings of a puzzle. Each time the player hits a set of elements, the set, is moved in smaller size, to the right of the screen, freeing up space on the board for the remaining pieces.

The game features themed levels, based on important concepts to children as Food, Transportation and Hygiene. The choice of the level is made by the player before starting the match. After fitting all the pieces of figures, the level is complete. Figure 6 shows a screenshot from the game in the theme Food.

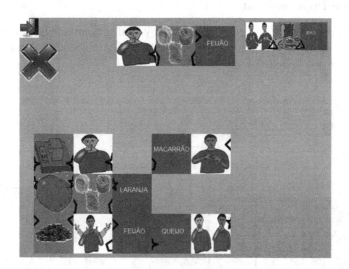

Fig. 6. Puzzle game of case study

For this game, just like the two games of the evaluation process, each guideline was checked in order to see if it was met, partially met, not met or not applicable. For each guideline that was partially met or not met, an adjustment to the game was made. The changes made are listed next:

- Guideline 4 states that the game's objectives need to be clear. Since the shaped pieces did not have resemblance to puzzle, they were changed into more adequate puzzle pieces.
- Guideline 5 says the game needs to have a tutorial for teaching the players how to play it. The game did not have one, so a video tutorial was recorded, showing how to play the game and how to react to the game's feedbacks.
- Guideline 7 concerns player's evaluation system, the game had no feature like that. In the improved version, an evaluation system consisting of a boy that receives clothes pieces when the player successfully matches the sets was inserted.
- Guideline 11 says the game needs to have difficulty levels. Two levels of difficulty are now present in the game: one with shaped pieces, one (harder) without it.
- Guideline 23 relates to interface colors and highlights. All the colors of the game were reworked in order to be more adequate to children.
- Guideline 28 concerns interface consistency. In order to guarantee it, all of the buttons and options in the interface have been renovated.

– Guideline 31 states the feedback must be adequate for Deaf children. To do this, the visual feedbacks for right, wrong, selected button, level complete were improved.

5.1   Game Improvement

After the application of the guidelines and a visual makeover, the game became more suitable for the education of Deaf children. Figure 7 contains a screenshot from the renewed version of the game.

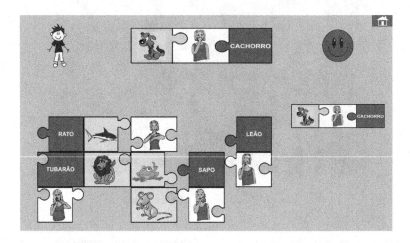

Fig. 7. Puzzle game of case study - After the guidelines application

6   Conclusions and Future Work

The application of the guidelines as an inspection tool was satisfactory. As a result of the tests, it was possible to identify points for improvement of existing educational games. This is a positive result, it is better for a developer to fix or to improve a game already developed, rather than developing a game from scratch. The improvement/adjustment can be made in a shorter time interval.

In the case study, with the improvement of the game based on the guidelines, the tool also proved suitable. The game has undergone many modifications. It is possible to see the significant evolution experienced by the application after the use of the guidelines.

Since the checklist's target audience are designers and teachers, a possibility of future work would be to adapt the checklist to other target audiences, for example, the users himself, in checking the quality of their games. Another possibility, would be having smaller checklists to evaluate each part of the game (interface, content and gameplay) separately.

Acknowledgments. We wish to thank CAPES foundation for granting the scholarship that made this study possible. We also want to thank professors Adriana Vaz, Francine A. Rossi and Andrea F. Andrade for the authorship of artistic drawings of the final interface of the game explored in the study case.

References

1. Bellugi, U., Poizner, H.: Language, Modality and the Brain. Trends Neurosci. **10**, 380–388 (1989)
2. Fernandes, S.F.: Avaliação em lingua portuguesa para alunos surdos: algumas considerações. Tese de Doutorado - Universidade Federal do Paraná (2007)
3. Stokoe, W.C.: Sign Language StructureLinstok Press. Silver Spring: Linstok Press, M.D. (1978)
4. García, L., Guimarães, C., Antunes, D., Fernandes, S.: HCI architecture for deaf communities cultural inclusion and citizenship. In: ICEIS (2013)
5. García, L., Guimarães, C., Antunes, D., Trindade, D., da Silva, A.: Structure of the brazilian sign language (libras) for computational tools: citizenship and social inclusion. World Summit Knowl. Soc. **112**, 365–370 (2010)
6. Canteri, R.P.: Diretrizes para o Design de Aplicações de Jogos Eletronicos para Educação Infantil de Surdos. Dissertação de Mestrado - Universidade Federal do Paraná (2014)
7. Virvou, M., Katsionis, G., Manos, K.: Combining software games with education: evaluation of its educational efectiveness. Educ. Technol. Soc. **8**(2), 54–65 (2005)
8. Bethke, E.: Game Development and Production: Wordware Game Developer's Library. Wordware Publications Inc., Plano (2003)
9. Squire, K., Jenkins, H.: Harnessing the Power of Games in Education. Insight **3**(1), 5–33 (2003)
10. Schcroter, B.A.F.: O Jogo e o Ensino de Linguas (2004)
11. Ibrahim, R., Jaafar, A.: Educational Games (EG) Design Framework - Combination of Game Design, Pedagogy and Content Modeling. Peter Lang Publishing, NewYork (2009)
12. Song, M., Zhang, S.: EFM - a model for educational game design. In: Pan, Z., Zhang, X., Rhalibi, E.A., Woo, W., Li, Y. (eds.) Edutainment 2008. LNCS, pp. 509–517. Springer, Heidelberg (2008)
13. Henderson, V., Lee, S., Brashear, H., Hamilton, H., Starner, T., Hamilton, S.: Development of an american sign language game for deaf children. In: Proceedings of the 2005 Conference on Interaction Design and Children (IDC 2005), pp. 70–79 (2005)
14. Lee, S., Henderson, V., Hamilton, H., Starner, T., Brashear, H., Hamilton, S.: A gesture-based american sign language game for deaf children. In: CHI 05 Extended Abstracts on Human Factors in Computing Systems, pp. 1589–1592 (2005)
15. Brashear, H., Henderson, V., Park, K.H., Hamilton, H., Lee, S., Starner, T.: American sign language recognition in game development for deaf children. In: Proceedings of the 8th International ACM SIGACCESS Conference on Computers and Accessibility (Assets 2006), pp. 79–86 (2006)
16. Korte, J., Potter, L.E., Nielsen, S.: Designing a mobile video game to help young deaf children learn auslan. In: Proceedings of the 26th Annual BCS Interaction Specialist Group Conference on People and Computers (BCS-HCI 2012), pp. 345–350. British Computer Society (2012)

Resonance: An Interactive Tabletop Artwork for Co-located Group Rehabilitation and Play

Jonathan Duckworth[1]([⊠]), Nick Mumford[6], Karen Caeyenberghs[6], Ross Eldridge[1], Scott Mayson[2], Patrick R. Thomas[3], David Shum[4], Gavin Williams[5], and Peter H. Wilson[6]

[1] School of Media and Communication, RMIT University, Melbourne, Australia
{jonathan.duckworth,ross.eldridge}@rmit.edu.au
[2] School of Architecture and Design, RMIT University, Melbourne, Australia
scott.mayson@rmit.edu.au
[3] School of Education and Professional Studies, Griffith University,
Brisbane, Australia
p.thomas@griffith.edu.au
[4] Behavioural Basis of Health, Griffith Health Institute and School of Applied
Psychology, Griffith University, Brisbane, Australia
d.shum@griffith.edu.au
[5] School of Physiotherapy, University of Melbourne, Epworth Hospital,
Melbourne, Australia
gavinw@unimelb.edu.au
[6] Faculty of Health Sciences, School of Psychology,
Australian Catholic University, Melbourne, Australia
{nimumford,karen.caeyenberghs,peterh.wilson}@acu.edu.au

Abstract. In this paper we describe the design and development of Resonance, an interactive tabletop artwork that targets upper-limb movement rehabilitation for patients with an acquired brain injury. The artwork consists of several interactive game environments, which enable artistic expression, exploration and play. Each environment aims to encourage collaborative, cooperative, and competitive modes of interaction for small groups (2-4) of co-located participants. We discuss how participants can perform movement tasks face-to-face with others using tangible user interfaces in creative and engaging activities. We pay particular attention to design elements that support multiple users and discuss preliminary user evaluation of the system. Our research indicates that group based rehabilitation using Resonance has the potential to stimulate a high level of interest and enjoyment in patients; facilitates social interaction, complements conventional therapy; and is intrinsically motivating.

Keywords: Interactive art · Group interaction · Tabletop display · Movement rehabilitation · Acquired brain injury

1 Introduction

The ability to enhance recovery of motor and cognitive function following brain injury remains a significant challenge for rehabilitation professionals. One of the greatest impediments to recovery is the patient's reduced capacity to engage in therapy and to

© Springer International Publishing Switzerland 2015
M. Antona and C. Stephanidis (Eds.): UAHCI 2015, Part III, LNCS 9177, pp. 420–431, 2015.
DOI: 10.1007/978-3-319-20684-4_41

persist with it in the face of significant impairment [1]. People with an acquired brain injury (ABI) caused mainly from stroke or traumatic brain injury (TBI), often experience a range of physical, cognitive, and psychological issues that can have long-lasting and devastating consequences, both for the sufferer and their families. The psychological problems including isolation, low self-esteem, reduced social support, apathy, chronic anxiety and depression, are often part and parcel of the psychosocial deficits experienced among people with neurological impairments [2, 3]. This presupposes the need to design solutions in therapy that encourage social interaction and a more playful orientation to participation in rehabilitation.

Group-based rehabilitation that is playful in nature, thematically appropriate, and engaging has been shown to enhance rehabilitation outcomes. For example, the work of Green and colleagues have designed a program to encourage children with hemiplegia to learn (bimanual) magic tricks involving assorted props (like cards), culminating in a magic show after a 3-week program [4]. This program has demonstrated significant improvements in motor function and, based on child and parent reports, improved interaction with typically developed peers and family members at home. Another recent group-based approach with hemiplegic children is the Pirates program of Aarts and colleagues [5]. This program is based on the fundamental premise that play is the primary means by which children interact, learn and derive meaning in their world. Here groups of children dress as pirates and are encouraged to role-play scenarios that involve bimanual and locomotor activity using a variety of props such as plastic swords, treasure chests, "booty", etc.

Both these programs demonstrate that playful interaction, role-play and performing with others provide opportunities for peer modeling, cooperation and friendly competition, all of which provide a fulcrum for goal-related activity and practice. Indeed, the rehabilitative effect of these group activities is regarded almost as an incidental outcome of the play itself. The playful and social context of these programs are inherently motivating, an essential aspect of therapy efficacy that is often neglected in the design of new rehabilitation systems [6].

Rehabilitation computer systems and custom off the shelf games (e.g. Nintendo Wii) commonly direct participants to focus attention on a wall-mounted vertical screen or head-mounted display but generally not on other participants [7]. These configurations can hinder social interaction and reduces opportunity for more complex interpersonal communication and vicarious learning [8].

Alternatively, with large format interactive walls and tabletop displays comes the possibility for computers to facilitate the work practices of small teams co-located around the same physical interface [9, 10]. In particular, tabletop displays can support face-to-face multiuser interaction through the physical affordances of the horizontal interface or the users' mental models of working around traditional tables [11]. The technology is able to support a broad range of user interactions such as multi-finger touch, hand gesture and simultaneous manipulation of physical objects [12, 13], has been shown to lead to collaborative learning in a group setting [14], and foster multimodal communication between healthy users [15] and clinical populations (such as children with Autism Spectrum Disorders [16]. How group work using tabletop technology can enhance motor rehabilitation of acquired brain injury is, however, relatively unexplored. Our research aims to design environments that may be exploited to enhance social aspects of group participation and physical affordances of tabletop displays.

2 The Resonance System

The Resonance system is designed to mediate small groups of people with a brain injury interacting with one another face-to-face, and enables an embodied, first person view of performance. We have created a suite of interactive environments that facilitate social interaction and group rehabilitation. Group participation is fundamental to the experience of Resonance and builds upon our prior work called 'Elements', which supports upper-limb rehabilitation for individuals with traumatic brain injury (TBI) patients [17–19]. Resonance utilizes a tabletop graphics display and four soft graspable objects used by the patients (i.e. tangible user interfaces, TUIs). We utilize the same tabletop platform and TUI's for Resonance and Elements to greatly extend the range of therapeutic options available to individuals and groups of patients. Resonance provides unimanual and bimanual game-like tasks and exploratory creative environments of varying complexity geared toward reaching, grasping, lifting, moving and placing tangible user interfaces on a tabletop display. Each environment aims to encourage collaborative, cooperative, and competitive modes of interaction for small groups of co-located participants.

Our design approach draws from principles of Computer Supported Cooperative Work (CSCW), a sub-field of Human Computer Interaction (HCI), to understand how computers can mediate and support collaborative work in a group environment (see [20] for a detailed discussion). Tabletop interaction supports an embodied, first-person experience of user interaction, one that capitalizes on our physical skills and our familiarity with real-world objects, which reflects the ecological approach of rehabilitation [21]. The ability of tabletop displays to support awareness of others' actions is often cited as one of the main benefits of collaborative face-to-face learning [14]. We considered how participants might observe, communicate, and learn from others, who are involved in playful activities [22]. Awareness of what others in a group are doing is essential in coordinating collaborative learning and achieving common goals around a shared activity. We considered a wide variety of collaboration styles, including working in parallel, working sequentially in tightly coupled activities, and working independently. We combine these ideas to design activities that support co-located participation and social engagement within motor rehabilitation contexts.

2.1 System Hardware

The Resonance system incorporates the latest advances in computing and visual tracking to maximize the level of user interaction. We are using a Multitaction™ 42" touch screen display with a fully integrated computer, multi-point touch screen, and marker-based tracking [23]. Multiple cameras are embedded in the unit below the LCD panel which sample at 200 Hz. The computer vision systems are able to see through the LCD panel using infrared light to identify multiple fingertips, finger orientation and complete hands. Physical objects can also be tagged with optical 2D markers.

By placing the marker on the base surface of the TUI's the computer vision system is able to identify each object and track its position and orientation when placed on the display. As an added advantage the system is compact, self-contained, and does not require calibration for ambient lighting conditions.

2.2   Tangible User Interface Design

A key feature of the Resonance tabletop display is its capacity to integrate and support the manipulation of physical objects such as TUIs in ways that are natural to the user's body and their environment [24]. The development of naturalistic interfaces for user interaction is essential to optimize performance and improve access for patients with cognitive and motor impairments [25]. TUIs can exploit multiple human sensory channels otherwise neglected in conventional interfaces and can promote rich and dexterous interaction [26].

TUIs placed on the tabletop are the primary means for users to control features and events within the Resonance system. The shape and physical weight of each TUI offers the patient varying perceptual motor cues for physical action. For example, the TUI design assists patients to relearn movement skills akin to lifting a cup, tumbler, or similar-sized object, and refine/adjust control while moving it. These simple actions offer some elements of real world human experience through the ways one might manipulate real world objects.

Movement performance in brain injured patients is constrained by a number of physiological and biomechanical factors including the increase in muscle tone that occurs as a result of hypertonia, reduced muscle strength, and limited coordination of body movement [27]. In response, we have created three sets of Additively Manufactured (3D printed) plastic fused filament fabricated TUI's of varying dimensions, with a soft flocked fiber covering (see Fig. 1). Participants with varying grasp width and strength can select the TUI most appropriate for their hand size and level of function. To provide additional feedback on object orientation, the TUI's have a variable internal material density that relates to size, thus increasing weight distribution at the base, making them more stable and orientating them toward the table surface.

The form factor of the interfaces has also taken into account the deficits typically experienced by brain-injured patients, including perceptual difficulties in visual functions, perception of objects, impaired space and distance judgment, and difficulty with orientation [27]. Therefore, high contrast colors and simple graspable shapes were used in the present design of the TUI's to assist a visually impaired user individuate each interface and ease cognitive load.

2.3   The Interactive Environments

We describe three environments called *Synchroshapes*, *Resonance*, and *Paint Wars* that offer co-operative, collaborative and competitive modes of playful user interactions, respectively. These environments have been developed using the Unity 3D game development software [28], and TUIO software protocol for object and touch event tracking [29]. An onscreen main menu enables the therapist to select up to four

Fig. 1. A range of TUI's of different size with a flocked fiber finish

participants from a database of users, select challenge options for each environment, and specify which side of the display each participant is using. To begin each player must manually select a TUI they will use for each hand before commencing. Players register their selection in the system software by placing the TUI's on a left and right hand graphic 'base station' next to their player name.

The *Sychroshapes* environment is a goal directed bimanual task for 2 participants who must *co-operate* with one another placing objects on targets to build a sequence of sounds. Players must attend to their target shape as well as the movements of the other player. To play, a pair of TUI's must be placed simultaneously on a sequence of targets when displayed (see Fig. 2).

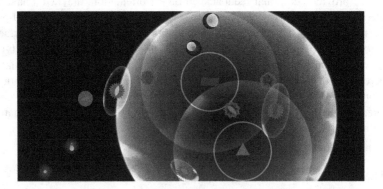

Fig. 2. A screen grab of the *Sychroshapes* environment. Participants must synchronously place the TUIs on the corresponding rectangular and triangular target. A colored circle that grows centrally from the target indicates successful placement. An animated visual entity that plays a looped musical sound is created for each successful attempt.

The targets are surrounded by an on-screen barrier. Players take turns to lift and move their pair of TUI's over the barrier and place them as accurately and simultaneously on the targets as possible. A visual link between the two targets highlights the level of synchrony between the placements of the TUI's. A short looped musical sound is created and visually represented on the screen if the objects are placed simultaneously. The distance between the targets increases and the reaching range varies over trials. Subsequent sounds are created and added to the sequence on successful placement of the objects, resulting in a procedurally generated musical soundtrack. Failure to place objects synchronously produces no sound. As the level of challenge increases players must cooperate in the placement of the TUI's. As the task progresses shapes from both players may appear on the screen at certain intervals. Both players must time the placement of TUI's on their target at the same time to create a new sound effect.

The *Resonance* environment is a **collaborative** musical tool to compose sounds using the position and orientation of the TUI's together with multi-touch. Here, groups of participants can mix and manipulate sound and colorful graphics in an aesthetically pleasing way (see Fig. 3). Complex soundscapes can be generated easily using a combination of simple gestures and movements. Each TUI produces a unique set of sounds we call *notes*, *pulses* and *atmospheres*. A number of colored lines emanate on a central axis from the base of each TUI when placed on the display. These lines visually subdivide the screen into colored polygonal fragments that produce an audiovisual *note* when touched.

Fig. 3. A participant using the *Resonance* environment to compose sounds

Additional fragments (approximate range 3-25) are created as more TUI's are placed on the display, enabling a larger range of *notes* that can be played concurrently. Single touch and multi-touch gestures generate softer and louder sounds respectively. Sliding the TUI's across the display changes the size of the fragments. The pitch of the *note* changes based on the fragment's position on the screen. Another feature includes a circular array of graphic buttons around the base of each TUI that generate glowing pulses at regular intervals when touch activated. These visual pulses travel outward along the lines emanating from the TUI and create a percussive sound when they cross an intersecting line. Moving the TUI so that the lines intersect at different points can vary the pitch of the sound. For example, intersecting lines nearer and further away from the base of the TUI raises and lowers the pitch of the *pulse* respectively. Finally, rapidly rotating the TUI controls the playback speed of an *atmosphere* sound (e.g. sound recordings of nature - wind, running water). Turning the TUI clockwise and anti-clockwise plays the atmosphere forward or backwards respectively. A circular ring around the base of the TUI represents this feature. The volume of the *atmosphere* can be adjusted using a pinch-like finger gesture over the ring. For example, pinching the ring inward reduces the volume. Using a combination of these simple gestures and movements described, participants can collaborate together easily to create complex soundscapes.

In *Paint Wars* players **compete** in a race to collect a number of shapes that match the color and shape of their TUI (see Fig. 4). The shapes are gathered into a corresponding colored circular home base assigned to each player in one of four locations around each edge of the display. Players shoot a set amount of colored paint from the base of their TUI by touching the TUI to activate the stream of paint. The shapes swim along and move toward the home base if the virtual paint color matches. Players can spread the paint using their fingers to create colored pathways for the shapes to swim. The paint moves and reacts to touch using a 2D fluid simulation that mixes and blends the colors in complex ways. More paint can be added to the scene by refilling the TUI at the players' home base.

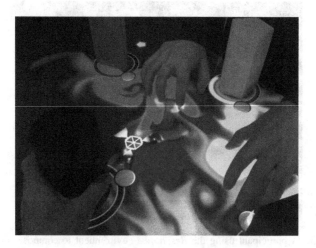

Fig. 4. Two participants playing *Paint Wars*

Players are instructed to create enough paint of their color to attract and guide the shapes they are collecting. Moreover, to increase the level of difficulty a series of virtual 'pests' can be added to the game to disrupt the player collecting their shapes. The pests include *Magnets* that momentarily draw shapes toward them, *Ink Drains* that attract and consume nearby paint, *Sprayers* that shoot out inverse paint color as they move, *Repulsors* that push the shapes away, *Whirlygigs* that mix the paint around, and *Foils* that use the paint to seek out a corresponding home base and steal shapes collected by players. Memorizing the functions of these entities is not important, but rather players should be able to dynamically respond to their influence on the shapes.

3   Preliminary User Evaluation

The current pilot study aimed to characterize the Resonance experience of patients with ABI and to determine the suitability and usability of the Resonance for this population. A total of 4 patients with ABI (Mean age = 41.5 years, SD = 21.73 years, 2 females, 2 males) were recruited for the pilot study, including one patient with acute demyelinating encephalomyelitis, two patients with TBI and one with stroke. A summary of the clinical and demographic information of the patients can be found in Table 1. The ABI patients were tested at least 4 months post-injury when neurological recovery was stabilized, corresponding to the sub-acute (> 2 weeks) stages of injury. The patients were still participating in the sub-acute phase of rehabilitation. The mean interval between the injury and our pilot session was 15 months. The mean age at injury was 40 years (SD 21.56 years). Exclusion criteria were pre-existing central neurological disorders, and musculoskeletal injury. The study was carried out in accordance with the principles of the Declaration of Helsinki and approved by the local ethics committee. Consent was obtained from all subjects.

Table 1. Summary of demographic and injury characteristics for the ABI group

Patient ID/Age/Gender/Handedness	Age at Onset	Condition	Hemiplegic Presentation	Level of Education	Clinical Presentation
ABI 1: KI 25/F/RH	23	Acute demyelinating encephalomyelitis	Left Side	Tertiary	a dense left hemi-paresis with dystonia
ABI 2: RE 50/F/RH	49	TBI – Traffic Collision Coma - 53 days	Left Side	Tertiary	GCS - 5 Subdural hematoma, diffuse axonal injury
ABI 3: IA 18/M/RH	17	TBI – Traffic Collision Coma – 110 days	Right Side	High School	GCS – 3 Left frontal parietal contusions, diffuse axonal injury
ABI 4: ER 73/M/RH	71	Stroke	Right Side	Tertiary	a dense right hemi-paresis

Participants were instructed to train for three sessions per virtual environment (i.e. Synchroshapes, Resonance, and Paint Wars), with approximately 12 min per session. For this pilot study, we divided the participants into pairs (Group 1 and Group 2). After experiencing each virtual environment, the participants were asked to complete an experience questionnaire and rate the following factors: (1) Engagement/enjoyment (e.g. Did you enjoy the musical sounds and/or sound effects?); (2) Feeling of control/usability (e.g. Did you know what to do with the objects?); (3) Effectiveness/success (e.g. Did you learn new ways to improve your movement?); and (4) Interaction with the other patient (e.g., How well did the system encourage you to interact with others while playing?). At the end of the procedure the participants were asked to fill in the Intrinsic Motivation Inventory [30] and they were asked which of the three environments they found the most enjoyable. The entire experimental procedure took place during a 60-min session for each pair in a room located in the rehabilitation center.

4   Results of the Evaluation

Synchroshapes. Individuals in Group 1 (KI and RE) and Group 2 (IA and ER) were engaged and enjoyed the environment. Both groups were able to perform the task. Despite a range of impairments (such as hemiplegia) all individuals were able to hold the objects (even with their hemiplegic hand) and perform the placement of the objects on the targets. They understood the task instructions. For instance, participant ER, who presented with more severe cognitive defects than the other three, took longer to understand the timing requirements of the task. This highlights the need for flexibility in the introduction of the VEs, to allow participants to learn at their own pace. Competency was mixed – consistent with the injury and cognitive loading. The environment allowed a level of co-operation between participants. For example, Group 1 verbalized a countdown together as a strategy to synchronize their movements, whereas Group 2 used visual timing because one of the participants was non-verbal and less able to communicate.

Resonance. There was initial willingness and interest to engage with the environment. However, there was a rapid drop off in interest and motivation. We attribute this to the exploratory, user-driven, interaction style of Resonance potentially being counter-intuitive to the patients, in comparison to their typical rehabilitation.

In conventional rehabilitation, patients are accustomed to receiving instructions on which actions to perform, and then performing them. With the Resonance VE, participants may have been confused by the user-driven interaction style. In future, a brief discussion on how the Resonance VE operates as a rehabilitation tool will be provided to patients. Nevertheless, all participants rated their experience with Resonance positively, in terms of usability, and audio and visual design. In addition to the data on participants' interaction with the system, we also considered the environmental constraints and influences on their experience. For instance, we noted that the ambient noise of the rehabilitation environment might have been distracting, as we were unable to exclude ambient noise from the training environment. This had a noticeable impact on the audio feedback quality in the Resonance environment and reduced their level of immersion.

Paint Wars. Group 1 competed well together and understood the task. They reported a sense of 'losing track of time', were immersed in the game's interactivity, were enthusiastic about using all of the game's features, and expressed a desire to play the game again. Participants KI and RE both rated their interaction with Paint Wars highly, in all areas.

Group 2 were not competitive in performing the task. Overall, they gave the impression of being two single-users operating on the same screen. Both participants had difficulty remembering the task parameters, and interface controls, and required constant prompting on how to interact with the environment. As stated above, the participants in Group 2 presented with greater cognitive and communicative impairment than KI, and RE. Thus, we have concluded that the design of Paint Wars may need to accommodate a more gradual learning curve. Alternatively, it may indicate a higher baseline for cognitive function required for successfully utilizing this environment. Assessing these possibilities will be part of the next stages of development and testing.

5 Conclusion

Overall our preliminary findings from the usability trial have produced positive results, which justifies its continued development and testing. Situating and testing the system in the actual working environment of the hospital was invaluable to our work. This allowed us to field test and gain insights into how patients used Resonance and how we may improve the system. We observed that each mode of play encouraged a range of social and physical interactions between groups of players. Players were able to observe others' success in accomplishing certain tasks, which in turn may provide a sense of self-efficacy to the observer that they might also have the ability to accomplish the task. Importantly, the participants were able to use the Resonance system to coordinate multiple everyday upper-limb movements related to fine motor control and touch, moving and orientating their arm in space, and modulating the force with which they are manipulating an object. These are functional motor skills that ABI patients struggle to perform and are able to practice in a fun, motivating, and engaging way using the Resonance system.

Based on the information gathered in this usability study, the next stages for the Resonance system will be to refine the design and the administration procedures. We will expand our research to include larger sample outcome studies, including pre-post designs, trialing Resonance over several sessions, and assessing near and far transfer effects from the training.

Resonance provides a novel multi-user solution that has the potential to maximize patients' potential to "learn from others", to develop social skills and confidence, and to instill motivation to work harder with fellow patients. Our study indicates that tabletop rehabilitation activities that incorporate co-located social play afford a powerful therapeutic tool to engage individuals with brain injury socially in rehabilitation and motivate them to participate in therapy.

Acknowledgements. This work is supported by an Australian Research Council (ARC) Linkage Grant LP110200802, and Synapse Grant awarded by the Australia Council for the Arts.

References

1. Murphy, T.H., Corbett, D.: Plasticity during stroke recovery: from synapse to behaviour. Nat. Rev. Neurosci. **10**(12), 861–872 (2009)

2. Esbensen, A.J., Rojahn, J., Aman, M.G., Ruedrich, S.: Reliability and validity of an assessment instrument for anxiety, depression, and mood among individuals with mental retardation. J. Autism. Dev. Disord. **33**(6), 617–629 (2003)
3. Starkstein, S.E., Pahissa, J.: Apathy following traumatic brain injury. Psychiatr. Clin. North Am. **37**(1), 103–112 (2014)
4. Green, D., Schertz, M., Gordon, A.M., Moore, A., Schejter Margalit, T., Farquharson, Y., Ben Bashat, D., Weinstein, M., Lin, J.P., Fattal-Valevski, A.: A multi-site study of functional outcomes following a themed approach to hand–arm bimanual intensive therapy for children with hemiplegia. Dev. Med. Child Neurol. **55**(6), 527–533 (2013)
5. Aarts, P.B., Hartingsveldt, M., Anderson, P.G., Tillaar, I., Burg, J., Geurts, A.C.: The pirate group intervention protocol: description and a case report of a modified constraint-induced movement therapy combined with bimanual training for young children with unilateral spastic cerebral palsy. Occup. Ther. Int. **19**(2), 76–87 (2012)
6. Tatla, S.K., Sauve, K., Virji-Babul, N., Holsti, L., Butler, C., Loos, H.F.M.: Evidence for outcomes of motivational rehabilitation interventions for children and adolescents with cerebral palsy: an american academy for cerebral palsy and developmental medicine systematic review. Dev. Med. Child Neurol. **55**(7), 593–601 (2013)
7. Pietrzak, E., Pullman, S., McGuire, A.: Using virtual reality and videogames for traumatic brain injury rehabilitation: A structured literature review. Games Health Res. Dev. Clin. Appl. **3**(4), 202–214 (2014)
8. Kruger, R., Carpendale, S., Scott, S., Greenberg, S.: How People use orientation on tables: comprehension, coordination and communication. In: GROUP 2003, AMC Press (2003)
9. Dietz, P., Leigh, D.: DiamondTouch: a multi-user touch technology. In: Proceedings of the 14th Annual ACM Symposium on User Interface Software and Technology, pp. 219–226. ACM, Orlando (2001)
10. Wellner, P.: Interacting with paper on the Digital Desk. Commun. ACM **36**(7), 87–96 (1993)
11. Scott, S., Grant, K., Mandryk, R.: System guidelines for co-located, collaborative work on a tabletop display. In: Proceedings of the 2003 Eighth European Conference on Computer-Supported Cooperative Work (2003)
12. Wu, M., Balakrishnan, R.: Multi-finger and whole hand gestural interaction techniques for multi-user tabletop displays. In: UIST 2003, pp. 193–202. AMC Press (2003)
13. Ullmer, B., Ishii, H.: The metaDESK: models and prototypes for tangible user interfaces. In: UIST 1997, pp. 223–232. ACM Press (1997)
14. Rick, J., Marshall, P., Yuill, N.: Beyond one-size-fits-all: how interactive tabletops support collaborative learning. In: IDC 2011, Ann Arbor (2011)
15. Fleck, R., Rogers, Y., Yuill, N., Marshall, P., Carr, A., Rick, J., Bonnett, V.: Actions speak loudly with words: unpacking collaboration around the table. In: ITS 2009, New York (2009)
16. Giusti, L., Zancanaro, M., Gal, E., Weiss, P.: Dimensions of collaboration on a tabletop interface for children with autism spectrum disorder. In: CHI 2011, AMC Press (2011)
17. Duckworth, J., Wilson, P.H.: Embodiment and play in designing an interactive art system for movement rehabilitation. Second Nat. **2**(1), 120–137 (2010)
18. Mumford, N., Duckworth, J., Thomas, P.R., Shum, D., Williams, G., Wilson, P.H.: Upper limb virtual rehabilitation for traumatic brain injury: initial evaluation of the elements system. Brain Inj. **24**(5), 780–791 (2010)
19. Mumford, N., Duckworth, J., Thomas, P.R., Shum, D., Williams, G., Wilson, P.H.: Upper-limb virtual rehabilitation for traumatic brain injury: a preliminary within-group evaluation of the elements system. Brain Inj. **26**(2), 166–176 (2012)

20. Duckworth, J., Thomas, P.R., Shum, D., Wilson, P.H.: Designing co-located tabletop interaction for rehabilitation of brain injury. In: Marcus, A. (ed.) DUXU 2013, Part II. LNCS, vol. 8013, pp. 391–400. Springer, Heidelberg (2013)
21. Dourish, P.: Where the Action is: The Foundations of Embodied Interaction. MIT Press, Cambridge (2001)
22. Gajadhar, B., de Kort, Y.A.W., Ijsselsteijn, W.A.: Rules of engagement: influence of co-player presence on player involvement in digital games. Int. J. Gaming Computer-Mediated Simul. **1**(3), 14–27 (2009)
23. Multitaction. Accessed from: http://www.multitaction.com
24. Ishii, H.: Tangible Bits: beyond Pixels, In: TEI 2008. 2008, AMC Press: New York. pp. xv-xxv (2008)
25. Rizzo, A.A.: A SWOT analysis of the field of virtual reality rehabilitation and therapy. Presence **14**(2), 119–146 (2005)
26. Ishii, H., Ullmer, B.: Tangible bits: towards seamless interfaces between people, bits and atoms. In: SIGCHI Conference on Human Factors in Computing Systems. ACM Press, Atlanta (1997)
27. McCrea, P.H., Eng, J.J., Hodgson, A.J.: Biomechanics of reaching: clinical implications for individuals with acquired brain injury. Disabil. Rehabil. **24**(10), 534–541 (2002)
28. Unity 3D. http://www.unity3d.com
29. TUIO. http://www.tuio.org
30. McAuley, E., Duncan, T., Tammen, V.V.: Psychometric properties of the intrinsic motivation inventory in a competitive sport setting: a confirmatory factor analysis. Res. Q. Exerc. Sport **60**(1), 48–58 (1989)

Increasing *Super Pop VR*^{TM} Users' Intrinsic Motivation by Improving the Game's Aesthetics

Sergio García-Vergara$^{(\boxtimes)}$, Hongfei Li, and Ayanna M. Howard

Electrical and Computer Engineering Department,
Georgia Institute of Technology, 85 5th Street NW,
Atlanta, GA 30332, USA
{sergio.garcia,hli311}@gatech.edu, ayanna.howard@ece.gatech.edu

Abstract. During physical therapy intervention protocols, it's important to consider the individual's intrinsic motivation to perform in-home recommended exercises. Physical therapy exercises can become tedious thus limiting the individual's progress. Not only have researchers developed serious gaming systems to increase user motivation, but they have also worked on the design aesthetics since results have shown positive effects on the users' performance for attractive models. As such, we improved the aesthetics of a previously developed serious game called *Super Pop VR*^{TM}. Namely, we improved the game graphics, added new game features, and allowed for more game options to provide users the opportunity to tailor their own experience. The conducted user studies show that participants rank the version of the game with the improved aesthetics higher in terms of the amount of interest/enjoyment it generates, thus allowing for an increase in intrinsic motivation when interacting with the system.

Keywords: Technological rehabilitation · Super Pop VR^{TM} · Physical therapy · Game aesthetics · Serious games

1 Introduction

In general, individuals with a motor skill disorder are required to engage in some form of physical therapy. Some common disorders include, but are not limited to: cerebral palsy, Parkinson's disease, and motor impairment due to stroke. Although the benefits of physical therapy are well-documented, many individuals fail to perform the recommended in-home exercises. For example, M. Shaughnessy et al. [1] reported that only 31 % of the 312 stroke survivors that participated in the study exercised four times weekly. They concluded that maintaining an exercise program has the potential to improve physical function in the target population. As such, clinicians use gaming platforms for serious games as part of intervention protocols to increase the individual's self-efficacy and intrinsic motivation to perform the recommended in-home exercises. In general, serious games are defined as "(digital) games used for purposes other than

© Springer International Publishing Switzerland 2015
M. Antona and C. Stephanidis (Eds.): UAHCI 2015, Part III, LNCS 9177, pp. 432–441, 2015.
DOI: 10.1007/978-3-319-20684-4_42

mere entertainment" [2]. More specifically, serious games for rehabilitation can affect the physiological and psychological outcomes for individuals in different scenarios. In this paper, we focus primarily on virtual reality (VR) rehabilitation games in physical therapy interventions. We have previously developed a VR game called *Super Pop VR^{TM}* [3,4]. It combines interactive game play for evoking user movement with an objective and quantifiable kinematic algorithm to analyze the user's upper-body movements in real-time. During game play, users are asked to move their arms to 'pop' virtual bubbles that appear on screen while a three-dimensional (3D) depth camera maps the user's movements into the virtual environment.

Previous studies have shown that physical appearance in the design aesthetics has a positive effect on the users' performance for attractive models [5]. We adhere to these results and focused this work on improving the game's aesthetics such that it increases the user's intrinsic motivation to interact with the *Super Pop VR^{TM}* game thus allowing for improvements in physical function. In addition to improving the game's appearance, we also modified the game's structure such that users have the option of selecting different combinations of game settings/features to allow for a more interactive experience.

In this paper, we present a set of new features that increases the users' intrinsic motivation to comply with their intervention protocols. Section 2 presents a short literary review on previously developed virtual reality gaming systems with a similar purpose. Section 3 discusses in detail the procedure taken to implement said features. Section 4 presents the results obtained in testing sessions with human participants. Finally, we analyze the results in Sect. 5, and make our concluding remarks in Sect. 6.

2   Background

Previous studies have identified the benefits of using virtual reality (VR) systems in the rehabilitation setting. The study conducted by Viau et al. [6] showed that both healthy individuals and those with motor deficits used similar movement strategies when performing different tasks in the virtual and reality environments. They concluded that the training of arm movements in virtual environments may be a valid approach to the rehabilitation of individuals with motor skills deficiencies. Holden et al. [7] conducted a study with two stroke patients who interacted with the telerehabilitation system they developed. They concluded that both individuals demonstrated an improvement on kinematic measures of upper-extremity trajectories performed in the real world, indicating that the training in the virtual environment was transferred to real-world performance.

Based on the positive results obtained from studies conducted on VR systems in the physical therapy setting, various serious games have been developed to aid physiotherapists and increase the efficacy of the intervention protocols. Ma et al. [8] developed a VR game that adapts to the user's needs in order to maintain the rehabilitation tasks at an appropriate level of challenge and thus maintaining the user's motivation to continue performing the recommended tasks. Moreover, an effective rehabilitation protocol must be early, intensive, and repetitive, which can lead to problems with patient motivation and engagement. In the spirit of developing more effective systems for stroke rehabilitation in terms of good user engagement, Burke et al. [9] identified different game design principles for stroke rehabilitation and developed several games that employ these principles. Finally, Reid [10] conducted a study using the Mandala Gesture Xtreme technology, which uses a video camera that maps the users movements to the presented virtual environment. Comments from the three children with cerebral palsy that participated in the study showed a high degree of motivation and interest, thus suggesting the viability of a VR play-based intervention as part of the children's intervention protocols.

Based on the benefits identified by previous studies, we improved the aesthetics of the *Super Pop VR^{TM}* game such that it provides an environment that encourages the users to perform the recommended exercises thus improving the effectiveness of their intervention protocols.

3   Methodology

3.1   Game Updates

As described in [3,4], the goal of the *Super Pop VR^{TM}* game is to 'pop' as many bubbles as possible in the allotted amount of time. The original version of the game employs colored circles as bubbles and provides no costumes or options for the users to choose from (Fig. 1). Among other modifications, we improved upon the gaming graphics by interchanging the colored circles for images that better resemble an actual bubble and introduced different 'hats' that follow the user's heads such that they (especially children) can enjoy seeing themselves 'wearing' various costumes throughout their interactions with the game (Fig. 2).

The costumes overlay and re-size according to the location of the patient and the distance between the patient and the camera. We implemented a linear model with a calibrated distance to size in order to adjust the width and height of the costume that is overlayed. Due to the fact that different costumes are worn with different style, relative position of the costume changes according to its type. For example a medieval knight helmet is positioned 15 pixels above the center of the player's head, while a wizard hat is positioned 45 pixels above the center point of the player's head. Chroma key compositing (green screen) is implemented to enable patients to customize the environment they want to play in. Having customizable gaming graphics motivates the patients and increases the gaming engagement.

The new game settings has been made much easier and safer to use for both patients and therapists. It contains the regular graphics settings and the advanced settings. The graphics settings allow patients to select their own costumes, game play music, and VR display brightness. The advanced setting window is password protected and is meant to be used by therapists only. This password protection layer ensures that patients can modify the game to make

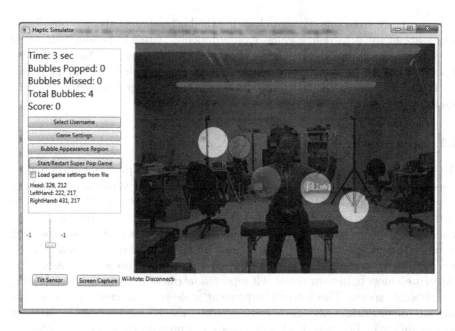

Fig. 1. Main interface of the *Super Pop VR*^{TM} game's original version showing colored circles as representation of the virtual bubbles (Color figure online)

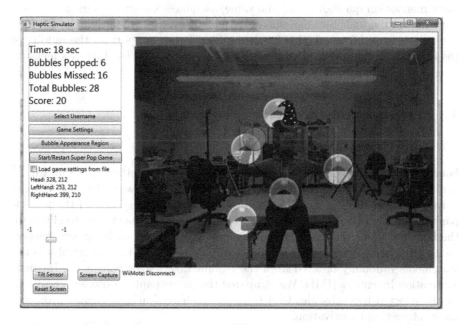

Fig. 2. Main interface of the *Super Pop VR*^{TM} game's updated version showing bubble images as representation of the virtual bubbles and the 'Wizard Hat' as an example of the available 'helmet' options (Color figure online)

the game more enjoyable without changing the backend analysis methods. Therapists are enabled to define game mode, difficulty, game duration, number of levels, game speed, good and bad bubble ratio, bubble size, bubble scores, etc. The game is highly customizable so that therapists can design completely different games for every single patient according to his/her up-body movement ability.

3.2   Assessment Methodology

We used the Intrinsic Motivation Inventory (IMI) to compare the participants' responses after interacting with the original and updated versions of the *Super Pop VR^{TM}* game. The IMI is a device intended to assess participants' subjective experience related to a target activity in laboratory experiments [11]. The instrument measures the participants' self-reported motivation by assessing several subscales. In this study, we focused on assessing the participants' interest/enjoyment, perceived competence, effort/importance, pressure/tension, and value/usefulness to measure their self-reported intrinsic motivation, thus yielding five subscale scores. The interest/enjoyment scale is considered the self-report measure of intrinsic motivation, thus we focus the better part of the analysis on this subscale. The perceived competence and pressure/tension sub-scales are theorized to be a positive and negative predictors of self-report of intrinsic motivation respectively. Effort is considered to be an additional relevant variable to some motivation questions, and the value/usefulness sub-scale is used to determine how individuals become self-regulating with respect to activities that they experience as useful or valuable for themselves. Strong support for the validity of the IMI was found in [12]. Thus, various studies have used the IMI as a measure of self-report of intrinsic motivation [13–15].

4   Experimental Results

4.1   Experimental Setup

Fourteen able-bodied adults were recruited to interact with the *Super Pop VR^{TM}* system. Nine females and five males ranging in age between 18 and 31 years played both the original and updated versions of the game. None of the participants had any previous interactions with any version of the system to eliminate the bias that their relative experience might provide. For each version, participants were asked to choose the most appropriate responses to a subset of selected statements randomly ordered from the 7-point Likert scale that is the Intrinsic Motivation Inventory (IMI). We compared the participants' responses organized by the selected five subscales to determine which version of the game promotes more interest and motivation.

Participants played two games for each version such that they could have enough experience to get familiarized with the system. When interacting with the original version of the game (Fig. 1), the virtual bubbles were represented as colored circles, no 'hats' were provided, the bubble popping sound was constant for the two games, and no game options were provided to the user. When interacting with the updated version of the game (Fig. 2), the virtual bubbles were represented with colored images that better resemble bubbles, four 'hat' options and four bubble popping sounds were provided for the users to choose from before each game, and users were allowed to select the size and appearance speed of the bubbles to better tailor their own experience. The order of the game versions they interacted with was randomized to reduce the bias of the participants' responses.

4.2   Qualitative Results

We compiled the answers of all participants and organized the scores by the selected five IMI subscales. Figure 3 shows the comparison of average IMI scores ± 1 std between the original and updated versions of the game for each subscale. Looking at the interest/enjoyment subscale, the average score for the original version of the game was **5.7 ± 0.52** while the average score for the updated version was **5.8 ± 0.51**. Similarly, looking at the value/usefulness subscale, the score for the original game was **5.5 ± 0.29** while the score for the updated version was **5.6 ± 0.42**.

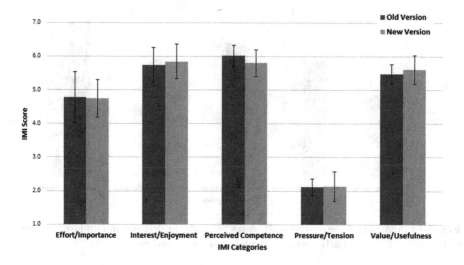

Fig. 3. Comparison of the average IMI scores from all participants between the original and updated versions of the game organized by the selected subscales

We also wanted to investigate if there were any trends related to the order in which the participants interacted with the *Super Pop VR^{TM}* game. Figures 4 and 5 show the average IMI scores ± 1 std for both versions of the game for the participants that interacted with the original version first and for the participants that interacted with the updated version first respectively.

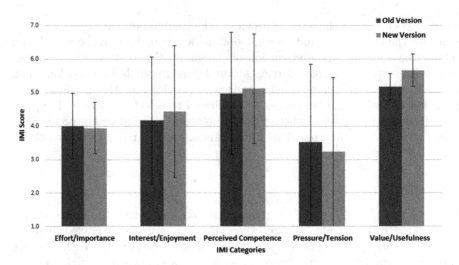

Fig. 4. Comparison of the average IMI scores between the original and updated versions of the game from the participants that played the original version first

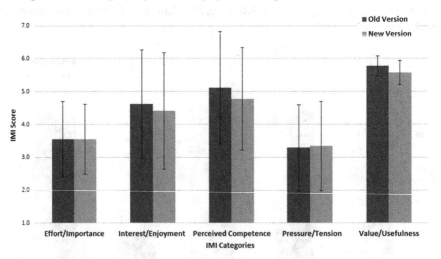

Fig. 5. Comparison of the average IMI scores between the original and updated versions of the game from the participants that played the updated version first

5   Analysis

Although not significant, the results shown in Fig. 3 suggest that participants favored the updated version of the Super Pop VR game over the original version. In terms of the interest/enjoyment IMI subscale, participants maintained their interest and better enjoyed the version of the game that provided more options and features to choose from. In terms of the value/usefulness subscale, they determined that the experience was useful and/or valuable for themselves.

Moreover, all participants gave the pressure/tension subscale a relatively low score for both versions making a positive prediction in the users' self-report of intrinsic motivation. These findings confirm our hypothesis that attractive models increase motivation and user performance thus allowing for an improvement in the efficacy of the recommended intervention protocol. It's important to keep in mind that the interest/enjoyment subscale is the one that assesses intrinsic motivation per se. As such, even though participants gave the original version a higher score in the effort/importance and perceived competence subscales, we can still conclude that updated version of the game promotes more interest than the original version. These results just mean that the participants put in more effort, and thought to be more competent when interacting with the original version of the game.

There is something to be said about the similar scores in all five subscales. Even though the results favor the updated version, it's not by much. This suggests that the original version of the *Super Pop VR^{TM}* game is still engaging and interesting as is. Future work can include a study that further increases the game's aesthetics to determine if there is a bound on how much more interest can the developed system promote.

Figures 4 and 5 show that the order in which users interact with the game matters. The trend in both figures determines that participants favored the second system which they interacted with in terms of the interest/enjoyment and value/usefulness. From Fig. 4, the participants that played the original version first favored the updated game. From Fig. 5, the participants that played the updates version first favored the original game. This trend may have surfaced because of inexperience given that none of the participants had interacted with the *Super Pop VR^{TM}* game before. It may be the case that participants did not fully enjoyed themselves in the first round of games because they were worrying about their initial performance. In general, the more they played the game, the more comfortable they got and the more they enjoyed it regardless of the added game features. However, it's also important to note that the standard deviation for the interest/enjoyment subscale is very high for both scenarios: ± 1.90 for the original game in the case where the original version was played first, and ± 1.78 for the updated version in the case where the updated version was played first. This suggests that the responses are not consistent. Possibly due to the fact that only half the population is considered in each group. As such, more data would help reduce the variation in responses.

6   Conclusion and Future Work

After improving the *Super Pop VR^{TM}* game's aesthetics and updating the game structure, the overall participants' self-reported motivation was slightly higher when interacting with the updated version of the game as determined by the Intrinsic Motivation Inventory (IMI). This suggests that, because of the improved game aesthetics, users can improve their performance when interacting with the system. However, it's important to keep in mind that the study's results are limited by targeted population. The volunteers that were recruited for this study were young adults even though the final system is targeted to children who have some form of motor skills disorder. As such, additional studies will need to be conducted in order to determine the level of self-reported motivation a child has when interacting with the *Super Pop VR*^{TM} game. Another item to keep in mind is that there is a possibility that the game users' self-reported motivation may vary as a function of their experience with the system.

In the meantime, we can conclude that the developed system has the potential to be used in the rehabilitation setting. By maintaining the user's interest and enjoyment while reducing the pressure and tension of complying with the recommended intervention protocol, the *Super Pop VR*^{TM} game can increase the efficacy of said protocol thus helping users make progress in their physical therapy.

Acknowledgments. This work was supported in part by the NSF Graduate Research Fellowship under Grant No. DGE-1148903, and NSF Grant 1208287. Any opinions, findings, and conclusions or recommendations expressed in this material are those of the author's and do not necessarily reflect the views of the National Science Foundation.

References

1. Shaughnessy, M., Resnick, B.M., Macko, R.F.: Testing a model of post-stroke exercise behavior. Rehabil. Nurs. **31**(1), 15–21 (2006)
2. Susi, T., Johannesson, M., Backlund, P.: Serious games: an overview (2007)
3. García-Vergara, S., Chen, Y.-P., Howard, A.M.: Super Pop VR^{TM}: an adaptable virtual reality game for upper-body rehabilitation. In: Shumaker, R. (ed.) VAMR 2013, Part II. LNCS, vol. 8022, pp. 40–49. Springer, Heidelberg (2013)
4. García-Vergara, S., Brown, L., Park, H.W., Howard, A.M.: Engaging children in play therapy: the coupling of virtual reality games with social robotics. In: Brooks, A.L., Brahnam, S., Jain, L.C. (eds.) Technologies of Inclusive Well-Being. SCI, pp. 139–163. Springer, New York (2014)
5. Sonderegger, A., Sauer, J.: The influence of design aesthetics in usability testing: Effects on user performance and perceived usability. Appl. Ergon. **41**(3), 403–410 (2010)
6. Viau, A., Feldman, A.G., McFadyen, B.J., Levin, M.F.: Reaching in reality and virtual reality: a comparison of movement kinematics in healthy subjects and in adults with hemiparesis. J. Neuroeng. Rehabil. **1**, 11 (2004)
7. Holden, M.K., Dyar, T.A., Schwamm, L., Bizzi, E.: Virtual-environment-based telerehabilitation in patients with stroke. Presence: Teleoperat. Virtual Env. **14**(2), 214–233 (2005)
8. Ma, M., McNeill, M., Charles, D., McDonough, S., Crosbie, J., Oliver, L., McGoldrick, C.: Adaptive virtual reality games for rehabilitation of motor disorders. In: Stephanidis, C. (ed.) UAHCI 2007 (Part II). LNCS, vol. 4555, pp. 681–690. Springer, Heidelberg (2007)
9. Burke, J.W., McNeill, M., Charles, D.K., Morrow, P.J., Crosbie, J.H., McDonough, S.M.: Optimising engagement for stroke rehabilitation using serious games. Vis. Comput. **25**(12), 1085–1099 (2009)

10. Reid, D.T.: Benefits of a virtual play rehabilitation environment for children with cerebral palsy on perceptions of self-efficacy: a pilot study. Dev. Neurorehabil. **5**(3), 141–148 (2002)
11. Deci, E., Ryan, R.: Intrinsic motivation theory (2000). Accessed 3 February 2015
12. McAuley, E., Duncan, T., Tammen, V.V.: Psychometric properties of the intrinsic motivation inventory in a competitive sport setting: a confirmatory factor analysis. Res. Q. Exerc. Sport **60**(1), 48–58 (1989)
13. Ryan, R.M.: Control and information in the intrapersonal sphere: an extension of cognitive evaluation theory. J. Personal. Soc. Psychol. **43**(3), 450 (1982)
14. Plant, R.W., Ryan, R.M.: Intrinsic motivation and the effects of self-consciousness, self-awareness, and ego-involvement: an investigation of internally controlling styles. J. Personal. **53**(3), 435–449 (1985)
15. Ryan, R.M., Connell, J.P., Plant, R.W.: Emotions in nondirected text learning. Learn. Individ. Differ. **2**(1), 1–17 (1990)

Games for Change: The Strategic Design of Interactive Persuasive Systems

Igor Revoredo Hosse[✉] and Rachel Zuanon

Sense Design Lab, PhD and Master's Design Program, Anhembi Morumbi University,
São Paulo, Brazil
igrhosse@anhembimorumbi.edu.br, igor.hosse@gmail.com,
rzuanon@anhembi.br, rachel.z@zuannon.com.br

Abstract. Games for Change are designed to promote positive social impacts leading to reflection and behavior change of the players. However, it is a challenge to develop games that are motivators and, at the same time, stimulate positive changes. Therefore, in order to help designers to achieve these objectives, thirteen (13) design elements divided into three (3) structural strategic foci were proposed. To validate these elements, the Games for Change Ecocity (Brazil) and Half The Sky – The Game (USA) were analyzed. As a result, the design elements proposal helped to identify which aspects of each one of the analyzed games were responsible for the performance regarding the players behavior change and ability to motivate.

Keywords: Game Design · Games for Change · Motivation to Play · Flow

1 Introduction

Currently the planet spends more than 3 billion hours played per week [1]. If on one hand the consumption of digital games is increasing, on the other there are societal concerns on the impact of these experiences on players. According to Bogost [2], games are an expressive media able to generate radical changes in the behavior of the players and society. In this regard, researchers agree there is room to develop games aiming to contribute positively to the society [3–5].

Among the various types of increasingly popular digital games, Games for Change (GfC) belong to a special category of games intended to make players to consider, reflect and act in social and political issues, helping to promote positive change in the society.

GfC are included in a larger group identified as Serious Games, which include all games that have other explicit objectives in addition to entertainment. Despite having a small fraction of researchers, there are more developers who are interested in creating games that promote social impact. However, many games in this category are unable to motivate the players.

However, it seems to be difficult to achieve this objective because there is some resistance to Serious Games in general - which include GfC – given that many of them fail to provide motivation [6, 7].

© Springer International Publishing Switzerland 2015
M. Antona and C. Stephanidis (Eds.): UAHCI 2015, Part III, LNCS 9177, pp. 442–453, 2015.
DOI: 10.1007/978-3-319-20684-4_43

Thus, a set of strategic design elements is proposed here with the goal of helping designers to create GfC that promote positive behavior changes and are motivators. Altogether, there are thirteen (13) elements divided into three (3) different structural strategic foci: definition of a social or political objective; selection and abstraction of a physical system; and development of a motivating game. The thirteen (13) elements are: objective; theme; scenario and relevance; context; selection of a physical system; abstraction of a physical system; validity; clear objectives; choices; appropriate challenge; immediate feedback; social connection and polishing.

Accordingly, the next section examines GfC as persuasive systems; the concept of procedural rhetoric is presented and its use in digital games. In the third section, the challenge of motivating the players is discussed through two theories – Flow and Self-Determination-Theory (SDT) – whose objective is to create intrinsic motivation in GfC. In the fourth section, three structural strategic foci and their design elements are proposed. In the last section, there is the comparative analysis between two games – Ecocity and Half The Sky Movement – The Game – with the results to the proposed design elements.

2   Games for Change as Persuasive Systems

For GfC to achieve their main objective, which is to promote reflection and positive behavior changes in players in the physical world[1], it is necessary that they have characteristics that persuade players to consider the social or political issue presented in the game.

In this regard, [2] states that digital games have the ability to create a special kind of rhetoric, the procedural rhetoric. According to him, games have a unique way of developing rhetoric through an abstraction of physical world systems, which are systems based on rules and interactions within the game, where players can experience the operation and thereafter interpret the system. Bogost [2] defines this unique type of game rhetoric as procedural rhetoric and classifies digital games as persuasive media. However, this rhetoric has specific characteristics compared to the traditional rhetoric: "I call this new form *procedural rhetoric*, the art of persuasion through rule-based representations and interactions rather than the spoken word, images, or moving pictures [2]".

In this sense, the procedural rhetoric is directly linked to the choices made by the digital game designers as to which elements of the physical world system they will use, which they will change and what they will create for the development of the game system. Depending on how the abstraction of the everyday world is developed, there is the possibility of persuading the players to reflect or positively change their behavior about a specific subject. Frank [8] argues that this abstraction should not mischaracterize the physical world because the players may have difficulty in applying their experiences in the game to the physical world. Consequently, there must be similarities between the game system and the physical world system.

---

[1] In this case, the term "physical world" is used to refer to the world outside the digital game.

3 The Motivation in Games for Change

Motivations can be divided into intrinsic and extrinsic [9]. While the intrinsic motivation activities refer to activities that are done regardless of any external reward because the making itself is the reward; extrinsic motivation activities are conducted considering some external factor and are usually considered less motivating when compared to the intrinsic activities [9, 10]. In this regard, Jull [3] states that digital games are usually played without the need for any external benefit. Therefore, the activity of playing digital games can usually be considered intrinsic.

Nevertheless, it is challenging to develop digital games that can create intrinsic motivation in the players. Thus, two theories have been used to support the proposal of design elements related to the creation of intrinsic motivation in GfC, they are: Theory of Flow and Self-Determination-Theory (SDT).

The Theory of Flow [10] is often employed [11, 12] as a tool for developing strategies aiming at increasing motivation in digital games. The Flow can be characterized as an experience of total absorption of the players in an activity in which there is the feeling of control and altered sense of time while they lose consciousness of "themselves". To achieve the Flow state, the activity has to have the chance of being completed, it has to have clear objectives and immediate feedback which allows total concentration [10]. As a result, GfC designers can provide the experience of total absorption of the players in the game by employing design elements aiming at ensuring the Flow.

Together, the SDT addresses three aspects not considered by the Theory of Flow: the need for autonomy; the importance of the relatedness; and the possibility of internalization of extrinsic motivation [9]. In this sense, this theory considers three basic needs for intrinsic motivation: competence, autonomy and relatedness.

Competence is an approach point between the Theory of Flow and SDT and highlights the need for challenge and the feeling of effectiveness as crucial elements for intrinsic motivation [13]. Consequently, the balance between the skills of the players and the challenges of the game is a priority in the development of current games [14]. On autonomy, Deci and Ryan [9] state this is one of the essential elements for intrinsic motivation and can be understood as the inverse of external control, in other words, a sense of freedom. Relatedness is another important point that may contribute to intrinsic motivation and to be understood as the experience of being connected with others [13]. These two aspects can contribute to the intrinsic motivation in GfC design in order to promote situations where the players have a greater chance of significant choices during the game, enhancing the player's experience variation, in addition to the connection tools with other players, allowing cooperation or competition among them.

4 Proposal of 3 Structural Strategic Foci for the Design of Games for Change

With the purpose of assisting GfC designers to overcome the challenge of creating a game that exploits a relevant issue for society and, at the same time, is motivating, three structural strategic foci are proposed: the definition of a social or political objective, selection and abstraction of a physical world system and the development of a motivating game. Each focus has a set of design elements specifying each point of attention in the game development.

The first focus - **definition of a social or political objective** - has four design elements: The **objective** (1) referring to the objective of the game as behavior change generator in the physical world; the **theme** (2) demonstrating the referred social or political issue; the **scenario and relevance** (3) that are connected to the environment developed for the game and their relevance regarding the game persuasion objective; and the **context** (4) discussing the relevance of the game to the social and political context of the physical world in which it is developed.

The second focus concerns the **selection and abstraction of a physical world system**. In this case the three design elements are: **Selection of a physical world system** (1) which identifies the physical system selected for the game and its alignment with the objective and theme of the game; the **abstraction of a physical world system** (2) which is related to the process of creating the game system and its similarity to the physical world system and **validity** (3) addressing the level of contribution of the game system with the theme and objective of the game.

The third focus – **development of a motivating game** - has six design elements directly related to the basic requirements for intrinsic motivation that are presented in the Theory of Flow and SDT, they are: **clear objectives** (1) referring to the clarity of the objectives in the game and its relation to the theme and objective of the game; **choices** (2) which relates to the level of freedom the game offers to the players; **appropriate challenge** (3) pointing to the difficulty presented by the game, which may result to the players motivation if balanced, or boredom and anxiety if it is unbalanced; **immediate feedback** (4) concerning the directions to the players on their position related to the objective of the game; **social connection** (5) dealing with the possibilities of the game in providing social connection tools for players and **polishing** (6) which addresses the use of visual or sound effects to further enhance the effectiveness of feedback.

5   Implementation, Results and Discussion

In order to validate the design elements of the three structural strategic foci presented, two GfC were analyzed. In order to ensure greater consistency in the analysis, there were chosen two games with characteristics as similar as possible to the platform and release date. Thus, the following games were selected: *Ecocity*[2] (Sioux[3], 2011) and *Half The Sky – The Game*[4] (Frima[5], 2013). Both are GfC on Facebook and they were released

---

[2] More information about the release of the Game for Change Ecocity available at: http://www.meioemensagem.com.br/home/midia/noticias/2011/06/01/20110530Fox-lanca-social-game-no-Dia-Mundial-do-Meio-Ambiente.html.

[3] More information available at: http://www.sioux.com.br/.

[4] More information about the release of Half The Sky – The Game available at: http://www.gamesforchange.org/2013/02/half-the-sky-movement-the-game-launches-march-4/.

[5] More information available at: http://www.frimastudio.com/.

with a gap of less than two years (June 2011 and March 2013), respectively. Both games obtained different performances regarding players access number and impact on the physical world. Regarding the ability to motivate the players, the site AppData[6] was used by the average position that is defined by the average number of accesses to the game compared to other games on Facebook in a given period of time. Accordingly, the most accessible game gets the first position. Thus, it can be noted that Half The Sky – the Game (HtS) had a weaker performance compared to Ecocity (Table 1) because they had lower average position in 2013, and still showed a greater tendency to drop on January 16th, 2014.

Table 1. Average position comparison between HtS and Ecocity with respect to *Facebook* accesses.

Game	2013	01/16/14
Ecocity	3921	4071
HtS	4322	5256

In order to measure the impact of the game HtS on the physical world, data provided by the game development team were used[7]. Consequently, by using tools within the game, such as direct links to provide cash aid or automatic donations by just playing the game, HtS got 250.00 donations of books, more than US$ 163.000 in donations for fistula surgeries and more than US$ 450.000 in direct donations to nonprofit organizations, representing a considerable impact on the physical world. However, Ecocity showed no tools in this regard, offering no directions to make the players act concretely in the physical world. As a side result, the game also showed no metric in that effect.

The results of each GfC, regarding the impact on the physical world and the players motivation, were used as a support for the analysis of games with respect to the proposed design elements. In addition to showing results similar to those presented by the website AppData and reports on the impact on the physical world, it was expected that the analysis also presented the main reasons why each game presented the respective results.

Therefore, the analysis of structural strategic foci was carried out as follows: for each design element, numerical values were assigned to classify how the game supports each one of them; zero indicates that it is not applicable because the game has not this feature to be evaluated; one means "partially meets"; and two represents "fully meets". In combination, the values of each element form an overall result for each structural focus. For easy reading, Table 2 shows the results for each focus.

---

[6] Website evaluating the popularity of online games through the number of accesses (www.appdata.com).

[7] Learn more at: http://www.gamesforchange.org/g4cwp/wp-content/uploads/2011/06/HTS_ImpactReport_October_web.pdf.

Table 2. Performance of GfC assessed according to the proposed design elements

Focus	HtS	Ecocity
(1) Definition of a social or political objective		
Objective	2	2
Theme	2	2
Scenario and relevance	2	1
Context	2	2
Average	**2**	**1.7**
(2) Selection and abstraction of a physical world system		
Selection of a physical system	2	1
Abstraction of a physical system	2	1
Validity	2	1
Average	**2**	**1**
(3) Development of a motivating game		
Clear objectives	2	2
Choices	1	2
Appropriate challenge	1	2
Immediate feedback	2	2
Social connection	2	2
Polishing	2	1
Average	**1.6**	**1.8**

5.1 Half the Sky Movement

HtS is part of a transmedia campaign (including a book, documentary, mobile games and game for Facebook) called Half the Sky Movement aiming to promote reflection and questioning of the women social oppression worldwide[8]. The player controls Radhika, an illiterate and poor woman who lives with her family in a modest house in India. Each game challenge is presented through a story related to several issues regarding women oppression, such as domestic violence and sexual exploitation. The first challenge the player faces, for an example, is when Radhika's daughter, Aditi, gets sick and the family does not have money to pay for her treatment. Thus, the player must

---

[8] More information available at: http://www.halftheskymovement.org/pages/movement.

find a way to earn money, but first, the player must face Radhika's sexist husband, Bhanu, who does not like the idea of his wife finding a solution by herself to help their daughter.

There are three possible ways to continue the game. First, there is a map in which the player picks his next quest (the quests are unlocked according to the player's performance). Second, there is the predefined dialogues interface in which the player must click on the answers they find most convenient leading to different results. Third, there is a collection mini-game (e.g. used to collect mangos), in which the player must connect the same elements and use them to continue.

HtS provides three essential resources, the **hope bonds**, **coins** and **energy**. Hope bonds are the fastest way to play, through the purchase of coins, energy and even other powers. They are rare in the game, but it is possible to buy them with the physical world money. The coins represent the money in the game and are earned through completion of some activities, such as selling fruit in the market. Energy is required to perform any task in the game, so it is the feature that runs out faster. When the energy goes out, the only solutions are to wait until it automatically recharges; buy it using the hope bonds or ask friends on Facebook who also play the game to donate energy. The quickest option is to buy the hope bonds with physical money, which is reversed in donations to NGOs involved with the cause. There are three other ways to make donations in the game. First, access a list of partners who are NGOs involved the same cause of the game, enter the website and look for a way to help, which can be, for example, sign a petition. Second, donate physical money to the cause directly by the game. Third, that is automatically, because as the player goes on and reaches a certain level, some partner companies provide donations to NGOs, for example, money for surgeries in the Fistula Foundation. Moreover, as it is on Facebook, the game encourages the player to provide information on the cause through posts.

Therefore, with respect to the focus number one, the game meets all the criteria. There is a social **objective**, which is to talk about the exploitation of women in developing countries. There is also a clear intention to lead the players to act for the cause, either through donations, unlock automatic donations, access partner NGOs or share information with friends. The **theme** has social background and is adequate for the objective of the game. The **scenario** chosen, some developing countries - India, Kenya, Afghanistan and Vietnam - is relevant to the objective of the game, given the conditions of oppression to which women are subjected in these countries. Finally, the **context** in which the game was released contributes to the objective and theme, since women oppression is currently a major issue in society.

In HtS, there is also compliance with focus number two. First, the chosen **physical world system**, which are the various social problems to be faced by women, complies with the theme and the objective of the game. Second, the **system developed for the game** does not mischaracterize the physical world system, as the quests deal with social problems often faced by women. Third, the system is **valid** because it contributes both to the theme of the game, which deals with the journey of Radhika against the problems that oppress women in developing countries, and for the social objective of the game, which is to talk about these social issues and also offer tools to conduct the largest number of players to actively participate in the cause.

With respect to focus number three, HtS achieved a varied performance. Regarding the **clear objectives**, HtS presents all the necessary elements. The game helps the player to understand what needs to be done through explanatory windows explaining from the general objective of the game to the objective of each quest. When there is more than a quest going on, the game has visual cues with animations to be clicked so that the player continues. In addition, all the quest objectives are aligned with the social objective of the game and, although they seem to be challenging, they are likely to be completed.

Nevertheless, concerning **choices**, HtS limits the options of the player, for though offering choices, they are not significant. For example, in a part of the first quest, the player must convince her husband to find a way to get money to pay for the treatment of their sick daughter. In this sense, the game offers two options to the player during the dialogue. The player can choose if Radhika will confront her husband or will agree with him and stay silent. Whatever the choice, the player must perform the same actions to complete the quest, including harvest mangos and sell them at the town market to earn some money. There are not other ways to get the money, which makes the quest poorly varied. The only difference between the answers is that the score received from remaining silent (3 points) is less than that score obtained for facing the husband (7 points). However, the missing points can be easily recovered by selling mangos at the market again.

Regarding the **appropriate difficulty level**, there are three game situations that only partially meet the issue. First, there is energy shortage. The energy runs out really fast and prevents the player from taking any action. To ask energy for Facebook friends is only a stopgap solution because they can only give little amount of energy (5 points) in large time intervals (1 h). Thus, for every action in the game, it is usually necessary 4 friends to donate energy. As friends are not always available, the player needs to wait for the points automatically increase or use physical money, which can frustrate or bore the player. Second, the penalty for the getting the wrong answer during the dialogues is low and does not affect the development of the game. The player is not challenged, which can take them to boredom. Third, there is the collection interface where the player must collect the highest number of points in a limited time. It also provides poor variation, preventing the player to create strategies to get more points. The player can buy powers, which increase the time available for collection or offer double points, but for that, the player needs the hope bonds, which are very rare. As to the **immediate feedback**, HtS is appropriate because it provides a number of indications to the player on their position related to the objective of the quest and the game. The player can check their current position in the quests through indicative windows. For every action in the game, there are windows that show the value of earned resources, and a wide range of sound effects for every action, including move your mouse over quests, complete quests and select items. On **social connection**, HtS works properly. The sense of competition is generated through the bar showing their friends who have accounts on Facebook and also play the game. It also indicates the level of each player for comparison. There is also the possibility of cooperation. An example is the quest in which Radhika gathers a group to search for her friend's aggressive husband, who is a fugitive. In this situation, the player can recruit Facebook friends to help and complete it faster. Another way is to wait for the game itself to free artificial helpers, which can take hours. As it is within Facebook, there is the possibility of communication and chat messages between the participants of the game, besides creation of groups. Regarding **polishing**, HtS has visual and sound effects appropriate to strengthen the feedbacks of the game. When the player wins or spends resources such as energy, they are displayed in the center of the graphic interface and then they move along with the sound effects, until reaching their respective resource bar indicating to the player the type of earned resource.

5.2 Ecocity

Facebook Ecocity was released on June 5th, 2011, the World Environment Day. Fully developed in Brazil, the game received the certification of the National Geographic Society[9] and aims to bring environmental discussions to the public, and also to have an impact in the physical world. The game does not have tools to direct the player to contribute directly to the cause, as donations. Therefore, there are no metrics available to verify the impact generated in the physical world.

The game is set in a fictional town that can be named by the player. The city faces problems like garbage in the streets, polluted river, abandoned buildings, air pollution and lack of energy. Through the resources offered by the game, the player must turn the city into an ecocity, that is, a sustainable city. In this regard, the player should pay attention to **quality of life** points. It begins negative, so the player's objective is to change it for positive points. With **ecocredits**, it is possible to buy other resources, such as energy, to go faster in the game. For each action or quest completed, **experience points** are awarded releasing new constructions for the player to use in the city. **Energy** is used to supply power to the buildings. Without it, the city does not produce money, products, waste or sewage. **Products** are needed to make the businesses work and can be produced in reforestation area or in the recycling stations. **Money** is needed to build and increase the city. **Waste** produced by homes and businesses needs to be stored in warehouses and then recycled. **Sewage** needs to be treated or it will be directed automatically by the game to the river, polluting it. There are **quests**, such as investing in public transportation, that help the player to win resources and increase experience points throughout the game. In **friends**, it is possible to visit their cities, help them to keep their cities in operation and also invite new friends. In the **construction** tab, it is possible to choose different types of interventions to increase the city and make it sustainable. There is the option of building homes concerned with the population growth; businesses that provide money to the city; infrastructure and decoration, which enhance the quality of life; structures for the power supply; structures for sustainability and expansion aiming to increase the size of the city.

Ecocity partially meets the requirements of focus number one. Regarding the definition of the **objective**, it is adequate because the objective of the game is to make the player aware and act positively concerning sustainability. The **theme** of the game,

---

[9] One of the largest scientific and educational non-profit institutions. Its interests include geography, archeology and natural science and environmental conservation promotion and also history. More information on: http://www.nationalgeographic.com/.

consisting of the management of a city for sustainability, is also consistent because it is aligned with the social objective of the game. The social and political **context** is also appropriate as the game works with sustainability, matter of great relevance curretly. The **scenario**, on the other hand, lacks important elements that are found in the physical world, such as floods, possibility of creating awareness programs, hydropower plants, and alternative transportation, such as subways and bicycles. These missing elements create a gap between the game world and the physical world, reducing the possibility of generating positive behavior change in the player. The game also lacks tools to drive the player to be aware of and act in relation to sustainability, such as the possibility of donations, tips about the sustainability or indication of organizations involved with the cause.

With respect to focus number two, GfC Ecocity only partially meets the requirements. The **physical world system,** chosen as a basis for developing the game system, was the operation and administration of a city. The choice of this system is appropriate because it is aligned with the objective and theme of the game. However, the system allows actions that mischaracterize the physical world. For example, in a certain game situation, the city has poor quality of life, represented by the value of -246 points. The ideal strategy would be to clean up the river, which would improve the quality of life of city dwellers in 960 points. However, there are not enough coins to build the river treatment plant costing 10,000 coins. It is possible to buy newsstands for the city though. Each newsstand costs 410 coins and adds 30 points in quality of life. Thus, after creating 9 newsstands in the same block, the city began to offer a satisfactory quality of life. As a prize, the player receives bonus in business. In the physical world, however, the construction of a city block with several newsstands would hardly make positive influence in the city's quality of life. The game also does not meet fully the criteria of **validity**, because as it mischaracterizes the physical world, it is difficult to establish a more direct relationship between the game system and the physical world system.

With respect to focus number three, Ecocity meets most of the criteria presented. On the issue of **clear objectives**, the game meets all the necessary elements. All active quests have a fixed position in the player interface, making it easy to identify which quests must be completed. By clicking on each of the quests, a window shows all the steps to complete it, including the itens that have already been completed. The graphical interface is complete and easy to understand, according to the informational point of view, by displaying the level of all resources. In addition, the objectives seem to be challenging, because they require several steps to be completed and resources are not always available. Game objectives always deal with a sustainability problem, for example, creation of public transport or disposal of waste, aligned to the social objective of the game. Concerning the **choices**, the game offers several ways of achieving the quality of life. For example, while a player can invest more in decoration elements, another player can first try to win many coins with pollutant facilities, increasing it initially, and then replace the coal plant with a less polluting one, such as wind power plant, improving the quality of life in the city. Another player may prefer to follow the game's quests, which are gradually contributing to a city with better quality of life. In this sense, there is no dominant strategy, the decision is up to the player, increasing the possibility of intrinsic motivation. In Ecocity, another important feature to be considered is the appropriate challenge. At the beginning, the player has a significant amount of coins and energy to build the city and win the first quests. Over time, however, the player needs to understand the most efficient means of maintaining a sustainable city while solving the quests and earning experience points. This progression is varied, containing the easiest and most difficult quests. Energy is scarce and can be purchased with physical money too. However, if it runs out, the player can do other things as moving the city buildings, collect resources, etc. Besides the player only needs to wait a few minutes to increase energy, preventing them to get frustrated by not being able to interact. As to the **immediate feedback**, the game also meets all the criteria, because the game interfaces have all the necessary information to the player. Thus, there are direct information on what player needs to do when choosing a quest, to complete it and also to level up. Regarding **polishing**, the game partially works. Although the interface responds to player interaction with animations that emphasize interaction, the game has no sound feedback, which, in addition to making the visual feedback lose sound reinforcement, requires the player to stay all the time looking at the interface. The competition is generated through a dropdown bar, which indicates experience level of Facebook friends, who are players also. There are cooperation tools to advance in some quests in the game. For example, there is a quest in which the player needs to create a health center and store vaccines, which must necessarily be delivered by the neighbors. Another way is to visit the city from a neighbor and help collecting coins, causing the two to gain resources. The game also allows communication via posts, chat, and the creation of communities using the tools of Facebook. Moreover, through the game page on this social network, it is possible to use the forum in order to answer questions, find new friends interested in social issues or write comments about the game.

Comparing both analysis on the three suggested foci and the impact of each game in the physical world, two main points were identified. First, there was similarity between the results of the analysis based on three structural strategic foci and the game performance with respect to the popularity and impact on the physical world, validating the proposal of the design elements. Secondly, the result of the analysis showed the possible reasons for their performances in each structural focus. In this regard, while HtS satisfactorily met the proposed elements in foci one and two, which are more related to the impact on the physical world, it did not reached the same result in the focus related to the players motivation mainly because it did not meet the design elements - appropriate challenge and choices. This result is mainly because HtC does not offer strategic ways to overcome the greatest difficulties of the game, making the players to repeat the same action several times, which makes it frustrating at times. Moreover, the choices available in the game were not significant because they did not offer very different results.

Ecocity achieved median performance mainly on focus two because the game system mischaracterized the physical world system, which resulted in inadequate contribution to the theme and objective of the game, affecting the transfer of the players experience in the game to the physical world. Conversely, Ecocity showed better performance in the elements related to the ability to motivate with average performance only in polishing, mainly for lack of audible feedback and visual effects.

6 Conclusion

Mainly through the study of procedural rhetoric and the Theory of Flow and SDT, thirteen (13) design elements divided into three distinct and strategic foci were proposed to assist GfC designers to develop games that cause positive social impact and that are motivators. Thus, Ecocity and HtS were analyzed to validate the proposed elements. As a result, the data related to the social impact and motivation of games through access data and social impact reports were similar to the results of the analysis by the proposed structural strategic foci, demonstrating the main reasons for each of the GfC performances. Consequently, through the results presented, it is possible to initially validate the proposed design elements, which are the main contribution of this research, with regard to the engagement and motivation, for the GfC development context, once it showed direct relationship between the application of design elements and the results of the user experience with these games. In future developments, there will be other tests with the above-mentioned design elements and also the development of games using them as a support.

References

1. Mcgonigal, J.: Reality Is Broken: Why Games Make us Better and How They Can Change The World. Penguim Press, New York (2011)
2. Bogost, I.: Persuasive Games: The Expressive Power of Videogames. MIT Press, EUA (2007)
3. Juul, J.: Half-Real: Video Games Between Real Rules And Fictional Worlds. MIT Press, EUA (2005)
4. Koster, R.: A Theory of Fun For Game Design. Paraglyph Press, Eua (2005)
5. Shaffer, D., Squire, K., Halverson, R., Gee, J.: Video Games And The Future of Learning. Phi Delta Kappan **87**(02), 104–111 (2005)
6. Resnick, M.: Edutainment? No Thanks. I Prefer Playful Learning. In: The Associazione Civita report on Edutainment. (2004)
7. Mattar, J.: Games Em Educação: Como os Nativos Digitais Aprendem. Pearson Prentice Hall, São Paulo (2010)
8. Frank, A.: Balancing three different foci in the design of serious games: engagement, training objective and context. In: Proceedings of Digra (2007)
9. Deci, E.L., Ryan, R.M.: The What And Why of Goal Pursuits: Human Needs And The Self-Determination of Behavior. Psychological Inquiry **11**, 227–268 (2000)
10. Csikszentmihalyi, M.: Flow: The Psychology of Optimal Experience. Harper Perennial, EUA (2008)
11. Schell, J.: The Art Of Game Design: A Book of Lenses. Morgan Kaufmann, EUA (2008)
12. Fullerton, T.: Game Design Workshop: A Playcentric Approach To Creating Innovative Games. Morgan Kaufmann, EUA (2008)
13. Ryan, R., Rigby, C.S., Przybylski, A.: The Motivational Pull of Video Games: A Self-Determination Theory Approach. Etr&D **53**(02), 67–83 (2006)
14. Przybylski, A., Rigby, C.S., Ryan, R.A.: Motivational model of video game engagement. Rev. Gen. Psychol. **14**(02), 154–166 (2010)

Developing a Digital Game for Domestic Stroke Patients' Upper Extremity Rehabilitation – Design and Usability Assessment

Lan-Ling Huang[1]([✉]), Mei-Hsiang Chen[2], Chao-Hua Wang[3], and Chang-Franw Lee[4]

[1] Department of Art and Design, Tan Kah Kee College, Xiamen University, Zhangzhou Development Zone, Zhangzhou 363105, People's Republic of China
Lanlingh@gmail.com
[2] Department of Occupational Therapy, Chung Shan Medical University/Chung Shan Medical University Hospital, No. 110, Sec. 1, Jianguo N. Rd., Taichung 40201, Taiwan
cmh@csmu.edu.tw
[3] Department of Multimedia Design, National Taichung University of Science and Technology, No.129, Sec. 3, Sanmin Rd., North Dist., Taichung 404, Taiwan
[4] Graduate School of Design, National Yunlin University of Science and Technology, 123 University Road, Sect. 3, Douliou 64002, Yunlin, Taiwan
leecf@yuntech.edu.tw

Abstract. Digital games have been proven effective in upper extremity rehabilitation for stroke patients in addition to arousing higher motivation and feelings of pleasure. A well designed upper extremity rehabilitation digital game should intentionally meet the purpose of rehabilitation. Therefore, it is desirable to dmestically develop digital upper extremity rehabilitation games for the local hospitals as well as individual users. We are proposing this research to develop such digital games for rehabilitation and their feasibility assessment. A questionnaire was designed to evaluate the usability and feasibility associated with using this game. The results of this study can be summarized as follows: (1) the set of upper extremity rehabilitation game was named as upper extremity rehabilitation gardening game (UERG game). It is special designed for domestic stroke patients. (2) This UERG game uses Kinect's skeletal tracking features and motion sensor to interaction with patients. (3) design features are as following: game contents include three difficult levels according to different upper limb motor function recovery stages; to record user's motor performance; to provide feedback information (for example: to record the completed the task time and to detect whether the user has compensatory action, etc.). (4) A total of 10 patients to assess this set of games. The results showed that 90 % of patients reported that using UERG game in treatment increased their treatment motivation.; 70 % of them reported that this games is very interactive; 80 % patients considered this game is conducive to recovery their upper extremity functions; 80 % patients considered the feedback information provided help them to

© Springer International Publishing Switzerland 2015
M. Antona and C. Stephanidis (Eds.): UAHCI 2015, Part III, LNCS 9177, pp. 454–461, 2015.
DOI: 10.1007/978-3-319-20684-4_44

understand their performance in each session after training; 60 % patients indicated the game interfaces were easy to operate and learning; 90 % of patients reported that this game is enjoyment and satisfied with this game for rehabilitation. They are willing to continue to use.

Keywords: Upper extremity rehabilitation · Stroke · Digital gaming design · Usability assessment

1 Introduction

Many daily living tasks are performed with the upper limbs. Upper limb motor deficit is one of the main symptoms of stroke patients, and up to 85 % of stroke patients experience hemiparesis immediately after stroke (Saposnik et al., 2010). Therefore, rehabilitation treatment of the upper limbs is very important for stroke patients.

Upper extremity rehabilitation equipment (UERE) is usually used for training the proximal upper extremity movement functions (Lee et al., 2010). They are essential tools in the occupational therapy (OT) practice. Most existing clinical UERP provides no feedback to the patients in Taiwan. Patients may find that repeating the same activity can be boring and monotonous and thus develop a negative attitude toward the therapy process. In order to increase the mental satisfaction and physical vitality of rehabilitation therapy, some therapists have using off-the-shelf video game systems in rehabilitation. Digital games have been proven effective in upper extremity rehabilitation for stroke patients in addition to arousing higher motivation and feelings of pleasure. However, only a few OT departments in Taiwan's hospitals have tried to adopt digital games in their OT programs. The main reasons may be summarized as following: a) the devices are expensive; b) the gaming interfaces are not in Chinese, hence easily causing operation errors and inconveniences; c) the gaming interfaces are complicated for patients to independently operate the games without help from the therapists; d) the games contents are design for normal person to leisure, not for Stroke patient. Their individual strengths and weaknesses may affect treatment effectiveness and safety for the patient. Therefore, digital games for stroke patient must be designed with users in mind. Such products that truly fit the users can increase user acceptance (Jacobs, 2008).

It is desirable to domestically develop digital upper extremity rehabilitation games for the local hospitals as well as individual users. The purpose of this study was to develop a digital game system for rehabilitation and to assess their feasibility. It is hoped that the results of this study could be used to improve existing UERE to meet the practical needs of practitioners providing treatment and quality care.

2 Methods

This study included three parts: 1) to conduct literature review and expert interviews to identify types of daily living activities that meet treatment purposes and then determine the priority of each task for patients' resumption to independent living; 2) to design a digital game for upper extremity rehabilitation, based on the selected daily living activities and the results of our previous research on improvement of game design; 3) a questionnaire was designed to evaluate the usability and feasibility associated with using this game. Further elaboration of the parts follows.

2.1   Expert Interviews to Identify the Game Contents for Rehabilitation

This part includes two items to identify the game contents for rehabilitation: 1) to interview the clinical occupational therapists, and 2) to reference previous research results.

Three clinical occupational therapists were interviewed. They proposed two most important suggestions for the system design: 1) Reaching-to-Grasp is one of the most important daily living activities. Also, note that, when patients do Reaching-to-Grasp activity, the compensatory movements easy occurred. Therefore, therapists suggested that an attention function of the Compensatory Movements design is needed in the digital gaming design for rehabilitation. 2) Rehabilitation-based game contents (such as usage situation and tasks)should conform to the actual task in life. It would make patients more familiar with the task of daily life.

Our previous study was to survey the therapeutic effectiveness, usage problems and needs of the commercial digital videogames (Wii and XaviX) applied in rehabilitation, then summarize a guideline for improvement design of the digital UERP. Design guidelines can be synthesized as follows, where items a to d are about software design, and items e to i about hardware (Chen et al., 2014): (a) To increase the response time of the games. (b) To increase difficulty levels of the games in order to better suit the various patients with different abilities of upper extremity functions. (c) To expand the sensor's sensing scope. (d) To be able to record movement data, such as: reaction time, operating time. (e) To improve the ways to fix the controller on the user's hand. (f) To fit the controllers size for different hand dimensions of the patients. (g) To provide better correspondence between the game and real-life movements. (h) To provide controllers for body control training, such as chest strap and belt. (i) To simplify the controller's operation. A systematic design process was then followed to create the digital UERP.

Considering these interviewed results and authors previous research results, we proposed a set of digital gaming.

2.2   A Digital Game Design for Upper Extremity Rehabilitation

According to the foregoing results, a digital game system for upper extremity rehabilitation was designed. It is especially designed for the patients with upper limb defect. In order to make the system context meet with the actual task in life, this study references some studies (Relf 1973, 2005; Relf and Dorn, 1995; Soderback et al., 2004) and clinical occupational therapists reported apply gardening tasks in rehabilitation can stable mood, establish self-confidence, and increase patients' therapy motivation. Therefore, this game system design was named as 'upper extremity rehabilitation gardening game (UERG game).'

UERG game is designed to use Kinect's motion sensors and skeletal tracking function, and to combine with the gardening activities (Fig. 1). Functions and contents of this system has been repeatedly discussed and revised with occupational therapy experts, digital media experts and product design experts. The design characteristics are described as following:

(a) Three difficulty levels of the games (Fig. 2): easy, medium, and difficult.

In easy level, the game includes three tasks: to dial the soil (Fig. 3), to pick up the seeds to sow, and to water the potting. These tasks are main training patient (Brunnstrom recovery stages of upper extremity in III-IV stages)(Sawner & LaVigne, 1992) to do reaching-to-grasp activity and expend forward movement. When patients operate smoothly and the posture correct, the seed would grow into seedlings in fresh green (this color means the seed is healthy growing). On the contrary, if the user's operation is on and off, or the posture not correct (e.g. the Compensatory Movements occur or body barycenter offset), the color of the seedlings will present in tan (this color refers to the seedling is not healthy).

For medium level, the game includes three tasks: weeding (Fig. 4), deinsectization, and photosynthesis. These tasks are main training patient (Brunnstrom recovery stages of upper extremity in IV-V stages) to do reaching-to-grasp activity, expend forward movement, abduction movement and adduction movement. The seedlings color also the same the foregoing situation.

For difficulty level, the game includes three tasks: to block the wind for little tree, to block the lightening, and receive sunlight (Fig. 5). These tasks are main training patient (Brunnstrom recovery stages of upper extremity in V-VI stages) to do compositionality movement, fine movement, balance and coordination movement by both hands. The little tree color also the same the foregoing situation.

(b) Navigation function: In order to avoid the patients get lost in the process of operating, this system provides navigation function to guide patients operating menu and each task. At the login screen (Fig. 6), patient can chose the voice guider speaks in Chinese or Taiwanese. Before task execution, patients could watch a animation with 3D virtual character to understand how to operate the task (Fig. 7).

(c) Feedback: to present operating time in one task, encourage slogans (Fig. 8) and the Compensatory Movement warnings (Fig. 9). Patients are asked to correct his/her posture, when the graphic warnings appear in screen. Once the posture is corrected, the graphic warnings will clear off, then the game starts.

(d) Recording movement data (Fig. 10): a single action of moving speed, spend time in complete one task, the time and date of user login the game, posture error times (e.g. the Compensatory Movements or body barycenter offset), and moving track of the each action. These data would help patients and therapists to know recovery progress situation in each therapy session.

Fig. 1. Usage situation

Fig. 2. Three difficulty levels of the games

Fig. 3. Easy level: to dial the soil

Fig. 4. Medium level: weeding

Fig. 5. Difficulty level: receive sunlight

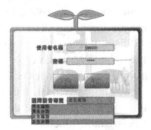

Fig. 6. The login screen

Fig. 7. Navigation

Fig. 8. Encourage slogans-good job!

Fig. 9. The compensatory movement warnings.   **Fig. 10.** Recording movement data

2.3 The Usability and Feasibility Assessment

In order to confirm whether the UERG game design is feasible used in clinical, we applied participatory design in this part. The occupational therapists and Stroke patients were invited to actual use this system, and proposed their suggestions. The stroke patients were asked to complete a total of 5 training sessions in 2 weeks, scheduled at three 20-minute sessions per week (excluding set-up time). After 5 training sessions, each patient also completed the questionnaire.

Stroke patients were recruited from an outpatient occupational therapy department of Chung Shan Medical University Hospital in Taiwan. Inclusion criteria were as follows: (a) hemiparesis with upper extremity dysfunction following a single unilateral stroke, (b) a history of first-time stroke (3-24 months post stroke), (c) a need for upper extremity rehabilitation to convalescent levels of Brunnstrom stages III to V, (d) ability to communicate, and to understand and follow instructions, and (e) ability to maintain sitting and standing balance unsupported for two minutes under supervision (score ≥ 3 on the Berg Balance Scale). Exclusion criteria were as follows: (a) engagement in any other rehabilitation studies during the study and (b) serious aphasia or cognitive impairment. Each patient gave informed consent. This study was approved by the Human Research Ethics Board of a local hospital.

A questionnaire is designed based on the technology acceptance model (TAM) multi-item and related literature (Tsai et al., 2012; Davis et al., 1986). The Technology Acceptance Model is an information systems theory that models how users come to accept and use a technology. This questionnaire contains two parts: 1) the basic subjects information and 2) the TAM included five major variables, such as Perceived Usefulness, Perceived Ease of Use, Attitude toward using, attitude to use, and perceived usefulness. According to these factors and the game features, the questionnaire was completed. Each item were listed on a 7-point Likert-type scale with 1 signifying "strongly disagree" and 7 being "strongly agree".

For the occupational therapists, they were invited to use the UERG game and propose suggestions.

2.4   Data Analysis

The collected data were analysed with an SPSS statistical package. For each question on the questionnaire, the mean and standard deviation were calculated.

3   Results

A total of ten stroke patients were recruited, four males and six females, with an average age of 52.9 years (SD: 14.7). For their upper extremity convalescent levels of Brunnstrom stages (proximal), five patients were in IV stage, and five patients in V stage. For their upper extremity convalescent levels of Brunnstrom stages (distal), two patients in III stage, three patients in IV, and five patients in V stage. All subjects were never use digital games for upper limb rehabilitation.

Stroke patients agreed the game is feasible and acceptable (mean 5.4). 90 % of patients reported that using UERG game in treatment increased their treatment motivation (mean 5.3); 70 % of patients reported that this games has high interactivity, they still want to use it in their rehabilitation (5.7); 80 % of patients considered that UERG game is conducive to recovery their upper extremity functions (mean 5.0); 80 % of patients considered that the recorded movement data can help to understand their performance of each session after training (mean 5.0); 60 % of patients indicated that the interfaces were easy to operate and learning (mean 5.1); 90 % of patients reported that this game is enjoyment and satisfied with this game for rehabilitation, and are willing to continue to use (mean 5.6). Overall, Stroke patients showed positive attitudes toward the UERG game in rehabilitation.

Three clinical occupational therapists proposed two suggestions as following: 1) the Compensatory Movement warnings is too sensitive to break off the game. They suggest that the motion sensor sitting should expand the area. 2) about the game's induction system, it is suggested that adjust the sensor high sensitivity and synchronization of action.

4   Conclusion

This study develops a upper extremity rehabilitation gardening game and to assess their feasibility. The results of this study can be summarized as follows: 1) the UERG game is special designed for patients with upper limb deficits. 2) This UERG game uses Kinect's skeletal tracking features and motion sensor to interaction with patients. 3) design features of UERG game include the following: game contents include three difficult levels according to different upper limb motor function recovery stages; to record user's motor performance; to provide feedback information (for example: to record the completed the task time and to detect whether the user has compensatory action, etc.). 4) A total of 10 patients to assess this set of games. The results showed that 90 % of patients reported that using UERG game in treatment increased their treatment motivation.; 70 % of patients reported that this games is more interactivity, they still want to use it in their rehabilitation; 80 % of patients considered that this game is conducive to recovery their upper extremity functions; 80 % of patients considered that the feedback information provided can help to understand their performance of each session after training; 60 % of patients indicate that the game interfaces were easy to operate and learning; 90 % of patients reported that this game is enjoyment and satisfied with this game for rehabilitation, and are willing to continue to use.

Acknowledgment. This study is supported by the the Ministry of Science and Technology with grant No: MOST 103-2221-E-040-009.

References

Chen, M.H., Huang, L.L., Lee, C.F.: Usability evaluation of digital games for stroke rehabilitation in taiwan, In: Proceedings of. IARIA, pp. 371–376 (2014)

Davis, F.D.: A Technology Acceptance Model for Empirically Testing New End-User Information Systems Theory and Results. Sloan School of Management MIT, Cambridge (1986)

Jacobs, K.: Ergonomics for Therapists. Mosby Elsevier, Louis (2008)

Lee, C.F., Huang, L.L., Chen, M.H.: An investigation of the upper extremity rehabilitation equipments for stroke patients. Journal of Science and Technology—Humanity and Sociology, **19**(2), 103–114 (2010)

Relf, P.D.: The therapeutic values of plants. Pediatr. Rehabil. **8**(3), 235–237 (2005)

Relf, P.D.: Horticulture: A therapeutic tool. J. Rehabil. **39**(1), 27–29 (1973)

Relf, P.D., Dorn, S.: Horticulture: meeting the needs of special populations. Technology **5**, 94–103 (1995)

Saposnik, G., Teasell, R., Mamdani, M., Hall, J., McIlroy, W., Cheung, D.: Effectiveness of virtual reality using wii gaming technology in stroke rehabilitation: a pilot randomized clinical trial and proof of principle. Stroke **41**, 1477–1484 (2010)

Soderback, I., Soderstrom, M., Schalander, E.: Horticultural therapy: The "healing garden" and gardening in rehabilitation measures at Danderyd Hospital Rehabilitation Clinic, Sweden. Pediatric Rehabilitation, **7**(4), 245–260 (2004)

Swarner, K.A., LaVigne, J.M.: Brunstrom's Movement Therapy in Hemiplegia: A Neurophysiological Approach, 2nd edn. J.B. Lippincott Company, Philadelphia (1992)

Tsai, T.H., Chang, H.T., Chang, Y.M., Huang, G.S.: Sharetouch: a system to enrich social network experiences for the elderly. J. Syst. Softw. **85**(6), 1363–1369 (2012)

An Integrated Playful Music Learning Solution

Kristoffer Jensen[✉] and Søren Frimodt-Møller

Architecture, Design and Media Technology, Aalborg University, Aalborg, Denmark
{krist,sfm}@create.aau.dk

Abstract. This paper presents an integrated solution using IT technologies to help a (young) musician learn a piece of music, or learn how to play an instrument. The rehearsal process is organized in sequences, consisting of various activities to be 'passed'. Several games are investigated that help in learning especially difficult parts, or in the learning of an instrument. The integrated solution, demonstrated on a tablet, proposed in this paper also includes tools that assist the musician in the rehearsal process. Feedback consists of computer tracking that supports self-assessment of rehearsal quality together with shared audio and video material that can be viewed by teacher and peers.

Keywords: Informal learning · Music rehearsal · Mobile applications · Gamification · Low-fidelity prototyping

1 Introduction

Recent developments in the theories of music learning point to the need for new tools to aid the learning processes of musicians. Drawing on insights from research in music pedagogy, the integrated digital toolkit proposed in this paper aims to provide especially young musicians with means for receiving feedback, and allow for playful interaction between musician and technology. For instance, part of the integrated solution is a game where the musician gets points for notes while playing, thereby simultaneously providing feedback to the music student and allowing for playful interaction [1, 2].

Younger music students typically learn music in a semi-autonomous environment [3, 4] in which the teacher interacts with the student less than half an hour a week, and the student works alone [5] most of the time, or with the help of family, e.g. on homework given by the teacher, or via self-motivation. The limited teacher interaction set-up is, however, potentially demotivating and can result in many errors on behalf of the student [6]. Errors can include forgetting what is to be played, as well as lack of expressiveness, e.g. when the score is seen as an exact representation of the music. It requires a high skill-level for a musician to be expressive on his or her own. The lack of organization and attention to expression in the traditional music school scenario is potentially harmful for the apprentice musician.

In addition to individual one-to-one teaching, many music teachers use group teaching, in which several students work together. While this enables more active participation, logistic problems often impede on the added motivation [3].

© Springer International Publishing Switzerland 2015
M. Antona and C. Stephanidis (Eds.): UAHCI 2015, Part III, LNCS 9177, pp. 462–471, 2015.
DOI: 10.1007/978-3-319-20684-4_45

In addition to the lack of learning due to miscommunication and other errors in the environment, the students may lose self-belief and self-efficacy (conviction of success), which is one of the key characteristics needed in order to be a successful musician [7]. According to [8], formal music training increases the self-assessment score, and this internalization of the evaluation process increases self-efficacy, hence the need for supporting and enhancing self-assessment.

McPherson [9] investigates skill development in music pupils. Five main skills are acquired when learning music: performing rehearsed music, sight reading, playing from memory, playing by the ear and improvising. In a large-scale study with 7-9 year old music pupils, improvements were found in all categories in three consecutive years. These were explained mainly by four strategies, organizational strategies, order of practice, practicing to improve and self-correction strategies. For all the skills, the strategy employed was a significantly more powerful indicator for the improvement than was the hours of practice. Conversely, lack of mental strategies can therefore be expected to impede on a pupil's progress in music learning.

Play as such has been studied as a learning resource, combining imagination and cognition at the same time, by researchers such as Bateson [10], Vygotsky [11], and Apter [12]. According to these researchers, players enact their play, reflecting upon the implications of their actions as in reality. E.g. [11] propose that children playing with tangible toys are transported to an imaginary world, in which they practice conceptual thinking, exploring what actions they could take and their implications. In the context of ECML, the integrated games can, in particular, enable serious musical performance attempts (i.e. in performances outside the game), e.g. in relation to parallel octave shifts on the piano, difficult key fingering in wind instruments, etc. Similarly, games helping musicians practice music theory can be made by transposition knowledge methods [13], in which knowledge is obtained by a user via interaction with seemingly disparate games into which relevant information has been inserted.

2   State of the Art

Several applications for aiding musicians in their learning process already exist, both for regular computers and portable devices. Apple's lite digital audio workstation, Garage Band [14] (available on both iOS devices and Mac) has long been able to offer step-by-step video lessons for purchase, where the user can then easily record his or her feedback within the program for later reference. The process of sharing such recordings with others, as well as a classic "music minus one" approach where the musician can play or sing along with accompaniment and practice sheet music are integrated into the iOS only app Tunemio [15]. However, neither of these platforms offers the gamification aspect, which ECML includes.

If one expands the scope of applications to involve platforms for collaborating on music as such (and not necessarily on the music learning process), many communities exist, such as those around the multi-platform services Indaba Music [16] or Kompoz [17], both of which offer social network style environments, in which music projects have 'pages' where collaborating users can upload sound files, lyrics, sheet music and other elements for use in a song, as well as comment on the process. Similar collaboration processes take place on the sound sharing service Soundcloud [18] (which, however, is nowadays also used by record companies to promote signed artists) and comparable platforms. A flashier collaborative tool is the iOS-based WholeWorldBand [19], which allows users to add tracks (in the sense of layers) to the songs of other users by means of video files, thereby gradually generating a multi-splitscreen music video.

What distinguishes ECML from the aforementioned platforms is the integration of collaborative tools, tools for music learning targeted towards the individual user, especially to aid the rehearsal process and the link between rehearsal and music lesson (with the music student's teacher), and again, the gamification aspect.

3 Design and Development

The target platform for the design of ECML is tablets, given the consideration that the integrated solution should be easily portable (as the music student usually shifts between different rehearsal spaces) and afford online communication with teachers or fellow students. Mobile devices in general, iOS, Android and Windows-based alike, make it possible to synchronize information quickly between users, in this case making it easy to ensure that e.g. a teacher's advice or other information for the student passes on effortlessly and stays up-to-date.

Another aspect of the tablet, as opposed to the smartphone or similar small mobile devices, is that the size of it (typically the size of a piece of paper or a book page, even though exact sizes vary) is sufficiently close to that of a traditional, physical piece of sheet music, to make the transition from rehearsing a piece of notated music via physical sheet music to rehearsing with the aid of a digital platform, as seamless as possible. For the present version of ECML, an Android-based tablet was used.

3.1 Design

In order to develop the initial ideas for the application further, a low fidelity prototype was used. This consists in designing the application in a paper version. The advantage is that it is easy to create functionalities at the conceptual level and test these in practice by moving pieces of paper. Thus, subjects see exactly what the ideas would look like in practice, and modifications are made directly. An example of the use of a low-fidelity prototype is seen in Fig. 1.

In order to assess the quality of the prototypes better, another approach used in the development process is the creation of scenarios, observations of, and interviews with apprentice musicians using the ECML in a given scenario. The chosen scenario presents the main functions of ECML: first a general presentation with the basic options (selection of a song, choice of instrument, play button…), secondly other useful options (metronome, tuning fork, access to Youtube, Facebook…), then the games, and finally the ECML messenger. Another created scenario focuses on the sequence of activities. The knowledge gained from this process is used in the iterative development process. An early prototype from this process is seen in Fig. 2.

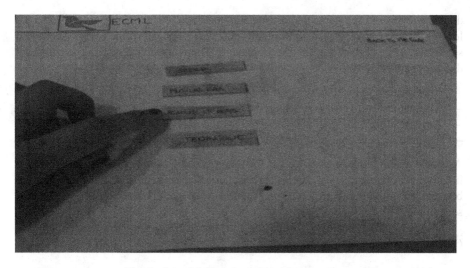

Fig. 1. Low fidelity prototype with interaction

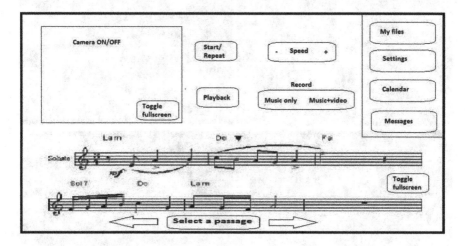

Fig. 2. Low-fidelity prototype of integrated solution

As general strategies for designing the games in ECML, the following basic principles from Salen and Zimmerman [20] were used:

- The game has to have clear goals
- The game has to have clear feedbacks
- The game must include challenges but not too hard

Also, the games had to be fun, but still supporting the main goal of learning to play an instrument or a piece of music. It was decided to base the game on the individual personal experience of learning music. A group of university interns helping with the development of ECML provided examples of exercises typically given to them by their own music teachers. These examples were transformed into different games. There are different levels in each game and the generic goal is to reach a higher score. To pass a level, the player has to reach a minimum score. For each game, the player has to first select a section of the song that he is playing. The team of interns first suggested 4 different games:

- "Speed": the goal is to play a part of the song as quickly as possible
- "Musical ear": the goal is to recognize the notes by ear
- "Note Reading": the goal is to learn to read the notes quickly and correctly
- "Technique": the goal is to play the part of the song with different rhythms

As stated above, the games as well as the integrated solution were developed using an iterative process using low-fidelity prototypes. Some examples of the relationship between the low-fidelity prototype and the final software version for one game can be seen in Fig. 3.

One example of the developed games, the note reading game, can be seen in Fig. 4 (screenshot from the end of one game).

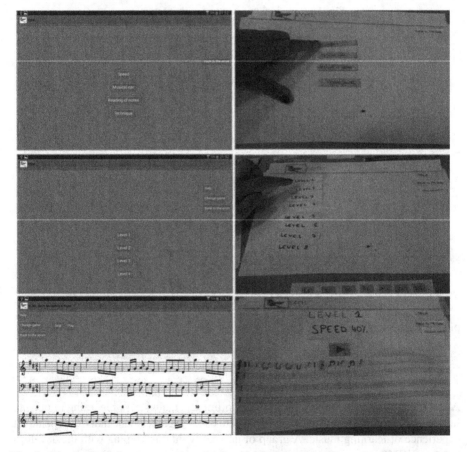

Fig. 3. The final version compared to the low-fidelity prototype for some functions of the software.

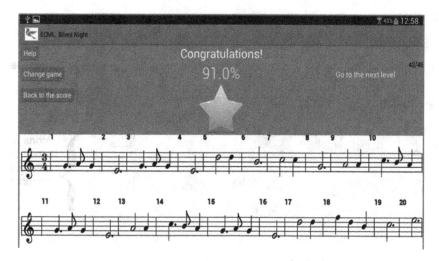

Fig. 4. Example of a learning game, the note reading game

3.2 Development

The development of ECML has been an iterative approach, with an initial low fidelity prototype, an early software prototype and a final beta version. About half of the development team had extensive music background (more than ten years) and many of the functions included were suggested and/or improved upon in the weekly meetings between the developers and the project responsible.

Functions developed started with notation visualization, calendar, communication, and games. The functioning prototype looked similar to the paper prototype of Fig. 2. Then an organization approach was initiated, and the sequence of activities was developed, along with music learning and practice games, and common music functionalities such as audio and video recording, metronome and tuning fork. The final version can be seen in Fig. 5. Other functionalities implemented include a mute button and delay before notation starts, so as to enable preparation time.

ECML is implemented on Eclipse [21] using the built-in Android Developer Tools. The main elements of this approach are the manifest (all the essential information about the application, permissions, main activity and the first activity to be launched), the layout (either statically in XML or dynamically), the menu (view and items in XML), the values (String (application name and other string variables) and Assets (files that will be included in package) and sources (Java files).

The development has been done with the Agile methodology [22], as it is often used in software development to enhance productivity, in respecting the Model-View-Controller architecture. This pattern separates the different components inside the architecture of the application. According to the discussions in the development team and information from low-fidelity prototypes, and from observations using the developed scenarios, an iterative approach, using information from the low-fidelity and scenarios experiment, has been taken, and development consists of bug fixes, feature additions and new functionalities.

Fig. 5. Final prototype of integrated solution.

The final integrated solution, dubbed ECML (Easy Coach for Music Learning) organizes the rehearsal process in sequences, consisting of various activities to be 'passed'. Activities are, for instance, warm-up, note-studying, playing from sheet music, and games, the latter to provide variation and opportunities for playful learning. Several games have been made that help in learning especially difficult parts of a piece of music, or in learning how to play an instrument as such. As an example, pianists often consider moving in parallel octaves difficult. If the note-following functionality detects many errors in this part, it is suggested that the player tries an associated game to improve upon this skill. Another example could be if the tracking mechanism detects errors in the musician's playing in relation to the sheet music: in this case, a game exists with this specific part of the music, having the musician perform the part correctly, gradually increasing the speed. ECML also includes tools that assist the musician in the rehearsal process, such as a calendar (for agreements, meetings, etc.), tools for communication (with the teacher, other musicians etc.), video (in order to observe an expert or studying one's own progress), tuning fork and metronome. Feedback consists of computer tracking that supports self-assessment of rehearsal quality together with shared audio and video material that can be viewed by teacher and peers.

4   Evaluation

A questionnaire was created based on the Technology Acceptance Model [23], [24] and the System of Usability Scale [25] in order to study the potential acceptance of the ECML application and its usability. The goal of this questionnaire was to evaluate the level of acceptance of the application by musicians, an evaluation made in the light of different hypotheses (what can influence the intentions of the musician to use the application). The questionnaire was given to students at the conservatory of Esbjerg. After careful examinations, it was decided to divide the questionnaire into three parts: The first part

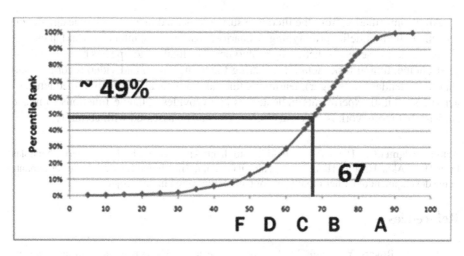

Fig. 6. System of usability scale score of the ECML prototype

is based on TAM and its aim is to collect some information about the perception of ECML. The purpose of the second section, which is based on SUS, is to evaluate the usability of the application. The third part is targeted towards the gathering of additional information on the habits of musicians, in order to improve the application, in other words, an element of actual interview in the, thus semi-structured, questionnaire.

Unfortunately, it was not possible to find enough subjects for the surveys. Consequently, only 8 interviews were conducted. Due to the limited number of responses to the questionnaire, the only reliable results are those coming from the second and the last part of the questionnaire consisting of SUS-score, which has been proven informative even for very small samples [26] using the qualitative documentation of the habits of musicians. The average result of the SUS-score is 66,9. In Fig. 6, taken from [27], we see the distribution of results from 500 SUS studies with different topics, for which the average score is 68, and 5 classes (A, B, C, D and F, alluding to the American grading system) defined for the usability of the scores (given in percentage on the y-axis). Plotting the score from the present SUS-questionnaire onto the graph, we see that it falls in class C: for the eight interviewed people, the ECML application is usable at approximately 50 %. This means that the usability is at this point acceptable (average), but could still be improved.

5   Conclusions

This study shows the iterative process of developing an integrated music learning tool. With an extensive literature survey to obtain information about habits of music students and the requirements of music students and music teachers, several defining aspects of the music learning tool was found. These include structuring and motivating the students, and making sure all necessary information about the current rehearsal topic is available, the attention to the development of different skills when learning music, and the variation of learning methods with both formal and non-formal (games) learning.

All the information from the literature survey was used in an iterative design development with low-fidelity prototyping, scenarios, observations, interviews and questionnaires, rendering several functioning prototypes. The final prototype has basic functions (metronome, tuning fork, notation), sharing functions (audio and video recording and sharing, calendar, messenger), learning games and organization function (sequence of activities). Initial experiments indicate this app provides valuable functions to music students but more work is necessary before this can be assessed with certainty.

Acknowledgments. The authors would like to thank Anaïs Tournois, Tessa Guérin, Nicholas Fruy, Hajar Akla, Hajar El Hammoumi, Thibaut Grandin, Brice Freund as well as the participants in the development of earlier prototypes for their participation in this project.

References

1. Price, S., Rogers, Y., Scaife, M., Stanton, D., Neale, H.: Using tangible to promote novels forms of playful learning. Interact Comput. **15**, 169–185 (2003)
2. Price, S., Rogers, Y.: Let's get physical: the learning benefits of interacting in digitally in augmented physical spaces. Comput. Educ. **43**, 137–151 (2004)
3. Gaunt, H.: One-to-one tuition in a conservatoire: the perceptions of instrumental and vocal teachers. Psychol. Music **36**(2), 215–245 (2008)
4. Kurkul, W.W.: Nonverbal communication in one-to-one music performance instruction. Psychol. Music **35**(2), 327–362 (2007)
5. Austin, J.R., Berg, M.H.: Exploring music practice among sixth-grade band and orchestra students. Psychol. Music **34**(4), 535–558 (2006)
6. Rostvall, A.L., West, T.: Interaktion och kunskapsutveckling. En studie av frivillig musikundervisning. KMH förlaget, Stockholm (2004)
7. McPherson, G.E., McCormick, J.: Self-efficacy and music performance. Psychol. Music **34**(3), 291–309 (2006)
8. Seddon, F.A., O'Neill, S.A.: How does formal instrumental music tuition (FIMT) impact on self- and teacher-evaluations of adolescents computer-based compositions? Psychol. Music **34**(1), 27–45 (2006)
9. McPherson, G.E.: From child to musician: skill development during the beginning stages of learning an instrument. Psychol. Music **33**(1), 5–35 (2005)
10. Bateson, G.: Steps to an ecology of mind. Jason Aronson Inc., Northvale (1972)
11. Vygotsky, L.: Mind in Society. Harvard University Press, Cambridge (1978)
12. Apter, M.: Reversal Theory: The Dynamics of Motivation, Emotion and Personality. Oneworld Publications, Oxford (2007)
13. Marchetti, E., Jensen, K., Valente, A.: Transposition of Domain Knowledge into Educational Games. Int. J. Technol. Knowl. Soc. **9**(4), 273–288 (2014)
14. Garageband (2015). https://www.apple.com/mac/garageband/ Accessed on 4 February 2015
15. Tunemio (2015). https://itunes.apple.com/fi/app/id849934448 Accessed on 4 February 2015
16. Indabamusic (2015). https://www.indabamusic.com Accessed on 4 February 2015
17. Kompoz (2015). http://www.kompoz.com Accessed on 4 February 2015
18. Soundcloud (2015). http://www.soundcloud.com Accessed on 4 February 2015
19. Wholeworldband (2015). http://www.wholeworldband.com Accessed on February 4, 2015
20. Salen, K., Zimmerman, E.: Rules of Play. Game Design Fundamentals. The MIT Press, Cambridge (2004)

21. Eclipse (2015). https://eclipse.org/ Accessed on 5 February 2015
22. Agile Manifesto (2015). http://agilemanifesto.org/iso/en/principles.html Accessed on 5 February 2015
23. Davis, F.D.: Perceived Usefulness, Perceived Ease Of Use, And User Acceptance of Information Technology. MIS Q. **13**(3), 319–340 (1989)
24. Shroff, R.H., Deneen, C.C., Ng, E.M.W.: Analysis of the technology acceptance model in examining students behavioural intention to use an eportfolio system. Australas. J. Educ. Technol. **27**(4), 600–618 (2011)
25. Davis, F.D.: User acceptance of information technology: system characteristics, user perceptions and behavioral impacts. Int. J. Man Mach. Stud. **38**, 475–487 (1993)
26. U.S. Dept. of Health and Human Services (2006). Web page summarizing *The Research-Based Web Design & Usability Guidelines, Enlarged/Expanded edition*. Washington: U.S. Government Printing Office. http://www.usability.gov/how-to-and-tools/methods/system-usability-scale.html Accessed 4 February 2015
27. Sauro, J.: Measuring Usability With The System Usability Scale (SUS) (2011). http://www.measuringu.com/sus.php Accessed on 4 February 2015

A Game-like Application for Dance Learning Using a Natural Human Computer Interface

Alexandros Kitsikidis[1], Kosmas Dimitropoulos[1(✉)], Deniz Uğurca[2], Can Bayçay[2], Erdal Yilmaz[2], Filareti Tsalakanidou[1], Stella Douka[3], and Nikos Grammalidis[1]

[1] Information Technologies Institute, ITI-CERTH, 1st Km Thermi-Panorama Rd, Thessaloniki, Greece
{ajinchv,dimitrop,filareti,ngramm}@iti.gr
[2] Argedor Information Technologies, Ankara, Turkey
{dugurca,can.baycay,erdlylmz}@gmail.com
[3] Department of Physical Education and Sport Science, Aristotle University of Thessaloniki, Thessaloniki, Greece
sdouka@phed.auth.gr

Abstract. Game-based learning and gamification techniques are recently becoming a popular trend in the field of Technology Enhanced Learning. In this paper, we mainly focus on the use of game design elements for the transmission of Intangible Cultural Heritage (ICH) knowledge and, especially, for the learning of traditional dances. More specifically, we present a 3D game environment that employs an enjoyable natural human computer interface, which is based on the fusion of multiple depth sensors data in order to capture the body movements of the user/learner. In addition, the system automatically assesses the learner's performance by utilizing a combination of Dynamic Time Warping (DTW) with Fuzzy Inference System (FIS) approach and provides feedback in a form of a score as well as instructions from a virtual tutor in order to promote self-learning. As a pilot use case, a Greek traditional dance, namely Tsamiko, has been selected. Preliminary small-scaled experiments with students of the Department of Physical Education and Sports Science at Aristotle University of Thessaloniki have shown the great potential of the proposed application.

Keywords: Dance performance evaluation · Natural human computer interface · Traditional dances

1 Introduction

Modern games tend to transcend the traditional boundaries of the entertainment domain giving rise to the proliferation of serious and pervasive games, i.e., games that are designed for a primary purpose other than pure entertainment. Exploiting the latest simulation and visualization technologies, serious games are able to contextualize the player's experience in challenging, realistic environments, supporting situated cognition [1, 2]. To this end, serious games are gaining an ever increasing interest in various domains such as defense, education, scientific exploration and health care. Especially

© Springer International Publishing Switzerland 2015
M. Antona and C. Stephanidis (Eds.): UAHCI 2015, Part III, LNCS 9177, pp. 472–482, 2015.
DOI: 10.1007/978-3-319-20684-4_46

in the field of education, serious games have the potential to be an important teaching tool because they can promote training, knowledge acquisition and skills development through interactive, engaging or even immersive activities. Therefore, by combining gaming and learning, serious games have introduced a new area in the educational domain.

In this paper, we focus on a special field of education, which is the preservation and transmission of intangible cultural heritage (ICH). Such expressions include music, dance, singing, theatre, human skills and craftsmanship. The importance of these intangible expressions is not limited to cultural manifestations, but it coexists with the wealth of knowledge, which is transmitted through it from one generation to the next [3]. As the world becomes more interconnected, many different cultures come into contact and communities start losing important elements of their ICH, while the new generation finds it more difficult to maintain the connection with the cultural heritage treasured by their elders. To this end, the advances in serious games technologies are expected to play a crucial role in the safeguarding of ICH by providing more engaging and, hopefully, effective learning environments.

A characteristic case of ICH is dance (either traditional or contemporary), which can convey different messages according to the context e.g., artistic, cultural, social, spiritual etc. A dominant factor towards this direction is the human body motion. Therefore, the capture, analysis, modelling and evaluation of dancer's motion with the help of ICT technologies could contribute significantly to the preservation and transmission of this knowledge. Dance analysis is an active research topic [4], while commercial products also exist, such as the Harmonix' Dance Central video game series [5], where a player tries to imitate the motion demonstrated by an animated character. Many research projects have been conducted on the topic of dance assistance and evaluation employing various sensor technologies. Saltate! [6] is a wireless prototype system to support beginners of ballroom dancing. It acquires data from force sensors mounted under the dancers' feet, detects steps, and compares their timing to the timing of beats in the music playing, thus detecting mistakes. Sensable project [7] also employs wireless sensor modules, worn at the wrists of dancers, which capture motions in dance ensembles. On the other hand, the VR-Theater project [8] allows choreographers to enter the desired choreography moves with a user-friendly user interface, or even to record the movements of a specific performer using motion capture techniques. Finally, in [9] different kinds of augmented feedback (tactile, video, sound) for learning basic dance choreographies are investigated.

In this paper, we propose a novel serious game aiming to enhance the learning of a Greek traditional dance through multi-sensing and 3D game technologies and evaluate the dancer's performance by means of sensorimotor learning. For the capturing of dancer's motion, multiple depth sensors are used to address the problems occurring due to self-occlusions by parts of dancer's body. Subsequently, the skeletal data from different sensors are fused into a single, more robust skeletal representation, which is used for both driving the user's avatar in the 3D environment and for his/her performance evaluation. The proposed evaluation algorithm is based on the estimation of motion similarity between the learner's movements and an expert's recording through a DTW/FIS-based approach in conjunction with an appropriate set of metrics. The 3D environment was developed based on Unity 3D engine [10], which is a popular multiple-platform gaming solution, and supports a set of activities and exercises designed in close cooperation with dance experts, in order to teach different variations of the dance.

2   The System Architecture

The architecture of the proposed game application consists of three modules, which communicate bilaterally with each other: the Body Capture Module, the 3D Game Module and the Web Platform, as illustrated in Fig. 1. Specifically, the Body Capture Module is used for the capture and analysis of motion data, which are subsequently transmitted to the 3D Game Module for visualization purposes. For motion capture, Kinect depth sensors are used [11]. Although it is possible to play the game using just a single Kinect sensor, multiple Kinect sensors are supported, which leads to improved motion robustness. Each sensor provides the 3D position and orientation of 20 predefined skeletal joints of the human body. A skeletal fusion procedure is performed to combine the data obtained from multiple sensors onto a single fused skeleton as described in Sect. 3. This fused skeletal animation data are transmitted via TCP/IP in the form of XML messages to the 3D Game Module, where they are used for animating the 3D avatar as well as for the evaluation of user performance. The 3D Game Module is implemented in the Unity game engine and is described in detail in Sect. 4. The game has bilateral communication with the Web Platform, which is responsible for user profile management and game analytics storage.

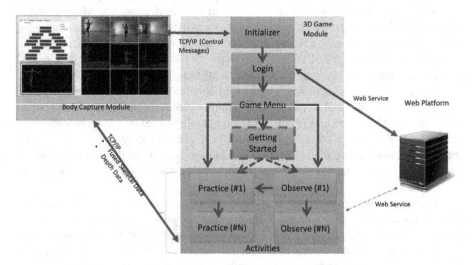

Fig. 1.   Tsamiko game architecture

3   Natural Human Computer Interface

To improve the performance of the markerless body motion capture, we apply skeleton fusion, which is the process of combining skeletal data captured by multiple sensors into a single, more robust skeletal representation [12]. This helps address problems occurring due to occlusions, in particular self-occlusions by parts of the dancer's body, e.g. when one raised leg hides other parts of the body from the field of view of a specific sensor. In addition, using multiple sensors results in a larger capturing area since the total field of view can be increased, depending on the placement of the sensors. We use three depth sensors placed on an arc of a circle in front of the dancer, thus allowing the dancer to move in a larger area. In addition, skeleton fusion decreases the noise inherent in skeletal tracking data of depth sensors.

Prior to fusion, sensor calibration procedure must take place in order to estimate the rigid transformation between the coordinate systems of each sensor and a reference sensor. For each sensor, we use the Iterative Closest Point algorithm [13] implementation from the Point Cloud Library (PCL, http://pointclouds.org/) [14] to estimate a rigid (Rotation-Translation) transformation, which is subsequently used to register the skeleton data captured by the sensor in the reference coordinate system. Registered skeletons corresponding to each sensors are then combined into a single skeleton representation using a skeletal fusion procedure, based on positional data (Fig. 2).

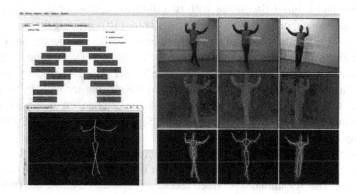

Fig. 2. Skeletal fusion from three Kinect sensors

Initially, the sum of all joint confidence levels of each (registered) skeleton is computed and the skeleton with the highest total is selected as the most accurate representation of the person's posture (base skeleton). Based on the joints of this skeleton, we enrich it with data provided by the remaining skeletons. Specifically, if the confidence of a joint of the base skeleton is medium or low, the joint position is corrected by taking into account the position of this joint in the remaining skeletons: if corresponding joints with high confidence are found in any of the remaining skeletons, their average position is used to replace the position value of the joint; otherwise, the same procedure is repeated first for joints containing medium confidence values and then for joints containing low confidence values. Finally, a stabilization filtering step is applied in order to overcome problems due to rapid changes in joint position from frame to frame which may occur because of the use of joint position averaging in our fusion strategy. The final result of this procedure is a more robust animation of the 3D virtual avatar of the user.

4   The Game-like Application

The main objective of the proposed game-like application is to teach two variations of the Greek traditional dance "Tsamiko" (i.e., the single style consisting of 10 steps and the double style consisting of 16 steps). Towards this end, two learning activities were designed and implemented, in close cooperation with dance experts, each one consisting of a number of specific exercises. The learner has to perform all of the exercises successfully to achieve the activity objective. Each exercise consists of several dance steps, which are presented to the learner one by one. In order to proceed to the next exercise, the learner must repeat the current exercise at least 3 to 5 times correctly. At the beginning of each exercise, a 3D animation of the virtual avatar of the expert performing the specific moves is shown to the learner. Afterwards, the learner is expected to imitate the same moves correctly. If the imitation is successful enough, the game progresses to the next exercise. Otherwise, the learner is expected to repeat the same exercise until she/he performs the moves correctly.

More specifically, the game consists of two *Activities* related to the two variations of the dance and a *Final Challenge* with two different options each: "Observe" and "Practice" in order either to observe the exercises or to start practicing the dance routines respectively. There is also a tutorial aiming at explaining to the learner the basics of how to play the game. In order to teach how to use each user interface element, a 2D virtual tutor presents both the sensors and the GUI to the learner. More specifically, the virtual tutor explains a) the basics of Tsamiko dance, b) the sensing technology used in this game, c) the Observe screen sub components and d) the Practice screen sub components. When tutorial finishes, the learner is expected to continue with the observe phase of the first activity, followed by the practice phase.

Both learning activities have an Observe screen (Fig. 3a), which shows the performance of the expert. In this screen, the learner can watch the moves repeatedly in order to learn them. The 3D animations, video recordings and dance music are presented to the user. The moves are all controlled via the animation player, which is located at the bottom center of the screen. The Observe screen consists of different visual and functional elements, such as the 3D expert view (central view), the animation player (bottom center), the exercise indicator (top center), a video of the expert performance (top-right) and two close-up camera views (center/bottom-right). Subsequently, the Practice screen is used to enable the learner to practice the moves that he/she observed in the Observe screen. The Practice screen (Fig. 3b) shows the expert's avatar at the central window from a backward view, so as to facilitate the learner to repeat his moves. It also contains: a) the animation controller (central-bottom), used both for recording of the performance of the learner as well as for its playback so that the learner can examine the mistakes he/she made, b) The exercise indicator (central-top), i.e. a panel where the learner can see the current exercise and the remaining exercises to complete the activity, c) a video of the expert performance (top-right), synchronized with the animation of the expert, d) the avatar of the learner (center-right) from a backward view and e) close-up view (bottom-right) of the expert avatar's legs from a backward view.

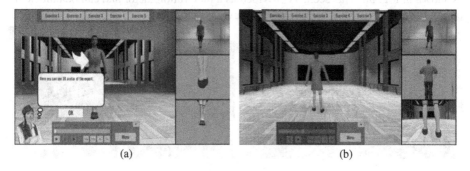

(a)   (b)

Fig. 3. a) Observe and b) Practice screen

The practice starts with an introduction from the virtual tutor. After providing some basic instructions, the virtual tutor asks the learner to get ready and a counter starts counting down. Then, the learner is expected to imitate the moves of the expert displayed on the screen. After the performance is completed, the evaluation process starts and the virtual tutor presents the evaluation score along with an appropriate message, e.g. "Outstanding performance! You are ready for the next exercise/activity!". If the learner goes beyond a pre-defined success threshold, the virtual tutor asks him/her to get ready for the next exercise. If the performance was not as good as expected, the learner is asked to repeat the exercise. Although the exercises progress sequentially, in some cases the learner has to repeat not only the previous exercise but also some of the previous ones. The flow graph of dance exercises for each activity is shown in Fig. 4, where each exercise is labeled (a)-(h). If all of the exercises are completed successfully, the activity is considered as completed and the next activity unlocks.

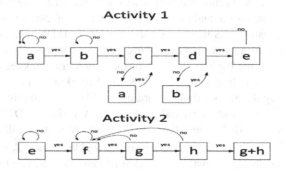

Fig. 4. The flow graph of dance exercises in each activity

Two 3D environments were created for the Tsamiko dance game. For the first and second activity, the 3D environment is a modern dance studio with parquet floor and a big mirror at the back wall (Fig. 5a). The mirror has the same functionality as in real dance studios and provides a reflected image of the dancer. For the final challenge activity, a 3D model of the famous "Odeon of Herodes Atticus" in Athens is designed, as shown in Fig. 5b. This scene is provided as a motivation factor and can be unlocked only when the learner has completed the previous activities.

Fig. 5. (a) Dance studio (left) and (b) Odeon of Herodes Atticus 3D environments (right)

4.1 Evaluation Metrics and Score Calculation

One of the most important elements of the game is the evaluation of the performance of the learner, which is based on the degree of similarity between his body movement and the moves performed by the expert. In order to perform this comparison, specific features are extracted from the learner and expert motion. Those features constitute two time series, which are compared by applying the Dynamic Time Warping (DTW). DTW is a well-known technique for measuring similarity between two temporal sequences that may vary in time or speed. The DTW algorithm calculates the distance between each possible pair of points/features of the two time series, constructing a cumulative distance matrix. It is used to find the least expensive path through this matrix, which represents the ideal warp, the alignment of the two time-series which causes the feature distance between their points to be minimized [15]. This is considered as a distance between the time series under comparison, and provides a good metric of their similarity.

We used three feature sets which are used as input to DTW separately in order to obtain three distinct distance measures. Taking into account that in Tsamiko dance the leg movements constitute the key elements of the choreography, knee and ankle joint positions were used. The first feature set consists of local ankle positions (relative to the waist). By taking the 3D positional coordinates of both left and right ankle relative to the waist, we obtain a 6-dimensional time series. A variant of DTW called multi-dimensional DTW is applied to these time series in order to provide a distance measure. For the 2nd and 3rd feature sets we derive the normalized knee and ankle distances [16]. Specifically, the relative (to waist) 3D position of knee (K_R, K_L) and ankle (A_R, A_L) joints for both left and right feet are used to measure the knee-distance D_K and the ankle distance D_A in each frame:

$$D_K = |K_L - K_R| \tag{1}$$

$$D_A = |A_L - A_R| \tag{2}$$

However, these distances both depend on the height of the dancer, so to ensure invariance to dancer's height a specific normalization process is applied. More specifically, normalized distances are calculated by dividing them by the distance of a "body path" connecting these joints. Thus, the normalized knee-distance $\hat{D}_K$ and ankle distance $\hat{D}_A$ are:

$$\hat{D}_K = \frac{D_K}{|K_L - H_L| + |H_L - R| + |R - H_R| + |H_R - K_R|} \text{ and} \tag{3}$$

$$\hat{D}_A = \frac{D_A}{|A_L - K_L| + |K_L - H_L| + |H_L - R| + |R - H_R| + |H_R - K_R| + |K_R - A_R|} \tag{4}$$

respectively, where H_L, H_R are the left/right Hip positions and R is the root(waist) position.

For each feature set, DTW provides a distance measure between the time-series of the user and the expert. These distances, one per feature set, are subsequently fed to a Fuzzy Inference System (FIS), which computes the final evaluation score (Fig. 6). The proposed FIS system is based on Mamdani method [17], which is widely accepted for capturing expert's knowledge and allows the description of the domain knowledge in a more intuitive, human like manner. The evaluation function produces a normalized scalar value between 0 and 1, which can also be translated into the appropriate text to be displayed by the virtual tutor.

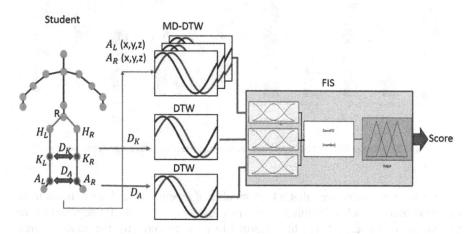

Fig. 6. Estimation of the evaluation score using the proposed DTW/FIS approach

5 Experimental Results

The proposed game-like application was evaluated by a class of students of the Department of Physical Education and Sports Science at Aristotle University of Thessaloniki.

More specifically, 18 students, both male and female, practiced Activity 1, i.e., the "single-step" style, consisting of five exercises. All students were beginners in Tsamiko dance and they were initially shown the "Getting Started" and "Observe" modes of the game. During the practice session, analytics were automatically gathered, such as the time of practice for each student, the number of repetitions for each exercise and the intermediate and final scores of students.

Figure 7 presents the average number of repetitions and the maximum average score per exercise. More specifically, as shown in Fig. 7a, students had less difficulty in passing exercises B and D. This is mainly due to the fact that these exercises have many similarities with their previous ones, i.e. exercise A and C respectively. As a consequence, students who had already practiced these exercises were familiarized with motion patterns, i.e. dance figures, appeared also in exercises B and D and, thus, it was easier for them to pass. As we can see in Fig. 7b, students achieved higher scores in exercise A and B, since these exercises are shorter and easier than the other three ones. It is worth mentioning that although exercise D has a great degree of difficulty, students achieved higher scores than in exercise C due to the reason described above. The lowest scores are appeared in exercise E, which is the most difficult one consisting of the dance figures of both exercise C and D.

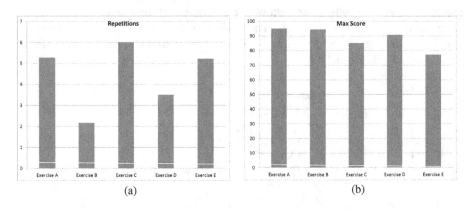

Fig. 7. a) The average number of repetitions and b) the maximum average score per exercise.

Moreover, it was noticed that a high number of repetitions lead many times to an increased score, which is justified by the fact that students gradually approached the movements of the expert, i.e. they learned to perform correctly the dance figures. Figure 8 presents the average number of repetitions for all exercises per student as well as the average score of each student. More specifically, the average score for all students was 85.56 %, while the number of repetitions for each student in all exercises was 4.4, which corresponds to an average practice time of 7.1 min per student.

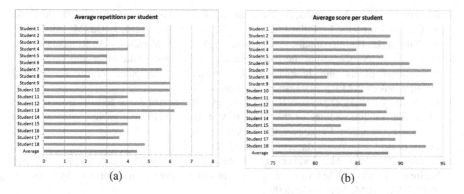

Fig. 8. a) The average number of repetitions and b) the average maximum score per student.

6 Conclusions

This paper presents a serious game application for transmitting ICH knowledge and specifically the Greek traditional dance "Tsamiko". The game is structured as a set of activities, each consisting of several exercises, aiming to teach different variations of the dance. One of the most important elements of the proposed game-like application is the evaluation of the performance of the learner, in order to provide meaningful feedback. To this end, the learner's movements are captured using a markerless motion capture approach, which aims to fuse skeletal data from multiple sensors into a single, more robust skeletal representation. Subsequently, the motion similarity between the learner's movements and an expert recording is performed through a set of appropriate performance metrics and a DTW/ FIS-based approach. Preliminary small-scale experiments with students of the Department of Physical Education and Sports Science at Aristotle University of Thessaloniki have shown the great potential of the proposed application.

Acknowledgement. The research leading to these results has received funding from the European Community's Seventh Framework Programme (FP7-ICT-2011-9) under grant agreement no FP7-ICT-600676 "i-Treasures: Intangible Treasures - Capturing the Intangible Cultural Heritage and Learning the Rare Know-How of Living Human Treasures".

References

1. De Gloria, A., Bellotti, F., Berta, R., Lavagnino, E.: Serious Games for education and training. Int. J. Serious Game **1**(1), 1–14 (2014)
2. Watkins, R., Leigh, D., Foshay, R., Kaufman, R.: Kirkpatrick Plus: Evaluation and Continuous Improvement with a Community Focus. Educ. Technol. Res. Dev. **46**(4), 90–96 (1998)

3. Dimitropoulos, K., Manitsaris, S., Tsalakanidou, F., Nikolopoulos, S., Denby, B., Al Kork, S., Crevier-Buchman, L., Pillot-Loiseau, C., Dupont, S., Tilmanne, J., Ott, M., Alivizatou, M., Yilmaz, E., Hadjileontiadis, L., Charisis, V., Deroo, O., Manitsaris, A., Kompatsiaris, I., Grammalidis, N.: Capturing the intangible: an introduction to the i-treasures project. In: Proceedings of the 9th International Conference on Computer Vision Theory and Applications (VISAPP2014), Lisbon, 5–8 January 2014

4. Raptis, M., Kirovski, D., Hoppe, H.: Real-time classification of dance gestures from skeleton animation. In: Proceedings of the 2011 ACM SIGGRAPH/Eurographics Symposium on Computer Animation, Vancouver, 05–07 August 2011

5. Dance central. http://www.dancecentral.com/

6. Drobny, D., Weiss, M., Borchers, J.: Saltate! - a sensor-based system to support dance beginners. In: CHI 2009: Extended Abstracts on Human Factors in Computing Systems, pp. 3943–3948. ACM, New York (2009)

7. Aylward, R.: Sensemble: A Wireless Inertial Sensor System for InteractiveDance and Collective Motion Analysis, Masters of Science in Media Arts and Sciences, Massachusetts Institute of Technology (2006)

8. VR-Theater project. http://avrlab.iti.gr/HTML/Projects/current/VRTHEATER.htm

9. Drobny D., Borchers, J.: Learning basic dance choreographies with different augmented feedback modalities. In: CHI 2010 Extended Abstracts on Human Factors in Computing Systems, ACM Press, New York

10. Unity. http://unity3d.com

11. Kinect for Windows | Voice, Movement & Gesture Recognition Technology. (2013) http://www.microsoft.com/en-us/kinectforwindows/

12. Kitsikidis, A., Dimitropoulos, K., Douka, S., Grammalidis, N.: Dance Analysis using Multiple Kinect Sensors. In: VISAPP2014, Lisbon, 5–8 January 2014

13. Besl, P., McKay, N.: A method for registration of 3-D shapes. IEEE Trans. Pattern Anal. Mach. Intell. **14**(2), 239–256 (1992). (Los Alamitos, CA, USA: IEEE Computer Society)

14. Rusu, B., Cousins, S.: 3D is here: point cloud library (PCL), In: IEEE International Conference on Robotics and Automation, 9–13 May 2011

15. Holt, G., Reinders, M., Hendriks, E.: Multi-dimensional dynamic time warping for gesture recognition. In: Thirteenth Annual Conference of the Advanced School for Computing and Imaging (2007)

16. Kitsikidis, A., Dimitropoulos, K., Yilmaz, E., Douka, S., Grammalidis, N.: Multi-sensor technology and fuzzy logic for dancer's motion analysis and performance evaluation within a 3D virtual environment. In: HCI International (2014), Heraklion, 22–27 June 2014

17. Mamdani, E.H., Assilian, S.: An experiment in linguistic synthesis with a fuzzy logic controller. Int. J. Man Mach. Stud. **7**(1), 1–13 (1975)

Augmentation of Board Games
Using Smartphones

Artūras Kulšinskas[✉], Cătălin Bălan, Nicholas Bukdahl,
and Anthony Lewis Brooks

Aalborg University Esbjerg, Niels Bohrs Vej 8, Esbjerg, Denmark
{akulsi11,cbalan11,nbukda11}@student.aau.dk, tb@create.aau.dk

Abstract. This paper contains details about research into the effect of digital augmentation on social presence in board games. A case study of the board game *Tobago* was performed during the project and a prototype application for smartphones was developed in order to compare the players' social presence in traditional and augmented versions. A repeated measures experiment was carried out with 15 subjects, during which both quantitative and qualitative data was collected. The results of the experiment show that while digital augmentation did not increase social presence in this board game, transferring some of the physical elements to digital medium is a viable game design choice.

Keywords: Board game · Smartphones · Digital augmentation · Social presence

1 Introduction

New types of board games combining physical and digital elements - hybrid board games - can be created using recent technological advancements such as smartphones and tablets. Previous research in the field of hybrid board games [1,2] looks at usability and new forms of interaction. Board games are primarily a social activity [3] and so, if any changes are to be made to them, it is important to investigate their effect on social elements as well.

The goal of the project is to investigate what effect digital augmentation has on social presence in traditional board games. The results of this research could potentially help board game designers both when designing new board games and adapting existing ones to new technologies.

1.1 Social Presence

Until recently, social presence was primarily associated with telecommunications and could be summarized as "the sense of being with another" [4]. However, as network bandwidth, processing power and the amount of smartphones increase, there is a need to expand the theory of social presence. Social presence theories can be divided into four categories [4].

© Springer International Publishing Switzerland 2015
M. Antona and C. Stephanidis (Eds.): UAHCI 2015, Part III, LNCS 9177, pp. 483–492, 2015.
DOI: 10.1007/978-3-319-20684-4_47

The *binary formulation* of social presence is the simplest one and treats another person as either present or not present [5]. However, it is strongly argued that social presence should be regarded as a continuum, not as a binary state [4].

The definition of social presence relating to *co-presence*, however, only covers sensing another body. It does not state that the body has to respond to anything or inhabit any kind of intelligence [4].

The body has to exhibit some signs of intelligence, which is defined as intentional and intelligent responses to the environment and others. The *psychological involvement* definition of social presence states that it is important to have access to another intelligence [6]. The users have to be able to project themselves and understand the projected other [7]. Other researchers argue that social presence is very closely related to two concepts: immediacy and intimacy [8]. Immediacy is described as "directness and intensity of interaction between two entities" [9, p. 325], while intimacy deals with "proximity, eye-contact, smiling, and personal topics of conversation etc." [10, p. 95].

The *behavioral engagement* dimension of social presence definitions is more recent than the others, mostly due to advances in communication and virtual reality systems. The researchers in this area state that reaction and interactivity are important, and the users can "effectively negotiate a relationship through an interdependent, multi-channel exchange of behaviors" [11, p. 291].

In order to make the project goal more clear, a definition of social presence had to be chosen. The definition created by [6] states that:

> "The minimum level of social presence occurs when users feel that a form, behavior, or sensory experience indicates the presence of another intelligence. The amount of social presence is the degree to which a user feels access to the intelligence, intentions, and sensory impressions of another." (p. 22)

This project took notion of this particular definition of social presence. The users would already be co-located and psychological involvement would be the important factor in social presence in a board game session, where players should react to other players' actions. It is thus expected that there will be a change in social presence in the hybrid version when compared to the traditional version.

1.2   State of the Art

Social presence in games is a topic of interest that only recently started emerging [12]. However, it is an important research angle because, while the social angle was not a focus in the early days of game development, it is now clear that games have more social richness than previously believed [12].

Reference [13] developed a prototype of a digitally augmented version of the classic game *The Settlers of Catan*. The idea of the research was that traditional board games could be improved by automating non-strategic actions such as board set up and resource distribution. This version was then compared to a traditional, fully physical version, and a fully digital version running on an

Apple iPad. The hybrid version was shown to have the highest scores in relation to players' social experience. However, the experiment was carried out in a laboratory setting with a stationary hybrid version.

Reference [1] also worked on a hybrid version of *The Settlers of Catan*. While the project did not explore the effects on social interaction, it provided an insight into what features could be transferred to a digital format. A survey carried out by the researchers showed that the players of hybrid board games would like to see:

- Randomly changing game board;
- Automatic rule enforcement and error detection;
- Virtual players.

The prototype was positively received by the test subjects. It was developed using a smartboard and was expected to be a viable solution for future board game enhancements.

Most board game digitization projects, such as the ones mentioned above, make use of tangible user interfaces (TUI) [14,15]. These interfaces are "concerned with providing tangible representations to digital information and controls, allowing users to quite literally grasp data with their hands" [14, p. 4]. Tangibles are an important part of board games, but the advantage of implementing tangibles directly into the digital interface comes at the cost of portability. TUIs generally imply that a bulky setup needs to be created for the interface to work [16,17].

As an alternative to TUIs, [2] digitized parts of the game *Power Grid* by using smartphones. Tedious tasks, calculations and trading mechanics were transferred to smartphones and tablets. These *tedious tasks* were operations which players tended to forget during a play session. The tracking of the game's state was achieved by scanning elements of the board by using built-in cameras on smartphones and tablets. Additionally, introducing object and board tracking via camera required modifications to the game board and made the players perform certain actions in both digital and physical space. This research focused on the usability of the smartphones in the context of a board game.

2 Methods

Tobago [18], an existing board game, was chosen to be augmented for the purpose of this project. It is a competitive game where players have to find treasures hidden on a map. The game is centered around *locating* and *collecting* treasure.

Players use clue cards to search for treasure (clue cards such as *the treasure is near a statue* or *the treasure is not in a forest*) (Fig. 1). When treasures are found, players race across the map to pick them up. When a player reaches a treasure and collects it, the game rewards all players who helped with finding that treasure, not just the person who collected it.

During gameplay, players use several artifacts: clue cards, treasure cards (points), the board, small cars (which mark the player's position on the board),

Fig. 1. Treasure view in the traditional version.

markers (which players use to indicate where a treasure might be), amulets (collectible objectives on the board) and landmarks (pieces which indicate special locations on the board and are set up at the beginning of the game).

2.1   Prototype Design

A prototype application for smartphones was created in order to augment *Tobago*. A subset of the game rules were digitized, based on an initial play test and on an analysis of the game rules.

The game rules were not altered during the design process.

For the design of the prototype, two groups of game pieces were transferred to the mobile interface: clue cards and treasure cards. The fact that all cards were digital meant that the following interactions took place using the mobile phone

1. Placing clue cards to find treasures.
2. Handling card draws and discarded cards.
3. Visualizing already played clue cards.
4. The entire treasure distribution process.

As a result, several tedious tasks were handled by the digital interface:

1. Players no longer needed to check if placing a card constituted a correct move or not, as the device did automatic rule checking.
2. Players no longer needed tokens to keep track of who played each card.
3. Players no longer needed to keep track of the treasure distribution process, and could focus more on which treasure they actually wanted to collect.
4. Players were reminded when they needed to add amulets to the map.

Amulets, resources used to make additional actions during a player's turn, represented a problem for the digitization process. The actions made using amulets could take place through either the physical or the digital interface. However, amulets could only be collected through the physical interface. The digital interface could not be made aware of how many amulets players had, unless modifications to the original game or setup were made. Asking players to collect amulets using both interfaces would have complicated the interaction, thus the amulets were kept only physical. The smartphone alerted players whenever they needed to use amulets, but trusted players to actually have a physical amulet to use.

All these decisions enabled the two interfaces to be synchronized during a gameplay session. Players were only required to set up the game at the start of the session using both interfaces. Afterwards, the smartphone was able to advance the state of the game without any information regarding to what was taking place on the physical board. Actions which took place in the physical interface did not affect the digital one.

The prototype was implemented in Python, using Kivy [19]. Kivy is a cross platform user interface toolkit for Python, designed for touch interfaces.

Digital Constraints. Mobile devices have a different set of affordances compared to physical cards. Affordances, as defined by [20], refer to "the perceived and actual properties of the thing, primarily those fundamental properties that determine just how the thing could possibly be used" (p. 9). For example, cards can be shuffled while a mobile device cannot.

The differences in affordances imposed constraints on the design of the prototype. The most significant such constraint was the small screen to visualize all the information which is normally available on the table. Therefore, the interaction was split across several different screens.

During initial play testing, players did not always chose a card and then chose the treasure they wanted to place it on. Sometimes they chose the treasure first. Therefore, the user interface was designed in such a way that both interactions were possible. Players could chose a card in the *card view* (Fig. 2a) and this choice was then reflected in the other views. Similarly, players could chose a treasure in the *treasure view* (Fig. 2b) or the *treasure detail view* (Fig. 2c), which was then reflected in the *card view*.

The interface was simpler for treasure distribution as everything could fit on one small screen. Players only needed to see one treasure card at a time and the order in which collection took place (Fig. 2d).

2.2 Experimental Design

Repeated measures experimental design was chosen as it allowed to compare the effect of the conditions within the group. A convenience sample of Aalborg University Esbjerg students and members of a local board game club was used for the experiment (five pre-formed groups of three people each), ages 18 to 35. For university students, the test venue was one of the rooms in the university, while board game club members performed the tests in their club. Firstly, the participants were asked pre-test questions regarding their experience and familiarity with both board games and smartphones. During the test the participants were

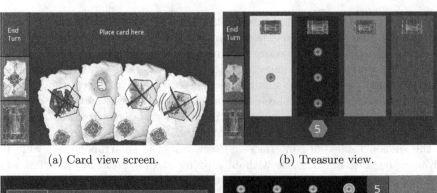

(a) Card view screen.   (b) Treasure view.

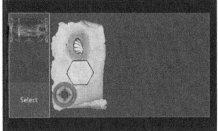

(c) Treasure detail view.   (d) Treasure distribution screen.

Fig. 2. Screen captures from the application.

filmed so that the video data could be later analyzed in-depth. After the users experienced the augmented version, they were asked questions about the use of the application. When a test group underwent both conditions, they were asked open-ended questions to reveal the users' thoughts on usability of the application and compare the two versions.

When the participants had completed playing each condition the test subjects were asked to fill out the social presence in gaming questionnaire (SPGQ) [12]. The questionnaire is designed to measure how aware and involved the players were with their co-players. It is a self-report measure, in which the players answer questions on a five point Likert scale and is divided into three sections: *empathy*, *negative feelings*, and *behavioral involvement*.

SPGQ is used to compare the players' scores between traditional and hybrid version players in order to determine the effects on social presence. It is expected that if social presence increased, empathy and behavioral involvement score would decrease, while negative feelings score decreased [13].

3   Results

The questionnaire data completed by the 15 participants was analyzed to determine if there was a consistent difference between the two conditions. A t-test was performed to measure if the change between the conditions was significant. Each of the three categories measured by SPGQ were summarized separately for both of the conditions. These results can be found in Table 1. The table shows means (along with standard deviations) for the measurements, as well as the scores for the t-tests. The distribution of the questionnaire results can be seen in Fig. 3.

Table 1. SPGQ results summary. Data is represented as mean (SD). All p values are noted for a two-tailed t-test.

Measurement	Condition		t	p
	Traditional	Hybrid		
Empathy	3.70 (0.62)	3.44 (0.80)	-1.82	0.090
Negative feelings	2.22 (0.68)	2.38 (0.61)	1.22	0.242
Behavioral engagement	3.90 (0.49)	3.88 (0.71)	-0.17	0.866

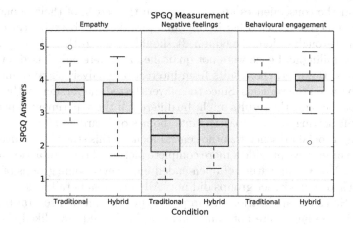

Fig. 3. SPGQ result distributions.

No significant change was measured in any of the three parameters. The measured increase in *negative feelings* and decrease in *behavioral engagement* were not statistically significant. However, *empathy* scores decreased on average by 0.26 points when players experienced the hybrid version of the prototype. Although not significant enough ($p = 0.09$), the measured p value indicated a decrease in social presence in the hybrid version.

4   Discussion

The five recorded gameplay sessions were also analyzed using interaction analysis [21] while looking for elements related to social presence, specifically gaze, smiling and personal topics of conversation [4], in order to triangulate with the quantitative results provided by SPGQ.

It was noticed that the players' behavior and conversations were similar between the two conditions. The participants joked in both versions of the game and the topics of these jokes were similar. The content of conversations that were not related to the game was observed to be heavily related to external factors such as the day of the week, or past and future events. Furthermore, the frequency of these conversations was similar between the conditions.

Smiling was another focus point while performing interaction analysis. Players were noticed smiling in both version when reacting to game events or other players. Gaze was also found to be related to social presence and for this reason it was observed. While playing the traditional version the players split their focus between their cards and the board. Similar behavior was noticed in the hybrid version, except instead of cards, participants looked at their mobile phones. The users looked at each other in both versions, but not as much as they did at board and cards (or phones) and generally when it was not their turn.

In the traditional version when one player made his turn, the others observed the action and its consequences. This did not happen in hybrid version as the actions and the consequences are only seen on the screen of their phones. Still, the players reacted to each other in the same way, despite observing the effects of the actions through different medium. It should be noted that the observations relating to smiling and gaze were not quantified and were only based on general observations. However, the results from interaction analysis show similar social presence between the versions. Since the players tested the versions of the game in a laboratory setting, the results might be different if the experiment is performed in a real life setting, such as participants' homes or board game clubs.

Although social presence was the central focus of this study, the video material and the interviews provide a more complete picture of the interaction and user experience. Due to the nature of open-ended interviews, some groups of participants touched topics other groups did not. All participants talked about usability issues. Since the application was in prototype stage, it had several bugs. The players said the bugs were not game breaking but would have liked the hybrid version better if they were fixed. Several participants noted they felt safer playing the augmented version since the computer kept track of most of the rules and it made it easier to play. It was also mentioned that since the game had less physical elements, it made the game more portable than the original. A suggestion was given to make the physical part of the game printable for even higher portability. Participants mentioned that they would not sacrifice portability in favor of full tracking of game state with bulky setup. An advantage of physical version, according to the players, was the better overview of the game. In the hybrid version the players had to navigate through different screens to see all the information, while in the physical version everything was on the table at the same time. A majority of the participants felt afraid that either they or another player would accidentally cheat while not knowing how to operate the application. This can be avoided by providing additional checks and an interactive help menu. Two groups of players said that having the application on their phone reduced the distraction caused by the device. As the application could not be minimized, the players could not do background tasks like messaging or browsing while playing the game.

An interesting behavior was observed in each of the groups. Players who had unused tangibles near them, like marker cubes and amulets, held them in their hands or played with them. When asked about this behavior, they could not find a reason why they did it. The players said it was something they did unconsciously and were unsure of how they would feel if this interaction was removed. Two of the participants who did not have such tangibles near them said they would have liked to play with the objects but did not want to reach to the other side of the table and take them.

5 Conclusion

The research shows that digital augmentation of board games using smartphones did not produce a statistically significant change in social presence. Some differences in social interactions were noticed in video material between the traditional and hybrid versions, however they did not seem to be related to social presence. Some players noted that the hybrid version felt safer to play and praised its portability. The results point to digital augmentation being a viable board game design choice.

In order to further validate and generalize the results of the study, the experiment should be repeated using a similar design process as previously but a different board game should be augmented for another case study.

Acknowledgements. We would like to thank the students of Aalborg University Esbjerg and members of the *Lords Assembly* board game club who helped test the prototype. Furthermore, the authors would like to thank Christian Petersen who was an integral part of this project.

References

1. de Boer, C.J., Lamers, M.H.: Electronic augmentation of traditional board games. In: Rauterberg, M. (ed.) ICEC 2004. LNCS, vol. 3166, pp. 441–444. Springer, Heidelberg (2004)
2. Thijs, G.: Electronic Augmentation of Board Games through Smartphones. Master's thesis, Katholieke Universiteit Leuven (2012)
3. Magerkurth, C., Engelke, T., Memisoglu, M.: Augmenting the virtual domain with physical and social elements: towards a paradigm shift in computer entertainment technology. Comput. Entertain. **2**(4), 12–12 (2004)
4. Biocca, F., Harms, C., Burgoon, J.: Toward a more robust theory and measure of social presence: review and suggested criteria. Presence **12**(5), 456–480 (2003)
5. Huguet, P., Galvaing, M.P., Monteil, J.M., Dumas, F.: Social presence effects in the stroop task: further evidence for an attentional view of social facilitation. J. Personal. Soc. Psychol. **77**(5), 1011–1025 (1999)
6. Biocca, F.: The Cyborg's Dilemma: Progressive Embodiment in Virtual Environments. J. Comput.-Mediat. Commun. 3(2) (1997)
7. Savicki, V., Kelley, M.: Computer mediated communication: gender and group composition. CyberPsychol. Behav. **3**(5), 817–826 (2000)

8. Rice, R.E.: Media appropriateness: using social presence theory to compare traditional and new organizational media. Hum. Commun. Res. **19**, 451–484 (1993)
9. Mehbabian, A.: Orientation Behaviors and Nonverbal Attitude Communication. J. Commun. **17**(4), 324–332 (1967)
10. Argyle, M.: Social Interaction, vol. 103. Atherton Press, New York (1969)
11. Palmer, M.T.: Interpersonal communication and virtual reality: mediating interpersonal relationships. In: Biocca, F., Levy, M.R. (eds.) Communication in the Age of Virtual Reality, pp. 277–299. L. Erlbaum Associates Inc., Hillsdale (1995)
12. Kort, Y.A.W., Ijsselsteijn, W.A., Poels, K.: Digital Games as Social Presence Technology: Development of the Social Presence in Gaming Questionnaire (SPGQ). In: Proceedings of PRESENCE 2007: The 10th International Workshop on Presence, pp. 195–203 (2007)
13. Ip, J., Cooperstock, J.: To virtualize or not? the importance of physical and virtual components in augmented reality board games. In: Anacleto, J.C., Fels, S., Graham, N., Kapralos, B., Saif El-Nasr, M., Stanley, K. (eds.) ICEC 2011. LNCS, vol. 6972, pp. 452–455. Springer, Heidelberg (2011)
14. Shaer, O., Hornecker, E.: Tangible user interfaces: past, present, and future directions. Found. Trends Hum.-Comput. Inter. **3**(1–2), 1–137 (2010)
15. Fitzmaurice, G.W., Ishii, H., Buxton, W.A.: Bricks: Laying the foundations for graspable user interfaces. In: Proceedings of the SIGCHI Conference on Human Factors in Computing Systems, pp. 442–449. ACM Press/Addison-Wesley Publishing Co., New York (1995)
16. Magerkurth, C., Memisoglu, M., Engelke, T., Streitz, N.: Towards the next generation of tabletop gaming experiences. In: Proceedings of the 2004 Graphics Interface Conference, pp. 73–80. GI 2004, Canadian Human-Computer Communications Society, School of Computer Science, University of Waterloo, Waterloo, Ontario, Canada (2004)
17. Leitner, J., Haller, M., Yun, K., Woo, W., Sugimoto, M., Inami, M.: IncreTable, a mixed reality tabletop game experience. In: Proceedings of the 2008 International Conference on Advances in Computer Entertainment Technology, pp. 9–16. ACM, New York (2008)
18. Allen, B.: Tobago (2009)
19. Virbe, M., Hansen, T., Pettier, G., Arora, A., Knapp, B., Pittman, J., Rousch, B., Kovac, J., Taylor, A., Einhorn, M.: Kivy (2014). http://kivy.org
20. Norman, D.A.: The Design of Everyday Things: Revised and Expanded Edition, Chap. 4. Basic Books, New York (2013)
21. Jordan, B., Henderson, A.: Interaction analysis: foundations and practice. J. Learn. Sci. **4**(1), 39–103 (1995)

Games Accessibility for Deaf People: Evaluating Integrated Guidelines

Ana L.K. Waki, Guilherme S. Fujiyoshi, and Leonelo D.A. Almeida$^{(\boxtimes)}$

Federal University of Technology - Paraná, Curitiba, Brazil
{alk.waki,gfuji1211}@gmail.com, leoneloalmeida@utfpr.edu.br

Abstract. The lack of accessibility in digital games imposes barriers for people with disabilities. Currently there is not a standardized set of guidelines however there are researches that consisted in integrating guidelines disperse in several sources as, for example, the integrated set of guidelines for games accessibility for deaf people proposed by Waki, Fujiyoshi and Almeida. In this study we propose and conduct a process for evaluating that set of integrated guidelines that is composed of two complementary evaluation techniques that articulates predictive evaluations with prospective game developers and workshops with deaf gamers. The results provided us with information: (a) on whether the set of integrated guidelines is sufficient for determining accessibility of digital games; and (b) for refining the set of integrated guidelines.

Keywords: Deaf people · Games · Accessibility · Evaluation · Guidelines

1 Introduction

Digital games often demand more cognitive and motor skills when compared to other common interactive applications due to specific input devices, complex interaction techniques, and emphasis on visual control and attention [5]. Thus, people with disabilities may face barriers to access and use digital games. Issues related to accessibility in the development of digital games have stimulated several improvements in current games e.g. closed captions for game characters, and visual representation of aural clues.

Studies have proposed approaches to alleviate or remove access barriers in digital games (e.g. [5,7,9,12]) and their contributions can be classified as [5]: (a) external Assistive Technologies (ATs) for data input or data display (e.g. [9,12]); (b) games designed for people with a specific disability (e.g. [7]); and (c) games designed to be universally accessible without requiring other ATs (e.g. [5]).

In addition to the aforementioned approaches, researches proposed sets of guidelines or suggestions to support the design or evaluation of accessible games (e.g. [2–4,6,8]). Commonly, guidelines vary regarding the scope of disability (i.e. specific or universal), game genre (e.g. adventure, puzzle, role-playing game), information about the issue approached by the guideline, impacts, and techniques for meeting the guidelines. Currently, there is not a standardized set of

© Springer International Publishing Switzerland 2015
M. Antona and C. Stephanidis (Eds.): UAHCI 2015, Part III, LNCS 9177, pp. 493–504, 2015.
DOI: 10.1007/978-3-319-20684-4_48

guidelines for games accessibility, as occurs in other areas, e.g. Web Content Accessibility Guidelines for websites [11]. However, there are preliminary initiatives to integrate existing guidelines (e.g. [2, 6, 10]).

Waki, Fujiyoshi, and Almeida [10] integrated some of the main sets of guidelines for games accessibility for deaf people. That study proposed a method that consisted of: normalization (i.e. breaking the guidelines into comparable units and identifying similarities, complements and contradictions among them) and consolidation of these guidelines (i.e. reorganization in a set that keeps references to the original guidelines). Besides, the guidelines' complementary information, when available, were organized into three categories (i.e. "What?", "Why?" and "How to apply?") aiming at providing clear information for designers and evaluators. In complement to the information integrated from the guidelines sets, [10] conducted a workshop involving two deaf professors (with little familiarity to digital games) for discussing the issues and preferences of deaf people in the context of digital games. The preliminary results of that workshop provided information for: supplying new complementary information for the integrated guidelines, and rearranging the guidelines in order to provide clear and unambiguous instructions. On the other hand, the preliminary evaluation was insufficient for providing clear information on how gamers and potential game developers could benefit or could directly use the integrated set of guidelines.

In this study we propose a process for evaluating sets of guidelines and conduct it on the set of guidelines integrated by Waki, Fujiyoshi and Almeida [10]. Our method involves two evaluation activities: workshops with deaf gamers and predictive evaluation by undergraduate Information Systems students (and potential game developers) using the integrated set of guidelines. The two evaluation activities provided us with information to analyse the coherence of the integrated guidelines to the deaf people' needs, and the usefulness of them for prospective game designers.

This paper is organized as follows: Section 2 reviews existing guidelines for accessible digital games. Section 3 describes the integrated set of guidelines. Section 4 reports the method and the results of the evaluation activities. Section 5 discusses the evaluations results. Finally, Sect. 6 concludes.

2   Reviewing Existing Guidelines

There are several studies that aim to increase accessibility on digital games (e.g. external ATs, games designed for people with a specific disability, and games designed to be universally accessible)[5]. This work focuses on studies that provide support by means of indications on how to design and/or evaluate specific features, considering one or more disabilities. Those indications are usually organized in sets of guidelines, recommendations, suggestions, and others. Despite of the different nomenclatures for the sets (usually based on how mature and prescriptive an indication is) the objective is to provide resources (e.g. texts, graphics, examples) for supporting the design and/or evaluation of digital games. Also, some works propose the integration of different sets of such indications, considering different contexts e.g. [2, 4, 8, 10].

Cheiran [2], in his master's thesis, approaches accessibility issues considering different types of disabilities. The survey conducted by him selected guidelines proposed by other five projects, and proposed an integrated set of guidelines based on the organization of the Web Content Accessibility Guidelines 2.0, from W3C [11].

Considering the access barriers found in digital games for deaf people, Waki et al. [10] present an integration of recommendations on games accessibility for deaf people. The integration involved sets of guidelines and suggestions from other five studies. In complement to the sets from the literature, Waki et al. also conducted an exploratory study involving deaf consultants for identifying additional issues.

Garber [4] describes the relevant aspects of people with disabilities and their relation to the games, such as the benefits from promoting accessibility for impaired individuals and barriers in the attempt to persuade the gaming industry to offer better accessibility. According to Garber, most of the accessible games are generated by small companies, individuals or researchers. This initiative is gradually stimulating some of the major producers of games, also influenced by organizations that advocate for the rights of people with disabilities, to increase accessibility of their products.

Despite the popularity of First-Person Shooter (FPS) games, this game genre is not very appreciated by the deaf community because of the difficulties faced, mainly, due to the need for fast reactions to succeed in the missions. Nogueira et al. [8] investigated how communication strategies were adopted by players, by the analysis of some FPS. The findings of that research provided reflections on the use of audio in projects of new games and its impact for players with hearing impairments.

Other initiatives such as the Able Gamers [1] and the International Game Developers Association (IGDA) [6] are non-profit organizations that promote the involvement of communities of game developers for proposing indications on how to provide accessibility resources for digital games. Able Gamers focuses on players with disabilities. In 2012 the foundation developed a manual of good practices for promoting the accessibility for players with several needs, such as visual and hearing impairments. The manual explains the most important accessibility options that can be included in a game and what each option means to the players. IGDA supports the investigation of general issues related to the creation of digital games. In 2004, the association launched the article "Accessibility in Games: Motivations and Approaches" that is intended to provide information about accessibility in games and addresses issues for different types of disabilities and limiting conditions.

This work focuses on the set of guidelines from Waki et al. [10] since (1) it is the most recent study to our knowledge, and (2) it approached both the sets of indications and the sets of integrated indications presented in this section.

3   Integrated Set of Guidelines

This section summarizes relevant aspects of the set of integrated guidelines from Waki et al. [10]. First we present the method for integration of the different set of guidelines, followed by some examples of guidelines. Finally, we present some results from the activity with deaf consultants.

The method for integration of the different sets of guidelines for digital games accessibility for deaf people consisted of 5 steps: (1) separation of the guidelines in smaller informational blocks, (2) codification of each block in order to be able to keep track of the original sets, (3) classification of the blocks in: guideline title and complementary information, organized in three topics i.e. "What is it?", "Why?", and "How to apply?", (4) refining and testing the integrated set by the researchers through the evaluation of 13 games from different genres [10], and (5) identification of possible issues still not covered through an activity with deaf consultants.

The resulting set is composed of 19 integrated guidelines. Table 1 presents some of these guidelines (only the title and respective sources from which they were extracted). Table 2 presents a complete example of guideline.

Table 1. Examples of guidelines titles from Waki et al. [10].

ID	Guideline title [source(s)]
01	Closed Captioning [2,3,6,8]
02	Subtitles [2,3,6,8]
06	Alternative representation of events [2,3,6,8]
07	Options for including environmental sounds as text output [2,3]
08	Enough time for understanding events [2,4,6]
10	Multi-player communication through sign language [8]
11	Instructions through sign language [8]
12	Translation of text and audio to sign language through videos [2,8]
15	Use of a more accessible vocabulary [8]
18	Configuration of alternative sound files [6]

Waki et al. [10] concluded that none of the original sets of guidelines fully covered all the integrated guidelines. Also, after the activity with deaf consultants they verified that the integrated set proposed by them covered all the aspects pointed.

4   Evaluation Activities

The method for evaluating the set of integrated guidelines consisted of four activities: (1) predictive evaluation of mainstream games by the researchers using the set of guidelines; (2) exploratory activity with deaf consultants using some of the games of the previous activity, and without the set of guidelines; (3) workshops with deaf gamers using only the games chosen in the activity 1, and without the

Table 2. Complete example of a guideline from Waki et al. [10].

Title	06. Alternative representation of events [2,3,6,8]
What is it?	Replicate events non perceptible for deaf gamers in alternative ways (e.g. visual effects and joystick vibration)
Why?	Replication of events non perceptible for deaf gamers helps them to be aware of what is happening. Graphical elements are also better understood by deaf gamers and are useful for children and adults to keep aware of the game dynamics.
How to apply?	Provide gamers with other resources for receive events notifications. Use images and animations as possible.

set of guidelines; and (4) predictive evaluation with (prospective) game developers using the set of integrated guidelines. After each of the evaluation activities the set of guidelines was iteratively refined.

The first two activities of the method are published in Waki et al. [10]. The evaluation of mainstream games was performed by the researchers of the project, aiming to define the preliminary set of consolidated guidelines to be used in other evaluations. In this first activity 13 games were evaluated: Battlefield 4, Borderlands 2, Child of Light, Don't Starve, GCompris, GRID Autosport, League of Legends, Magic 2014, Resident Evil 6, Show do Milhão, Sudoku Pro, The Sims 2, and Valiant Hearts. The results were analysed and used for determine which game would be evaluated in the next activities.

The second activity analysed some of the games that presented interesting results in the previous activity (i.e. Battlefield 4 and Resident Evil 6) with deaf consultants. The consultants were invited to explore the games and think aloud while they experienced issues. The consultants provided another information regarding the deaf culture, since they are active researchers on the social inclusion of deaf people. The detailed results of the first two evaluations are described in Waki et al. [10].

Next subsections describe the results of the two last evaluations of our method i.e. workshops with deaf gamers and predictive evaluations with game developers.

4.1 Workshops with Deaf Gamers

We conducted two workshops with different participants. In the first workshop there were three participants, while there were six participants in the second. All the participants were deaf and in both the workshops, when necessary, the communication was mediated by a sign language interpreter. Both the workshops were organized in three steps: the first step was the presentation of the workshops' purpose, a brief conversation with the participants and the application of a questionnaire to assess the participants' familiarity with games, and filling a Informed Consent; in the second step, the researchers presented the games that could be used in the next step and the participants were invited to choose the games they would like to experience; and in the third step, the participants had the opportunity to experience the chosen games and discuss with the whole group their perceptions and issues while playing the games.

The games (followed by the respective genders) presented to the participants were: Valiant Hearts (puzzle / strategy), Don't Starve (adventure / survival), Battlefield 4 (FPS), Show do Milhão (puzzle), The Sims 2 (simulation), Sudoku Pro (puzzle), League of Legends (on-line action) and Resident Evil 6 (Third Person Shooter). The game chosen by the participants for the first workshop was Battlefield 4; The Sims 2 and Resident Evil 6 were selected for the second workshop.

In the **first workshop** the participants experienced some difficulty about the questionnaire. The words "rarely" and "time" (in Brazilian Portuguese) were initially misinterpreted. The correct meaning of the words in the phrases were explained to the participants and those problems were solved in the second workshop.

In respect to tutorial game modes, usually presented before the beginning of the game, the participants informed that the some basic details need to be better explained, such as "Who is the enemy?" and "What is the color used to represent a specific element of the game?". According to them, it is necessary just a short explanation, indicating colors and subtitles of what is important in the gameplay. One participant informed that it is important to not rely only the written language, since not all deaf people domain it, reiterating the importance of visual elements for supporting the player.

Other participant also suggested the use of closed captioning so that the player could be aware of possible events that may be taking place in the game.

One of the participants briefly played the game Battlefield 4. In the first actions, the participant found it too difficult to jump the obstacles in the scenario. The instructions on how to perform the action appears in the right side of the screen and it is not clear to the player that he must press two keys simultaneously. After overcome this first issue with support from the researchers, the participant faced another problem: he did not realize that he needed to enter in a room through a door. The game provided a white circle on the door handle so that the player could use that hint to discover the way that must be followed. However, the visual representation was very subtle and passed unnoticed by the participant. After some time, the participant perceived the information on the door handle and continued the game, but not for long. Just after he crossed the door a mission was assigned to the player. The mission consisted in to pick up munition in a box in a corner of the scenario. The participant did not understand what was to be done, and only after being aided by the researchers of where to go he could continue the mission. In this part of the game the characters were talking all the time that the player needed to grab the munition in the box, but the subtitle was in English (the participants were Brazilian Portuguese native speakers). After getting the munition, the player should protect a fellow being attacked by enemies. The game shows the instructions very briefly, so that the participant did not perceived this information, and took a while to realize how to use the keys and buttons to complete the goal. This experience lasted about 15 min.

After that the participants were invited to discuss in group about the game. The first question raised was related to the location of the indicator of the amount of available ammunition since it was not realized by any of the participants. The participant noticed when he was hit by a shot, but did not realize where it was the indicator of "remaining life". The indicators of available ammunition and remaining life were in the periphery of the screen, in the lower right corner.

The participants also did not notice the instructions to "crouch" or "jump" over obstacles that had to be explained by the researchers to continue the game. The participant who played the game also said that if the basic movements of the game, such as walking forward, back and sides were not explained before the experience with the game, he would not know how to start. He suggested the inclusion of a tutorial mode, unaware that he had played the introduction, which plays the role of a tutorial in this game. Another participant suggested that these basic movements should be shown on separated screens, with the possibility of using sign language to explain certain concepts. The importance of visual representation and the use of sign language were considered valuable in this part of the workshop.

After a brief discussion, the participants received a sheet of paper containing a screenshot of the game and were invited to draw on it the aspects they would like to change for improving the game accessibility for deaf gamers. Figure 1 presents the screenshot annotated by the participants. After that the researchers created an adjusted design of the annotated screenshot. The result is presented in the Fig. 2. Elements for notification of events as steps of other players, sounds of helicopters, tanks, and others are presented in the top center of the screen. Also, other players received a contour different for fellows (blue) and enemies (red). Information about remaining life and munition are located in the top left corner of the screen. In contrast to the original indications the suggested indications to use graphical representations.

The **second workshop** with deaf gamers was organized as the first work-shop. We only changed the available games to avoid repetition in relation to the first workshop. Before the discussion of the game The Sims 2, the first point raised by the participants was the translation of texts to sign language. One of the participants argued that it would not be feasible, since sign language is not unified, so that it would be the need for translating to several languages.

Some of the participants considered the game The Sims 2 good and easily understandable, while others pointed that improvements were needed. One of the participants, who already knew the game, reported that in a previous game match he did not hear a baby character complaining about something, which resulted in the death of the character.

In a situation of the game testing, the home phone started ringing. That event were presented by audio cues and an animation representing sound waves. However, none of the participants realize until one of the researchers inform them. One participant suggested the inclusion of an option to the player enable the screen vibration to events like that, thus, non-deaf players could disable this option. In addition to the vibration, the game could also use colors together to represent each type of event, for example, a color for the phone, other for car horns, and others.

Fig. 1. Screenshot of the game Battlefield 4 annotated by the participants of the first workshop.

Fig. 2. Representation created based on the annotations of the participants.

When asked about the use of texts in the game, the participants agreed that the use of sign language is necessary for long texts. The participants suggested an icon to be placed on text blocks where there was the translation to sign language, so that the player could click on it to see the translation. For small texts, there was disagreement among participants. Some of them agreed that there is no need for any type of translation, while others thought it was necessary. One participant suggested the use of images next to short texts to represent them, thus avoiding a translation to sign language.

The second game evaluated in the second workshop was Resident Evil 6. When performing the first moves of the character, one of the participants suggested the use of sensors on the players' body to control the moves in the game.

Another point discussed was the lack of notification of events taking place in the game when he was playing on the keyboard of a computer. An example that demonstrates this issue occurred when there were enemies approaching and the brightness of the scenario was intentionally low. Figure 3 presents that scenario and highlights (red rectangles) hidden enemies due to the low brightness.

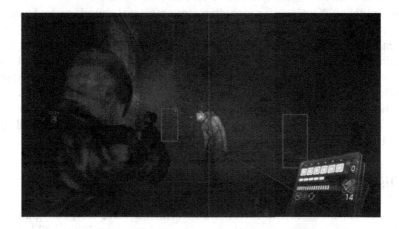

Fig. 3. Example of issue related to events notification in the Resident Evil 6.

One of the participants suggested that texts about objects to be translated to sign language in the beginning of the game (e.g. a glossary). Some participants supported the idea of using joystick vibration, since they believe it could be an incentive to keep playing or as a tool for better understanding the gameplay.

4.2   Predictive Evaluation with (Prospective) Game Developers

After the workshops we conducted two evaluation sections involving undergraduate Information Systems students. Those students were selected based on their proficiency with digital games and potential of becoming game developers. The activity consisted in the evaluation of the games investigated in the workshops with deaf gamers, using the set of integrated guidelines. The students were also invited to review and suggest improvements to the set of guidelines.

At the beginning of the activity, each participant received a copy of the set of integrated guidelines (in a version already refined based on the workshops with deaf gamers) and a Informed Consent form. The researchers briefly introduced the project objectives to the students and explained the purpose of the activity.

The activity involved two different sessions, with different students as well. For the first session the researchers provided a notebook with Battlefield 4 installed (the same used in the first workshop) so they could play at any time they needed to collect some information. For the second activity it was available the game The Sims 2 and Resident Evil 6 (the games used in the second workshop).

We observed that most of students' contributions focused on the guidelines that required less programming effort. Fact that could be related to the point of view of a game programmer. The guidelines that usually require more complex programming effort (e.g. Communication through sign language) received less contributions from the students. Examples of guidelines that were adjusted based on the comments of the students are 7 and 08 (see Table 1).

The guideline "Options for including environmental sounds as text output", deals with inclusion of textual representations of sounds in the game environment. Students complemented the respective informative text by arguing that a good place to apply the guideline would be centralized on the screen edges, so that it would be easily noticeable but, at the same time, not disruptive. Another suggestion was on the guideline "Enough time for understanding events", that raises the question of the providing enough time for perceiving and understand events. The students argued that the guideline is not applicable to all game genres. However it should be applied whenever it is needed.

5 Discussion

As a result of the literature review we identified several incipient guides and sets of indications. Furthermore, there is no standard accessibility guidelines for digital games. The integration process conducted by Waki et al. [10] is an attempt to organized different sources of relevant information spread across the literature and on-line communities. Also, information was added for each guideline aiming at facilitating the understanding and application of the guidelines. After the integration process of the guidelines, Waki et al. proposed a set of 19 guidelines. The set was iteratively refined by our evaluation process.

Our evaluation process focused on gathering information from different points of view (representatives of the target audience and prospective game developers). Each of the activities brought different perspectives and experiences that encouraged thinking on the integrated set of guidelines. All the evaluation process was done prioritizing the direct participation of the target group, composed of volunteers.

In the activity performed with deaf consultants, Waki et al. [10] reported the benefits from better understanding the social perspective of deaf people. That activity provided some indications that opposed some of the initial guidelines e.g. the use of a simplified language, since they considered that games could be a relevant mean for learning written languages.

The workshops with the deaf gamers discussed more intensively the aspects involving alternative representation of audio cues. Also, the participants debated about the interference of visual pollution on the gameplay. The participants agreed that the visual and tactile perceptions are of great relevance for the immersion in any game. They also emphasized that these aspects should receive more attention from mainstream gaming industry.

Deaf players could be benefit from notifications, warnings and instructions, necessary for the progress in the game, to be presented next to the focus of their attention (usually in the center of the screen). When this information is passed quietly and/or briefly in periphery of the screen, they often go unnoticed, as occurred in situations in the game Battlefield 4, in which it showed the commands to jump and crouch to overcome objects, or when the player should not realize the circle on the door was indicating that he had to interact with the object.

Despite of not being directly related to deafness, the arrangement of certain instructions also hindered the interaction. For example, in the game Battlefield 4, the representation of types of munitions that could be chosen, afforded the movement keys (see Fig. 1). The deaf players also proposed the use of a movement assessment sensor (e.g. Kinect) and the use of tactile perception (e.g. joystick vibrations), arguing that it would make games more stimulating and easier for deaf gamers get immersed.

The evaluation of the integrated set of guidelines by the Information Systems students provided us with information about issues in understanding the guidelines. They asked about the meaning of some terms as "closed caption" and "alternative representation of events". The participation of students resulted in changes in fourteen out of the nineteen guidelines. Most of the changes were related to the understanding of the guidelines, and the results of this evaluation were used as an input for supplementing the guidelines' contents.

We believe that, despite the main contribution of this work is the integrated set of guidelines for supporting games developers in designing and evaluating digital games, our participatory evaluation process is a relevant approach for evaluating emerging sets of guidelines. The results of the evaluation activities were satisfactory regarding the ability for revealing aspects that could the underestimated by activities based only on predictive evaluations with experts on IT. It is also relevant to emphasized that we believe accessibility evaluations should not be limited to sets of guidelines. The direct involvement of people with disabilities is essential for any software development and is not different for digital games.

6   Conclusions

This paper proposed an evaluation process for the set of integrated guidelines for designing and evaluating accessible digital games to deaf people, from Waki et al. [10]. The process involved four evaluation activities, two of them presented in this study: two workshops with the participation of deaf gamers, and two predictive evaluations with (prospective) game developers, with the intent to asses the guidelines upon a game development process view.

The workshops with deaf gamers were useful to collect information that allowed us to improve the set of guidelines. Some examples of the results are: positioning of subtitles in the screen, the way that events should be handled (e.g. environment noises, steps), ways to display blocks of text translated to sign language.

The predictive evaluation with students collected information mostly related on how the set of guidelines should be adopted in the development of a digital game. After those activities, based in the opinion of the students, we were able to detect which of the guidelines in the set would be the most complex ones to implement, which tend to be the ones that involves sign language in any way (e.g. translation of texts to sign language, multi-player communication via sign language). Also, we collected information to improve the guidelines e.g. the ways that the game sounds could be exhibited to deaf gamers.

Future research involves: applying the evaluation process to other sets of guidelines, evaluate other games genres using the set of integrated guidelines of Waki et al. [10], make the set of integrated guidelines publicly available, and invite the community of games developers to collaborate to the sets of guidelines and to the evaluation process.

References

1. Barlet, M.C., Spohn, S.D.: Includification: A pratical guide to game accessibility (2012)
2. Cheiran, J.F.P.: Jogos Inclusivos: diretrizes de acessibilidade para jogos digitais. Master's thesis, University of Federal do Rio Grande do Sul (2013)
3. Deaf Gamers: (2000–2013). http://www.deafgamers.com
4. Garber, L.: Game accessibility: enabling everyone to play. Computer **46**(6), 14–18 (2013)
5. Grammenos, D., Savidis, A., Stephanidis, C.: Designing universally accessible games. Comput. Entertain. **7**(1), 29 (2009). Article 8
6. IGDA: On auditory disabilities (2003–2014). http://igda-gasig.org/about-game-accessibility/development-frameworks/auditory/
7. Miller, D., Parecki, A., Douglas, S.A.: Finger dance: a sound game for blind people. In: 9th ACM SIGACCESS, pp. 253–254. ACM (2007)
8. Nogueira, D.N., Coutinho, F.R.S., Soares Jr., W.A., Prates, R.O., Chaimowicz, L.: Analyzing the use of sounds in fps games and its impact for hearing impaired users. In: Proceedings of SBGames SBC, pp. 127–133 (2012)
9. Ossmann, R., Thaller, D., Nussbaum, G., Veigl, C., Weiß, C.: Making the playstation 3 accessible with AsTeRICS. In: Miesenberger, K., Karshmer, A., Penaz, P., Zagler, W. (eds.) ICCHP 2012, Part I. LNCS, vol. 7382, pp. 443–450. Springer, Heidelberg (2012)
10. Waki, A.L.K., Fujiyoshi, G.S., Almeida, L.D.A.: Consolidation of recommendations on games accessibility for deaf people. In: XIII Brazilian Symposium on Human Factors in Computer Systems (IHC 2014) (2014)
11. World Wide Web Consortium: Web content accessibility guidelines (wcag) 2.0 (2008). http://www.w3.org/TR/WCAG20/
12. Yuan, B., Folmer, E.: Blind hero: enabling guitar hero for the visually impaired. In: 10th ACM SIGACCESS, pp. 169–176. ACM (2008)

Enhancing Self-Motivation Through Design of an Accessible Math App for Children with Special Needs

J. MacCalla, Jin Xu, and Ayanna Howard[(✉)]

Zyrobotics, LLC, Atlanta, GA, USA
{jmaccalla,jxu,ahoward}@zyrobotics.com

Abstract. The inclusion of learning activities using tablet devices in the classroom environment continues to grow. Unfortunately, this corresponding increase has not correlated with a growth in accessible content for children with special needs. In fact, most children with a reported disability take fewer science and math courses than mainstream students primarily due to the unavailability of information in accessible formats. In this paper, we discuss an educational App that makes math engaging to students while being accessible to children with special needs. We then present a pilot study to collect empirical evidence on how well the app self-motivates the user. Results from the study, which involved thirty-four participants, show significant measures of self-motivation when using the educational math app.

Keywords: Accessible math · Special needs · Gamification · Intrinsic motivation

1 Introduction

Tablet devices are known to provide an interactive experience that has revolutionized learning for children. Unfortunately, while these tablet devices are intuitive to utilize and easy for many children, those with motor limitations tend to have difficulties due to the fine motor skills required for interaction. Thus, as tablet devices are increasingly being integrated into the classroom environment, there is a measurable demographic of school-age children, such as those with motor disabilities, that are not being given equal access [1].

To enable general access to computing platforms, children with motor impairments typically use a physical device, such as a switch, to gain access. Switch types of devices range from hand switches, head switches, foot switches, mouth switches, and even switches that can detect muscle movement. Software applications that enable access through switches to mobile tablets are called switch-accessible Apps. Based on the emerging appeal of tablets, there has been a slow influx of switch-accessible Apps being created [2]. Unfortunately, of the 675,000 Apps listed as native to iPad in October 2014, less than 0.02 % of them were switch-accessible. Despite the popularity of Apps, only a few have considered accessibility, especially in the context of motor impairments [3, 4]. In fact, in a recent survey [5], it was noted that very few Apps could support accessibility with respect to motor limitations - 24 % required two-handed input, 50 % required complex

© Springer International Publishing Switzerland 2015
M. Antona and C. Stephanidis (Eds.): UAHCI 2015, Part III, LNCS 9177, pp. 505–513, 2015.
DOI: 10.1007/978-3-319-20684-4_49

surface gestures such as swiping or two-finger pinch, and 10 % used motion gestures—all of which have important implications for motor-impaired accessibility.

Given that the societal adoption of tablet devices continues to grow and access continues to remain unequal for children with movement disorders, our objective is to increase access to educational content for children with motor disabilities that support their goals in the classroom environment. In the K-12 space, approximately 11 % of children between the ages of 6 to 14 have a reported disability [1, 6], and yet these students took fewer science and mathematics courses than those without disabilities. Since these differences are generally due to the unavailability of information in accessible formats [6], our emphasis in this paper discusses the inclusion of math content into switch-accessible Apps for children with motor disabilities. In this paper, we discuss elements of the math App that make it engaging to students while being accessible to children with special needs. We then present a pilot study to collect empirical evidence on how well the app self-motivates the user. Results from the study, which involved thirty-four participants, show that these types of apps are enjoyable and self-motivating based on the Intrinsic Motivation Inventory [7], a validated multidimensional measurement device used to assess participants' subjective experience related to a target activity.

2   Description of Accessible Math Apps

Intrinsic motivation (or self-motivation) is shown to be a vital factor in learning. Intrinsic motivation involves an individual engaging in various learning opportunities because they are seen as enjoyable, interesting, or relevant to meeting one's core psychological needs [10]. There are three inherent sources of intrinsic motivation that have been highlighted by researchers [11] - the need for developing competence, the need for relatedness, and the need for autonomy. With respect to children's learning, the need for developing competence can be achieved by ensuring learning activities are set right above the learner's skill level so that the child feels success after accomplishing a task. For children with special needs, where traditional educational materials are not always provided in alternative, accessible formats, relatedness can be achieved by creating learning activities that are accessible and enjoyable to all, thus creating meaningful connections based on common activities shared with their peers. Autonomy for children with disabilities can be accomplished by ensuring learning materials are accessible based on the student's needs and abilities and thus can be used independently. Students who feel like they have a choice and are provided a sense of control are more likely to engage in the learning activity. Thus, any education app that is designed for children with special needs should incorporate these factors into their design to enhance intrinsic motivation.

In the early child development literature, cause-and-effect refers to a child's understanding that an action can produce a result to control the environment. Through play, a child typically learns the concept of cause-and-effect, which is an important step in their developmental process [8]. For many children with disabilities, purposeful movement across space will not occur until they understand this concept of cause-and-effect. Thus, many special education teachers that use mobile apps with children with special needs, tend to use cause-and-effect apps and/or apps that require visually attending to objects of interest [9]. As such, we focus on designing accessible math apps based on this cause-and-effect framework that incorporates the three factors for enhancing intrinsic motivation as discussed above. The need for competence is addressed by incorporating different learning settings that can be selected based on the current knowledge level of the child. The need for relatedness is addressed by gamifying the education math app such that it is engaging to all children with or without special needs. The need for autonomy is addressed by incorporating adjustable settings that makes the education app accessible to children with differing abilities.

OctoPlus is a math adaptation of a cause-and-effect gaming app called Turtle Invaders [12]. OctoPlus places the user in an underwater water world where the user has to battle turtles to score points (Fig. 1). OctoPlus reinforces key addition math skills within an interactive gaming environment through the inclusion of both a drill and challenge mode. Through adjustable learning settings (such as a beginner, advanced, and expert mode), students can learn and be assessed based on their own individual learning skills. OctoPlus is also switch-accessible and is designed to enhance motor skills for young children and kids with motor or cognitive delays. OctoPlus incorporates the common core math standards associated with Operations and Algebraic Thinking, namely:

- CCSS.MATH.CONTENT.K.OA.A.3 - Decompose numbers less than or equal to 10 into pairs in more than one way
- CCSS.MATH.CONTENT.K.OA.A.4 - For any number from 1 to 9, find the number that makes 10 when added to the given number
- CCSS.MATH.CONTENT.K.OA.A.5 - Fluently add and subtract within 5.

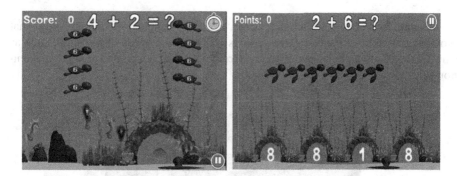

Fig. 1. OctoPlus Game Scenes. The left image shows the OctoPlus Drill Mode in which different equations that add up to the same number are sequentially presented. The right image shows the OctoPlus Challenge Mode at the beginner level in which the user must select the correct answer to solve the equation.

ZyroMath City Count is a math app based on the runner game concept. The runner game concept is simple; you run until you die. Despite its simplicity, runner games are among the most popular gaming Apps on mobile devices. ZyroMath City Count places the user in a city environment where the user must jump to collect stars to score points, while also jumping over obstacles to survive (Fig. 2). Just as with OctoPlus, ZyroMath is designed to be switch-accessible and accessible to children with motor or cognitive delays. ZyroMath City Count incorporates the common core math standards associated with Counting and Cardinality, namely:

- CCSS.MATH.CONTENT.K.CC.A.1 - Count to 100 by ones and by tens
- CCSS.MATH.CONTENT.K.CC.A.2 - Count forward beginning from a given number within the known sequence
- CCSS.MATH.CONTENT.K.CC.A.3 - Represent a number of objects with a written numeral 0-20 (with 0 representing a count of no objects)

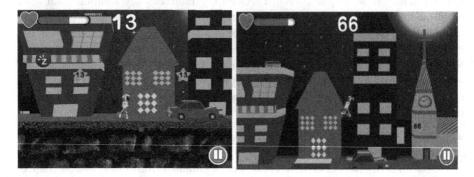

Fig. 2. Example of the ZyroMath City Count Scene, where the user must jump to collect stars to count and earn points.

In addition to being switch-accessible, each app employs a settings menu that provides the ability to adjust game settings based on the needs of the child, such as slowing or speeding up the game avatars or removing the background to improve attention (Fig. 3).

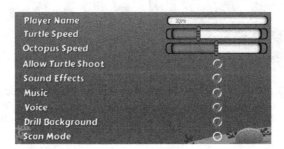

Fig. 3. Adjustable game settings for the OctoPlus math app allows, for example, changing the speed of the game characters or removing background, voice, or sound effects.

3   Experimental Setup

To evaluate self-motivation of users when using the accessible math gaming app and confirm that the factors we selected in the design can enhance intrinsic motivation, we employ the Intrinsic Motivation Inventory (IMI) instrument [11], which has been used in several experiments related to intrinsic motivation and children [13, 14]. In IMI, the interest/enjoyment subscale is considered the self-report measure of intrinsic motivation; thus, it is the only subscale we use in this study.

3.1   Participants

Thirty-four (34) adult participants were recruited and the study conducted using Amazon's Mechanical Turk service. In prior studies, Mechanical Turk was shown to provide a sufficiently diverse participant pool necessary for conducting high-quality studies involving human participants [15, 16]. Three different math games were selected for play and randomly assigned. The opening instructions provided were as follows:

We are studying how accessible math games can motivate children with special needs. The results from this study will enable us to design more effective mobile applications for children with disabilities. In this study, you will play two iterations of a math game. It shouldn't take you any longer than 10-15 min. After playing the games, you will need to fill out a survey.

3.2   Testing Scenario

There were three different math games employed in this study – *You Do the Math*, *OctoPlus*, and *Math Game*. Group 1 (*G1*) was randomly assigned to play the math game called *You Do the Math* (Fig. 4) in which each participant used a calculator-type interface to answer addition equations. Group 2 (*G2*) was randomly assigned to play the accessible math game *OctoPlus* in which each participant had to answer addition equations by shooting turtles when in the arch with the correct answer (Fig. 1). Group 3 (*G3*) was randomly assigned to play the math game called *Math Game* in which each participant answered addition equations by selecting the correct answer via touch (Fig. 4). For these game scenarios, the math equations focused on adding two numbers, summing up to 10.

Participants in each group played two iterations of their game. The self-report measure of intrinsic motivation was calculated based on the interest/enjoyment subscale of the IMI, as shown in Table 1. The score for the IMI instrument is calculated by first reversing the score of the items for which a (*) is shown in Table 1 and then using the resulting number as the item score. The self-report measure of intrinsic motivation is then calculated by averaging across all of the items on that subscale.

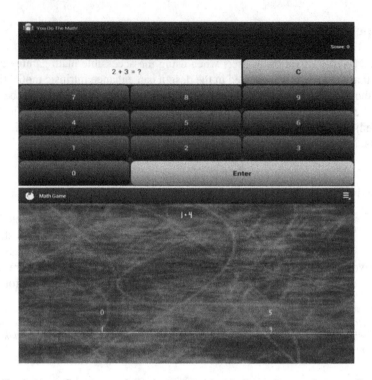

Fig. 4. Top image – Game scene from the *You Do the Math* app; Bottom image – Game scene from the *Math Game* app.

Table 1. Interest/enjoyment subscale of the Intrinsic Motivation Inventory. This subscale is considered the self-report measure of intrinsic motivation.

	1 not at all	2	3	4 somewhat true	5	6	7 very true
I enjoyed doing this activity very much							
This activity was fun to do.							
I thought this was a boring activity. (*)							
This activity did not hold my attention at all. (*)							
I would describe this activity as very interesting.							
I thought this activity was quite enjoyable.							
While I was doing this activity, I was thinking about how much I enjoyed it.							

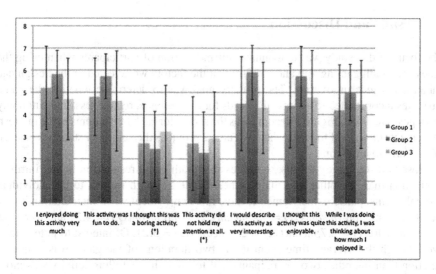

Fig. 5. Decomposition of participant averages for the interest/enjoyment subscale of the IMI used to assess self-motivation.

Table 2. Study statistics correlated with evaluating intrinsic motivation associated with each of the math gaming apps.

	Group 1 - *You Do the Math*	Group 2 *OctoPlus*	Group 3 *Math Game*
Age			
<21	1	1	2
21-30	6	6	6
31-40	3	4	5
Gender			
Male	7	8	10
Female	3	3	3
No. Participants	10	11	13
Avg. Time Played (min)	8.7	17.6	14.0
Average IMI Score	4.81	5.64	4.67
Stdv IMI Score	1.75	0.97	1.70

4   Results and Discussion

The focus of this study was to evaluate self-motivation of participants when using the accessible math gaming app and confirm that the factors we selected in the design can enhance intrinsic motivation. The primary goal was to determine whether the game attributes incorporated to address the needs for competence, relatedness, and autonomy had a positive effect. Figure 5 decomposes the scores for each of the items in the interest/enjoyment subscale of the IMI whereas Table 2 provides the summary statistics on each of the participant groups.

Based on the survey results, the accessible math game resulted in higher intrinsic motivation than the other two math games (Table 2). With respect to the individual subscale items, participants seemed to have more enjoyment when interacting with the OctoPlus math app $\{mean(G1) = 5.2; mean(G2) = 5.8; mean(G3) = 4.7\}$ and were less bored $\{mean(G1) = 2.7; mean(G2) = 2.5; mean(G3) = 3.2\}$. Of interest to note is that, even though the average time spent doing two iterations of the game was longer in duration than the other two, participants still felt that the OctoPlus activity was more fun to do $\{mean(G1) = 4.4; mean(G2) = 5.7; mean(G3) = 4.8\}$. Although, based on the sample size, these results only indicate trends in the data, it does show some evidence that the accessible math app can enhance self-motivation in participants.

5   Conclusions

The pilot study discussed in this paper was designed to investigate elements of an accessible math app and collect empirical evidence on how well the app enhances intrinsic motivation. Although the study involved adult participants, this work lays the foundation in understanding how an accessible math app can be designed to address the needs of competence, relatedness, and autonomy. To further build an evidence base, future studies will expand to include children and children with various disabilities. Another future study will also investigate the impact on math skills and whether gains in math knowledge are achieved. These future studies are necessary to fully validate the effectiveness of math education apps, especially with respect to engaging children with disabilities in additional learning opportunities.

Acknowledgments. This work was supported in part by NSF SBIR Grant IIP-1447682. Development of the ZyroMath application is sponsored by the National Institute on Disability and Rehabilitation Research (NIDRR) of the U.S. Department of Education under grant number H133E110002. Any opinions, findings, and conclusions or recommendations expressed in this material are those of the author's and do not necessarily reflect the views of the National Science Foundation or the National Institute on Disability and Rehabilitation Research.

References

1. U.S. Department of Education, National Center for Education Statistics, Digest of Education Statistics, 2010 (NCES 2011–015) (2011)

2. Farrell, J.: Switch Accessible Apps for iPad and iPhone Growing Apace. http://www.janefarrall.com/blog/2012/08/12/switch-accessible-apps-for-ipad-and-iphone-growing-apace/ Accessed February 2014

3. Mustaquim, M.M.: Assessment of universal design principles for analyzing computer games' accessibility. In: International Conference on Computers Helping People with Special Needs, pp. 428–435 (2012)

4. Yuan, B., Folmer, E., Harris, F.C.: Game accessibility: a survey. Univers. Access Inf. Soc. **10**(1), 81–100 (2011)

5. Kim, Y., Sutreja, N., Froehlich, J., Findlater, L.: Surveying the accessibility of touchscreen games for persons with motor impairments: a preliminary analysis. In: 15th International Conference on Computers and Accessibility ACM SIGACCESS, New York (2013)

6. Bech-Winchatz, B., Riccobono, M.: Advancing participation of blind students in Science, Technology, Engineering, and Math. Adv. Space Res. **42**(11), 1855–1858 (2008)

7. Guyton, G.: Using toys to support infant-toddler learning and development. YC Young Child. **66**(5), 50–56 (2011)

8. Saylor, G.M., Rodriguez-Gil, G.: Using the iPad and a sequence of apps for young children with multiple disabilities. ReSources **17**(2), 33 (2012)

9. Intrinsic motivation inventory. Self-Determination Theory Questionnaires. http://www.psych.rochester.edu/SDT/measures/intrins_scl.html Accessed November 2014

10. Froiland, J.M., Oros, E., Smith, L., Hirchert, T.: Intrinsic motivation to learn: the nexus between psychological health and academic success. Contemp. Sch. Psychol. **16**, 91–101 (2012)

11. Ryan, R.M., Deci, E.L.: Self-determination theory and the facilitation of intrinsic motivation, social development, and well-being. Am. Psychol. **55**(1), 68–78 (2000)

12. Howard, A., MacCalla, J.: Pilot study to evaluate the effectiveness of a mobile-based therapy and educational app for children. In: ACM Sensys Workshop on Mobile Medical Applications, Memphis, November 2014

13. Vos, N., Van der Meijden, H., Denessen, E.: Effects of constructing versus playing an educational game on student motivation and deep learning strategy use. Comput. Educ. **56**, 127–137 (2011)

14. Xie, L., Antle, A.N., Motamedi, N.: Are tangibles more fun? Comparing children's enjoyment and engagement using physical, graphical and tangible user interfaces. In: Conference on Tangible and Embedded Interaction, pp. 191–198. ACM Press (2008)

15. Buhrmester, M., Kwang, T., Gosling, S.D.: Amazon's mechanical turk a new source of inexpensive, yet high-quality, data? Perspect. Psychol. Sci. **6**(1), 3–5 (2011)

16. Paolacci, G., Chandler, J., Ipeirotis, P.: Running experiments on amazon mechanical turk. Judgment Decis. Making **5**(5), 411–419 (2010)

The Use of Multisensory User Interfaces for Games Centered in People with Cerebral Palsy

Eliza Oliveira, Glauco Sousa, Icaro Magalhães, and Tatiana Tavares[(✉)]

Federal University of Paraíba, João Pessoa, Brazil
{eliza,glauco,icaro,tatiana}@lavid.ufpb.br

Abstract. The evolution of user interfaces has improved the user experience, especially the sensory features. Also, the sensory aspect is crucial for the interaction, mainly for the development of effective assistive technologies. This study presents a game for people with Cerebral Palsy (CP). CP refers to a range of clinical syndromes characterized by motor disorders and postural changes that may or may not be associated with cognitive impairment and speech disorders. Due to restricted motor condition, sports and games become difficult for people with CP. Our challenge is to offer an alternative to people with PC based on tangible and multisensory devices. The use of a robotic ball allowed remote manipulation, which makes this solution useful for people with physical disabilities. Also, an user centered design process was adopted. The game encourages people to interact by using different control devices, making it an important resource for promoting play in these users.

Keywords: Assistive technology · Multisensory devices · Cerebral palsy · Games · User study · Tangible interfaces

1 Introduction

Human-Computer Interaction (HCI) is related to the functionality, design and evaluation of computer systems, to provide an effective and enjoyable user experience for individuals. To achieve these objectives is taken into account the process of communication between man and the computer system. Also you need to have knowledge about the characteristics of users, the contexts of the tasks that will be necessary for interaction to occur and the environments in which systems will be used. Human factors are therefore extremely important for the development and production of effective and efficient computational systems [1–3]. Currently, computer systems are increasingly dedicated to providing users with more sophisticated sensory experiences. Therefore, user interfaces and, consequently, computing systems are increasingly approaching ubiquity within our reality and our physical world. This fact is tangibly observable due to the proximity of physical elements, as the sensations of everyday life, such as playing, talking and listening [4].

Assistive technology (AT) is defined as the use of resources, products and services that work to provide independence and autonomy to people who show any dysfunction [5]. According to the Act the Americans with Disabilities (American with Disabilities

© Springer International Publishing Switzerland 2015
M. Antona and C. Stephanidis (Eds.): UAHCI 2015, Part III, LNCS 9177, pp. 514–524, 2015.
DOI: 10.1007/978-3-319-20684-4_50

Act), Assistive Technology is "any piece of equipment, product system, whether acquired commercially, modified or customized, used to increase, maintain or improve functional capabilities of individuals with disability" [6–8]. Also hardware or software can be consider as assistive devices of high performance in order to address the special needs of people with disabilities. That way they could fit within the TAs [9].

Several studies have been performed using TUI's in Assistive Technology with rehabilitate people with special needs A wide range of resources, products, and services that work to provide independence and autonomy for people who show any dysfunction have been developed [5]. The use of these technological devices may provide disabled children with enjoyable experiences in safe environments, in turn, enabling the patient to take risks and fearlessly try to achieve their goals. It is thought that this will ultimately cause a greater motivation and a higher engagement level during the child's rehabilitation. One use of these devices is to treat people with motor disabilities, such as cerebral palsy (CP).

Cerebral Palsy (CP) refers to a series of clinical syndromes characterized by motor disorders and postural changes which may or may not be associated with cognitive impairment and speech disorders. This ailment occurs from a significant lack of oxygenation of the brain cell within the first two years of life. The most common causes of this is the malformation of the central nervous system, in addition to genetic factors such as congenital infections [10]. Currently, the treatment of individuals with CP occurs with a multidisciplinary team with a focus on promoting the role of independence for the individual through the use of a large number of activities, based on the severity of the disorder. It is important to conduct a review of this subject matter in order to identify the areas with which these children have problems, in which ways they need to be assisted, and to what context their personal involvement is impaired. Additionally, to establish priorities for an intervention, environmental adaptations of objects should be performed to promote autonomy, prevent deformities and increased functionality. Early treatment is essential and leads to better outcomes and, consequently, greater independence of the subject [11, 12]. Stimulus is crucially important for the development of people with CP. Games can promote a therapeutic process for people with CP, as well as for people without physical disabilities and it provides the opportunity to try out new games while engaging in fun activities [13, 14]. Such games are, thus, a way to increase the motivation and engagement, to provide a greater social interaction, and to promote playing in patients who are in the process of motor rehabilitation [15–17]. The main goal of this paper is present a game for people with CP. We intend to put together the needs of a CP-users with the playability of a robotic ball. The robotic ball is a robotic device that allows remote control of its functions as movements and colors [18]. The use of a robotic device allows manipulation of the ball remotely, which makes this feature helpful for people with disabilities. For the development of this project, we need a multidisciplinary approach involving professional from occupational therapy, and computing. In the first section, our main interest is to present theoretical background. In the second section related work is detailed. After that the game is presented and also preliminary results achieved from an experience with an individual PC.

2   Theoretical Background

In literature we can find statements about the use of interactive technologies that explore multisensory qualities and help people to participate through their senses. Urbanowicz [19] emphasizes the power of these interactive technologies as important tools, which have the ability to enhance the perception of individuals. The same author also emphasizes that knowledge of the human senses led to the conclusion that sensory systems have a crucial role in the life of all beings, from the moment they allow the development of perceptual capacity of the environment in which we live [19]. The computer systems are dedicated to provide to its users sensory experiences. Besides intrinsic attributes of perception of shared environments, applications transcend the barrier of pixels and make the user part of it. Ishii [4] explains the concept of "radical atoms" through an analogy with icebergs and the ocean, as seen in Fig. 1. In this illustration, the iceberg is the interface that interacts with the user, the water is the digital world and outside of the water is the physical world. So, the first part of the figure, where the iceberg is totally submerged, shows a GUI (Graphical User Interface). The interaction with this interface/the forms below this surface is made through remote controls; such as a mouse, keyboard, or touchscreen. The second unit of the iceberg analogy refers to Tangible User Interfaces (TUI's) as they act as physical manifestations of Computing. Similar to the iceberg, with TUI's, there is a portion of the digital world reaching into the physical world, allowing a direct interaction with the tip of the iceberg/interface. The rightmost portion of Fig. 1 corresponds to the concept of "radical atoms." It is as if the iceberg emerged from the depths to reveal the mass that was submerged. This is the futuristic vision of Ishii, where he defines hypothetical dynamic materials that are computationally convertible and reconfigurable.

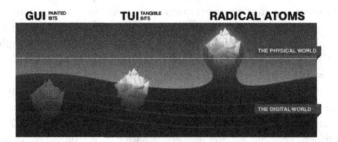

Fig. 1. Radical atoms [4]

Conceptually, all digital information contained in those dynamic materials has a physical manifestation that can be directly interacted with it.Additionally computational systems that develop user/computer relation from objects and environments in the physical world are made. In this sense, there are tangible interfaces (IT), which are based on the concept of tangible digital device, or touchable, that will ensure a realistic interaction between man and computer. The use of physical objects by ITs allows users to employ a wider range of actions and regain skills and knowledge acquired in the form of data manipulation [20, 21]. The day-to-day life of every individual is filled with objects whose functions, textures and shapes, determine specific ways to catch, carry, throw, throw, and thus build practices that shall be recovered in other situations. Within this perspective, the mediations between the individual and his environment are key determinants for the production of meanings. The action is considered a prerequisite for perception. Thus, the sensory inputs, such as the recognition of the environment only start to have meaning the extent to which actions are performed and the space around the individual is explored [20, 21]. In addition, systems that include interaction by tangible interfaces has not only a software structure, but also a physical structure, represented by physical space and objects. Thus, this systems are embedded in real space and physically embodied. Applications can offer a framework which includes facilitation, prohibiting or hindering of the actions in the moment that directs user behavior. This way, it can influences human behavior and patterns and emerging social interactions. This makes the tangible interactions really embody facilitation [22].

3 Related Work

Works that uses some kind of interaction resources to improve assistive technology have often been the focus for investigations, for example [16, 17, 23]. In all three studies, the authors put conditions to improve games in order to maintain the motivation of the players with respect thereto. Furthermore, it is emphasized that the interest of the subject at stake is an essential factor to be used in rehabilitation. The gameplay is therefore present in all studies, with a view that all studies show an interest in maintaining the quality of the user interaction with the games. In the first work the author puts as attractiveness factor of the games, the fact that the movements are assisted by computer. The second puts the guesses of the therapist and patients to improve the quality of the system and increase the interest of the subject. This system is based on Microsoft Kinect [24], which is a device with two cameras and peripheral complement

Table 1. Related work comparison.

	[17]	[23]	[16]
Devices	*Joystic* + mecanic arm	Kinect Xbox	*Wiimote/Wii Balance Board*
Interaction	TUI	NUI	TUI
Participants	18 people with CP	1 person with CP e 1 with muscular atrofy	10 people with CP
Gameability	Well-known games as spacecraft, balloons, sharks and football	Kinect games	Games with difficult levels

of the Xbox 360. The suggestions are related to the increased number of games offered by the system and the ability to play with another person, increasing social interaction. The third study puts, using guidelines, basic attributes for the development of digital games for CP users. The author states that the intention is to develop games in which players will maintain the high level of interest in the game. Four interactive games were produced. On those games the players used the Wii Balance Board [25] to navigate in the virtual environment Table 1.

4   Game Outline

Regarding the development of digital games, the user/game interaction is important to be analyzed. The gameability concept is related to the quality of the user interaction with the games. In this way, characteristics to determine criteria that define the quality of digital games have been developed [28]. The presented game also considered gameplay issues. The analysis of the above concepts becomes crucial in this project, since the proposal is the development of games, from assistive technologies for patients with PC. The characteristics that afford gameplay should be taken into consideration in order to achieve a good relationship between the user (patient) and the game [26–28].

4.1   Game Idea

The purpose of this study is to use multisensory devices to develop a game designed to promote the play in people with CP. In the conception phase of the project, we thought how can we develop games that can simulate real games that are common for children without Cerebral Palsy, but uncommon for children with the condition. So it was found the Sphero [18], a robotic ball that its movements can be manipulated by many different devices, detailed in the following sections. So, using the Sphero as a tangible device we focus on games that use a ball as the main object of the game, such as football and bowling. The main idea was to make the users with CP have the thrill with the movement of the ball that they may have never had, like kicking or throwing a ball. The next step was to think how the user will be able to manipulate the Sphero. So we came up with several ideas, such as a projector to project a scenario of the game (like a virtual crowd) to induce the fantasy property as suggested in [28]. This feature could collaborate for the immerse of the user into the game. And different ways to control the ball. Some possibilities are eye trackers, mobile devices or natural interaction devices as Leap Motion [29].

4.2   Game Design

For developing the proposed game we used an user centered design approach. This approach puts the disabled person as an active part of the team, contributing to the development of adaptations of interfaces according to their needs. Thus, user interaction with the devices will be efficient and effective. The user-centered design relates to the production of a customized computer system, i.e. facing the demands of a single user. In this way, the specific attributes that must be in games in way to get a high jogability are easier to achieve. The main phases of the followed processed are conceptual view, architecture view and user experience. Depending on the embodiment, the service will aggregate professionals with different backgrounds to serve users of TA [6]. This team will develop the product according to the demands of each person in order to meet the needs of them and avoid disuse of technology. Still about the production of a TA product, the prescription of a TA feature demand the following set of actions: (1) review the state of the client; (2) evaluation of devices being used; (3) evaluation of customer needs and the family; (4) prescription item; (5) development of the project; (6) user training; (7) monitoring of the use; (8) reviews changes in framework [5].

4.3 Devices

The Sphero device is a robotic ball manufactured by Orbotix and is equipped with various internal motors which allows it to roll on a surface in any direction. The control of the robot is made mostly from applications for mobile devices with Android [31] and IOS [32] operational systems. Communication between devices is done via Bluetooth. But there are already programming libraries that allows the development of applications for other platforms such as Windows, Arduino and others. It can move at a speed of up to one meter per second, approximately, and also has an internal lighting system, which, by combining the colors of the lights it can shine in about sixteen million different colors. The Sphero also has a set of sensors, including an accelerometer, a magnetometer and a gyroscope, which enables the robot to know which direction it is being rotated. The Sphero is shown on Fig. 2 (a). One of the promising application areas of Sphero is the digital games. We have a lot of games using Sphero as Sphero Pet and Sphero Draw N' Drive from Orbotix Inc. [33]. Another devices used in games is the Leap Motion Controller [29], as shown in Fig. 2 (d). The Leap Motion was developed in 2012 by the company Leap Motion Inc, is a recognition device that uses light and infrared motion sensors to map the position, movement and gestures made with the hands and fingers of the user. The focus on capturing the hands promoted by the device provides a high rate of data obtained under high precision. It works in both Windows and IOS operational systems. In order to adapt keyboard devices to people with special needs, products were specifically designed to help them to use computers. The pull and click mouse's (see Fig. 2 (c)) and also the pressing buttons (see Fig. 2 (b)) are example of that. Included with all joystick products is a 'soft ball' and T-bar handle for those who find it difficult to use a conventional joystick. All the used products are PC and MAC compatible, 'plug and play' with auto detecting PS2 and USB protocols [30].

4.4 Storyboards

The players should have the ability to understand the proposal and how the games will be handled the ball. Fig. 3 shows the storyboard for the proposed soccer game. In Fig. 3 (a) the desire of playing soccer controlling a ball. Fig. 3 (b) the explicit goal of the proposed game: the goal. In addition, it's possible to spice up the game by adding new levels of difficulty that will work with the driving characteristics of the user in order to exercise him too. So, Sphero can be used as the ball and it keeps the integration with other interactive devices which are used to control Sphero. This feature highlights the flexibility of this work. Once the project uses a user-centered design, the devices can be used in accordance with the user needs and capacities.

(a)   **(b)**

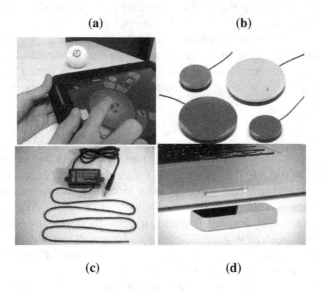

(c)   **(d)**

Fig. 2. Devices. In (a) Sphero, in (b) pressing buttons, in (c) pull and click mouses and in (d) leap motion.

Fig. 3. Storyboards.

4.5 Early User Feedback

According with the used design process to have an early user feedback was one of our goals. For do that, we had the opportunity to realize user experiments in the Clinic School in the Departament of Occupational Therapy (TO) of Federal University of Paraíba (UFPB). A patient with 19 years old with spastic quadriplegic cerebral palsy participated of the design process as a team member representing our endusers. It is important to point out that the presented solution fits our patient needs. Other patients with the same disease could have different solutions, so why the flexible options of controller is so important to us. In the beginning, the patient and their parents were invited to participate in the process, which occurred in meetings with distinct goals: one for evaluate the devices and other to get the impressions about the game. Sphero was introduced to our patient in order to validate it as a multisensory device. And for do that, we performed simple tasks with Sphero, small movements and color changes. We moved the ball around the patient so he could follow its movements and understand how it works. The patient was placed in a way so that he could view the ball moving in the ground. The patient uses wheelchair. So, one thing that called our attention was the best ergonomic position to set up the game. Next step was introducing the game. Soccer is very common in Brazil, especially during the World Cup. So, understand the game goal was quite easy. The game set up included a small green field and the goalkeeper. We put the field in the ground. The wheelchair was placed in a way that the patient could control the ball but keep the visual connection with the Sphero. The Sphero could be controlled by using the tablet and the pull and click mouse. During this experience, we evaluate how the control devices fits with the user physical abilities. Such movements in the Tablet were performed with the patient's finger. Also, the boy was positioned in a way that could see the whole scenario of the game so that he could show good performance. The difficulty level used was minimal and the playful environment included a goal and two side chains extending from the goal posts on each side barriers. Such barriers had the intention of not allowing the ball to go in another direction than the goal direction. In this way, some instructions was given for the patient related to the game.

The realized experiments included the participation of the occupational therapist of the patient. When we used the tablet, the patient was instructed to just direct his finger in the direction of the goal and helped by his therapist. About the pull and click, the patient was instructed only to pull the cord that was aggregated to the mouse. This would be enough to move the Sphero. After the instructions, the game was initiated. The parents decided to stay in the room what made this experience a fun activity for the patient. It is important to affirm that the user was an active part of the team and the tangibles interfaces was used in order to provide the best interaction according to his needs. Figure 4 show the game objects: goalkeeper, the field limited by side barriers and the Sphero.

5   Discussion

From informal observation and parents' reports were possible to identify that the patient correctly understood the purpose as well as the instructions of the game, as it managed to manipulate the Sphero from Tablet towards goal, as well as pull the cord of the click mouse device. Moreover, another important point was the fact that he managed to achieve the goal of the game to make a goal when he used the pull and click mouse. The patient recognized the participants and remembered how manipulated the Sphero ball in the meeting that followed its presentation. More difficulty was observed to direct the ball towards the goal using the Tablet. Because its needed higher dexterity to manipulate the Tablet itself and the ball through the screen, the user failed to achieve the goal of the game.

Fig. 4. User experience.

Moreover, the fact of having to perform the movement in Tablet with greater precision and strength made it difficult to driving the ball. However it can be used other applications, like one which the ball goes only into one direction. This way, the player do not have to worry about drive the Sphero into a exactly direction. In the meantime the patient has shown satisfactory performance and good interaction with the Tablet, because it was possible to try out a game that he could never have done before. From this it can be stated that there was interaction between the individual and the Sphero. Also the participation in a game in which the objective is to score, was made possible because of the effective interaction between the user and the technological devices, mediated by the use of a tangible interface. Some attributes that makes a good gameplay, like the main objective of the game is presented to the player from the beginning; the challenge of the game can be adjusted according to the player's skill; the player should be rewarded for their achievements in a clear and immediate way and controls should be clear, customizable and physically comfortable has been achieved. This means that the interaction between the user and the game was satisfactory.

The different user interfaces allow several adaptations that meet the needs of different users. The tangible user interfaces, therefore, correspond to a potential alternative to promote greater independence and autonomy for people with special needs, including persons with CP. That way the user interfaces play an important role in the rescue of function to people with physical dysfunctions. From the moment we can develop a customized computer system according to the capabilities of a user skills, facilitation of interaction and hence greater chances of achieving personal goals occurs. Thus we can produce a more efficient and personalized TAs product. This feature demystifies the series production of TA's, which are not centered on the capabilities of each individual user. Therefore, tangible user interfaces can be used as high technology, which Incorporate electronics and computers.

After all the considerations, it is recommended, that interventions be performed in order to validate the use of multisensory devices in promoting play in individuals with cerebral palsy. It is recommended also that the games offered are graduates and adapted according to the cognitive and motor skills of the patient.

Acknowledgements. Thanks the Assistive Technology Lab of occupational therapy department in UFPB. In addition we would like to thanks all the children that have been participate of the research.

References

1. Karray, F., Alemzadeh, M., Saleh, J.A., Arab, M.N.: Human-computer interaction overview on state of the art. Int. J. Smart Sens Intell. Sys. **1**(1), 137–159 (2008)
2. Harper, R., Rodden, T., Rogers, T., Sellen, A.: Being Human: Human-Computer Interaction in the year 2020. Microsoft Research Ltd, England (2008)
3. Mauri, C., Granollers, T., Lorés, J., García, M.: Computer Vision Interaction for people with Severe Movement Restrictions. Hum. Technol. **2**, 38–54 (2006)
4. Ishii, H., Lakatos, D., Bonanni, L., e Labrune, J.: Radical atoms beyond tangible bits, toward transformable materials. Mag. Interact. **19**(1), 38–51 (2012)
5. Bersch, R.: Introdução à Tecnologia Assistiva. Centro Especializado em Desenvolvimento Infantil, Porto Alegre (2008)
6. Reis, N.M.M.: Introdução à Tecnologia Assistiva. In: Anais do III Seminário Internacional Sociedade Inclusiva. Belo Horizonte (2004)
7. Brummel-Smith, K., Dangiolo, M.: Assistive Technologies in the Home. Clin. Geriatr. Med. **25**, 61–77 (2009)
8. Leung, P., et al.: Assistive Technology: Meeting the Technology Needs of Students with Disabilities in Post-Secondary Education. Institute of Disability Studies Deakin University, Geelong (1999)
9. Chang, Y., Chen b, S., Huang, J.: A Kinect-based system for physical rehabilitation: a pilot study for young adults with motor disabilities. Res. Dev. Disabil. **32**, 2566–2570 (2011)
10. Cavalcanti, A., Galvão, C.: Terapia ocupacional, fundamentação e prática, Rio de Janeiro (2007)
11. Rotta, N.T.: Paralisia cerebral, novas perspectivas terapêuticas. Jornal de Pediatria. **78**, 371–374 (2002)
12. Scalha, T.B., Souza, V.G., Boffi, T., Carvalho, A.C.: A importância do brincar no desenvolvimento psicomotor: relato de experiência. Revista de Psicologia da UNESP. **9**, 79–92 (2010)
13. Ferland, F.: O Modelo Lúdico: o brincar, a criança com deficiência física e a terapia ocupacional. São Paulo (2006)
14. Reid, D., Campbel, K.: The use of virtual reality with children with cerebral palsy: a pilot randomized trial. Ther. Recreation J. **40**, 255–268 (2006)
15. Reid, D.: The influence of virtual reality on playfulness in children with cerebral palsy: a pilot study. Occup. Ther. Int. **11**, 131–144 (2004)
16. Hernandez, A.H., Ye, Z., Graham, N.T.C., Fehlings, D., Switzer, L.: Designing action-based exergames for children with cerebral palsy. In: Proceedings of the SIGCHI Conference on Human Factors in Computing Systems, pp. 1261–1270 (2013)
17. Weightman, A., Preston, N., Levesley, M., Holt, R., MonWilliams, M., Clarke, M., Cozens, A.J., Bhakta, B.: Home-bases computer-assistes upper limb exercise for yung children with cerebral palsy: a feasibility study investigating impact on motor control and functional outcome. J. Rehabil. Med. **43**, 359–363 (2011)
18. Sphero. http://www.gosphero.com/sphero-2-0/
19. Urbanowicz, K., Nyka, L.: Media architecture – participation through the senses. In: Proceedings of the Media Architecture Biennale, pp. 15–17, Aarhus (2012)

524   E. Oliveira et al.

20. Paraguai, L.: Interfaces multisensoriais: espacialidades híbridas do corpoespaço. Revista Famecos **37**, 54–60 (2008)
21. Paraguai, L.: Interfaces multisensoriais: corpo e espaço. In: XXXI Congresso Brasileiro de Ciências da Comunicação (2008)
22. Hornecker, E.: A design theme for tangible interaction: embodied facilitation. In: Conference on Computer Supported Cooperative Work, pp. 18–22, Paris
23. Chang, Y., Chen b, S., Huang, J.: A Kinect-based system for physical rehabilitation a pilot study for young adults with motor disabilities. Res. Dev. Disab. **32**, 2566–2570 (2011)
24. XBOX 360. http://www.xbox.com/pt-BR/xbox360/why-xbox-360?xr=shellnav&xr=shellnav
25. Wii Balance Boar. http://wiifitu.nintendo.com/
26. Barcelos, T.S., Carvalho, T., Schimiguel, J., Silveira, I.F.: Análise comparativa de heurísticas para avaliação de jogos digitais. In: Proceedings of the 10th Brazilian Symposium on Human Factors in Computing Systems 5th Latin American Conference on Human-Computer Interaction (2011)
27. Costa, G., Barcelos, T., Oliveira, C., Muñoz, R., Nöel, R., Silveira, I.: Construindo jogabilidade: como a percepção dos jogadores afeta o desenvolvimento de jogos em um contexto escolar. In: XII SBGames, pp. 16–18 (2013)
28. Malone, T.W.: Heuristics for designing enjoyable user interfaces: lessons from computer games. In: Proceedings of the ACM and National Bureau of Standards Conference on Human Factors in Computer Systems, Gaithersburg, pp. 15–17, March 1982
29. Leap Motion. https://www.leapmotion.com/product
30. Mouse's as assistive technologies. http://www.clik.com.br/clik_01.html#prodcomp
31. Android. http://www.android.com/phones-and-tablets/
32. IOS. https://developer.apple.com/devcenter/ios/index.action
33. Sphero games. http://www.gosphero.com/games/

SPELTRA: A Robotic Assistant
for Speech-and-Language Therapy

Vladimir Robles-Bykbaev[1,2(✉)], Martín López-Nores[2], Juan Ochoa-Zambrano[1],
Jorge García-Duque[2], and José Juan Pazos-Arias[2]

[1] GI-IATa, Centro de Investigación, Desarrollo e Innovación en Ingeniería (CIDII),
Universidad Politécnica Salesiana, Calle Vieja 12-30, Cuenca, Ecuador
vrobles@ups.edu.ec, jochoaz@est.ups.edu.ec
[2] Department of Telematics Engineering, AtlantTIC Research Center for Information
and Communication Technologies, University of Vigo, Vigo, Spain
{mlnores,jgd,jose}@det.uvigo.es

Abstract. The Speech and Language Therapy (SLT) is an area focused on the
rehabilitation of people suffering from different kinds of disorders and disabilities
related with language and communication. According to latest estimates of the
World Health Organization, most countries do not have appropriate structures to
provide healthcare and rehabilitation services for those people. This problem
becomes more complex on developing countries, due the lack of professionals
and ICT-based tools to support the several activities that must be performed by
the Speech and Language Pathologists (SLPs). On those grounds, this paper
presents a robotic assistant with the aim to help SLPs during the therapy activities.
This approach is based on an integrative environment that relies on mobile ICT
tools, an expert system, a knowledge layer and standardized vocabularies. This
proposal has been tested on 26 children suffering from different kind of disabilities, and the results achieved have shown important improvements in some activities related with SLT like reduction of the time required to prepare patients for
therapy, and better response of children to perform tasks.

Keywords: Speech-language therapy · Mobile applications · Expert system ·
Robotic assistant

1 Introduction

The language and communication constitute one of the cornerstones of cognitive development of children, since they provide a set of skills that any individual can use to
interact with his/her environment, or express his/her needs, ideas, thoughts, and feelings.
However, currently an important number of people in the world (children and adults)
suffer from different kind of disabilities that can affect their language and communication
skills.

Some of the latest world estimates present a complex overview, with 15 % of the
world's population living with some form of disability, whereas 60 million people live
with disabling hearing loss and 15 million suffer from stutter. In the same line, the

© Springer International Publishing Switzerland 2015
M. Antona and C. Stephanidis (Eds.): UAHCI 2015, Part III, LNCS 9177, pp. 525–534, 2015.
DOI: 10.1007/978-3-319-20684-4_51

number of existing SLP confirms a lack of personnel to provide adequate healthcare and rehabilitation services [1]: in sub-Saharan Africa there is 1 SLP for every 2–4 million people, while in the US, UK, Austria, and Canada there is 1 SLP for every 2500–4700 people.

Commonly, the People with Communication Disorders (PWCD) can be affected by a disability. The range of the existent disabilities is large, and a disability can appear in any stage of the person's life. In the early life stages, a delay in meeting developmental milestones may be secondary to perinatal events, involving complicated interactions between mother and fetus during delivery. Maternal factors including weight, diet, and morbidities can affect neonatal adaptation and later development. Prematurity, low birth weight, and previous intrauterine insults as well as complications during delivery of a previously normal fetus increase the risk for perinatal stress [2]. Some of the most common speech and language disorders are the following [3]:

- *Speech disorder* is present when a person is not able to produce speech sounds correctly or fluently, or has problems with his/her voice.
- *Language disorder* appears when a person cannot understand in a proper way other people (receptive language) or cannot share thoughts, ideas or feelings (expressive language).
- *Swallowing disorder* can occur during some of the three phases of swallowing process (oral, pharyngeal or esophageal).
- *Hearing disorder* appears when damage exists in the auditory system. This disorder can be one of these three types: conductive hearing loss, sensorineural hearing loss, or mixed hearing loss.

These disorders can be related or not with several types of disabilities/diseases like cerebral palsy, Alzheimer's disease, Parkinson's disease, bacterial meningitis, intellectual disabilities, autism spectrum disorder, etc. [3]. On those grounds, in this paper we present a comprehensive approach to support the different activities conducted by SLP, with the aim of providing better healthcare and rehabilitation services for PWCD. Our approach uses an integrative ICT layer of robotic, mobile and web tools that relies on formal knowledge model and standardized vocabularies. In the next sections we will describe in detail the most important features of the Robotic Assistant for Speech and Language Therapy (SPELTRA).

This paper is organized as follows. In Sect. 2 are presented some relevant researches related to ICT tools and SLT. A general overview of the proposed approach and the details related with the robotic assistant and the mobile environment are described in Sect. 3. The pilot experiments conducted in order to validate and analyze the patient's response to SPELTRA are shown in Sect. 4. Finally, the Sect. 5 presents conclusions and some lines of future work.

2   Related Work

During the last decade several researches have been conducted with the aim of improving different activities conducted during the SLT sessions. Some robots have been developed to assist in the rehabilitation of patients suffering disabilities due strokes. A research example of this area is uBot-5, a humanoid robot capable of providing physical therapy and speech therapy for people suffering from aphasia and hemiparesis [4], allowing to analyze how the intervention in one domain of therapy affects the progress in others domains. Likewise, several elderly people suffering from dementia have shown recovery from depression, reduction of agitation, and recovery from speech disorders during therapies conducted with support of PARO robot (a seal pup) [5].

The interaction between children with special needs and robotic interviewers is another field of study. In this field, a research was conducted in [6] with the aim of analyzing the children behavior during the interviews conducted by a robot compared to interviews performed by a human interviewer. The results reveal very similar outcomes in the children responses for both cases (number of words, filler words and key words). Other approaches propose the use of robots to support therapy sessions and improve the social interaction skill in children with autism spectrum disorders [7, 8], motivate children with communication disorders to learn the sign language [9] or provide support for Mexican patients suffering from motor speech disorders (dysarthria) [10].

The aforementioned proposals do not pay attention to important issues as the domain-knowledge modeling as well as the storage, sharing and querying of electronic healthcare records through international standards and vocabularies.

3   Support Model for SLT

Our proposed approach has the aim of providing a complete support for SLT, considering all people involved during the different rehabilitation and assessment stages and activities. The model helps doctors and SLPs with different kind of activities related with therapy and health care like report generation, support during therapy sessions, patients monitoring, and multisensory stimulation. The relatives can use several mobile applications to conduct reinforcement activities in home and help with patient's monitoring, whereas students (future SLPs) can be trained using real cases and automated tests. Some of the most important elements of SPELTRA are the following (Fig. 1):

- The **knowledge layer** is based on seven main areas of speech and language: hearing, voice, swallowing, receptive language, expressive language and articulation, oral structure and function, and linguistic formulation. Each of these areas allows defining the skills, development milestones, knowledge, assessments and tests that must be considered during the rehabilitation process of PWCD. Through the use of OpenEHR archetypes (www.openehr.org), ontologies, and standardized vocabularies is possible to represent, manage and share all information related with patients/subjects (stored in a **database**). The left hand side of Fig. 2 shows a partial screenshot of the protocol (template) to conduct a Pure Tone Audiometry test (PTA) test. This template is based on an archetype that allows assessing the patient's response to sound stimulation and voice commands, and determine whether he/she is able to localize sound sources without visual stimuli. The right side of Fig. 2 shows a partial view of the archetype that captures the information related with speech fluency patient's evaluation.

- **SPELTRA** incorporates a set of functionalities (described in the next section) that allow building a wide range of **software tools to support** different activities of SLT. Some of most relevant examples are the following: an application to assess and help patients suffering from disabilities related with speech production, a tool to present exercises to develop/rehabilitate gross and fine motor skills, a set of exercises to stimulate visual and auditory memory, and a special application to control the robot remotely.
- The model integrates an **expert system** to automatically generate therapy plans for long term periods (6 months). The expert system uses an approach based on multi-level clusters (see more details in [11]), and performs an analysis the patient's profile (medical condition, initial speech-language screening, skills affected, disorders/disabilities suffered by patient, etc.).

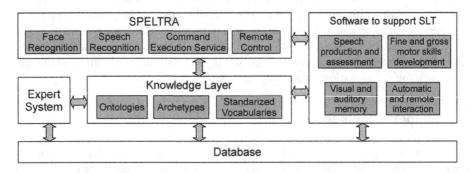

Fig. 1. The SPELTRA robot and its relation to a knowledge model of SLT, the support software and the expert system.

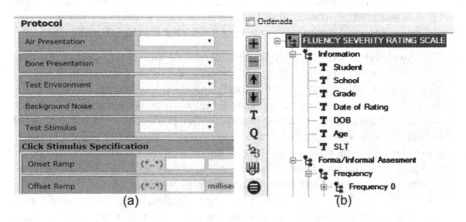

Fig. 2. (a) Partial view of the protocol (template) required to conduct a Pure Tone Audiometry Test (developed with OpenGENEHR: https://code.google.com/p/open-ehr-gen-framework). (b) Partial view of the archetype modeled to store the information of fluency evaluation on patients (developed with OpenEHR Archetype Editor).

3.1 Speltra

The robot is an intelligent environment that uses mobile devices to provide support during the SLT process. Basically, it relies in a set of mobile applications and on a robotic assistant consisting in two elements: a central processor (an Android-based smartphone or tablet) and a displacement platform (electronic device). The robot can perform several activities and provide the following services to SLP:

- Provide exercises and activities to assist in therapy activities like visual stimulation (colors, geometric forms, etc.) and motor skills acquisition (painting, virtual puzzles, etc.).
- Recognize four different hand gestures: fist, open hand, closed hand, and semi-closed hand.
- Detect and recognize faces of several system users.
- Tell stories, play songs, execute commands like searching words or sentences in Internet, and read emails.
- Hold objects using a clip.

The most complex tasks performed by the robot are related to facial recognition and gesture recognition. For the first one we use the Local Binary Patterns (LBP) approach, due it is a less expensive technique for mobile devices [12]. In order to recognize the hand gestures, we require the patient to wear a glove of a uniform color (typically, red, blue or green) and apply two techniques that had obtained good results convex hull with polygonal approximation descriptors [13, 14]. With this combination we have achieved around 90 % of precision in gesture recognition.

The SPELTRA control software can work independently of the displacement platform, and be installed on any version of Android from 2.3 to 4.4. The requirements on the devices include 256 MB of RAM memory, a Qualcomm processor and around 10 MB of storage space. It can be controlled remotely through a graphical user interface to allow the SLTs to have complete control of the therapies. The power consumption is low, and an energy supply system is included for 8 h of uninterrupted operation.

In order to recognize the hand gestures, the patient must to wear a glove of a uniform color (typically, red, blue or green). Once the image is captured, we extract and combine two shape descriptors to perform the recognition: convex hull and polygonal approximation. With this combination we have achieved around 90 % of precision in gesture recognition. Figure 4 shows a patient that suffers from cerebral palsy interacting with the robot.

In the other hand, the mobile complementary applications allow to conduct several kinds of exercises related with articulation (phonemic awareness, sentence construction, phonation ...). Likewise, these applications provide support during the patient's articulation assessments (repetitive and spontaneous). Figure 3 depicts the robotic assistant, his displacement platform and two screen captures of the mobile application to provide support during breathing exercises.

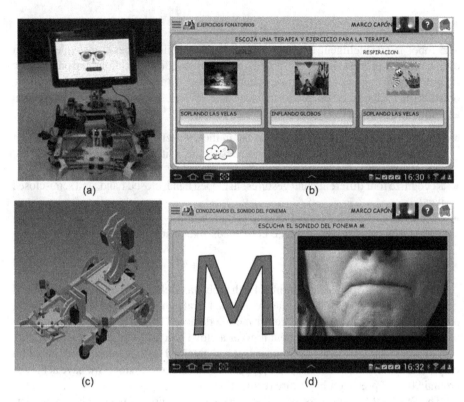

(a)   (b)

(c)   (d)

Fig. 3. The assembled robot (a), the design of the displacement platform (b), a screen capture that shows the main menu of the breath exercises (blowing candles, inflating balloons, etc.) (c) and a screen capture of the visual menu to help in utterance productions (phoneme/m/) (d).

Table 1. Groups of children that participated in the experiment (the column "disability" includes the standard code provided by [3]).

Patients	Disability
2	Mild intellectual disability (F70)
15	Moderate intellectual disability (F71)
1	Severe intellectual disability (F72)
1	Autistic disorder (F84)
2	Attention-deficit hyperactivity disorder (F90)
1	Cerebral palsy (G80)
4	Down syndrome (Q90)

4 Experiments and Results

In order to assess the functionalities and the advantages of SPELTRA, we have conducted two preliminary experiments in the "Jesus for Children" foundation of Cuenca, Ecuador. This foundation is a public institution that provides different services as counseling, rehabilitation (SLT, physical therapy, occupational therapy, and psychological support), and provides an environment where children with disabilities can be integrated. The participants of this experiment were 26 patients (23 children between 5 and 17 years, and 3 adults with an average age of 24 years) suffering from different kind of disabilities (see Table 1).

4.1 Relaxation Activities to Prepare Children for Therapy

This experiment was conducted with the aim to measure the required time to perform some relaxation activities and exercises as previous stage of SLT. During this process we have worked with the aid of two clinical psychologists, two speech-language pathologists, one occupational therapist and one educational psychologist. The main goals of this experiment were measure response time of children to activities proposed/conducted by robot, and verify the robot's integration with the database of profiles and therapy plans.

Likewise, some of the most relevant activities carried out with the guidance of robot were related to auditory stimuli production (listening stories, maintaining a basic conversation, etc.), performing actions when the robot shows a specific color in the screen (jumping, raising the hands, etc.), executing simple commands (playing "Simon says"), among others.

All of the experiments thus far have provided very positive and encouraging results. Among other achievements, the time needed to conduct the relaxation activities and initial therapy has shrunk from 40 min to 25, all the specialists have agreed on the usefulness of SPELTRA as a supporting tool for their work, and children have shown high levels of motivation during their interactions with the robot.

4.2 Level of Interest

In this experiment, we asked the team of experts to provide a subjective rating of the level of interest shown by each group of patients during the activities described above. To achieve this task, we have used a Likert scale in order to characterize each level: very low $= 1$, low $= 2$, medium $= 3$, high $= 4$, very high $= 5$.

Table 2 shows the results of subjective evaluation, according to each group of patients aforementioned. It is important to mention that lowest values of interest are present in groups of patients where the interaction with the robot is a more complex task, due to nature of the disability (cerebral palsy, autistic disorder and severe intellectual disability). Conversely, the patients suffering from intellectual disabilities (mild and moderate), attention-deficit and Down syndrome present high levels of interest.

Table 2. Level of interest according to each group of patients

Disability	Average level of interest
Attention-deficit hyperactivity disorder (F90)	4,5
Autistic disorder (F84)	3
Cerebral palsy (G80)	4
Down syndrome (Q90)	4,75
Mild intellectual disability (F70)	4,5
Moderate intellectual disability (F71)	4,47
Severe intellectual disability (F72)	3
Overall average	**4,3**

Figure 4 shows some examples of stimulation activities to develop memory, motor skills and creativity. On the left hand side of the figure, when the subject closes his hand, the "virtual" hand grabs a geometric figure and allows him/her drag it across the screen. The other pictures show a child using a painting application.

Fig. 4. Some pictures taken during a therapy session with the SPELTRA robot

5   Conclusions and Future Work

The results obtained with this research show that is possible to automate several activities related with SLT, with the aim to provide a better service to patients suffering from several kinds of disabilities. In the same way, mobile applications constitute important backing tools, allowing SLPs to perform their activities anywhere and in a more comfortable way.

In general, the use of robotic assistant to guide several activities related with SLT can achieve an important motivation in specific groups of patients suffering from Down syndrome, intellectual disabilities and attention-deficit disorder. It is important preparing special therapy sessions for patients suffering from autistic disorder, since they require establish bounds of confidence with the robot.

As lines of future work, we intend to develop more specific activities and routines for treatment, considering a spectrum of the most common types of disabilities.

Acknowledgements. The authors from the Universidad Politécnica Salesiana have been supported by the "Sistemas Inteligentes de Soporte a la Educación CIDII-010213" research project. The authors from the University of Vigo have been supported by the European Regional Development Fund (ERDF) and Xunta de Galicia under project CN 2012/260 "Consolidation of Research Units: AtlantTIC", and by the Ministerio de Educación y Ciencia (Gobierno de España) research project TIN2013-42774-R (partly financed with FEDER funds). We would like to thank the support provided by the following institutions of special education: Unidad Educativa Especial del Azuay (UNEDA), and Fundación "Jesús para los niños".

References

1. McAllister, L., Wylie, K., Davidson, B., Marshall, J.: The World Report on Disability: an impetus to reconceptualize services for people with communication disability. Int. J. Speech-Lang. Pathol. **15**(2), 118–126 (2013)
2. Ergaz, Z., Ornoy, A.: Perinatal: early postnatal factors underlying developmental delay and disabilities. Dev. Disabil. Res. Rev. **17**(2), 59–70 (2011)
3. American Speech-Language-Hearing Association: International Classification of Diseases, Tenth Revision - Clinical Modification, Related to Speech, Language, and Swallowing Disorders (2014)
4. Choe, Y.K., Jung, H.T., Baird, J., Grupen, R.A.: Multidisciplinary stroke rehabilitation delivered by a humanoid robot: interaction between speech and physical therapies. Aphasiology **27**(3), 252–270 (2013)
5. Shibata, T.: Therapeutic seal robot as biofeedback medical device: qualitative and quantitative evaluations of robot therapy in dementia care. Proc. IEEE **100**(8), 2527–2538 (2012)
6. Wood, L.J., Dautenhahn, K., Lehmann, H., Robins, B., Rainer, A., Syrdal, D.S.: Robot-mediated interviews: do robots possess advantages over human interviewers when talking to children with special needs? In: Herrmann, G., Pearson, M.J., Lenz, A., Bremner, P., Spiers, A., Leonards, U. (eds.) ICSR 2013. LNCS, vol. 8239, pp. 54–63. Springer, Heidelberg (2013)
7. Villano, M., et al.: DOMER: a wizard of oz interface for using interactive robots to scaffold social skills for children with autism spectrum disorders. In: Proceedings of the 6th International Conference on Human-Robot Interaction, pp. 279–280. ACM Press (2011)
8. Vanderborght, B., et al.: Using the social robot probo as a social story telling agent for children with ASD. Interaction Studies **13**(3), 348–372 (2012)
9. Kose, H., Akalin, N., Uluer, P.: Socially interactive robotic platforms as sign language tutors. Int. J. Humanoid Rob. **11**, 1450003 (2014)
10. Morales, S.O.C., Enríquez, G.B., Romero, F.T.: Speech-based human and service robot interaction: an application for mexican dysarthric people. Int. J. Adv. Robotic Sy **10** (2013)
11. Robles-Bykbaev, V., López-Nores, M., Pazos-Arias, J.J., Arévalo-Lucero, D.: Maturation assessment system for speech and language therapy based on multilevel PAM and KNN. Procedia Technol. **16**, 1265–1270 (2014)
12. McCool, C., Marcel, S., Hadid, A., Pietikainen, M., Matejka, P., Cernocky, J., Cootes, T.: Bi-modal person recognition on a mobile phone: using mobile phone data. In: IEEE International Conference on Multimedia and Expo Workshops (ICMEW), Melbourne, Australia. IEEE (2012)

13. Nieto, O., Shasha, D.: Hand gesture recognition in mobile devices: enhancing the musical experience. In: 10th International Symposium on Computer Music Multidisciplinary Research, Marseille, France. Springer (2013)
14. Xu, R., Dai, H., Wang, F., Jia, Z.: A convex hull-based optimization to reduce the data delivery latency of the mobile elements in wireless sensor networks. In: IEEE International Conference on Embedded and Ubiquitous Computing (EUC), Zhangjiajie, China. IEEE (2013)

Multimodal Videogames for the Cognition of People Who Are Blind: Trends and Issues

Jaime Sánchez[1], Ticianne Darin[2(✉)], and Rossana Andrade[3]

[1] Department of Computer Science, University of Chile, Blanco Encalada, 2120 Santiago, Chile
`jsanchez@dcc.uchile.cl`
[2] Virtual University Institute, Federal University of Ceará, Humberto Monte, S/N,
Fortaleza, Brazil
`ticianne@virtual.ufc.br`
[3] Department of Computer Science, Federal University of Ceará, Humberto Monte, S/N,
Fortaleza, Brazil
`rossana@great.ufc.br`

Abstract. Multimodal serious games are attractive tools for achieving this goal and helping people with visual disabilities to perceive and to interpret the surrounding world. However, it is fundamental to ensure that the games can stimulate cognitive development. The purpose of this study was to investigate the role of multimodal components in the development and evaluation of games and virtual environments targeting the enhancement of cognitive skills in people who are blind. We analyze the state-of-the-art concerning approaches and technologies currently in use for the development of mental maps, cognitive spatial structures, and navigation skills in learners who are blind by using multimodal videogames. Besides, we identify the current approaches used for designing and evaluating multimodal games in this context. In this paper, we discuss the results on these and related topics and draw from them some trends and issues.

Keywords: Accessible games · Multimodal interfaces · Cognition · Blind people

1 Introduction

One of the most significant cognitive issues for people who are blind is the development of orientation and mobility skills, so the person can become autonomous. Frequently the absence of vision adds unnecessary complexity to easy tasks that require spatial representation [1]. The absence of information about the environment leads people who are blind to choose a certain route based on safety concerns, instead of in the efficiency of the route. It happens due to the less risk of tripping or bumping into anything, although the distance may be longer [2]. In an unfamiliar environment such as an airport or a hotel, this experience is commonly far more complex and dynamic [1]. In these environments either autonomous aid would be essential, for example guide dog or cane.

However, the limitations of conventional aids when facing some obstacles, like escalators and rotation doors, difficult guiding the user to choose the best possible route to a given destination [4]. In order to navigate in an efficient manner it is necessary to have a

© Springer International Publishing Switzerland 2015
M. Antona and C. Stephanidis (Eds.): UAHCI 2015, Part III, LNCS 9177, pp. 535–546, 2015.
DOI: 10.1007/978-3-319-20684-4_52

mental representation of the environment, so one can develop orientation skills and mobility techniques. To assemble this mental image a person needs to gather information about the surroundings. Besides, it is necessary to be able to detect items and places, and to keep a trail of the relationships between the objects within an environment [5]. The visual channels are responsible for collecting most of the information required for such a mental representation [6, 7]. In order to gain spatial information and generate a cognitive map of the surroundings a blind person needs to use non-visual stimuli to perceive the environment. Receiving space information via complementary sensors collaborates with the creation of an adequate mental representation of the environment. There are evidences that audio-based and haptic interfaces can foment learning and cognition in blind children [8, 9].

Since children and young people widely use games as part of their daily routine [10] multimodal serious games can be attractive tools to stimulate cognitive improvement. There are several experiences with the design and use of video games for stimulating the development of various abilities in people with visual impairment [11, 12]. Video games and virtual environments with this purpose should meticulously combine different sources of perceptual inputs, as audio and haptics [13]. Once cognitive skills have been developed or improved, a multimodal game can still help to transfer them to a real environment and, ultimately, to everyday life.

However, it is fundamental to ensure that these games can stimulate cognitive development. It is crucial to promote a better understanding and adequate, relevant and meaningful use of the multimodal elements in a serious game. The purpose of this work is to investigate the role of multimodal elements in the development and evaluation of games and virtual reality environments, whose target is to enhance cognitive skills of blind people. We analyze the state of the art about approaches and technologies currently in use for the development of mental maps, cognitive spatial structures and navigation skills in blind learners, through video games. Besides, we identify the selected solutions for conducting multimodal evaluation and usability in this context. In order to perform the analysis it was adopted a protocol that defined the study procedures. The results are discussed in this paper and summarized in a table containing the game name, its capability of enhancing cognitive skills, the type of evaluation performed, its interface and interaction characterization (available on http://1drv.ms/1zW6vlY).

2   Methodology

The study was carried out based on the Systematic Review approach [14, 15], from July to November in 2014. A systematic literature review is a secondary study method that goes through existing primary studies, reviews them in-depth and describes their methodology and results [14]. There are three main phases in a systematic review: planning, conducting and reporting the review [15]. In this research, we used the tool StArt [16] to support to the application of this technique to the three stages of the review.

The first step of this research was the definition of the protocol to describe the conduction of the study. The protocol guided the research objectives and clearly defined the research questions and planning how the sources and studies selected will be used to answer those issues. Two researchers and two experts performed incremental reviews to the protocol. We revisited the protocol in order to update it based on new information collected as the study progressed. The research questions are: Q1: What strategies[1] have been used for the design of multimodal games for blind learners in order to enhance cognition[2]? Q2: What strategies have been used to evaluate usability and quality of multimodal games for blind learners? Q3: What technologies have been used for the development of multimodal games for blind learners, in order to enhance cognition?

We selected eight digital libraries as sources: ACM Digital Library, Engineering Village, IEEE Xplore, Scopus, Science Direct, Springer Link, PubMed, and Web of Science. We refined the search string by reviewing the data needed to answer each of the research questions, as well as the relevance of the results returned for each test of the string. Figure 1 presents the final search string submitted to the eight sources addressing the research questions Q1, Q2 and Q3. A set of selection criteria filtered the suitable studies, according to the goals of the research. It consists of four inclusion criteria and eleven exclusion criteria. The large set of exclusion criteria is due to the variety of knowledge fields that this study covers.

```
(
    ((Evaluation AND (usability OR quality)) OR Design OR
    Development)
    AND
    (Serious AND (Videogame OR Game))
)
AND
(
        ("blind learners" OR (("eyes-free" OR "visually
        impaired" OR blind) AND ("education" OR "learning")))
    AND
        (Multimodal OR haptic OR audio OR auditory OR
        vibrotactile OR device OR "I/O" OR gadget OR
        technology)
    AND
        ("cognition" OR "Cognitive spatial structures" OR
        "Navigation Skills" OR "Mental map" OR "Walking
        Simulation")
)
```

Fig. 1. Search string applied to the eight selected sources

The obtained result of submitting the search string to the eight selected bases was a first set of 446 papers. Then, using the snowballing sampling technique [17] we manually added a set of 52 papers to the initial sample. The new sample resulted from the references in the first round of articles and the investigation of the DBLP pages of the principal authors. From the total of 498 studies obtained, there were 48 papers from ACM (9.6 %), 136 from IEEE (27.3 %), 28 from Scopus (5.6 %), 181 from ScienceDirect (36.3 %), 50 from Springer (10 %), 4 papers from Web of Science (0.8 %), 1 paper from Pubmed (0.2 %) and 52 added manually (10.5 %). It is important to note that, although Science-Direct has had most of the results, there were not many outcomes related to the desired area. It happened because this source returned a vast amount of articles related to cognition and/or blind people, but under the medical point of view.

---

[1] A formal methodology comprehending the whole process of conception and development or evaluation and quality measurement of a multimodal game.

[2] Concerning to mental models, cognitive spatial structures, and/or navigation skills.

In order to choose the most suitable studies to answer the research questions we filtered the papers. The first filter (F1) consists of removing the duplicated and short papers, i.e. less than four pages; secondary studies and articles published before 1995. The F1 excluded 172 papers (34.5 %), so that 326 studies went to the second filter. The second filter (F2) consists of the application of the specific purpose exclusion criteria and the inclusion criteria, after the reading of papers title and abstract. F2 excluded 216 papers (43.4 %) and included 68 papers (13.7 %), that went to the third filter (F3), intending to refine the initially accepted set of studies. F3 consisted of the examination of the full text of the 68 articles and the review of the assigned inclusion and exclusion criteria. F3 excluded 34 articles by criteria and four duplicated papers (7.6 %) and included 30 papers (6 %). Most eliminated papers related to cognition, but not to multimodal games for blind people. From the 30 papers finally selected for data extraction, one paper was from ACM, two from IEEE, four from Scopus, two from ScienceDirect, two from Web of Science. Finally, 19 papers were added manually, through a snowballing sampling. The relevant papers are from 1999 to 2014, being 80 % of the papers from 2008 on.

We considered studies describing multimodal video games or navigational virtual environment. We also examined studies describing no application but introducing a model for the design or the evaluation of multimodal game or environment for blind people. The selected papers were: [6, 13, 18–45]. Among these, 25 papers described 21 distinct applications: 17 multimodal games and 4 multimodal navigation virtual environ- ronment. Some papers discussed the same application, but from another point of view, or executing a complementary research or evaluation method. There was four proposals of models to design multimodal games for blind learners.

3   Trends and Issues on Multimodal Games for Blind Learners

3.1   Design and Development of Multimodal Games

The selected papers showed that there is not a widespread process for the design of this particular kind of application. Most of the papers use some traditional software engi- neering process. However, given the specificities of this type of implementation and the limitations of the public, several factors must be taken into consideration, such as context of use and desired skills. The typical development cycles do not cover these aspects. Thus, each author adapts the development process, according to the goals of the game in question. Nevertheless, four papers [27, 31, 32, 34] introduce models for the design and development of games for enhancing cognition of blind people. Each model relates to a specific context of use, audience and/or desired cognitive skill.

The work of [34] introduces a model for the development of videogame-based appli- cations designed to assist the navigation of blind people. While [32] is a video game development model to serve as a framework for designing games to help learners who are blind to construct mental maps. These maps are for the development of geometric- mathematical abilities and orientation and mobility (O&M) skills. The second process modifies the first one, improving and extending it in terms of the cognitive abilities implied by O&M and geometric thinking. The study [31] introduces a novel technique using concept maps for the design of serious video games, in Ejemovil Editor. The goal is that teachers can be able to define the storyline of the video game, incorporating the concepts that they want to teach in a structured way. The proposed process guides the teacher in transforming a conceptual map into a video game model. Finally, [27] presents a complete model for developing virtual learning environments for learners with visual disabilities. The model is cyclic and includes various steps and recommendations by discussing critical issues for conceptualization and implementation. The result is the input to generate a suitable user-adapted aural output.

3.2 Interface and Interaction Characterization

Although the proposed methodologies are not yet widely used, there are several common elements in the design of the 21 applications. It shows some trends in interface characterization and the interaction style. All of the applications use at least one aural interface element, although most of the cases combine two or more aural elements. The prevailing combination is between iconic and spatialized sound, in 3D environments. Iconic sounds are the most common type of sonorous feedback, occurring in 16 applications (76 %) followed by spatialized sounds, present in 11 (52 %) applications. The spoken audio is more prevalent than the speech synthesis, what may cause more empathy to the interface. The first one occurs in 11 applications (52 %) while the second appears in seven (33 %). However, five applications combine the two approaches. Stereo sound is another option, present in five applications (23 %). Only one application uses music/tones to represent different objects.

Twenty applications (95 %) present a graphic interface in addition to the aural elements. The interfaces can be 2D or 3D graphics combined with images or text. Contrary to what one might imagine, the results do not point to sound-only interfaces. Three of the applications (14 %) allow users to navigate only by sound (no graphics mode) and uses a graphic interface only for configuration. It happens because these interfaces aim to include not only blind users, but also visually impaired and sighted users, especially the teachers. However, only one interface assure that shows no relevant information in colors (for color-blind people). Although some papers may have omitted this information; it is an essential issue to attempt, in order to ensure that this public will be able to use interface correctly. Other basic features that demand more consideration are the adaptation of the size of the elements and the use of a high contrast mode. Only 9 % of the applications allows the resize of interface elements and 23 % of the applications offers a high contrast mode. Both of these functionalities should be typical in such applications since they are crucial to people with partial blindness.

The most common interaction pattern is the keyboard, used by 15 applications (71 %) especially in those whose feedback is mainly sonorous. The second more used interaction form is the joystick, present in seven applications (33 %). The joystick interaction always has an alternative interaction mode, usually the keyboard. The interaction with joystick occurs in interfaces with 3D environments that commonly use some haptic feedback. Two applications (9 %) allows the use of mouse together with the keyboard and one claim the mouse as the primary interaction mode. However, this application main audience is not total blind users. Although natural language might be expected to be an easier and instinctive way to interact, only two games allows the user to give natural language commands. The reasons are not clear in the papers, but it can be due to it is not a trivial task to recognize and process the natural language accurately. Besides, blind users who have any experience with technologies are used to utilizing the keyboard in other applications, what may facilitate the interaction.

3.3 Evaluation of Multimodal Games

None of the resulting papers addressed a model for usability evaluation of multimodal games. There is no apparent standardization about the elements to evaluate, nor the methodology, instruments and measures. Some of the evaluations described in the studies are very formal, while it seems to be ignored in a number of studies. Between the 18 applications aiming to enhance blind people cognition, only 9 (50 %) performed a cognitive impact evaluation. From the 25 papers that presented applications 16 (64 %) performed at least one type of usability evaluation. It shows that usability evaluation is the most frequent type of quality evaluation, performed more often than cognitive impact evaluation. However, in this context both evaluations are essential.

Sixteen papers presented at least one kind of measure of quality, but none related to any formal standard. From these, 10 were measures specifically related to usability, one was about efficiency (number optimal of steps/number of steps taken in an interface) and there was 6 measures specific to the context of the paper. Some of the specific measures are user performance (percentage of achievement, based on the total number of steps to complete a task), learner performance and level of progress.

The instruments used for the usability evaluation were mainly specialized questionnaires, especially in the more formal evaluations. The most frequently used questionnaires are the Software Usability for Blind Children Questionnaire (SUBC) [46] and the End-user and Facilitator Questionnaire for Software Usability (EUQ) [47]. Both instruments applied in four distinct evaluations. Two evaluations utilized the Software Usability Elements Questionnaire (SUE) that quantifies the degree to which the sounds are recognizable. These three instruments seems to fit very appropriately in the context of multimodal games for blind learners. In addition, two evaluations applied the Open Question Usability Questionnaire (OQU). Other less common specialized instruments used in only one evaluation each are the Heuristic Evaluation of the Videogame (HEV), the Heuristic Evaluation Questionnaire (HEQ) and the Initial Usability Evaluation (IUE). It is interesting to point out that none of the papers reference these instruments, except for SUBC and EUQ. It may be a reason these other specialized instruments have such a small use. Although some evaluations combine the questionnaires, there is no identifiable pattern for it.

The third more common instrument was a survey with Likert Scale items, used in three distinct evaluations. In this case, the authors created the instruments, and they do not claim to base it on any validated instrument or particular formalization. The surveys are mainly based on the context of the application and are applied personally or via email. The other evaluations use simple observations, non-specified usability questionnaires, open questionnaires, prototype interface questionnaires or even give no details about the instruments used in usability evaluation. We found no information about the efficiency, advantages or limitations of using these instruments to evaluate multimodal interfaces in the context of cognitive enhancement of blind learners.

3.4   Technologies for the Development of Multimodal Games

From the 25 papers that presented applications four (16 %) did not describe any of the technologies used. Between the articles that described its technologies, not the same kind of information was available in every one. There were articles describing in details the programming environment, libraries and modules used while other papers described only the hardware used for the interaction with the game. Figure 2 summarizes the technologies utilized in the development of the applications, in order to allow the interaction and interfaces described in Sect. 3.2. We grouped the technologies into Development Environments, Software Development Kits (SDKs) and Toolkits, Programming Languages and Parsers. Besides, there are other specific software utilized, joysticks and devices and technologies relate to Text to Speech. These were the technologies identified in some of the papers. There were cases when the applications claimed to provide functionality, but did not describe the technology used.

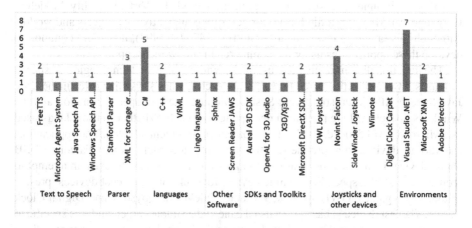

Fig. 2. Technologies used in the multimodal games or environments

Concerning to development environments, Visual Studio.NET was the most used one (7 applications); it is an Integrated Development Environment (IDE) developed for the .NET software framework. Another utilized environment was Microsoft XNA Framework + Game Studio (two applications). Microsoft XNA is a set of tools with a managed runtime environment that aims to facilitate video game development and management. XNA is also based on the .NET Framework. Both environments being based on the .NET framework explains the extensive use of the languages C# and C ++, the use of XML for storage and the need for parsers, such as DOM and Stanford Parser. These results point that the .NET framework and its related technologies seem to offer a better support for developing multimodal video games and environments. One application used Macromedia Director (currently Adobe Director); that is a multimedia application authoring platform, initially designed for conceiving animation sequences.

The papers showed a considerable variety of Software Development Kits (SDKs) and Toolkits related to spatialized audio. Two applications applied the Microsoft DirectX SDK library. It is a set of application programming interfaces (APIs) for handling tasks related to multimedia, principally game programming, and video, on Microsoft platforms. These applications also used with Microsoft's DirectSound that provides diverse capabilities such adding effects to sound (e.g., reverb, echo, or flange) and positioning sounds in 3D space. Two applications used the Aural A3D SDK. It is similar to an improved DirectSound, featuring hardware accelerated 3D positional audio, providing three-dimensional sound quality to an ordinary pair of speakers. OpenAL for 3D Audio appears in one application and allows a developer to produce high-quality audio output, specifically multichannel output of 3D arrangements of sound sources around a listener. In addition, one application utilized Xj3D, a Java toolkit to develop X3D applications. It displays the 3D modeling standard formats VRML97 and X3D.

The most used programming languages are C# (5 applications) and C ++ (2 applications), due to the significant use of the .NET framework. The one application that used Adobe Director also used Lingo, an object-oriented programming language, embedded into this environment. Besides, one application used the Virtual Reality Modeling Language (VRML). It is a file format for describing interactive 3D objects and worlds. Although this language is a standard (ISO/IEC 14772-1:1997), it is more common to develop these applications using the commercial frameworks support.

The functionality implemented using the wider range of technologies is speech synthesis. Two applications used FreeTTS, a speech synthesis system written in the Java. Java Speech API, Microsoft Agent System Module's text-to-speech function and the Windows Speech API are present in one application each. Whether to use a Java-based or a Microsoft API depends on the development environment adopted. The applications use various devices to allow the function of haptic feedback. Novint Falcon, a USB haptic device, is the most popular one (4 applications). It seems to exist an attempt to reduce the cost of a specialized haptic device. Joysticks and low-cost devices, present in four video games: OWL joystick, Wiimote, SideWinder joystick and Digital Clock Carpet. The last device is based on a usual cane and a simple carpet, and it is specific to one application, but could be reutilized. Among the 21 applications there are only three (14.3 %) designed for the mobile paradigm. It seems to be a quite unexplored area since only among these applications takes advantage of the benefits that mobile offers, such as GPS, sonar, and the sound compass.

4 Discussion and Conclusion

The purpose of multimodal software is to deal with the problems of the human-computer interaction through the adaptation of a computer to the user's needs [48]. While developing one must carefully consider several factors, such as context of use, the desired skills to be developed and the severity of visual impairment. Although the papers analyzed show that audio is a mandatory interface element, other important issues remain neglected, such as the adaptation of the elements size and the use of color-blindness safe colors. Developers could reduce this type of problem if they used proper models for the design of this kind of application, instead of using a traditional software engineering process whose development cycle do not cover these aspects.

We verified that half these video games do not perform any cognitive impact evaluation. In these cases, one cannot assure that a particular application can actually develop or enhance any cognitive skills in children and youth with visual disabilities. We identified a number of validated instruments to evaluate the usability in the context of blind learners and video games. Developers and researchers should apply more often these tools to improve the quality of the usability evaluation. It is clear that usability is an important aspect of quality of the game. There are though other aspects to considerate, as the satisfaction of blind users, the learnability of the interface, application reliability, and so on. There is an opportunity for the academy to develop works in this area, towards creating instruments and evaluating the effectiveness of the existing ones, in the context of multimodal video games for blind learner's cognition enhancement.

There is a huge variety of technologic options for implementing these games. The mobile paradigm should be more explored to the construction of this type of games. It is possible to take advantage of the resources available in the mobile context to provide contextual information that may help in orientation and mobility of legally blind users.

It is crucial to promote a better understanding and adequate, relevant and meaningful use of the multimodal elements in a serious game. In order to help achieving this purpose, this work provides a holistic comprehension of the approaches and technologies currently in use for the development of cognitive skills in learners who are blind, by using multimodal videogames.

Acknowledgment. This report was funded by the Program STIC-AmSud-CAPES/CONYCIT/MAEE, project KIGB-Knowing and Interacting while Gaming for the Blind, 2014.

References

1. Kolb, B., Whishaw, I.: Neuropsicología Humana 5a edición. In: Editorial Médica Panamericana 2006, p. 555 (2006)
2. Pressl, B., Wieser, M.: A computer-based navigation system tailored to the needs of blind people. In: Miesenberger, K., Klaus, J., Zagler, W.L., Karshmer, A.I. (eds.) ICCHP 2006. LNCS, vol. 4061, pp. 1280–1286. Springer, Heidelberg (2006)
3. Kulyukin, V., Gharpure, C., Nicholson, J., Pavithran, S.: FID in robot-assisted indoor navigation for the visually impaired. In: IEEE/RSJ Intelligent Robots and Systems (IROS 2004) Conference, September - October 2004, Sendai Kyodo Printing: Sendai, Japan, pp. 1979–1984 (2004)
4. Sánchez, J., Elias, M.: Guidelines for designing mobility and orientation software for blind children. In: Baranauskas, C., Abascal, J., Barbosa, S.D.J. (eds.) INTERACT 2007. LNCS, vol. 4662, pp. 375–388. Springer, Heidelberg (2007)
5. Loomis, J.M., Klatzky, R.L., Golledge, R.G.: Navigating without vision: Basic and applied research. Optom. Vis. Sci. **78**(5), 282–289 (2001)
6. Lahav, O., Mioduser, D.: Haptic-feedback support for cognitive mapping of unknown spaces by people who are blind. Int. J. Hum.-Comput. Stud. **66**, 23–35 (2008)
7. Sánchez, J., Zúñiga, M.: Evaluating the Interaction of Blind Learners with Audio-Based Virtual Environments. Cybersychol. Behav. **9**(6), 717 (2006)

8. Lahav, O., Schloerb, D.W., Kumar, S., Srinivasan, M.A.: BlindAid: A learning environment for enabling people who are blind to explore and navigate through unknown real spaces. In: Proceedings Virtual Rehabilitation 2008 Conference, Vancouver, Canada, pp. 193–197 (2008)

9. Sánchez, J., Tadres, A.: Audio and haptic based virtual environments for orientation and mobility in people who are blind. In: Proceedings of the 12th International ACM SIGACCESS Conference on Computers and Accessibility (ASSETS 2010), pp. 237–238. ACM, New York (2010)

10. Mayo, M.: Games for science and engineering education. Commun. ACM **30**(35), 30–35 (2007)

11. Yuan, B.: Towards generalized accessibility of video games for the visually impaired. Ph.D. Dissertation. Univ. of Nevada, Reno, Reno, NV, USA. Advisor (S Frederick C. Harris and Eelke Folmer. AAI3355610) (2009)

12. Yuan, B., Folmer, E.: Blind hero: enabling guitar hero for the visually impaired. In: Proceedings of the 10th International ACM SIGACCESS Conference on Computers and Accessibility, pp 69–176 (2008)

13. Westin, T.: Game accessibility case study: terraformers – a real-time 3D graphic game. In: Proceedings of the 5th International Conference on Disability, Virtual Reality and Associated Technologies, ICDVRAT 2004, Oxford, UK, pp. 95–100 (2004)

14. Petersen, K., Feldt, R., Mujtaba, S., Mattsson, M.: Systematic mapping studies in software engineering. In: EASE 2008, Proceedings of the 12th International Conference on Evaluation and Assessment in Software Engineering, University of Bari, Italy (2008)

15. Kitchenham, B., Charters, S.: Guidelines for performing systematic literature reviews in software engineering. Technical report EBSE 2007–001, Keele University and Durham University Joint Report (2007)

16. Fabbri, S., Hernandes, E., Di Thommazo, A., Belgamo, A., Zamboni, A., Silva, C.: Managing literature reviews information through visualization. In 14th International Conference on Enterprise Information Systems, ICEIS, Wroclaw, Poland, June 2012. Scitepress, Lisbon (2012)

17. Lewis-Beck, M.S., Bryman, A., Liao, T.F.: The SAGE Encyclopedia of Social Science Research Methods (2004)

18. Connors, E.C., Chrastil, E.R., Sánchez, J., Merabet, L.B.: Action video game play and transfer of navigation and spatial cognition skills in adolescents who are blind. Frontiers in Human Neuroscience (FNHUM) 8, article 133, Frontiers (2014)

19. Sánchez, J., Saenz, M., Garrido, J.M.: Usability of a multimodal video game to improve navigation skills for blind children. In: ACM Transactions on Accessible Computing, Proceedings of the 11th International ACM SIGACCESS Conference on Computers End Accessibility, pp. 35–42 (2010)

20. Dulyan, A., Edmonds, E.: AUXie: initial evaluation of a blind-accessible virtual museum tour. In: Proceedings of the 22nd Australasian Computer-Human Interaction Conference, Brisbane, Australia, pp. 272–275 (2010)

21. Espinoza, M., Sánchez, J., Campos, M.B.: Videogaming interaction for mental model construction in learners who are blind. In: Proceedings of 8th International Conference, UAHCI 2014, Held as Part of HCI International, Crete, Greece, pp. 525–536 (2014)

22. Guerrero, J., Lincon, J.: AINIDIU, CANDI, HELPMI: ICTs of a personal experience. In: 2012 Workshop on Engineering Applications (WEA), Bogotá, Colombia, pp. 1–7 (2012)

23. Lahav, O, Schloerb, D.W., Srinivasan, M.A.: Virtual environment system in support of a traditional orientation and mobility rehabilitation program for people who are blind. In: Presence, vol. 22, pp. 235–254. MIT Press (2013)

24. Lahav, O., Mioduser, D.: Construction of cognitive maps of unknown spaces using a multysensory virtual environment for people who are blind. Comput. Hum. Behav. **24**(3), 1139–1155 (2008)
25. Lumbreras, M., Sánchez, J.: Interactive 3D sound hyperstories for blind children. In: Proceedings of the SIGCHI Conference on Human Factors in Computing Systems, Pittsburgh, USA, pp. 318–325, May 1999
26. Mccrindle, R.J., Symons, D.: Audio space invaders. In: Proceedings of the Third International Conference on Disability, Virtual Reality and Associated Technologies, pp. 59–65 (2000)
27. Sánchez, J.: A model to design interactive learning environments for children with visual disabilities. In: Education and Information Technologies, vol. 12(3), pp. 149–163. Kluwer Academic Publishers-Plenum Publishers (2007)
28. Sánchez, J.: Development of navigation skills through audio haptic videogaming in learners who are blind. In: Proceedings of the Software Development for Enhancing Accessibility and Fighting Info-Exclusion (DSAI), July 2012. Douro, Portugal, pp. 102–110 (2012)
29. Sánchez, J., Aguayo, F.: AudioGene: mobile learning genetics through audio by blind learners. In: Kendall, M., Samways, B. (eds.) Learning to Live in the Knowledge Society. IFIP, vol. 281, pp. 79–86. Springer, Heidelberg (2008)
30. Sánchez, J., Campos, M.B., Espinoza, M., Merabet, L.B.: Audio haptic videogaming for developing wayfinding skills in learners who are blind. In: Proceedings of the ACM International Conference on Intelligent User Interfaces (ACM IUI), February 2014, Haifa, Israel, pp. 199–208 (2014)
31. Sánchez, J., Espinoza, M.: Designing serious videogames through concept maps. In: Kurosu, M. (ed.) HCII/HCI 2013, Part II. LNCS, vol. 8005, pp. 299–308. Springer, Heidelberg (2013)
32. Sánchez, J., Espinoza, M., Campos, M.B., Leite, L.L.: Modeling videogames for mental mapping in people who are blind. In: Proceedings of 8th International Conference, UAHCI 2014, Held as Part of HCI International 2014, Crete, Greece, pp. 605–616 (2014)
33. Sánchez, J., Espinoza, M., Campos, M.B., Merabet, L.B.: Enhancing orientation and mobility skills in learners who are blind through videogaming. In: Proceedings ACM Creativity and Cognition (ACM C&C), June 2013, Sydney, Australia, pp. 353–356 (2013)
34. Sánchez, J., Guerrero, L., Sáenz, M., Flores, H.: A model to develop videogames for orientation and mobility. In: Miesenberger, K., Klaus, J., Zagler, W., Karshmer, A. (eds.) ICCHP 2010, Part II. LNCS, vol. 6180, pp. 296–303. Springer, Heidelberg (2010)
35. Sánchez, J., Mascaró, J.: Audiopolis, navigation through a virtual city using audio and haptic interfaces for people who are blind. In: Stephanidis, C. (ed.) Universal Access in HCI, Part II, HCII 2011. LNCS, vol. 6766, pp. 362–371. Springer, Heidelberg (2011)
36. Sánchez, J., Flores, H.: Virtual mobile science learning for blind people. Cyberpsychology & Behavior: the Impact of the Internet, Multimedia and Virtual Reality on Behavior and Society, vol. 11(3) (2008)
37. Sánchez, J., Sáenz, M.: 3D sound interactive environments for blind children problem solving skills. In: Behaviour & IT. From the 7th International ACM SIGACCESS Conference on Computers and Accessibility, Baltimore, USA, vol. 25(4), pp. 367–378 (2006)
38. Sánchez, J., Sáenz, M.: Video gaming for blind learners school integration in science classes. In: Gross, T., Gulliksen, J., Kotzé, P., Oestreicher, L., Palanque, P., Prates, R.O., Winckler, M. (eds.) INTERACT 2009. LNCS, vol. 5726, pp. 36–49. Springer, Heidelberg (2009)
39. Sánchez, J., Sáenz, M.: Metro navigation for the blind. Computers and Education (CAE) **55**(3), 970–981 (2010) (Elsevier Science, Amsterdam, The Netherlands)
40. Sánchez, J., Tadres, A., Pascual-Leone, A., Merabet, L.: Blind children navigation through gaming and associated brain plasticity. In: Virtual Rehabilitation International Conference 2009, June 29–July 2, 2004, Haifa, Israel, pp. 29–36 (2009)

41. Sánchez, J., Sáenz, M., Pascual-Leone, A., Merabet, L.B. Enhancing navigation skills through audio gaming. In: Proceedings of the ACM Conference on Human Factors in Computing Systems (CHI), April 2010, Atlanta, GA, USA, pp. 3991–3996 (2010)
42. Sánchez, J., Sáenz, M.: Three-dimensional virtual environments for blind children. CyberPsychol. Behav. **9**(2), 200 (2006)
43. Torrente, J., Blanco, Á., Serrano-Laguna, Á., Vallejo-Pinto, J.Á., Moreno-Ger, P., Fernández-Manjón, B.: Towards a low cost adaptation of educational games for people with disabilities. Comput. Sci. Inf. Syst. **11**(1), 369–391 (2014)
44. Torrente, J., Blanco, A., Moreno-Ger, P., Martinez-Ortiz, I., Fernandez-Manjon, B.: Implementing accessibility in educational videogames with e-adventure. In: Proceedings of the 1st ACM International Workshop on Multimedia Technologies for Distance Learning, Beijing, China, pp. 57–66 (2009)
45. Trewin, S., Hanson, V.L., Laff, M.R., Cavender, A.: PowerUp: an accessible virtual world. In: Proceedings of the 10th International ACM SIGACCESS Conference on Computers and Accessibility, Halifax, Canada, pp. 177–184 (2008)
46. Sanchez, J.: Software Usability for Blind Children Questionnaire (SUBC). Usability evaluation test, University of Chile (2003)
47. Sánchez, J.: End-user and facilitator questionnaire for Software Usability. Usability evaluation test. University of Chile (2003)
48. Alba, J.: Introducción a las Interfaces Multimodales. Revista Bit, No.157, 2006, pp. 56–58. Disponible en (2006). http://dialnet.unirioja.es/servlet/articulo?codigo=2034916 (Last Accessed 13 November 2014)

Designing Accessible Games with the VERITAS Framework: Lessons Learned from Game Designers

Michael James Scott[1], Fotios Spyridonis[1], and Gheorghita Ghinea[1,2(✉)]

[1] Department of Computer Science, Brunel University London, Uxbridge UB8 3PH, UK
[2] Westerdals Oslo School of Arts, Communication and Technology, 0178 Oslo, Norway
george.ghinea@brunel.ac.uk

Abstract. Testing is important to improve accessibility. However, within the serious games area, this can sometimes rely on minimal testing with the use of heuristics and external assistive devices, with limited input from impaired users. Efficiency would be improved if designers could readily evaluate their designs with the assistance of virtual users. The VERITAS framework simulates and presents data on the impact of a virtual user's impairments; thus, facilitating a more efficient approach to inclusive design. This article reports insights into the use of the framework by 31 evaluators from the serious games field. A log-file analysis highlights key areas of concern, which are then further explored through a questionnaire. The findings suggest that the background knowledge of designers should be considered in order to improve acceptance and usability. Specifically, by addressing challenges comprehending interface elements, following the simulation workflow, and reacting to feedback.

Keywords: Accessibility · Universal design · Inclusion · Games · Simulations · VERITAS framework · Designers

1   Introduction

It is important for game designers to consider the accessibility of their products. According to census data, almost 11 % of the population in the United States [1] and 15 % of the population in the European Union [2] have some form of cognitive, motor, or sensory impairment. Many such individuals want to play games, but cannot [1]. Yet, enabling them to do so would likely improve their quality of life [3] and need not be difficult to achieve [4, 5].

However, designers can encounter several challenges such as: understanding the constraints associated with specific impairments; evaluating designs in terms of those constraints; and selecting designs [6–9]. The Virtual and Augmented Environments and Realistic User Interactions to Achieve Embedded Accessibility Designs (VERITAS) project helps to overcome these challenges by simulating impairments and using data to help designers assess their designs. A previous study demonstrates adequate acceptance and usability [10], but the participants were recruited from many different industries and so the specific challenges encountered by game designers were not explored. A particular concern is the diversity of employees in the games industry.

© Springer International Publishing Switzerland 2015
M. Antona and C. Stephanidis (Eds.): UAHCI 2015, Part III, LNCS 9177, pp. 547–554, 2015.
DOI: 10.1007/978-3-319-20684-4_53

As no domain-specific qualification is needed for a career in games design, designers in this field can possess a wide range of skills as a result of their diverse backgrounds. This means that any individual designer could have a broad range of technical competence. Thus, this article aims to addresses the following question:

– *What are the key challenges that game designers encounter while using the VERITAS framework to design GUI-based games?*

In answer, this article will illustrate three themes and their associated implications for the design of future accessibility testing tools that are better suited for the serious games industry.

2   The VERITAS Simulation Framework

The VERITAS approach to accessibility is driven by simulations and metrics. The process incorporates three phases: (i) virtual user modeling; (ii) simulation scenario definition; and (iii) the simulation of an impaired virtual user. Three tools are used to achieve this: the User Model Generator (VerGen), to specify the nature of the virtual user's impairments; the Simulation Editor (VerSEd-GUI), to define the actions to test; and the Simulation Viewer (VerSim-GUI), to simulate the experience of the impaired virtual user. These form a workflow that includes the tasks listed below in Table 1:

Table 1. Tasks involved in the VERITAS assessment workflow

ID	Task	Tool
1.1	Initialize Virtual User Model	VerGen
1.2	Select Population Distribution	
1.3	Adjust Disability Parameters	
1.4	Generate Virtual User Model	
1.5	Export Virtual User Model	
2.1	Select GUI Design	VerSEd-GUI
2.2	Capture Product	
2.3	Set Hot Areas	
2.4	Set Before After Images	
2.5	Set Flags and Export Scenario	
3.1	Load Virtual User Persona	VerSim-GUI
3.2	Open Simulation Scenario	
3.3	Perform Simulation	

Figure 1 on the next page illustrates this process. It is important to note that designers have two sources of information on the accessibility of their design: the post-simulation metrics, providing support for criterion-based assessment and comparison; as well as the experience within the simulation itself, providing the designer with insight into the impact of a proposed design on a particular user.

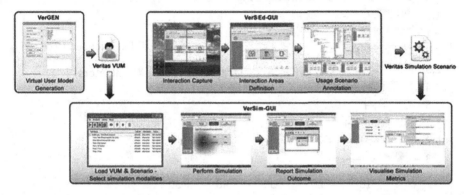

Fig. 1. Workflow of the VERITAS framework for evaluating the accessibility of GUI-based digital games (from [10])

3 Methodology

To assess the usability of the framework, each tool in the VERITAS framework was assessed using an empirical user testing approach in which expert users use the tool under observation in a lab setting (based on [11, 12]). A group of 31 evaluators from the serious games community, with a high level of task-related design expertise, were recruited. They used each tool to assess the accessibility of a sample game provided by the research team. A mixed-methods approach to data collection was adopted in order to identify areas of key concern, while providing rich insights. As such, while the participants used the tool, log-files were generated. Descriptive statistics, such as the number of click events and total duration required to complete each task, were compared to a benchmark set by an experienced user to identify those tasks which were problematic. The designers then made comments on each tool using an open-ended questionnaire (derived from well-known heuristics, e.g., [13]), thereby enabling a thematic analysis to elicit insight into each challenge that emerged.

4 Findings

4.1 Log File Analysis

Figure 2 below shows the mean duration, measured in seconds, that the evaluators needed to perform each task, listed in Table 1, when compared to the experienced user:

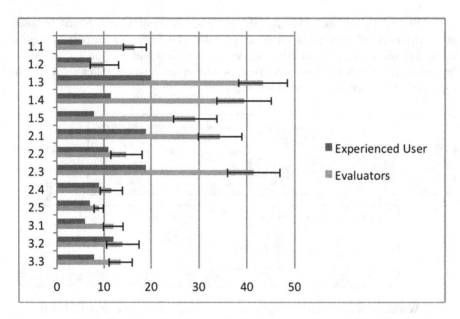

Fig. 2. Mean total duration required to complete each task ($N = 10$)

As expected, the evaluators were consistently slower compared to the experienced user. Of the users that successfully completed tasks, they were only marginally slower in eight (~62 %) of the tasks. Areas of concern include the definition of the user model (1.3–1.5), which typically required approximately more than 15 s to setup the user model compared to the experienced user for each task. Additionally, they were also approximately 20 s slower at setting the hot areas (2.3).

Figure 3 below shows the mean count of click events needed by the evaluators to complete each task compared to the experienced user:

In many cases, the evaluators required a greater number of clicks to complete tasks compared to the experienced user, suggesting lower efficiency. It is interesting to note, however, the fewer clicks during the initialization of the user model (1.2–1.3), which hints at less sophisticated models being defined. The evaluators were also less efficient at setting hot areas (2.3) and there was notably less interaction during the analysis of the simulation results (3.3), suggesting challenges in setting up the test scenario and then reviewing the results.

4.2 Thematic Analysis

Qualitative data procured through the questionnaires were analyzed using two types of thematic analysis, following the initial stages posed in [14] and [15]. Figure 4 shows an example of a VOSviewer visualization of the frequency and relatedness of terms used by evaluators. Figure 5 shows an example of a thematic map constructed through the inductive and deductive coding (see [16] for more details) of the questionnaire responses in nVIVO and Microsoft Excel.

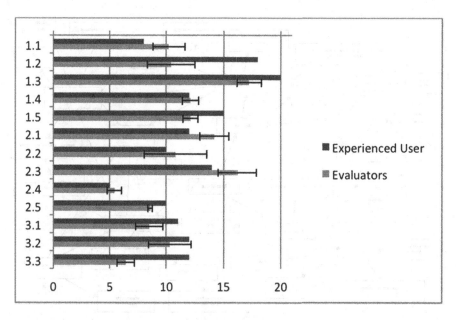

Fig. 3. Mean count of click events to complete each task ($N = 10$)

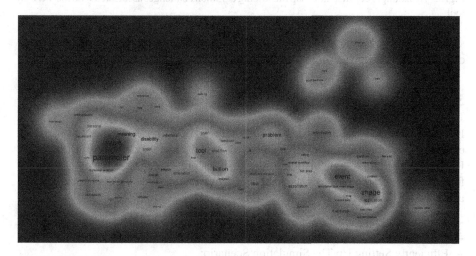

Fig. 4. An example of a VOSviewer heat map visualization showing the frequency and relatedness of words in questionnaire responses

As can be seen in Fig. 4, the meanings of the values required to setup the virtual users parameters appear quite prominently on the left. Likewise, on the right, the setup of events and assigning hot areas to images were raised frequently. To a lesser extent, the workflow of the tools and finding buttons also appeared frequently.

Figure 5 expands on these issues, providing greater insight into specific issues such as unclear units of measurement. Here, potential reasons behind some of these issues,

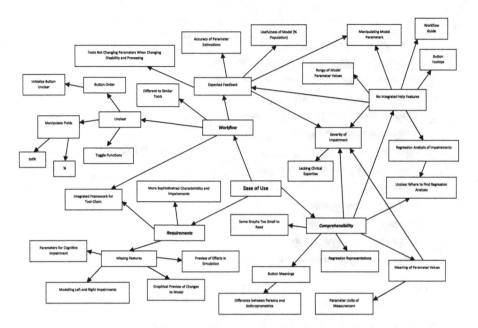

Fig. 5. An example of a thematic map illustrating common challenges associated with the VerGen tool

such as unclear feedback in the way evaluators know that a model parameter values have changed, begin to appear more prominently.

5   Conclusion

In general, the feedback provided by the users was positive in nature. Furthermore, evaluator performance was comparable to an experienced user for most of the tasks. However, based on a triangulation of the analyses presented in the previous sections, four themes are proposed as key challenges that game designers can encounter while using the VERITAS framework:

- Comprehending Model Parameters and Interface Features;
- Understanding the Workflow of the Simulation Tools;
- Efficiently Setting Up The Simulation Scenario;
- Responding to Feedback Provided by the Tools

In order to overcome these challenges, it is recommended that additional features be incorporated to better meet the background knowledge of designers as well as the demands of their work environment. In particular, incorporating support features that: guide designers through the terminology and interface used in each tool to improve comprehension; address low familiarity with simulation tools to improve ease of use; streamline the workflow with as much automation as possible to reduce complexity and time required to complete tasks; and present clearer feedback in order to facilitate the setup of realistic virtual users while better supporting decision making between different design features.

Nevertheless, the VERITAS framework has received an encouraging evaluation, paving the way for a radical change in how accessibility concerns are addressed in serious games. With further improvements, in line with these recommendations, it is hoped that adoption of the framework will increase and subsequently enable improved access to games, thereby enhancing the quality of life of those with impairments.

Acknowledgements. The work presented in this paper forms part of the VERITAS Project which was funded by the European Commission's 7th Framework Programme (FP7) (Grant Agreement # 247765 FP7-ICT-2009.7.2). All sites involved in the study received ethical approval from both their regional ethics committee as well as the EU VERITAS ethics committee.

References

1. Yuan, B., Folmer, B., Harris Jr., F.C.: Game Accessibility: A Survey. Univ. Access Inf. Soc. **10**(1), 81–100 (2011)
2. European Union: Report of the Inclusive Communications (INCOM) Subgroup of the Communications Committee (COCOM) (2004)
3. Barbotte, E., Guillemin, F., Chau, N.: Prevalence of impairments, disabilities, handicaps and quality of life in the general population: a review of recent literature. Bull. World Health Organ. **79**(11), 1047–1055 (2001)
4. Scott, M.J., Ghinea, G., Hamilton, I.: Promoting inclusive design practice at the global game jam: a pilot evaluation. In: Proceedings of IEEE Frontiers in Education, pp. 1076–1079. IEEE Press, New York (2014)
5. Scott, M.J., Ghinea, G.: Promoting game accessibility: experiencing an induction on inclusive design practice at the global games jam. In: Proceedings of the Inaurgural Workshop on the Global Games Jam, pp. 17–20. SASDG, Santa Cruz (2013)
6. Keates, S., Clarkson, P.J., Harrison, L.-A., Robinson, P.: Towards a practical inclusive design approach. In: Proceedings of the Conference on Universal Usability, pp. 42–52, ACM, New York (2000)
7. Choi, Y.S., Yi, J.S., Law, C.M., Jacko, J.A.: Are universal design resources designed for designers? In: Proceedings of the 8th International ACM SIGACCESS Conference on Computers and Accessibility, pp. 87–94. ACM, New York (2006)
8. Law, C.M., Yi, J.S, Choi, Y.S., Jacko, J.A.: Are disability access guidelines designed for designers? Do They Need To Be? In: Proceedings of the 18th Australian Conference on Computer-Human Interaction, pp. 357–360. ACM, New York (2006)
9. Stephanidis, C., Akoumianakis, D.: Universal design: towards universal access in the information society. In: Extended Abstracts on Human Factors in Computing Systems, pp. 499–500. ACM, New York (2001)
10. Spyridonis, F., Moschonas, P., Touliou, K., Tsakiris, A., Ghinea, G.: Designing accessible ICT products and services: the VERITAS accessibility testing platform. In: Proceedings of the International Working Conference on Advanced Visual Interfaces, pp. 113–116. ACM, New York (2014)
11. Nielsen, J.: Usability inspection methods. In: Proceedings of the International ACM Conference on Human Factors in Computing Systems, pp. 413–414. ACM, New York (1994)

12. Gould, J.D., Lewis, C.: Designing for usability: key principles and what designers think. Commun. ACM **28**(3), 300–311 (1985)
13. Nielsen, J.: Finding usability problems through heuristic evaluation. In: Proceedings of the International ACM Conference on Human Factors in Computing Systems, pp. 373–380. ACM, New York (1992)
14. Van Eck, N., Waltman, L.: Text mining and visualisation using VOSviewer. ISSI Newsletter **7**(3), 50–54 (2011)
15. Braun, V., Clarke, V.: Using thematic analysis in psychology. Qual. Res. Psychol. **3**(2), 77–101 (2006)
16. Fereday, J., Muir-Cochrane, E.: Demonstrating rigor using thematic analysis: a hybrid approach of inductive and deductive coding and theme development. Int. J. Qual. Methods **5**(1), 80–92 (2008)

Gaze Interaction and Gameplay
for Generation Y and Baby Boomer Users

Mina Shojaeizadeh, Siavash Mortazavi, and Soussan Djamasbi[(⊠)]

User Experience and Decision Making Research Laboratory, Worcester
Polytechnic Institute, 100 Institute Road, Worcester, MA 01609, USA
{minashojaei, smortazavi, djamasbi}@wpi.edu

Abstract. As high quality eye tracking devices become more readily available
and affordable, gaze interaction is becoming a viable and fun way to interact
with games. Because we direct our eyes toward objects that we choose to attend
to, gaze is likely to provide a natural way to manipulate objects in certain types
of games. However, little work has been done to design and test games that use
gaze as an interaction method. Despite the popular belief that the majority of
gamers are young, research shows that Baby Boomers also like to play games.
Thus, understanding possible differences in interaction preferences of these two
generations provides valuable insight for developers who are planning to design
gaze-enabled games for these two populations. In this study, we examine the
gaze interaction experience of Baby Boomer and Generation Y users by
comparing them to the familiar mouse interaction experience.

Keywords: Gaze enabled interactions · Gaze interaction · User experience ·
Game play · Baby boomers · Human technology interaction · HCI

1 Introduction

Despite the popular belief that the majority of gamers are young, research shows that
Baby Boomers also like to play games. Both Generation Y (people born between 1977
to 1994) and Baby Boomers (people born between 1946 to 1964) form a sizable portion
of gamers in the United States. Recent reports by the entertainment industry show that
about 32 % of gamers in the United States are between the age of 18 and 34, and 26 %
of gamers in the United States are at least 50 years old [2–4]. With the advances in
manufacturing high quality eye tracking devices, gaze is increasingly becoming an
interesting interaction method in video games [5, 11]. However, little work has been
done to test if there is a difference between Generation Y and Baby Boomer users in
reacting to games that use gaze as an input method. Understanding preferences of the
older and younger users can provide valuable insight for game developers who are
planning to design for this growing target market.

In a recent study, we contrasted the reaction of Baby Boomer and Generation Y
users for several gaze interaction methods [11]. In this current study, we examine the
gaze interaction experience of the two generations by comparing it to an interaction
experience that is familiar to them, namely the mouse interaction experience. To
conduct this experiment, we used a gaze-enabled version of the single player memory

M. Antona and C. Stephanidis (Eds.): UAHCI 2015, Part III, LNCS 9177, pp. 555–564, 2015.
DOI: 10.1007/978-3-319-20684-4_54

game, Simon, that was developed in our lab. In the following sections, we provide a brief review of the relevant literature as well a short description of the memory game used in our study.

2 Background

Our recent gaze interaction study showed that older users did not enjoy gaze as a way to interact with game objects in a single player PC memory game as much as their younger counterparts. Baby Boomers did not like to use blink as an activation method and rated the likability and naturalness of gaze as a selection/activation method much less favorably than younger users did [11].

Recent research, however, suggests that gaze interaction is likely to serve as a natural method for selecting objects on a computer screen. Because we use our foveal vision to look at objects that we wish to attend to, we naturally use our eyes to select objects that we wish to view on a computer screen (e.g., text, images, links, etc.) [6]. Research also suggests that gaze may also serve as a natural activation strategy in digital environments. For example, we often use gaze in social interactions to initiate, stop, or control the flow of our conversations [1]. Similarly, in certain situations, gaze may serve as an intuitive activation trigger or control in digital media. Thus, examining the impact of gaze interaction on user experience can help to identify situations that gaze can serve as a suitable, natural, and/or fun input method. Such an investigation can provide insight for designing more appealing gaze interaction experiences for both younger and older users.

In order to address this need, in this study, we compared users' gaze and mouse interaction experiences for younger and older users. This comparison allows us to gauge a new method of interaction against a familiar and commonly used method of interaction for both user groups.

2.1 Simon Memory/Puzzle Game

The game developed for this project was a gaze-enabled version of Simon, a single player memory/puzzle game. In this game, there are four game objects (squares) that can be activated by a user. To play, a user is required to remember and repeat a sequence that is played by the computer in a specific order. First, the computer plays a sequence by highlighting a series of colorful squares and their corresponding sounds and then the player repeats the same sequence. Every time a user activates a sequence of objects correctly, the computer increases the length of the sequence by one and thus makes the game harder for the user. If the player fails to remember the correct sequence, the player loses the game. The user can restart the game or exit it if he/she does not wish to continue playing.

We developed four different versions of the game so that players could select and activate objects using four different methods: (1) Gaze Only interaction method (gaze was used for both selecting and activating an object), (2) Mouse Only interaction method (the mouse was used for both selecting and activating an object), (3) Gaze &

Click interaction method (gaze was used for selecting an object and a left mouse click was used for activating an object), and (4) Mouse & Click interaction method (a left mouse click was used for selecting an object and gaze was used for activating an object). Figure 1 displays a screenshot of our Gaze Only interaction method.

Fig. 1. A screenshot of the gaze-enabled Simon game. The colorful squares are the objects of the game. Each object has a distinct color and an associated sound. The red circular dot represents a user's gaze point during the gameplay. A video of some of the gameplay of the gaze-enabled version of the game is available at http://youtu.be/2Sp4vHFOrw8.

2.2 Generation Y, Baby Boomers, and Gaze Interaction Experience

It is commonly believed that Generation Y is more comfortable using new technologies because this generation has been exposed to video games and other similar technologies since childhood. Because of its exposure to technology during childhood, Generation Y has a different expectation and interaction with technology as compared to Baby Boomers who started using technology at later ages [7, 8]. Grounded in this point of view, a number of studies show that the two generations react differently to different technologies. For example, Baby Boomer and Generation Y users show significant differences when they need to click on a link on a webpage or when they browse a webpage [6, 9]. These differences that stem from Baby Boomers' late start with technology, does not mean they have not embraced digital environments [6–8]. In fact, recent data shows that the number of older users who use digital media, particularly digital games, is growing rapidly [2, 3]. Thus, designing fun experiences that can engage both older and younger users becomes increasingly important in the gaming industry.

Recent trends in developing low-cost high quality eye tracking devices make it possible to introduce novel experiences, such as gaze interaction, in video gaming [6]. Because using gaze to play video games is still an untapped area in research and development, investigating users' reactions to gaze interaction is of significant importance to both theory and practice. Additionally, because Baby Boomers and Generation Y users form a healthy portion of gamers, it is important to understand possible differences between older and younger users in experiencing gaze enabled games.

One way to assess new experiences is by comparing it to familiar experiences. Thus, in this study, we compare the gaze interaction experience of our participants against their mouse interaction experience. To achieve this goal, we designed four different interaction methods to play a memory game. In this paper, we refer to these interaction methods as Gaze Only, Gaze & Click, Mouse Only, and Mouse & Click. The Gaze Only interaction method uses gaze for selecting and activating an object. A user can select an object by looking at it. The user can activate an object by keeping his or her gaze on the object for a predetermined short amount of time (e.g., 500 ms). The Gaze & Click interaction method uses gaze to select an object and a mouse click to activate it. In the Mouse Only interaction method, a user can select and activate an object by hovering the mouse over it. In Mouse & Click interaction method, a user can select an object by hovering the mouse over it; the user can activate the selected object by clicking on it.

3   Methodology

We collected a sample of 40 sets of data from 10 participants (4 Baby Boomer and 6 Generation Y) users. The study had a within subjects design, i.e., each participant played the games with the 4 different interaction methods specified above. The order by which the users were exposed to the above mentioned interaction methods were randomized to avoid possible order effects.

3.1   Measurements

In order to compare the differences in gaze activation methods, we adopted interview questions from the ImmersiveNess of Games (ING) instrument by Norman [10]. The interview questions in our experiment required users to report their subjective experiences on a 7-point scale. We used only the items that were related to reactions to interaction methods because our goal was to examine the difference between the four interaction methods among Baby Boomers and Generation Y users. The following interview questions were used to measure users' experiences of the different interaction strategies that we used in our study on a 7-point scale:

1. **Perceived control** measured the degree to which users were able to control their interaction with the game. Higher scores indicated better control.
2. **Perceived naturalness** measured the degree to which interactions felt natural to users. Higher scores indicated experiences that were more natural.
3. **Involvement** measured the degree to which players felt that they were involved with the game. The higher the involvement scores the less distracting the interaction method.
4. **Frustration** measured the degree to which users experienced frustration when interacting with the game. The higher the score the more frustrated the user.
5. **Interaction Experience** measured the general degree of users' subjective interaction experience. Higher scores indicated a better interaction experience.

3.2   Procedure

The experiment was conducted in a laboratory setting. Upon arrival, participants were provided with a brief explanation of the game and a short practice period for the gaze enabled interaction methods. Each participant was then involved in a 15 s calibration procedure. The Tobii x30 eye tracking system and the Tobii SDK were used to develop the Simon game used in our study.

Each participant played the game four times, each time with a different interaction method. The interaction methods were assigned to participants in a random order. Users played each game as long as they wanted to or until they were unable to remember the sequence to repeat. The experiment was not timed. Each user played at his or her own pace. After each game, users were interviewed by the same experimenter using the measures discussed in the previous section. Users rated their interaction experience during the interview after each game.

4   Results

As in a prior study, average scores for each measure were calculated and displayed in a chart to provide a summary of user reactions per interaction method per user group [11]. In order to better understand the span of reactions, the charts were denoted with low, medium, and high "ranges" for participants' average scores: low ($1 \leq$ scores < 3), medium ($3 \leq$ scores < 5), and high ($5 \leq$ scores ≤ 7) [11].

As shown in Fig. 2, Mouse & Click and Mouse Only methods were rated most favorably in both user groups. The average scores for these interaction methods for perceived control, naturalness, involvement, and interaction experience were well above 5 (high range). The average ratings for frustration for Mouse & Click and Mouse Only interaction methods were less than 3 (low range). Except for perceived control, Baby Boomers' average ratings for naturalness, involvement, and interaction experience for Mouse & Click and Mouse Only interactions were slightly higher than those ratings for the same interaction methods by Generation Y (Fig. 2.a–e).

While both user groups' ratings for frustration were in the low range for Mouse & Click and Mouse Only interactions, Generation Y users exhibited more frustration with these two interaction methods than their older counterparts did. For example, the frustration ratings by Generation Y for Mouse & Click and Mouse Only interactions were closer to the medium range (2.67 and 2.50), while Baby Boomers' ratings for the same variable were quite low, 1.5 and 1.0 for Mouse & Click and Mouse Only interactions respectively.

For the Gaze & Click interaction method, Baby Boomers' frustration level was on the high end of the low range (2.75), which was relatively higher than their frustration levels for the mouse dominant interaction methods (1.5 and 1 for Mouse & Click and Mouse Only respectively). Generation Y, however, seemed to have experienced somewhat equal levels of frustration during the Gaze & Click, Mouse & Click, and Mouse Only interactions (2.33, 2.67, 2.50 respectively).

Both user groups rated the Gaze & Click interaction method more favorably than the Gaze Only interaction method for the variables control, naturalness, involvement,

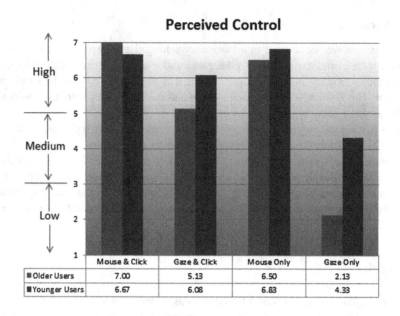

a

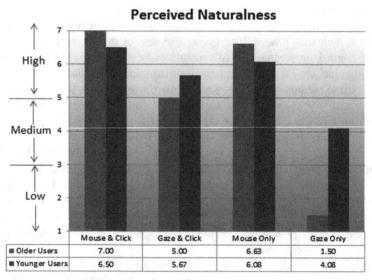

b

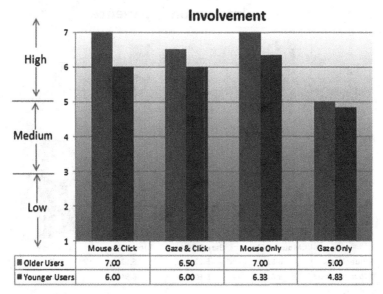

c

	Mouse & Click	Gaze & Click	Mouse Only	Gaze Only
Older Users	7.00	6.50	7.00	5.00
Younger Users	6.00	6.00	6.33	4.83

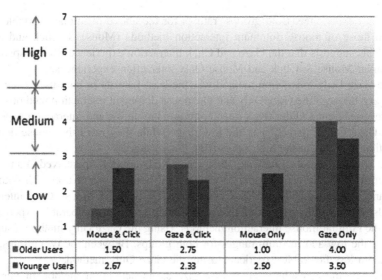

d

	Mouse & Click	Gaze & Click	Mouse Only	Gaze Only
Older Users	1.50	2.75	1.00	4.00
Younger Users	2.67	2.33	2.50	3.50

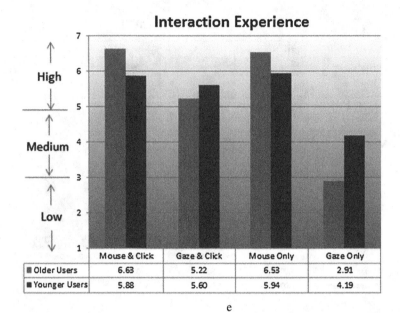

e

Fig. 2. Average values of Perceived Control, Naturalness, Involvement, Frustration and Interaction Experience for Generation Y and Baby Boomers using different interaction methods.

and overall experience. Both groups' ratings for the above mentioned variables were close to those of mouse dominant interaction methods (Mouse & Click and Mouse Only). This suggests that the Gaze and Click interaction experience was comparable to the familiar Mouse & Click and Mouse Only interaction experiences.

The Gaze Only interaction method was the least favorite in both user groups. The largest gap between the Gaze Only and the mouse dominant interaction methods was in the older user group. Older users rated control, naturalness, and interaction experience for the Gaze Only interaction in the low range while they rated the mouse dominant interaction methods in the high range (Fig. 2.a–c, and d).

The overall results indicate that perceived control, perceived naturalness, involvement and interaction experience scores for both groups of users fall within the high range when using Mouse & Click, Gaze & Click and Mouse Only interaction methods. These results suggest that Gaze & Click provided a comparable experience to that of the familiar mouse interaction methods. Using the Gaze Only method resulted in scores in the low and medium ranges for both groups. Between the two groups, older users had a less favorable experience using the Gaze Only method.

Together, these results suggest that gaze as an activation method in our study provided less satisfactory experience for both user groups. However, when gaze was used as a selection method and was combined with the familiar mouse click as an activation method, it enhanced the control and naturalness of the gaze-enabled method and reduced the level of the frustration, particularly for the older users.

5   Discussion and Conclusion

As discussed earlier, the familiar Mouse & Click and Mouse Only interaction methods were used as benchmarks for evaluating the Gaze & Click and Gaze only interaction methods. As expected, the ratings for the familiar methods of selecting and activating an object with a mouse were in the high range for perceived control, perceived naturalness, involvement, and interaction experience (Fig. 2.a–d), and in the low range for frustration (Fig. 2.b). Our results showed that both Generation Y users and Baby Boomer users rated the Gaze & Click interaction method in the high range. These ratings were similar to their ratings for the Mouse Only and Mouse & Click interaction methods. Frustration levels for the Gaze & Click interaction were low and were similar to frustration levels for the Mouse Only and Mouse & Click interaction methods. The Gaze Only interaction method, however, was not rated as favorably as the Gaze & Click interaction method, particularly by the older users.

The results show that, overall, the Gaze & Click interaction method provided an interaction experience comparable to that of the Mouse Only and Mouse & Click interaction methods for both generations. However, the similarities of these interaction experiences were more pronounced for the younger users.

These results contribute to gaze interaction research [11] and to prior research that examines generational differences in user experience of a technology [6, 13–16]. While more research is needed to extend this study, these initial results suggest that gaze interaction may provide a natural, fun, and challenging way to play games.

6   Limitations and Future Research

In this study, the games were not timed. Participants could play as long as they wanted. Applying a time limit could affect our results. If we would have required users to play the game in a limited amount of time and achieve a desired level of performance, the results may have been different. In addition, the sample size was small and the participants were new to the gaze enabled games. If participants were to gain experience in using gaze as an interaction method, they (especially Baby Boomers) may feel more comfortable playing gaze-enabled games. Future studies are needed to test these possibilities.

7   Contribution

The results of our study have important theoretical and practical implications. From a theoretical point of view, the results extend gaze interaction studies [11–13], as well as those studies that focus on generational differences in user experience design [8, 12–15]. The results also provide insight into gaze activation methods for gaming [11, 12]. From a practical point of view, the results provide valuable insight for developing a more successful gaze interaction experience for Baby Boomers as well as Generation Y users.

References

1. Abele, A.: Functions of gaze in social interaction: communication and monitoring. J. Nonverbal Behav. **10**(2), 83–101 (1986)
2. Entertainment Software Association (2013). Essential facts and the computer & video game industry. Washington, DC: Authors. http://www.theesa.com/facts/pdfs/esa_ef_2013.pdf. Accessed 13 June 2014
3. The Entertainment Software Rating Board (ESRB), How Much Do You Know About Video Games? http://www.esrb.org/about/video-game-industry-statistics.jsp. Accessed 13 June 2014
4. Pearce, C.: The truth about baby boomer gamers a study of over-forty computer game players. Games Cul. **3**(2), 142–174 (2008)
5. Djamasbi, S.: Eye tracking and web experience. AIS Trans. Hum. Comput. Interact. **6**(2), 37–54 (2014)
6. Djamasbi, S., Siegel, M., Skorinko, J., Tullis, T.: Online viewing and aesthetic preferences of generation Y and baby boomers: testing user website experience through eye tracking. Int. J. Electron. Commer. (IJEC) **15**(4), 121–158 (2011)
7. Prensky, M.: Digital natives, digital immigrants. On the Horizon, 9(5). MCB University Press (2001a). http://www.marcprensky.com/writing/Prensky%20-%20Digital%20Natives,%20Digital%20Immigrants%20-%20Part1.pdf. Accessed 13 June 2014
8. Prensky, M.: Digital natives, digital immigrants, part II: Do they really think differently? On the Horizon, 9(6). MCB University Press (2001b). http://www.marcprensky.com/writing/Prensky%20%20Digital%20Natives,%20Digital%20Immigrants%20-%20Part2.pdf. Accessed 13 June 2014
9. Chadwick-Dias, A., McNulty, M., Tullis, T.: Web usability and age: How design changes can improve performance. In: Kurniawan, S., Zaphiris, P. (eds.) Proceedings of the 2003 Conference on Universal Usability, pp. 30–37. Idea Group, Hershey (2003)
10. Norman, K.L.: Development of instruments to measure immerseability of individuals and immersiveness of video games. Technical Report LAPDP-2010-03, HCIL Technical Report 12-5-10, University of Maryland, College Park, MD 20742 (2010)
11. Djamasbi, S., Mortazavi, S.: Generation Y, baby boomers, and gaze interaction experience in gaming. In: Proceedings of the 48th Hawaii International Conference on System Sciences (HICSS), Computer Society Press (2015)
12. Isokoski, P., Joos, M., Spakov, O., Martin, B.: Gaze controlled games. Univ. Access Inf. Soc. **8**(4), 323–337 (2009)
13. Schneider, N., Wilkes, J., Grandt, M., Schlick, C.M.: Investigation of input devices for the age-differentiated design of human-computer interaction. In: Proceedings of the Human Factors and Ergonomics Society Annual Meeting, vol. 52(2), pp. 144–148. Sage (2008)
14. Loos, E.F., Romano Bergstrom, J.: Older adults. In: Romano Bergstrom, J., Schall, A.J. (eds.) Eye Tracking in User Experience Design, pp. 313–329. Elsevier, Amsterdam (2014)
15. Loos, E.F.: Generational use of new media and the (ir) relevance of age. In: Colombo, F., Fortunati, L. (eds.) Broadband Society and Generational Changes, pp. 259–273. Peter Lang, Berlin (2011)
16. Loos, E.: In search of information on websites: a question of age? In: Stephanidis, C. (ed.) Universal Access in HCI, Part II, HCII 2011. LNCS, vol. 6766, pp. 196–204. Springer, Heidelberg (2011)

Ludic Educational Game Creation Tool: Teaching Schoolers Road Safety

Nikolas Vidakis[1], Efthymios Syntychakis[1], Kostantinos Kalafatis[1],
Eirini Christinaki[1], and Georgios Triantafyllidis[2(✉)]

[1] Department of Informatics Engineering, Technological Educational Institute
of Crete, Heraklion, Crete, Greece
nv@ie.teicrete.gr, kalafatiskwstas@gmail.com,
echrist@ics.forth.gr
[2] Medialogy Section, AD:MT, Aalborg University, A.C.Meyers Vænge 15,
Copenhagen, Denmark
gt@create.aau.dk

Abstract. This paper presents initial findings and ongoing work of the game creation tool, a core component of the IOLAOS(IOLAOS in ancient Greece was a divine hero famed for helping with some of Heracles's labors.) platform, a general open authorable framework for educational and training games. The game creation tool features a web editor, where the game narrative can be manipulated, according to specific needs. Moreover, this tool is applied for creating an educational game according to a reference scenario namely teaching schoolers road safety. A ludic approach is used both in game creation and play. Helping children staying safe and preventing serious injury on the roads is crucial. In this context, this work presents an augmented version of the IOLAOS architecture including an enhanced game creation tool and a new multimodality module. In addition presents a case study for creating educational games for teaching road safety, by employing ludic interfaces for both the game creator and the game player, as well as ludic game design.

Keywords: Educational game · Road safety · Open authorable framework · Ludic game design

1 Introduction

Educational games for children have been widely used in supporting learning inside and out of school and as a result a growing interest has appeared for the potential of digital games to deliver effective and engaging learning experiences [5]. There is a variety of computer games and software that intend to assist users to achieve various educational goals. Educational gaming is a great platform that helps in motivating students to learn and is designed to teach students about a specific subject and/or skills. Prensky in [3] argues that children are naturally motivated to play games. Educational games are interactions that teach students goals, rules, adaptation, problem solving, interaction, all represented as a narrative. Such games give them the fundamental needs of learning by providing enjoyment, passionate involvement,

M. Antona and C. Stephanidis (Eds.): UAHCI 2015, Part III, LNCS 9177, pp. 565–576, 2015.
DOI: 10.1007/978-3-319-20684-4_55

structure, motivation, ego gratification, adrenaline, creativity, interaction and emotion. "Play has a deep biological, evolutionarily, important function, which has to do specifically with learning" [3].

In general, computer games and other digital technologies such as mobile phones and the Internet seem to stimulate playful goals and to facilitate the construction of playful identities. This transformation advances the ludification of today's culture in the spirit of Johan Huizinga's homo ludens [4]. In this context, this ludification of today's culture can be also used in educational activities to strengthen the motivation and the engagement of the students.

In this paper, we introduce the game creation tool of the IOLAOS platform [1, 2] which is an open authorable framework for educational games for children. IOLAOS aims to employ ludic elements to provide efficient educational gaming for children.

IOLAOS suggests a fully authorable editor, with which, educational experts can create templates and teachers can shape and customize the template-based games according to specific needs for a more personalized education. It's important that such customizations can be performed easily and without the reliance on software developers. The editor is also open. This means that new templates can be added easily for creating new games serving new educational goals.

Regarding the ludic approach, IOLAOS game creation tool features ludic elements for creating games, which support the use of natural user interface (NUI) for the playing. A NUI is a human-computer interface that allows humans to communicate with the computer using standard modes of human communication such as speech or gestures, and to manipulate virtual objects in a fashion similar to the way humans manipulate physical objects. During the last few years, technology has been improved rapidly and allowed the creation of efficient and low-cost applications featuring NUIs. One of the characteristics of a successful NUI is thus the reduction of cognitive load on people interacting with it. This is an important feature that makes NUI a suitable interface in developing successful learning applications. In our approach NUI focuses on the kinesthetic factor (gestures, movements, etc.), which is an important element in achieving the required playfulness of a ludic interface. For example, it is much more "fun" in a game to drive a car with your hands naturally, compared to pressing some keyboard keys. And this is even more important and critical when the target group is children.

Besides the ludic interface, ludic design for the game has been also employed in the game creation tool in order to improve playfulness, make the educational games more attractive for the children and aim to improve the learning procedure.

As a proof of concept for the IOLAOS game creation tool, a work scenario is presented in this paper, for creating an education game for teaching schoolers about road safety.

The rest of the paper is organized as follows. In Sect. 2, a brief presentation of similar existing work and the context of relevant educational games in road safety is presented. Section 3 focuses on the proposed architecture of the IOLAOS game creation tool. To illustrate the concepts of the proposed architecture, Sect. 4 presents the scenario for teaching schoolers road safety and how is this possible by using the IOLAOS framework. Finally, Sect. 5 describes conclusions and discusses future work.

2   Background Work in Road Safety Education

The pedestrian accidents are considered as one of the most serious of all health risks facing children in developed countries with United Kingdom (U.K.) leading Europe in the rate of child pedestrian fatalities [6]. In United States (U.S.), the fifth leading cause of unintentional injury death to children aged 1–14 years is also the pedestrian injury [7]. In 2012, more than one in every five children between the ages of 5 and 15 who were killed in traffic crashes were pedestrians [8].

Young children are most susceptible to pedestrian injury as they are not capable of making decisions concerning their safety. The perception of road danger depends on cognitive development, which may impose limitations on the children's ability to make decisions when negotiate crossing traffic-filled roads. Crossing a street safely is a cognitively difficult task for them as it requires planning and multiple steps. The several functions required for safe pedestrian ability are developed through early and middle childhood [9].

For safe street-crossing, children must develop a wide range of abilities such as cognitive, perceptual and decision making skills. They must be able to choose the appropriate location to judge the traffic, to accurately perceive the speed and the distance of oncoming traffic and finally to determine the safest root to cross the road. Oxley et al. [10] conducted a research to evaluate the effectiveness of a targeted and practical training program for primary school children aged between 6 and 10 years using a simulated road environment. In this study, the children had to make road-crossing decisions in a simulated road environment in which time gap and speed of approaching vehicles were manipulated. Their results suggested that children predominantly made decisions based on distance gap and that younger children (6–7 year olds) were 12 times more likely than older children (8–10 year olds) to make critically incorrect (or unsafe) crossing decisions. Factors found to be associated with incorrect crossing decisions included lower perceptual, attentional, cognitive and executive performance, and independent travel.

Several scholars have previously considered ways to teach children relevant skills for pedestrian road safety. Different type of interventions have been proposed such as interactive classroom training, computer-based training, virtual reality training, film or video training and verbal instruction training. Many school-based training programs have been implemented in order to increase children's knowledge of road safety. These initially training programs revealed that there are many variables that can affect the judgments of children and have been considered broadly ineffective because they often do not include behavioral training techniques and rely on parents to implement practice outside of the classroom [11]. Classroom approaches are also criticized for focusing on increasing children's knowledge about road safety rather than providing practical skills to use in real situations in order to improve traffic behavior. Zeedyk et al. [12] conducted a classroom-based study that employed commercially marketed products, a three-dimensional model of the traffic environment, a road safety board game and illustrated posters and flip-chart materials for teaching children about road safety. They showed that although classroom training succeed in increasing children's knowledge, children who received such training failed to automatically transfer these knowledge to behavior and performed no better in a real-traffic environment than children in their control group.

Alternative solutions have been used for children pedestrian safety through the use of virtual reality training. Bart et al. [13] examined street crossing behavior of children in real and virtual environments. In this study, typical developed children between 7 and 12 years old were trained to cross the street safely using a virtual reality environment. The results showed that the simulation employed in this study had a positive effect on children's street crossing behavior. This intervention was effective as the children improved not only their street crossing behavior in the virtual environment but could successfully transfer this improvement into the real street crossing environment. More recently, researchers suggested the development of virtual reality programs that might be disseminated broadly over the internet such as the internet-based virtual system that was proposed as an environment to train 7–8 year old children in pedestrian safety [14]. This program was developed using Unity 3D software and runs on any internet-connected computer and could also be adapted for mobile devices. The preliminary results indicated that this program offered a feasible environment for pedestrian training, it was educational and entertaining and children remained engaged and attentive while playing the game. Another study [15] examined the efficacy of widely available videotapes and websites used as training tools that require no or minimal adult support to implement in order to teach children safe pedestrian route selection skills. They compared these interventions to alternative pedestrian safety training strategies, including one-on-one training with an experienced adult pedestrian that was focused primarily on gap selection but also addressed route selection. In this study children 7–8 years old were trained in route selection and results suggested that children improved their pedestrian route selection somewhat over time. However, children trained with videos and websites did not learn route selection more quickly or better than children who received no training, or than children in either of their active comparison groups. Furthermore, computer-based interventions can offer repeated practice but fail to address other aspects of pedestrian safety. Thus, these methods may be more effective when supplemented with other learning modes that teach basic road safety rules. A recent systematic review and meta-analysis that evaluates behavioral interventions to teach children pedestrian safety where authors discuss the importance of using theories of child development to design interventions can be found in [16]. In this review authors propose further research with attention to child development and point the importance to provide interventions according to the global needs that can be disseminated broadly at low cost. As pedestrian safety represents a significant global health issue it is important to consider the need for innovation in measurement of children's pedestrian behaviors and how to focus intervention efforts internationally.

3   The IOLAOS Platform

The design of IOLAOS platform focuses on setting up the operational model for carrying out the codification of educational theories and learning styles, the generation of ludic, narrative, and educational games according to needs, abilities and educational goals and the evaluation of an inclusive educational session. This design exhibits several novel characteristics, which differentiate an IOLAOS-based game from other forms of educational computer games and platforms. Our approach is not only concerned with educational computer games, but instead, it seeks to provide a guided learning environment for both educators and children, that is story-telling and play-based by combining narrative and ludic for harnessing knowledge. Consequently, its primary focus is to enable educators and children with the use of ludology to perform learning tasks and provide an effective and engaging learning experience.

3.1 The Architecture

The proposed architecture has been designed in order to support a game platform that fulfils the requirements of customized narratives, ludic interfaces and ludic game designing. The system architecture consists of four distinct components that collaborate together to: (a) codify all different elements of educational theories and learning styles available and to create templates which are then offered to game developers, (b) compile games through a three step process, namely *template customization, game creation* and *utilization definition*, (c) manage inclusive learning session and play room attributes and (d) administer all necessary elements, modalities, users and their roles, game engine parameters etc. Peripheral to the system architecture are knowledge derived from educational theories, learning styles, evaluation models, pedagogical methods and classroom practices. The main components of our architecture are the *"Template Codifier"*, the *"Game Compiler"*, the *"Inclusive Education Training"*, the *"Multimodality Amalgamator"* and the *"System Administration"* as shown in Fig. 1.

The *"System Administration"* component of the platform is responsible for managing system attributes, template parameters, game elements, artifacts and behaviors, session attributes, input/output modalities, and user accounts and roles.

The *"Template Codifier"* component is accountable for systemize/codify the various elements of the educational theories, evaluation models, pedagogical theories and learning styles. This is achieved by imprinting the theory's elements using a tabbed stepwise process by the expert.

The *"Inclusive Education Training"* component of the system is responsible for setting up the appropriate space for playing and evaluating games. It consists of the "Learning Session Compilation", the "Class-Play Room Compilation", the "Evaluation Compilation", the "Observation Center Compilation" and the "Play Area(s)".

More details about the *"System Administration"*, the *"Template Codifier"* and the *"Inclusive Education Training"* components can be found in [1, 2].

3.2 The Game Compiler Tool

The "Game Compiler" component (see and Fig. 2) of the system consists of the "Template Customization" the "Game Creation" and the "Utilization Management". It is responsible for providing the "Educator" with the necessary tools to set up a ludic educational game. In other words, it gives the "Educator" the possibility to (a) customize the generic template set up by the "Expert" at the "Template Codification" component in such a way that suits the specific game requirements according to target

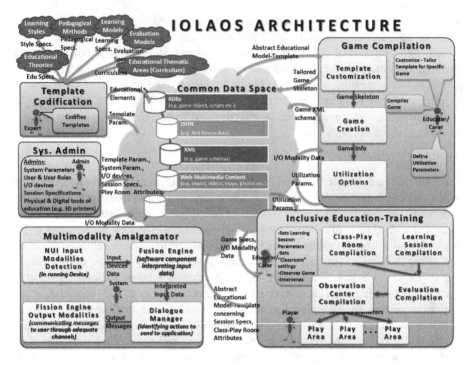

Fig. 1. System architecture

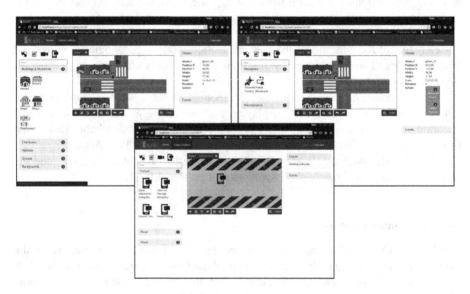

Fig. 2. IOLAOS game compiler component

user group abilities and educational goals to be achieved, (b) create a ludic game with the use of the tools provided by IOLAOS platform (see Fig. 2) and (c) to define game utilization parameters such as: Free Use, Registered User Only, etc.

Figure 2 exhibits selected elements of the game creation component based on our representative scenario described in Sect. 4. In more details, the top left screenshot of the tool demonstrates the construction of the game from predefined and filtered game objects (see the left area from the game canvas) according to our representative scenario game template, namely the "Minimum body movement template". Furthermore, the placement of the game object is performed by drag and drop user actions using a mouse pointing device or a touch screen device. At the bottom of the game area there is a tool bar with appropriate tools for the manipulation of the game objects in respect to their attributes i.e. position, size, rotation, etc. The top right screenshot illustrates game object details in respect to object attributes and containing scripts. Finally the bottom screenshot describes the rewarding scene(s) of the game and their content. A rewarding scene encompass game objects such as (a) textual, visual and sound feedback, (b) game artefacts and scripts and (c) evaluation object i.e. score, time etc. The rewarding scene canvas is activated by game creation completion according to the chosen educational game template.

Multimodal interaction systems aim to use naturally occurring forms of human communication as a way for human computer interaction [17]. In our system, the "Multimodality Amalgamator" component (see Figs. 1 and 3) uses modalities with very different characteristics such as speech, hand gestures and body movement, in addition with more commonplace input methods, in order to allow the user to have a more natural interaction with the application.

The "NUI Input Modalities Detection" sub-component perceive input modalities through the appropriate input devices (e.g. microphone, web cam, etc.). Its results are then passed to the "Fusion Engine" sub-component, a software component responsible for providing a common interpretation of the input data. The various levels of which the data can be fused is beyond the scope of this paper. When "Fusion Engine" reaches an interpretation, it is communicated to the "Dialogue Manager", in charge of identifying the action to communicate to the given application, and/or the message to return through the "Fission Engine Output Modalities" sub-component. The "Fission Engine Output Modalities" is finally in charge of returning a message to the user through the most adequate channel of communication (output modality), depending on the user profile.

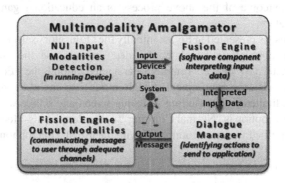

Fig. 3. Multimodal system component

4 Representative Scenario

To illustrate some of the concepts described so far and to provide insight into the Ludic Educational Game Creation Tool, we will briefly describe a representative scenario emphasizing on ludic, multimodal, narrative and authorable game creation for educating children. Our reference scenario is summarized in Exhibit 1.

Exhibit 1: The game begins at paused and a dialogue at the bottom of the screen shows the main character talking to the player. Through this dialogue the main character passes information to the player concerning (a) the purpose and goal of the game, (b) interaction possibilities and (c) motion guidelines. Having being informed the player closes the instruction dialogue and the game begins. She/he can use any input modality that is available on her/his device and permitted by the game. In our reference scenario the permitted input modalities are "keyboard" and "microphone". An available modality bar with appropriate icons is displayed on the top right corner of the screen. When the player uses a modality its representing icon is highlighted by background color changes (green color means modality in use and red color means modality is idle). The player must cross the road only on the zebra crossings in order to reach the end destination, in our reference scenario the "Shop". If the main character crosses from anywhere else but the zebra crossings then either there is a car present and the character collides with it or there is no car present. In both cases the game produces an appropriate text alert as feedback, for the wrong movement, to the main character and restarts. When the player gets to the final destination successfully, the game ends and the rewarding screen comes forth, informing the player on her/his achievement and the rewards gained.

4.1 Game Compilation

According to our reference scenario the "Educator" creates the game by performing the following steps in IOLAOS platform: (a) Select appropriate template, (b) Customize template according to scenario requirements, (c) Generate game framework upon which, the "Educator", will construct/fabricate the game, by defining artifacts and behaviors. The outcome of the above process is an educational game for teaching schoolers road safety.

In more details, as presented in Fig. 4, initially the "Educator" selects "Game Create" and chooses the appropriate template provided, in our case the "Minimum body movement template". At step 2 "Template Parameterization", the "Educator" applies our representative scenario requirements which in our case are: a) the number of game scenes-levels are limited to 1 excluding welcome screen and final rewarding screen(s), b) the color scheme option is "Normal Coloring", c) the Peripherals-Modalities for game navigation is performed via voice commands with the use of a microphone and keyboard strokes.

Feedback is passed to player (a) through light coloring for the modality used (see top right corner of Fig. 5) (b) through text alerts during game execution according to player moves and (c) as concluding feedback-rewarding at the end of the game.

At step 3 "Game Basic Info", the platform allows the "Educator" to provide game info such as "game name", "game visibility" and "game type" according to her/his desires and boundaries set up at step 2. In our reference scenario game name is "Road Safety", game visibility is "In Session" and game type is "Multidirectional".

4.2 Play Game

The game begins paused and a dialogue at the bottom of the screen shows the main character "Gary" talking to the player. Through this dialogue the main character passes information to the player concerning (a) the purpose and goal of the game, (b) inter-action possibilities and (c) motion guidelines (see Fig. 5). When the child feels ready, she/he can choose to start the game.

To enlighten the different aspect of the game we describe three different playing scenarios namely the "Wrong Crossing" scenario (see Fig. 6), the "Collision with Car" scenario (see Fig. 7) and the "Successful Crossing" scenario (see Fig. 8). The goal of the main character "Gary" is to go to a shop safely.

In more detail at the "Wrong Crossing" scenario the player navigates Gary", with the use of voice commands to cross the road from the wrong place outside the zebra crossing. The active modality (voice command) is highlighted at the top right corner of the scene where the microphone device icon is turned to light green color (see Fig. 6 a, b). As a result of the wrong actions of "Gary" the game (a) provides the appropriate feedback, and (b) resets and urges "Gary" to use one of the zebra crossings (see Fig. 6 c).

At the "Collision with Car" scenario the player navigates "Gary", with the use of voice commands to cross the road from the zebra crossing but without checking if there is a vehicle passing. The active modality (voice command) is highlighted at the top right corner of the scene where the microphone device icon is turned to light green color (see Fig. 7, left screenshots). As a result of the negligent action of "Gary" the

Fig. 4. Game template customization

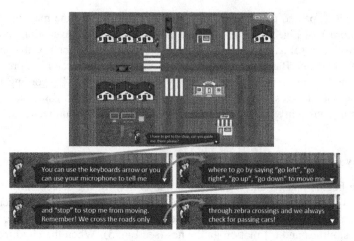

Fig. 5. Game instruction start screen

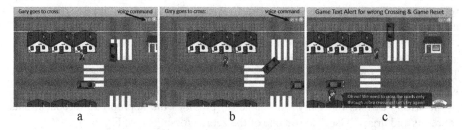

Fig. 6. Play scenario: wrong crossing (Color figure online)

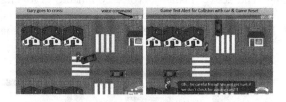

Fig. 7. Play scenario: collision with Car (Color figure online)

game (a) ends and the player lose, and (b) resets and urges "Gary" to be more careful with passing cars (see right screenshot of Fig. 7).

Moving on with our play time scenarios, at the "Successful Crossing" scenario the player navigates "Gary", with a different modality from the other two scenarios namely keyboard strokes to cross the road from the zebra crossing after checking for passing vehicles. The active modality (keyboard strokes) is highlighted at the top right corner of the scene where the keyboard device icon is turned to light green color (see Fig. 8, left screenshots). As a result of the correct road crossing attribute of "Gary" the game

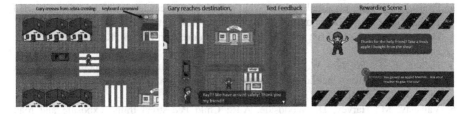

Fig. 8. Play scenario: successful crossing (Color figure online)

(a) ends successfully with "Gary" reaching his destination, and (b) informs "Gary" about his achievement (see right screenshot of Fig. 8). The game concludes with the appropriate rewarding scene.

5 Conclusion and Future Work

In this paper we have attempted to sketch the organizational underpinnings of the IOLAOS platform, a pilot effort aiming to build an open authorable framework for educational games for children by combining ludology and narratology. Our primary design target is to set up an operational model for carrying out the codification of learning styles, educational theories, pedagogical methods and evaluation models as well as the generation of ludic, narrative, and educational games according to needs, abilities and educational goals and to support this model with appropriate software platform and tools.

Ongoing work covers a variety of issues of both technological and educational engineering character. Some of the issues to be addressed in the immediate future include: (a) Elaborate on the Inclusive Educational-Training module, (b) Further exploration of learning styles, educational theories, pedagogical methods and evaluation models in collaboration with expert and educator professional associations, (c) Run various use cases in vivo with the guidance and involvement of expert and educator professional associations (d) Enhance ludology aiming not only to children experience, but also to experts and teachers, and (e) Elaborate further on the Multimodality Amalgamator module to involve more input and output modalities so that the roles between game player and machine are reversed and the player performs gestures, sounds, grimaces etc. and the machine responds.

References

1. Vidakis, N., Christinaki, E., Serafimidis, I., Triantafyllidis, G.: Combining ludology and narratology in an open authorable framework for educational games for children: the scenario of teaching preschoolers with autism diagnosis. In: Stephanidis, C., Antona, M. (eds.) UAHCI 2014, Part II. LNCS, vol. 8514, pp. 626–636. Springer, Heidelberg (2014)
2. Christinaki, E., Vidakis, N., Triantafyllidis, G.: A novel educational game for teaching emotion identification skills to preschoolers with autism diagnosis. Comput. Sci. Inf. Syst. J. **11**, 723–743 (2014)

3. Prensky, M.: Fun, play and games: What makes games engaging. In: Prensky, M. (ed.) Digital Game-Based Learning, pp. 1–31. McGraw-Hill, New York (2001)
4. Huizinga, J.: Homo Ludens: A Study of the Play-elements in Culture. Routledge & K. Paul, London (1949)
5. Hwang, G.-J., Po-Han, W.: Advancements and trends in digital game-based learning research: a review of publications in selected journals from 2001 to 2010. Br. J. Educ. Technol. **43**, E6–E10 (2012)
6. Vaganay, M., Harvey, H., Woodside, A.R.: Child Pedestrian traffic exposure and road behaviour. In: European Transport Conference, Strasbourg (2003)
7. Centers for Disease Control (2015). WISQARS (Web-based Injury Statistics Query and Reporting System). http://www.cdc.gov/injury/wisqars/. Accessed 15 February 2015
8. Department of Transportation (US), National Highway Traffic Safety Administration (NHTSA). Traffic Safety Facts 2012: Pedestrians. Washington (DC): NHTSA. http://www-nrd.nhtsa.dot.gov/Pubs/811888.pdf. Accessed 15 February 2015
9. Barton, B.K., Morrongiello, B.A.: Examining the impact of traffic environment and executive functioning on children's pedestrian behaviors. Dev. Psychol. **47**(1), 182 (2011)
10. Oxley, J.A., Congiu, M., Whelan, M., D'Elia, A., Charlton, J.: The impacts of functional performance, behaviour and traffic exposure on road-crossing judgements of young children. In: Annual Proceedings/Association for the Advancement of Automotive Medicine, vol. 51. Association for the Advancement of Automotive Medicine, p. 81 (2007)
11. Cross, R.T., Pitkethly, A.: Concept modification approach to pedestrian safety: a strategy for modifying young children's existing conceptual framework of speed. Res. Sci. Technol. Educ. **9**(1), 93–106 (1991)
12. Zeedyk, M.S., et al.: Children and road safety: increasing knowledge does not improve behaviour. Br. J. Educ. Psychol. **71**(4), 573–594 (2001)
13. Bart, O., Katz, N., Weiss, P.L., Josman, N.: Street crossing by typically developed children in real and virtual environments. OTJR: Occup. Participation Health **28**(2), 89–96 (2008)
14. Schwebel, D.C., McClure, L.A., Severson, J.: Usability and feasibility of an internet-based virtual pedestrian environment to teach children to cross streets safely. Virtual Real. **18**(1), 5–11 (2014)
15. Schwebel, D.C., McClure, L.A.: Children's pedestrian route selection: efficacy of a video and internet training protocol. Transp. Res. Part F: Traffic Psychol. Behav. **26**, 171–179 (2014)
16. Schwebel, D.C., Barton, B.K., Shen, J., Wells, H.L., Bogar, A., Heath, G., McCullough, D.: Systematic review and meta-analysis of behavioral interventions to improve child pedestrian safety. J. Pediatr. Psychol. **39**, 826–845 (2014)
17. Dumas, B., Lalanne, D., Oviatt, S.: Multimodal interfaces: a survey of principles, models and frameworks. In: Lalanne, D., Kohlas, J. (eds.) Human Machine Interaction. LNCS, vol. 5440, pp. 3–26. Springer, Heidelberg (2009)

Employing Ambient Intelligence Technologies to Adapt Games to Children's Playing Maturity

Emmanouil Zidianakis[1(✉)], Ioanna Zidianaki[1], Danae Ioannidi[1],
Nikolaos Partarakis[1], Margherita Antona[1], George Paparoulis[1],
and Constantine Stephanidis[1,2]

[1] Institute of Computer Science, Foundation for Research and Technology –
Hellas (FORTH), 70013 Heraklion, Crete, Greece
{zidian,izidian,ioanidi,partarak,antona,groulis,
cs}@ics.forth.gr
[2] Department of Computer Science, University of Crete, Rethimno, Greece

Abstract. Play development is part of the child's growth and maturation process since birth. Games in general, and technologically augmented games in particular, can play a fundamental role in this process. This paper introduces the design, implementation and deployment of a new version of the popular Tower Game integrated within an Ambient Intelligence (AmI) simulation space, based on knowledge stemming from the processes and theories used in occupational therapy. An augmented interactive table and a three-dimensional avatar are employed in order to extend the purpose and objectives of the game, so that its applicability expands to the age group of preschool children from 3 to 6 years old. Various augmented artifacts, such as force-pressure sensitive interactive surface, and augmented pen, and a digital dice are integrated in the environment, aiming to enhance children's play experience. Through such augmented artifacts, the game becomes capable of monitoring and following the progress of each young player, adapt accordingly and provide important information regarding the abilities and skills of the child and his development growth progress over time.

Keywords: User and context modeling and monitoring · User interface adaptation · Ambient intelligence · Computer games · Design for children

1 Introduction

Development is usually considered as a process of growth and maturation that an individual undergoes throughout the life span. Children are naturally inclined to create play situations and explore their environments. Through play they learn, practice and improve skills, involve in social roles and experience emotions. Play is widely used in therapy to treat children's emotional and behavioral problems because of its responsiveness to their unique and varied developmental needs [6].

Nowadays interactive technologies provide the means to achieve a radical transformation of play much beyond desktop computers games. According to [4], a large

© Springer International Publishing Switzerland 2015
M. Antona and C. Stephanidis (Eds.): UAHCI 2015, Part III, LNCS 9177, pp. 577–589, 2015.
DOI: 10.1007/978-3-319-20684-4_56

number of products that incorporate interactivity is available to young children, such as musical keyboards, programmable and radio-controlled toys, etc. This range of toys and devices is part of a move towards pervasive or ubiquitous computing in which technology blends into the environment and is not necessarily visible. Ambient Intelligence (AmI) refers to electronic environments that are sensitive and responsive to the presence of people. According to [1], the AmI paradigm builds upon pervasive computing, ubiquitous computing, profiling, context awareness, and human-centric computer interaction design. AmI environments offer opportunities for supporting the playing needs of children and examine a variety of ways in which ICT can be integrated into playing situations.

Designing and creating playing experiences under the perspective of AmI has the potential to provide enhanced gaming experience to users and in particular to children. Such games are facilitated by systems and technologies that: (a) are embedded in the environment, (b) can recognize children and their situational context, (c) are personalized to their needs, (d) are adaptive in response to young children interaction and (e) are anticipatory to children's desires without conscious mediation.

2 Background and Related Work

2.1 Augmented Artifacts for Play and Play Environments

Embedding interactivity into physical objects allows supporting traditional exploratory play with physical objects that can be extended and enhanced by the interactive power of digital technology [168]. A literature review revealed various smart artifacts targeted to support young children's play through enriched interaction and enhance their learning skills. For instance, I-Blocks are physical artifacts that support not only learning by construction, but also programming by building [12]. 'Cube to learn' is a tangible user interface for the design of a learning appliance [20]. It provides a general learning platform that supports test-based quizzes where questions and answers can be text or image based, employed in a common shape cube. Smart Puzzle, a two-dimensional puzzle, enhances the ability of students to solve mathematical and scientific problems [19]. Similarly, the Smart Jigsaw Puzzle Assistant [5] uses miniature RFID tags and a RFID scanner in order to provide to each puzzle piece its unique ID. Another approach to augmented artifacts in children entertainment and education is the Farm Game, a tangible tabletop application for children [13]. The main objective of the Farm Game is to contribute enhancing both motor-skills and cognitive development. FaTe [8] allows young children to play, communicate, explore, build their own stories and create their own narrative flows in a collaborative environment. Similarly, Kidpad [10] is a collaborative storytelling tool for children, which allows them to create their own hyperlinked story scenes and link them together in a two dimensional space. Along the same lines, Story Toy [7] lets the children play with linear and branched narrations on a toy farm with electronic sensors making use of voice but not of images, whereas SIDE Project [14] aims to improve the social skills of adolescents with Asperger's Syndrome.

2.2 Tangible User Interfaces for Play

Tangible interfaces have the potential to provide innovative ways for children to play and learn through novel forms of interaction [15]. Example of such a tangible interface is the I/O Brush, where children play using special paintbrushes which they can sweep over the picture of Peter Rabbit in the classic storybook [17]. Chromarium is a mixed reality activity space that uses tangibles to help children aged 5–7 years experiment and learn about color mixing [16]. The Telltale system is a technology enhanced language toy which aims to aid children in literacy development [2]. It consists of a caterpillar-like structure and children can record a short audio clip in each segment of the body and can rearrange each segment to alter the story.

2.3 Occupational Therapy and Technology

Occupational therapy (OT) is a client-centered health profession concerned with promoting health and well-being through occupation. Play is one of the areas of human occupation that OT focuses on, and appropriate activities for children are widely used in order to evaluate and facilitate the development of their skills and abilities. Technological advancements continually influence occupational therapy practice methods and create new tools for intervention. Nowadays, there is a large range of software solutions that promote the development of a child and monitor potential developmental issues, as well [3, 11, 21].

3 Technological Infrastructure

In the context of Ambient Intelligence, a set of augmented artifacts was developed to extend the "means" that the child can use during playing such as: (a) force-pressure sensitive table surface, (b) augmented pen, and (c) digital dice. These artifacts supplement existing technological infrastructure including an augmented interactive table called Beantable [22] and a cross-platform remotely-controlled three-dimensional avatar called Max [23]. Beantable supports preschool children development and it is made up of technological components that offer to the child the opportunity to engage in virtual (–based) play situations either alone or with the presence of the Max virtual partner. Max can act as a guide, assistant or information presenter for novel, cross-platform Ambient Intelligence (AmI) edutainment scenarios. The role of Max depends on the client-application's requirements. In order to achieve natural communication channels, both non-verbal and verbal behavior are essential. Non-verbal communication includes full body animation and facial expressions.

3.1 Force Pressure Sensitive Interactive Surface

A force pressure sensitive interactive surface can be used as an alternative medium for communication and multimodal interaction. Firstly, it can act as an alternative joystick, and secondly, it can be used to identify the psychological and physiological state of the

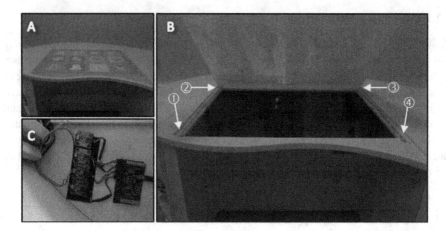

Fig. 1. Deployment of force resistors to recognize pressure during interaction

children through monitoring somatic and behavioural components. Beantable has a horizontally vision based-back projection interactive surface. This setup allows the installation of four force pressure sensitive resistors beneath it, as shown in Fig. 1 (A, B). Each sensor varies its resistance depending on how much pressure is being applied to the sensing area. Despite the fact that these sensors are not extremely accurate, a software module uses them as a scale to capture information about the pressure exerted by the user during interactions. Every single sensor is attached to a FlexiForce adapter[1] which provides analog input to the Phidget Interface Kit,[2] as shown in Fig. 1(C).

The software module receives the analog values from the Phidget Interface Kit (connected via usb to the pc) and calculates the two-axis position of the exerted pressure using torque and rotational motion equations. Additionally, it measures the total force in pounds (lbs) by summing the applied force that each sensor receives. Because of the weight of the translucent Beantable's surface, as well as the sensor's inability to return always to the initial condition (as was before user's touching), the software module runs internally an auto-reset algorithm for calibration purposes. The latter ensures that whenever the interactive surface is empty (no touches, no physical objects, etc.), the captured data are used as a starting point for the next user interaction.

3.2   Augmented Pen

Children's drawing is a way to improve physical, social, emotional, cognitive development, and at the same time a way to have a lot of fun. The manipulation of a pencil reveals numerous indications of the maturity level of children's writing skills. As a result, the augmentation of a pen is considered very important in order to measure the

---

[1] http://www.phidgets.com/products.php?product_id=1120.

[2] http://www.phidgets.com/products.php?product_id=1018.

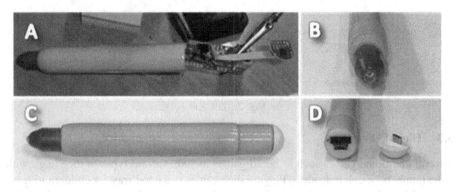

Fig. 2. Augmented pen assembly

applied pressure, the position and the orientation of the pen on the writing surface. The augmented pen allows developers to create new and innovative pen-centric user interfaces and learn how users are affected by them. It is a custom made pen in which all necessary hardware micro-electronic parts fit together while the measured dimensions do not exceed 2cm (L) × 2cm (W) × 16cm (H). The augmented pen (see Fig. 2) was designed with SolidWorks and came to reality via a 3D printer.

As Fig. 2(A) depicts, various micro-electronic parts are used for measuring the applied pressure weight, the position and orientation on the screen, and the movement acceleration. In details, the pen consists of: (a) an infrared led which lights automatically when the stylus is pressed on its tip against any surface, (b) a force sensitive resistor in a specific embodiment in order to directly receive the pressure exerted by the user during writing, (c) a small, thin, and low power triple axis accelerometer, (d) a small microcontroller (i.e., Arduino Pro Mini), and (e) an RF link transmitter at 315 MHz. Embedding the aforementioned hardware infrastructure into the pen does not impact negatively its weight, which remains under 20 gr.

The augmented pen uses no ink, but infrared light to make drawings. Due to the use of the infrared led, the augmented pen is suitable for interactive surfaces monitored by infrared spectrum cameras as in the case of Beantable. The force sensitive resistor is attached to a custom made adapter which provides analog input to the microcontroller. The latter gathers input from every sensor and transmits them as raw data wirelessly to the RF receiver attached to another microcontroller connected to the computer. Moreover, an appropriate software module runs in the background in order to receive augmented pen's transmitted raw data. Such module computes the rotation matrix using the accelerometer values as well as the total force in Newton classifying the applied pressure as soft, normal or hard.

The augmented pen is powered with an ultra-small lithium rechargeable battery with a capacity of 40 mAh and by utilizing the microcontroller's low power consumptions settings it can run continuously for almost a week. Nevertheless, the battery can be easily recharged via a micro usb socket placed beneath the cap (see Fig. 2(D)).

Fig. 3. DICE+

3.3 Digital Dice

Several traditional games such as board games include various types of dice (e.g., with dots, numbers or colored sides). Playing dice games is a good way for children to learn game skills like taking turns, staying on task, mentally adding numbers, observing others' game, etc. An augmented physical dice allows the system to be able to recognize its motions and identify its top side. This approach allows children to continue using a typical dice in a traditional way, while the results of a roll can be automatically retrieved by the system.

DICE +[3] is an interactive gaming dice already available on the market (see Fig. 3). The choice of DICE + was made to give children the affordance of using traditional-looking dice while supporting the wireless communication of the rolling results to the registered clients. DICE + provides: (a) an accelerometer with the magnetic field sensor resulting in 3D orientation, (b) 6 independent touch sensitive faces, (c) 6 independent LEDs that can glow in any color, (d) a battery that gives 20 h of game playing, (e) a micro-USB for easy charging, and (f) a thermometer. Due to the fact that DICE + communicates only with mobile devices, an iOS device (i.e., iPad) was selected to host a service application acting as the mediator between the AmI environment and the dice. The implemented iOS service employs a middleware network layer in order to expose its functionality to the network clients.

4 Tower Game

The Tower Game has been designed based on OT expertise, so as to meet the needs of OT common practice. Moreover, it has provided the knowledge needed in order to support the monitoring and adaptation logic employed by the game. The Tower Game builds upon sound developmental theories and the definition of expected skills and tools to provide the scientific basis for the rationale of the game [9, 18]. The game is organized into four levels, each targeting a specific age within the range from 3 to 6 years old, following the developmental expectations for child's play performance in specific age related activities. Each level of the game includes different activities required by young children.

The Tower Game is tailored to the needs of preschool children and supports playing through tangible interaction with augmented artifacts. More specifically, the game allows children to learn, identify and compare six different colors on each side of the

---

[3] http://dicepl.us/.

dice with those illustrated on the path of the game. Using the aforementioned technological infrastructure this game extends the age range supported by the original game. This is achieved by increasing the difficulty and playing demands according to developmental standards, while providing runtime adaptation based on the child's level of performance.

4.1   Adaptation Logic

The main adaptation concept employed by the game during play, is that the game is responsible to monitor and evaluate the play performance and commit a representative score to the Adaptation infrastructure mechanism (ADAM). The latter provides the child's profile, which consists of basic information such as name, surname, birthdate, etc., as well as problems involving functions and structures of the body, activity limitations and participation restrictions. Furthermore, ADAM analyzes the play performance of the child at the current game's level and makes appropriate adaptation suggestions back to the game. The analysis is conducted using time series methods (i.e., weighted moving average). Using this analysis, the recorded data are imported to the time series in order to generate the developmental curve of the targeted specific activity of the currently active game level. Through statistical analysis, ADAM can not only isolate possible errors and extract the current developmental capacity, but also it makes a prediction about the developmental rate. As a result, the adaptation logic is able to identify children whose development deviates significantly from the one expected at their age. This implies that further investigation is recommended to determine if there are any problems that require treatment. Additionally, using this information, the game can adapt to the child's evolving skills so as to choose the most appropriate level according to child's estimated abilities.

4.2   Design

Tower Game has simple rules and offers opportunities to promote knowledge and practice fundamental skills such as color and number recognition, counting and writing. During play the child can acquire knowledge of concepts such as seriation, counting and ordering and at the same time practicing fine hand use and other skills related to numeracy and the use of writing implements. The child also learns to integrate sets of actions so as to follow rules and coordinate movements.

Starting Point of the Game. The game is started through the Beantable's startup screen by selecting the image of the "Tower". At the beginning of the game, Max asks the child to place his identity card on the surface (see Fig. 4 Left, Fig. 5 Left). The system recognizes the card and remotely requests the child's profile from ADAM. The system initializes the game, by using the received profile, and Max welcomes the child with his/her name. At this point, Max asks the child to find and place the "Tower Box" on the Beantable's surface (see Fig. 5 Right). Thereafter, the game will be started at a level corresponding to the child's profile, while Max explains by giving relevant

Fig. 4. Tagged "identity cards" with lanyards (Left). Interactive gaming dice (Right).

Fig. 5. Waiting for the identity card (Left). Waiting for the "Tower Box" (Right)

instructions. If no action is performed, after waiting a period of time, Max says a "Good bye" message, and the game is terminated.

Gameplay. Regarding the gameplay, the child rolls the colored dice (see Fig. 4 Right) and moves forward until he reaches the first tile of the same color. In the case of a numbered dice, the child must recognize the number that he rolled and move forward that number of spaces. Two sets of numbers are used, 1–6 and 7–12 according to child's maturity. If the performed action is correct, he rolls the dice again and continues the previous procedure. If the dice roll is white, a card appears; this card has a random position on the path to which the young child should move. In case he reacts correctly, the card will be added to a staple of similar cards next to the display. The last tile of the path represents the entrance into the tower, however if the player rolls too high, he has to move backwards. The round is over when the rolling result is the exact color or number needed to land in the tower and the player has gathered all the cards. If the child lands at the tower but some cards are missing, Max asks him to continue playing by rolling the dice again and explains him the reason why (i.e., "You haven't selected all of your cards, throw the dice again").

At the first game level (from age 3 to 4), the child has to move over the path-maze by touching the tiles one after the other using his finger until he reaches the tile with the same color as the rolling result of the colored dice (see Fig. 6 Left). If the child does not

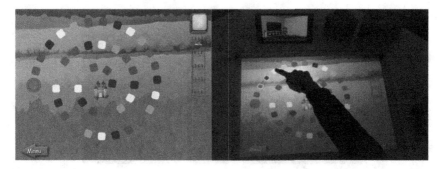

Fig. 6. An indicative instance of the first level (Left). Player has to drag his finger (Right)

understand Max instructions (i.e., "roll your dice"), the first tile of the path starts blinking followed by an appropriate voice message. If the rolling result is white, the player has the opportunity to save a random positioned animal by moving forwards or backwards to its position.

While playing the system counts errors, or unsuccessful user performance, for each rolling result. The child's progress and potential errors are continually reported to ADAM for further analysis. When finishing the game, the adaptation logic is informed and the next two phases are initiated as following:

- **Congratulation phase:** Max congratulates the child by saying a random message such as, "Congratulations", "Bravo", "Very well", etc.
- **Free play mode:** At the end of the "congratulation phase", the free play mode starts. During this mode, the child can interact with the system without errors being signaled. The child can freely roll the dice and interact with the game. In this way, the child can create his own play situation and enjoy the game undisturbed. When the child stops interacting for a few seconds, this mode is disabled.

At the second level (from age 4 to 5) the system has similar functionality as in the first. The child has to move over the path by dragging his finger over the tiles one after the other as drawing a line until he reaches the color-name (see Fig. 6 Right). During the game, if the child faces a significant difficulty or makes wrong movements, the system repeats the color name in order to help him move on. Following the same concept as at the first level, when the child drags his finger over the tiles they illuminate for a few seconds.

At the third level (from age 5 to 6) the dice depicts numbers. After rolling the dice, the system reads the number and instructs the child to count as many tiles on the path in order to land on the tile that corresponds to that number. While the child drags his finger over the tiles, they lighten as long as his movements are correct.

Finally, at level four (from age 6 to ~7) the functionality of the system remains exactly the same as at the previous levels, apart from the fact that the child has to move over the path by dragging the augmented pen over the tiles as drawing a line in a maze (see Fig. 7).

Fig. 7. The use of the augmented pen over the tiles

Fig. 8. The entire setup

5 Deployment Setup

The Tower Game has been deployed in vitro within the AmI classroom simulation space of the FORTH-ICS AmI Research Facility as shown in Fig. 8. The deployed technological infrastructure includes Beantable, and the avatar Max both as a playmate running on an iPad mini installed on top of Beantable and as a standalone avatar on a large 55" display. Furthermore, within the AmI simulation space the adaptation logic is deployed to capture interaction data and produce the appropriate adaptation.

6 Evaluation

A preliminary evaluation of the augmented artifacts and the Tower game was conducted involving expert walkthroughs with three accessibility and usability experts from the Human-Computer Interaction Lab of FORTH-ICS. The main objective was to assess the overall system usability and provide recommendations on how to improve the design. The experts were asked to play the developed Tower game and use the developed augmented artifacts in order to uncover any potential violations of usability standards in the design, as well as identify any areas of the design that could potentially cause problems specifically to children.

Overall, the experts found the design of the Tower game intuitive and engaging and pointed out some minor problems. Experts noticed that on the one hand Max was very slow in his reactions and additionally that the game's idle time was expiring too early without allowing children to think or plan how to play. They also expressed their concern about the size of the secondary screen presenting Max and expresses the opinion that it should be bigger. Furthermore, experts found that the monitoring and adaptation logic of the fourth level should not be as tolerant as it was. They suggested that the voice of the Max should be louder and less computerized. They also suggested that Max should always announce the rolling result after every dice roll. Regarding the physical design of the augmented pen, the experts found it ergonomic, although they recommended that it should be slightly lighter and considerably smaller. Finally, the experts commented very positively both the design of the game and the adaptation mechanism used to dynamically adapt the game to the developmental characteristics of children while playing.

7 Discussion and Future Work

This paper presented the design and implementation of novel augmented artifacts which can be used to enhance children's play experience, influence occupational therapy practice methods and create new tools for intervention, through popular traditional games implemented in AmI environments. These artifacts are: (a) a force-pressure sensitive interactive surface that can be used to identify the psychological and physiological state of the children and additionally it can be used as an alternative medium for interaction, (b) the augmented pen which measures the applied pressure, the position and the orientation of the pen on the writing surface, and (c) a digital dice that facilitates traditional board games. Through the augmented artifacts, the game became capable of monitoring and following the progress of young players, adapting accordingly and providing important information regarding the abilities and skills of the child and his inferred development progress over time. This was achieved by employing OT knowledge aiming to form the adaptation logic employed by the game. Apart from the developed artifacts, the game involved the use of an interactive table for preschool children and a remotely-controlled three-dimensional avatar. The presented artifacts as well as the introduced game will be evaluated in the future in the context of a small-scale study with children of the aforementioned age group, their parents, and early intervention professionals.

Acknowledgments. This work is supported by the FORTH-ICS internal RTD Programme 'Ambient Intelligence and Smart Environments'.

References

1. Aarts, E.H.L., Marzano, S.: The New Everyday: Views on Ambient Intelligence. 010 Publishers, Rotterdam (2003)
2. Ananny, M.: Supporting children's collaborative authoring: practicing written literacy while composing oral texts. In: Proceedings of the Conference on Computer Support for Collaborative Learning, Boulder, pp. 595–596 (2002)

3. Baranek, G.T., Barnett, C., Adams, E., Wolcott, N., Watson, L., Crais, E.: Object play in infants with autism: methodological issues in retrospective video analysis. Am. J. Occup. Ther. **59**(1), 20–30 (2005)
4. BECTA 2001. Keyboard Skills in Schools. (Information sheet.) British Educational Communications and Technology Agency, Covertry. http://www.becta.org.uk/technology/ infosheets/index.html
5. Bohn, J.: The Smart Jigsaw Puzzle Assistant: Using RFID Technology for Building Augmented Real-World Games. Institute for Pervasive Computing, Zurich, Switzerland (2004)
6. Bratton, S.C., Ray, D., Rhine, T., Jones, L.: The efficacy of play therapy with children: a meta-analytic review of treatment outcomes. Prof. Psychol. Res. Pract. **36**(4), 376 (2005)
7. Fontijn, W., Mendels, P.: StoryToy the interactive storytelling toy. In: The Second International Workshop on Gaming Applications in Pervasive Computing Environments at Pervasive 2005 (2005)
8. Garzotto, F., Forfori, M.: FaTe2: Storytelling edutainment experiences in 2D and 3D collaborative spaces. In: Proceedings of the 2006 Conference on Interaction Design and Children, Tampere, Finland, pp. 113–116 (2006)
9. Hurlock, E.B.: Child Growth and Development. Tata McGraw-Hill Education, New Delhi (1978)
10. Hourcade, J.P., Bederson, B., Druin, A., Taxen, G.: KidPad: collaborative storytelling for children. In: CHI 2002 Extended Abstracts on Human Factors in Computing Systems, Minneapolis, Minnesotta, USA, pp. 500–501 (2002)
11. Lehman, J.F.: Toward the use of speech and natural language technology in intervention for a language-disordered population. In: Third International ACM Conference on Assistive Technologies (1998)
12. Lund, H.H., Vesisenaho, M.: I-blocks for ICT education development - case iringa tanzania. In: Proceedings of 33th International Symposium on IGIP IEEE / ASEE, pp. 364–371. University of Applied Science of Western Switzerland, Switzerland (2004)
13. Marco, J., Cerezo, E., Baldassarri, S.: Bringing tabletop technology to all: evaluating a tangible farm game with kindergarten and special needs children. Pers. Ubiquit. Comput. **17**(8), 1577–1591 (2013)
14. Piper, A.M., O'Brien, E., Morris, M.R., Winograd, T.: SIDES: a cooperative tabletop computer game for social skills development. In: Proceedings of the 2006 20th Anniversary Conference on Computer Supported Cooperative Work (2006)
15. Price, S., Rogers, Y., Scaife, M., Stanton, D., Neale, H.: Using 'tangibles' to promote novel forms of playful learning. Interact. Comput. **15**(2), 169–185 (2003)
16. Rogers, Y., Scaife, M., Gabrielli, S., Smith, H., Harris, E.: A conceptual framework for mixed reality environments: designing novel learning activities for young children. Presence: Teleoperators Virtal Environ. **11**, 667–686 (2002)
17. Ryokai, K., Marti, S., Ishii, H.: I/O brush: drawing with everyday objects as ink. In: Proceedings of the ACM SIGCHI Conference on Human factors in Computing Systems (CHI 2004), pp. 303–310. ACM Press, Vienna (2004)
18. Salkind, N.J.: An Introduction to Theories of Human Development. Sage, Thousand Oaks (2004)
19. Scarlatos L.L.: Puzzle Piece Topology: Detecting Arrangements in Smart Objects Interfaces; Brooklyn College (1999)
20. Terrenghi, L., Kranz, M., Holleis, P., Schmidt, A.: A cube to learn: a tangible user interface for the design of a learning appliance. Presented at Personal and Ubiquitous Computing, pp. 153–158 (2006)

21. WHO: International Classification of Impairments, Disabilities, and Handicaps. World Health Organization, Geneva (1980)
22. Zidianakis, E., Antona, M., Paparoulis, G., Stephanidis, C.: An augmented interactive table supporting preschool children development through playing
23. Zidianakis, E., Papagiannakis, G., Stephanidis, C.: A cross-platform, remotely-controlled mobile avatar simulation framework for AmI environments. In: SIGGRAPH Asia 2014 Mobile Graphics and Interactive Applications, p. 12. ACM (2014)

Cognitive Disabilities and Cognitive Support

Augmenting Speech-Language Rehabilitation with Brain Computer Interfaces: An Exploratory Study Using Non-invasive Electroencephalographic Monitoring

Abeer Al-Nafjan[1,2(✉)], Areej Al-Wabil[2], and Yousef Al-Ohali[2]

[1] College of Computer and Information Sciences, Imam Mohammed Bin Saud
University, Riyadh, Saudi Arabia
alnafjan@ccis.imamu.edu.sa
[2] College of Computer and Information Sciences,
King Saud University, Riyadh, Saudi Arabia
{aalwabil,yousef}@ksu.edu.sa

Abstract. The design and development of Brain Computer Interface (BCI) technologies for clinical applications is a steadily growing area of research. Applications of BCI technologies in rehabilitation contexts is often impeded by the cumbersome setup and computational complexity in BCI data analytics, which consequently leads to challenges in integrating these technologies in clinical contexts. This paper describes a framework for a novel BCI system designed for clinical settings in speech-language rehabilitation. It presents an overview of the technology involved, the applied context and the system design approach. Moreover, an exploratory study was conducted to understand the functional requirements of BCI systems in speech-language rehabilitation contexts of use.

Keywords: Brain Computer Interface (BCI) · Speech language pathology · Rehabilitation · Electroencephalography (EEG)

1 Introduction

A Brain Computer Interface BCI offers an alternative to natural communication and control [1–5]. Instead of depending on peripheral nerves and muscles, a BCI directly measures brain activity associated with the user's intent and translates the recorded brain activity into corresponding control signals for BCI applications [2]. Applied BCI research in clinical and interaction design contexts is an interdisciplinary field that seeks to explore this idea by leveraging recent advances in neuroscience, signal processing, machine learning, and information technology. Many recent projects developed systems based on BCIs for patients with cases such as Amyotrophic Lateral Sclerosis (ALS), brainstem stroke, brain or spinal cord injury, cerebral palsy, muscular dystrophies, multiple sclerosis, and numerous other degenerative diseases that impair the neural pathways that control muscles or impair the muscles themselves [3, 4].

© Springer International Publishing Switzerland 2015
M. Antona and C. Stephanidis (Eds.): UAHCI 2015, Part III, LNCS 9177, pp. 593–603, 2015.
DOI: 10.1007/978-3-319-20684-4_57

In the healthcare contexts, innovative BCI applications have been developed such as cursors and word spellers for communication used by locked-in patients suffering from ALS or stroke. BCIs have also been designed for controlling wheelchairs for individuals with physical disabilities (e.g. [3] and [6]). Furthermore, there are promising signs of contributions for BCIs designed for addressing the onset of dementia, Alzheimer's and Parkinson's disease in the elderly [7].

Our proposed system aims to use EEG-based BCI in the context of clinical settings for speech pathology. In this research, we conduct exploratory studies of using BCI technologies in clinical settings to understand the requirements and computational processing constraints for designing systems to support speech- language therapy. We propose the use of an electroencephalography (EEG) device to detect user emotions via brainwaves to augment speech therapy session by providing insights and visualizations of brain activity during the session and in post-session analysis.

This paper is organized as follows. Section 2 describes the clinical context's background and applied concepts of BCI monitoring. Section 3 proposes a framework of EEG systems designed to solve the computational processing problems with BCI in speech language pathology. Section 4 describes an exploratory study conducted to gather preliminary information that will help identify the functional requirements of the system, define problems in the clinical settings for BCI solutions, and suggest hypotheses for further investigation in clinical contexts. Finally, we conclude with a summary of findings and BCI design considerations.

2 Background

2.1 Speech-Language Pathology

A speech disorder refers to a problem with the actual production of sounds. It includes: articulation disorders, fluency disorders, resonance or voice disorders, and dysphagia/oral feeding disorders. A language disorder refers to a difficulty comprehending words or combining words to form expressive sentences/phrases or communicate ideas. A speech disorder can be either receptive disorders or expressive disorders [8, 9].

Speech-language pathology is the study of developmental and acquired communication and swallowing disorders. It includes the assessment and management of such disorders. Speech-language pathologists are concerned with the study, assessment, and treatment of a broad range of disorders of speech and language. Such impairments may result from structural or functional causes, and may have developed over time or have resulted from medical conditions such as stroke, head injury or cancers of the head and neck. Assessment of an individual with a speech sound disorder may involve the use of a wide variety of diagnostic procedures by the speech-language pathologist as well as by medical and/or related professionals [9, 10].

Although the treatment procedures vary, and may involve group or individual approaches, the accurate diagnosis and assessment of patients with speech-sound disorders often presents challenges for speech-language pathologists. Therefore, our system aims to provide an observation and assessment tool that records and monitors the brain activity and provides longitudinal information about the patients in clinical contexts to determine if language and speech evolved over time.

2.2 Emotion

Emotion is an affective state induced by a specific stimulus. Emotion typically arises as reactions to situational events and objects in one's environment that are relevant to the needs, goals, or concerns of an individual. Emotion is one of the key elements involved in learning and education; it also affects decision-making, communication and the ability to learn [11]. Research studies found that an emotional state has the potential to influence one's thought and thinking. For example, the child may learn and perform better when they feel secure, happy, and excited about the subject matter. On the other hand, emotions such as sadness, anxiety, and anger have the potential to distract students' learning efforts by interfering with their ability in attending to the tasks at hand. Recent developments in BCI technologies have facilitated emotion detection and classification [12].

2.3 EEG-Based BCI

Electroencephalography (EEG) is one of the non-invasive techniques for recording signals from the brain using electrodes placed on the scalp. EEG predominantly captures electrical activity in the cerebral cortex [5]. The EEG headset is capable of detecting changes in electrical activity in the brain on a millisecond-level. It is one of the few techniques available that has such high temporal resolution; however it has been reported to have poor spatial resolution.

EEG is often used in BCI research experimentation because the process is non-invasive to the research subject and minimal risk is involved. Moreover, the devices' usability, reliability, cost effectiveness, and the relative convenience of conducting studies and recruiting participants due to their portability have been cited as factors influencing the increased adoption of this method in applied research contexts [1–7].

3 The Proposed EEG-Based BCI System

Our proposed system aims to use EEG-based BCI in the context of clinical settings for speech pathology. It is designed to measure brain activity to provide a detailed recording of the temporal dynamics of brain activity related to language. The system is designed to provide an intuitive interface for exploring rich datasets of brain visualizations, activity and quantitative measurements. These insights aim to assist professionals in uncovering the mechanisms underlying information processing by applying electrophysiological, imaging, and computational approaches to conscious thoughts and intent, emotions, facial expressions and attention processes and its implications for speech and language disorders.

Our system is designed to provide an observation and assessment tool which can record and monitor brain activity, and provide the required information that reveals if the subject's language and speech evolves over time. There is potential for this EEG-based BCI application to enhance speech therapy sessions by providing insights and visualizations of brain activity during the session and in post-session analysis.

Figure 1 illustrates our proposed framework; the patient is wearing an EEG headset where the electrodes detect electrical signals from brain activity which are recorded on the machine. The brain signals are amplified and digitized. The machine then extracts relevant signal characteristics. This detailed recording of the temporal dynamics of brain activity related to language provide important clues about the mechanisms that allow the speech-language therapy processing to be more effective.

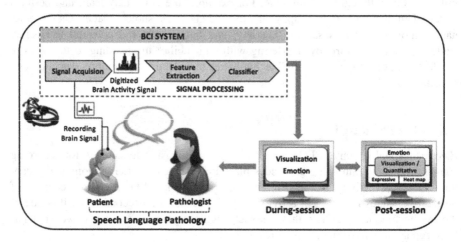

Fig. 1. Framework diagram for a BCI system in a speech-language therapy sessions

Our proposed system is designed to be used in clinical settings with a series of test cases of children who have fluency disorders' problems in speech-language rehabilitation such as stuttering, in which the flow of speech is interrupted by abnormal stoppages, repetitions (st-st-stuttering), or prolonging sounds and syllables (ssssstuttering). In this context, there are many theories about why children stutter and the factors behind it. Also, the emotional state of the patient changes in different ways (e.g. visible frustration when the patient is trying to communicate or exhibiting signs of being tense during speech). Furthermore, the child may avoid speaking due to a fear of stuttering [9].

4   Exploratory Study

We conducted an exploratory study of applying BCI applications in clinical settings. The purpose of the study was to investigate the effects and feedback on the perceived ease-of-use and the control of the EEG neuroheadset, specifically when speech language pathologists use the headset on the patients during different tasks in a typical therapy session.

We also aimed to study the effects of this system on task speed, task performance (efficiency and effectiveness), subjective measures such as comfort and ease of use, and learning curves. Moreover, we are interested in determining whether or not there is any relationship between the emotional states identified by EEG headset and the emotional states reported by the pathologists using observation-based assessment.

4.1 Materials

4.1.1 EEG Headset

In this study, we used the Emotiv EPOC headset. It is a lightweight wireless EEG device that allows greater flexibility than traditional EEG devices. EPOC has been used in various BCI research studies in the context of emotion detection. In [13], T. Pham and D. Tran (2012) used EPOC to find the relationships between EEG signals and human emotions based on emotion recognition experiments that are conducted while participants are watching emotional video segments. Their recognition results have shown that the low-cost Emotiv EPOC headset is good for implementing emotion recognition applications for recommender systems in e-commerce and entertainment. Petersen et al. (2011) used the EPOC to distinguish between emotional responses reflected in different scalp potentials when viewing pleasant and unpleasant pictures compared to neutral content [14]. The EPOC headset is comprised of 14 electrodes that are located around the head, and it also has a two-axis gyro for detecting head movements following the "10–20 system".

4.1.2 BCI Prototype

The EPOC device can detect five different types of emotions: short term excitement, long term excitement, meditation, engagement and frustration. The EPOC scores each channel on a scale from zero to one where a higher channel score corresponds to a greater intensity of the emotion. Table 1 represents the definitions and explanations of the different types of emotions [15].

We developed an application to collect data from the EPOC device during a clinical session for speech-language therapy. Our application processes four emotions: excitement, meditation, engagement, and frustration. Basically, we developed an information visualization interface that represents a real-time emotional spectrum tool. We score each channel on a scale from zero to ten where a higher channel score corresponds to a greater intensity of the emotion as depicted in Fig. 2.

The Emotiv control panel was used to ensure that good sensor contact was established. The experimenter constantly monitored the control panel during the experiment to ensure that good signal quality was maintained. To control the experiment, a program was written using C# to determine the task type and timestamp, collect data from the EPOC, visualize the detected emotions, and calculate the average of each emotion after every session. Our program used the Emotiv SDK to integrate a .net application with the EmoEngine in order to read values directly from the EPOC headset.

Table 1. Definitions and explanations of the different types of emotions

Emotion	Definition	Explanation
Excitement	A feeling or awareness of physiological arousal in a positive sense	Short-term excitement determines the instantaneous excitement for example a sudden distraction. Whereas long-term excitement measures the mood, rather than short events. It takes a sustained period of excitement before it transitions to higher states of excitement
Engagement/Boredom	The alertness experienced by a person and the conscious direction of attention towards a task-relevant stimulus	Higher score means the person is more engaged. In contrast, lower scores indicate a bored affective state
Meditative state	The state that determines the calmness level of a person	Determine the relaxation (un-stressing) state. The higher the score, the calmer they are. Lower scores reflect increased anxiety
Frustration	A feeling of anger or annoyance caused by being unable to do something, or a perceived resistance to the fulfillment of individual desire and/or will.	A higher score on frustration represents a higher level of affective states of irritation or anger

4.2   Procedure

In this study, seven participants were recruited. Three girls and four boys, ages ranging between 7-10 years (Mean = 8.71 years, SD = 1.11). All participants were typically developing children (healthy) and none had any previous experience with EEG or BCI technologies. The experiment was conducted in two sessions. Both sessions were video recorded. The experiment started with a short explanation to ensure that the participant had a clear understanding of the required tasks. Following that, the Emotiv EPOC headset was fixed on the participant's head and electrodes were adjusted until a clear EEG signal was acquired from all electrodes by using the EPOC control panel to ensure that each of sensor nodes have a good signal, and the participant confirmed feeling comfortable in wearing the device.

In the first session, the participant was asked to read a selected story out loud for three minutes. The story was chosen to invoke the child's emotions and ensure that he/she would be engaged both cognitively and visually (see Fig. 3).

Fig. 2. Arabic story used in the reading task

The second session was conducted after a short break (1-2 min), the experimenter asked the participant to think out loud, tell and discuss the story while the pathologist filled-in an observation-based assessment sheet regarding the participant's emotional state. The assessment sheet and range of values is depicted in Fig. 3.

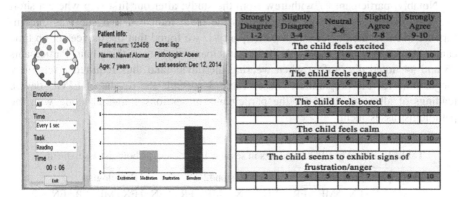

Fig. 3. **Left:** Emotions' monitoring application; **Right:** Pathologist assessment sheet

The experimenter sat directly in front of the participant observing the participant's actions during the session and monitoring the status of the headset and the detection of emotions from the application. During each session, the speech-language pathologist sat on the side monitoring and evaluating the participant's cognitive-affective states.

4.3   Results and Discussion

The results are presented in Table 2, where the duration refers to the sessions' length in minutes. Duration of the setup and preparation time that was needed for connecting the headset to the computer ranged between 2 and 10 min (M = 5:42 min, SD = 2.99). The duration of the observation sessions (i.e. reading and discussion sessions) ranged between 1:00 and 2:05 min (M = 1:19 min, SD = 0.028). The initial setup for the EPOC headset in regards to preparation of the headset where each of the sensor nodes are hydrated with saline solution and then clicked in to place on the headset takes 10 to 15 min.

Table 2. Results obtained from the BCI exploratory study (Session 1: Reading, Session 2: Discussion).

Participant	Age	Preparation Step up (min)	Duration (min)	
			Session 1	Session 2
1	**9**	**10**	**1:40**	**1:05**
2	8	5	2:00	1:15
3	10	8	1:50	1:30
4	8	7	2:05	1:55
5	10	3	1:00	0:55
6	9	2	1:12	2:00
7	7	3	0	0

Notably, participant #7 withdrew from the study; after our first step where a short overview of the session was presented as the child indicated that she was uncomfortable in using the device. With participant #1, we found that the device set up time can be particularly long especially if the participant has long or thick hair. Participants #3 and #4 noted discomfort when wearing the device and thus required a relatively longer time for the preparation phase. Table 3 presents the results of EPOC device readings of affective states for the participants in sessions 1 and 2, along with the pathologist assessment.

Table 3. Result of EPOC readings in session 1 and 2 and pathologist assessments

Participant	Session#1				Session#2				Pathologist			
	EX	ME	FR	EN	EX	ME	FR	EN	EX	ME	FR	EN
1	1	3.27	4.27	5.65	0.05	3.2	4.64	5.6	1	4	4	7
2	2.7	3	0.2	6.4	5.00	3.1	0.6	7.2	4	3	7	7
3	5.68	3.26	7.86	5.67	5.79	3.22	6.36	5.78	5	4	3	7
4	5.25	3.26	6.49	8.00	7.00	3.21	2.25	8.7	8	3	3	6
5	3.81	3.27	7.63	5.66	4.85	3.25	1.73	5.71	4	4	5	6
6	6.23	3.27	0.71	5.65	8.92	8.92	3.47	5.58	7	7	2	6

Excitement (EX) Meditation (ME) Frustration (FR) Engagement (EN)

Comparing the EPOC results with the pathologist's evaluation, we can notice that there are some differences in their values. Such as with participant #1, the EPOC frustration levels in session one and two are 0.2 and 0.6 points whereas the pathologist assessment was 7 points. Moreover, the EPOC meditative state level of participant #6 was 3.27 whereas the pathologist assessment was 7.

Therefore, The relationship between EPOC values and the pathologist evaluations values was investigated using Spearman's rank correlation coefficient. In Table 4, we found that there was a strong positive correlation between EPOC excitement values and the pathologist excitement evaluations values. Moreover, from the coefficient of determination, we found that EPOC excitement values help to explain nearly 86.1 % of the variance in pathologist excitement evaluations. By the same token, we found that same strong correlation emerges with the meditation values. Where 74.1 % of the variance in EPOC meditation values is shared with the pathologist meditation evaluations values. On the other hand, we found that there is no significant correlation between the EPOC frustration values and the pathologist frustration evaluations values. Similarly, there is no significant correlation between the EPOC engagement values and the pathologist engagement values.

Table 4. Spearman's correlation of EPOC values and the pathologist evaluation (N = 4)

EPOC values of (session 1 and session 2) and pathologist evaluation				
	Excitement	Meditation	Frustration	Engagement
Spearman's Correlation	0.928	0.861	-0.116	-0.098
P value	*0.008	*0.028	0.827	0.854
Coefficient of determination	86.1 %	74.1 %	1.34 %	0.96 %

* Correlation is significant at the 0.05 level (2-tailed)

Table 5. Spearman's correlation of EPOC values in task 1 and task 2 (N = 4)

EPOC values of session 1 and session 2				
	Excitement	Meditation	Frustration	Engagement
Spearman's Correlation	0.886	0.617	0.486	0.982
P value	*0.019	0.192	0.329	*0.000
Coefficient of determination	78.5 %	38.1 %	23.7 %	96.4 %

* Correlation is significant at the 0.05 level (2-tailed)

Moreover, we compared the EPOC values in task 1 with values in task 2. The comparison is listed in Table 5. We found that excitement values from the reading task in the first session and excitement values from task 2 have a high correlation. Notably, 78.5 % of the variance on task 1 is shared with task 2. The same strong correlation emerges with the engagement values from the reading task in the first session and engagement values from task 2 where 96.4 % of the variance on task 1 is shared with task 2.

Reflecting on using our BCI systems in clinical contexts, we faced a variety of challenges. Some of these challenges are technology-related, whereas other challenges are user-related. Technology-related challenges include impedance with sensors, system usability, real-time constraints, and the perceived obtrusiveness of the device.

User-related challenges deal with unfamiliarity of participants with the BCI technology, discrepancy between readings, and time of the preparation setup which require assistance from the facilitator to apply the electrodes. The results shown are only preliminary but demonstrate the potential of embedding BCI monitoring in speech-language therapy sessions to objectively measure cognitive-affective states of patients.

5 Conclusion

EEG-based BCI has rapidly grown in the recent years due to the portability, ease of use, and relative safety compared to other neuroimaging techniques currently used in research facilities and hospitals. Advances in these techniques have facilitated the observation of activities or abnormalities within the human brain in clinical settings, without invasive procedures. BCIs have been shown to be effective in providing insight into the brain activity of a patient in a clinical context. In this paper, we proposed an EEG-based BCI framework in the context of clinical settings for speech pathology to enhance speech therapy sessions. Preliminary evidence from our exploratory study suggests that the system can sufficiently provide insights into cognitive activity and affective states in situ during speech-language therapy sessions, and augment that with visualizations of brain activity during the session and in post-session analysis.

Acknowledgements. We extend our appreciation to the Deanship of Scientific Research at King Saud University (KSU) for funding the work through the research group project number RGP-VPP-157. We would like to express our thanks to Dr. Maha Omair from Department of Statistics and Operations Research for assistance with statistical analysis. We would also like to express our appreciation for the assistance provided by speech-language pathologist Mr. Abdurrahman Ashore at King Abdulaziz University Hospital (KAUH). Finally, we would like to thank all the children who participated in our research.

References

1. Wolpaw, J.R., Birbaumer, N., McFarland, D.J., Pfurtscheller, G., Vaughan, T.M.: Brain–computer interfaces for communication and control. Clin. Neurophysiol. **113**, 767–791 (2002)
2. Graimann, B., Allison, B., Pfurtscheller, G.: Brain-Computer Interfaces: A Gentle Introduction. In: Brain-Computer Interfaces: Revolutionizing Human-Computer Interaction, pp. 1–27. Springer (2010)
3. Rao, R.P.: Brain-Computer Interfacing: An Introduction. Cambridge University Press (2013)
4. Mak, J.N., Wolpaw, J.R.: Clinical applications of brain-computer interfaces current state and future prospects. IEEE Rev. Biomed. Eng. **2**, 187–199 (2009)
5. Nicolas-Alonso, L.F., Gomez-Gil, J.: Brain computer interfaces, a review. Sensors **12**, 1211–1279 (2012)
6. Postelnicu, C., Talaba, D., Toma, M.: Brain computer interfaces for medical applications. Bull. Transilvania Univ. Braşov **3**, 99–106 (2010)

7. Shih, J.J., Krusienski, D.J., Wolpaw, J.R.: Brain-computer interfaces in medicine. Mayo Clin. Proc. **87**, 268–279 (2012)
8. Ullman, M.T.: Language and the brain. In: An Introduction to Language and Linguistics, vol. 3, pp. 235–272. Cambridge University Press, Cambridge (2006)
9. Schnelle, H.: Language in the Brain. Cambridge University Press, Cambridge (2010)
10. Brumberg, J.S., Nieto-Castanon, A., Kennedy, P.R., Guenther, F.H.: Brain-computer interfaces for speech communication. Speech Commun. **52**, 367–379 (2010)
11. Boekaerts, M.: Being concerned with well-being and with learning. Educ. Psychol. **28**, 149–167 (1993)
12. Shirazi, A.S., Hassib, M., Henze, N., Schmidt, A., Kunze, K.: What's on your mind?: mental task awareness using single electrode brain computer interfaces. In: Proceedings of the 5th Augmented Human International Conference. ACM (2014)
13. Pham, T.D., Tran, D.: Emotion recognition using the emotiv EPOC device. In: Huang, T., Zeng, Z., Li, C., Leung, C.S. (eds.) ICONIP 2012, Part V. LNCS, vol. 7667, pp. 394–399. Springer, Heidelberg (2012)
14. Petersen, M.K., Stahlhut, C., Stopczynski, A., Larsen, J.E., Hansen, L.K.: Smartphones get emotional: mind reading images and reconstructing the neural sources. In: D'Mello, S., Graesser, A., Schuller, B., Martin, J.-C. (eds.) ACII 2011, Part II. LNCS, vol. 6975, pp. 578–587. Springer, Heidelberg (2011)
15. Emotiv EPOC user manual. http://wiki.emotiv.com/tiki-index.php?page=Getting+Start+Document&structure=Getting+Start+Document&page_ref_id=449

Usability Heuristics for the Design of Interactive Attention Assessment and Rehabilitation Technologies

Layla Al-Salhie, Weaám AlRashed, and Areej Al-Wabil[✉]

Software Engineering Department, College of Computer and Information
Sciences, King Saud University, Riyadh, Saudi Arabia
aalwabil@ksu.edu.sa

Abstract. Emerging technologies are beginning to find their way in different health care centers and clinics worldwide for the purpose of assessment and rehabilitation for people with attention deficit disorders. And due to the variation in the practitioners and patients' requirements and preferences for using these technologies, understanding the usability issues has become essential for further development in this domain. In particular, addressing issues of selecting usability evaluation methods and their effectiveness in identifying usability problems. A bespoke heuristic set for the context of intervention programs for developing sustained attention is proposed and tested. In this study, we conducted usability heuristic evaluations on three sustained attention assessment and rehabilitation programs that involve emerging technologies; which are Neurofeedback and eye tracking. The heuristic evaluation was conducted by five evaluators, and the results showed that the proposed heuristic inspection evaluation method was effective in finding major usability problems in programs designed for sustained attention assessment and rehabilitation. Moreover, recommendations were presented regarding the evaluators' experience with the evaluated interactive programs, the contexts of usage, target user communities, and the technical background knowledge of the interaction modalities.

Keywords: Attention · Usability · Heuristic evaluation · Eye tracking · Neurofeedback

1 Introduction

During the recent decade, a plethora of tools, methods and tests have been developed and utilized for the diagnosis and assessment of sustained attention problems in individuals, and in particular people with Attention Deficit Hyperactivity Disorders ADHD and Attention Deficit Disorders ADD. These tools and methods range from manual assessments, to more complex adaptive and intelligent computerized tests. Moreover, during the last few years, this field showed incredible increases in adopting emerging technologies for the purpose of diagnosis, assessment and rehabilitation of people with sustained attention difficulties. These technologies include: Neurofeedback detection and brainwaves analysis, Brain Computer Interfaces BCI, eye tracking, virtual and augmented reality applications. Furthermore, for the purpose of measuring sustained

© Springer International Publishing Switzerland 2015
M. Antona and C. Stephanidis (Eds.): UAHCI 2015, Part III, LNCS 9177, pp. 604–615, 2015.
DOI: 10.1007/978-3-319-20684-4_58

attention, there are common features that are applied and implemented in these methods, regardless of the different formats that are presented to the target patients. However, tests for measuring the sustained attention of an individual require the patient to perform a number of tasks that involve directing his/her attention to one or more targets for specified periods of time; and during this time the patient is expected to respond to a number of stimuli [1]. These responses often vary from one technology to another. For instance, in the technologies that use brain waves, the response is measured and monitored by evoking cognitive activities like concentration and paying attention, and for the technologies that use gaze interaction the response is measured and monitored by performing activities that involve directing the user's visual attention to specific areas of interest displayed on the interface. And despite the ongoing debate among researchers and scientists about the effectiveness, efficiency and the convenience of these methods, some of which are beginning to find their way in different health care centers and clinics worldwide. Furthermore, some characteristics of these methods are perceived as issues that may hinder their usability and accessibility to a wider range of audiences. These issues include availability and mobility of the method, accuracy of information that is obtained during or after the session, patient self-dependency, cost effectiveness and user entertainment. As a result, giving more insight and focus on the usability issues of the current sustained attention assessment methods and technologies is valuable for both specialists and patients. Meanwhile, usability inspection methods that address the specific contexts of attention assessment and rehabilitation are scarce. Therefore, we worked on developing a heuristic inspection method and applied it in the context of evaluating the usability of three selected sustained attention assessment and rehabilitation computer applications that use emerging technologies (i.e. eye tracking and neurofeedback) as input modalities. These selected applications are deployed for interventional programs that support users with ADHD and ADD in local service centers in Saudi Arabia. The usability heuristic evaluation was conducted by a number of evaluators who had prior experience in assistive technologies' usability evaluation and Human Computer Interaction (HCI) design experience. The aim was to examine the usability issues with such methods that adopt emerging technologies and determine the efficacy of the proposed heuristic inspection method for these technologies. In heuristic evaluations, the evaluators often review the methods/technologies, and then determine their compliance with pre-defined usability principles known as heuristics. However, this evaluation method tends to focus on identifying problems in interaction with technologies rather than solutions [2]. Nonetheless, it is often considered effective when combined with other usability evaluation tools and when conducted by subject-matter experts [3].

The remainder of the paper is organized as follows; first we describe the study design and the three selected interventional interactive programs that have been evaluated in the study. Following that, we provide an overview about the participants who conducted the usability heuristic evaluations. And then we describe the usability evaluation sessions followed by the obtained results and discussion. Then we conclude the paper in the last section with implications of our key findings on the design of interactive sustained attention rehabilitation technologies.

2 Study Design

Three attention assessment and rehabilitation programs were selected for evaluation. These programs were characterized as interventional programs which are designed with persuasive aspects and novel interaction modalities. Persuasive technologies are designed with behavior modification strategies that promote healthy behaviors [4]. These technologies are often designed in a way that ensures behavior changes and user's likelihood of long-term adoption, as noted by [4]. And considering the fact that the custom and more specialized heuristic is more effective and can reveal more usability issues, we adopted the list of specialized heuristics for persuasive health technologies developed by [4]. This list is comprised of 10 heuristics that have been shown to be effective in finding more relevant usability issues related to the persuasive aspects of the technologies being examined when compared to the basic heuristics of [2]. In our adaptation, we made some modification on these heuristics to make it more applicable to the nature of the attention assessment and rehabilitation technologies. The revised set of persuasive health heuristics is listed in Table 1.

Furthermore, it is noted that all the three programs examined in this study have been developed and designed as serious gaming systems for cognitive/behavioral therapy purpose. Therefore, we examined the gaming usability heuristics and guidelines that could be adopted for evaluating the usability of the three selected programs. Authors in [5] have developed heuristics for evaluating the usability of children's e-learning applications that involve games for educational purposes. Four of these heuristics were perceived to be relevant to the cognitive rehabilitation games. Also, they were found to be complementary to the persuasive health technologies heuristics described in Table 1. The revised subset of gaming heuristics is described in Table 2. Also, we referred to the work in [6] which includes general principles and guidelines for the accessibility and usability of educational gaming environment for students with disabilities. These principles have been combined in an aggregated usability heuristics set, specific to the context of attention assessment and rehabilitation technologies. This was used to ensure comprehensive coverage of heuristics for persuasive health aspect, serious gaming, and accessibility for users with disabilities.

3 Technologies Under Evaluation

In this study, we selected three therapeutic programs for sustained attention assessment and rehabilitation. One of them involves neurofeedback as a main input modality to control objects in a number of games designed for users who have difficulties in concentration and sustaining visual and auditory attention. The other two programs use eye tracking technologies to control objects in therapeutic games designed for users with ADHD or ADD. In the following subsections, we provide a brief overview about each program.

Table 1. Persuasive health technology heuristic

1- Appropriate Functionality:

- The technology functionalities should meet usability, mobility and visibility of target users' needs; considering the settings in which this technology might be used in
- The technology should function effectively in the user's own environment and allows the daily use as part of an individual life's routine
- The technology functionalities should be exactly reflecting the purpose that it has been developed and intended for without any extra features that might confuse the target users

2- Not Irritating or Embarrassing:

- The technology devices shouldn't irritate or embarrass the target users during the usage
- The technology shouldn't be embarrassing when it is present in the users' environment
- The technology should be easily customized in order to fit the different needs of the target users

3- Protect Users' Privacy

- The technology should allow the users to keep their information private
- The technology should allow the users to define which information can be shown and shared with others

4- User Motivation

- The technology should provide frequent feedback that indicates the progress in the user's behavior in order to meet the target goals
- The technology should use positive motivation strategies to promote the user's progress

5- Usable and Appealing Design

- The interface design should be simple and adhere to the basic usability standard with main consideration to the different usability and accessibility needs of the target users
- The interface design should be attractive and appealing promoting more user interest and engagement

6- Accuracy of Information

- The technology should obtain an accurate and comprehensive user's data
- The technology should avoid any misrepresentation of the data because of inability to use the device in one of the environments or due to certain user's conditions

7- Appropriate Time and Place

- The technology should provide the information and the feedback in effective way that helps the users to achieve the intended purpose
- The technology should provide the help when and where needed

8- Visibility of User's Status

- The technology should keep the user updated and informed about his progress toward the goals by using appropriate feedback
- The technology should provide accurate clear feedback that easily understood by the users

9- Customizability

- The technology should allow the user to customize some aspects of the technology to create personalized settings/goals
- The various interface components can be customized by switching its visibility to on or off according to the different users preferences

(Continued)

Table 1. (*Continued*)

• The technology implies cultural aspects by considering the diversity of its users. Including the different languages, race, gender, etc.
10- Educate Users
• The technology should increase the user understanding of the actions that led to his/her cognitive abilities improvement, by knowing which behavior leads to the target goal
• The technology should allow the users to learn all the information and skills that are relevant to the intended goals

Table 2. Gaming heuristics

1- Multimedia Representations
• All information should be presented in a variety of multimedia format: such as text, audio, and video… etc.
• The multimedia representation should assist the rehabilitation process
• The games should provide sound and visual feedback which are meaningful, and give hints that evoke emotions
• The system should avoid unnecessary multimedia as they may confuse the user
2- Use Appropriate Hardware Devices
• The games should be designed in a wide range of input/output devices
• The devices should be easily customized to suit the different users' capabilities
• The devices can be used effectively for their intended purpose
• There should be consistency between the motor effort needed to interact with the device and the user skill
3- Challenging the Users
• Enough information and guidelines should be available and provided in a clear way before starting the games, so users can start playing the game with full knowledge and confidence
• In the games, there should be different difficulty levels, so the user has greater challenge when he/she upgraded and moved from one level to the next one
• The game challenging levels should consider the users' different cognitive abilities
6- Evoke Mental Imagery
• The games should allow the user to evoke his/her imagination during the interaction with the different games elements in a way that support the cognitive rehabilitation process
• The games should encourage the user to use his/her own interpretation of the different games context and characters which increase his/her motivation toward the games' goals
• The games should be designed based on an interesting story/plot

3.1 Play Attention (Neurofeedback)

Play Attention is one of the programs that was designed for children and adults with attention problems. It has been used globally in different environments such as health care centers, clinics, schools and homes [7]. It uses neurofeedback technology that allows the user to control the elements of computer games with cognitive activity involving attention. The main concept in this technology is that when the user is actively paying attention, the brain generates streams of brainwave signals that are processed to interact with the interface. These signals are monitored by the system's body-wave armband or headset that transmits the signal wirelessly to the computer, so the user can interact with the games [7]. The Play Attention program aims to develop the patients' abilities to focus, filter out distractions, and improve memory skills. Therefore, the program has been designed and built with several games that train the user to develop the skills mentioned earlier. This program is designed for PC platforms, and the setup involves having the user to wear an armband or a helmet to allow the program to monitor his/her brainwaves.

3.2 Tarkeezy (Eye Tracking)

Tarkeezy is a cognitive/behavior therapy PC program with games controlled through movement of the eyes [8]. It has been designed to help users with ADHD to improve their focus, attention, learn how to ignore distractions and decrease impulsive behavior. This program facilitates controlling the games by using eye tracking technology instead of using the mouse, keyboard or joystick. The eye tracking device provides an insight into what the individual is looking at, and facilitates controlling the screen objects if the stability of eye gaze remains above a predefined threshold [8].

3.3 Attentive I (Eye Tracking)

Attentive I is a cognitive therapy game designed for users with ADHD and ADD. It was developed to improve the visual attention of users and strengthen their visual memory skills with gaze-based serious gaming scenarios. Gaze-based technologies enable the users to use their eyes as an input modality to control the objects in the games. Also, the program generates reports that help specialists in tracking patients' progress [9].

4   Participants

The number of participants who conducted the expert heuristic inspections and evaluation was five. Four of them evaluated Tarkeezy and Attentive I programs. And three evaluators applied the heuristic inspection method on the Play Attention program. The evaluators experience ranged from 1 to 6 years of experience with HCI design and/or usability engineering. All evaluators had prior experience in applying heuristic inspection methods in the design and development of assistive technologies.

5   Evaluation Sessions

To evaluate the three attention assessment and rehabilitation programs, a heuristic template sheet was created. However, for every program the evaluator received a sheet that contains the list of the heuristics along with their corresponding descriptions. The evaluators were requested to indicate the severity rating for every usability issue identified. The severity rating is used to identify the range of usability issues for these technologies and to examine the most serious usability problems in depth. In this study, we followed Nielsen's severity scale recommendations [10]. Nielsen suggested to have 0 to 4 rating scale as it is shown in Table 3.

Table 3. Severity scale

Rating	Description
0	I don't agree that this is a usability problem at all
1	Cosmetic problem only: need not be fixed unless extra time is available on project
2	Minor usability problem: fixing this should be given low priority
3	Major usability problem: important to fix, so should be given high priority
4	Usability catastrophe: imperative to fix this before product can be released

The evaluator can specify the usability severity rating based on a combination of three factors [10]:

- The frequency of the problem: Is it a common problem or rare?
- The impact of the problem: Is it easy for the user to overcome this problem and continue using the program or is it preventing him/her from completing certain tasks?
- The persistence of the problem: Is it a one-time problem (assumption is that once users are aware of the problem, they will know how to overcome it), or will users repeatedly be bothered by this problem?

All the severity rating scale details and factors' information were presented and discussed with the evaluators before starting the evaluation sessions. All the evaluation sessions followed a consistent scenario to control for variations in inspections.

First, the evaluators took part in a briefing session that was comprised of a description about the purpose of the study, the duration of the session and the method that will be used during the evaluation. In this briefing, it was ensured that a succinct explanation of the heuristic list and the severity rating scales were presented and discussed prior to examining the programs. Following that, evaluators were handed the heuristic sheet to obtain a quick overview of the list and the response recording methods. Next, a brief description about the program under study was provided. This included the main purpose of the program, its target user population, the environment that the program is intended for, and relevant specifications and features used in these programs. During this phase, the evaluators were allowed to observe and examine the devices or hardware peripherals such as the eye tracker device. After that, a demo of the software program was provided covering all the gaming scenarios. The important features and design considerations were highlighted during the demo to give the evaluators more insights about the program's objectives (especially if the evaluators did not have prior experience with the interaction modality or hardware). In addition, other materials and resources were provided during the session such as videos that demonstrate the usage scenarios of the program by the target user population. Furthermore, screen shots for the different program interfaces were presented and discussed to highlight design objectives. After the demo, a Q&A session with the evaluators is conducted so as to give the evaluators the chance to raise any questions or concerns about the software programs or the technologies that are being examined. Following that, individually, each evaluator completes the heuristic sheet with the usability issue (s) that they identify. During this phase of the evaluation, the evaluators are allowed to go through the program's interfaces, re-examine the videos or presentation slides to recall cues or issues noted in the interface, specifications, or scenarios of the gaming programs. Once all the evaluators are finished, the debriefing session is conducted and evaluators are given the opportunity to discuss their views and findings with the other evaluators. In the debriefing session, all the usability issues that have been identified and their severity rating are shared and discussed; and the lead evaluator notes variation in views and assessment. Findings and usability issues from all the evaluators were consolidated and combined in one list. Priority listings, based on the frequency and severity ratings were collated and described in Sect. 6.

6 Results

After conducting all the evaluation sessions using qualitative heuristic usability inspections, the key findings were compiled and classified into two main categories usability problems and issues, and usability strength points.

The usability problems have been identified with severity ratings ranging between 0 and 4. And the usability strength points have been identified by indicating the area that supports the skill-development ot rehabilitation purpose for users with sustained attention difficulties. The usability issues that have been identified were listed, and their corresponding severity ranged from cosmetic problems to major usability issues. Furthermore, variation on the evaluators' opinions in determining the severity level was noted. For example, in the evaluations of the Play Attention system, two evaluators reported that the systems' hardware (either the headset or the armband used for detecting and monitoring the brainwaves) were perceived as obtrusive. This was especially relevant for the armband that needs to be wrapped tight around the arm to ensure sufficient readings. The severity rating of this issue was defined as a cosmetic problem with a severity score of (1) by one evaluator, while other evaluators rated it as a minor usability problem with a severity score of (2). Evaluators also seemed to agree on heuristics that were considered as clear and concise; for example, two evaluators indicated that the program doesn't support the local language which is the Arabic language under "Customizability" heuristic and noted that this is could cause some difficulties with non-specialized users who don't speak other languages other than Arabic language. Moreover, for the two programs that use eye tracking technology as a main input modality, the effectiveness and accuracy of the eye tracker device was one of the main issues that were identified by the evaluators. However, evaluators varied in their perception of how this influences usability based on their familiarity with eye tracking technologies. This was evident in the assessment of the "Appropriate Functionality" heuristic where two evaluators indicated that the eye tracking device's functionality and its quality of detection were influenced by several factors (e.g.

changes in the environment illumination, the need to have fixed position for the device during the interaction with the games). Furthermore, three evaluators stated that the availability of the eye tracker device is considered a usability issue. The device's cost was perceived as prohibitive; hindering its accessibility and limiting its availability to healthcare clinics or specialized rehabilitation centers. All the three evaluators found this as a major usability problem with a severity score of (3). The specific heuristics related to daily usage of the technology for patients and users facilitated a succinct description of the scope of usability assessment of this aspect of interaction. Evaluators were also requested to note strengths of the interactive systems to address the insufficient support of solution discovery by heuristic evaluation. For example; one evaluator reported that the two programs, Tarkeezy and Attentive I, effectively considered the cultural aspects in their design; considering the Arabic language and cultural-inspired elements in the games, since the programs are designed for users with ADHD/ADD in the local context of Saudi Arabia. In Table 4 we summarized all the usability issues that were identified after conducting the heuristic evaluation sessions.

Table 4. Heuristic evaluation results

Severity	{0}	{1}	{2}	{3}	{4}	Total
Play Attention	1	5	9	7	0	22
Tarkeezy	2	0	13	14	1	30
Attentive I	0	0	9	13	2	24
Total	3	5	31	34	3	76
Percentage %	3.9 %	6.5 %	40.7 %	44.7 %	3.9 %	100 %

7 Discussion

The analytic usability heuristic evaluation method has revealed a comprehensive list of usability issues in this study. This method was conducted by a relatively small group of five evaluators, who examined three sustained-attention assessment and rehabilitation programs and judged their compliance with two sets of usability heuristics. The majority of the usability issues that have been identified were considered major usability problems with a severity score of (3), which accounted for approximately 44.7 % of the total usability issues identified. This is followed by minor usability problems that had a severity score of (2), which accounted for approximately 40.7 % of the total usability issues. The cosmetic problems were about 6.5 %; and the usability catastrophe-rated type of problems were reported at 3.9 % of the overall usability issues. These results have been obtained from five evaluators; 4 of them were in Tarkeezy and Attentive I evaluation sessions, and 3 evaluators took part in the Play Attention evaluation session. It is noted that the number of evaluators was an important factor for conducting effective heuristic evaluations as it seems to impacts the quality and accuracy of issues identified during the session. According to [11], the recommended number of evaluators in heuristic evaluations is between 3 and 5. Furthermore, the combined group of evaluators is able to find the largest number of usability problems, which is often more than 50 % of the total usability problems found [12].

In the evaluations reported in this study, it is noted that the problems were mapped to the heuristics by directly checking the program's compliance with the heuristic or by relying more on the evaluator's prior experience with the software or the technology that was examined. It was interesting to note that the evaluator's prior experience with a specific program seemed to influence the type of the usability issues identified. For example evaluators who had experience with the product seemed to uncover more minor usability issues and reported more usability issues ranging in severity scores (0-2) than major usability issues. In contrast, evaluators with little or no experience with the products reported less minor usability when compared to experienced users, and were able to identify major usability problems with severity scores (3-4). Table 5 lists the total number of usability issues in relation to the evaluators' experience level.

Table 5. Usability issues per evaluators' experience

Evaluator	Experience	Number of Programs Under Evaluation	{0}	{1}	{2}	{3}	{4}
E1	High	3	3	8	15	9	0
E2	Low	3	2	0	14	22	4
E3	Low	2	4	5	12	12	2
E4	Medium	2	5	5	7	3	0
E5	Low	1	2	1	1	3	4

We found that this result could be obtained because the evaluators who have experience with the product and who were involved with the software development team are more aware of the technical limitations on the design or in the technology that led to some usability issues. Thus, the evaluators either didn't see it as usability problem or they identified it, but with low severity score. In contrast, authors in [13] found different results in a case study conducted to assess the complementarity and convergence of heuristic evaluation and usability testing. During the study, they conducted heuristic evaluation on a software product by two evaluators with different experiences. And the results showed that the evaluator with more familiarity with the product/tool tended to identify more major usability problems than the other evaluators who were less familiar with the product/tool, and seemed to be focused more on minor usability problems. They stated that this result has been found because the evaluator, who had previous exposure to the software and know its development details, may have lower sensitivity to minor usability problems.

The severity of the usability issues that have been obtained after conducting the usability evaluation sessions are listed in Table 4. The majority of the issues identified are the most serious problems with 44.7 % and the minor usability problems were about 40.7 %. Thus, in this study the heuristic evaluation generated a comprehensive list of the most serious problems within the evaluated programs in addition to reporting a large number of low priority problems. This result is in-line with previous findings reported in [12] and [13] who have noted that the heuristic evaluation method is a cost effective method that can find the most serious problems with the least amount of effort. In addition, heuristic evaluations are widely known for their ability to generate large number of low priority usability problems. Authors in [12] stated that the loosely structured methods like heuristic evaluation can find many usability problems that are considered minor problems which may not the high important to correct. In general, during the heuristic evaluation, the HCI specialist studies the software different interfaces deeply and then searches for properties that lead to usability problems. As a result, heuristic evaluation often falls short in identifying positive findings. Notably, authors in [13] highlighted that the main aim of heuristic evaluation is to identify key problems in interacting with the systems. To address this concern, during our study, the five evaluators were asked to identify usability problems as well as strength points or positive aspects of the design that effectively support the specific objective of cognitive rehabilitation. These strength points were effective in eliciting design recommendations for developing sustained attention assessment and rehabilitation programs.

8 Conclusion

In this study, we conducted usability heuristic evaluations for three sustained attention assessment and rehabilitation programs that involve emerging technologies of Neurofeedback and eye tracking. A heuristic evaluation inspection method was introduced in the context of sustained attention technologies and applied by a team of HCI specialists. The majority of the usability issues that have been identified with this inspection method were major usability problems. The aggregate heuristic evaluation method was found to be effective as a tool for usability inspections of sustained attention assessment and rehabilitation systems and technologies. Findings suggest that this method was effective in identifying usability issues that affect the users' performance and acceptance. However, two factors emerged that seem to impact the rigour in eliciting design recommendations and uncovering interaction problems, that we have noticed during our study. First, recruiting specialized evaluators with HCI experience and familiarity with the contexts of usage of these technologies is important to achieve insights mapped directly to the contexts of usage. Second, understanding the specifications of the hardware and software involved in these systems was found to be essential to facilitate rapid and accurate identification of the usability issues related to user experience and the developed product's functionality. Future work involves applying the bespoke heuristics on iterative software development cycles of sustained attention rehabilitation software using brain-computer interfaces,

Acknowledgement. This work was partially funded by King Abdulaziz City for Science and Technology (KACST). The authors extend their appreciation to the Deanship of Scientific Research at King Saud University for funding the work through the research group project number RGP-VPP-157.

References

1. Ballard, J.C.: Computerized assessment of sustained attention: a review of factors affecting vigilance performance. J. Clin. Exp. Neuropsychol. **18**(6), 843–863 (1996)

2. Nielsen, J., Rolf, M.: Heuristic evaluation of user interfaces. In: Proceedings of the SIGCHI Conference on Human Factors in Computing Systems. ACM (1990)
3. Nielsen, J.: Usability inspection methods. In: Conference Companion on Human Factors in Computing Systems. ACM (1994)
4. Kientz, J.A., et al.: Heuristic evaluation of persuasive health technologies. In: Proceedings of the 1st ACM International Health Informatics Symposium. ACM (2010)
5. Alsumait, A., Asma A.-O.: Usability heuristics evaluation for child e-learning applications. In: Proceedings of the 11th International Conference on Information Integration and Web-Based Applications & Services. ACM (2009)
6. Hersh, M.A., Barbara, L.: Accessibility and usability of educational gaming environments for disabled students. In: ICALT (2012)
7. Walker, J.M., Achilles N.B.: Review: play attention interactive learning tool, by Freer, P. J. Attention Disord (2008)
8. Al-Shathri, A., Al-Wabil, A., Al-Ohali, Y.: Eye-controlled games for behavioral therapy of attention deficit disorders. In: Stephanidis, C. (ed.) HCII 2013, Part I. CCIS, vol. 373, pp. 574–578. Springer, Heidelberg (2013)
9. AlOmar, A., et al.: Interactive therapy of attention deficit disorders with gaze-based games. In: Proceedings of the 10th Pacific Conference of Computer Human Interaction. ACM (2012)
10. Nielsen, J.: Severity ratings for usability problems. Papers and Essays (1995)
11. Nielsen, J.: Usability inspection methods. In: Conference Companion on Human Factors in Computing Systems. ACM (1995)
12. Jeffries, R., et al.: User interface evaluation in the real world: a comparison of four techniques. In: Proceedings of the SIGCHI Conference on Human Factors in Computing Systems. ACM (1991)
13. Law, L.-C., Thora Hvannberg, E.: Complementarity and convergence of heuristic evaluation and usability test: a case study of universal brokerage platform. In: Proceedings of the Second Nordic Conference on Human-Computer Interaction. ACM (2002)

The Effect of Dyslexia on Searching Visual and Textual Content: Are Icons Really Useful?

Gerd Berget[1(✉)] and Frode Eika Sandnes[1,2]

[1] Faculty of Technology, Art and Design, Institute of Information Technology, Oslo and Akershus University, College of Applied Sciences, Oslo, Norway
gerd.berget@hioa.no
[2] Faculty of Technology, Westerdals Oslo School of Arts, Communication and Technology, Oslo, Norway
frode-eika.sandnes@hioa.no

Abstract. Little is known about how dyslexia affects online information seeking. This study addresses the search performance of 21 users with dyslexia and 21 controls in textual versus visual displays. The aim was to investigate whether visual content enhance search performance. Participants were presented with 24 icons and 24 words and asked to locate a target item. Eye-tracking data revealed no differences in performance in visual or textual content in the dyslexia group. There were no significant differences between the user groups on visual tasks. However, users with dyslexia performed significantly slower on textual tasks than controls, mainly due to longer fixation durations. Users in the control group took much less time solving textual tasks than visual tasks. The results indicate that there may be no advantages in replacing textual content with icons for users with dyslexia. However, replacing text with icons may be counterproductive for users without dyslexia.

Keywords: Dyslexia · Information search · Icons · Eye-tracking

1 Introduction

Dyslexia is a reading and writing impairment, which affects the abilities to recognize and comprehend written words [1]. This cognitive impairment is found in at least 3–10 % of any population [2], and it often entails a reduced short-term memory capacity, concentration difficulties, reduced sequencing skills and impairments in word retrieval [3–7].

Although dyslexia is most often discussed in relation to educational settings, users with this impairment may experience difficulties in other areas, such as online information searching [8]. For instance, browsing result lists may be a challenge due to the large amounts of textual content which needs to be assessed. Consequently, slow reading speeds and decoding errors, which are common among users with dyslexia [1], may affect the information search negatively.

The inclusion of visual content in result lists may reduce the workload associated with reading large amounts of text and thus enhance the search process for users with reading impairments. However, dyslexia is often associated with visual perceptual

© Springer International Publishing Switzerland 2015
M. Antona and C. Stephanidis (Eds.): UAHCI 2015, Part III, LNCS 9177, pp. 616–625, 2015.
DOI: 10.1007/978-3-319-20684-4_59

deficits [9], and several studies have addressed the visual search skills among users with dyslexia. Most of this research follow the traditional visual search paradigm, where the user is presented with an odd target item, and then asked to decide whether the item is present or not in a display with several distractor items [10]. Performance measurements are typically reaction times and error rates.

Several experiments with standard visual search tasks have concluded that users with dyslexia are impaired in visual search tasks [10, 11]. This impairment is found both in children [12] and adults [13]. Vidyasagar & Pammer [14] found a set-size effect on feature tasks, where users with dyslexia performed significantly poorer than the controls in tasks with a large number of distractors.

Some studies have suggested that only certain users with dyslexia are impaired in visual search, or that the deficit is related only to some types of tasks. Iles, Walsh and Richardson [15] suggested that impairments in visual search tasks are related to specific characteristics in dyslexia. Moreover, they found that participants with dyslexia with a motion coherence deficit were impaired in serial search tasks, while the users with normal motion coherence were not impaired in any of the visual tasks in their study. Prado, Dubois & Valdois [9] concluded that although users with dyslexia had atypical eye movements during reading, such eye movements were not found in visual search tasks in letter-based stimuli. Consequently, atypical eye movements had no impact on the performance on visual search tasks.

This article presents the findings from a study where 21 students with dyslexia and 21 students in a matched control group conducted 12 search tasks each in textual and visual content. The aim was to investigate whether visual content facilitated the search process. The hypotheses were that users with dyslexia would perform better when searching for icons than for words, and that the control group would perform better in the textual tasks than the users with dyslexia.

2   Method

2.1   Participants

The participants comprised 42 volunteering students, 21 diagnosed with dyslexia and 21 controls. Three people were diagnosed with ADHD or ADD (two users in the dyslexia group, one in the control group). Comorbidity of dyslexia and AHDH is quite common [16].

A Norwegian word chain test [17] confirmed group affiliation. Low scores are indicative of dyslexia where adults who score below 43 are recommended further diagnostic tests. The students with dyslexia scored significantly lower $(M = 39.7, SD = 10.2)$ than the control group $(M = 60.3, SD = 9.7)$, $t(40) = 6.7, p < .001$.

The control group was matched with the dyslexia group according to gender, age, field of study and year of study. Both groups were evenly distributed according to gender, with 57.1 % females and 42.9 % males. The mean values of age were 24.0 years for the dyslexia group and 23.4 for the controls. The participants followed bachelor programmes or master programmes in nursing, engineering, educational training, social sciences and humanities. The mean year of study was 2.3 for both groups (bachelor students counted as year 1–3, master students as 4–5).

Visual acuity tests using Landolt C charts ensured that the participants had normal vision, since reduced visual acuity could affect the outcome of the experiment. All students were tested on 4 m for far sight and 40 cm for near sight, which is the European standard [18]. The students had at least an acuity of 0.6 on each eye separately and 0.8 with both eyes open on both tests, which is considered within the range of normal vision [19].

2.2 Procedure

Each participant completed 24 search tasks; 12 in visual content and 12 in textual content. In addition, the students were given one rehearsal trial for each stimulus type. The tasks were presented in sections of six of each type. If an icon or a word had been the target of a search task, it did not reappear in later tasks as distractors to ensure that the students with reduced short-term memory would not get confused regarding which target to search for. The consequence of using this research design was that all participants were presented with the tasks in the same order. All tasks were completed in one session, and the participants were not spoken to except if they asked a question to the experimenter. The participants commented on specific searches during debriefing where unusual behaviour was observed.

2.3 Apparatus

Eye movements were recorded with an SMI RED remote eye-tracker at 250 Hz. A chin rest was used to reduce the head-motion during the session. Stimuli files were created in Adobe Photoshop CS4. The experiment was created and run in the visual presentation software SMI Experiment Center 3.2.11. A 21' flat screen Dell LED monitor was used to display the stimuli with the screen resolution set to 1680 × 1050 pixels. The behavioural and eye tracking software SMI BeGaze 3.2 and the statistical analysis software IBM SPSS Statistics 22 were used for data analysis.

2.4 Materials

For each trial, the participant was presented with three views: an instruction of search target, a fixation cross and the search task (see Fig. 1). The instructions were presented in pre-recorded sound files using speech synthesis. The verbal instructions prevented spelling of the textual targets to be revealed. The instruction was followed by a fixation cross, which appeared either in one of the corners or the middle of the screen in random order. The fixation cross was a trigger area of interest, so that the search task was not displayed until the participant had fixated directly on the cross for 1000 ms. The purpose of the fixation cross was to ensure that all the participants fixated on the same place on the screen at the start of each task to enable comparisons of scan path lengths and navigation patterns. When the target was located, the participants were asked to fixate on the target and push a button on the keyboard.

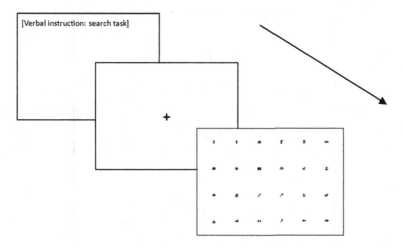

Fig. 1. Sequence of visual stimuli

The search tasks comprised of either visual stimuli containing icons (see Fig. 2) or textual stimuli containing words (see Fig. 3).

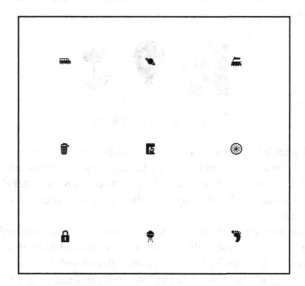

Fig. 2. Section from visual stimuli

All the displays included 24 items; one target item and 23 distractor items laid out in grids of six times four items. The visual stimuli contained black icons representing nouns (see Fig. 4) from the Noun Project (http://thenounproject.com/) released into the public domain under a Creative Commons license. The icon bank consisted of 99 icons, which had been screened by 64 library and information science students during the pilot testing. Only icons with a 100 % rater agreement were included as target icons.

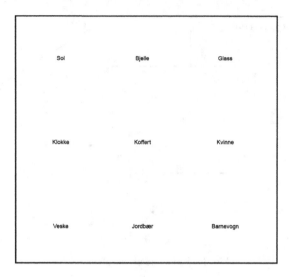

Fig. 3. Section from textual stimuli

The purpose of the screening was to avoid errors in the search tasks due to misinterpretations of the icons.

Fig. 4. Examples of icons

The textual stimuli contained Norwegian words equivalent to the nouns represented by the icons. All words consisted of 2 to 21 letters, written in black ink with 18 point Arial regular sharp font. The shortest and longest words were not included as targets, since they would stand out significantly from the rest of the words, which could potentially influence search times.

The icons and words were extracted randomly from an icon/word bank. Words and icons could appear in several stimuli, but icons or words used as targets were not used in subsequent tasks. The items in the displays were placed with a distance to ensure that the participants could not process more than one item per fixation (see Fig. 5).

2.5 Analysis

One of the icon tasks was removed in its entirety because several participants chose the wrong target (a calculator was misinterpreted for a telephone). Consequently, the matching word-task was removed to ensure an equal set of trials for each stimuli type. In addition, ten trials from each stimuli type were removed due to insufficient data quality. The final data set consisted of 904 trials; 452 for each stimulus, equally, distributed in the two participant groups.

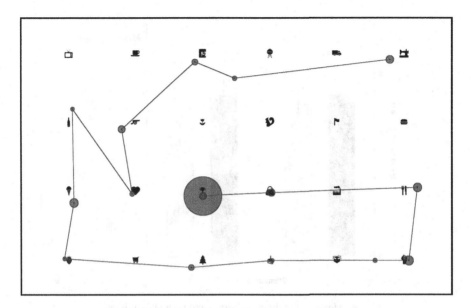

Fig. 5. Example of scan path in visual search task

3 Results

Search times in the icon displays were similar for both groups, $t(40) = 0.98$, $p = .33$. However, the students with dyslexia spent significantly longer time searching the textual stimuli ($M = 5.19$ s, $SD = 2.24$ s) than the control group ($M = 3.88$ s, $SD = 0.92$ s), $t(40) = 2.49$, $p < .02$, $d = 0.79$ (see Fig. 6). There were no significant differences in time usage between visual and textual tasks within the dyslexia group, $t(40) = 0.16$, $p = .84$. In contrast, the control group found the target significantly faster in the textual content ($M = 3.88$ s, $SD = 0.92$) compared to the visual content ($M = 4.93$ s, $SD = 1.16$), $t(40) = 3.28$, $p < .003$, $d = 1.04$ (see Fig. 6).

There were no significant differences in the eye data between the two groups in the visual tasks. However, in the textual tasks the dyslexia group had on average longer fixations ($M = 233.5$ ms, $SD = 40.1$ ms) than the control group ($M = 202.1$ ms, $SD = 3.8$ ms), $t(40) = 2.66$, p $< .02$, $d = 0.84$ (see Fig. 7). Except for the differences in fixation duration, the number of fixations and the saccades were similar in the two groups.

The users with dyslexia did not exhibit any differences in eye movements in the visual and textual tasks. In contrast, significant differences were found in both the fixations and saccades in the control group. Participants in the control group had significantly fewer textual stimuli fixations ($M = 15.3$, $SD = 3.8$) than in the icon stimuli ($M = 19.8$, $SD = 4.1$), $t(40) = 3.68$, $p < .002$, $d = 1.16$. Consequently, the number of saccades was correspondingly higher in the icon stimuli. Moreover, the average scan-path lengths were significantly longer in the icon task ($M = 5810.1$ px, $SD = 1286.3$) than the textual task ($M = 4370.2$ px, $SD = 1244.7$), $t(40) = 3.68$, $p < .002$, $d = 1.16$.

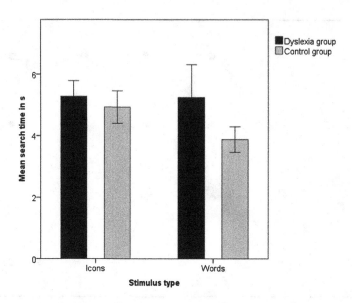

Fig. 6. Mean search times for visual and textual search tasks

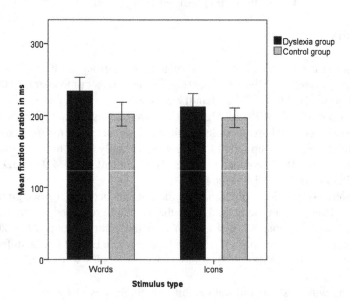

Fig. 7. Mean fixation duration for textual and visual search tasks

To get an indication of the effectiveness of the participants' eye movements, areas of interest (AOIs) were defined in the displays as either content or white space. There were no significant differences in percentage dwell times in these two types of AOIs between the users with dyslexia and controls in either icon tasks, $t(40) = 0.94$, $p = .35$ or textual tasks, $t(40) = 0.22$, $p = .83$. The participants in both groups fixated on approximately the same number of icons per task in the visual stimuli, $t(40) = 0.83$, $p = .41$.

Moreover, there were no significant differences in the number of words fixated on per task in the textual tasks, $t(40) = 0.72$, $p = .48$.

4   Discussion

Results from this study indicate that eye movements and performance levels between users with dyslexia and controls are quite similar in visual search tasks. Moreover, the users with dyslexia did not perform better in the visual tasks than the textual tasks. This finding contradicts the first hypothesis which assumed that users with reading impairments would perform best on the visual tasks.

Eye movements and time usage in the textual tasks were significantly different between the two groups. This result supports the second hypothesis, namely that controls would perform better than users with dyslexia in textual tasks. These findings may be partly explained by differences between processing images and reading. While perception of icons primarily depends on visual strategy, word identification also involves language decoding [12]. It is not surprising that the main differences are found in the textual tasks, since dyslexia mainly affects recognition and comprehension of written words [2]. The results from this study indicates that replacing text with icons will not reduce search times for users with dyslexia, but may be counterproductive for users without dyslexia.

Previous research has found that people with dyslexia usually exhibit longer fixation durations than users without dyslexia, both in reading sentences and single words [9], which is in accordance with this study. No significant differences were found between the two groups in the visual tasks, which may indicate that eye movements are more similar in the two user groups in such tasks. These findings contradict several studies which conclude that users with dyslexia are impaired in visual search tasks [10–15]. However, these differences may be due to experimental design, since this study did not follow the traditional search paradigm, but applied stimuli designed to resemble an icon-based graphical user interface.

Overall search times could possibly have been reduced if the participants were familiar with the icons before the trials. However, Greene & Rayner [20] suggested that if a user is presented with target and distractor items which are both either familiar or unfamiliar, the search rates are not affected. These findings may imply that familiarity with icons would not affect search times in this study.

Although this study indicate that searching visual stimuli is not more effective for users with dyslexia than searching text, it is possible that a combination of icons and text could facilitate the search process. A small set of recursive icons representing different media could be added to the textual content in result lists to enhance the browsing process. For instance, icons such as a news-paper representing news pages or speakers implying sound files could be included in search engines result lists. However, it has been suggested that the search performance among users with dyslexia decreases with an increasing set size [14]. Therefore, the consequences of introducing several modalities and an increased amount of content in a result list must be balanced against the benefit of introducing visual content. However, since most users seem to evaluate result lists linearly and only consider the top results [21, 22], it is possible that reducing the results per page may compensate for some size effect. More research is needed to conclude on the efficiency of such an interface.

5   Conclusion

The results from this study indicates that replacing textual content with visual content such as icons will not affect search performance among users with dyslexia. However, users without dyslexia will use more time on visual tasks than textual tasks. In visual search tasks such as those described in this experiment, users with dyslexia do not seem to be impaired compared to users without dyslexia, which contradicts findings in the more traditional visual search paradigm. However, this may be related to a task effect. More research is needed to investigate whether a combination of visual and textual content may enhance the search performance among users with dyslexia without reducing the search experience for users without dyslexia.

Acknowledgements. This project has been financially supported by the Norwegian ExtraFoundation for Health and Rehabilitation through EXTRA funds grant 2011/12/0258. The authors are grateful to the participants for their helpful cooperation and to Dyslexia Norway for assisting with recruiting students.

References

1. Shaywitz, S.E., Shaywitz, B.A.: Dyslexia (specific reading disability). Biol. Psychiatry **57**(11), 1301–1309 (2005)
2. Snowling, M.J.: Dyslexia. Blackwell, Malden (2000)
3. Jeffries, S., Everatt, J.: Working memory: its role in dyslexia and other specific learning difficulties. Dyslexia **10**(3), 196–214 (2004)
4. Hiscox, L., Leonavičiūte, E., Humby, T.: The effects of automatic spelling correction software on understanding and comprehension in compensated dyslexia: improved recall following dictation. Dyslexia **20**(3), 208–224 (2014)
5. Snowling, M.J.: From language to reading and dyslexia. Dyslexia **7**(1), 37–46 (2001)
6. Mortimore, T., Crozier, W.R.: Dyslexia and difficulties with study skills in higher education. Stud. High. Educ. **31**(2), 235–251 (2006)
7. Smith-Spark, J.H., Fisk, J.E.: Working memory functioning in developmental dyslexia. Memory **15**(1), 34–56 (2007)
8. Macfarlane, A., Al-Wabil, A., Marshall, C.R., Albrair, A., Jones, S.A., Zaphiris, P.: The effect of dyslexia on information retrieval: a pilot study. J. Documentation **66**(3), 307–326 (2010)
9. Prado, C., Dubois, M., Valdois, S.: The eye movements of dyslexic children during reading and visual search: impact of the visual attention span. Vision. Res. **47**(19), 2521–2530 (2007)
10. Sireteanu, R., Goebel, C., Goertz, R., Werner, I., Nalewajko, M., Thiel, A.: Impaired visual search in children with developmental dyslexia. Ann. N. Y. Acad. Sci. **1145**, 199–211 (2008)
11. Boer-Schellekens, L.D., Vroomen, J.: Sound can improve visual search in developmental dyslexia. Exp. Brain Res. **216**(2), 243–248 (2012)
12. Huang, X., Jing, J., Zou, X.-B., Wang, M.-L., Lin, A.-H.: Eye movements characteristic of Chinese dyslexic children in picture searching. Chin. Med. J. **121**(17), 1617–1621 (2008)

13. Jones, M.W., Branigan, H.P., Kelly, M.L.: Visual deficits in developmental dyslexia: Relationships between non-linguistic visual tasks and their contribution to components in reading. Dyslexia **14**(2), 95–115 (2008)
14. Vidyasagar, T.R., Pammer, K.: Impaired visual search in dyslexia relates to the role of the magnocellular pathway in attention. NeuroReport **10**(6), 1283–1287 (1999)
15. Iles, J., Walsh, V., Richardson, A.: Visual search performance in dyslexia. Dyslexia **6**(3), 163–177 (2000)
16. Germanò, E., Gagliano, A., Curatolo, P.: Comorbidity of ADHD and dyslexia. Dev. Neuropsychol. **35**(5), 475–493 (2010)
17. Høien, T., Tønnesen, G.: Ordkjedetesten [The Word Chain Test]. Logometrica, Bryne (2008)
18. International Organization for Standardization: ISO 8596 Ophthalmic optics: Visual acuity testing – standard optotype and its presentation. International Organization for Standardization, Geneva (2009)
19. Zhang, P., Bobier, W., Thompson, B., Hess, R.F.: Binocular balance in normal vision and its modulation by mean luminance. Optom. Vis. Sci. **88**(9), 1072–1079 (2011)
20. Greene, H.H., Rayner, K.: Eye movements and familiarity effects in visual search. Vision. Res. **41**(27), 3763–3773 (2001)
21. Klöckner, K., Wirschum, N., Jameson, A.: Depth and breadth: first processing of search result lists. In: CHI 2004 Extended Abstracts on Human Factors in Computing, pp. 1539–1539. ACM (2004)
22. Cutrell, E., Guan, Z.: What are you looking for: an eye-tracking study of information usage in web search. In: Proceedings of the SIGCHI Conference on Human Factors in Computing Systems, pp. 407–416 (2007)

Defining an Interaction Model for Users with Autism: Towards an Autistic User Model

Andrés Mejía-Figueroa[(✉)] and J. Reyes Juárez-Ramírez

School of Chemical Sciences and Engineering,
Autonomous University of Baja California, Tijuana, Baja California, Mexico
{mejia.andres,reyesjua}@uabc.edu.mx

Abstract. The consideration of Human Factors is an integral part of the design and development of any software system. User Models are used to represent the user's characteristics in a computational environment, forming an integral part of Adaptive Interfaces, by enabling the adaptation of the interface to the user's needs and attributes. In this paper we describe a proposed user model based on Executive Functions and a description of the planned case study, being users with Autism Spectrum Disorder.

Keywords: User modelling · Adaptive interfaces · Usability · Accessibility · Autism spectrum disorder · Executive functions

1 Introduction

Currently, the consideration of Human Factors has become of extreme importance in the design and specification of any software system for the reason of the huge impact that they have on the usability of the software and the efficiency in which the user can accomplish the tasks in the software.

All human beings have a series of attributes or characteristics, being: physical, cognitive, demographic, among others; that in one form or another affect how we perceive and interact with the world around us, including electronics and software. This is especially true for users with some form of disability, since it is necessary a profound understanding of the user's impaired capabilities and how will they affect interaction with the software or electronic device, in order to achieve a user experience adapted to that particular user. Such is the case with persons with Autism, which have some of these abilities impaired, such as generativity, motor, and attention. In addition to having a series of impairments, no two persons with Autism are the same, making the development of software for them especially difficult for the reason that it not might be usable for many, if not most, of them.

Due to the varying degree of user capabilities, a software can me more or less usable in comparison to another user, resulting in being impossible to achieve a uniform level of usability, accessibility and user satisfaction. One of the ways of dealing with the problem of usability and user experience is the integration of usability engineering practices in to the software development life cycle, such as the activities of user and task analysis, and prototyping [1].

Another possible solution is the use of Adaptive User Interfaces, which are capable of adapting itself to the user's characteristics and needs [2]. One of the essential parts of

M. Antona and C. Stephanidis (Eds.): UAHCI 2015, Part III, LNCS 9177, pp. 626–636, 2015.
DOI: 10.1007/978-3-319-20684-4_60

an Adaptive Interface is the User Model. User Models can be considered the abstract representation of the user characteristics in a computational environment [3], which is used in order to achieve the adaptation needed. Due to the wide variety of electronic devices and users with differing characteristics, there hasn't been a single generic user model definition, although there is research towards that goal [4, 5]. Also there is no consensus on what are the elements of the user interface to be adapted, what design patterns, what characteristics to consider of the user and how it affects the adaptivity of the interface, each software developer implements their own interaction rules based on experience and some guidelines.

In this paper we present the proposal of a PhD thesis that presents a user model that focuses on Executive Functions, adapting the user interface to measurements of said functions, and the subsequent reasoning for the case of study being developed.

2 Adaptive Interfaces

As software systems become more complex with added functionality, the diversity of the user base also increases, which means accommodating all the wide range of user characteristics becomes a daunting task, impacting usability and acceptance of the software and general user satisfaction. Adaptive Interfaces were first developed as an answer to this predicament by dealing with four mayor concerns [6]:

- A system is used by users with different requirements.
- A system is used by a user with changing requirements.
- A user works in a changing system environment.
- A user works in different system environments.

The architecture of Adaptive System can vary to a certain degree depending on the range of adaptation decided. As shown in [7], an Adaptive System consist of three basic models, each one having a direct impact of the adaptability of the system:

1. *User Model*. Represents the characteristics of the users, such as cognitive characteristics and domain knowledge.
2. *Domain Model*. Represents the functionality and tasks that the user can accomplish.
3. *Interaction Model*. Defines what are adaptations possible based on Domain Model, system characteristics and the User Model.

Depending on the system being developed it is possible for the need of more than one of each model. There is no requirement for Adaptive Systems to possess the three modules or to have only one of each.

Although Adaptive User Interfaces do help deal with the problems preciously mentioned, they have their own pros and cons when using them. According to Lavie et al. [10], in order for an Adaptive Interface to achieve the level of adaptivity desired, it is necessary to consider the following factors:

- *The task that the user must accomplish.* Analysis of the task and all the actions needed for the user to accomplish said task.
- *The user and his characteristics.* User attributes that are considered necessary for the task and interaction with the software system.

- *Level of adaptivity that wants to be achieved.* It can range from manual to fully adaptable and customizable, to fully adaptive and the level in between.

Of particular importance is the definition of what are going to be considered routine tasks, since Adaptive Interfaces are not optimal for non-routine tasks, since the user must relearn the interface each time that the interface is adapted. Another drawback concerns on how the system collects user feedback in order to adapt, and the fact that there is no methodology to determine when and how the adaptation should take place [10].

There is room for improvement in Adaptive User Interfaces by enhancing the predictability (if the user can predict the adaptation) and accuracy (percentage of time that UI elements are contained in the adaptive area) of the adaptivity algorithms used. In [11] it is shown that improving those two factors greatly affected user's satisfaction, but accuracy only affected user performance or utilization of the adaptive interface. The study showed the importance of the adaptivity algorithm as an essential element in contributing toward system usability and user satisfaction.

With the focus on user characteristics it is easy to see why Adaptive Interfaces can help in solving the problem of usability with a varied user base, but first, an important part of any adaptive system must be defined: the User Model, in order to determine what user characteristic will be considered, and more importantly, what adaptations are possible based on the data contained in the User Model.

3 Executive Functions

Executive Functions are an umbrella term for the set of cognitive processes necessary to accomplish goal-oriented tasks, this includes: planning, sustained attention, working memory, inhibition, self-monitoring, self-regulation and initiation carried out by the frontal lobes of the brain.

The concept of Executive Functions is one that defies a formal definition, since research in this area often gives contradictory results, generating lack of clarity and controversy when trying to define the nature of executive functions [12]. Although there are discrepancies researching the nature of Executive Functions, the definitions proposed coincide in the fact that Executive Functions function as processes where cognitive abilities are used in goal oriented tasks [12].

3.1 Overview of Some Executive Function Definitions

One of the earliest notions of Executive Functioning was by Pribam [13] in studies related to the function of the pre-frontal cortex, and later by Baddeley and Hitch [14] as the term "central executive" when referring to a part of their proposed Working Memory Model. Previous work by Luria [15] gives support of the importance of the frontal cortex and frontal lobes in Executive Functions by analyzing the abnormalities present in patients with frontal lobe damage, such abnormalities included: impaired ability to evaluate their behavior and actions, and goal directed mindset.

In subsequent years, numerous studies and research was done pertaining the pre-frontal cortex and frontal lobes and Executive Function. Numerous definitions were proposed, but with some research yielding opposing results a formal definition has not been possible. For example: In Godefroy et al. [16] puts in doubt the notion that all the control processes for Executive Functions were in the frontal lobes by submitting patients with lesion of the pre-frontal or posterior cortices to a series of conflicting and combined tasks. Although the results give additional evidence of the prominent role of the frontal lobes in Executive Functioning, it also shows evidence that Executive Functions depends of multiple, separate, and modular control processes because of the fact that certain patients with frontal lobe injury performed well on tests designed to assess Executive Functioning while others did not.

Delis [17] defines Executive Functions as the ability to manage and regulate one's behavior in order to achieve a desired goal. This author also denotes that neither a single ability nor definition captures the conceptual scope of executive functions, in reality, executive functioning is the sum of a collection of higher level cognitive skills that enable the individual to adapt and thrive in a social environment.

Similar to Delis, Miller and Cohen [18] suggest that Executive Control involve the cognitive abilities needed to perform goal oriented tasks.

Lezak [19] describes Executive Functioning as collection of interrelated cognitive and behavioral skills that are responsible for goal-directed activity, includes intellect, thought, self-control, and social interaction.

As we can see, although there is some controversy on the nature of Executive Functioning and the great number of definitions of Executive Functioning, there is the general consensus that it involves the cognitive processes that manage goal directed behavior.

3.2 Executive Functions and Software Interaction Design

There isn't much research done about the effect of Executive Functions on how it affects software or device usage.

In Mizobuchi et al. [20] a study was made to measure multitasking performance across several device interfaces and the relationship between task performance and three Executive Functioning processes (shifting, inhibition and updating). The experiments yielded that higher levels of the Executive Function improved multitasking performance, however when touch input with visual and audio output was used, the impact of cognitive demand was reduced.

In Reddy et al. [21] a study was made in order to determine some of the effects of cognitive ageing and prior experience with technology on user interfaces intuitively. The study included 37 participants, between the ages of 18 to 83. All participants were assessed for their cognitive abilities and experience with technology. The results showed a strong negative correlation between Sustained Attention (part of Working Memory), the time to complete the task and the number of errors made by the users.

4 Autism Spectrum Disorder

According to the Diagnostic and Statistical Manual of Mental Disorders (DSM-V) [22] and the International Classification of Diseases and Related Health Problems (ICD-10) [23], autism affect two core areas of neurodevelopment:

- Impairment in reciprocal social interaction and communication.
- Restricted repetitive and stereotyped patterns of behavior, interest and activities.

Because of the nature of Autism, being considered a spectrum, each person with Autism is unique, since the level of severity of the afflictions in the core areas vary from person to person, even worse, usually other cognitive abilities show signs of impairment also [24]. With proper therapy and early detection, the prognosis of an autistic person can be improved in most if not all of the symptoms of autism he may have [24].

With new technologies accessible to the general public, new options for therapy emerge, serving as tools for the betterment of their quality of life, including for persons with Autism. One example is the use of tablets and smartphones. Persons with Autism, especially children, seem to have a knack for computers and other devices, making tablets the device of choice for most autistic children.

4.1 Executive Dysfunction Theory

There are several theories on what causes the symptoms of Autism that try to explain the traits that characterize Autism and what originates them. One of the theories, which has grown in prevalence in the past couple of years, relates to Executive Functions.

A growing body of work [25, 26] suggests that many, if not all, of the symptoms of Autism originate with problems in the Executive Functions, such as working memory, planning, cognitive flexibility, generativity, self-monitoring and inhibition. Some of the difficulties of a person with Autism with Executive Functioning are as follows [25, 26]:

- *Working Memory.* A temporary system where we can store and manipulate information in the short term memory. Persons with deficit in working memory have difficulty following more than one instruction. There are signs that information is absorbed but the ability to manipulate said information may be impaired.
- *Cognitive Flexibility.* Ability to shift to a different thought or action in response to a situation change. One of the symptoms of Autism is the stereotypical and repetitive behavior showing significant difficulty to adapt or respond to unexpected events such as conversations and the environment.
- *Planning.* The operation to plan a sequence of actions for a certain goal where this sequence is monitored, evaluated and updated. Tied to cognitive flexibility, persons with Autism show difficulty in organizing a sequence of tasks and completing them within the allotted time, such as homework, household chores and planned events.
- *Generativity.* Ability to generate novel ideas or behaviors. Persons with Autism have been shown to have difficulty generating new knowledge based on information presented.
- *Self-monitoring.* Ability to monitor one's own thoughts and actions. Necessary for other Executive Functions such as planning and organizing ideas.
- *Inhibition.* Ability to suppress irrelevant or interfering information or impulses. Persons with Autism have a hard time controlling impulses and emotions that interfere with current actions or tasks.

4.2   Technology Applied to Autism Spectrum Disorder Therapy

With new consumer electronics, comes new opportunities for applications for the therapy of the symptoms of Autism, such as Augmentative and Alternative Communication (AAC) [27] and Computer Assisted Instruction (CAI) software [28]. However designing this specialized software brings certain challenges. The nature of Autism, being a spectrum, makes the interaction design a very difficult task since each autistic user is unique with great variance in their characteristics, making the software more usable for some more than others. In order for the software to be an effective tool, it must be specially designed for that particular autistic user [28].

Putnam et al. [8] suggests that the main point in the development of technology based solutions for autistic users was understanding them. Some of the questions that motivated the research were:

1. What types of software and technology have users already tried?
2. What has been their experience with those products?
3. What do users report as desirous in software and technology?
4. What are end-user's attitudes and behavior toward technology?
5. What other common proclivities, interests, behaviors and talents might also help future design efforts?

As can be seen the main challenges for the development of proper special needs software and technology for autistic users has been analyzing and understanding how their particular characteristics will affect the interaction and use of the software or device, even more so since it is considered a spectrum there are no base level of characteristics to consider, each child can have the same basic traits, but the varying degree of affliction on each trait makes each person with autism unique.

5   Related Works

One of the core parts of the architecture of an Adaptive Interface is the User Model. In order to develop an adaptive system we must first determine what will be the user characteristics that will compose the user model. With this model, the user interface can be adapted based on the values of the characteristics that are being considered of the user.

Most software applications that use user models often just consider some aspects of the user that they deem relevant to the application, there is no generic solution to be used, although there is research towards achieving that goal [4, 5].

Some works center on what user characteristics must be considered for interactive systems, such as Zhang et al. [1] where it is proposed a methodology to integrate Human Computer Interaction practices in the software development life cycle, Zudilova-Seinstra [31] which notes what human factors must be taken into consideration based on the Wagner's Ergonomical Model [32] when designing software using the Yule's coefficient of colligation [33] and Biswas et al. [34] proposed a user model to be used in the design of personalized interfaces for motor impaired users taking into consideration certain related characteristics (Table 1).

Table 1. User characteristics considered in different models

Author	User characteristics
Zhang et al. [1]	Demographic (Age, gender, education, occupation, cultural background, special needs, computer training and knowledge, experience with similar systems/products), Traits and intelligence (Cognitive styles, affective traits, skill sets), Job or task related factors (Job characteristics, knowledge of application domain, rate of computer use)
Biswas et al. [34]	Experience (With the software and similar software), Age (Actual age), Occulomotor characteristics (Vision), Gender, Language level (Language medium, interaction language), Education Level, Personality (Motivation)
Zudilova-Seinstra [31]	Gender, Age, Learning abilities, Verbal and non-verbal IQ's, Locus of control, Attention focus, Cognitive strategy

Kaklanis et al. [5] present one of the most recent advances towards a standardization of a user model to be used across different platforms for simulation and adaptation purposes. The VUMS (Virtual User Modelling and Simulation Standardization) cluster of projects that works toward the development of an interoperable user model as a generic solution for the modelling for able-bodied users and users with disabilities. Currently the model includes a myriad of user attributes but for the moment no actual adaptation rules based on the attributes.

Because Adaptive Interfaces can adapt to the user characteristics, they can be used in software systems designed for special needs users, but for some reason there is not much. An example is the AVANTI project [9], in which the user interface provides views of adaptive multimedia web documents, adapting itself in a dynamic way to the characteristics and preferences of the users as they interact with the system by considering users with light or severe motor disabilities and blindness. Also research is being made toward improving accessibility for all users, especially older users, using adaptive and adaptable interfaces and multi-modal interaction, although it is still considered that there is much work to be done before a definitive methodology for the development of said systems and for the different measures to improve accessibility to be adopted [29, 30].

As we can see, there has been work on work on improving usability by integrating HCI and usability engineering practices in the software development life cycle and consideration of user characteristics. There is significant advancement towards a standardized user model but there is still much work to be done before we can have a generic solution with a standard rule set for each user characteristic.

6   Problem Definition

As we proposed in previous work [4] in order to improve usability in interactive systems it is necessary to relate software functionalities with user characteristics.

In order to establish this relation, we formulated the following statement: A software S is a set of functionalities operated by the user. This is expressed as follows:

$$S = \{F_1, \ldots, F_n\} = F \tag{1}$$

The functionality F_i involves a set of actions to be executed by the user. This is expressed as follows:

$$Fi = \{A_1, \ldots, A_n\} = A \tag{2}$$

Each action A_i can be of the type: input, indication, interpretation, etc. From the perspective of the user, an input and indication action can involve using fingers, voice, etc. in order to insert or indicate data. An interpretation action can involves processes such as perception, attention, and information processing. A perception action involves employing the senses, such as eyesight and hearing. An information processing action involves employing working memory and cognitive processor. Taking into account these assumptions, an action A_i can be expressed as follows:

$$A_i = \{t, \{C\}\} \tag{3}$$

Where t is the type of action, and C is a set of user attributes employed to interact with the software application. In this case C represents the Executive Functions (Ef) needed to interact with the software. Based on this, the functionality F_i is expressed as follows:

$$F_i = \{\{t, \{Ef\}\}_1, \ldots, \{t, \{Ef\}\}_n\} \tag{4}$$

The problem with usability arises when your user base has a very varied set of characteristics, in this case Executive Functions levels, affecting usability, adoption and user satisfaction across the board. In the case of persons with Autism, this problem is of special consideration because of the very nature of the disorder, requiring specially adapted software for each user [28].

7   Towards an Interaction Model for Users with Autism: A Proposal in Progress

In this paper we present a proposal of a potential user model based on some Executive Functions, as continuation of progress of previous work [35], that we consider necessary for the proper interaction and user of software applications. The Executive Functions we are considering are as follows:

1. *Working Memory*. Our ability to store information in the short term memory and manipulate said information.
2. *Planning*. Ability to plan a sequence of actions which involves other cognitive functions and Executive Functions, such as self-monitor, evaluation and update.

3. *Cognitive Flexibility*. Ability to shift one attention to a different thought or event in response to stimuli.
4. *Inhibition*. Suppression of conflicting impulses or external elements.

As Executive Dysfunction is shown to happen to people with other disabilities apart from Autism, it is possible that modelling Executive Dysfunction can be a generic model for any number of users.

In order to measure the Executive Functions of the model we will be using the NEPSY II battery of neuropsychological tests [36] for planning, inhibition, and cognitive flexibility. In the case of working memory we can measure it with the Wechsler Intelligence Scale for Children (WISC) [37].

In order to establish an interaction model we must first determine the impact of the different levels of the measurements of the Executive Functions and determine optimal usability patterns and interaction styles. In order to determine this, we are currently designing a variety of usability testing of software applications in tablets with different combinations of usability patterns and interaction styles for different tasks, in order to detect the best way for the user to accomplish the type of tasks being presented with his particular Executive Function levels (Fig. 1).

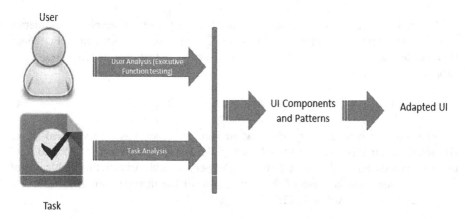

Fig. 1. Adapted UI process

8   Conclusions and Future Work

In this paper we presented a doctoral thesis proposal for a user model based on Executive Functions for adaptation purposes of the interface. A case study was proposed for Autistic users, since with their particular characteristics, provide an excellent chance to test the interaction model. Currently we are in the process of designing usability tests on software applications, where the user tries to complete a series of tasks in a different manner each time, with different usability patterns and interaction styles. Once an interaction style is determined we will test it in a broader audience by developing an AAC application with adaptive interface and determine the impact on usability and user satisfaction.

References

1. Zhang, P., Carey, J., Te'eni, D., Tremaine, M.: Integrating human-computer interaction development into the systems development life cycle: A methodology. Commun. Assoc. Inform. Syst. **15**(1), 29 (2005)
2. Schneider-Hufschmidt, M., Malinowski U., Kuhme T.: State of the art in adaptive user interfaces. In: Adaptive User Interfaces: Principles and Practice, p. 13. Elsevier Science Inc. (1993)
3. Fischer, G.: User modeling in human–computer interaction. In: User Modeling and User-Adapted Interaction, vol. 11(1), pp. 65–86. Springer (2001)
4. Mejía, A., Juárez-Ramírez, R., Inzunza, S., Valenzuela, R.: Implementing adaptive interfaces: a user model for the development of usability in interactive systems. In: Proceedings of the CUBE International Information Technology Conference, pp. 598–604. ACM (2012)
5. Kaklanis, N., Biswas, P., Mohamad, Y., Gonzalez, M. F., Peissner, M., Langdon, P., Jung, C.: Towards standardization of user models for simulation and adaptation purposes. In: Universal Access in the Information Society, pp. 1–28, Springer (2014)
6. Schneider-Hufschmidt, M., Malinowski U., Kuhme T.: State of the art in adaptive user interfaces. In: Adaptive User Interfaces: Principles and Practice, pp. 3–4. Elsevier Science Inc. (1993)
7. Benyon, D.: Adaptive systems: a solution to usability problems. In: User modeling and User-adapted Interaction, vol. 3(1), pp. 65–87. Springer (1993)
8. Putnam C., Chong L.: Software and technologies designed for people with autism: what do users want? In: Proceedings of the 10th International ACM SIGACCESS Conference on Computers and Accessibility, pp.3–10. ACM (2008)
9. Stephanidis, C., Paramythis, A., Sfyrakis, M., Stergiou, A., Maou, N., Leventis, A., Karagiannidis, C.: Adaptable and adaptive user interfaces for disabled users in the AVANTI project. In: Trigila, S., Mullery, A., Campolargo, M., Vanderstraeten, H., Mampaey, M. (eds.) Intelligence in Services and Networks: Technology for Ubiquitous Telecom Services. LNCS, vol. 1430, pp. 153–166. Springer, Heidelberg (1998)
10. Lavie, T., Meyer, J.: Benefits and costs of adaptive user interfaces. Int. J. Hum.-Comput. Stud. **68**(8), 508–524 (2010) (Elsevier)
11. Gajos, K.Z., Everitt, K., Tan, D.S., Czerwinski, M., Weld, D.S.: Predictability and accuracy in adaptive user interfaces. In: Proceedings of the SIGCHI Conference on Human Factors in Computing Systems, pp. 1271–1274. ACM (2008)
12. Jurado, M.B., Rosselli, M.: The elusive nature of executive functions: a review of our current understanding. Neuropsychol. Rev. **17**(3), 213–233 (2007)
13. Pribram, K.H.: The primate frontal cortex - executive of the brain. In: Pribram, K.H., Luria, A. R. (eds.) Psychophysiology of the Frontal lobes, pp. 293–314. Academic, New York (1973)
14. Baddeley, A., Hitch, G.: Working memory. In: Bower, G.H. (ed.) Recent Advances in Learning and Motivation, vol. 8. Academic, New York (1974)
15. Luria, A.R.: The Working brain: An introduction to neuropsychology. Basic, New York (1973)
16. Godefroy, O., Cabaret, M., Petit-Chenal, V., Pruvo, J.-P., Rousseaux, M.: Control functions of the frontal lobe: Modularity of the central-supervisory system. Cortex **35**, 1–20 (1999) (Elsevier)
17. Delis, D.C.: Delis rating of executive functions. Pearson, Bloomington (2012)
18. Miller, E.K., Cohen, J.D.: An integrative theory of prefrontal cortex function. Annu. Rev. Neurosci. **24**(1), 167–202 (2001)

19. Lezak, M.D.: Neuropsychological Assessment, 3rd edn. p. 49. Oxford University Press, New York (1995)
20. Mizobuchi, S., Chignell, M., Suzuki, J., Koga, K., Nawa, K.: Central executive functions likely mediate the impact of device operation when driving. In: Proceedings of the 3rd International Conference on Automotive User Interfaces and Interactive Vehicular Applications, pp. 129–136). ACM (2011)
21. Reddy, G.R., Blackler, A., Mahar, D., Popovic, V.: The effects of cognitive ageing on use of complex interfaces. In: Proceedings of the 22nd Conference of the Computer-Human Interaction Special Interest Group of Australia on Computer-Human Interaction, pp. 180–183. ACM (2010)
22. American Psychiatric Association: Diagnostic and Statistical Manual of Mental Disorders, 5th edn. American Psychiatric Publishing, Arlington (2013)
23. World Health Organization. The ICD-10 classification of mental and behavioral disorders: diagnostic criteria for research. World Health Organization (1993)
24. Rapin I., Riva D.: Autism Spectrum Disorders. John Libbey Eurotext (2005)
25. Robinson, S., Goddard, L., Dritschel, B., Wisley, M., Howlin, P.: Executive functions in children with autism spectrum disorders. In: Brain and Cognition, vol. 71(3), pp. 362–368. Elsevier (2009)
26. Hill, E.L.: Executive dysfunction in autism. Trends Cogn. Sci. 8(1), 26–32 (2004) (Elsevier)
27. Mirenda, P.: Autism, Augmentative Communication, and Assistive Technology What Do We Really Know? In: Focus on Autism and Other Developmental Disabilities, vol. 16(3), pp. 141–151. Sage Publishing (2001)
28. Ploog B.O., Scharf A., Nelson D., Brooks P.J.: Use of computer-assisted technologies (CAT) to enhance social, communicative, and language development in children with autism spectrum disorders. Journal of Autism Dev. Disord. 43(2), 301–322 (2013) (Springer)
29. Jorge J.A.: Adaptive tools for the elderly: new devices to cope with age-induced cognitive disabilities. In: Proceedings of the 2001 EC/NSF workshop on Universal Accessibility of Ubiquitous Computing: Providing for the Elderly, pp. 66–70. ACM (2001)
30. Sloan D., Atkinson M.T., Machin C., Li, Y.: The potential of adaptive interfaces as an accessibility aid for older web users. In: Proceedings of the 2010 International Cross Disciplinary Conference on Web Accessibility (W4A), p. 35. ACM (2010)
31. Zudilova-Seinstra, E.: On the role of individual human abilities in the design of adaptive user interfaces for scientific problem solving environments. In: Knowledge and Information Systems, vol. 13, pp. 243–270. Elsevier (2007)
32. Wagner E.: A system ergonomics design methodology for HCI development. In: Brusilovsky, P. (ed.) Proceedings of the East–West International Conference on Human–Computer Interaction (EWHCI 1992), pp. 388–407 (1992)
33. Bishop, Y.M., Feinberg, S.E., Holland, P.W.: Discrete multivariate analysis: theory and practice. MIT Press, Cambridge (1975)
34. Biswas, P., Bhattacharya, S., Samanta, D.: User model to design adaptable interfaces for motor-impaired users. In: TENCON 2005, pp. 1–6. IEEE (2005)
35. Figueroa, A.M., Juárez-Ramírez, R.: Towards a user model for the design of adaptive interfaces for autistic users. In: Computer Software and Applications Conference Workshops (COMPSACW), pp. 264–269. IEEE (2014)
36. Brooks, B.L., Sherman, E.M., Strauss, E.: NEPSY-II: A developmental neuropsychological assessment. Child Neuropsychol. 16(1), 80–101 (2009) (Taylor & Francis)
37. Wechsler, D.: Wechsler Intelligence Scale for Children-WISC-IV. Psychological Corporation (2003)

Analysis and Design of Three Multimodal Interactive Systems to Support the Everyday Needs of Children with Cognitive Impairments

Stavroula Ntoa[1], Asterios Leonidis[1], Maria Korozi[1], Eleni Papadaki[1], Ilia Adami[1], George Margetis[1], Margherita Antona[1(✉)], and Constantine Stephanidis[1,2]

[1] Institute of Computer Science, Foundation for Research and Technology – Hellas (FORTH), N. Plastira 100, Vassilika Vouton, 700 13 Heraklion, Crete, Greece
antona@ics.forth.gr
[2] Department of Computer Science, University of Crete, Crete, Greece
cs@ics.forth.gr

Abstract. The autonomy and independence of users with cognitive impairments can be fostered through cognitive technologies. The use of traditional computer interfaces has however proved to be difficult for these users. This paper proposes three innovative systems to train children with cognitive impairments in three fundamental everyday life activities: (a) familiarizing with the home environments, its objects and activities; (b) learning about money and practicing shopping skills; and (c) learning how to prepare and cook simple meals. All three systems feature multimodal interaction and support multimedia output.

Keywords: Multimodal interactive systems · Children with cognitive impairments · Card-based interaction · Touch · Cooking · Monetary transactions · Learning the home environment

1 Introduction

Cognitive impairment is an inclusive term used to describe deficits in intellectual functioning, and entails limitations in specific operations, such as conceptualizing, planning, and sequencing thoughts and actions, remembering, interpreting social cues, and understanding numbers and symbols [1]. Although the specific functionality limitations may vary from profound mental retardation with minimal functioning to mild impairment with difficulties in specific operations, a common problem among people with cognitive impairments is self-management and carrying out everyday tasks, such as bathing, eating, preparing simple meals, etc. To this end, cognitive technologies have the potential to help individuals with cognitive disabilities to be more independent and enhance their quality of life [1].

However, accessing a computer and using a typical GUI can be a challenging task for users with cognitive disability. For example, simple interface actions such as double-clicking, using scroll bars, or reading menu items and button labels can present barriers [2]. In this respect, alternative interaction means and multimodal input may benefit

© Springer International Publishing Switzerland 2015
M. Antona and C. Stephanidis (Eds.): UAHCI 2015, Part III, LNCS 9177, pp. 637–648, 2015.
DOI: 10.1007/978-3-319-20684-4_61

cognitive impaired users, while multisensory output may alleviate difficulties in comprehending written text.

This paper presents three systems that have been designed to train children with cognitive disabilities in learning the home environment, money and monetary transactions, as well as preparing simple meals. The systems support multimodal interaction and multimedia output and are intended to be used by trainers of the Rehabilitation Centre for Children with Disabilities in Heraklion (Crete, Greece) to train children with disabilities in the aforementioned domains.

The remaining of this paper is structured as follows: Sect. 2 discusses related work, Sect. 3 introduces the three systems and the process that was followed for their design and implementation, while Sect. 4 describes the requirements elicitation phase that preceded the design of each system. Sections 5, 6 and 7 introduce each one of the three systems. The evaluation that has been carried out for one of the systems is described in Sect. 8. Finally, the paper concludes with discussion and future work in Sect. 9.

2   Related Work

Technology has been claimed to improve performance and independence of individuals with disabilities in comparison to more traditional means, such as pictorial prompts, tactile prompts or auditory prompts [3, 4]. Common assistive technologies include software for reminding and prompting, task guidance, way-finding assistance, remote assistance from caregivers, computer assisted learning and communication [1, 2, 5].

Meal preparation is an important skill to acquire for individuals with cognitive disabilities in order to increase their independence. Several traditional and technological approaches have emerged, while comparative studies have also been carried out. Lancioni et al. [6] introduce a palm-top computer involving pictorial instructions as well as auditory and vibratory mechanisms for preparing four different meals, compare it with a card system and conclude that participants had higher performance with the computer system and preferred it. Mechling et al. [7] studied the use of a self-prompting PDA system using video, picture and auditory prompts to instruct individuals with autism for preparing three cooking recipes and found that it can be an effective assistive medium for performing multi-step tasks. Giroux et al. [8] describe a smart home environment aiming to assist individuals with cognitive impairments in cooking tasks, by presenting the recipe steps through pictures or video and assisting them in locating objects or ingredients in the kitchen.

Money management and purchasing skills constitute another important subject to teach to individuals with cognitive impairments to sustain their autonomy. Lagnone et al. [9] introduce a multimedia environment employing video-based instruction and an interactive CD-ROM providing students with a virtual shopping experience. Several studies have been carried out [e.g., 10, 11] examining the use of the aforementioned computer-based program by students with intellectual disabilities in order to learn fundamental shopping skills, suggesting that computer-based video models can be used to effectively teach functional skills. A suite of serious games has been proposed by Lanyi and Brown [12], including a virtual supermarket to teach students money management skills, where students have to buy virtual products based on a given shopping list and pay using their virtual wallet.

On the other hand, learning the home environment including objects, activities and behavioral rules is a topic that has not been extensively addressed through computer-based media.

The three proposed systems aim at teaching through playing the aforementioned topics which are considered important for daily activities and independent living of individuals with intellectual disabilities. To achieve their objectives the systems employ novel multimodal interaction techniques and deliver multimedia output.

3 The Three Multimodal Interactive Systems

3.1 Overview

Based on the requirements specified by the employees of the Rehabilitation Centre, learning the home environment, learning about money and monetary transactions, and learning how to cook simple meals were selected as fundamental steps in order to enhance the autonomy of children with cognitive impairments and improve their everyday living.

Each one of the three systems has been analysed separately in order to define its main objectives and specific functionality. Furthermore, each system employs a different setup (see Fig. 1) and supports interaction through various input modalities (see Table 1). In more details, the three interactive systems were defined as follows:

Table 1. Input modalities for each one of the three interactive systems

	Home	Money & Shopping	Cooking
Cards	[X]	[X]	[X]
IR pointing device			[X]
Touch	[X]		
Mouse		[X]	

- **Learning the home environment (The "Home" game).** The system includes a variety of exercises and mini-games aiming to instill which are the main house rooms, which are the most important objects one can find in each room, as well as what activities are usually carried out in each room. Furthermore, the system instructs children regarding dangerous behaviors that should be avoided, as well as good behavior patterns for everyday activities at home, through multiple-choice mini quizzes. Interaction with the system is possible through touch via the provided touch screen, or through printed cards representing objects and activities placed on a large board depicting specific rooms. The system features a touch screen, computer, and a high resolution camera overlooking the board (see Fig. 1a).

- **Learning about money and monetary transactions (The "Money" game).** The system's objectives are to teach children the coins and bills of Euro as well as their value, assist them in learning to identify euros and cents for a given amount, support familiarization with monetary transactions through virtual shopping and promote good behavior regarding shopping and monetary transactions in general. Interaction with the system is achieved through mouse and printed cards (representing coins and bills) placed on a tabletop surface [13]. The system setup consists of a laptop and a high resolution camera (see Fig. 1b)

- **Learning how to cook simple meals (The "Cooking" game).** The system includes a variety of exercises and mini games, aiming to instruct children: (i) which foods are appropriate for breakfast, lunch, and dinner, (ii) how to cook simple meals (e.g., bread with butter and honey, lettuce salad, pasta with tomato sauce, etc.), and (iii) fundamental rules of safety and hygiene that should be applied during food preparation. Interaction with the system is achieved through printed cards representing various dishes, recipe ingredients and kitchen utensils, as well as through a custom-made IR pointing device (see Sect. 3.2). The system consists of a computer, a high-resolution projector, a simple wooden table, an RGB-D depth camera, a high-resolution camera, speakers and the custom IR input device [14]. The system will be installed in the actual kitchen of the Rehabilitation Centre. With the aim to support an immersive user experience, the hardware equipment will be hidden inside a kitchen board, leaving visible only the plain wooden table. (see Fig. 1c)

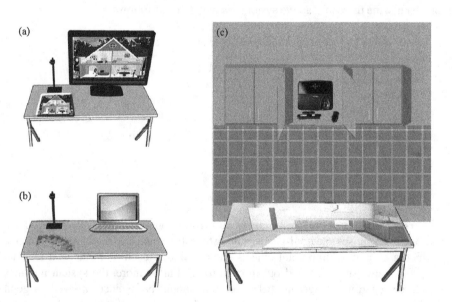

Fig. 1. Representation of the system setups: (a) Learning the home environment (b) Learning about money and monetary transactions (c) Learning how to cook

One key characteristics of the aforementioned interactive systems is the ability to frequently update their content to be harmonized with the current educational activities of the Rehabilitation Center. To this purpose, a full-scale content management tool has been developed through which the trainers will be able to update: (i) the **"Home" game** by adding new or modifying existing rooms, objects and activities, and determining their associations (e.g., object X belongs in room Y, etc.), (ii) the **"Money" game,** by editing the available products for purchase (e.g., add a new product, change a product's price, create a new shopping list, etc.), (iii) the **"Cooking" game** by adding new ingredients, tools, utensils, or even recipes along with detailed directions about their preparation and (iv) all the **quizzes** used in the games.

Furthermore, with the aim to support user management, the Student Profiler application has been implemented, allowing trainers to register new students, update or delete existing ones, and also to generate student identification cards. Student identification cards are used by the system to identify the current player and adapt each system according to the user's interaction preferences (e.g., provision of audio prompts, use of symbols along with text, etc.).

3.2 The Custom IR Device

The interaction paradigm of the cooking game could be summarized as follows: a student firstly collects the recipe's ingredients by laying the respective physical cards on the table's surface, and then mixes them by interacting with their virtual counterparts. Clearly such process poses some unique requirements: during its first half the interaction mimics the physical actions that someone would perform in a real kitchen, while during its second half the user has to interact in a manner that would not disrupt the natural flow of the whole process.

To that end, a custom IR 3D printed stamp that supports wireless charging (Fig. 2) has been designed, through which students can "tap" on virtual interactive elements. Internally it features a pressure-sensitive bottom which, when pressed, lights up the infrared LED mounted on its topside. Whenever that happens, the computer vision subsystem that monitors the table's surface through the high-resolution camera (Fig. 1c) propagates an artificial mouse event back to the main game [15]. However, the innovative feature of the stamp is its physical design rather than its functionality, as similar devices can be found in the market.

Fig. 2. A 3D reconstruction of the stamp and its different handles

The stamp's design employs many of Norman's rules for designing good and usable everyday things [16] in order to accommodate the special needs of the target user group. In terms of materials, the stamp's main body is made of lightweight plastic, while its bottom side is covered with rubber to satisfy a threefold purpose: (a) increased friction to discourage dragging, (b) minimized noise generation when "hitting" the desk and (c) increased durability. Regaring appearance, its exterior shape features a "pointy" design to implicitly guide the user where to direct the light, while the embedded handle contributes to its stamp-like look and enhances the natural relationship that couples function and control: while holding it a user can only "stamp" interactive elements. Three different handles were built to accommodate different grip sizes (i.e., small, medium, large), while a fourth option is available for students with motor disabilities where the stamp can be strapped on the student's fist.

3.3 The Design Process

The design and implementation of the three interactive systems has followed an iterative approach, involving multiple evaluations, as shown in (Fig. 3). In more details, for each one of the three systems, functional and non-functional requirements were specified with the collaboration of the Rehabilitation Centre's personnel (see Sect. 4). The requirements analysis and documentation was followed by an evaluation of the requirements specification by the Rehabilitation Centre experts who will be using the systems together with the children. A detailed design was then produced for each system, which was again evaluated by the Rehabilitation Centre experts. Following, a preliminary prototype was implemented for each system, featuring at least half of the provided functionality. Next, an evaluation experiment involving children of the Rehabilitation Centre will be conducted, with the aim to assess the produced designs as well as the various interaction modalities and system setups. Finally, based on the results of the evaluation, each system will be fully implemented and installed at the Centre for pilot use and evaluation.

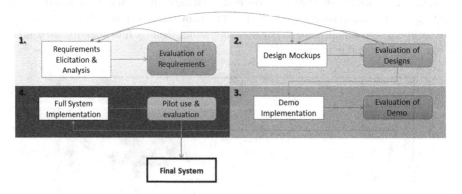

Fig. 3. The iterative design process of the three interactive systems

Currently, the following phases have been competed for each one of the three systems: requirements elicitation and analysis, mockups' design, as well as demo implementation. An evaluation experiment has been conducted for the "Cooking" game (see Sect. 8), while the experiments for the remaining two systems are being planned. All three systems are expected to be installed at the Rehabilitation Centre for pilot use within the next six months.

4   Requirements Elicitation

Requirements elicitation has been carried out through questionnaire and interviews with the Rehabilitation Centre's personnel in order to identify the characteristics and needs of the target users (children with cognitive impairments visiting the Centre for rehabilitation). Furthermore, the detailed functionality of each system has been analyzed through focus groups with the participation of the Rehabilitation Centre's personnel, as well as system designers and developers. The Rehabilitation Centre participants have professional expertise in various domains, including speech therapist, psychologists, occupational therapists, nursery staff, pediatrician, and a health visitor.

In summary, the users of the interactive systems were defined as children with cognitive age of at least three years old, with a variety of characteristics and skills. More specifically:

- Children's physical age ranges from preschoolers (3-4 years old) to teenagers, with the corresponding variations in physique.
- Reading skills may vary from minimum to excellent. Children with deteriorated skills may recognize short phrases, individual words, texts read aloud, images and symbols.
- All children can successfully understand when text is read aloud, especially if the reading rate is appropriate and the text language is simple.
- Upper limb mobility varies from no use of upper limbs at all, to difficulties in separating fingers, to satisfactory gross motor skills, or sufficient mobility.
- The most common visual problems include color blindness and difficulties in reading small size fonts.
- Eye-hand coordination problems are common.
- Children exhibit a variety of individual traits, such as placing objects in mouth, spitting, and carrying out involuntary movements.

As a result, each system should be able to accommodate a large variety of skills, by: (i) supporting information presentation through text, audio and images, concurrently available if needed, (ii) allowing customization of font size, (iii) employing a minimalistic approach towards graphic design, (iv) providing context-sensitive help in each individual exercise, and (v) supporting two levels of content, a simple one for students with severe cognitive problems and a more advanced one, allowing teachers to switch to any of the two levels at runtime.

5   Learning the Home Environment

The system includes nine exercises, namely: (1) **Presentation** of the primary house rooms (kitchen, living room, dining room, master bedroom, child's bedroom, bathroom) and secondary house areas (storage room, corridor, balcony, terrace, yard, garage). Users can receive information about a room as well as the most common objects located in it, upon its selection. (2) **Locate the room**, where children are asked to locate a specific room in the house. (3) **Find the correct room**, where children are asked to find the room to which a specific object belongs. (4) **Locate an object** in a specific room, where users have to indicate the most appropriate location of an object (e.g., pot) in a specific room (e.g., kitchen) (see Fig. 4a), for all the primary house rooms. (5) **Find mismatches**, where users have to indicate which objects should not be found in a specific room (see Fig. 4b), for all the primary house rooms. (6) **Place in the correct order the steps of an activity**, in which cards representing the steps of a specific activity carried out in the house (e.g., brushing teeth) are used. (7) **Place in the correct order the activities of a routine**, cards representing activities carried out during a specific time of the day (e.g., what do we do at night before going to sleep) are used. (8) **Dangerous behaviors exercise**, where users have to select the correct between two behaviors, one of which is dangerous (e.g., I ask an adult to plug a device in the power socket vs. I plug myself devices in the power socket). (9) **Social behaviors exercise**, where users have to select the correct behavior between two possible answers, one of which is socially inappropriate (e.g., I knock the bathroom door when there is someone else inside vs. I can open the bathroom door when there is someone else inside).

Fig. 4. Indicative screenshots (a) Place the objects correctly in a room (b) Indicate objects that should not be found in a specific room

6   Learning About Money and Monetary Transactions

The system comprises seven main thematic areas, as follows: (1) **Learn coins and bills**, where children are: (a) presented coins and bills and taught about their value (see **Fig. 5a**), (b) asked to place a coin/bill in the correct location according to its value, and (c) asked to identify a specific coin/bill among three provided options (e.g., "which coin is 1 Euro?"). (2) **Order coins and bills**, where users are asked to order six cards representing different coins and bills, from the smallest to the largest. (3) **Amount comparison**, where users are asked to identify the largest (or smallest) of two amounts. (4) **Amount analysis**, in which users are asked to identify and separate the cents and the euros for a given amount. (5) **Amount synthesis**, in which users are requested to create a given amount using specific coins and bills (see **Fig.** 5b). (6) **Shopping**, where users select a specific store (i.e., super market, bakery, bookstore, toy store, clothes store, shoes store) and are asked to: (a) shop products, pay with virtual money in a virtual wallet and indicate whether they should receive any change back (b) purchase products of a given shopping list, pay with virtual money in a virtual wallet and indicate whether they should receive any change back (c) pay with virtual money the price of a given shopping basket (d) indicate which products they can buy with a given amount in their virtual wallet. (7) **Find the correct behavior**, where users have to select the correct answer between two options, one of which is inappropriate in a monetary transaction context (e.g., I don't eat something I took from the shelves unless I pay for it first vs. I can eat it in the store before paying it).

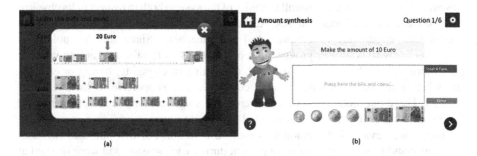

Fig. 5. (a) Learning coins and bills (b) Amount synthesis exercise

7 Learning How to Cook Simple Meals

The system features five individual exercises. More specifically: (1) **Meal appropriateness**, in which students have to select appropriate meals for a specific time of the day (morning, noon, afternoon) among several options. (2) **Cooking**, which aims to teach students the steps needed for preparing a simple meal. Meal recipes are presented step by step. In each step the user is asked to carry out a specific action (e.g., place the lettuce in a bowl), as shown in Fig. 6a. As soon as a step is completed, the recipe automatically advances to the next one. (3) **Collecting recipe ingredients**, in which users are presented with various ingredients and are asked to select only the ones that will be needed for executing the recipe. (4) **Collecting the utensils needed for a recipe**, in which users are presented with various kitchen utensils and are asked to select only the ones that will be needed for executing the recipe (Fig. 6b). (5) **Safety and hygiene rules**, where users have to select the correct answer between two options, one of which is inappropriate behavior during meal preparation (e.g., I wash my hands before cooking vs. I cook with dirty hands).

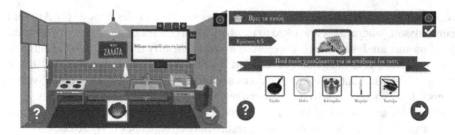

Fig. 6. Cooking game (a) Recipe step (b) Collect the utensils

8 Evaluation

A first round of user-based evaluation was conducted for the "Cooking" game. A working prototype of the system was set up at the Rehabilitation Centre's kitchen, where children are actually taught to prepare simple meals. The goal of the evaluation was primarily to examine the overall usability of the system both in respect to its physical attributes and its functional features. At the same time, it also aimed at assessing the overall user experience of children and their teachers. Since this technology is completely new to both user groups, a lot of questions were raised regarding whether the children would find it fun or stressful, distracting or engaging, boring or exciting and whether the teachers would find it conducive and supportive to their teaching strategy. These questions cannot be answered in a single evaluation session per child, therefore a long-term evaluation is planned in the near future.

The chosen evaluation method was user observation. For this purpose, two user experience and usability experts were present during each session and were situated at a distance from the child and the teacher so as not to distract the child. During each session the experts paid close attention to the way both the child and the teacher interacted with the system. A video camera recorded each session to allow further analysis. The experts did not interrupt or speak during the session, allowing for the teacher and the child to use the system freely. Prior to the experiment, the teachers were thoroughly trained on how to use the system and its interaction modes. An observation protocol form was used by the observers to easily mark down specific interaction behaviors and user preferences, as well as the performance of the system features.

A total of nine children participated in the evaluation. The children that were selected to participate had a wide range of cognitive impairments and functional limitations (from level 0-3, with 0 being severe functional limitations and 3 few functional limitations, as shown in Table 2). Five of the children were male and four female. Their parents were asked to sign a consent form. In addition, four teachers participated in the experiment, a speech therapist, a special education teacher, and two occupational therapists.

This phase of the experiment allowed drawing some general conclusions about the system and the user experience in the form of qualitative data. Overall, the system fared well with the children and the teachers. The children's initial reaction to the system was mainly that of excitement and curiosity, but not to a degree that was distracting them from the focus of the game. The children with more severe impairments (level 0 and 1), had to be guided continuously by their teachers on how to interact with the system, as expected due to the level of their disability. The children with less severe impairments (level 2 and 3) were able to follow what was actually going on with the exercises and could use the pointer device independently. In fact, the design of the pointer device proved to be very intuitive, as all those children immediately grabbed the handle and started moving it around the table and over various elements before any instructions was given by the teacher. At the beginning of the game most children would use unnecessary force to select an element, but gradually applied less force once they realized that the device was responsive even with a gentler tap. These children were able to distinguish the interaction elements that were displayed on the table and understood right away that they had to use the device to select them. However, they did seem to miss a lot of the questions that were given verbally by the system, and as a result the teachers had to often repeat them. This is an area that has to be further investigated in order to identify the source of the problem and whether it is due to speech and voice quality (a synthetic speech engine has been used to automatically transform text to speech) or rather to the combination of visual and verbal cues creating a mental overload for the children. In addition, it was observed that the children with psychomotor impairments had more trouble to accurately point and hold the pointer device over a selection.

Table 2. Disabilities and level of functionality

Disability	Children	Level of functionality
Autism	4	0, 1, 1, 2
Down syndrome	2	2, 2
Paraplegic	1	2
Psychomotor impairment	2	3, 3

9   Conclusions and Future Work

This paper has presented three innovative interactive systems enhancing the independence of everyday activities of children with cognitive impairments, each employing a variety of modalities along with card-based interaction: mouse and cards, touch and cards, custom IR pointing device and cards. Furthermore, the systems support multimedia output, personalized according to each individual child's needs and preferences. A preliminary usability evaluation has been conducted for one of the three systems indicating positive results and revealing a few problems with the input device and audio output. Future work will include extensive long-term evaluation of each system, as well as a comparative evaluation of the various interaction combinations.

Acknowledgements. The authors would like to thank the Rehabilitation Centre for Children with Disabilities in Heraklion, Crete, for the valuable contribution during the requirements elicitation and the evaluation of the produced mockups and interactive prototypes. The graphics design for the "learning to cook" system was carried out by Elias Giannopoulos. The custom IR pointing device has been constructed by Elias Giannopoulos and Thanasis Toutountzis. Finally, the Content Editor and the Student Profiler have been implemented by Nikolaos Louloudakis, Evangelos Poutouris, Parthena Basina and Evropi Stephanidi.

References

1. Braddock, D., Rizzolo, M.C., Thompson, M., Bell, R.: Emerging technologies and cognitive disability. J. Spec. Educ. Technol. **19**(4), 49–56 (2004)
2. Scherer, M.J.: Assistive Technologies and Other Supports for People with Brain Impairment, pp. 175–176. Springer Publishing Company, Heidelberg (2011)
3. Mechling, L.C.: Assistive technology as a self-management tool for prompting students with intellectual disabilities to initiate and complete daily tasks: A literature review. Education and Training in Developmental Disabilities, 252–269 (2007)
4. Lopresti, E.F., Mihailidis, A., Kirsch, N.: Assistive technology for cognitive rehabilitation: State of the art. Neuropsychological Rehabil. **14**(1–2), 5–39 (2004)
5. Lopresti, E.F., Bodine, C., Lewis, C.: Assistive technology for cognition Understanding the Needs of Persons with Disabilities. IEEE Eng. Med. Biol. Mag. **27**(2), 29–39 (2008)
6. Lancioni, G.E., O'Reilly, M.F., Seedhouse, P., Furniss, F., Cunha, B.: Promoting independent task performance by persons with severe developmental disabilities through a new computer-aided system. Behav. Modif. **24**(5), 700–718 (2000)
7. Mechling, L.C., Gast, D.L., Seid, N.H.: Using a personal digital assistant to increase independent task completion by students with autism spectrum disorder. J. Autism Dev. Disord. **39**(10), 1420–1434 (2009)
8. Giroux, S., Bauchet, J., Pigot, H., Lussier-Desrochers, D., Lachappelle, Y.: Pervasive behavior tracking for cognitive assistance. In: Proceedings of the 1st international conference on PErvasive Technologies Related to Assistive Environments, p. 86. ACM, July 2008
9. Langone, J., Clees, T.J., Rieber, L., Matzko, M.: The future of computer-based interactive technology for teaching individuals with moderate to severe disabilities: Issues relating to research and practice. J. Spec. Educ. Technol. **18**(1), 5–16 (2003)
10. Ayres, K.M., Langone, J., Boon, R.T., Norman, A.: Computer-based instruction for purchasing skills. Educ. Training Dev. Disabil. **41**(3), 253–263 (2006)
11. Hansen, D.L., Morgan, R.L.: Teaching grocery store purchasing skills to students with intellectual disabilities using a computer-based instruction program. Educ. Training Dev. Disabil. **43**(4), 431–442 (2008)
12. Lanyi, C.S., Brown, D.J.: Design of serious games for students with intellectual disability. IHCI **10**, 44–54 (2010)
13. Korozi, M., Leonidis, A., Margetis, G., Koutlemanis, P., Zabulis, X., Antona, M., Stephanidis, C.: Ambient educational mini-games. In: Proceedings of the International Working Conference on Advanced Visual Interfaces, pp. 802–803. ACM, May 2012
14. Margetis, G., Zabulis, X., Ntoa, S., Koutlemanis, P., Papadaki, E., Antona, M., Stephanidis, C.: Enhancing education through natural interaction with physical paper. Universal Access in the Information Society, 1–21
15. Margetis, G., Zabulis, X., Koutlemanis, P., Antona, M., Stephanidis, C.: Augmented interaction with physical books in an Ambient Intelligence learning environment. Multimed. Tools Appl. **67**(2), 473–495 (2013)
16. Norman, D.A.: The design of Everyday Things, pp. 13–28. Basic books, New York (2002)

Toward a Piano Lesson System that Gives People with Reduced Cognitive Functioning a Sense of Accomplishment

Chika Oshima[✉], Kimie Machishima, and Koichi Nakayama

Saga University, Saga, Japan
chika-o@ip.is.saga-u.ac.jp

Abstract. Creative activities provide elderly people with reduced cognitive functioning with a sense of accomplishment in nursing care facilities. Music therapists and their clients usual sing songs and play percussive musical instruments. However, they may not provide a feeling of accomplishment from these kinds of music therapy. Then, we aim to construct a piano lesson support system that can give people with reduced cognitive functioning a sense of accomplishment through playing the piano. In this paper, we conducted experiments in which a participant with higher brain dysfunction took piano lessons using video educational materials. The results of the experiments showed that she participated with enthusiasm and got better at playing the piano. On the other hand, we found several issues to consider. We discussed these issues with consideration of the symptoms according to the depression of cognitive function.

1 Introduction

Most nursing care facilities hold leisure activities on a daily basis. Elderly people with reduced cognitive functioning often exercise, play games, craft products, play and listen to music, do housework, and so on. Although most elderly people with memory problems cannot remember their activities, they often retain memories of the pleasant feelings associated with such activities. The care staff at such facilities often say that elderly people begin to talk significantly more, do more by themselves, and have fewer problem behaviors as a result of leisure activities. Hence, we can expect to improve their quality of life (QOL) and prevent their behavioral and psychological symptoms of dementia (BPSD).

Creative activities, including cooking, handicraft work, gardening, and ceramic artwork, provide them with a sense of accomplishment. These activities require them to execute a series of small tasks. They are quite willing to continue in such activities, as they find them enjoyable.

Most elderly people with reduced cognitive functioning also participate in music therapy, which is one of the leisure activities offered in the facilities where they attend. In Japan, they play percussive musical instruments like the tambourines and castanets in an ensemble and achieve a feeling of togetherness. Many researchers [1–4] have demonstrated that music therapy allows people with

© Springer International Publishing Switzerland 2015
M. Antona and C. Stephanidis (Eds.): UAHCI 2015, Part III, LNCS 9177, pp. 649–659, 2015.
DOI: 10.1007/978-3-319-20684-4_62

dementia to reduce their aggressive behavior, a BPSD. However, it is difficult for the participants of music therapy to achieve a sense of accomplishment. Many specialized lessons taught by a professional teacher are required to achieve technical growth in playing these musical instruments.

On the other hand, keyboard instruments have a high threshold [5]. A performer has to learn how to read music scores and hit the appropriate keys using all ten fingers. Professional teachers are needed to give them individual guidance and support. Hence, the leisure activities in nursing care houses do not include playing the piano. However, we believe that even elderly people with reduced cognitive functioning can try to play the piano when given appropriate support for performance and lessons. The most important thing is that the people in such a facility become willing to continue playing the piano with a sense of accomplishment.

There are many systems that assist people in learning how to play musical instruments. "The Piano Tutor [6]" provides computer-based instruction to beginning piano students. The system can follow people's performances and analyze their performance and select appropriate remedial actions. "Piano Tutor for iPad [7]" is an application for learning the piano. The system teaches mistakes in performances by high-score tracking. "Piano Marvel [8]" shows where people should hit on a small picture of a keyboard. The system also shows people where they made mistakes. "Lighted Keys [9]" is a keyboard that includes the 3-Step Lesson System and lights the key the performer should hit next. In a piano learning system [10], the projector is set above a keyboard. The system refers to the next key that is to be pressed and each next key is outlined in color to provide keying information. These systems may be useful for adult piano beginners. However, it is difficult for most elderly people with reduced cognitive functioning to find the position of the correct key that the system shows on the display. They cannot learn fingering numbers and hit the keys with the correct fingers shown on the display. Our research aims to help people with reduced cognitive functioning continue being motivated in playing the piano rather than that to gain skills.

In the first step of this research, we conducted an experiment in which an elderly woman with "higher brain dysfunction" took piano lessons using educational video materials. She was asked to play an electronic piano following the instructions in the educational videos. In general, a student has a face-to-face piano lesson with a teacher. However, we employ the educational videos because we aim to construct a piano lesson support system that such elderly people can use pianos alone in the future. We show her progress on the piano and that she gained a sense of accomplishment. Then, we discuss improvements in a construction of a display and a system to provide a sense of accomplishment for people with reduced cognitive functioning.

2   Experiment 1

2.1   Participant

The participant is a woman in her 70s with higher brain dysfunction due to a brain contusion. The higher brain dysfunction includes impaired cognitive functioning caused by a brain contusion, aprophoria, apraxia, agnosia, and dementia. The occurrence of these symptoms depends in part on her brain contusion. She has constructional and ideational apraxia and a reduction in skilled behavior due to her injured frontal lobe and temporal lobe. She cannot move her hands skillfully now, although she was a professional sewer when she was young. She may have semantic paraphasia. Her score of the revised version of Hasegawa's Dementia Scale (HDS-R) was 14/30. In particular, the temporal orientation score was low. In activities of daily living, she needs a little help to eat a meal, change her clothes, and take a bath, although she is independent in toileting. She has not played the piano so far. She likes Hibari Misora, who was a very famous singer in Japan, and often sings her songs.

2.2   Informed Consent

The participant in this experiment was informed about the intentions of the experiment and the treatment of personal information. Moreover, she was informed that she could withdraw from the experiment at any time. No reward was prepared for her. Then, we obtained written consent from her.

The second author, who is a nurse, observed the experiment. If she had estimated that the participant was tired, felt bad, and was mentally hard, the experiment would be terminated early.

2.3   Method

Experiments were carried out three times in twelve days. Figure 1 shows that the participant played an electronic piano (YAMAHA NP-30) that has 76 keys while watching an educational video on a 27-inch display. The video showed not musical scores, but the hands of model performances. Because the target of our research is elderly people with cognitive dysfunction, it is difficult for them to learn and memorize each key position corresponding to each note. The participant was asked to play the piano as a help for us because she might be nervous to play the piano for the first time.

The musical piece used in this experiment was "Kawa no nagare no yoni (like a flowing stream)," a Hibari Misora song. The participant liked the piece very much. One of the authors wrote down the hook-line of this piece in a score. The participant could play this part using only eight white keys: G3, A3, B3, C4, D4, E4, F4, and G4. She used both hands to play the piece. Her thumbs did not need to pass through other fingers or other fingers did not need to pass over her thumbs.

As shown in Fig. 2, colorful seals were put on eight keys. Seals whose colors corresponded to each key were also placed on the participant's and the video performer's fingers.

The performer in the video repeated each phrase six times (model performance). First, the participant listened to the phrase one time. Then, she played each phrase five times along with the model performances like shadowing.

Fig. 1. The participant plays the keyboard while viewing the display.

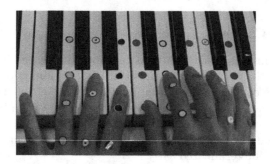

Fig. 2. Each finger is assigned a key.

2.4   Video Educational Material

One of the authors made three educational videos for the participant's lessons. Figure 3 shows three practice phases as examples. The hook-line was divided into many parts (phrases). Example 1 shows the start of the hook-line. The first note should be played using the participant's left hand, and the second note should be played using her right hand. First, the participant practiced a very short phrase. Then, she practiced a slightly longer phrase. The phrase in Example 3 includes that of Example 2. After the participant practiced Example 2, she then practiced Example 3.

The videos for the second and third lessons were made after the first lesson and the second lesson, respectively. The phrases used on three lessons were the same. In the video for the second lesson, the performer said the color of the key (see Fig. 2) immediately before playing the key. For example, the performer said "Red" immediately before hitting the red key. We expect that the participant can find the correct key more quickly.

In the video for the third lesson, the way the hook-line was divided into the phrases differed from that of the first and second lessons. For the first and second lessons, we divide the hook-line into nine phrases and ten phrases for the third lesson. A shorter phrase allows the participant to practice with less of a mental burden.

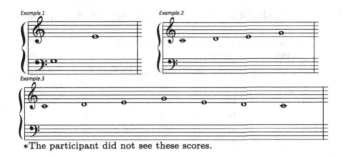

*The participant did not see these scores.

Fig. 3. Examples of the phrases for practicing.

2.5   Method of Analysis

We recorded the participant's performance and counted the errors in pitches and fingerings. Rhythm is also an important element for music. The participant knew the musical piece very well because she often sang it. Therefore, she understood the correct rhythm of this piece. However, she had a difficult time physically hitting the keys in the correct rhythm. Therefore, in this experiment, we analyzed only the pitches and the fingerings.

The pitch errors are divided into "wrong," "missing," "extra," and "holding keys." Wrong means that the participant hit the wrong key. Missing means that she did not hit any keys. Extra means that she hit an extra key. The holding key means that she held down some keys since before starting to play a phrase.

Moreover, we considered a hitting a key "incorrect fingering" when she hit the key with a finger that did not correspond to the finger that the performer in the video used to hit the key.

2.6   Result

Performance. Table 1 shows the results of her performances (three lessons). The numbers of all notes that the author played in the videos are 280 (the first and second lessons) and 270 (the third lesson). The ratios of hitting the keys to the number of all notes are 80 % (224/280), 81 % (228/280), and 87 % (236/270) in the three lessons.

The number of pitch errors gradually decreased. Although "wrong" decreased in the second lesson from 43 to 19, it increased in the third lesson from 19 to 27.

"Correct keying" means the number of correct keys hit with the correct fingerings. The number in the second lesson is smaller than that of the first lesson although the number of the wrong keys hit decreased.

Table 2 shows the number of fingering errors. The number of "incorrect fingerings" increased in the second lesson from 64 to 149. Therefore, the ratio of the incorrect fingerings to the correct pitches decreased in the second lesson. The participant was apt to play the keys with one finger in the second lesson.

Observation. The participant played each phrase along with the model performances as though she was shadowing. As the lessons progressed, she continued

Table 1. The results of the participant's performances (Experiment 1).

Day	Phrase	The number of all notes (5 times)	The number of keys hit	Pitch errors				Correct keying
				Wrong	Missing	Extra	Holding keys	
1st	1	10	10	2	1	1	10	7
	2	15	16	0	4	5	2	7
	3	20	18	3	5	2	9	11
	4	35	31	5	8	4	8	16
	5	45	32	8	19	4	2	8
	6	25	21	7	4	0	4	9
	7	30	27	4	9	6	11	8
	8	45	34	9	13	2	14	12
	9	55	35	5	24	4	4	10
	Sum	280	224	43	87	28	64	88
2nd	1	10	10	0	0	0	3	5
	2	15	19	0	0	4	1	0
	3	20	23	0	0	3	0	5
	4	35	33	0	2	0	0	13
	5	45	35	5	13	3	0	9
	6	25	18	2	8	1	3	3
	7	30	27	6	5	2	0	2
	8	45	31	3	16	2	0	2
	9	55	32	3	24	1	0	6
	Sum	280	228	19	68	16	7	45
3rd	1	10	9	1	1	0	1	4
	2	15	14	0	1	0	0	6
	3	25	25	7	1	1	0	9
	4	20	22	2	0	2	0	18
	5	25	25	0	1	1	0	7
	6	30	29	2	3	2	0	14
	7	35	36	2	0	1	0	11
	8	45	34	8	13	2	0	17
	9	10	10	0	0	0	0	10
	10	55	32	4	23	0	0	20
	Sum	270	236	27	43	9	1	116

playing the phrase even after the model performance had finished. Moreover, when she made extra type errors, she hummed a tune and replayed the correct key. She may have hit the keys while judging whether each key was correct or not relying on remembering what she heard.

She forgot that she had played the piano on the night of taking the first and second lessons. Soon after the second lesson, she said "I could play the piano a little" with a smile. After the third lesson, we observed her cleaning up the dust on the edge of the piano although the author had already cleaned the piano.

Moreover, she complained that it was difficult to find the same key as the key the performer played in the video.

Table 2. The results of fingering errors.

	Correct pitch	Incorrect fingering	Incorrect fingering / Correct pitch(%)	Correct pitch / The numbers of all notes(%)
1	151	64	37.5	57.8
2	193	149	77.5	76.5
3	201	85	39.3	81.2

2.7 Discussion

The finding that the ratio of hitting the keys to the number of all notes was greater than 80 % shows that she played the piano with enthusiasm. Even elderly people with reduced cognitive functioning can try to play the piano with support. Moreover, the results show that the number of pitch errors gradually decreased. She said, "I could play the piano a little" after the second lesson. The motion of her cleaning up the dust on the edge of the piano may show her affection for the piano. Therefore, we recognized that she gained a sense of accomplishment through the piano lessons.

On the other hand, the number of correct notes with correct fingering decreased in the second lesson. We thought that she focused on touching the correct keys because the performer in the video said the color of the key. She had hardly watched the display, but saw the color of the keys and found the correct key one after another. Therefore, she might have hit most of the keys with her index finger.

In general, students who learn to play the piano know that the numbers from one to five are assigned to the fingers from the thumb to the little finger, respectively. Some notes in musical scores indicate the number of fingers that the piano player should use. However, it is difficult for elderly people with reduced cognitive functioning to recognize the fingering number on the score and hit the key with the finger applied to the designated number. Even if we were to indicate the next key by coloring or lighting the key [9] without a voice, she would have hit all of the keys using one finger.

Furthermore, the participant complained that it was difficult to find the same key as the key the performer played in the video. The eight keys of the piano that the participant and the performer played had colorful seals placed on them. However, it must have been difficult for her to find the same color on the piano as the key in the video because of her symptoms.

3 Experiment 2

3.1 Display Setup

In Experiment 1, it was difficult for the participant to find the same key as the key the performer played in the video. Therefore, we abandoned putting the seals on the keys as well as the participant's and the performer's fingers.

Fig. 4. Model performance that the participant can watch like a mirror.

As shown in Fig. 4, we calibrated the length of the keyboard in the video. Each key in the video corresponded to the same pitch key on the real piano. Moreover, we improved the appearance of the video so that the participant could find the correct keys easily. The model performance appeared like a mirror.

3.2   Method

Two months after Experiment 1, the same participant was asked to play the same electronic piano as in Experiment 1. The musical piece used in the experiment was the hook-line of the same piece. However, only five phrases were prepared and the time of the educational video was ten minutes.

There were two experimental conditions. In the first condition, the model performance in the video appeared as shown in Fig. 4. The performer in the video played the piano facing the participant like a mirror.

Figure 5 shows the second condition. As a comparative condition of the first condition, the performer in the video played the piano looking ahead in the same direction as the participant was playing. The experiment of the second condition was conducted after the experiment of the first condition.

3.3   Result

Table 3 shows the results of the participant's performances. The number of all notes that the author played in the videos is 145. The ratios of hitting the keys to the number of all notes are 99 % (144/145) and 100 % (145/145), respectively.

There is a significant difference between the two conditions in the item "extra (p=0.04)." This result might be not be due to the differences between the two conditions, but rather the learning effect.

We can see the number of "wrong" errors is very high. In Experiment 1, the ratio of wrong errors to the number of keys hit are 19 % (43/224), 8 % (19/228), and 11 % (27/236) in the three lessons. On the other hand, in Experiment 2, those are 72 % ((104/144) and (104/145)) in both conditions.

Fig. 5. Examples of the phrases for practicing.

Table 3. The results of the participant's performances (Experiment 2).

Condition	Phrase	The number of all notes (5 times)	The number of keys hit	Pitch errors			Correct keying
				Wrong	Missing	Extra	
1	1	25	26	8	5	6	9
	2	20	22	19	0	2	0
	3	35	38	32	0	5	1
	4	10	10	10	0	0	0
	5	55	48	35	9	7	2
	Sum	145	144	104	14	20	12
2	1	25	22	18	3	0	1
	2	20	21	16	0	0	0
	3	35	37	22	0	0	8
	4	10	10	5	0	0	5
	5	55	55	43	7	4	1
	Sum	145	145	104	10	4	15

Table 4 shows the number of correct fingerings in the wrong hittings. The ratios of the number of correct fingerings to the wrong keys hit are very high. Namely, the participant hit the keys with the correct fingering although most of the keys were wrong. Fig. 6 illustrates an example in which the participant hit the wrong keys with the correct fingerings. The figures below each note indicate the number for each finger. We can see that the participant played the piano with much the same motion of fingers as that of the performer in the video.

3.4 Discussion

The result that the ratio of hitting the keys to the number of all notes is almost 100 % shows she played the piano with enthusiasm. In this experiment, we improved a composition of the video as shown in Figs. 4 and 5. However,

Table 4. The number of correct fingerings when the wrong keys were hit.

Condition	Phrase	The number of correct fingerings in the wrong keys hit (cf-wh)	cf-wh / wrong keys hit (%)
1	1	6	75.0
	2	14	73.6
	3	20	62.5
	4	5	50.0
	5	20	57.1
2	1	8	44.4
	2	16	100.0
	3	19	86.3
	4	5	100.0
	5	22	51.1

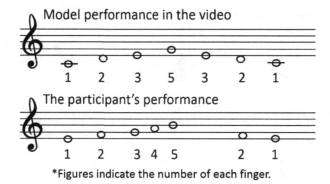

*Figures indicate the number of each finger.

Fig. 6. Examples of the correct fingerings while hitting the wrong keys.

the number of "wrong" errors was very high although most of the wrong keys were played with the correct fingerings. She might find it easier to consider the fingerings because of the calibration of the keyboard's length. It is difficult for the participant to find the correct keys corresponding to the keys that the performer hit in the video. The first reason is that she has constructional apraxia. For example, people with constructional apraxia cannot make the reconstruct a model with blocks. Namely, they may not be good at estimating the correct key as a real object in comparison with a key on a screen image.

The second reason is that the quality of experimental materials was low. The frame of the display might interrupt her exploration of the correct keys. If the display connected to the keyboard of the piano seamlessly, she would find the keys more precisely. Moreover, it might be hard for her to determine the position of the key the performer hit in the video. We find it hard to determine whether each key is going down because the color of the keys' surface is white and that of keys' sides are light brown.

4   Conclusion

We aimed to construct a piano lesson support system that gives the people with reduced cognitive functioning a sense of accomplishment. We conducted an experiment in which an elderly woman with "higher brain dysfunction" took piano lessons using educational video materials. The results of Experiment 1 showed that the participant could try to play the piano in spite of being a beginner. She became skillful and gained a sense of accomplishment through the piano lessons. However, when the performer in the video said the color of the key each time, the participant hit any keys with only her index finger.

The results of Experiment 2 showed that the participant hit many of the wrong keys although she played with the correct fingerings. We thought that she might find it easier to consider the fingerings because of the calibration of the keyboard's length. However, we considered that people with reduced cognitive functioning might find it hard to find the correct keys in comparison with keys on a screen image. The participant might have had a hard time knowing the position of the key in the video because the frame of the display interrupted her exploration, and it was hard to know when each key was going down.

As the next step, we will develop a model performance with computer graphics and use a frameless display.

References

1. Svansdottir, H.B., Snaedal, J.: Music therapy in moderate and severe dementia of Alzheimer's type: a case-control study. Int. Psychogeriatr. **18**, 613–621 (2006)
2. Park, H., Pringle Specht, J.K.: Effect of individualized music on agitation in individuals with dementia who live at home. J Gerontol. Nurs. **35**(8), 47–55 (2009)
3. Vink, A.C., Zuidersma, M., Boersma, F., de Jonge, P., Zuidema, S.U., Slaets, J.P.: The effect of music therapy compared with general recreational activities in reducing agitation in people with dementia: a randomised controlled trial. Int. J. Geriatr. Psychiatry. **28**(10), 1031–1038 (2013)
4. Sepehry, A., Yang, L., Hsiung, G.-Y.R., Jacova, C.: Music therapy, global affect and behavior in Alzheimer's disease: a meta-analytic perspective on outcomes and on music therapy methodologies, Alzheimer's & Dementia. J. Alzheimer's Assoc. **9**(4), 665 (2013)
5. Oshima, C., Nishimoto, K., Hagita, N.: A piano duo support system for parents to lead children to practice musical performance. ACM Trans. Multimedia Comput. Commun. Appl. **3**(2), 9 (2007)
6. Dannenberg, R.B., Sanchez, M., Joseph, A., Capell, P., Joseph, R., Saul, R.: A Computer-Based Multi-Media Tutor for Beginning Piano Students. Interface. **19**(2–3), 155–173 (1990)
7. SmileyApps: Piano Tutor in iPad. http://www.smileyapps.com/
8. PianoMarvel. http://www.pianomarvel.com/
9. Casio: Lighted Keys. http://www.casio.com/home
10. Takegawa, Y., Terada, T., Tsukamoto, M.: A Piano Learning Support System considering Rhythm. In: Proceedings of International Computer Music Conference, pp. 325–332 (2012)

Jurojin: Designing a GPS Device
for People Living with Dementia

Mark Palmer[1(✉)] and Jude Hancock[2]

[1] University of the West of England, Bristol, UK
Mark.Palmer@uwe.ac.uk
[2] Avon and Wiltshire Mental Health Partnership NHS Trust, Bristol, UK
jhancock1@nhs.net

Abstract. Memory loss is the most common symptom of dementia. The impact is such that people living with dementia (PLWD) lose the ability to find their way to previously familiar locations, such as local amenities, and without the aid of others, find themselves confined to home. PLWD report they would like to be able to live unsupported for as long as possible [3] and in this regard the ability to walk to amenities also provides exercise which has been shown to be particularly beneficial for PLWD. This paper presents the Jurojin project which arose out of the Dress/Sense competition to design wearable technology that would positively impact on an individual's health. It details the challenges of the design process, examines PPI (Patient and Public Involvement) feedback and considers whether there might be lessons to be learnt beyond simply designing for PLWD.

Keywords: Dementia · GPS · Exercise · Design

1 Introduction

1.1 Living with Dementia

The number of people living with dementia [PLWD] worldwide is estimated to be 35.6 million [1]. Memory loss is the most common symptom of dementia [2]; however, it is the loss of independence due to increased reliance on others that PLWD find most difficult to cope with [3]. The impact of memory loss is such that PLWD lose the ability to find their way to what used to be familiar locations, such as local amenities; and without the aid of others, they find themselves confined to home. PLWD report that they would like to be able to live unsupported for as long as possible [3], and in this regard the ability to walk to local shops and amenities would have added benefits to an individual's well-being. Exercise is part of a healthy lifestyle across the lifespan [4], and is important for PLWD [5]. Exercise programmes designed for PLWD have had positive results [6, 7]. Exercise can aid cognition, reduce apathy, aid sleep, muscle strength and balance, which in turn can prevent falls [5, 8, 9]. Based on existing evidence, feedback from PLWD, and those supporting PLWD, there appears to be a need for developing wearable, user-friendly GPS technology designed for PLWD.

© Springer International Publishing Switzerland 2015
M. Antona and C. Stephanidis (Eds.): UAHCI 2015, Part III, LNCS 9177, pp. 660–668, 2015.
DOI: 10.1007/978-3-319-20684-4_63

1.2   Developing a Wearable GPS Technology for PLWD

The EPSRC funded Interdisciplinary Research Collaboration Sphere (http://www.irc-sphere.ac.uk/) is focused upon addressing a range of healthcare needs by utilizing 'non-medical networked sensors in a home environment.' As a part of their activities they held the Dress/Sense competition in 2014 looking for teams 'to design a wearable item that will have an impact on an individual's health'. Through a series of three workshops participants drawn from disciplines as broad as science, medicine, engineering, art and design worked together to identify potential projects and then form teams to create a prototype to address a particular issue. Workshops were provided introducing participants to technological and health issues and teams were provided with a basic kit that included the Arduino Lilypad development board, a range of basic sensors and conductive thread.

The authors' of this paper were members of one of the teams formed as a part of this process who alighted upon the need for a wearable GPS system for PLWD as described above. Whereas many pieces of new technology foreground their novelty and innovation, what became one of the most interesting aspects of the challenge was that the memory loss affecting PLWD make it difficult for them to learn new skills; this can also result in them being wary of trying anything new. This presents an interesting set of circumstances for anyone designing for PLWD because the novelty and choice so often prioritized by new technologies now becomes a barrier to its use. Given that there is currently no known cure for dementia, if there is to be 'design for all' there is a clear need to address systems that can be used by the 35.6 million PLWD. But this is a need not just affecting those immediately living with the condition given that the proposed freedoms afforded by the device should not be at the cost of already pressed carers having to deal with complexities hidden from the user.

The Jurojin prototype was the result of the team's examination of these issues. In itself this demanded the consideration of alternative strategies in for the systems inputs and outputs. This led to a development process which moved away from screen based interfaces, and the consideration of alternatives that prioritized simplicity that could be incorporated into a wearable. This had to deal with the means by which destinations were input into the device as well as the way routes would be conveyed. Beyond this consideration was also given to strategies that might make the system itself more familiar. This paper will discuss the approaches taken by the team and the initial responses of feedback from people currently supporting, and who have previously supported PLWD as well as the initial responses of PLWD. It will then go on to consider what guidance might be provided for those seeking to design systems for PLWD.

2   Method

2.1   Design Process and Challenges

The initial design for Jurojin arose from discussion between team members (whose skills included clinical experience of PLWD). As a part of this process there was also input from advisors who were a part of the Dress-Sense workshops and who possessed medical or technical expertise. These discussions highlighted what were initially quite different approaches to the use of technology. Although many technologists are increasingly involved with user centered design, the discipline often begins with technology, with the result that it can often become a 'solution' that is looking for a problem.

As noted above the team had identified the need to move away from screen based interfaces and wished to prioritize simplicity. Arguably, this is a challenge faced by all satellite navigation systems because of the dangers that can be caused through split attention. From a technological perspective this broader problem informed ideas that sought to make use of haptic feedback/vibration in each arm to inform users of the need for changes in direction (in as much that it would address any potential issues of confusion between left and right). This approach was also encouraged by one of the technology advisors because it was felt that such an approach had the potential to address the question of split attention for all users. However, input from those with experience of PLWD quickly highlighted the problematic nature of such an approach. This was because if a garment suddenly started to vibrate, its 'novelty' would most likely upset the user who would then be inclined to discard the wearable. In this way it rapidly became apparent that the novelty we have so often considered to be a defining virtue in new technology would most likely be detrimental to the creation of a device for PLWD. To this extent it could be argued that in some circumstances the design of a 'natural user interface' should avoid the inclusion of novel features.

As a result of these discussions it became apparent that despite a desire to innovate audio was the most appropriate form of feedback. In order to appropriately address the safety of users a single ear piece would be used and preferably a bone conductive device so that spatial nature of environmental events reaches the ears unhindered. Whilst everyday users might consider GPS for a range of activities its use for PLWD would be limited to a small range of 'regular' destinations such as local cafes, supermarket, post office/post box and of course home. Given that what us becoming an increasingly unfamiliar world the familiar can be a comforting point of reference for PLWD, the use of tailored audio also provided an opportunity for carers to be able to add messages/prompts along a route thereby providing a familiar touchstone for users. This is important and as the Alzheimer's Society points out in its *Dementia-friendly technology charter* 'it is very important to personalize technology for each individual and not present it as part of a 'set menu' or 'dementia package'.' [10].

2.2   GPS Accuracy

Before deciding what kind of instructions would be provided it was important to ascertain the limitations of GPS tracking. Consumer devices based around single receivers are reported to have around 5-10 m precision (ordinance survey [11]) and high accuracy devices 3.5 m. The exactitude of this data can be further affected by environmental conditions that impact on the propagation of GPS signals. These factors can include the weather and signal reflection off of buildings, particularly within urban and city environments. Given that development was based around the use of Arduino and an AdaFruit GPS 'break out' board, the accuracy of the device was tested against known location data and to check the accuracy of an additional function written to provide point to point measures of distance (however this did assume the earth was a perfect sphere). The purpose of this function was to measure the user's distance from waypoints and to use this to trigger the delivery of instructions. A fine tuning of this distance was built into the prototype through the use of potentiometer to adjust this parameter. Despite the manufacture's claim that the board possessed the accuracy similar to or greater than other devices (3 m) testing within Bristol confirmed a precision of around 5-10 m with a relatively stable output within this range, however this was achieved with the board's passive antenna. The use of an active antenna would increase the number of satellites detected and boost the accuracy of position finding. However in many ways working to a lower accuracy meant that instructions would need to take this into consideration by providing an appropriate set of environmental references for users such as buildings or features that provide local reference points and this might provide a more user friendly means of delivering instructions.

Having examined the data provided by GPS systems it was found that the device can be used to detect the direction that somebody is moving (using the same method as most commercial GPS devices) and through this infer the orientation of the user. Whilst this might work quite well in devices such as vehicle satellite navigation systems this would become problematic if somebody on foot became confused and was turning on the spot. Although the prototype utilized the assumed orientation provided by the GPS sensor it was decided that the incorporation of a compass into the system would be important at a later date.

Given that the project was developed over a relatively short timeframe the prototype used simple routes hardcoded into the device; however that this was a prototype built on the Arduino platform future development would examine increasing onboard storage or the utilization of an SD card, something that was present on the prototype due to the use of a wav shield to deal with delivery of instructions to users.

2.3 Context

Designing a wearable GPS system for PLWD meant that many of the features that would be expected of other systems would not be a requirement for the system. Although all GPS systems are used to help people move around unfamiliar locations, the unfamiliarity experienced by PLWD is of a different kind to those of us who might be traveling to an unfamiliar city. Commercial devices have to content with a multitude of potential destinations and routes. Instead of this we were looking to support PLWD to make the local journeys that those of us who do not live with dementia take for granted; as we have noted this would be limited to a small range of 'regular' destinations such as local cafes, supermarket, post office/post box and home. Although the device would be tailored for a set of destinations the inclusion of mobile GSM technology could be utilized to draw down data from facilities such as Google Maps if users were to stray off of route. The potential disadvantage might be that a switch from a familiar voice to the automated systems associated with GPS device might be disconcerting for the user. Alongside this the addition of GSM into the device would allow notifications of position to be utilized. Devices capable of tracking PLWD are available and although welcomed by carers, their reception by PLWD hasn't been as positive and has been compared with the electronic tagging of offenders. Tracking is perceived as a loss of independence [12] so its inclusion would most likely be perceived as a feature contrary to the very thing that the device is intended to promote. As it stands the use of tracking systems has an ethical dimension that should include the informed consent of 'users'. Although it wasn't included in the initial prototype if this feature was included it would ideally be something that is enabled by the user when they wish to obtain assistance.

2.4   Route Selection

On one level the limited set of routes provided by the system simplified the requirements of the user interface but once again the tendency towards technological innovation drove initial suggestions within the team. Initially, the need to incorporate this into a wearable appeared to complicate this; however, the incorporation of a natural interface into a wearable began to reframe the teams thinking around this issue. Having discussed the requirements of an interface for PLWD the use of symbols presented itself as an appropriate way forward. When this was considered against the range of conductive materials available for wearable technology a simple solution became apparent. Given that the decision had been made to make use simple icons for the destinations the use of conductive ribbon and press studs presented the opportunity to use the visual metaphor of the road provide to provide a simple switch to each destination (Fig. 1). These could be embroidered or transferred into garments. Given that conductive ribbon provides a number of conductive tracks the design of a press stud capable of distinguishing between these tracks might provide additional opportunities to tailor functionality.

2.5   Evaluation Strategy

This exploratory study used purposive sampling to gather feedback on the Jurojin concept and subsequent prototype.

2.6   Participants and Procedure

Phase one was to gather feedback about the design concept of Jurojin. Emails outlining the concept with accompanying pictures were emailed by the co-author to six individuals who have previously supported PLWD in either a paid or non-paid role. The email content was analyzed to explore common themes regarding the concept. In addition feedback was received as a part of the Dress/Sense competition.

  Phase two was to gather feedback about the Jurojin prototype. A DVD was produced by the lead author showcasing the prototype. This DVD was sent to PLWD and their carers for feedback.

Fig. 1. User interface design

3   Results

Phase one results of email feedback had all those who were contacted stated that wearable GPS technology could be useful for PLWD to allow greater independence outside the home. Feedback indicated the importance of having personalized clothing with this technology embedded, for example, one carer suggested that if the technology were embedded in a body warmer this might be the type of garment that is put on daily on top of any other clothing. This would minimize the risk of the PLWD forgetting to put on a different piece of clothing that housed the device. Similarly one of the professionals suggested building the device into a shirt, as males in particular often wear shirts daily and therefore could have a series of shirts with the device. Another professional indicated that it would be important to identify which piece or pieces of clothing the PLWD wear most often and adapt these with the device.

In terms of user interface, the importance of the 'home' function was felt very significant. Two individuals felt that a device which only had a 'home' button could be a basic device available for PLWD. One professional noted that as part of a local project raising awareness of dementia in local shops, a PLWD had been able to go out alone more as shopkeepers were directing the PLWD home as they were leaving their premises. A wearable GPS would allow the PLWD to safely reach their destination as well as return home again without reliance on others.

One professional felt that a device which was ultimately linked to, for example, a spouses smartphone, so that the spouse to track where the PLWD was if they hadn't returned home for some time would be useful. As has been noted the team had discussed building in this feature, but felt in the given timescales it was better to work on a simple device. However, this feedback suggested the importance of this monitoring in future developments of the device.

Some feedback questioned the use of a single ear piece and how this would fit with PLWD with hearing aids. This had been considered in the design stage, it was felt for the purposes of developing a prototype the single ear piece would be used as this was cheap to purchase. However, alternative audio bone headphones could be used which sit behind the ear if this suited the needs of the PLWD.

It was also noted that one of the difficulties experienced with dementia is the lack of insight into changes in oneself. Consequently timing of promoting use of wearable technology would be key to the PLWD accepting the need for the device, and subsequently integrating it into activities of daily living.

Feedback was also received from the Dress/Sense competition focused on the positive aspects of the device; however a more critical evaluation was sought by the authors. This raised two issues concerning technical aspects of the device; one being that of battery life and the other being the device's use in buildings.

Phase two results at the time of writing are yet to be received. These are of importance to the project given that we are seeking the input of PLWD themselves and will be featured when the paper is presented.

4   Discussion

Initial feedback has lent support to the notion of a wearable GPS device for PLWD. The choice as to which garment the device is embedded within remains although this is an issue that has been dealt with in a different way by the products that have made it to the market. These have tended to be wearable in the sense of jewelry. Almost all of these products have been a smart watch or a variation on it such as the jawbone activity tracker and the Nike FuelBand, each of which takes the form of a bangle. Other wearables have experienced faltering development, as has been seen with the Google Glass and other smart glasses being withdrawn from the market. Indeed the viability of such devices has been questioned by Apple's chief executive Tim Cook who stated that 'We always thought that glasses were not a smart move, from a point of view that people would not really want to wear them'.

Although wearables that are embedded into garments reduce the visibility of the device in question the danger is that this would restrict it to one garment. To this extent it would make sense for a modular system to be developed whereby some elements become a part of the garment, such as the root selection, and others could be switched between garments as the seasons or taste required. Given the importance of appropriately integrating its use into the lives of PLWD one would suspect that the device should be as unobtrusive as possible so as not to label the user. Being able to fit this technology into familiar clothing would also be a positive feature.

Whilst tracking was seen as benefit by some there are still ethical issues concerning this matter. This is often seen as a positive feature for carers, who have the reassurance of being able to locate the PLWD if something were to happen. It has been noted that the device could have a 'panic button' so that users could request assistance; but such feedback also prompts the question as to whether the device might make use of a timer, such that tracking could become active after an agreed period of time.

The issue of battery life has been examined and the fact that the interface does not make use of a LCD display dramatically increases this. In fact the reported battery life of tracking devices that are commercially available for PLWD can be up to a week of use. The use of active antenna with the GPS can increase power consumption because they have a built-in low-noise amplifier. To this extent it would need to be questioned whether increasing the degree of accuracy provided through the addition of an active antenna is worth sacrificing battery life. The issue of the devices use indoors does present issues. The devise is intended to be used by PLWD to make local journeys and increase their independence and to a large extent the assumption had been made that the device would be used to get to local amenities. At this stage the PLWD would not be driving or using public transport independently. As a result the larger 'mall' style shopping environments are not likely to be a destination however this does raise the issue of how destinations that possess multiple exits might be dealt with.

5 Conclusion

Although it is still an ongoing process, the initial stage of PPI (Patient and Public Involvement) evaluation has demonstrated a perceived value in the development of a wearable GPS system for PLWD. The development of such a system brings with it a range of issues that will benefit from user input and as always users should be at the center of the design process, although the extent to which this is possible is different when dealing with conditions such as dementia where the demands that are placed on participants needs particular consideration.

The issue of consent is also important given the ethical issues concerning the data generated by such devices. Such considerations also need go beyond the immediate issues such as the active tracking of PLWD. This is because GPS devices (including the one used) have data logging facilities hardcoded into the device that store location data every 15 s for approximately 16 h. However it is also clear that solutions can be created that ethically address the concerns of diverse interests, particularly if these concerns are tackled as a part of the design process rather than being a 'bolt on' consideration that is dealt with at a later date.

In many cases it's the case that 'innovation' foregrounds technology, in this instance a different approach was required. The move towards natural interfaces has often featured new technologies and arguably, it is often the case of technologies in search of a solution. The creation of natural interfaces should push technology to the background, so that as far as possible, the interface is not perceived. PLWD face particular challenges concerning processes that involve concentrating, planning or organization that mean any interface should ideally provide simple and direct options for the user. Although it might be argued that designing a wearable GPS system for PLWD is a special case, the use of any technology should advantage the user and place them and the things they are engaged with first, rather than making technology the center of attention. To this extent the lessons learnt when designing systems for PLWD might be of value to us all in our engagement with technology.

References

1. World Health Organization and Alzheimer's Disease International. Dementia: A public health priority (2012). http://www.who.int/mental_health/publications/dementia_report_2012/en

2. McKhann, G.M., Knopman, D.S., Chertkow, H., Hyman, B.T., Jack Jr., C.R., Kawas, C.H., Klunk, W.E., Koroschetz, W.J., Manly, J.J., Mayeux, R., Mohs, R,C., Morris, J.C., Rossor, M.N., Scheltens, P., Carrillo, M.C., Thies, B., Weintraub, S., Phelps, C.H.: The diagnosis of dementia due to Alzheimer's disease: Recommendations from the National Institute on Aging-Alzheimer's Association workgroups on diagnostic guidelines for Alzheimer's disease. In: Khachaturian, Z. (eds) Alzheimer's & Dementia, vol. 7(3), pp. 263–269. Elsevier, Amsterdam (2011)

3. Marshall, A., Spreadbury, J., Cheston, R., Coleman, P., Ballinger, C., Mullee, M., Pritchard, J., Russell, C., Bartlett, E.: A pilot randomised controlled trial to compare changes in quality of life for participants with early diagnosis dementia who attend a 'Living Well with Dementia' group compared to waiting-list control. In: Aging & Mental Health, online first, pp 1–10. Taylor and Francis (2014). http://www.tandfonline.com/doi/abs/10.1080/13607863.2014.954527#.VO7w-_msWSo

4. Hamer, M., Lavoie, K.L., Bacon, S.L.: Taking up physical activity in later life and health ageing: The English longitudinal study of ageing. Brit. J. Sports Med. **48**, 239–243 (2014) (BMJ Journals, London)

5. Alzheimer's Society. Exercise and physical activity for people with dementia (2011). http://www.alzheimers.org.uk/factsheet/529

6. Chu, D.C., Fox, K.R., Chen, L.J., Ku, P.W.: Components of late-life exercise and cognitive function: an 8-year longitudinal study. In: Prevention Science, vol. 10, pp. 1–10. Springer, Heidelberg (2014)

7. Wu, E., Barnes, D.E., Ackerman, S.L., Lee, J., Chesney, M., Mehling, W.E.: Preventing loss of independence through exercise (PLIE): Qualitative analysis of a clinical trial in older adults with dementia. In: Aging & Mental Health, vol. 19(4), pp. 1–10. Taylor and Francis (2014). http://www.tandfonline.com/doi/full/10.1080/13607863.2014.935290#abstract

8. Fox, B.B., Hodgkinson, B., Parker, D.: The effects of physical exercise on functional performance, quality of life, cognitive impairment and physical activity levels for older adults aged 65 years and older with a diagnosis of dementia: a systematic review. In: The JBI Database of Systematic Reviews and Implementation Reports, vol. 12(9), pp. 158–276. The JBI Database of Systematic Reviews and Implementation Reports, Adelaide (2014)

9. Stubbs, B., Eggermont, L., Soundy, A., Probst, M., Vandenbulcke, M., Vancampfort, D.: What are the factors associated with Physical Activity (PA) participation in community dwelling adults with dementia? A systematic review of PA correlates. In: Archives of Gerontology and Geriatrics, vol. 59(2), pp. 195–203. Elsevier, Amsterdam (2014)

10. http://www.alzheimers.org.uk/site/scripts/download_info.php?fileID=2256

11. http://www.ordnancesurvey.co.uk/business-and-government/help-and-support/navigation-technology/gps-beginners-guide.html

12. Landau, R., Werner, S.: Ethical aspects of using GPS for tracking people with dementia: recommendations for practice. In: Lautenschlager, N (eds) International Psychogeriatrics, vol. 24(3), pp. 358–366. Cambridge University Press, Cambridge (2012)

Understanding and Improving Collaborative Skills Among Individuals with ASD in a Distributed Virtual Environment

Arpan Sarkar[1], Joshua Wade[2(✉)], and Zachary Warren[3,4]

[1] University School of Nashville, Nashville, USA
[2] Electrical Engineering and Computer Science, Nashville, USA
joshua.w.wade@vanderbilt.edu
[3] Treatment and Research Institute for Autism Spectrum Disorders (TRIAD),
Nashville, USA
[4] Pediatrics, Psychiatry and Special Education, Vanderbilt University,
Nashville, TN 37212, USA

Abstract. Individuals with Autism Spectrum Disorders (ASD) evidence core impairments regarding social interaction and communication. These impairments can inhibit the ability of individuals with ASD from effectively engaging with peers and collaborating on goal-oriented tasks. Recently collaborative virtual environment (CVE) in which individuals with ASD can interact with one another or with a therapist to achieve some common goal has been proposed for social competence interventions (SCI) for these individuals. In this paper, we present the design of a distributed CVE for playing the classic video game pong to be used for SCI. This collaborative game can be played at several different modes ranging from one player against an artificial agent in one computer to two players against each other in two different computers. The system functionality and robustness were validated through a small user study. In the future, this CVE will be evaluated with children and adolescents with ASD.

Keywords: Collaborative Virtual Environment (CVE) · Autism Spectrum Disorder (ASD)

1 Introduction

The Centers for Disease Control and Prevention estimates 1 in 68 children in the United States has an Autism Spectrum Disorders (ASD) [1]. Individuals with ASD evidence core impairments regarding social interaction and communication [2–6]. These impairments can inhibit the ability of individuals with ASD from effectively engaging with peers and collaborating on goal-oriented tasks, which in terms can contribute to further social isolation, distress, and impairment. Various implementations of social competence interventions (SCI) have emerged that try to address this problem. Recently, many of these interventions have taken the form of a collaborative virtual environment (CVE) in which individuals with ASD interact with one another or with a therapist to achieve some common goal [7–11]. SCIs based on CVE technology are highly flexible and have some advantages over alternative intervention methods.

M. Antona and C. Stephanidis (Eds.): UAHCI 2015, Part III, LNCS 9177, pp. 669–680, 2015.
DOI: 10.1007/978-3-319-20684-4_64

Users of CVEs may communicate verbally or non-verbally with one another [12] with no restrictions on the physical distance between individuals and administrators as there are in clinic-based interventions. Personal interaction in CVEs may feel "safer" than in the real world for individuals with ASD [11], and CVEs are capable of creating interactive scenarios that would not otherwise be possible in the real world.

Recent work on SCIs using CVEs have utilized the strengths of CVEs to deliver targeted interventions to individuals with ASD. Stichter et al. [7] deployed iSocial: a distributed, 3D virtual learning environment which was designed as a SCI for individuals with ASD in a distance learning format. ISocial contained collaborative tasks including one in which students worked together to design and build a restaurant in the virtual world, requiring students to talk with one another and coordinate their actions in order to complete tasks. Hourcade et al. [8] designed an array of tablet-based activities designed to encourage social interaction and face-to-face collaboration among children with ASD. The activities provided on the tablets included drawing (to create and/or express how they feel), music authoring (to create different kinds of media), puzzle-solving (to test communication, collaboration, coordination, and visuo-spatial reasoning), and a photo-distorting app (to explore emotions on faces). Cheng et al. [10] developed a CVE aimed at increasing empathy in individuals with ASD by showing them scenarios intended to elicit empathic responses such as witnessing a person cutting in line or slipping and falling on the floor.

In this work, we present the design of a distributed CVE based on the game pong to understand and eventually improve the collaborative skills of individuals with ASD. The system that we designed records quantitative, objective data from users regarding measures of performance—both individual and collaborative—as well as conversation through recorded audio.

In this paper, we discuss the design decisions made in the development of this system as well as a series of validation tests of the system to ensure its correctness and efficiency. The remainder of the paper is organized as follows. Section 2 details the hierarchical, hybrid automata model of computation used in implementing the software. Section 3 discusses the preliminary evaluation of the system with volunteers. In Sect. 4, we provide the results from both the throughput analysis and the validation study. Section 5 concludes the paper with a discussion of the limitations of the current system and proposed future work.

2   System Design

2.1   Overview

Pong is a classic video game with a simple interface and is based on the game of ping pong in which two players use paddles to hit a ball back and forth trying to cause their opponent to miss the ball. Figure 1 shows an example pong interface. We selected pong as the basis for a collaborative game because it is simple to understand, easy to implement, and offers a variety of ways in which collaboration can be introduced into the game. We chose to implement the element of collaboration through the control of a single game paddle by more than one user—two users in this case. The subsections that follow elaborate on the design of gameplay, overall architecture, models of computation used to create system components, and our method of converting the models into software.

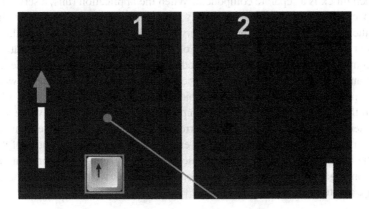

Fig. 1. Basic pong interface

2.2 Game Design

Our version of the pong game consists of a collection of *matches* which we refer to as a *session*. A match is defined as an interval of time beginning when the ball is deployed and ending when one player misses the ball. Sessions can be played in one of several different types of *configurations*. The following configurations were implemented: (1) single human *vs.* artificially intelligent agent (AI) on a single PC, (2) human team *vs.* AI on a single PC, (3) human team *vs.* AI on separate PCs, (4) human *vs.* human on a single PC, and finally (5) human *vs.* human on separate PCs. Matches in a session are presented sequentially with a 3 s countdown before the match starts and a period of feedback following the end of a match. This feedback is presented as both text and audio and either congratulates the player for scoring, encourages them if they do not score, or remains neutral in the event of a draw.

The AI was designed with three different difficulty settings: easy, medium and hard. In the easy setting, the AI follows an oscillating trajectory based on the triangle wave function with a period of 2 s (1).

$$p(t) = 2(-1)^{\left|t+\frac{1}{2}\right|}\left(t - \left|t + \frac{1}{2}\right|\right) \tag{1}$$

This behavior is considered easy because the AI effectively demonstrates random movement without any consideration of the ball's trajectory. In the medium and hard settings, the AI predicts the destination of the incoming ball and moves towards this goal with a speed controlled by a scalar k and a linear interpolation function l_2, where the value of k is larger in the hard setting (i.e., faster) and smaller in medium setting (i.e., slower). In order to guarantee that the AI fails to reach the goal occasionally, a random error within a reasonable range was applied to the calculation of the goal position.

2.3   Architecture

There are several components of this work which comprise the overall application architecture. Figure 2 gives a representation of the architecture as a block diagram where each block is a separate component. When the application runs, a server or client role is specified. The blocks shaded in grey are executed only when the role chosen is that of the server and are disabled otherwise. The Main Controller is the central component of the application—regardless of role—and handles synchronization of all the adjacent components. The Network Module takes on the behavior of either a server or client and manages all sending and receiving of messages over the network. The messages passed over the network are objects serialized as JSON strings. Messages sent from the client to the server contain input from the human player while messages from the server to the client contain the current state of the CVE. The Session Manager executes in either server or client role and ensures that the client instances of the CVE reflect the true state of the server instance. In the System Configuration Module, information regarding IP addresses and port numbers as well as the session configuration to execute is specified.

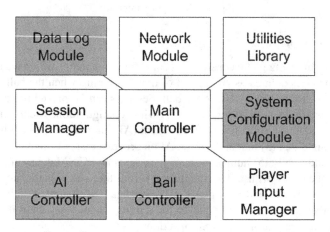

Fig. 2. Block diagram of the overall architecture (server-exclusive components shaded in grey)

The remaining components' functions should be evident based on their names. The Data Log Module records several different types of data. Time series data including the velocity and position of the ball, velocity and position of both paddles, and player input are recorded with a timestamp at the fastest possible rate. Data related to various predefined events are also logged such as at the beginning and ending of matches, at the beginning and ending of feedback, and for collisions of the ball with other objects. In addition, audio is recorded from two separate microphones for offline analysis of speech. The Ball Controller simply updates the position of the ball during matches while the AI Controller updates the position of the AI player. The Player Input manager obtains player input on the client side and applies changes to the player's paddle on the server side.

2.4 Models of Computation (MoC)

The nontrivial components of the system were first modeled using formal models of computation (MoC) and then converted to software. The latter step is discussed in the next subsection. The MoCs chosen were finite state machines (FSM) and hybrid automata (HA). More specifically, the FSMs in this system are composed hierarchically in what is referred to as a hierarchical state machine (HSM). The syntaxes for FSMs, HSMs and HA used here are in the style found in Lee and Seshia [13]. Since there are so many components of this architecture, a full description of each one is not possible, so we instead focus on the MoCs involved in the AI player's behavior.

At a certain level of abstraction, the AI has only three distinct states: (1) idle because the match has not started, (2) idle because the match configuration type is human *vs.* human, and (3) playing. This behavior is captured formally in the FSM shown in Fig. 3. The initial state *GameNotStarted* indicates that a match has not yet begun and the AI is idle. The state *GameStartedAgentPlaying* is arrived at when a match begins *and* the match configuration type is not human *vs.* human. Conversely, the FSM transitions to *GameStartedAgentNotPlaying* if a match begins and the match configuration type *is* human *vs.* human. If a match ends while the FSM state is either *GameStartedAgentPlaying* or *GameStartedAgentNotPlaying*, then the FSM transitions back to the *GameNotStarted* state and remains there until the next match begins.

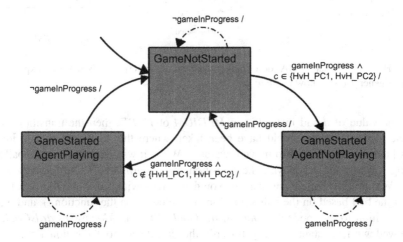

Fig. 3. FSM defining the general behavior of the AI player

Of course, this level of abstraction does not capture all of the complex behavior of the AI such as how it behaves under different difficulty settings or when the ball's trajectory changes and the AI must re-calculate its goal position. For this level of detail, we designed the HA shown in Fig. 4 which is an expansion of the AI's FSM state *GameStartedAgentPlaying*. Upon entering the HA in Fig. 4, a junction determines which transition is taken first based on the specified difficulty level d. If d is equal to the value *EASY*, then the transition to the discrete mode named *Oscillating* is taken and the AI follows the triangle wave trajectory described earlier. While in this mode, the velocity of the AI is constant $[v(t) = 1]$ and—as with all of the discrete modes in this particular HA—the rate of change of time is assumed to be constant as well $[\dot{s}(t) = 1]$.

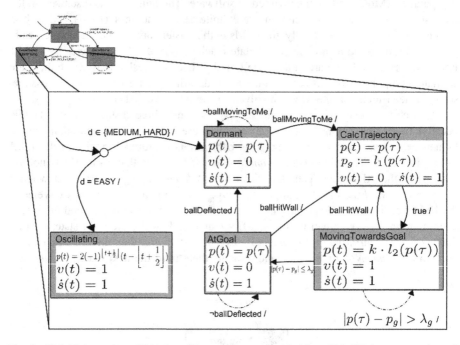

Fig. 4. Hybrid Automaton (HA) describing movement of AI player. This HA is an expansion of the more general FSM shown in Fig. 3.

If the value of d had instead been *MEDIUM* or *HARD*, then the transition to the discrete mode *Dormant* would have been taken where the AI would remain idle $[v(t) = 0]$ until the ball began to move towards it. When it was detected that the ball was moving towards the AI player, the transition from *Dormant* to *CalcTrajectory* was taken. Within *CalcTrajectory*, the AI would predict—with some random error—the path of the ball based on the ball's position and velocity via the function l_1, and would then transition to the mode *MovingTowardsGoal*. While in *MovingTowardsGoal*, the AI moved with constant velocity towards the calculated goal position until it was within some small distance threshold λ_g of the goal. Once arrived at the goal, the AI would remain there until either the ball was deflected successfully or the ball's direction changed due to hitting a wall.

The hierarchy shown in Fig. 4 is only a small view of the total hierarchy involved in the system. At the highest level there is the Main Controller's FSM which includes states for obtaining the network role from the user as well as starting and stopping sessions. Below the Main Controller's FSM is the Session Manager's FSM whose states deal with setting up matches, performing the match countdown, executing the match, and giving feedback. All of the AI behavior is below the Session Manager's FSM. Next we describe how we implemented this 4-layer HSM in software.

2.5   Implementation

The authors used their own method of converting formal MoCs into programming code. A base class called *Automaton* maintained state variables and provided a state transition function:

```
public class Automaton {
  private int m_currState;
    ⋮
  public void Transition( int NextState ) {
    m_currState = NextState;
  }
}
```

Each formal MoC was then implemented as a derived instance of this *Automaton* object. For example, the HA shown in Fig. 4 was defined thusly:

```
public class MotionPlanningAutomaton : Automaton {
  public const int DORMANT = 0;
  public const int CALCULATING_TRAJECTORY = 1;
  public const int MOVING_TOWARDS_GOAL = 2;
  public const int AT_GOAL = 3;
  public const int OSCILLATING = 4;

  public MotionPlanningAutomaton() : base() {
    this.Transition(DORMANT); //default transition
  }
}
```

In most cases, each MoC was implemented in a separate file in order to maximize isolation which simplified the development process. The logic of each MoC was written in an if-then-else branching structure and was updated at the fastest rate that the system would allow. All of the code was written in C# using the Unity3D game engine (www.unity3d.com).

Figure 5 shows a stack of graphs which give the state values of the HSM from the AI's motion planning HA up to the Main Controller's FSM during a sample run of the system. A selection of discrete events is represented by the vertical lines. Table 1 gives details about the events as well as the responses of each relevant component of the system due to the events. The reader can see clearly from the graph that between events e_2 and e_3, the AI player is performing the triangle wave oscillating behavior. From event e_7 until the end of the graph, the AI player is using the intelligent method of play where it moves based on the ball's trajectory.

3   Procedures

3.1   Network Throughput Analysis

In order to assess the reliability and performance of the system, we analyzed the network throughput of the system defined here as the number of serviced requests from

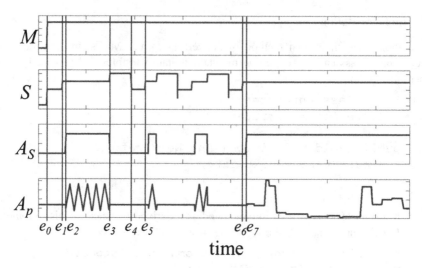

Fig. 5. AI Behavior HSM state values over time: the Main Controller FSM (M), Session Manager FSM (S), general agent FSM (A_S), and agent position (A_p).

Table 1. Events corresponding to HSM output graph in Fig. 5

Event	Description of system changes
e_0	M: session begins
	S: match countdown begins
e_1	S: countdown complete and match begins (*EASY* match)
e_2	A_S: AI becomes active
	A_p: AI begins **oscillating** trajectory
e_3	S: match ends and feedback begins
	A_S: AI becomes inactive
	A_p: AI stops moving
e_4	S: feedback done and countdown starts again
e_5	S: countdown complete and match begins (*EASY* match)
e_6	S: countdown complete and match begins (*MEDIUM* match)
e_7	A_S: AI becomes active
	A_p: AI begins **intelligent** trajectory

the perspective of the client(s) during regular gameplay. In order to provide a smooth experience to users, the update rate on the client side needed to be sufficiently fast so as not to show lag—in gaming, this value is often 60 frames per second (FPS), but can be as low as 30 FPS. We performed this analysis on two different network configurations: (1) a server and client running on the same PC, and (2) a server and client running on one PC while another client ran on a second PC. Note that there is no requirement that the server must be run on the same PC as any client. Both PCs had 3.7 GHz processors with at least 20 GB of RAM and NVIDIA Quadro K600 GPUs. Each configuration type was evaluated 5 times each and the results are presented in Sect. 4.

3.2 Human Validation Study

A small validation study was conducted with 2 pairs of volunteers—3 females (age, M 25.7 y, SD 1.7 y) and 1 male (age, 25)—to verify that the system was robust and complete. Each of the participants first completed a practice session consisting of 9 matches in which he/she played against the artificial agent to become acclimated to the system. Predetermined pairs of participants then completed a collaborative session on the same PC followed by a collaborative session on separate PCs. The goal was, contrary to the original pong game where each player plays to defeat his/her opponent, to play collaboratively with one's partner to defeat the AI player. All three sessions consisted of 9 matches with 3 easy, 3 medium, and 3 hard match difficulties. For side-by-side collaborative play, both participants sat at the same computer and shared a keyboard to control the paddle. One person used the up and down arrow keys of the keyboard to control the paddle while the other used the "W" and "S" keys. For collaborative play on 2 separate PCs, participants sat at adjacent desks and could speak to one another. In both types of collaborative play, 2 separate directional microphone devices captured the speech of the participants.

4 Results and Discussion

4.1 Network Throughput Analysis Results

Table 2 gives the results of the two analyses of the network throughput. In both cases, all of the involved clients demonstrated a throughput rate sufficiently high enough to avoid any noticeable image stuttering or lag. Since Client 1 ran on the same PC as the server in both evaluations, it had a very high throughput rate greater than 300 Hz while Client 2, which ran on a separate PC, had a throughput rate just under 60 Hz.

4.2 Human Validation Results

Table 3 gives the results of the user validation study for individual practice and collaboration for the two pairs of participants. Participants P0 and P1 performed comparatively well both individually and collaboratively. Nothing can be generalized from this small dataset, but it seems reasonable that player performance would drop from individual play to collaborative play since the sense of control is lessened. The player score indicates the number of times that the AI player failed to deflect the ball. Similarly, AI score indicates the number of times that the human player or players were unable to deflect the ball. A draw occurred if, after 1 min of play, no player, neither the human player(s) nor the AI player, scored.

Table 2. Network throughput rates in Hz

Trial number	Single client	Two clients	
	Client 1*	Client 1*	Client 2
1	340.14	319.85	59.83
2	327.25	309.86	59.65
3	339.94	318.63	59.84
4	344.12	275.08	59.88
5	341.55	332.48	57.20
Mean	338.60	311.19	59.28
SD	6.56	21.74	1.17

*Executed on the same PC as the server.

Table 3. User performance results

	P0	P1	P2	P3	P0, P1 Collaboration		P2, P3 Collaboration	
	Individual practice				Same PC	Diff. PC	Same PC	Diff. PC
Player Score	6	6	3	2	3	4	3	4
AI Score	3	2	5	7	3	3	6	4
Draws	0	1	1	0	3	2	0	1

4.3 Discussion

The network throughput analysis results provide significant evidence that the system is fast enough to handle one or two clients and therefore all of our proposed gameplay configurations. In fact, scaling up the number of clients in the future would likely contribute to relatively minor declines in system performance. The sample used for the validation test is obviously too small to draw any performance-related conclusions from, but it does show that our system is capable of collecting the data needed in order to assess whether an individual's performance varies when playing alone or in a team as well as whether the various configuration types affect performance.

5 Conclusion

We have developed a distributed CVE, based on the video game pong, to understand, analyze, and eventually address the collaborative and communicative skills of individuals with ASD. This system records quantitative and objective data regarding both individual and collaborative performance through analysis of recorded audio and gameplay.

There were some limitations regarding the experiment. First, we conducted a small user study with typically developed individuals to validate the system, but they are not the target group for this research. Second, we only implemented one form of input for the paddle (i.e., keyboard-based). And third, we used a wired connection for recording audio. In future work, we intend to address all of these issues. We plan to conduct a pilot user study on individuals with ASD, in order to determine differences in collaborative gameplay from that of typically developed individuals and also to determine any long-term effect that our system has on the collaborative skills of individuals with ASD. We intend to add other forms of input besides keyboard, such as joysticks or mobile devices (i.e., iPhone, Android, etc.). We also aim to implement some form of audio streaming to allow increased separation, while playing collaboratively, between participants in experiments. In addition, we intend to implement a "rally" mode which would allow a more sophisticated kind of collaboration game, instead of pure competitive gameplay. A rally mode would involve two players, each controlling their own paddle, playing with each other, instead of against each other, and the goal would be to continuously pass the ball from paddle to paddle. In this scenario, to succeed, users would have to accurately gauge their paddle movements and the effect their actions will have on the other player. We believe that this will provide highly accurate data regarding participation and collaboration between users.

Acknowledgment. This work was supported in part by the National Institute of Health Grant 1R01MH091102-01A1, National Science Foundation Grant 0967170 and the Hobbs Society Grant from the Vanderbilt Kennedy Center.

References

1. Wingate, M., Kirby, R.S., Pettygrove, S., Cunniff, C., Schulz, E., Ghosh, T., Robinson, C., Lee, L.C., Landa, R., Constantino, J., Fitzgerald, R., Zahorodny, W., Daniels, J., Nicholas, J., Charles, J., McMahon, W., Bilder, D., Durkin, M., Baio, J., Christensen, D., Van, N. Braun, K., Clayton, H., Goodman, A., Doernberg, N., Yeargin-Allsopp, M., Monitoring, A. D.D.: Prevalence of autism spectrum disorder among children aged 8 years - autism and developmental disabilities monitoring network, 11 Sites, United States, 2010. Mmwr Surveillance Summaries, vol. 63, March 28 2014

2. Senju, A., Johnson, M.H.: Atypical eye contact in autism: models, mechanisms and development. Neurosci. & Biobehav. Rev. 33, 1204–1214 (2009)

3. Bekele, E., Crittendon, J., Zheng, Z., Swanson, A., Weitlauf, A., Warren, Z., Sarkar, N.: Assessing the utility of a virtual environment for enhancing facial affect recognition in adolescents with autism. J. Autism Dev. Disord. 44, 1641–1650 (2014)

4. Bekele, E., Zheng, Z., Swanson, A., Crittendon, J., Warren, Z., Sarkar, N.: Understanding how adolescents with autism respond to facial expressions in virtual reality environments. IEEE Trans. Vis. Comput. Graph. 19, 711–720 (2013)

5. Lahiri, U., Bekele, E., Dohrmann, E., Warren, Z., Sarkar, N.: Design of a virtual reality based adaptive response technology for children with autism. IEEE Trans. Neural Syst. Rehabil. Eng. 21, 55–64 (2013)

6. Kuriakose, S., Sarkar, N., Lahiri, U.: A step towards an intelligent human computer interaction: physiology-based affect-recognizer. In: 2012 4th International Conference on Intelligent Human Computer Interaction (IHCI), pp. 1–6 (2012)

7. Stichter, J.P., Laffey, J., Galyen, K., Herzog, M.: iSocial: Delivering the social competence intervention for adolescents (SCI-A) in a 3D virtual learning environment for youth with high functioning autism. J. Autism Dev. Disord. 44, 417–430 (2014)

8. Hourcade, J.P., Bullock-Rest, N.E., Hansen, T.E.: Multitouch tablet applications and activities to enhance the social skills of children with autism spectrum disorders. Pers. Ubiquit. Comput. 16, 157–168 (2012)

9. Montoya, M.M., Massey, A.P., Lockwood, N.S.: 3D collaborative virtual environments: exploring the link between collaborative behaviors and team performance. Decis. Sci. **42**, 451–476 (2011)
10. Cheng, Y., Chiang, H.-C., Ye, J., Cheng, L.-H.: Enhancing empathy instruction using a collaborative virtual learning environment for children with autistic spectrum conditions. Comput. & Educ. **55**, 1449–1458 (2010)
11. Cheng, Y., Moore, D., McGrath, P., Fan, Y.: Collaborative virtual environment technology for people with autism. In: Fifth IEEE International Conference on Advanced Learning Technologies, ICALT 2005, pp. 247–248 (2005)
12. Nguyen, T.T.H., Fleury, C., Duval, T.: Collaborative exploration in a multi-scale shared virtual environment. In: 2012 IEEE Symposium on 3D User Interfaces (3DUI), pp. 181–182 (2012)
13. Lee, E.A., Seshia, S.A.: Introduction to embedded systems: A cyber-physical systems approach. Lee & Seshia (2011)

Presence of Autism Spectrum Disorders in University Students: Implications for Education and HCI

Debra Satterfield[1(✉)], Christopher Lepage[2], and Nora Ladjahasan[3]

[1] California State University Long Beach, Long Beach, CA, USA
debrasatterfield@gmail.com
[2] Sutter Neuroscience Institute, Sacramento, CA, USA
[3] Iowa State University, Ames, IA, USA

Abstract. The Center for Disease Control (CDC) in 2014 estimates a prevalence rate of 1 in 68 for persons with an autism spectrum disorder (ASD). It is five times as prevalent in boys than girls and crosses all racial, ethnic and socioeconomic groups [1]. Therefore, there is a critical need for the HCI community to better understand the educational and informational needs for persons with ASD. This research identifies persons with ASD in higher education using a recognized autism diagnostic tool and correlates that data to their gender, major field of study, and their indicated preferences with regard to course content, content delivery preferences, and evaluation strategies. The significance of this information applies both to students in HCI who are on the autism spectrum and to university educators with regard to the design of educational materials and courses suitable for both students with and without ASD to achieve academic success.

Keywords: Autism · Academic success · Engineering · Design · Higher education

1 Introduction

An initial pilot study of 19 (n) graduate students from Human Computer Interaction (HCI), Graphic Design, and Engineering at Iowa State University in spring 2013 identified a 21.1 % rate of autism in that population based on the Ritvo Autism Asperger Diagnostic Scale-Revised (RAADS-R.) Scores above the threshold score of 65 are considered indicative of an autism spectrum disorder [2]. In addition, in this study those students above this threshold showed preferences for specific types of course design, content delivery methods and evaluation strategies distinctly different from those who scored below this threshold.

Therefore, **there is a critical need to identify university students with personality traits associated with ASD who are enrolled in higher education and better understand their educational and information needs** regarding best practices in curriculum design and course delivery methods. This second phase of research was sent to the entire student body of university students. This survey found 41.1 % of the graduate and undergraduate students who responded met or exceeded RAADS-R

© Springer International Publishing Switzerland 2015
M. Antona and C. Stephanidis (Eds.): UAHCI 2015, Part III, LNCS 9177, pp. 681–688, 2015.
DOI: 10.1007/978-3-319-20684-4_65

cut-off scores for autism phenotype. This observation and the current national CDC prevalence rate for ASD prompted this study.

2   Methodology

Approximately 33,241 students ages 18-years and older from eight colleges at Iowa State University were contacted by email for possible inclusion in this SurveyMonkey study. Demographic information was provided by each student. At their own time, location, and pace, the students evaluated preferred course content, delivery methods, and course evaluation techniques. Preferences were rated on a likert scale (1 being not preferred to 5 highly preferred).

They also completed the RAADS-R self-assessment (63 symptom-based questions and 17 non-symptom based responses). ASD traits were measured by the student's score on the 80 question RAADS-R survey tool. A reliability test was done. The overall Cronbach's alpha was .94 which is highly acceptable. A RAADS-R score of 65 and higher is consistent with ASD. Respondent RAADS-R scores were used to establish two unique groups 1) RAADS-R score $\geq$ 65, consistent with ASD traits and 2) RAADS-R score < 65, inconsistent with ASD traits.

University IRB Requirement. Full approval was obtained from the Iowa State University Institutional Review Board (IRB).

2.1   Hypothesis

Students enrolled in the Human Computer Interaction (HCI), Graphic Design, or Engineering university programs may show preferences for course content and delivery methods that vary according to their RAADS-R scores and other variables such as gender and major. Therefore the following hypothesis were developed:

H1: Some university students will have RAADS-R scores of 65 and higher indicating a presence of ASD associated personality traits.
H2: University students will exhibit unique and definable personality traits based on a RAADS-R scale and those traits will vary predictably according to their degree programs or majors and gender.
H3: University students will exhibit different preferences in course delivery methods based on two groups as identified by the RAADS-R of those scoring at or above the research-validated threshold of 65 and those scoring below.

2.2   Procedure/Data Analysis

Each student was asked to evaluate their preference in university courses based on delivery methods (i.e. face-to-face, online, group discussion, video recording, etc.), type of assignments (i.e. individual vs. group, topic selection, who determines the timeline and completion of assignments), and student learning evaluation techniques.

All of these issues were rated in a likert scale (from 1 to 5; 1 being not preferred to 5 highly preferred).

Students completed a self-assessment via the RAADS-R. Based on the scoring criteria discussed in the original RAADS-R publication, the symptom-based questions were coded as follows: 0 = never true; 1 = true only when I was young; 2 = Only true now; and 3 = True now and when I was young. The non-symptom based responses or normal behavior questions were coded reversely (i.e. 3 = never true, 2 = True only when I was young, 1 = Only true now and 0 = True now and when I was young). The RAADS-R survey instrument measures four scales: social relatedness, circumscribed interest, sensory-motor, and social anxiety.

3   Results

The survey generated 653 responses (226 males, 420 females). The mean RAADS-R score, for males was 74.8, for females 61.2. All scores combined ranged from 4 to 215 with a standard deviation of 37.9. The mode was 57. Based on a T-Test, no significant relationship was shown in the demographic data for the variables of age and employment.

Findings for H1. H1 hypothesized that high rates of university students will have RAADS-R scores of 65 and higher, indicating previously unidentified presence of ASD associated personality traits. Of the 653 respondents, 204 had a RAADS-R at or above the threshold score of 65, thus indicating a dramatic trend (44.1 %) toward ASD phenotype in at least those that completed this online survey. This supports the support the first hypothesis.

Findings for H2. H2 hypothesized that university students exhibiting ASD personality based traits will vary predictably according to: (1) degree track and college major; and (2) gender.

Findings by Degree Track and College Major. Students scoring above the RAADS-R threshold were present in all colleges. This finding is inconsistent with the hypothesis that specific major tracks or colleges would have higher prevalence. However, mean scores above the RAADS-R threshold were present in two colleges and the HCI program. The mean scores were: Human Computer Interaction (HCI), 76.14; Engineering College, 74.51; and Design College, 71.82. The graduate college also had a mean score higher than the RAADS-R threshold at 69.70. The colleges with mean RAADS-R scores below the ASD threshold were Liberal Arts and Sciences (LAS), 64.28; Human Sciences, 59.37; Agriculture, 58.16; Veterinary Medicine, 57.54; and Business, 55.55. Based on college data, of those students with a RAADS-R score above the threshold of 65, Engineering had a significantly higher mean score (.05 level) at 109.34 over Human Sciences at 88.95.

Findings by Gender. Based on gender, males had a higher mean score (significant at .01 level) of 74.84 over the mean score of females at 61.23. The male mean score exceeded the ASD threshold while the female mean score did not. In addition, of only those students with a RAADS-R score above the threshold of 65, males had higher mean threshold score at 107.08 compared to females with a mean threshold score of 95.2. Males also had higher scores on each of the subscales created based on RAADs scoring with the one exception of the social anxiety scale which did not showing a statistically significant difference between mean gender scores (Fig. 1).

RAADS-R sub-scale comparisons by gender

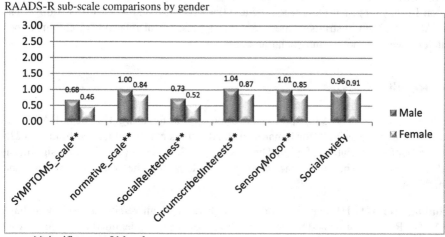

**significant at .01 level
*significant at .05 level

Fig. 1. Mean RAADS-R score based on gender across the RAADS-R sub-scales

Lecture and Discussion Preferences by Gender. Females showed a preference over males at a .05 level (Fig. 2) for group discussions through e-mail or blogs. Males showed a preference over females at a .01 level for real time discussions via Skype or live video both with peer groups and with their professor over females. Males also showed a preference at .01 level over females for phone calls with the professor. Both males and females indicated a higher preference for face-to-face interactions over other online or other asynchronous interaction methods.

When just considering gender, females showed a preference (at the .01 level) over males (Fig. 3) for individual projects, projects where students can select their own research topics, and professor assigned deadlines. Males showed a similarly significant (at the .01 level) preference for group projects over female students.

Once again when just considering gender, males showed a preference (significant at the .01 level) over females for designing physical models for assignments (Fig. 4), delivering team presentations of project research, delivering live presentations of projects, and phone or skype class discussions. Females showed a similarly significant preference over males for writing papers on assigned topics (Fig. 5).

Findings for H3. H3 hypothesized that University students scoring at or above the RAADS-R research-validated threshold of 65 will exhibit different preferences in course delivery than those scoring below 65, regardless of other demographics.

Lecture and class discussion method comparisons by gender

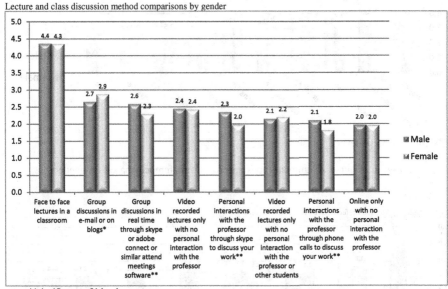

**significant at .01 level
*significant at .05 level

Fig. 2. Lecture and class discussion method preferences based on gender.

Student directed project content and deadlines

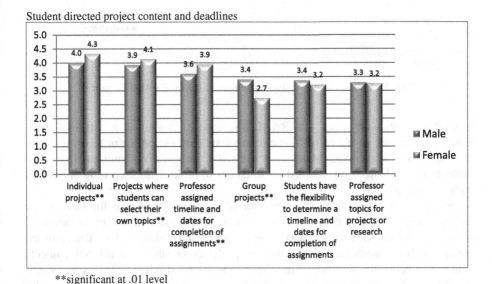

**significant at .01 level

Fig. 3. Preferences in course assignment groups and timelines based on gender assignment and project Preferences based on gender

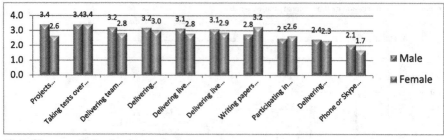

**significant at .01 level

Fig. 4. Course assignment types and format preferences based on gender

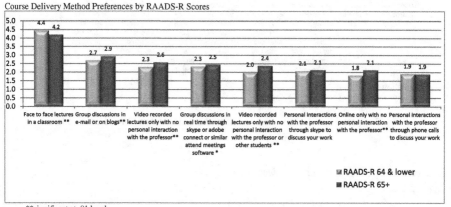

**significant at .01 level
*significant at .05 level

Fig. 5. Course content delivery methods based on RAADS-R scores

In content evaluation, males with RAADS-R score ≥ 65 showed a statistically significant preference on phone or Skype discussions with the professor to demonstrate the knowledge acquisition. Males also showed a statistically significant ($p < .05$) preference over females on recorded presentations of projects/research without any live audience present (Fig. 6).

Students with a RAADS-R score over 65 had less preference for face-to-face lectures in a classroom than did students who scored 64 and below. In addition, students with a RAADS-R of 65 and above had more of a preference for video recorded lectures with no interactions with either the professor or other students than students who scored below this threshold. Those scoring above 65 also had more of a preference for skype and other online meeting rooms for course meetings than did students who scored 64 and below. All of these findings were significant at the .05 level.

Deadlines and Timetables. Students with a RAADS-R score above 65 showed a greater preference to have deadlines and timetables given to them by their professor

Course Evaluation Method Preferences by RAADS-R Scores

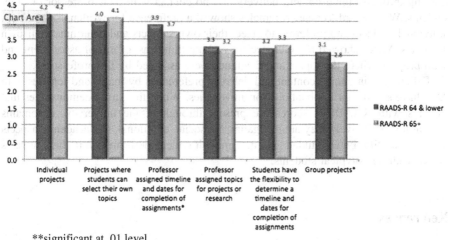

**significant at .01 level
*significant at .05 level

Fig. 6. Course evaluation preferences based on RAADS-R scores

rather than imposing their own deadlines. They also preferred group projects. These were both significant at the .05 level.

Students with scores above the RAADS-R threshold had less preference (statistically significant at the .05 level) for both professor assigned deadlines and for group projects.

4 Discussion

This research identified that persons with ASD were present in every college in this university. The programs of HCI, Engineering, Graduate College, and Design were identified as having the highest mean scores on the RAADS-R assessment. Interestingly, these programs all have significant involvement in many HCI degree programs. Therefore, there is a critical need for the HCI community to better understand the educational and informational needs of persons with ASD. In addition, significant differences were identified between males and females with regard to course content, delivery methods, and assessment strategies. These differences are of specific interest to programs that have a high number of students of one gender over the other such as engineering or industrial design. It is unclear if these differences impact academic success and further study needs to be done.

Lecture and Class Discussion Implications. In general, males and females rated face-to-face lectures higher than other forms of online communication such as blogs, e-mail, Skype, and phone calls. However, students who scored above the RAADS-R threshold for ASD consistently showed a statistically significant preference at the .01 level for online content delivery methods over those students who scored below the threshold. Students with a RAADS-R above 65 showed a greater preference for online learning through digital content delivery and no contact with their professor or other students. With regard to gender, females showed a preference for written assignments, individual projects and preferred to select their own subjects and determine their own deadlines. Males showed a preference for making things as a form of assessment and team projects where the topics and deadlines were assigned by the professor.

Differences in course content and delivery preferences by males and females with ASD have significant implications for universities. While this study demonstrates that students with RAADS-R scores are present throughout the university, it remains unclear how effectively they are navigating the social, emotional, and academic aspects of university life. Future studies will determine if college performance in these areas is on par with neurotypical students.

References

1. Center for Disease Control and Prevention (2014). http://www.cdc.gov/ncbddd/autism/data.html
2. Ritvo, R., Ritvo, E., Guthrie, D., Ritvo, M., Hufnagel, D., McMahon, W., Tonge, B., Mataix-Cols, D., Jassi, A., Attwood, T., Eloff, J.: The Ritvo Autism A sperger Diagnostic Scale-Revised (RAADS-R): a Scale to Assess the Diagnosis of Autism Spectrum Disorder in Adults: An International Validation Study. J. Autism Dev. Disord. **41**, 1076–1089 (2011)

A Virtual Reality Driving Environment for Training Safe Gaze Patterns: Application in Individuals with ASD

Joshua Wade[1(✉)], Dayi Bian[1], Jing Fan[1], Lian Zhang[1], Amy Swanson[2], Medha Sarkar[5], Amy Weitlauf[2,3], Zachary Warren[2,3], and Nilanjan Sarkar[1,4]

[1] Electrical Engineering and Computer Science, Nashville, USA
{joshua.w.wade,nilanjan.sarkar}@vanderbilt.edu
[2] Treatment and Research Institute for Autism Spectrum Disorders (TRIAD), Nashville, USA
[3] Pediatrics, Psychiatry and Special Education, Nashville, USA
[4] Mechanical Engineering, Vanderbilt University, Nashville, TN 37212, USA
[5] Computer Science, Middle Tennessee State University, Murfreesboro, TN 37132, USA

Abstract. It has been well established that adolescents with Autism Spectrum Disorders (ASD) present social and behavioral characteristics that differ significantly from those of their peers without ASD. A growing number of recent studies have begun to look closely at automobile operation characteristics in individuals diagnosed with ASD. Some of this work has suggested that certain driving behaviors demonstrated by those with ASD may pose significant safety concerns to both themselves and other drivers. Expanding on previous work, we designed and tested a gaze-contingent driving intervention system in which drivers were required to not only perform well, but also to look at key regions of interest in the environment such as traffic lights, stop signs, pedestrians and side-view mirrors. We present preliminary results from a study comparing performance outcomes and eye gaze patterns in a group using the gaze-contingent system and a group using a gaze-insensitive, performance-based system.

Keywords: Virtual reality · Eye gaze · Autism intervention

1 Introduction

The steady increase in the rate of diagnosis of Autism Spectrum Disorders (ASD) in the United States continues to persist. The Centers for Disease Control and Prevention released figures in 2014 suggesting this rate is now 1 in 68 children [1]. It has been well established that adolescents with ASD present social and behavioral characteristics that differ significantly from those of their peers without ASD. To note just a few of the more widely known examples, individuals with ASD may have trouble with motor coordination tasks [2], perform repetitive motions like rocking back and forth [3], and avoid eye contact during communication with others [4].

A growing number of recent studies have begun to look closely at automobile operation characteristics in individuals diagnosed with ASD [5–11]. Some of this work has suggested that certain driving behaviors demonstrated by those with ASD may pose significant safety concerns to both themselves and other drivers [5, 6, 9]. Two studies

© Springer International Publishing Switzerland 2015
M. Antona and C. Stephanidis (Eds.): UAHCI 2015, Part III, LNCS 9177, pp. 689–697, 2015.
DOI: 10.1007/978-3-319-20684-4_66

reported finding gaze patterns among individuals with ASD that differed significantly from TD controls that may be problematic for optimally safe driving [7, 10]. Specifically, the average gaze positions of individuals with ASD, compared to controls, tended towards the top of the driving viewing area as well as further to the right. Reimer *et al.* [7] offered potential explanations for these patterns: (1) the vertical difference in gaze may be the result of relocating one's gaze from areas of higher complexity (e.g., the roadway with cars coming and going) to areas of lower complexity (e.g., the sky), and (2) the horizontal difference may result from the driver being distracted by objects such as buildings and parked cars, since they are nearer to the driver than those on the left side of the road. Our previous research [10] comparing driving performance and gaze-patterns of people with ASD to TD controls, found this same pattern of gaze in the ASD sample. In addition, our previous work showed that ASD participants performed significantly higher numbers of driving errors than their TD peers, warranting the investigation of a possible link between driving performance and eye gaze patterns.

We tried to answer this question by creating a task-based, driving simulation system in which users cannot progress through tasks without looking at objects identified as key regions of interest (ROI) *in addition* to driving without performance errors. We expanded on our previous driving simulation platform (Fig. 1) to create such a system. In this paper, we present the design of the proposed system as well as preliminary results from a user study comparing two groups: one where task-progression depended on both performance and proper eye gaze, and another group in which task-progression depended only on performance. The rest of this paper is organized as follows. Section 2 discusses the process of expanding our previous system to produce the new gaze-contingent system. Section 3 describes the experimental procedure of the comparison study and Sect. 4 assesses the preliminary results of this study. Section 5 concludes the paper with a review of both the contributions and limitations of this work as well as future directions for this research.

Fig. 1. A typical example of the driving interface

2   System Design

The system presented in this paper is an extension of our previous work [10, 11] with two major updates. The current system now includes a gaze-contingent operating mode in which the user must not only perform driving tasks without error, but he/she must also look at key regions of the environment while driving. Failing to look at these regions will result in a failure of that particular trial. The second update to this system is the integration of an electroencephalography (EEG) data acquisition module that logs brain activity information from the user during driving sessions. We focus our discussion in this section on these new developments.

2.1   System Components

There were five major components of the system that we developed. We refer to these as the VR driving module (VDM), gaze data acquisition module (GDM), physiological data acquisition module (PDM), EEG data acquisition module (EDM), and observation-based assessment module (OAM). The overall architecture is shown in Fig. 2. The VDM ran the driving simulation program and managed networking with all of the other modules. The GDM, PDM, and EDM each logged relevant participant data at 120 Hz, 1000 Hz, and 128 Hz, respectively. The OAM managed a program for logging an observer's subjective assessment regarding a driver's affective state in real time.

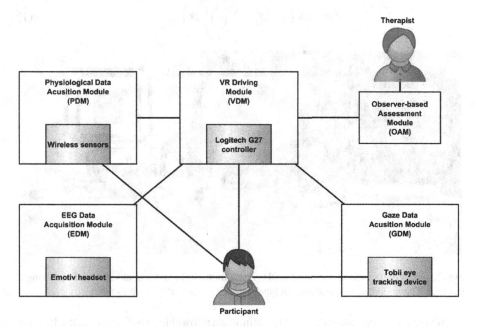

Fig. 2. Overall architecture of the driving platform

2.2   Online Gaze-Monitoring

Eye gaze information was collected using a Tobii X120 remote eye tracker. The GDM queried this information from the device and streamed the data to the VDM via TCP sockets. With this data, the VDM computed the amount of time that users spent looking at the key ROIs in the virtual environment. Henceforth, we refer to this gaze duration time as fixation duration (FD). For each driving trial (e.g., stopping at a stop sign or decreasing speed in a road work area), a predefined set of ROIs were chosen by the researchers based on what were deemed to be the most important elements of the environment. For example, when arriving at a four-way stop, it is obvious that the driver must notice the stop sign, therefore the stop sign was chosen as an ROI for that task. As another example, when a driver enters an area of road work, he/she must be aware of the change in speed (i.e., they must look at the speed limit signs and the vehicle's speedometer), as well as the presence of any road work signs. In this manner, ROIs were carefully selected for each of the more than 100 trials defined in the system.

For each type of ROI, a bounding cube was defined that would completely envelope the ROI. This bounding cube was used during gameplay to find the extents of the ROI, which allowed us to project the 3D object onto the 2D screen space in order to compute gaze intersections (Fig. 3). Given the position $p \in \mathbb{R}^3$ and extent $e' \in \mathbb{R}^3$ of a particular ROI and a world-to-screen space transformation function $T:\mathbb{R}^3 \rightarrow \mathbb{R}^2$ (provided by the game engine Unity3D), we calculated a screen space radius r as shown in Eq. 1

$$r = \max \left(\left\| T\left[p\right] - T\left[e'\right] \right\|, k \right) \tag{1}$$

Fig. 3. Bounding boxes shown for 2 ROIs (i.e., a traffic light and a truck) in a trial involving a left turn. The bounding box is shown in black and the extents are shown as white circles.

Where k is a constant indicating the minimum allowable radius and e' is the furthest extent in the set of extents E from p in the screen space (see Eq. 2). We chose a value of k equivalent to 1 cm because we found that smaller values of k reduced the accuracy of intersection detection below 80 %.

$$e' = \arg\max_{e \in E} \left\| T[p] - T[e] \right\|$$ (2)

A hashtable data structure was used to monitor FDs for each ROI in a given trial, where the *key* was the identifier of the ROI (e.g., "traffic light") and the *value* was the current FD for that ROI in seconds. To compute FD, the driver's current gaze position $g \in \mathbb{R}^2$ was compared against the position of each ROI relevant to the current trial. If the inequality shown in (Eq. 3) evaluated to *true*, then the FD for that particular ROI was incremented by the time elapsed between the current and previous frames as reported by the game engine.

$$\|g - T[p]\| \leq r$$ (3)

When a trial began, each ROI was loaded into the hashtable, and all of the FD values were initialized to 0. If the trial was failed, then all of FD values were reset to 0. If the participant successfully completed the trial, then the hashtable was cleared and the next set of ROI were loaded.

2.3 Gaze-Contingent Operating Mode

For the purposes of this study, the system operated in one of two distinct modes. Performance-based mode behaved exactly the same as described in Wade *et al.* [10] where progression through tasks depended only on driving performance. A new operating mode—gaze-contingent mode—has been introduced in which participants are required to perform without error, while also looking at key ROIs.

Regardless of operating mode, drivers progressed through the driving game by completing *assignments* or *missions*, which are comprised of eight different driving trials. At the beginning of an assignment, the first trial was presented to the driver whose goal was to complete as many trials as possible without accruing too many driving-related errors or *failures*. Under performance-based mode, the driver was permitted three failures and any number of failures more than three would result in the termination of the assignment without the possibility of a reattempt. In gaze-contingent mode, on the other hand, the driver was permitted three performance-related failures *and* three gaze-related failures. If the driver experienced more than three failures in either category, then the assignment was deemed a failure. Following a failure of any kind, drivers were presented with feedback, in the form of both text and audio, instructing them about the reason for the failure and how to avoid errors of that kind moving forward. When drivers successfully completed all eight trials of an assignment, then a congratulatory audio message was presented.

In gaze-contingent mode, when drivers failed to look at all of the relevant ROIs for a particular trial, the trial would restart and all of the relevant ROIs were highlighted with a fluorescent green light to draw the driver's attention to that specific region (Fig. 4). Upon the second attempt of the trial, the highlighting effect would be removed once the participant looked at the associated ROI.

Fig. 4. Scenes from the gaze-contingent system: feedback is presented for a gaze-related failure (left) and ROIs are highlighted to draw the attention of the driver during gameplay (right).

2.4 Integration of EEG Data Acquisition Module (EDM)

The EDM was defined by an Emotiv EEG headset and accompanying data acquisition program. The device sampled from 14 channels at 128 Hz and the data was streamed wirelessly to a custom application for logging. Additionally, this program received event messages from the VDM, which it used to label epochs of data based on the type of event (e.g., "trial started," "trial failure," and "trial success"). This information was logged and kept for offline analysis.

3 Experimental Procedure

3.1 Participants

Twelve individuals diagnosed with ASD were recruited to participate in this study, with ages ranging from 13 to 18 years, all of whom were male. Two of the participants had a learner's permit to drive within the state of Tennessee and only one participant had a driver's license. Each participant visited the lab facilities for a total of six sessions on different days, except for one participant who completed two sessions at each visit due to long distance traveling. Participants were reimbursed at each visit for their time spent. This study was approved by Vanderbilt's Institutional Review Board.

3.2 Experiment

Participants were randomly assigned to either a gaze-contingent group or a performance-based group in order to compare the effects on driving performance and gaze pattern of the different systems. Participants in the gaze-contingent group had a mean age of 14.65 years (SD 1.38) with one participant holding a driver's license, while participants in the performance-based group had a mean of 15.93 years (SD 1.26) with two participants holding learner's permits. Each participant attempted a total of three driving assignments (24 trials) at each visit for a total of 18 assignments (144 trials) for all six visits.

On the first visit, participants completed a pre-test session that consisted of a variety of difficulty levels. During the next four visits, participants completed sets of three assignments in which the difficulty increased from one visit to the next. On the sixth and final visit, participants completed a post-test session identical to that of the first visit's pre-test. We hypothesized that we would see improvement in terms of performance in both groups as well as a reduction in gaze-related failures from pre- to post-test in the gaze-contingent group.

4   Preliminary Results and Discussion

4.1   Results

Statistical significance was evaluated using a standard two-tailed t-test. We compared the gaze position patterns of participants in both groups considering only the valid data collected by the GDM (i.e., not including blinks or off-screen gaze). The average gaze position was computed for both horizontal and vertical (x and y, respectively) components of gaze for the two groups. Participants in the performance-based group showed an average vertical component of gaze that was significantly higher ($p < 0.01$) than that of the gaze-contingent group by 0.81 cm. Similarly, the performance-based group also showed a pattern of gaze significantly further to the right side of the screen ($p < 0.01$) than that of the gaze-contingent group by 1.44 cm.

In the performance-based group, every participant showed a decrease in trial failures from the pre-test to the post-test (see Table 1). As a group, this change was statistically significant ($p < 0.01$). In the gaze-contingent group, however, this pattern did not arise for performance-related trial failures. For three of the gaze-contingent group participants, the number of performance-related trial failures decreased, but for the other three participants, this value either remained the same, or, in one case, actually increased. In terms of gaze-related trial failures, all but one participant experienced either fewer, or the same number of gaze-related failures from pre-test to post-test.

4.2   Discussion

Reimer et al. [7] and Wade et al. [10] showed that drivers with ASD demonstrated patterns of gaze that were both higher vertically and further to the right horizontally compared to TD controls. The result of lowered and left-shifted average gaze position in the gaze-contingent group may indicate a shift in gaze pattern towards one more representative of the TD population. While this is not itself a mark of improved driving performance, it is a very interesting result that justifies further inspection.

In terms of failure-related results, it is difficult to draw major conclusions from this small sample. Two of the participants in the gaze-contingent group (i.e., participants G2 and G6) demonstrated some unwillingness to participate in the study and often intentionally crashed the virtual vehicle, resulting in unrealistic failure data. None of the participants in the performance-based group demonstrated this kind of behavior. It seems reasonable to assume, then, that given a larger and more evenly distributed sample, both groups would have seen some kind of decrease in performance-related failures.

Table 1. Comparison of results between the performance-based and gaze-contingent groups

Visit #	Fail Type	Performance Group						Gaze-contingent Group					
		P1	P2	P3	P4	P5	P6	G1	G2	G3	G4	G5	G6
Visit 1 (Pre-test)	Perf.	6	9	10	7	7	10	6	12	7	3	5	12
	Gaze	–	–	–	–	–	–	2	0	3	10	9	1
Visit 2	Perf.	5	0	4	3	2	8	1	12	3	2	5	12
	Gaze	–	–	–	–	–	–	4	4	4	6	3	3
Visit 3	Perf.	3	2	7	7	4	8	7	12	7	10	2	11
	Gaze	–	–	–	–	–	–	0	2	3	2	6	5
Visit 4	Perf.	4	2	3	5	1	10	0	9	6	2	2	8
	Gaze	–	–	–	–	–	–	3	4	6	7	2	4
Visit 5	Perf.	6	4	6	5	5	14	10	12	6	7	1	11
	Gaze	–	–	–	–	–	–	2	2	5	4	4	2
Visit 6 (Post-test)	Perf.	2	0	1	3	2	6	2	12	4	6	1	12
	Gaze	–	–	–	–	–	–	1	0	4	0	5	1

5 Conclusion

The work presented in this paper expands on previous work to understand and improve the driving performance of individuals diagnosed with ASD. We extended our previous driving simulation system to include an EEG data acquisition module in order to gain additional insight into the state of the drivers using our system. More importantly, we designed, implemented, and tested a new operating mode of the system in which drivers are required to not only perform well, but also look at regions of the environment deemed to be essential for optimal driving. We evaluated this system in a small comparison study and found encouraging, preliminary results.

A major limitation of this work is the size of the sample studied. The number of participants evaluated is quite small and therefore these results may not be entirely representative of the general ASD population. We plan to address this issue by continuing the study discussed in this paper until a more substantial sample is obtained. Additionally, a more in-depth analysis of the data collected is required. The results of this work will also be used to improve the current system in order to develop a more targeted and effective intervention system in the future.

Acknowledgment. This work was supported in part by the National Institute of Health Grant 1R01MH091102-01A1, National Science Foundation Grant 0967170 and the Hobbs Society Grant from the Vanderbilt Kennedy Center.

References

1. Wingate, M., Kirby, R.S., Pettygrove, S., Cunniff, C., Schulz, E., Ghosh, T., Robinson, C., Lee, L.C., Landa, R., Constantino, J., Fitzgerald, R., Zahorodny, W., Daniels, J., Nicholas, J., Charles, J., McMahon, W., Bilder, D., Durkin, M., Baio, J., Christensen, D., Van, K., Braun, N., Clayton, H., Goodman, A., Doernberg, N., Yeargin-Allsopp, M., A. D. D.: Monitoring, Prevalence of Autism Spectrum Disorder Among Children Aged 8 Years - Autism and Developmental Disabilities Monitoring Network, 11 Sites, United States (2010) Mmwr Surveillance Summaries, vol. 63, March 28 (2014)
2. Weimer, A.K., Schatz, A.M., Lincoln, A., Ballantyne, A.O., Trauner, D.A.: Motor impairment in Asperger syndrome: evidence for a deficit in proprioception. J. Dev. Behav. Pediatr. **22**, 92–101 (2001)
3. Lewis, M.H., Bodfish, J.W.: Repetitive behavior disorders in autism. Ment. Retard. Dev. Disabil. Res. Rev. **4**, 80–89 (1998)
4. Klin, A., Jones, W., Schultz, R., Volkmar, F., Cohen, D.: Visual fixation patterns during viewing of naturalistic social situations as predictors of social competence in individuals with autism. Arch. Gen. Psychiatry **59**, 809–816 (2002)
5. Sheppard, E., Ropar, D., Underwood, G., van Loon, E.: Brief report: driving hazard perception in autism. J. Autism Dev. Disord. **40**, 504–508 (2010)
6. Cox, N.B., Reeve, R.E., Cox, S.M., Cox, D.J.: Brief Report: Driving and young adults with ASD: Parents experiences. J. Autism Dev. Disord. **42**, 2257–2262 (2012)
7. Reimer, B., Fried, R., Mehler, B., Joshi, G., Bolfek, A., Godfrey, K.M., Zhao, N., Goldin, R., Biederman, J.: Brief report: examining driving behavior in young adults with high functioning autism spectrum disorders: a pilot study using a driving simulation paradigm. J. Autism Dev. Disord. **43**, 2211–2217 (2013)
8. Classen, S., Monahan, M.: Evidence-based review on interventions and determinants of driving performance in teens with attention deficit hyperactivity disorder or autism spectrum disorder. Traffic Inj. Prev. **14**, 188–193 (2013)
9. Daly, B.P., Nicholls, E.G., Patrick, K.E., Brinckman, D.D., Schultheis, M.T.: Driving behaviors in adults with autism spectrum disorders. J. Autism Dev. Disord. **44**, 3119–3128 (2014)
10. Wade, J., Bian, D., Zhang, L., Swanson, A., Sarkar, M., Warren, Z., Sarkar, N.: Design of a virtual reality driving environment to assess performance of teenagers with ASD. In: Stephanidis, C., Antona, M. (eds.) UAHCI 2014, Part II. LNCS, vol. 8514, pp. 466–474. Springer, Heidelberg (2014)
11. Bian, D., Wade, J.W., Zhang, L., Bekele, E., Swanson, A., Crittendon, J.A., Sarkar, M., Warren, Z., Sarkar, N.: A novel virtual reality driving environment for autism intervention. In: Stephanidis, C., Antona, M. (eds.) UAHCI 2013, Part II. LNCS, vol. 8010, pp. 474–483. Springer, Heidelberg (2013)

Digital Play Therapy for Children
with Developmental Disorders

Yukako Watanabe[1,2], Yoshiko Okada[1,2], Hirotaka Osawa[2(✉)],
and Midori Sugaya[1,2]

[1] Engineering, College of Engineering, Shibaura Institute of Technology,
Tokyo, Japan
{doly, okada}@shibara-it.ac.jp
[2] Engineering, Information and Systems, University of Tsukuba, Tsukuba, Japan
osawa@iit.tsukuba.ac.jp

Abstract. Children suffering with learning and developmental disorders require daily training to develop their social skills. However, such daily training is sometimes not provided because it requires interactive help from therapists, and lots of programs required for the training. In this paper, we propose a digital dollhouse that enhances traditional psychological play therapy with digital sensors and computer graphics (CG). The digital dollhouse provides immersive space for children, which develops their communication skills through their imaginary play through the complement of CG for enhancing the understanding of their situation. In this paper we present details of this prototype digital dollhouse. We also categorize requirements for digital play therapy, which are given by psychological viewpoints based on the prototype. Interdisciplinary design processes collaborating with engineers and psychologists show the possibility that digital dollhouses will be used for enhancing the communication, and providing the variety of training program that was difficult to prepare compared with the existent normal therapy devices.

Keywords: Developmental disorders · Children · Digital play therapy · Digital play therapy method · Digital play therapy device

1 Introduction

Learning and developmental disorders in children are intrinsic to the individual, presumed to be due to central nervous system dysfunction, and may occur across a life span [1]. These brain's disabilities will cause not only learning difficulties, but also communication difficulties, and physical difficulties in various situations. To moderate these difficulties, it requires daily training of social skills in terms of interaction and communication with others. To improve social skills, play therapy has been acknowledged as a major method by which to help children communicate and express their emotion with counseling [2]. Play therapy is a "here and now" approach to play therapy that is considered similar to a behavioral approach in which children practice new behaviors to prepare for real-life settings [3]. However, there are problems: these settings are expensive, and need trained therapists for supporting enrolment and

© Springer International Publishing Switzerland 2015
M. Antona and C. Stephanidis (Eds.): UAHCI 2015, Part III, LNCS 9177, pp. 698–708, 2015.
DOI: 10.1007/978-3-319-20684-4_67

immersing the settings interactively. Sometimes, it requires coming to a special care-center, therefore it is difficult to train their skills by using this method with settings in daily-life. In the therapy method that could improve social skills, it is important to listen to others, and express their emotion about their imminent environment with their language. Since daily training is required, the device should not be large and hopefully not be installed any specific place, and it is desirable to have a theme that children want to get involved with spontaneously.

Based on the above requirements, we present a digital dollhouse that enhances traditional psychological play therapy with sensors and computer graphics. For the children, it is similar to a house environment like their home, so it is possible for them to immerse themselves into doll play space in their pretend role play as a family member. We consider that this environment is suitable to train the children to improve the required social skills. To accelerate the basic effect of the dollhouse and compensate to meet the requirements, various sensors are installed to sense their physical world, to share the feeling and emotion with one another; the result would be visualized in the screen of the computer to share information more easily (Fig. 1).

Fig. 1. Orange roof's dollhouse and CG

A psychologist who uses play methods for children told us that there are important social skills which should be trained as follows: Firstly, we consider (1) basic training for hearing and speaking. Next, (2) training for choosing the appropriate word for explaining a particular situation.

To realize functionality with our digital dollhouse, we provide the following functions. (1) In the dollhouse, we installed temperature sensors, and a light sensor (photo detector), and these sensed the changing of physical situations that reflects to the virtual room illustrated on the screen. (2) We installed a switch that could change the situation of the room. We assume that the reactive system could change to help children to express the situation by their operation. Further, in the room that is illustrated in a computer graphic, we prepare a window that shows the changing of seasonal views. We assume that that encourages training into words' subtle changes in seasons. Though they share the sense of the physical world in the dollhouse and the augmented reality in the computer with visual appeal, we assumed that children easily immerse the play and express their word by sharing the situations visually and sensuously with the trainee.

As the first stage of the discussion, we discuss the idea with an expert, who has experience in play therapy, and organize the requirements for the device, and we have developed a prototype. In this paper, we will describe the design and prototype implementation, and describe how to apply in the discussion, and also about the challenges of the future.

The sections are organized as follows. In Sect. 2, we describe the related work for digital therapy and clears required issues. In Sect. 3, we describe the prototype implementation. In Sect. 4, we show the result of the discussion and factors for enhancing empathy resulting from the evaluation of a prototype. We conclude this paper in Sect. 5.

2   Requirement for Digital Play Therapy

2.1   Related Work of Play Therapy

In the case of children with disabilities of hearing in the lower grades of elementary school, it is recognized as the pre-operational stage of cognitive development, which is suggested by the Piaget's theory of cognitive development [4]. Since it is difficult for the children who were in the state of pre-operation to treat something logically just in their brain, it is important to give some specific things to treat at training. For these children to train hearing ability, a kind of games that are required to hear carefully from others are generally used (such as street hint game, flag up game etc.), and also widely used are social skill training games that involve the element of hearing such as sugoroku (Japanese backgammon) talk, and storytelling [5, 6, 7]. These games are used easily, since these are generally used in children's play, and are not only used for this specific purpose. On the other hand, these games are too general to focus on the training of specific abilities consciously. To satisfy the requirement especially for the improvement of hearing ability, the training by the expert and the teachers that have knowledge and experience of hearing and cognitive linguistics, and need to understand the elements of hearing that is included in the training and gaming materials.

Play therapy and Sand-play therapy are used for children who have communication disabilities [8, 9]. Play therapy has an advantage in that it provides education for the children to have experience of touching some play objects within the therapy. Particularly, the therapy is considered as an effective method for the children that could not see the environment objectively, since it is required to reproduce an objective environment in their play, by using an agent and surrounding devices. On the other hand, these therapies require experts to support, and sometimes require the use of large equipment such as therapy-balls and trampolines, and expensive dollhouses.

In these years, teaching devices have emerged that are supported by various computers such as the personal computer, PDA, smart phone or something. However, these may then require responsive reaction with keyboard and touching the screen by the children that provides some stimulus materials [10, 11]. These ways of training would be effective for typing and seeing the screen repeatedly. However, since this information is limited in the screen, it is difficult to increase the motivation to communicate with others for the children who are in the pre-operational stage, where it is difficult to have a concrete image without experience of treating actual object. In the HCI research area, like Tangible Computing, that are proposed by Prof. Ishii, novel interaction is provided through physical environment with digital information. However these are not taking advantage of the immersion agent [12].

2.2 Issues

Our proposed interactive devices have been aimed at training for children who suffer learning and developmental disorders, for the purpose of improving specific functions in their brain. Here we mean that "training" is brain function training through the growth of language and communication skills. In this training, we consider the ages to be about three years to eight years old who are undergraduate and lower graduate in primary school, since it is expected to obtain the effect easier than with elders. In the instruction of language and communication, there are mainly two target social skills that should be trained for improvement, being speaking and listening. We firstly consider the requirement for the training tools that improve these two social skills. The most important requirement for the device is that it gives a motivation to the children for having fun and being evolved in spontaneously and continuously without being bored, since the practices are necessary to be repeated in the same situation.

3 Design and Implementation

3.1 Proposal

We propose a digital dollhouse that enhances traditional psychological play therapy with digital sensors and computer graphics. For the children, it is familiar with the house environment; it is possible to immerse them in doll play space in their pretended roles. We consider this environment is suitable to train the children to improve required social skills that we discussed in the previous section. We prepare a dollhouse device that is possible to treat in small space and their roof will be opened with their small hand, since it is important for these children, who are in the stage of pre-operational age, that tend to think intuitively through concrete devices and to have a interest for the "touch" itself. Based on this idea, we installed the following features of the device that have the purpose to improve the three social skills that we discussed in Sect. 2.2.

3.2 Support for the Therapy

In the Fig. 2, we illustrate the abstract image of training in the therapy. We assume that a trainer trains the child. Between the two, our proposed device will be set (Fig. 2). Here we treat the therapist and trainer as having the same meaning. Through the training in conversation and interaction with the proposed device's functionalities, the abilities of the child are promoted so that they can choose appropriate words for explaining the feelings that were aroused in the house by different situations (Fig. 3).

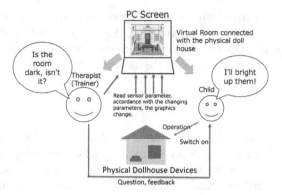

Fig. 2. Sharing the visual and tactile through the screen of a personal computer

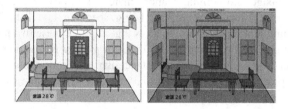

Fig. 3. Inside the room on the screen, Right: Without Light/Roof, Left: Natural Light

3.3 System Design

Our prototype is controlled with Arduino, [13] which is an open-source electronics prototyping platform. On the board, we installed a temperature sensor, light sensor, and switches. Through the sensors, the microcomputer read the changing analog and digital values, and it was possible to operate them to show the result on the screen. We developed a program that reads the analog values from the board, and analyzes them to select appropriate computer graphics interfaces that were illustrated as virtual rooms.

We assume that there are four states that may change in the room according to the combinations of parameters from the sensors as follows. (1) Roof (on/off) from the light sensor (2) Light (on/off) from switch (3) Air conditioner (on/off) from switch (4) Temperature in the room (analog value) from temperature sensor. There are two switches on the board, and each of them reacts according to the user input that changes the status of light, and the air conditioner. These four states indicate the status of the room to reflect to the physical environment and interaction from the children (Fig. 4).

We use LM35 temperature sensors to output a voltage (the analog of which is proportional to the Celsius temperature conversion formula that is output in accordance with (Vout_LM35 (T) = 10 mV /Celsius × T Celsius). The optical sensor (Photo resistor) is a sensor for detecting the intensity of light. With the electric resistance decreasing, the intensity of the incident light is increased, it is assumed that this quantifies the amount of light, corresponding to the brightness of the current room, it is possible to adjust the brightness of the room on the CG.

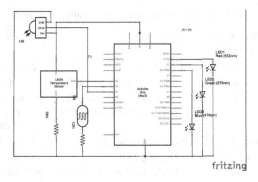

Fig. 4. Connections of sensors on the board

3.4   Software Design

Based on the idea of the changing status of the room being read and changing the CG on the screen, we designed the software program that decides which picture on the virtual room combined with the parameters from the microcomputer-board. Like other microcomputer programs, this program's flow chart in the figure consists of two phases. The first one is initialization phase (setup() in Arduino syntax), and loop phase (loop() in Arduino syntax). In the loop, the microcomputer reads sensors' values through their I/O connected sensors such as switches and light and temperature sensors, then these parameters firstly show on the screen (with appropriate values convered), since sometimes microcomputers only provide the limited range of parameter such as 0-255, therefore programmers need to map the value to the familiar parameter that should be understandable for the average person that ranges from 15-32c in temperature. In the case of deciding the brightness with light, we previously set two ranges of parameters that show "bright" and "dark" in our evaluation, then, the program could decide which picture should show on the screen in terms of reading the analog values from the sensor. Switches are simpler than the light and temperature sensors, because they just read on/off status from the sensor. To work correctly, we just set pull-up registers on the board.

3.5   Training Program

According to the functionalities we proposed, we consider the new training program using the proposed device.

To consider the training program to promote the ability of child, we use the classification metrics of LC-Scale (Language Communication Developmental Scale) [16]. It provides observable assessment of language communication behaviors of the typically developing children who are from 0 to 6 years old, and classifies these behaviors into different areas. According to the LC-Scale areas, we picked up appropriate functionalities of our device and programs, and classified each of them into an area as the training program. In the Table 1, we show the training program. In the first column we show a function that the device proposed, the second is the area of the LC-Scale,

Table 1. Device functions and training programs

Device Functions	Area of the LC-Scale	Social skill (Detail)	Training Program
Optical Sensor: Detect the brightness of the room. w/o Roof	Vocabulary and related skill	Basic Hearing Skill; Point a position of an object, and understand the instructions of the trainer	(1) Give a instruction which is "would you put the roof on the top of the house?" (2) Request the reaction for the instruction
Temperature Sensor: Show the temperature of the room	Vocabulary and related skill (Advanced)	Basic Speaking and Hearing Skill; Understand the words that represent the number of the objects, nature and quantity	(1) Using the number and amount, ask the child, such as "What's the temperature in the room?",(2) Give a instruction that uses the number or amount, such as "Please increase /decrease the temperature of the room?" depending on the current temperature
Infrared Sensor, remote controller: turn on/off the light of the room, air conditioner control	Word chain (two, three), Syntactic	Understand the complex instructions and syntactic	(1) Give instructions such as "What would you do after turning on the light of the room, then increase the temperature of the room to 25 degrees?". (2) Ask the child to make a question for the trainer. The trainer should deliberately give the wrong answer, then, ask the child to point out the mistake. The conversation should be longer, depending on the development level of the child
All of the functions	Discourse, Word operations	Understand the concept (such as seasons) and picture of the situation. Reasoning Infer the word from several hints. Explain the picture that expressed some situation	(1) Expected to reply to understand the intent of the question. For example, "that is, now, outside the house, wonder if any season?" "Spring /Summer /Fall / Winter!" (2) Ask the reason, such as "Why did you think the season is Spring /Summer / Fall /Winter?"

and the third is the obtained social skills that are assumed, and the last is the provided training program that contains detailed instructions from the trainer to the child.

The optical sensors were considered to perform training of promoting an understanding of the operation instruction of the position of the object, since it requires the ability to detect the presence or absence of the roof of the house on the top. This is the area of vocabulary of the LC scale.

Next, temperature sensor has the function of detecting temperature of the surrounding environment. Therefore, associating training of promoting an understanding of the vocabulary that represents the quantity by asking the temperature degree. The remote control using infrared light has the ability to switch the electricity and air conditioner ON /OFF in the room as well as in the room interior of the CG image being displayed on the PC screen. It is considered to perform training to understand the complex instructions, since the controller gives various operations. We assign the function to understand the word chain and syntactic area of the LC scale.

In the entire training materials, there is a function to change the scenery outside the window of the room inside of the CG image in the spring /summer /autumn /winter. This is because it can be used to train the mental function that classifies the understanding of temperature change was assigned a discourse-word operation area of the LC scale.

Training for choosing appropriate words to explain the changing situation: we installed a switch that could change the situation of the room. The change will be the result of the operation of the child pushing the button. We assume that the reactive system could help children to express the changing situation through performing this operation. Training for choosing an appropriate word for the more complex instructions is thus given. In the room that is illustrated in the computer graphics, we prepare a window that shows changing seasonal views. Though they share the sense of the physical world in the dollhouse and the augmented reality in the computer with visual appeal, we assumed that children easily immerse in the play and express their emotions by sharing the situations visually and sensuously with the trainee.

4 Discussion

We developed a prototype of our proposed system, and demonstrated it in front of an experienced expert. We discussed the issues and detected the problems with digital play therapy that are given from psychological viewpoints. We categorized the four issues about the device into four areas.

1. Using the Method of Play Therapy. We prepared a dollhouse device that is possible to treat the parts of device, since it is important for these children, who are in the stage of pre-operational age, who tend to think intuitively through physical devices and to have an interest for the "touch" itself. From the viewpoint of the expert, it is also preferable. Further, the "house" is a good device as also used in sand-play therapy; there is an advantage that is associated with the space in which they are living on a daily basis, in that it is easy to image the specific results from their operations. It is evaluated that it is easy to train and enjoy the play on words of everyday life by using it, to reproduce the behavior of them. It may also be effective even for children with no developmental disabilities.

2. Providing Functions According to the Development of Skills. In this research, we propose a novel device that has a purpose for development of three social skills. According to the recognition, we developed the device to have functionalities with sensors and CGs. These facilities are interesting; it should be needed to consider the evaluation of the effectiveness of the functionalities. Moreover, it may give a good motivation to speak the words "good morning" and "good night" naturally with easily understandable pictures. We also discuss the idea that, if there is a character that is preferable for the children, its use would be more effective to promote the motivation to speak.

3. CG Supports the Immersive Augmented Reality. The expert evaluates positively the CG support for visualization of the reactive operation and changing situation on the screen, since it can share the feeling easily through the screen between them. In the training, it is important to share the feeling with the therapist and children. The effectiveness of the CG support can be evaluated such as for the following example. When the room temperature is 20 degrees, we compare the two cases. The first one is where experts tell the children "It feels warm, do you?" and the second case is where the CG shows the cherry blossoms fall in the window of the room in accordance with the parameters of the temperature sensor on the CG. We consider that it is possible to imagine the specific meaning of that season as being more realistic. In other cases, children enjoy the changing result of their operation that causes the change of the situation in the room, to see the temperature will go down after their push of the switch.

CG representation is also the embodiment of the real world, thus, the extension is possible. It is believed to be able to stimulate the empowerment of operational feeling of operation, and give a pleasure to share and expand the world. In particular, it is considered to be very important that they can check the result of their operation in visual world (CG) that is an extension of the real world. These studies have been proposed as Blended Reality, and other names, [14] however, it has not been sufficiently discussed yet.

4. Augmented Reality and Development Empathy with an Agent. During the discussion between engineers and a psychologist, we found the process of our system enhances the ability of empathy for the child. Rogers noted in his work that the key factor of empathy is to feel the other's viewpoint "as if it were your own" [15]. Our proposed three devices support the enhancement of the ability to shift one's viewpoint to another location.

Based on the above discussions, we hypothesized that a character in a digital dollhouse enhances feeling of empathy. Children tend to talk to a character that seems to be familiar with them. These activities will be expected to encourage development of their ability to speak to the others. Moreover, these activities would develop the ability to select the most empathetic method of speech to others.

For example, if there is a character that seems to be almost cold, children talk to the character, such as "Are you cold? I will push the button to warm up the room". It is good training for developing the abilities of empathy and selects the appropriate words to express, and selects the appropriate actions to improve the situation of others. Thus, it is important to evolve the functions that can encourage sharing feelings with others and to have empathy with others, and develop their abilities to talk to others naturally through the changing of seasons and temperature. Moreover, in the future, we need to place a character. This would give a subject to talk about.

5. Contributions and Limitation. The contribution of our work is to show why digital technology supports children abilities in terms of a psychological viewpoint. We conducted interdisciplinary discussion between engineers and psychologists. The result of discussion with real prototype reveals that digital dollhouses will support children's abilities to shift viewpoints. It also suggests that our approach is also improved by applying human-agent interaction technologies. Our interdisciplinary works are just a start point. Further research will be required to verify our hypothesis.

5 Conclusion

In this paper, we propose a digital dollhouse for children who are suffering with learning and developmental disabilities, who require daily training to develop their social skills. It may enhance traditional psychological play therapy with digital sensors and computer graphics.

The digital dollhouse provides an immersive space for children that grows their abilities to hear and speak through their imaginary play. In this paper, we showed details about the digital dollhouse prototype. We also categorized requirements for Digital Play therapy, from psychological viewpoints, as the first stage of our research.

In the discussion we categorized the requirements and became aware of a new requirement character that would promote the training effectively. In the future, we will try to improve the house based on this discussion and include how multimodal interaction environments are effective for children from the viewpoint of those with neuroscience backgrounds [17]. We currently associate the relationship of communication and language as being based on empathy. From the viewpoint of computer science, we consider the effective support in the use of agents.

References

1. National Joint Committee on Learning Disabilities: Learning disabilities: Issues on definition. Asha, 33,(Suppl. 5), pp. 18–20 (1991)
2. Dale, M.A., Lyddon, W.J.: Sandplay: an investigation into a child's meaning system via the self-confrontation method for children. J. Constructivist Psychol. **16**, 17–36 (2000)
3. Russo, M., Vernam, J., Wolbert, A.: Sandplay and storytelling: Social constructivism and cognitive development in child counseling. Arts Psychother. **33**, 229–237 (2006)
4. Tanimura, S., Hamada, S.: Birth of the intelligence, Kyoto, Minerva Shobo (1978), (Piaget, J. La naissance de l'intelligence chez l'enfant, Delacchaux et Niestlé, Paris (1936)
5. Takeda, K., Ota, N., Yuka, N., Tabata, T.: Support program for children with learning disabilities, Bunka Kagakusha, Tokyo (2000)

6. Ueno, K., Okada, K.: Special Needs Education [Practice] Social Skills Manual. Meiji Tosho, Tokyo (2006)
7. Honda, K.: Social Skills Education for Short-Tempered kids: Activities for the Classroom and Practical Examples. Honnomori Press, Tokyo (2007)
8. Yamauchi, K., Tanaka, M., Kato, T., Onishi, N.: The effect of play therapy on a Japanese child suffering from expressive language disorder brought on by early english education. Nurs. J. Kagawa Univ. 12(1), 65–75 (2008)
9. Toyama, M., Takatsuka, T., Sogawa, N.: The therapeutic process for a child with language retardation: the second report. Bull. Tsukuba Dev. Clin. psychol. 13, 1–14 (2001)
10. Uchida, M.: Cooperation between resource rooms and regular classrooms in the guidance for children with developmental disabilities: through ICT utilization. Japan society of educational information, pp. 25–26 (2012)
11. Yoshino, K., Takata, M., Tenpaku, S., Joe, K.: Development of the handwriting training software on Nintendo DS. IPSJ SIG Technical report,19, pp. 81-84 (2007)
12. Hiroshi, I., Brygg, U.: Tangible Bits: towards seamless interfaces between people, bits and atoms. In: Proceedings of the ACM SIGCHI Conference on Human Factors in Computing Systems (CHI 1997), pp. 234–241(1997)
13. Arduino: http://www.arduino.cc/
14. Robert, D., Breazeal, C.: Blended reality characters. In: Proceedings of the Seventh Annual ACM/IEEE International Conference on Human-Robot Interaction (HRI 2012), pp. 359–366 (2012)
15. Rogers, C.R.: The necessary and sufficient conditions of therapeutic personality change. J. Consult. Psychol. 21(2), 95–103 (1957)
16. Kumise, A., Hayashi, A., Hashimoto, S.: The Study of the Relation of the Language Communications Skills by LC Scale, and Language Behavior and Group Participation of the Infants with Normal Development, Department of Center for the Research and Support of Education Practice, Bulletin of Tokyo Gakugei University. General Pedagogy, 63(2): 295–302
17. Giannopulu, I.: Multimodal interactions in typically and atypically developing children: natural vs. artificial environments. Cognitive Process. 14(4), 323–331 (2013)

Multimodal Fusion for Cognitive Load Measurement in an Adaptive Virtual Reality Driving Task for Autism Intervention

Lian Zhang[1]([✉]), Joshua Wade[1], Dayi Bian[1], Jing Fan[1],
Amy Swanson[2], Amy Weitlauf[2,3], Zachary Warren[2,3], and Nilanjan Sarkar[1,4]

[1] Electrical Engineering and Computer Science Department, Vanderbilt University,
Nashville, TN 37212, USA
lian.zhang@vanderbilt.edu
[2] Treatment and Research in Autism Spectrum Disorder (TRIAD), Nashville, USA
[3] Pediatrics and Psychiatry Department, Nashville, USA
[4] Mechanical Engineering Department, Vanderbilt University,
Nashville, TN 37212, USA

Abstract. A virtual reality driving system was designed to improve driving skills in individuals with autism spectrum disorder (ASD). An appropriate level of cognitive load during training can help improve a participant's long-term performance. This paper studied cognitive load measurement with multimodal information fusion techniques. Features were extracted from peripheral physiological signals, Electroencephalogram (EEG) signals, eye gaze information and participants' performance data. Multiple classification methods and features from different modalities were used to evaluate participant's cognitive load. We verified classifications' result with perceived tasks' difficulty level, which induced different cognitive load. We fused multimodal information in three levels: feature level, decision level and hybrid level. The best accuracy for cognitive load measurement was 84.66 %, which was achieved with the hybrid level fusion.

Keywords: Autism · Virtual reality · Multimodal fusion · Cognitive load measurement

1 Introduction

Autism spectrum disorder (ASD) is a common disorder that impacts 1 in 68 children in the US [1]. Although at present there is no single accepted intervention, treatment, or known cure for ASD, there is a growing consensus that appropriately targeted individualized behavioral and educational intervention programs have the potential to positively impact the lives of individuals with ASD and their families [2, 3]. However the availability of trained autism clinicians is limited and the cost associated with traditional therapies is enormous. As a result, the development of economical and effective assistive therapeutic tools for autism intervention is urgent.

© Springer International Publishing Switzerland 2015
M. Antona and C. Stephanidis (Eds.): UAHCI 2015, Part III, LNCS 9177, pp. 709–720, 2015.
DOI: 10.1007/978-3-319-20684-4_68

A growing number of studies have investigated the application of technology, specifically computer and virtual reality (VR) systems, to autism intervention. There are numerous reasons why incorporating VR technology into intervention may be particularly relevant for children and adolescents with ASD. The VR-based intervention platform is characterized by malleability, controllability, modifiable sensor stimulation, individualized approach, safety, and the potential to reduce problematic aspects of complex adaptive life skills [4]. These systems could not only help children with ASD generalizing learned skills to the real world, but also provide more control over how the basic skills are taught.

At present, most VR-based platforms have been designed to improve social skill deficits in ASD population [5, 6]. However, other activities of daily life that are important for functional independence for individuals with ASD have not received similar attention. In this work, we focus on VR-based driving since independent driving is often seen as a proxy measure for functional independence and quality of life for adults across a variety of disability and non-disability groups. It is noted that many individuals with ASD fail to obtain driving independence [7]. In addition, an emerging literature suggests that individuals with ASD display processing differences in driving environments that may be linked to unsafe driving behaviors. Despite its importance, to our knowledge, only two studies have investigated driving interventions for teenagers with ASD [8, 9].

Previous work has investigated the use of technological interventions for driving skills in people with ASD, but no studies have developed a closed-loop individualized system to the best of our knowledge. Reimer and colleagues (2013) and Classen and colleagues (2013) presented participants with a set of driving scenarios using a driving simulator paradigm within a real vehicle that was converted into a simulation tool [8, 9]. Classen and colleagues found a higher error in driving performance for teens with ASD or Attention Deficit-Hyperactivity Disorder (ADHD) compared with typically developing (TD) group [9]. Reimer and colleagues found different gaze patterns and physiological signals, such as heart rate and skin conductance level (SCL), between the TD control group and individuals with autism [8]. They also found the variation of heart rate in TD group under different cognitive condition. These related research work highlighted the need for deeper research in individualized driving system for autism intervention.

We plan to develop an individualized intervention system that can maximize a participant's long-term performance by adapting the difficulty level of a driving task. Task difficulty directly affects a participant's cognitive load [10]. A lot of studies modulated cognitive loads using different task difficulties [11, 12]. An appropriate cognitive load could maximize individual's long-term performance [13]. An individualized system, which can measure the user's current cognitive load and modulate the cognitive load to its optimal level by adjusting the task difficulty, has the ability to effectively improve the user's performance.

This paper measured cognitive load from multimodal signals, including performance data and three classes of psycho-physiological signals: peripheral physiological signals (heart rate, SCL etc.), EEG signals, and eye gaze signals. Performance-based measure was traditional way for cognitive load measurement [14]. Performance features, including reaction time, accuracy and error rate, indicated a participant's cognitive load [11].

Psycho-physiological measurement have been shown to provide real time information about cognitive load [15–17], which in turn can be used to our individualized difficulty level adjustment. For example, eye gaze offers rich physiological information, such as blink rate and pupil diameter, to reflect a user's cognitive state [18, 19]. EEG are sensitive and reliable data for memory load measurement [20, 21]. Peripheral physiological signals, such as electrocardiogram (ECG), photoplethysmogram (PPG), electromyogram (EMG), respiration (Resp.) and skin temperature (SKT), can reflect the variation of cognitive load [22, 23] as well as affective states [24, 25].

Integrating such psycho-physiological signals with performance data has the potential to increase the robustness and accuracy for cognitive load measurement [26]. Son and colleagues integrated performance with physiological data to estimate a driver's cognitive workload and got the best result with selected performance features and physiological features [27]. Koenig and colleagues have quantified the cognitive load of stroke patients with both psycho-physiological and performance data and applied in a closed-loop system [12]. Although other work has studied applications of cognitive load in individualized intelligent systems with multimodal information fusion techniques, this has not yet been done for individuals with ASD to the best of our knowledge.

The multimodal information fusion techniques could be presented in three levels: feature level, decision level and hybrid level [28]. The feature level fusion was an easily accomplished approach because it required only one learning phase on the combined feature vector [29]. However, the synchronization from multimodal information was found to be more challenging [30]. Decision level fusion combined the sub-decisions of each modality to arrive at a more robust decision [31]. However, it was not good at reflecting the correlation between features of different modalities [32]. Hybrid level fusion methods seek to combine the advantages of feature level fusion and decision level fusion [28].

In our previous work [33, 34], we presented a novel VR driving environment with the ultimate aim of developing an intervention platform capable of enhanced teaching of driving skills to teenagers with ASD. In this paper, we present our current work in fusing multimodal information to assess one's cognitive load during driving. We evaluated multiple classification methods for multimodal fusion and compared three levels of fusion in this paper. The long term goal is to close the loop in such a way that the driving task can be autonomously adapted to one's cognitive load to optimize performance, which is beyond the scope of this current paper.

2   Methods

2.1   Experimental Setup

The virtual driving system was designed with three components: a driving simulator, a data acquisition module and a therapist rating module, shown in Fig. 1. Participants used the driving simulator to engage in driving tasks. The data acquisition module acquired their psycho-physiological information and performance data in real time. One therapist observed and rated participants' emotional state and cognitive state from another room. All the data collected were synchronized by time stamped events from the driving simulator via a local area network (LAN).

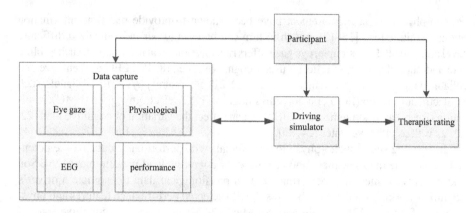

Fig. 1. The framework of the VR-based driving system

The driving simulator was composed of a virtual environment and a Logitech G27 steering wheel controller, shown in Fig. 2. The models in the virtual environment (e.g., the city, the car, and pedestrians) were realized with the modeling tools ESRI CityEngine (www.esri.com/cityengine) and Autodesk Maya (www.autodesk.com/maya). The game engine Unity3D (www.unity3d.com) was used to manipulate the logic of the system. The system was composed of six different levels of difficulty to invoke different cognitive loads. Each level included three driving assignments. Each assignment included a series of eight driving tasks in order to train the specified driving behaviors, such as stopping properly at a stop sign, yielding to pedestrians, merging lanes, and turning left.

Fig. 2. The driving simulator and environment

Participants controlled a vehicle in the virtual environment using the controller. Their driving behaviors and task performance were logged within the system. In addition to recording performance data, the data acquisition system recorded psycho-physiological data with psycho-physiological sensors shown in Fig. 3. A Tobii X120 remote eye tracker (www.tobii.com/) was used to track the participant's eye gaze. Biopac MP150 (www.biopac.com) sensors recorded ECG, EMG, Resp., SKT, PPG, and galvanic skin response (GSR)signals wirelessly [35, 36]. The GSR and PPG sensors were attached on the participant's toes instead of fingers to reduce the motion artifact from driving [37]. An Emotiv EEG headset (www.emotiv.com) recorded 14 channels of EEG signals.

Fig. 3. The psycho-physiological sensors [37]

In the therapist rating module, a therapist observed and rated the participant's affective state and the apparent difficulty of the assignment using a 0-9 Likert scale. The rating categories included difficulty level, engagement, enjoyment, boredom, and frustration. The module electronically recorded the rating in two ways: (1) the observer continuously rating affect and difficulty level during assignments, and (2) the observer providing an overall rating as a summary at the end of each assignment.

A total of 10 teenagers with ASD, with ages from 13 to 17 years, were involved in the experiment. We recruited teenagers with ASD through an existing university clinical research registry. The participants had a clinical diagnosis of ASD with scores at or above clinical cutoff on the Autism Diagnostic Observation Schedule [38]. Their cognitive functioning was measured using either the Differential Ability Scales [39] or the Wechsler Intelligence Scale for Children [40].

Each participant completed six visits on different days. The duration of each visit was approximately one hour including device setup, baseline measurement, driving practice, and the main task completion. As part of each visit, three researchers organized the sensors and carried out eye tracker calibration. After a three-minute period used for recording baseline physiological and EEG data, participants practiced driving for three minutes in a free-form practice mode. Finally, participants completed three driving assignments, which were unique except for the first and the last visit.

2.2   Feature Extraction

Eye Gaze Features. Eye gaze data was tracked by the eye tracker with a frequency of 120 Hz. The eye tracker had an average accuracy of 1 cm for gaze position tracking when the participants sat approximately 70 cm away from the monitor. In addition to gaze position, the eye tracker also measured the pupil diameter and blink.

The eye gaze data was preprocessed by reducing the noise with the median value method [41]. The blink rate and pupil diameter were calculated from the preprocessed eye tracker data. For the blink rate, the closure duration used a range from 75 to 400 ms [42]. The eye gaze features included mean and standard deviation of blink rate, pupil diameter, and fixation duration.

Physiological Features. The physiological signals were recorded with a 1000 Hz sample rate. The physiological features were preprocessed as shown in Fig. 4. First, we removed the outliers of physiological signals. Then, we removed signal noise with different high/low pass filters and notch filters [35, 36].

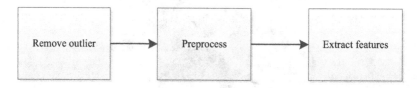

Fig. 4. Physiological signal analysis process

Sixty physiological features were calculated including sympathetic power, para-sympathetic power, very low-frequency power and ratio of powers of ECG, Mean Interbeat Interval of ECG, mean and standard deviation of the amplitude and peak values of PPG. The details of the physiological features can be found in [37].

EEG Features. The Emotiv EEG headset recorded signals from 14 channels from positions AF3, F7, F3, FC5, T7, P7, O1, O2, P8, T8, FC6, F4, F8, and AF4, defined by the 10-20 system of electrode placement [43]. There were two additional reference electrodes at locations P3 and P4. The bandwidth of the EEG headset was from 0.2 Hz to 45 Hz and the recorded sampling rate was 128 Hz.

After removing outliers, EEG signals were first filtered between 0.2 Hz and 45 Hz. We then removed eye blink, eye movement, and muscle movement artifacts by applying EOG-EMG artifact correction algorithm provided by EEGLab [44]. After this preprocessing, spectral features - averaged power of each channel on alpha (8-13 Hz), beta (13-30 Hz), and gamma (30-45 Hz) bands-were then extracted from the clean signals [20]. A total of forty-two EEG features were extracted.

Performance Features. Performance features were extracted from the driving behavior data and task performance data. Performance features included the number of failure during one assignment, the score achieved during one assignment, the levels of accelerating acceleration and braking, and the average speed.

2.3   Data Fusion Methods

In order to evaluate cognitive load, features from different modalities were input into classifiers The classifiers in Matlab (http://www.mathworks.com/) and Machine Learning Toolbox (MLT) (http://mirlab.org/jang/matlab/toolbox/machineLearning/) were used, including Support Vector Machine (SVM), Naïve Bayes (NB), Gaussian Mixture Models (GMM), K-Nearest Neighbors with (KNN), Quadratic Classifier (QCL), Decision Tree (DT), and Linear Classifier (LCL).

The therapist's overall rating of difficulty level was used as the ground truth for cognitive load classification methods. The 0-9 Likert scaled difficulty level rating was grouped and relabeled as low (difficulty level less than five) and high (difficulty level larger than five) to reflect a binary-level cognitive load. In brief, we hypothesized based on prior published research [12] that a participant in a high difficulty level task had high cognitive load; while a participant in a low difficulty level task had low cognitive load.

Three level fusion approaches were implemented to fuse multimodal information: feature fusion, decision fusion and hybrid fusion. Figure 5 (a) showed the feature level fusion. All features were input into the preprocess module, which normalized features and reduced their dimension with principal component analysis. The cognitive load was evaluated with the preprocessed features.

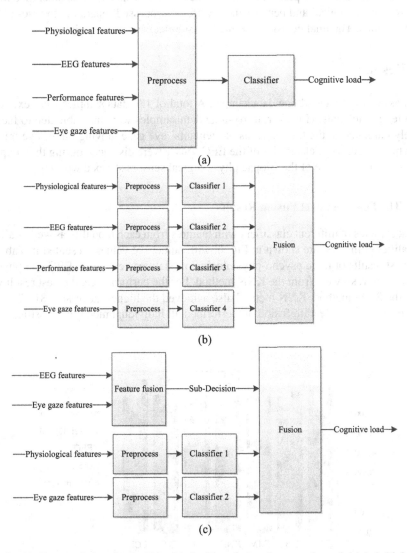

Fig. 5. (a) Feature fusion framework; (b) decision fusion framework; and (c) hybrid fusion framework.

Figure 5 (b) showed decision level fusion. We preprocessed the features from each modality separately and then input them into different classifiers. Each classifier output a cognitive load as a sub-decision. The fusion part summed all sub-decisions (D_1, D_2, D_3, D_4) with weights for the final cognitive load (D_{final}) as shown in Eq. (1).

$$D_{final} = w_1 D_1 + w_2 D_2 + w_3 D_3 + w_4 D_4 \tag{1}$$

Figure 5 (c) gave one example of hybrid level fusion. Hybrid level fusion combined the feature level fusion and decision level fusion. Features from more than one modality (EEG and eye gaze) were preprocessed to make one sub-decision; while other modalities features (physiological and performance) were preprocessed separately to assess other sub-decisions. The final decision summed all sub-decisions with weights.

3   Results

Each assignment yielded one data sample. A total of 180 data samples were extracted from ten participants. However, thirty-nine data samples were unusable due to factors largely unrelated to the task, such as participants' eye gaze moving out of eye tracker detection range, some electrodes of the EEG sensor were displaced during their experiments, or one instance of the Biopac physiological sensors stopped working.

3.1   The Feature Level Fusion Results

The accuracies of different classifiers with features from each modality as well as all the modalities combined are shown in Fig. 6, with numerical values presented in Table 1. The best results of three psycho-physiological modalities– eye gaze, EEG and physiological features - were from the KNN method. For the performance, the best result was from the SVM method. KNN method also achieved the highest accuracy, 81.57 %, for feature fusion. The feature fusion outperformed all individual modality classification.

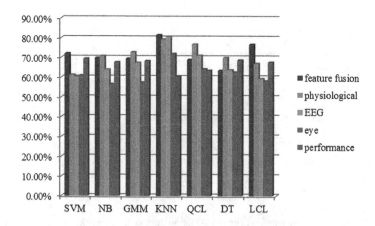

Fig. 6. The accuracies of different classifiers

Table 1. Accuracies of each modality and all modalities with different methods

	Feature fusion	Physiolog-ical	EEG	Eye	Performance
SVM	72.03 %	61.32 %	60.35 %	60.99 %	**69.41 %**
NB	69.90 %	70.86 %	63.97 %	56.62 %	67.71 %
GMM	69.51 %	72.77 %	67.44 %	57.60 %	68.38 %
KNN	**81.57 %**	**79.29 %**	**80.58 %**	**71.92 %**	60.49 %
QCL	68.92 %	76.73 %	71.07 %	64.28 %	63.48 %
DT	63.50 %	69.99 %	63.79 %	62.62 %	68.67 %
LCL	76.65 %	67.03 %	59.29 %	58.24 %	67.71 %

3.2 The Decision Level Fusion and Hybrid Level Fusion Result

For the decision level fusion, we tested all classifiers for every modality to get the sub-decision. We then tested various combinations of weights for every sub-decision. The best accuracy was achieved when using SVM for performance modality features and KNN for all three psycho-physiological modalities features. The weight for a sub-decision of one modality was proportional to the best accuracy of the modality. The results indicated that for one modality, the best method for decision fusion was consistent with the best method for its individual classification. The best decision fusion accuracy was 80.95 %, which was similar to the best accuracy of the feature fusion.

Hybrid level fusion outperformed the feature level and decision level fusion with a best accuracy of 84.66 %. The best accuracy was achieved when eye gaze and EEG features were combined for one sub-decision with KNN method and weight w_1, physiological features for one sub-decision with KNN method and weight w_2, and SVM method and weight w_3 for performance features ($0.5 > w_1 > w_2 > w_3$ and $w_1 + w_2 + w_3 = 1$).

4 Conclusions

This paper focused on multimodal fusion for cognitive load measurement during driving intervention for individuals with ASD. The signals for the cognitive load measurement were composed of physiological signals, EEG signal, eye gaze, and performance data.

Seven machine learning methods were explored to classify individual modality features and multimodal fusion. The KNN method yielded the best results for all the psycho-physiological related features, features from physiological signal, EEG data, and eye gaze. The SVM method yielded the highest accuracy for performance features.

This paper compared three levels multimodal information fusion approaches, feature level fusion, decision level fusion and hybrid level fusion, for cognitive load measurement. The multimodal fusion approaches outperformed individual modalities in cognitive load measurement. Hybrid fusion had the best result of 84.66 % compared to other fusion methods.

The results will be used to choose an optimal game difficulty level for individuals with ASD to provide a more challenging yet fruitful skill development opportunity in the future.

Acknowledgment. This work was supported in part by the National Institute of Health Grant 1R01MH091102-01A1, National Science Foundation Grant 0967170 and the Hobbs Society Grant from the Vanderbilt Kennedy Center.

References

1. Wingate, M., Kirby, R.S., Pettygrove, S., et al.: Prevalence of autism spectrum disorder among children aged 8 years-autism and developmental disabilities monitoring network, 11 sites, United States, 2010. MMWR Surveillance Summaries, vol. 63, p. 2 (2014)
2. Rogers, S.J.: Empirically supported comprehensive treatments for young children with autism. J. Clin. Child Psychol. 27(2), 168–179 (1998)
3. Cohen, H., Amerine-Dickens, M., Smith, T.: Early intensive behavioral treatment: Replication of the UCLA model in a community setting. J. Dev. Behav. Pediatr. 27(2), S145–S155 (2006)
4. Strickland, D.: Virtual reality for the treatment of autism. In: Studies in Health Technology and Informatics, pp. 81–86 (1997)
5. Tartaro, A., Cassell, J.: Using virtual peer technology as an intervention for children with autism. In: Towards Universal Usability: Designing Computer Interfaces for Diverse User Populations, vol. 231, p. 62. John Wiley, Chichester (2007)
6. Lahiri, U., Bekele, E., Dohrmann, E., et al.: Design of a virtual reality based adaptive response technology for children with autism. IEEE Trans. Neural Syst. Rehabil. Eng. 21(1), 55–64 (2013)
7. Cox, N.B., Reeve, R.E., Cox, S.M., et al.: Brief Report: Driving and young adults with ASD: Parents' experiences. J. Autism Dev. Disord. 42(10), 2257–2262 (2012)
8. Reimer, B., Fried, R., Mehler, B., et al.: Brief report: Examining driving behavior in young adults with high functioning autism spectrum disorders: A pilot study using a driving simulation paradigm. J. Autism Dev. Disord. 43(9), 2211–2217 (2013)
9. Classen, S., Monahan, M.: Evidence-based review on interventions and determinants of driving performance in teens with attention deficit hyperactivity disorder or autism spectrum disorder. Traff. Inj. Prev. 14(2), 188–193 (2013)
10. Galy, E., Cariou, M., Mélan, C.: What is the relationship between mental workload factors and cognitive load types? Int. J. Psychophysiol. 83(3), 269–275 (2012)
11. Hussain, M.S., Calvo, R.A., Chen, F.: Automatic cognitive load detection from face, physiology, task performance and fusion during affective interference. Interacting with computers, p. iwt032 (2013)
12. Koenig, A., Novak, D., Omlin, X., et al.: Real-time closed-loop control of cognitive load in neurological patients during robot-assisted gait training. IEEE Trans. Neural Syst. Rehabil. Eng. 19(4), 453–464 (2011)
13. Engström, J., Johansson, E., Östlund, J.: Effects of visual and cognitive load in real and simulated motorway driving. Transp. Res. Part F: Traffic Psychol. Behav. 8(2), 97–120 (2005)
14. Paas, F., Tuovinen, J.E., Tabbers, H., et al.: Cognitive load measurement as a means to advance cognitive load theory. Educat. Psychol. 38(1), 63–71 (2003)

15. Taelman, J., Vandeput, S., Spaepen, A., et al.: Influence of mental stress on heart rate and heart rate variability, pp. 1366–1369
16. Zhai, J., Barreto, A.: Stress Recognition Using Non-invasive Technology, pp. 395–401
17. Mehler, B., Reimer, B., Coughlin, J.F., et al.: Impact of incremental increases in cognitive workload on physiological arousal and performance in young adult drivers. Transp. Res. Rec.: J. Transp. Res. Board **2138**(1), 6–12 (2009)
18. Palinko, O., Kun, A.L., Shyrokov, A., et al.: Estimating cognitive load using remote eye tracking in a driving simulator, pp. 141–144
19. Pomplun, M., Sunkara, S.: Pupil dilation as an indicator of cognitive workload in human-computer interaction
20. Zarjam, P., Epps, J., Lovell, N.H., et al.: Characterization of memory load in an arithmetic task using non-linear analysis of EEG signals, pp. 3519–3522
21. Zarjam, P., Epps, J., Chen, F., et al.: Classification of working memory load using wavelet complexity features of EEG signals, pp. 692–699
22. Novak, D., Mihelj, M., Munih, M.: A survey of methods for data fusion and system adaptation using autonomic nervous system responses in physiological computing. Inter. with Comput. **24**(3), 154–172 (2012)
23. Wilson, G.F., Russell, C.A.: Performance enhancement in an uninhabited air vehicle task using psychophysiologically determined adaptive aiding. Hum. Factors: J. Hum. factors Ergon. Soc. **49**(6), 1005–1018 (2007)
24. Sarkar, N.: Psychophysiological control architecture for human-robot coordination-concepts and initial experiments, pp. 3719–3724
25. Rani, P., Sarkar, N., Smith, C.A., et al.: Affective communication for implicit human-machine interaction, pp. 4896–4903
26. Chen, F.: Robust Multimodal Cognitive Load Measurement, DTIC Document (2014)
27. Son, J., Park, M.: Estimating cognitive load complexity using performance and physiological data in a driving simulator
28. Atrey, P.K., Hossain, M.A., El Saddik, A., et al.: Multimodal fusion for multimedia analysis: a survey. Multimedia Syst. **16**(6), 345–379 (2010)
29. Snoek, C.G., Worring, M., Smeulders, A.W.: Early versus late fusion in semantic video analysis, pp. 399–402
30. Wu, Z., Cai, L., Meng, H.: Multi-level fusion of audio and visual features for speaker identification. In: Zhang, D., Jain, A.K. (eds.) ICB 2005. LNCS, vol. 3832, pp. 493–499. Springer, Heidelberg (2005)
31. Koelstra, S., Muhl, C., Soleymani, M., et al.: Deap: A database for emotion analysis; using physiological signals. IEEE Trans. Affect. Comput. **3**(1), 18–31 (2012)
32. Liu, E.S., Theodoropoulos, G.K.: Interest management for distributed virtual environments: A survey. ACM Comput. Surv. (CSUR) **46**(4), 51 (2014)
33. Wade, J., Bian, D., Zhang, L., Swanson, A., Sarkar, M., Warren, Z., Sarkar, N.: Design of a virtual reality driving environment to assess performance of teenagers with ASD. In: Stephanidis, C., Antona, M. (eds.) UAHCI 2014, Part II. LNCS, vol. 8514, pp. 466–474. Springer, Heidelberg (2014)
34. Bian, D., Wade, J.W., Zhang, L., Bekele, E., Swanson, A., Crittendon, J.A., Sarkar, M., Warren, Z., Sarkar, N.: A novel virtual reality driving environment for autism intervention. In: Stephanidis, C., Antona, M. (eds.) UAHCI 2013, Part II. LNCS, vol. 8010, pp. 474–483. Springer, Heidelberg (2013)
35. Liu, C., Conn, K., Sarkar, N., et al.: Physiology-based affect recognition for computer-assisted intervention of children with Autism Spectrum Disorder. Int. J. Hum.-Comput. Stud. **66**(9), 662–677 (2008)

36. Liu, C., Rani, P., Sarkar, N.: An empirical study of machine learning techniques for affect recognition in human-robot interaction, pp. 2662–2667

37. Bian, D., Wade, J., Swanson, A., et al.: Physiology-based affect recognition during driving in virtual environment for autism intervention. In: 2nd international conference on physiological computing system (Accepted, 2015)

38. Lord, C., Risi, S., Lambrecht, L., et al.: The Autism Diagnostic Observation Schedule— Generic: A standard measure of social and communication deficits associated with the spectrum of autism. J. Autism Dev. Disord. 30(3), 205–223 (2000)

39. Elliott, C.D.: Differential Ability Scales-ll. Pearson, San Antonio (2007)

40. Wechsler, D.: Wechsler intelligence scale for children (1949)

41. Komogortsev, O.V., Gobert, D.V., Jayarathna, S., et al.: Standardization of automated analyses of oculomotor fixation and saccadic behaviors. IEEE Trans. Biomed. Eng. 57(11), 2635–2645 (2010)

42. Benedetto, S., Pedrotti, M., Minin, L., et al.: Driver workload and eye blink duration. Trans. Research Part F: Traffic Psychol. Behav. 14(3), 199–208 (2011)

43. Klem, G.H., Lüders, H.O., Jasper, H., et al.: The ten-twenty electrode system of the International Federation," Electroencephalogr. Clin. Neurophysiol. 52 (suppl.), 3 (1999)

44. Delorme, A., Makeig, S.: EEGLAB: an open source toolbox for analysis of single-trial EEG dynamics including independent component analysis. J. Neurosci. Methods 134(1), 9–21 (2004)

Design of a Computer-Assisted System for Teaching Attentional Skills to Toddlers with ASD

Zhi Zheng[1(✉)], Qiang Fu[1], Huan Zhao[1], Amy Swanson[2], Amy Weitlauf[2],
Zachary Warren[2], and Nilanjan Sarkar[3,1]

[1] Electrical Engineering and Computer Science Department, Nashville, TN, USA
zhi.zheng@vanderbilt.edu
[2] Vanderbilt Kennedy Center Treatment and Research Institute for Autism Spectrum Disorder,
Nashville, TN, USA
[3] Mechanical Engineering Department, Vanderbilt University, Nashville, TN, USA

Abstract. Attentional skill, which is considered as one of the fundamental elements of social communication, is among the core areas of impairment among children with Autism Spectrum Disorder (ASD). In recent years, technology-assisted ASD intervention has gained momentum among researchers due its potential advantages in terms of flexibility, accessibility and cost. In this paper, we proposed a computer-assisted system for teaching attentional skills to toddlers with ASD, using the "response to name" skill as a specific example. The system was a fully closed-loop autonomous system capable of both providing name prompting from different locations of a room and detecting the child's attention in response to his name prompt. A preliminary user study was conducted to validate the proposed system and the protocol. The results showed that the proposed system and the protocol were well tolerated and were engaging for the participants, and were successful in eliciting the desired performance from the participants.

Keywords: Computer-mediated attention skills teaching · Toddlers with ASD

1 Introduction

Autism spectrum disorder (ASD) is a common disorder that impacts 1 in 68 children in the US [1]. Evidence suggests that early detection and intervention is critical to optimal treatment for ASD [2, 3]. Given the resource limitations in the healthcare system, technology-assisted approaches are being considered as potential intervention platforms due to their flexibility, controllability, duplicability, and cost effectiveness [4–9].

Previous work has examined technological interventions for older children with ASD. Feil-Seifer et al. [10] and Greczek et al. [11] proposed graded cueing mechanism for teaching imitation skills to children with ASD. Zheng et al. [12] studied adaptive gestures imitation training with fully autonomous robotic systems. Lahiri et al. [13], Wade et al. [8], and Herrera et al. [9] designed adaptive virtual reality response technologies for children with ASD in terms of conversation, a driving game, and symbolic game playing, respectively. While most of the existing technology-assisted intervention platforms target

© Springer International Publishing Switzerland 2015
M. Antona and C. Stephanidis (Eds.): UAHCI 2015, Part III, LNCS 9177, pp. 721–730, 2015.
DOI: 10.1007/978-3-319-20684-4_69

preschool or school-aged children, very few systems [14, 15] have been designed for potential applications to infants and toddlers, an age when the brain is still considered quite malleable. Robust systems capable of addressing meaningful core skill deficits during this time of neuroplasticity and prior to the full manifestation of ASD impairments could therefore have powerful impacts on children's long-term development.

We present a computer-assisted intervention system ultimately designed for use with infants and toddlers at risk for ASD. This system will address early social communication and social orienting skills, specifically response to name (RTN). Many children with ASD fail to orient to their names when called, nor do they share other core social attention bids with their caregivers as infants. These early orienting deficits often result in numerous lost social learning opportunities. The ultimate goal of the RTN protocol is to have the child successfully respond to caregiver's attempts to garner attention by calling his/her name from a variety of locations within the learning environment. The novel learning environment consists of:

- A spatially distributed name prompting system;
- A wide range attention detection system;
- An attractor that can help shift the child's gaze from the current location to the target location;
- A feedback mechanism to encourage the child. The integrated system works autonomously, and provides numerous practice sessions.

This paper is organized as follows. Section 2 introduces the system design. Section 3 presents the experimental setup. The experimental results are discussed in Sect. 4, and Sect. 5 draws conclusions about this work.

2   System Design

2.1   System Architecture

The proposed system was integrated as shown in Fig. 1. A supervisory controller (SC) controls the global execution logic. SC initializes the prompting sub-system and activates the name prompting or attractors as needed. It simultaneously receives the participant's gaze response from the attention tracking sub-system as feedback to make future decisions.

Figure 2 shows the experiment room layout. Five monitors in the name prompting sub-system covered a large range of the room to generate name calling prompts and provide attention attractors. The participant's attention was tracked by the 4 cameras in the Attention tracking Sub-system. If the child did not look at the target monitor, then a bouncing ball appeared in a monitor closest to his/her gaze direction and bounced towards the target monitor. If the participant still looked away, then special motion and sound effects were added to the bouncing ball to enhance the attractor's effect. If the participant looked at the target screen (target hit) during this procedure, then a reward video was displayed with a firework animation. We hypothesized that the attractor would reorient the participant towards the name calling location since children with ASD were shown to be attracted to inanimate objects. Such repeated practice and reward could

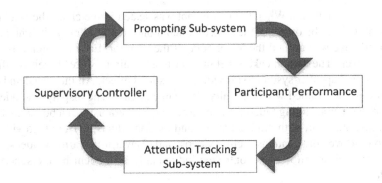

Fig. 1. Global system structure

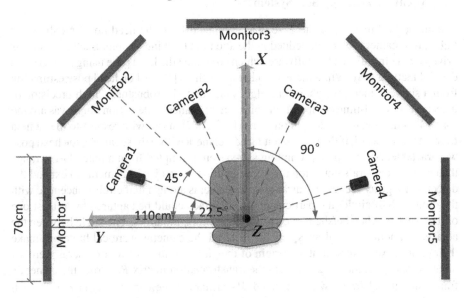

Fig. 2. Experiment room layout

teach children to develop an association between their names being called and looking towards the person, which may eventually lead to the development of RTN skills.

2.2 Name Prompting Sub-System

As shown in Fig. 2, the name prompting system consisted of 5 monitors positioned in a half circle. The participant was seated in the chair in the center of the circle. The center of Monitor1 to the center of Monitor5 created a view of 180° in yaw angle from the perspective of the participant. The radius of the monitor circle was 110 cm and the length of the monitor was 70 cm, so the display region was about 34° across for each monitor. The origin of the whole system was the center of the monitor half circle with a height of 120 cm. The *X, Y,* and *Z* axes in Fig. 1 are marked with the half-transparent wide arrows. Z axis points up. When the participant was seated in the chair, the head of the participant was on the origin of the system. Each monitor was 43 cm in height, and the participant's eye was around the lower edge of the monitor. Each monitor was linked with a speaker. The five speakers behind the five monitors were driven by the 5.1 surround sound speaker system to provide stereo sound effect. All the visual and audio displays were programed with the Unity [16] game engine. The displays included: (1) a prerecorded name calling video from an experienced therapist; (2) a bouncing ball as the attention attractor, with different sound and motion effects; (3) a reward video and animation; (4) welcome and instruction videos; and (5) warm-up cartoon videos. Those displays on each monitor were controlled individually as a client by the supervisory controller.

2.3   Attention Tracking Sub-System

The attention direction, or the gaze, was computed from the head pose. As shown in Fig. 2, four cameras were embedded in the attention tracking system. Each camera was driven by the IntraFace [17] software, which computed the head pose using a supervised descent method [18]. While there are other algorithms [19, 20] on head pose estimation from a single camera, we chose this algorithm due to its robustness, high precision of detection, and real-time computation ability. Each camera's detection range was around [-40°, 40°] in yaw, [-30°, 30°] in pitch and [-30°, 30°] in roll with respect to the camera frame. In other word, if the participant faced a camera within those ranges, the head pose was tractable. As the name prompting sub-system prompted from a much larger range than a single camera's detection range, we applied an array of 4 cameras to expand the detection range as needed. By arranging the cameras along a half circle concentric with the monitor half circle, the participant's frontal face could be captured by at least one of the cameras when he/she looked toward any of the monitors. The angle between the adjacent cameras' optical axes was 45°, and all the cameras were calibrated to make their optical axes intersect at the origin of the global frame. All four cameras were set up at the same height of 120 cm and the transformation matrix R_{GC} from the camera's frame and global frame was computed. By arranging the cameras as in Fig. 2, each individual camera's detection was transferred and seamlessly merged in the global frame. The actual detection range used for the system was [-17°, 197°] from the right to the left side in yaw, [-30°, 21°] from up to down in pitch and [-30°, 30°] from lower left to lower right in roll. This range covered the full display space.

If more than one camera detected the head pose at the same time, the result from the camera with the smallest detected yaw angle was chosen for transformation. A vector V_{face}^{camera}, which represents the frontal face orientation in the camera frame was then transformed as $V_{face}^{global} = R_{GC} V_{face}^{camera}$ in the global frame. We found that the participant's sidewise gaze direction was usually larger than the sidewise head turn, therefore the horizontal component of the angle between V_{face}^{global} and the X axis was amplified by 120 % to approximate the gaze to the side. The ratio of 120 % was found to be reasonable with a small study with 3 adults. If the extended line from V_{face}^{global} crossed with the target monitor's region, then a target hit was detected.

3   Experimental Setup

3.1   Task and Protocol

The flowchart for the user study is shown in Fig. 3. Each participant completed a single experimental session consisting of the following steps. First, a welcome video was played, followed by a fun video (Sesame Street) displayed on all five monitors, (one at a time). This helped participants understand that a video could be displayed on those positions. After 5 trials of RTN another fun video was shown to prevent the participants from getting bored. Another 5 trials followed the break and finally the whole experiments ended up with a "Good-bye" video.

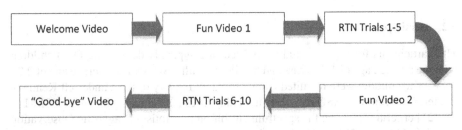

Fig. 3. Experimental procedure

The prompting levels of a RTN trial are listed in Table 1. The first level of prompt was a prerecorded name calling video displayed on the target monitor, where a therapist called the name of the participant twice. From prompt Level 2, a red bouncing ball appeared as the attention attractor. If the participant did not look at the target monitor within their name being called two times, the red ball started bouncing, starting at the direction of the participant's gaze and moving towards the target monitor. At the same time, the name calling video display was repeated at the target monitor. If the participant still did not look at the target monitor, the prompt Level 3 was introduced. Level 3 was the same as Level 2, except that the red ball bounced at the participant's gaze direction for 2 s before repeating the steps of Level 2. This initialized bouncing on the fixed position was designed to help the participant notice and focus on the attention attractor. If the participant still did not find the target monitor successfully, Level 4 was provided as the last level of prompting. Level 4 added a sound effect to the Level 3 prompts to make the bouncing ball more attractive. At any time during the 4 levels of prompts, if the participant looked at the target at any time, the prompting would be stopped and a reward video was displayed with a firework animation. The reward video was prerecorded by the same therapist in the name calling video saying, "Good job! You found me!" Even if the participant never looked at the target monitor, the rewards were still displayed for encouragement.

Table 1. Name Prompting Levels

Prompt level	Content
Level 1	Name calling on the target monitor
Level 2	Level 1 + Attractor bouncing from the gaze direction to the target monitor.
Level 3	Level 1 + Attractor *first bouncing at the gaze direction for 2 s*, and then bouncing from the gaze direction to the target monitor.
Level 4	Level 1 + Attractor first bouncing at the gaze direction, and then bouncing from the gaze direction to the target monitor *with special sound effect*.

3.2 Participants

The participants for the user study consisted of 5 typically developing (TD) children with the average age of 1.38 years and 5 children with ASD with an average age of 2.26 years. The children were recruited from a research registry of the Vanderbilt Kennedy Center. Children with ASD had confirmed diagnoses by a clinician based on DSM-IV-TR [21] criteria. They met the spectrum cut-off on the Autism Diagnostic Observation Schedule (ADOS) [22], and had existing data regarding cognitive abilities (Intelligent Quotient, or IQ) in the registry. Parents of participants in both groups completed the Social Responsiveness Scale– Second Edition (SRS-2) to index current ASD symptoms. The study was approved by the Vanderbilt University Institutional Review Board. The characteristics of the participants are listed in Table 2.

Table 2. Participant Characteristics

Mean (SD)	ADOS Raw Score	ADOS C2. Imagina-tion/Crea-tivity	IQ	SRS-2 Raw Score	SRS-2 T score	Age (Years)
ASD	22.40	2.88	55.00	92.80	69.60	2.26
	(3.65)	(0.45)	(8.49)	(22.69)	(8.85)	(0.24)
TD	NA	NA	NA	41.40	49.80	1.38
				(23.04)	(8.93)	(0.44)

The age range of the participants with ASD in this study was consistent with the age that many young children are able to be reliably diagnosed [23]. Therefore, this group provided the data regarding practicality of the proposed system for early intervention for children with ASD. Given that research has highlighted the importance of early screening and intervention for ASD in children, particularly those in high risk groups (such as infant siblings) [3], we recruited the TD group with an average age lower than the typical age of ASD diagnosis to test its use with younger infants. Note that since the TD group was younger than the group with ASD, the results from each group were not directly comparable due to developmental differences. Instead, the results of each group were analyzed separately.

4   Experimental Results

All participants successfully completed all parts of the experiment. Their parents, the supervisory therapist as well as the engineers qualitatively noted that the participants were engaged in the tasks and seemed to enjoy the procedures. We investigated 2 important aspects of the participants' responses:

- The prompt level that the participants needed to hit the target. This signified how well the participant performed in the RTN tasks.
- How long the participants took from the start of the name calling until they looked at the target monitor.

4.1   Results of Participants with ASD

All participants with ASD eventually hit the target across all trials. 41 target hits were on prompt Level 1 and 9 target hits were on prompt Level 2. Table 3 lists the mean and standard deviation of the target hit prompt level and the time spent from the start of the name prompting to the target hit. On average, this group needed a prompt level of 1.18 to hit the target. The average time spent to hit the target was 1.85 s. Given that one name calling period from the name prompt video was around 2 s, we can see that the participants with ASD generally responded to their names the first time it was called.

Table 3. Results of Participants with ASD

	Prompt level needed	Time spent to hit the target
Mean	1.18	1.85
SD	0.39	0.95

4.2   Results of TD Participants

The TD participants hit the target in 49 trials in the whole experiment. 40 target hits were on prompt Level 1 and 9 target hits were on prompt Level 2. Table 4 lists the average and standard deviation of the target hit prompt level and the time spent from the start of the name prompting to the target hit of TD group. We can see that on average, this group needed a prompt level of 1.26 to hit the target. The average time spent to hit the target was 2.87 s. Overall, TD participants responded to their names on the second call.

Table 4. Results of TD participants

	Prompt level needed	Time spent to hit the target
Mean	1.26	2.87
SD	0.66	2.54

5   Discussion and Conclusion

In this paper, we proposed a computer-assisted system to help infants and toddlers with, and at risk of, ASD learn response to name skills. The system consisted of a name prompting sub-system and an attention tracking sub-system. The name prompting sub-system covered a wide range (over 180° yaw angle) in space to simulate a free and natural name calling environment. To detect the participant's response within this broad environment, we formed a closed loop system by introducing a wide range attention tracking sub-system that collaborated with the name prompting system.

The proposed system prompted name calling in a reinforced pattern and with an assistive attention attractor. During the name prompting training trials, if the participants could not respond to their names being called at a low prompting level, a higher prompting level was introduced with a red bouncing ball attractor to help shift the participant's gaze toward the target.

A user study was conducted to test the effectiveness of the proposed system on toddlers with ASD and infants. This allowed us to test the system on children with existing diagnoses as well as children who could be considered at risk of later diagnosis. The experimental results showed that the system and task protocol were well tolerated by the participants. They showed engagement during the intervention and performed well in response to name calling. Meanwhile, we found that the participants mainly utilized prompt Level 1 and Level 2. This revealed that the difficulty level of the name calling stimuli can be increased to scaffold the learning procedure and take advantage of advanced attention attractors. Based on these preliminary results, we will further investigate the children's response to more difficult name calling stimuli, such as audio only prompts from different directions. Furthermore, we will study the effect of the advanced attention attractor (Level 3 and Level 4) in the upgraded prompting environment.

Acknowledgement. The authors are grateful to the participants and their parents for their participation in this study. This study was supported in part by a grant from the Vanderbilt Kennedy Center (Hobbs Grant), the National Science Foundation under Grant 1264462, and the National Institute of Health under Grant 1R01MH091102-01A1 and 1R21MH103518-01. Work also includes core support from NICHD (P30HD15052) and NCATS (UL1TR000445-06).

References

1. Autism Spectrum Disorders Prevalence Rate. Autism Speaks and Center for Disease Control (CDC) (2011)
2. Dawson, G., Rogers, S., Munson, J., Smith, M., Winter, J., Greenson, J., et al.: Randomized, controlled trial of an intervention for toddlers with Autism: the early start denver model. Pediatrics 125(1), e17–e23 (2010)
3. Warren, Z.E., Stone, W.L.: Best practices: Early diagnosis and psychological assessment. In: Amaral, D., Geschwind, D., Dawson, G. (eds.) Autism Spectrum Disorders, pp. 1271–1282. Oxford University Press, New York (2011)
4. Bekele, E., Lahiri, U., Swanson, A., Crittendon, J.A., Crittendon, Z., Sarkar, N.: A step towards developing adaptive robot-mediated intervention architecture (aria) for children with Autism. IEEE Trans. Neural Sys. Rehabil Eng. 21(2), 289–299 (2013)
5. Greczek, J., Atrash, A., Matarić, M.: A computational model of graded cueing: robots encouraging behavior change. In: Stephanidis, C. (ed.) HCII 2013, Part II. CCIS, vol. 374, pp. 582–586. Springer, Heidelberg (2013)
6. Zheng, Z., Zhang, L., Bekele, E., Swanson, A., Crittendon, J., Warren, Z., et al.: Impact of Robot-mediated interaction system on joint attention skills for children with Autism In: Presented at the International Conference on Rehabilitation Robotics, Seattle (2013)
7. Lahiri, U., Bekele, E., Dohrmann, E., Warren, Z., Sarkar, N.: Design of a virtual reality based adaptive response technology for children with Autism spectrum disorder. In: D'Mello, S., Graesser, A., Schuller, B., Martin, J.-C. (eds.) ACII 2011, Part I. LNCS, vol. 6974, pp. 165–174. Springer, Heidelberg (2011)
8. Wade, J., Bian, D., Zhang, L., Swanson, A., Sarkar, M., Warren, Z., Sarkar, N.: Design of a virtual reality driving environment to assess performance of teenagers with ASD. In: Stephanidis, C., Antona, M. (eds.) UAHCI 2014, Part II. LNCS, vol. 8514, pp. 466–474. Springer, Heidelberg (2014)
9. Herrera, G., Alcantud, F., Jordan, R., Blanquer, A., Labajo, G., De Pablo, C.: Development of symbolic play through the use of virtual reality tools in children with autistic spectrum disorders Two case studies. Autism 12, 143–157 (2008)
10. Feil-Seifer, D., Matarić, M.: A simon-says robot providing autonomous imitation feedback using graded cueing. In: Poster paper in International Meeting for Autism Research (IMFAR), Toronto, May 2012
11. Greczek, J., Kaszubksi, E., Atrash, A., Matarić, M.J.: Graded Cueing Feedback in Robot-Mediated Imitation Practice for Children with Autism Spectrum Disorders. In: Proceedings of 23rd IEEE International Symposium on Robot and Human Interactive Communication (RO-MAN 2014), Edinburgh, August 2014
12. Zheng, Z., Das, S., Young, E.M., Swanson, A., Warren, Z., Sarkar, N.: Autonomous robot-mediated imitation learning for children with Autism. In: IEEE International Conference on in Robotics and Automation (ICRA), pp. 2707–2712 (2014)
13. Lahiri, U., Warren, Z., Sarkar, N.: Dynamic gaze measurement with adaptive response technology. In: Virtual Reality Based Social Communication for Autism. In: presented at the International Conference on Virtual Rehabilitation (ICVR) (2011)
14. Shic, F., Chawarska, K., Bradshaw, J., Scassellati, B.: Autism, eye-tracking, entropy. In: 7th IEEE International Conference on Development and Learning (ICDL), pp. 73–78 (2008)
15. Feil-Seifer, D., Mataric, M.: Robot-assisted therapy for children with Autism spectrum disorders. In: Proceedings of the 7th International Conference on Interaction Design and Children, pp. 49–52 (2008)
16. Unity Game Engine. Unity Game Engine-Official Site. http://unity3d.com

17. Xiong, X., De la Torre, F.: Supervised Descent Method for Solving Nonlinear Least Squares Problems in Computer Vision. arXiv preprint arXiv:1405.0601 (2014)
18. Xiong, X., De la Torre, F.: Supervised descent method and its applications to face alignment. In: IEEE Conference on Computer Vision and Pattern Recognition (CVPR), pp. 532–539 (2013)
19. Murphy-Chutorian, E., Trivedi, M.M.: Head pose estimation in computer vision: a survey. IEEE Trans. Pattern Anal. Mach. Intell. **31**, 607–626 (2009)
20. Fanelli, G., Gall, J., Van Gool, L.: Real time head pose estimation with random regression forests. In: IEEE Conference on Computer Vision and Pattern Recognition (CVPR), pp. 617–624 (2011)
21. Diagnostic and Statistical Manual of Mental Disorders: Quick reference to the Diagnostic Criteria from DSM-IV-TR, Fourth ed. Washington D.C.: American Psychiatric Association (2000)
22. Lord, C., Rutter, M., DiLavore, P., Risi, S., Gotham, K., Bishop, S.: Autism Diagnostic Observation Schedule. Torrance, Western Psychological Services (2012). (ADOS-2)
23. Johnson, C.P., Myers, S.M.: Identification and evaluation of children with autism spectrum disorders. Pediatrics **120**, 1183–1215 (2007)

Author Index